ISBN: 9781313033107

Published by:
HardPress Publishing
8345 NW 66TH ST #2561
MIAMI FL 33166-2626

Email: info@hardpress.net
Web: http://www.hardpress.net

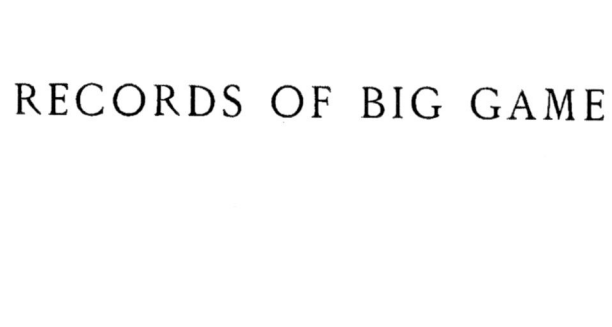

RECORDS OF BIG GAME

Yours faithfully
Rowland Ward

RECORDS OF BIG GAME

WITH

THEIR DISTRIBUTION, CHARACTERISTICS,
DIMENSIONS, WEIGHTS, AND

MEASUREMENTS OF HORNS

ANTLERS, TUSKS, & SKINS

THIRD EDITION

By ROWLAND WARD, F.Z.S.

AUTHOR OF 'THE SPORTSMAN'S HANDBOOK' ETC.

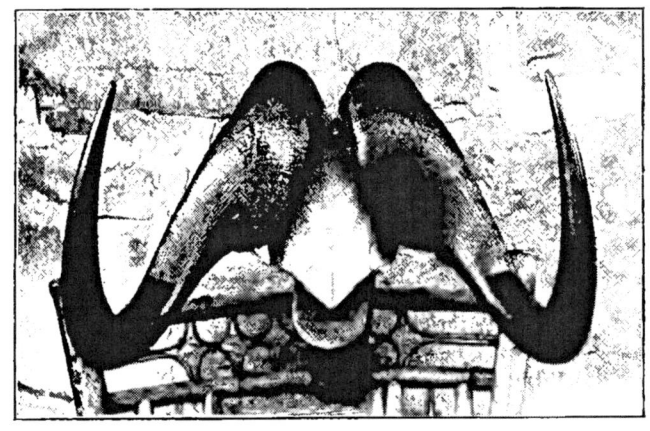

*WITH ABOUT **217** ILLUSTRATIONS*

LONDON
ROWLAND WARD, LIMITED
"THE JUNGLE," 166 PICCADILLY, W.
1899

THIS BOOK IS DEDICATED

TO THE

SPORTSMEN OF THE WORLD

WITHOUT WHOSE DETERMINED PLUCK AND LOVE OF TRAVEL THESE RECORDS

COULD NOT HAVE BEEN PRODUCED, NOR COULD THE AUTHOR

HAVE SPENT A LIFETIME IN THE ART HE HAS

TRIED TO ADVANCE

PREFACE TO THIRD EDITION

In the present edition, the finest known specimens of antlers, horns, tusks, and skins are, so far as possible, recorded. It has been found impracticable in some instances to verify the measurements of trophies in distant parts of the world; and such records must accordingly be taken on the responsibility of their respective owners or other persons who have been good enough to measure them. It is much to be regretted that one pair of hands and a steel-tape are not responsible for the measurements of all the actual "records." One of the many difficulties in connection with this compilation is due to the circumstance that different measurements of the same specimen are often sent me; this sometimes arising from the use of common tapes or string, which are absolutely unreliable unless checked at the time by a steel measure. In this connection I may mention that I shall at all times be pleased to cause such measurements to be carefully verified at my establishment in Piccadilly. With the horns of freshly killed hollow-horned ruminants an allowance for shrinkage should be made when comparing with older trophies. An average specimen of an *Ovis ammon* horn, for instance, will frequently shrink half an inch in length and proportionately in girth after it has left the field.

With the *Cervidæ* many difficulties have arisen as to comparison; and I may point out that although length of antlers is invariably put at the top of the list, other particulars such as *number of tines, general symmetry, spread,* and *weight of antler,* are in many instances the making of a good trophy. Small specimens are frequently noted in order to include measurements from different localities, as well as to record horns of certain species, such as *Ovis poli,* etc., in which recently shot specimens do not approach those of the record example.

I have to thank many sportsmen and naturalists all over the world for the help they have afforded me.

To Mr. A. O. Hume, and Prince Henry of Liechtenstein, my special thanks are due.

In the present volume great care has been taken with regard to the accuracy of the numbers; and, considering that there are so many thousand measurements, it will be readily understood the task attempted has been one of no ordinary difficulty.

The new illustrations, numbering over fifty in the present volume, are nearly all produced direct from photographs of notable examples.

A new feature in this edition is the introduction of a short description of the leading characteristics and the exact geographical distribution of each species and race. This, it is hoped, will render the volume of additional value as a work of reference to the sportsman.

ROWLAND WARD.

PREFACE TO SECOND EDITION

SINCE the publication of the first edition of this work under the title of " Horn Measurements," I have been successful in collecting much new and valuable data bearing upon the measurements of horns and other statistics of Big Game. For this information I am to a considerable extent indebted to numerous sportsmen, and to the curators of some of the most important museums of the world, who have been kind enough to measure all the finest specimens in the collections under their charge. In addition to this valuable help, for which I desire to express my grateful acknowledgment, I have had a record carefully prepared of all the most remarkable specimens registered, as well as those that have from time to time passed through our hands. I am indebted to Mr. H. A. Bryden for much of the descriptive matter of the South African game. There will also be found embodied with all these new records numerous illustrations of typical heads, skulls, and horns drawn especially for this new edition.

In addition to this supplementary information, the new edition will be found to contain more exact localities than have hitherto been recorded, and we continue in constant correspondence with sportsmen in almost every part of the world with a view of still further completing our records.

R. W.

PREFACE TO FIRST EDITION

MY object in producing this book is to start a record of Horn
Measurements of the Great Game of the World. I only regret
that it was not commenced at an earlier date, as in that case it
would have been more complete. In my earlier life I had but
little help, and often worked thirty hours at a stretch ; my work
necessitated attention to specimens that demanded immediate
treatment, and my love for reproducing life-like studies prevented
me from keeping records.

The measurements presented here have been taken prin-
cipally by one hand, and, for that reason, I value them the more.
The dimensions from acknowledged authorities I naturally am
not responsible for. This work is not designed to be in any
way a scientific treatise, but is prepared for sportsmen and
scientific men who are interested to see comparable measurements at a glance. I think these have not been produced in
like form before. These records can be added to, and I shall
feel indebted to sportsmen who will contribute any authentic
record measurements. It must be borne in mind that many
trophies which have passed through my hands are now scattered
all over the world, and the dimensions of them, for the time, are

not recorded here. Some that I give now are fine measurements, some are only ordinary statistics, many are of new species altogether; these last being mainly a result of the quite recent opening up of Africa. The advice noted as to the way to measure must be dealt with strictly, for many persons measuring by different methods produce untrustworthy record. We have tried to be fair in producing the statistics, taking them rather under than over the mark; and the tape has not been pressed into corrugations of horns, but carried outside, over all inequalities.

R. W.

ABBREVIATIONS AND SIGNS

— Owner's measurements or other known authority.

♂ Male.　　　　　♀ Female.　　　　　... Unrecorded.

R, Right horn or antler.　　　L, Left horn or antler.

Measurements are on the outside of the longest horn from base to tip ; with Deer from the bottom edge of burr, or coronet, to the highest tip point, except where notified to the contrary.

Circumference is at the base ; with Deer above brow tine ; in the Red Deer and Wapiti group between bez and trez.

Length is expressed in inches, when not otherwise noted.

Weights taken in the field should be accepted as approximate, and, unless mentioned, are of adult males.

Heights are in most cases taken at the shoulder of adult males (see p. 480).

P.Z.S. = Proceedings of the Zoological Society of London.

LIST OF ILLUSTRATIONS

RECORDS OF BIG GAME

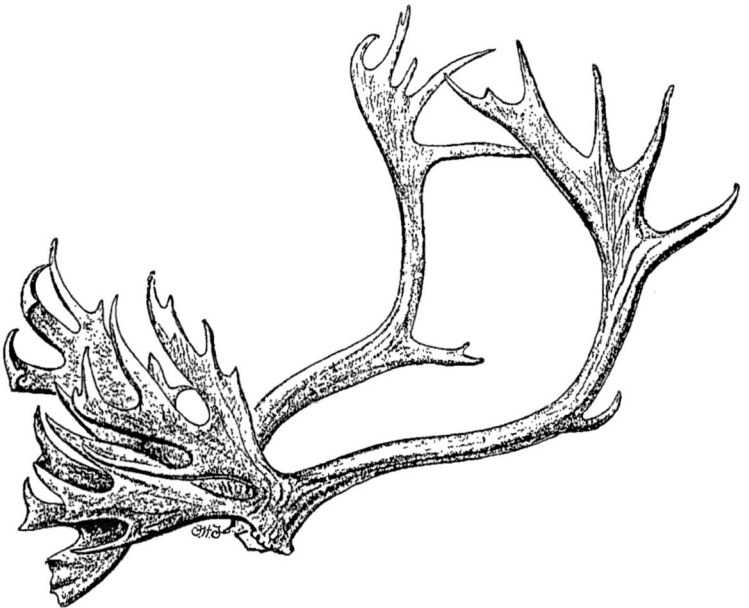

Antlers of Male Woodland Reindeer.   From a specimen in the British Museum.

REINDEER or CARIBOU (Rangifer tarandus).

DISTINGUISHED from all other deer by the presence of antlers in both
sexes ; those of males being complex, with the brow tines palmated
and often unsymmetrical, and the bez, or second tine, also generally
expanded.   The muzzle is entirely covered with hair, the ears and tail
are short, the throat has a fringe of long hair, and the coat is very
thick and of a nearly uniform clove-brown colour, with some white in
the region of the tail, and on the under parts and legs.   The false or
lateral hoofs are unusually large and spreading ; and there is a patch

of long white hair covering a gland on the hock, but none on the hind cannon-bone. Height at shoulder reaching to 4 feet 10 inches (Newfoundland); weight of a full-grown Scandinavian stag 30 stone, clean (Abel Chapman); antlers average about 30 lbs. per pair.

Reindeer inhabit the circumpolar regions of both hemispheres, in Europe including Scandinavia, Lapland, and Northern Russia; their

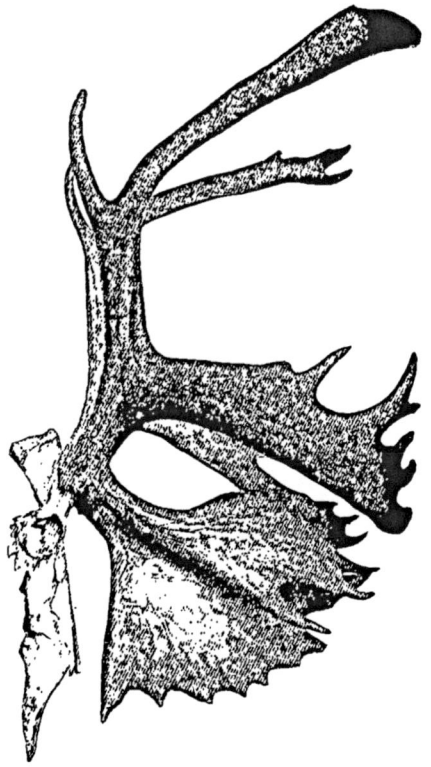

Antlers of Male Woodland Reindeer from Nova Scotia.
From a specimen in the British Museum.

southern limit varies from 52° to 54° N. latitude, while they extend to between 80° and 81° northwards.

Six varieties, or local races, of reindeer are recognised : (1) the Scandinavian reindeer (*R. tarandus typicus*) of Northern Europe and Asia, which is a rather small animal with moderately expanded antlers ; (2) the Spitzbergen reindeer (*R. tarandus spetzbergensis*), characterised by the peculiar form of the nasal bones of the skull ; (3) the woodland reindeer (*R. tarandus caribou*) of the forest districts of Arctic America, distinguished by its large bodily size and the short, much-palmated antlers; (4) the Newfoundland reindeer (*R. tarandus terræ-novæ*),

Side view of Antlers of Male Barren-Ground Reindeer.   From a specimen in the British Museum.

which is closely allied to the last, but with even more complex antlers and some differences in coloration; (5) the Greenland reindeer (*R. tarandus grænlandicus*), which is apparently very similar to the sixth variety; and (6) the barren-ground reindeer (*R. tarandus arcticus*), from the open country north of the forests in America, a very distinct animal, characterised by its small bodily size, and the great length and simple form of the antlers, in which, except on the brow tine, there is scarcely any palmation. Reindeer heads are probably some of the most difficult to measure, owing to the different curves the top points frequently present. Females have smaller and lighter antlers than males.

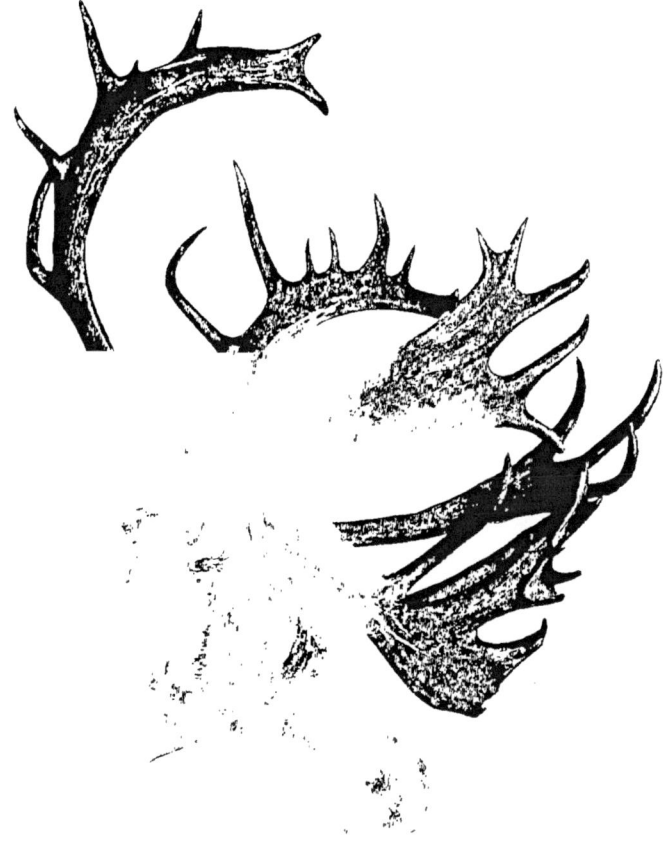

Head of Male Newfoundland Reindeer. From Dr. J. A. Allen.

Abel Chapman, writing in the *Field*, says two or three year old bucks run between 16 and 20 stone; but one big stag he shot was made out (perhaps erroneously) to scale well over 30 stone, clean. The measurements of the antlers have been separated for the convenience of sportsmen.

REINDEER or CARIBOU (Rangifer tarandus)—*continued.*

Length on outside curve.	Circumference.	Tip to Tip.	Widest inside.	Points.	Locality.	Owner.
62	5½	39	49¼	20 + 17	Canada . .	Mrs. Macintosh.
57⅝	5¼	13⅜	...	13 + 7	Arctic Region . .	British Museum.
57¼	5¼	33½	44½ (outside)	20 + 16	Do. .	Sylvester Browne.
54⅜	4⅞	20¼	...	11 + 13	N. America	The late Captain Sir John Franklin, British Museum.
-54	6¾	21¼	32¾	12 + 11	?	Paris Museum.
52½	5¼	15	26½	17 + 12	N. Canada	J. Talbot Clifton.
52	4⅝	28½	38	7 + 7	Do. .	David T. Hanbury.
[1]51⅜	4⅞	40⅞	48⅜	17 + 14	Hudson Bay .	Sir Edmund G. Loder, Bart.
49	4⅛	24⅝	32⅜	7 + 9	N. America . .	Hon. Walter Rothschild.
[2]48	6½	11⅞	25½	17 + 15	Newfoundland	Sir Edmund G. Loder, Bart.
47⅜	5⅛	32⅛	...	19 + 12	N. America .	A. Murray, British Museum.
46½	6½	16½	28	32	British Columbia	J. Turner-Turner.
45½	5½	31¼	33½	13 + 12	Newfoundland	F. C. Williamson.
45½	4¼	19¾	31	15 + 13	N. Canada . .	David T. Hanbury.
44⅜	5⅛	34	37	...	Newfoundland	C. H. Akroyd.
44	5½	18¼	30	18 + 13	Do. .	Vice-Admiral Sir William Kennedy.
44	5¾	19	26½	17 + 14	Do. . .	Lieut. A. E. Allgood, R.N.
43¾	5⅜	40	41⅞	16 + 11	Do. .	St. George Littledale.
-42½	7¼	33¼	38½	22 + 18	Do. . .	R. Gordon Smith.
-42½	...	...	49⅛ (outside)	24	Do. .	General R. L. Dashwood.
42	6½	...	18½	33	Alaska . .	Earl of Lonsdale.
42	5½	36½	39½	20 + 12	Newfoundland	Q. C. Colmore.
41	5½	20½	28	15 + 9	Do. . .	Lieut.-Col. Hon. W. Coke.
41	6	35	33	20	British Columbia .	Major C. C. Ellis.
40	6	31½	35½	19 + 14	Newfoundland .	Vice-Admiral Sir William Kennedy.
39	5⅝	...	23¼	17 + 14	Do. . .	Sir Victor Brooke's Collection.
39	6	31	30½	15 + 10	Do. . . .	Captain C. E. Stracey.
39	7	28	31	20 + 19	Do. . . .	Vice-Admiral Sir William Kennedy.

[1] Woodland Caribou. [2] Barren-ground.

REINDEER or CARIBOU (Rangifer tarandus)—*continued.*

Length on outside curve.	Circumference.	Tip to Tip.	Widest inside.	Points.	Locality.	Owner.
39	7	29	31¼	18 + 16	?	Duke of Westminster.
39	5¾	...	...	11 + 11	British Columbia	Sir Peter Walker, Bart.
39	4¾	26	26¾	15 + 15	Newfoundland	. D. F. Moir, R.N.
-39	7⅝	33	31⅞	29 + 22	Do. .	. Lord Thurlow.
38	5¾	19½	21½	17 + 14	British Columbia	. T. P. Kempson.
38	6	36	35½	39	Newfoundland	. Lieut. F. C. Osborne, R.N.
37¾	6¼	23	23	11 + 10	British Columbia	. W. S. Power.
37½	5¾	12	20	14 + 12	Canada . .	. J. W. Osborne.
37½	5½	...	29	...	?	Otho Shaw.
37¼	5⅝	...	24	27	Newfoundland	. Dr. Wm. Tait.
37	5¾	21½	25	12 + 12	British Columbia	. H. G. Walker.
-37	...	...	40 (outside)	43	Newfoundland	. General R. L. Dashwood.
37	4¼	14¾	25	15 + 13	Do. .	. Captain H. H. Grenfell, R.N.
36½	5½	28	25	8·9	British Columbia	. H. G. Walker.
36½	5½	19	22	10 + 9	Newfoundland	. V. L. A. Campbell, R.N.
36½	6¾	30	31¾	19 + 18	Do. . .	. A. Wilson, R.N.
36½	6⅛	26¼	28½	17 + 15	British Columbia	. Sir Peter Walker, Bart.
36	5⅝	44	...	15 + 12	Do. .	. J. V. Colby.
36	5	23	27½	12 + 11	Do. .	. Captain F. Molyneux.
35½	6¾	18¼	29½	13 + 11	New Brunswick	. P. N. Graham.
35½	5¼	32¼	34½	12 + 10	Newfoundland	G. C. W. Crispin, R.N.
33½	5¼	23	26	15 + 11	British Columbia	. Sir Peter Walker, Bart.
-32½	8½	12¼	18	17 + 10	Canada . .	. James J. Harrison.
32½	5½	32½	...	12 + 12	?	Major R. Hallowes.
-32	5½	...	..	14	British Columbia	. Theodore Roosevelt.

REINDEER or CARIBOU (Rangifer tarandus)—*continued.*

Length on outside curve.	Circumference.	Tip to Tip.	Widest inside.	Points.	Locality.	Owner.
[1]60	5⅝	38⅝	41⅛	22+15	?	Sir V. Brooke's Collection.
-59½	7	38	44	15+16	Norway . . .	J. Whitaker.
-59	4½	42½	46 (outside)	7+5	Do. . .	H. J. Elwes.
-58	6	30½	37	33	Jotunheim, Norway .	S. Ratcliff.
-55⅛	6½	38	43⅛	18+8	Sundal Fjelds, Norway	Capt. Gerard Ferrand.
54½	4⅞	33¼	40¾	15+13	Norway . . .	J. H. Thomas.
54	5	22	41¾	16+11	Do. . . .	Kenneth M'Douall.
-51	6 1/10	...	...	...	Rundane, Norway .	Capt. John Marriott.
-51	5¼	29	...	25	Norway . . .	Abel Chapman.
50⅜	4⅞	24	29 (outside)	16+13	?	H.R.H. the Duke of Saxe-Coburg and Gotha.
-49½	4⅞	20¾	34¼	13+12	Norway . . .	H. J. Elwes.
49	4¼	25	36½	18+15	Do. . .	J. H. Barnard.
♀ 47	4⅝	23	29	17+9	Do. . . .	Kenneth M'Douall.
46½	6	21½	26½	37	Do. . .	Hon. Walter Rothschild.
-46	5	29	38	42	Jotunheim, Norway .	S. Ratcliff.
44	4¼	20¼	32½	12+9	Norway . . .	Col. C. B. Harvey.
-42	6	26	40¾	22+13	Do. .	R. Rankin.
41⅛	4¾	...	24½	12+9	Spitzbergen . .	W. D. James.
41	4½	26½	30¾	12+12	Do.	Sir W. Martin Conway.
-40½	4½	29	30	11+8	Norway . . .	Lewis J. Cadell.
38¾	4	25¼	...	7+5	Do. . . .	British Museum.
38	5½	21½	...	15+13	Do. . . .	Do.
37	4¼	18	20½	15+11	E. Spitzbergen .	Arnold Pike.
36	4¼	24	26	17+11	Do. . .	Do.
-36	6½	34	33½	23+20	Lapland . .	Dublin Museum.
[2]-34½	6¾	31	...	33	Norway . . .	Abel Chapman.
-31	5½	23	20	19+18	Do. . . .	J. Benett-Stanford.

[1] Perished antlers. [2] A very old buck.

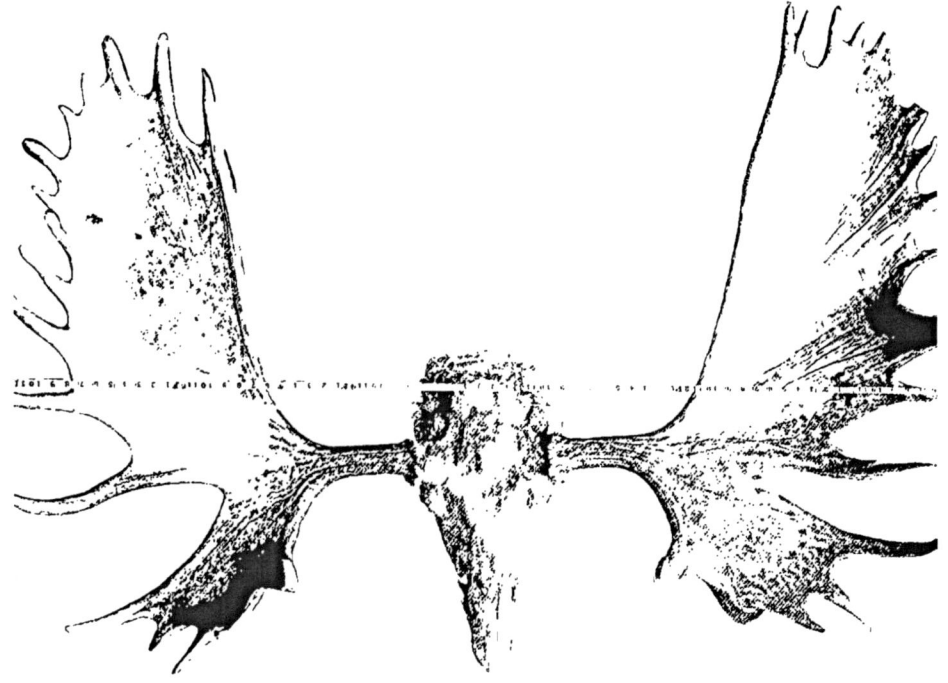

Skull and Antlers of Male Elk.
From an Alaskan specimen in the possession of the Duke of Westminster.

ELK or MOOSE (Alces machlis).

The largest member of the deer tribe, distinguished by its ungainly form, long limbs, broad, produced, and flabby muzzle (all of which, except a small triangular patch below the nostrils, is covered with hair), the presence of a pendulous hairy organ (the so-called " bell ") on the throat of the males, and the form and position of the antlers in that sex. These latter are set on the skull with their bases at right angles to the middle line of the face, the beams having neither brow nor bez tines, but expanding after a short distance into a broad palmation, carrying a number of snags on the outer border ; in young elk each antler is divided in a fork-like manner into a small front and a larger hind portion. The main hoofs are long and pointed, and the lateral pair large : there is a gland and tuft of hair both on the hock and hind cannon-bone, the latter being situated high up. The tail is very short. From birth to old age elk are uniformly coloured ; the general tint of the hair, which is long, coarse, and somewhat brittle, varying from yellowish gray to deep blackish brown, and being usually darker in American than in European examples. The height varies from 5 feet 9 inches at the shoulder in Scandinavian examples (Sir H. Pottinger) to as much as 6 feet 6 inches in American specimens (General R. L. Dashwood); the weight from 900 to 1400 lbs., that of the antlers being about 60 lbs.

Elk inhabit the forests and marshy districts of Scandinavia, Eastern Russia, Siberia, Northern Russia, and thence eastwards through Siberia

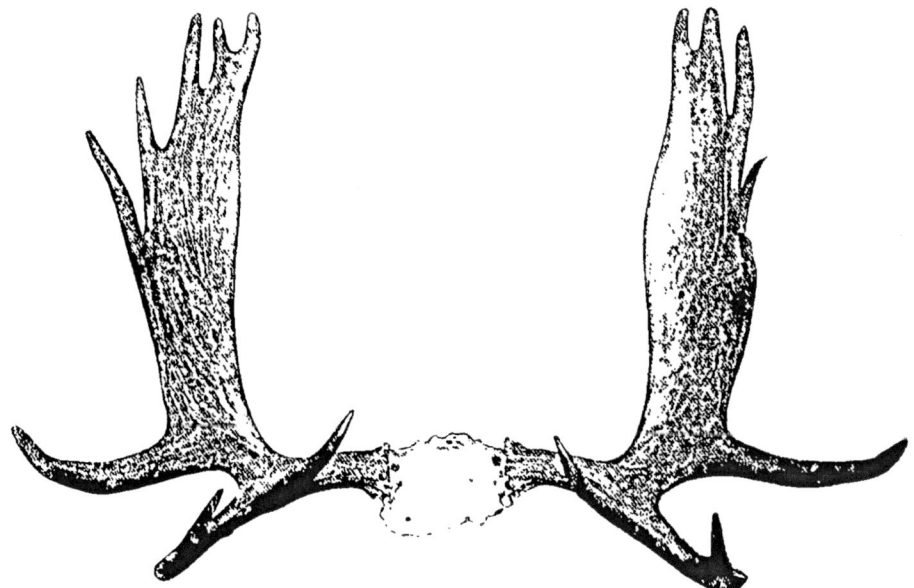

Antlers of Male Elk.

north of about latitude 50° N. to Amurland; while in America (where they are invariably known as moose) at the present time they are found in Alaska, Montana, Nova Scotia, and New Brunswick. Although many sportsmen say they can be distinguished by the antlers and the colour of the skin, the European and American elk appear so similar that they do not seem worthy of being regarded as even distinct local varieties, but for convenience in comparing the European and American measurements are separated.

An elk killed at Meswiez, Lithuania, by Count Scheibler measured

	Feet.	Inches.
Length tip of nose to tip of tail . .	9	$\frac{1}{2}$
„ „ „ „ root . .	8	6

	Feet.	Inches.
Crest to nose	2	7
Height at withers .	5	9
„ „ quarters . .	6	$5\frac{1}{2}$
Girth quarters .		$19\frac{3}{4}$
Round thigh .		$7\frac{1}{2}$
Below knee . . .	3	$6\frac{1}{2}$
Round neck near the ears . .	4	9

Estimated weight 1500 lbs. See antlers, $27\frac{1}{2}$, etc.

Length to longest tine.	Circumference above burr.	Tip to Tip.	Greatest width.	Breadth of Palm.	Points.	Locality.	Owner.
[1]$-55\frac{1}{2}$	$7\frac{1}{2}$	...	$70\frac{1}{4}$	29 ?	...	Alaska . .	W. W. Hart.
-55	11 ?	37	69	21	21	Do. . .	F. B. Tolhurst.
-49	...	...	$78\frac{1}{2}$	18	40	Yukon .	W. F. Sheard.
[2]-48	10	...	69	15	32	Do. .	Dall De Weese.
$-47\frac{1}{4}$	$9\frac{1}{4}$	$37\frac{1}{2}$	72	$16\frac{1}{4}$	20 + 17	Do. .	Duke of Westminster.
$44\frac{1}{2}$	$10\frac{1}{8}$	$49\frac{1}{2}$	66	14	17 + 14	Kenai Mts. .	Viscount Powerscourt.
-44	...	...	$61\frac{1}{2}$	...	...	Canada .	General R. L. Dashwood.
$43\frac{1}{4}$	$8\frac{1}{2}$	40	$59\frac{1}{4}$	$14\frac{1}{2}$	14 + 13	Manitoba .	G. H. M. Banks.
43	$9\frac{1}{2}$	$22\frac{1}{2}$	$47\frac{1}{2}$	12	11 + 11	Canada . .	Viscount Powerscourt.
$-42\frac{3}{4}$	10	$35\frac{3}{4}$	56	$13\frac{1}{4}$	12 + 11	N. America .	T. W. Wood, Jun.
-41	$8\frac{1}{2}$	...	...	$21\frac{3}{4}$	27	Chesincook, M.E.	Col. Hoselton.
-41	...	...	$54\frac{1}{2}$	...	12 + 11	Canada . .	General R. L. Dashwood.
-41	...	...	65	24	14 + 13	Manitoba .	Otho Shaw.
40	8	38	60	13	11 + 10	Canada . .	Viscount Powerscourt.
40	8	35	$55\frac{1}{2}$	13	12 + 11	Maine . .	J. S. Braithwaite.
$39\frac{7}{8}$	$6\frac{1}{2}$	...	$51\frac{3}{8}$	$15\frac{1}{8}$	13 + 12	N. America .	British Museum.
$-39\frac{1}{2}$	$8\frac{1}{2}$	...	$39\frac{7}{8}$	$13\frac{3}{4}$	...	Do. . .	Otho Shaw.
$39\frac{1}{2}$	7	38	$54\frac{1}{2}$	16	13 + 12	Canada . .	Sylvester Browne.
$39\frac{1}{2}$	$7\frac{3}{4}$	37	$56\frac{1}{2}$	$13\frac{1}{2}$	14 + 11	British Columbia	Sir Peter Walker, Bart.
$39\frac{1}{4}$	$7\frac{5}{8}$	$33\frac{1}{2}$	$49\frac{5}{8}$	$11\frac{1}{2}$	12 + 10	N. America .	J. Carr Saunders.
$39\frac{1}{8}$	$7\frac{5}{8}$	$36\frac{1}{4}$	$51\frac{3}{4}$	$9\frac{1}{2}$	8 + 7	E. slopes of the Rockies	J. C. L. Knight-Bruce.
39	$8\frac{1}{4}$	$38\frac{1}{2}$	57	$12\frac{1}{2}$	15 + 12	N. America .	Sir Edmund G. Loder, Bt.

[1] Height at shoulder, 8 ft. 2 in.?; skull horns, 68 lbs.; estimated weight, 2600 lbs.
[2] Height at shoulder stated to be 7 ft. 8 in.?

ELK or MOOSE (Alces machlis)—*continued.*

gth to igest ine.	Circumference above burr.	Tip to Tip.	Greatest width.	Breadth of Palm.	Points.	Locality.	Owner.
38½	7	...	52⅞	10⅞	11+10	N. America .	British Museum.
...	...	...	67	...	23	Yukon . .	J. H. Whitehouse.
38½	9½	44	66	14	28	New Brunswick	S. Decatur.
38¼	6⅛	34	49½	9¾	9+9	N. America .	Sir Victor Brooke's Collection.
38	7⅝	30½	47	12	12+12	British Columbia	Sir Peter Walker, Bart.
38	6½	...	59¼	9¾	11+11	?	H.R.H. the Duke of Saxe-Coburg and Gotha.
38	8	21½	57½	14	18+15	Manitoba . .	C. H. Akroyd.
38	11	50	61	14	26	New Brunswick	J. Bodkin.
37¾	8	...	51½	11¼	14+13	Canada . .	F. Ashby.
37½	8½	...	49½	11	21	?	Ernest Farquhar.
37¼	7⅛	35	50⅝	11⅝	13+10	New Brunswick	Hon. Charles Ellis.
35¾	7½	33½	47¾	11	12+11	Canada .	James J. Harrison.
35½	8¼	...	42 1/16	...	10+9	Do. . .	Paris Museum.
34½	8	39½	49½	10½	9+9	New Brunswick	P. N. Graham.
34¼	6⅝	42	51⅛	9½	10+9	Canada . .	G. Marchetti.
33½	7	28	44	11	13+13	N. America .	Dublin Museum.
33	6	30	44	10	10+10	Manitoba . .	Major C. S. Cumberland
32½	7	29¼	44	8	11+9	N. America .	Charles Makin.
31¾	7	...	...	...	14	Do. . .	A. Rogers.
31½	...	...	51½	12½	...	?	Earl of Lonsdale.
30	5½	...	40½	13	22	Montana . .	Theodore Roosevelt.
28¾	7⅜	35	49⅞	12½	11+11	New Brunswick	Hon. Charles Ellis.
27	5⅞	28	42	6¾	6+7	Eastern slopes of the Rockies	Hon. F. Thellusson.
26½	6¾	30	40	6	6+6	N. of Manitoba	P. B. Vander-Byl.

ELK or MOOSE (Alces machlis)—*continued.*

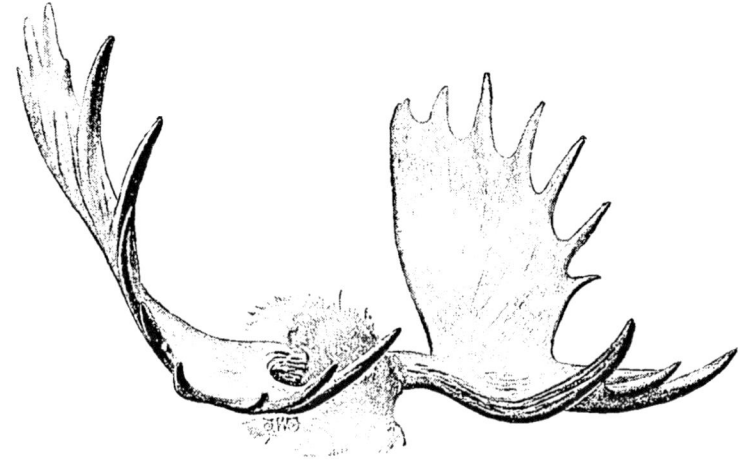

Antlers of Male Elk.

Length to longest tine.	Circumference above burr.	Tip to Tip.	Greatest width.	Breadth of Palm.	Points.	Locality.	Owner.
$37\frac{3}{4}$	8	$35\frac{3}{8}$	$57\frac{3}{4}$	$11\frac{1}{2}$	11 + 13	Norway . .	Thomas Bate.
33	$8\frac{1}{2}$	$36\frac{1}{4}$	$51\frac{3}{4}$	$15\frac{1}{4}$	10 + 10	Do. . .	Capt. Gerard Ferrand.
33	9	34	35	...	9 + 10	E. Prussia .	H.R.H. the Duke of Saxe-Coburg and Gotha.
$32\frac{1}{2}$	$7\frac{1}{2}$	33	46	$11\frac{1}{2}$	10 + 10	Sweden . .	Capt. Gerard Ferrand.
32	6	...	$43\frac{3}{4}$	$9\frac{1}{2}$	7 + 8	Russia . .	Sir Edward Caley, British Museum.
32	$8\frac{3}{4}$	$37\frac{1}{2}$	48	$11\frac{1}{2}$	10 + 9	Nr. St. Petersburg	Prince Demidoff.
32	7	...	52	9	9 + 9	Norway . .	} H. J. Elwes.
...	7	35	$42\frac{1}{2}$	...	9 + 7	Do. . .	
31	7	28	45	...	17	Do. . .	S. Ratcliff.
$30\frac{3}{4}$	$6\frac{1}{2}$	43	46	$10\frac{1}{2}$	15	Do. . .	Abel Chapman.
$30\frac{1}{2}$	8	27	$40\frac{1}{2}$	$9\frac{1}{2}$	10 + 7	Do. . .	Lieut.-Col. G. D. F. Sulivan.
$30\frac{1}{8}$	$7\frac{1}{8}$	$29\frac{1}{2}$	$44\frac{1}{2}$	10	9 + 8	Do. . .	Sir Victor Brooke's Collection.
29	6	$30\frac{1}{2}$	$42\frac{1}{2}$	$7\frac{1}{2}$	11 + 9	Do. . .	Sir H. Pottinger, Bart.
29	$6\frac{1}{2}$	$31\frac{1}{2}$	$39\frac{1}{2}$	$6\frac{1}{2}$	10 + 9	Do. . .	Do.
29	$7\frac{1}{2}$	...	$43\frac{1}{2}$	$10\frac{1}{2}$	24	Do. . .	Sir Peter Walker, Bart.
$28\frac{1}{2}$	$7\frac{1}{2}$	$24\frac{3}{4}$	42	$9\frac{1}{2}$	10 + 9	Do. . .	Sir H. Pottinger, Bart.

¹ Estimated weight, 90 stone.

ELK or MOOSE (Alces machlis)—*continued.*

Length to longest tine.	Circumference above burr.	Tip to Tip.	Greatest Width.	Breadth of Palm.	Points.	Locality.	Owner.
$-28\frac{1}{2}$	6	$33\frac{1}{4}$	$43\frac{1}{4}$	11	$12+10$	Lithuania	Prince Radziwill.
28	$6\frac{1}{4}$	32	47	9	$8+8$	Norway .	Sir H. Pottinger, Bart.
28	$7\frac{1}{2}$	$31\frac{1}{2}$	38	10	$12+10$	Sweden . .	Viscount Powerscourt.
$-27\frac{1}{2}$	7	$25\frac{1}{2}$	33	$8\frac{3}{4}$	$5+5$	Lithuania	Count Scheibler.
-27	$6\frac{3}{4}$	30	39	...	20	Norway . .	S. Ratcliff.
27	$6\frac{1}{2}$	40	$43\frac{1}{2}$	...	$8+7$	Do. . .	J. H. Barnard.
27	$6\frac{1}{2}$	$20\frac{1}{2}$	38	9	$8+6$	Nr. St. Petersburg	Prince Demidoff.
$-26\frac{3}{4}$	$8\frac{1}{4}$	$28\frac{1}{2}$	$41\frac{3}{4}$	$9\frac{1}{8}$	$8+8$	Norway . .	Sir H. Pottinger, Bart.
$26\frac{1}{2}$	$6\frac{1}{4}$	25	38	6	$9+7$	Russia .	Lieut.-Col. Hon. W. Coke.
$26\frac{1}{8}$	$6\frac{1}{2}$	...	$39\frac{3}{8}$	$6\frac{7}{8}$	$5+4$	S. Russia .	British Museum.
26	6	$27\frac{1}{4}$	$42\frac{1}{2}$	7	$7+6$	Norway .	Lord Delamere.
26	$6\frac{1}{2}$	29	37	5	$6+5$	Do. . .	Sir H. Pottinger, Bart.
$23\frac{1}{2}$	$5\frac{3}{4}$	...	$35\frac{3}{4}$	5	$5+3$	Do.	E. N. Buxton.
23	6	$27\frac{1}{2}$	36	6	$7+6$	Sweden . .	Sir H. Pottinger, Bart.

Antlers of Caspian Red Deer. From a Hungarian specimen in the collection of Viscount Powerscourt. Counting from the skull upwards, the first tine is the brow, the second the bez, and the third the trez, above which come the surroyals, or crown. The main shaft is termed the beam.

RED DEER (Cervus elaphus).

The red deer of Western Europe is the typical representative of the genus *Cervus*, in which the antlers of the males are set on the skull at an oblique angle to the middle line of the forehead, and always have a brow tine, while they are generally more or less nearly cylindrical, although sometimes palmated. There is always a large bare portion on the muzzle, the face is long, the ears are generally large, and the tail is comparatively short, often extremely so. Although there is almost always a gland and tuft on the hind cannon-bone, usually situated high up, there is none on the hock itself. The coat may be spotted.

In the red deer the antlers are subcylindrical and complex, generally with a bez tine, and always with a trez, the number of points exceeding five, and the crown frequently forming a cup. The tail is relatively long and pointed, and there is a distinct light-coloured patch on the buttocks, which includes the tail ; the general colour of the adult summer coat being reddish brown, and that of the winter dress grayish brown, while the young are profusely spotted.

Red deer, in the widest sense of the term, are inhabitants of Europe, North Africa, Asia Minor, and Northern Persia. In the typical red deer (*C. elaphus typicus*) of Western, Northern, and Central Europe, the antlers attain their maximum degree of complexity, sometimes having twenty or even more points, although in many Scotch examples the bez tine is wanting. In a park red deer killed at Spetchley Park the weight was 419 lbs. gross, and 216 when cleaned; while in one shot at Knowsley many years ago the clean weight was no less than 424 lbs. The height at the shoulder now reaches about 4 feet. H.R.H. the Duke of Braganza saw a continental stag shot which scaled 41 stone 10 lbs. two years ago, and last year H.R.H. shot a 10-pointer with a spread of 55 inches.

The Corsican red deer (*C. elaphus corsicanus*), of Corsica and Sardinia, is a very small race, with the bez tine of the antlers wanting, and the general colour of the upper parts dark brown in summer and blackish in winter. Nearly allied is the North African red deer (*C. elaphus barbarus*), which is of rather larger dimensions, with a grayish-brown streak down the middle of the back, and small irregular whitish spots on the flanks and sometimes on the back; traces of such spots being occasionally observable in the summer coat of does of the typical race. The bez tine seems to be very generally wanting.

The Caspian red deer (*C. elaphus maral*) is a large variety, described on page 33.

Lord Tweedmouth furnishes the following dimensions of his fine Scotch stag:—

Widest span over all, 39¼ inches; span inside below cups, 34 inches; span outside below cups, 37 inches.

Right antler.—Length, 39 inches; length of brow, 10¼ inches; of bez, 10 inches; of trez, 13 inches. Length of tines in cup, 10, 7, 4¼ inches. Circumference at coronet, 8½ inches; between bez and trez, 7¼ inches; above trez, 6 inches.

Left antler.—Length, 38 inches; of brow, 10 inches; of bez, 8 inches; of trez, 11 inches. Length of tines in cup, 8, 6, and 4 inches. Circumference at coronet, 9 inches; between bez and trez, 7½ inches; above tray, 6¼ inches.

Shot, October 9, 1880. Weight, 21 stone 9 lbs.; clean, but stag was much run.

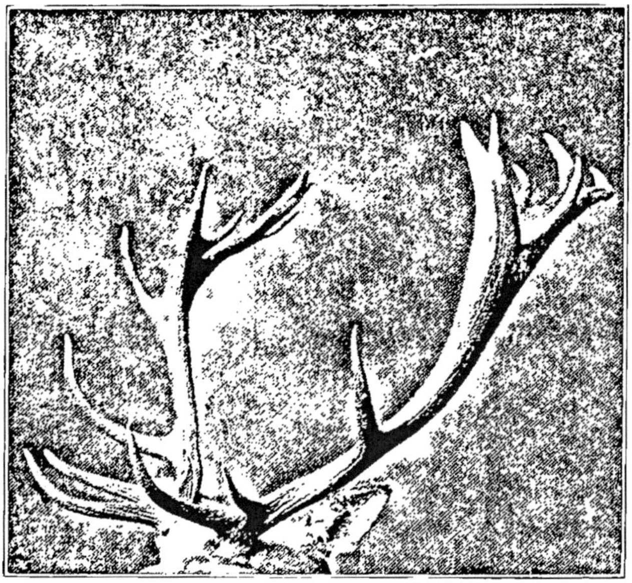

From a Photograph by Whyte.

Antlers of Red Deer killed by Lord Burton, with fully developed cups.

a.—SCOTCH RED DEER.

Length on outside curve.	Circumference between bez and trez.	Tip to Tip.	Widest inside.	Spread.	Points.	Weight.	Locality.	Owner.
						st. lbs.		
-41	7	22½	35	...	7+7	...	Inverness (1794)	W. H. Walker.
[1]-40	6	...	30	...	10	14.7	Glentilt	Duke of Atholl.
-39	7¼	...	34	39¼	6+6	21.9	Guisachan	Lord Tweedmouth.
-37⅝	...	20⅜	26½	...	7+7	...	?	Sir Humphrey de Trafford, Bart.
37⅜	5⅝	14¾	26⅛	...	6+7	...	?	H.R.H. the Duke of Saxe-Coburg and Gotha.
37¼	5	14¾	24¾	...	6+5	...	?	Do.
[1]-36½	...	...	35	12	...	...	Glenmoriston	Col. W. Gordon-Cumming.
36½	5	34	39½	41	5+6	...	Glenstrathfarrar	Viscount Powerscourt (shot by the late Roualeyn Gordon-Cumming).
36½	6½	31½	32½	...	6+6	...	?	Sir Humphrey de Trafford, Bart.
36¼	7	22¾	28	...	7+7	...	?	Do.
-36	...	...	36	42	13	...	Monymusk (1795)	The late Capt. Johnstone Grant.
36	5½	16¼	28	36	7+7	...	?	Duke of Portland.

[1] Recorded by J. G. Millais.

SCOTCH RED DEER—*continued.*

Length on outside curve.	Circumference between bez and trez.	Tip to Tip.	Widest inside.	Outside spread.	Points.	Weight. st. lbs.	Locality.	Owner.
36	4¼	21½	27	...	6+6	...	Caenlochan .	Henry Tate.
35½	4¾	27½	34	36⅜	4+3	...	Do.	Do.
35½	5½	...	25½	...	6+6	17 6	Sutherland .	Abel Chapman.
35½	6	...	...	29	12	19	Auchnashellach	The late Lord Alexander Paget.
35¼	4½	17½	30	...	5+6	17 6	Glenisla, Forfarshire	Viscount Powerscourt.
-35½	7	...	26½	...	20	...	Glenquoich .	Lord Burton. (See illustration.)
35½	4¾	27½	34	36⅜	4+3	...	Caenlochan .	Henry Tate.
-35¼	4⅞	31$\frac{7}{16}$	30	...	6+6	...	Deanich, Ross-shire	G. Percy V. Aylmer.
35	4¾	22	28	...	7+6	...	Talladh-a-Bheithe, Rannoch	E. Weller-Poley.
-35	...	...	...	34	10	16 1	N. Morar .	Capt. T. W. Gill.
-35	...	...	29	41¼	7+6	...	?	Sir Arthur Grant, Bart.
[1]-35	5¾	26	33½	37½	12	...	Guisachan .	Lord Tweedmouth.
[2]-35	4½	...	...	27½	8	...	Cairn Thomais Gaick	John Hargreave.
-34¾	...	...	...	31½	3+2	16 12	Cluanie .	Hon. T. A. Brassey.
34½	5¼	37½	34½	...	12	...	Braemore .	Sir John Fowler, Bart.
34½	4¼	18¼	27	...	6+5	...	N. Morar .	J. R. Hutchison.
[2]-34½	5	...	...	34½	12	16 7 (clean)	Glentilt .	Duke of Atholl.
34½	6	17¾	25	31¼	5+4	15 12	Caenlochan .	Mrs. Henry Tate.
34¼	4⅛	16¼	24⅜	...	5+5	...	Auchnasheen	F. Devas.
-34	5½	...	...	30	Switch	...	Letterewe .	Hon. T. A. Brassey.
34	4⅛	17¼	26¾	29	5+4	...	Caenlochan .	W. A. L. Fletcher.
34	...	...	30	...	11	17 2	N. Morar	Capt. T. W. Gill.
34	4	28½	30¾	...	5+4	...	Glenmuick .	J. Ponsonby.
34	4¼	12	23½	...	5+4	...	?	C. A. Grenfell.
34	4	16⅜	...	...	5+4	...	Blair-Atholl	Captain A. W. E. Count Gleichen.
-34	4⅜	19	28	...	6+5	...	Rothiemurchus, Inverness	A. Basil Brooke.
[1]-34	...	...	...	...	11	...	Braemar	Col. Gordon-Cumming.
[1]-34	4¾	...	...	36½	12	...	Glenbruar, Perthshire	Sir W. Ogilvie Dalgleish.

[1] Above trez.   [2] Recorded by J. G. Millais.

SCOTCH RED DEER—*continued.*

Length on outside curve.	Circumference between bez and trez.	Tip to Tip.	Widest inside.	Outside spread.	Points.	Weight.	Locality.	Owner.
						st. lbs.		
2-34	4⅞	...	...	30	10	...	Morar	W. Stirling.
2 34	7	...	...	26	14	...	Glenartney	Earl of Ancaster.
33¾	5½	19½	25½	...	5+5	...	?	H. S. O'Brien.
-33½	5	...	34½	...	5+5	20	Dalness	J. G. Millais.
33½	4	16½	25	29	5+5	...	Caenlochan	H. C. Pilkington.
-30½	4½	...	27	...	12	...	Kintail	Sir Edmund G. Loder, Bart.
33	4⅛	8⅛	20¾	24¾	4+4	...	Ben Alder	Julius Wernher.
33	4¼	24¾	28½	33½	5+4	15 12	Do.	F. C. Selous.
33	4¾	21½	28¾	33	4+4	...	Kintail	R. P. Page.
-32¾	5	25¾	29¼	...	6+6	...	Ardverikie	W. H. Walker.
32¾	4½	...	28	...	5+4	...	?	Sir Charles Tennant, Bart.
32½	4¼	16½	26¼	...	5+5	...	Auchnashellach	G. Webster.
32¼	4¾	20¾	28	...	5+5	...	Morar	J. R. Hutchison.
32	4	25¾	25	28	5+5	...	Invercauld	Otto Beit.
32	5	...	22½	...	5+4	19	Rannoch	Sir W. G. Pearce, Bart.
1 32	4½	31	29½	40	7+9	...	Rhidorrach	Viscount Powerscourt.
32	4	24½	29	...	4+4	...	Braulen	J. K. Fowler.
-32	...	...	...	34	10	...	Kintail	Sir Edmund G. Loder, Bart.
31¾	3¾	...	26½	...	4+4	...	Rhidorrach	Captain F. Cookson.
31¾	4¾	18	24¾	...	6+5	14	Inchgrundle	Countess of Dudley.
31½	4½	16	21	23½	6+5	...	Shank	R. K. Micklethwait.
31½	4¾	22	28¾	31¼	3+3	...	Caenlochan	E. L. Fletcher.
31½	4	12½	21½	25¼	6+4	...	Do.	W. W. Gossage.
31½	5	...	26½	...	12	17	Auchnasheen	J. F. Laycock.
31½	4	22	26¼	32½	7+6	...	Kintail	R. P. Page.
31½	4	24½	29	...	5+4	...	Braulen	J. Talbot Clifton.
31½	4¼	21	25½	...	4+4	15 3	Invermark	W. S. M. Burns.
31½	4⅜	20¼	25¾	...	3+3	...	Dalnacardoch	Hon. T. A. Brassey.

Above trez.   2 Recorded by J. G. Millais.

SCOTCH RED DEER—*continued.*

Length on outside curve.	Circumference between bez and trez.	Tip to Tip.	Widest inside.	Outside spread.	Points.	Weight. st. lbs.	Locality.	Owner.
31⅜	4⅜	8⅝	24	...	5+5	...	Glenmuick	C. Lawrence.
-31¼	5½	25½	29	...	Switch	...	Achdalien	M. K. North.
31¼	4⅛	16	24⅛	...	7+5	...	Rhidorrach	Capt. F. Cookson.
31¼	4⅝	24⅞	32	...	5+3	...	Ross-shire	E. Lort-Phillips.
31¼	4	...	40¼	...	6+6	...	?	Dr. Fancourt Barnes.
31¼	4	15	25	...	5+4	...	Auchnashellach	W. Maxwell Lyte.
31	4¾	24	25	...	5+5	...	Morar	J. R. Hutchison.
-31	5½	32½	...	38	5+4	...	Inverlochy	Mrs. J. E. Platt.
-31	5¼	20¼	24	...	10	...	?	C. V. A. Peel.
31	4¾	19¼	23¼	33¼	8+6	...	S. Harris	Earl of Dunmore.
31	4⅝	24½	28¼	...	5+4	...	Caenlochan	F. W. Robinson.
-31	4½	20	15	...	8+7	...	?	J. Benett-Stanford.
31	4½	16½	23½	29	6+5	...	Inversanda	J. Hamilton Leigh.
30⅞	4⅜	25⅞	28⅛	...	5+6	...	Rhidorrach	W. R. Cookson.
30¾	5	19½	24	...	6+5	...	Arisaig	J. R. Hutchison.
30¾	4¼	13	23¼	...	5+4	14	Invergarry	Guy Stephenson.
30½	3⅞	24¾	31	33¼	3+3	...	Inversanda	J. Hamilton Leigh.
30½	4⅛	13½	23½	...	6+6	...	Letterewe	Gordon Wood.
30½	4¼	17¼	24¾	...	7+6	...	Rhidorrach	J. Talbot Clifton.
30½	4½	18½	24	...	4+3	14	Glen Tana	Major Hon. A. H. Henniker.
30½	4	25½	28¾	...	4+3	...	Auchnashellach	Capt. H. Reynolds, R.N.
30½	4¼	22¼	29	31	3+3	...	?	L. Breitmeyer.
30¼	4⅛	20	25½	...	6+5	...	?	H.R.H. le Duc d'Orléans.
30	4⅜	...	25½	...	5+5	15	Blackmount	J. G. Millais.
29¾	4	32½	...	...	5+5	16	Do.	Do.
29½	4½	24¾	29	...	4+5	...	?	Marquis Camden.
29¼	6½	...	27⅞	...	...	16 11	Blackmount	Marquis of Breadalbane.
29	4	...	29	31	6+6	...	Inverness	H. Seton-Karr.

The widths of the six widest heads in the Duke of Fife's collection are as follows :—

| 40 | 38 | 37 | 35 | 35 | 35 |

The six longest antlers of this celebrated collection are respectively—

| 37 | 36 | 35½ | 35½ | 35 | 35 |

The antlers of one of the red deer in Mr. Lucas's Park at Warnham Court, Sussex, in 1889, had 34 points ; 1890, 34 points ; 1891, 37 points ; 1891, 47 points and weighed 17 lbs. ; 1893, 45 points, 16½ lbs.

For an interesting account of many fine specimens the reader is referred to *British Deer and their Horns*, by J. G. Millais.

b.—IRISH RED DEER.

Length on outside curve.	Circumference between bez and trez.	Tip to Tip.	Widest inside.	Points.	Weight.		Locality.	Owner.
					st.	lbs.		
1-42½	...	...	...	12	22	7	Colebrooke .	Sir Douglas Brooke, Bart.
-41	6	17½	23	10+9	23	3	Do.	Do.
-40	5½	28	29½	8+8	25	5	Do. .	Do.
39⅝	5¼	14½	26⅜	7+7	26	11	Do. . .	Do.
38	5⅜	20	30⅝	10+8	25	0 (clean)	Do. .	Do.
35	4¾	...	30	9	...		Ireland	Hon. A. Charteris.
35	5⅛	19⅝	26¾	6+5	20	2	Powerscourt Park	Viscount Powerscourt.
35	5¼	21¼	29	5+5	{ 24 st. as he fell 18 st. clean		Do. .	Do.
34½	5	12½	22½	5+5	{ 24 st. as he fell 18 st. clean		Do. . .	Do.
34	4½	25½	28½	6+6	{ 26 st. as he fell 20 st. clean		Do. .	Do.
34	5	20½	26	6+6	20 st. clean		Do. .	Do.
34	4¾	...	31½	6+5	26	8	Muckross .	Ralph Sneyd.
34	4⅛	13⅛	25	5+5	...		Colebrooke · .	Capt. J. M. Rogers.
33¾	5	...	26	5+5	22	0	Muckross .	Hon. Mrs. Bourke.
31	4¾	11	20¾	7+7	...		Do. .	Ralph Sneyd.
-31	4¾	18½	22	5+7	...		?	Dublin Museum.
30¼	4	...	26½	5+5	19	10	Muckross .	Geoffrey Carr-Glyn.
29¾	4¾	21¼	24½	6+6	...		Colebrooke . .	Montrose Cloete.

1 See Millais's *British Deer and their Horns*.

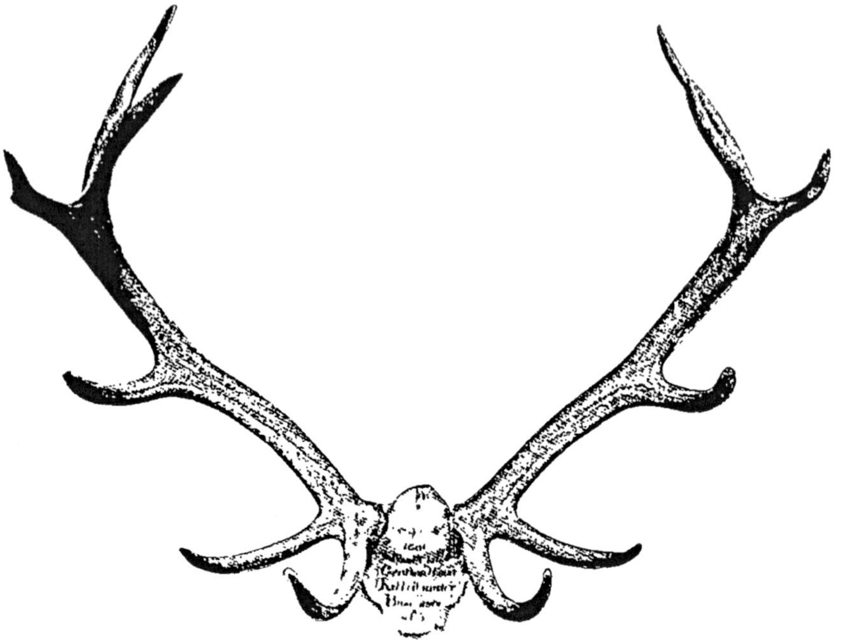

Antlers of Exmoor Stag.

c.—WEST OF ENGLAND RED DEER.

Length on outside curve.	Circumference between bez and trez.	Tip to Tip.	Widest inside.	Points.	Locality.	Owner.
[1]41	5¼	21½	32¼	5 + 5	Exmoor . .	Sir John Heathcoat-Amory, Bart.: killed in 1897 with the Devon and Somerset Stag-hounds.
39	5¾	15¾	28½	6 + 6	Do. . . .	R. A. Sanders.
38½	5⅛	17⅞	31½	6 + 6	Quantock Hills .	Viscount Ebrington; killed in 1885.
37½	5	22¼	30¼	7 + 7	Exmoor . . .	C. Nelder; killed in 1803.
36¾	6	21½	28⅞	6 + 7	Do. . . .	Sir A. Acland-Hood, Bart.: killed in 1893.
35½	5	20⅞	27½	6 + 6	Do. . . .	Earl Fortescue; killed in 1812.
35	5	15¾	27	6 + 5	Do. . . .	Com. G. F. Inglefield, R.N.
35	4⅞	25½	32¾	5 + 6	Do. . . .	Sir C. T. D. Acland, Bart.; killed in 1893.
34⅝	5⅝	23¼	31¼	6 + 6	Do. . . .	Viscount Ebrington; killed in 1881.
[2]–33	6½	...	29	6 + 6	Do. . . .	The late Sir T. D. Acland, Bart.; killed in 1788.
[3]–33	5¼	...	29½	9 + 7	Do. . . .	,, ,, 1792.
–33	5⅜	39	32	7 + 7	Do. . . .	,, ,, 1877.
33	5⅜	13	25	8 + 7	Do. . . .	Viscount Ebrington; killed in 1881.
32	5⅛	30⅜	30¾	7 + 4	Do. . . .	Earl Fortescue; killed in 1814.
32	4½	15¾	26	6 + 6	Do. . . .	Col. J. F. Hornby.
30½	5	24½	29½	6 + 6	Do. . . .	Earl Fortescue.

1 Weight 333 lbs., clean. Length of brow-tine, 17 inches. 2 Weight, 17 stone 2 lbs.
3 See *Red Deer* in Fur and Feather Series.

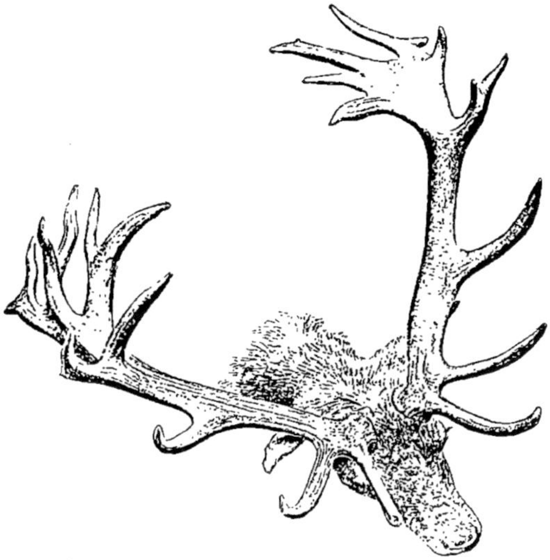

Head of Stoke Park Red Deer.

d.—ENGLISH PARK RED DEER.

Length on outside curve.	Circumference between bez and trez.	Tip to Tip.	Widest inside.	Spread.	Points.	Weight.	Locality.	Owner.
-42½	6¾	..	..	40	12	...	Melbury, Dorset	Earl of Ilchester.
41¼	5	[1] 22¾	32	...	7 + 6	...	Langley Park	J. G. Millais.
-40	...	..	...	41	7 + 7	...	?	Sir Greville Smyth, Bart.
-37½	7½	29½	27½	36½	10 + 9	...	Welbeck .	Duke of Portland.
-37	7¾	...	...	37	23	31 st. (clean)	Warnham .	T. Lucas.
-36	6½	24	30	...	6 + 6	...	Vaynol, North Wales	G. W. D. Assheton-Smith.
36	[1] 5½	19	28½	...	9 + 11	...	Woburn .	Duke of Bedford.
-35	6	14½	24	...	6 + 6	...	Vaynol, North Wales	G. W. D. Assheton-Smith.
34½	7	33	26¾	...	20 + 20	.	Warnham .	W. H. Lucas.
34¼	[1] 5½	18½	26	...	8 + 8	...	Woburn .	Duke of Bedford.
34	4½	...	23	...	6 + 6	..	Stowe . .	H.R.H. la Comtesse de Paris.
34	5⅝	21¾	28½	...	7 + 7	...	Dorset . .	Earl of Ilchester.
34	6½	...	...	48 (about)	45	...	Warnham .	C. T. Lucas.
33½	4⅞	...	33	...	6 + 6	...	Stowe . .	H.R.H. le Duc d'Orléans.
33½	5¼	21½	28½	...	9 + 9	...	Woburn .	Duke of Bedford.
33	7 above trez	...	...	45½	44	...	Warnham .	C. T. Lucas.

Some of the above measurements are recorded by J. G. Millais in *British Deer and their Horns.*

[1] White Stag.

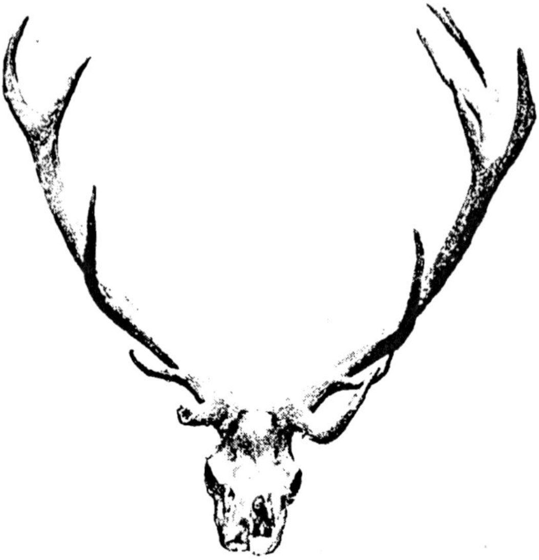

Skull and Antlers of Old English Red Deer.
(Found in cutting the Manchester Ship Canal.)

C.—ANCIENT BRITISH RED DEER.

Length on outside curve.	Circumference between bez and trez.	Tip to Tip.	Widest inside.	Spread.	Points	Where dug up.	Owner.
47½	8	35	...	...	5+8	Manchester Ship Canal excavations	Sir R. M. Brooke, Bart.
40	7½	22¼	28½	43¼	12+9	Combermere .	Duke of Westminster.
38½	5	18	30	39¼	8+6	Ireland . .	Viscount Powerscourt.
36½	5	24	25	35½	8+8	Do. . .	Do.
36	5½	23	27	37½	10+9	Kerry, Ireland .	Do.
[1] 36	5⅞	...	...	42½	23	South Ireland .	Sir Douglas Brooke, Bart.
35½	5¼	26½	32⅜	42½	13+11	Do. .	Sir Victor Brooke's Collection.
35¼	5⅛	31¼	27¾	...	12+10	Ireland . .	Viscount Powerscourt.
35	7	...	21	24	9+11	England . .	C. G. Burrow.
34½	5	22	30	...	10+10	Ireland . .	Viscount Powerscourt.
33	4¾	27	28¼	35¼	9+8	Do. . .	Do.

[1] Recorded by J. G. Millais.

f.—NORWEGIAN RED DEER.

"Hitteren may still be considered the headquarters of the red deer in Norway. These animals (unlike the elk, which would appear to be diminishing) are increasing in numbers, and are now found in districts where they were previously unknown. Of 138 killed in the whole country last year fifteen were shot in South Bergenhus, twelve in Romsdal, and thirty-one in North Bergenhus Amt" (SNOWFLY, *Field*, 11th December 1897).

Length on outside curve.	Circumference between bez and trez.	Tip to Tip.	Widest inside.	Spread.	Points.	Weight.	Locality.	Owner.
–34	...	...	...	...	7	...	Norway . .	J. H. Thomas.
31¾	4¾	...	25½	...	6+5	...	Do. . .	A. Brassey.
31½	4½	...	24½	...	5+5	...	Do. .	H. Seton-Karr.
31½	4¾	...	28	...	4+3	...	Do.	E. M. Denny.
31	4¼	23	25	29½	6+6	..	Do. .	J. H. Thomas.
30	5	...	29	...	12	20 st.	Do. .	E. M. Denny.
–30	4¼	...	28	33	5+4	...	Do. . .	H. Seton-Karr.
30	4¼	29¼	30¾	...	5+4	...	Do. .	Do.
29½	4⅞	18½	23¼	...	5+5	...	Do. .	J. H. Thomas.
29¼	4⅝	26	30¼	...	6+5	...	Do.	G. L. Denmar.
28¼	4	27	25	...	4+4	...	Do. .	H. F. Kemp.
–28	5⅛	Single Antler			5	...	Do.	H. Seton-Karr.
27½	5	26	26	...	5+6	...	Do. .	J H. Thomas.
26¼	4¼	19¾	21¾	...	4+4	...	Do.	Do.
26	4½	...	30	32½	6+5	20 st. 9 lbs.	Do. . .	H. Seton-Karr.
24¾	3½	21	20¼	...	2+2	...	Do. .	A. Henderson.

g.—SPANISH RED DEER.

[1]–40	...	...	36½	...	17	Sierra Morena, Spain	Abel Chapman.
–37½	...	...	34½	...	15	Sierra Morena .	Do.
36	5½	37	...	...	15	South Spain . .	The late Lord Lilford.
–32½	...	...	...	...	13	Plains of Andalucia .	W. J. Buck.
–29	5¼	...	25	...	12	Andalucia . .	Abel Chapman.
–28½	5¼	...	26¼	...	13	Do. . .	Do.

[1] A mountain head.

Some of the specimens in this list from Eastern Europe probably belong to the Maral, or Caspian, race.

Number of Points.	Weight in lbs. Avoirdupois.	Length along Curve.	Circumference of Burr.	Circumference above Burr.	Circumference above Middle Point.	Circumference below Crown.	Circumference between Bez and Trez.	Tip to Tip.	Widest inside.	Spread.	Weight of Stag.	Locality.	Owner.
- 18	over 20	53 9/16	11 1/4	10	...	15 1/2	10	...	...	...	206 kilos or 32 stone 5 lb.	Galicia	H.R.H. D. Miguel, Duke Braganza.
- 16	23.36	53.54	10.04	8.47	7.28	8.20	8.75	11 1/2	32	41 1/2	250 kilos	Zemplen Comitat	Count Géza Andrassy.
- 18	20.5	52	...	...	...	...	7.25	...	32.75	45	36 stone, cut up	Galicia	E. N. Buxton.
- 14	23	51	11	8 1/2	7	9	7.20	27	38	47	236 kilos	Zemplen Comitat	Count Géza Andrassy.
- 11	...	51	...	...	...	...	5.5	38.5	42.5	45.25	...	Hungary	Viscount Powerscourt (a).
[1] 14	...	51	...	...	...	...	7.25	23.5	39.5	50	...	Do.	Do.
- 14	...	50	...	...	...	...	6	42	40	...	...	La Mandria	J. J. S. Whitaker.
- 21	21.3	50.4	...	6.08	...	...	...	30	...	55.9	...	Pilis Mountains	Duke of Ratibor.
- 14	31 and an oz. or two	49 11/15	...	...	...	...	...	...	39 3/4	...	...	Radauc	Prince Lulu Rohan.
- 18	...	49 3/8	10 1/4	9 1/16	6 1/16	9 1/8	...	...	...	48 3/4	354 lbs.	Hungary	Count Joseph Hoyos.
- 12	21	49	10 3/16	...	...	...	...	...	...	...	...	Do.	Prince Philip of Saxe-Coburg and Gotha.
- 16	...	49	...	...	...	...	...	...	...	43	...	Carpathians	Prince Henry of Liechtenstein.
- 20	25.3	48.8	...	...	...	...	...	...	...	...	...	?	Prince Hugo Windischgraetz.
- 14	...	48 1/2	...	...	...	...	6 3/4	34	30	37 1/2	...	Carpathians	Lieut.-Col. L. Marshall.
- 19	...	48	8 7/8	...	...	...	...	...	...	...	...	Do.	Prince Henry of Liechtenstein.
- 19	...	48	9	...	...	...	...	...	27	48	...	Gotha	H.R.H. the Duke of Saxe Coburg and Gotha.
- 20	...	48	...	...	...	...	6 1/2	33 3/4	41 1/2	51 3/4	...	Germany	Viscount Powerscourt (c).
[1] 18	...	48	...	...	...	...	?	38	43	58	...	Hungary	Do.

[1] Dug up.

OTHER CONTINENTAL RED DEER—*continued.*

Number of Points.	Weight in lbs. Avoirdupois.	Length along Curve.	Circumference of Burr.	Circumference above Burr.	Circumference above Middle Point.	Circumference below Crown.	Circumference between Bez and Trez.	Tip to Tip.	Widest inside.	Spread.	Weight of Stag.	Locality.	Owner.
– 14	23	48	10	9½	7¼	12	7½	13	25	32	37 stone 1 lb.	Galicia	H.R.H. D. Miguel, Duke of Braganza.
– 16	20·57	47·84	11·21	9·25	7·87	7·87	...	...	...	...	...	Hungary	Prince Philip of Saxe-Coburg and Gotha.
15	...	47½	...	...	...	...	5¾	30	40	50	...	Do.	Viscount Powerscourt.
– 16	...	47¼	11½	8 11/16	7⅛	8½	...	35¾	25¼	29 9/16	242 kilos	Do.	Count Ferdinand Trauttmansdorff.
13	...	47	...	...	...	...	6¼	12¾	31½	...	...	Galicia	A. von André.
8	...	47	...	...	...	...	6½	23	38½	...	...	Germany	Viscount Powerscourt (*a*).
– 20	20·79	46·46	9.84	7·87	7·09	7·87	...	...	...	...	...	Hungary	Count Fery Nádasdy.
– 16	20·68	46·46	11·02	9·45	8·07†	6·89	...	...	...	...	...	Do.	Prince Victor Ratibor.
– 22	...	46¼	9 11/16	9½	6¾	8 11/16	...	52⅞	39¾	42⅞	479 lbs.	Do.	Count Max Hoyos.
– 16	19·91	46·06	11·81	9·25	6·89†	7·28	...	...	...	...	...	Do.	Count Mittrovszky.
– 20	22·55	46·06	10·63	9·05	6·69	8·46	...	...	...	...	...	Do.	Count Bela Szechenyi.
– 14	...	46	...	...	...	...	...	...	36	...	...	Carpathians	Prince Henry of Liechtenstein.
16	...	46	...	...	...	...	6¾	38	42¼	53	...	Hungary	Viscount Powerscourt (*e*).
13	...	46	9	...	...	...	7¾	19¾	31	...	...	N. Germany	Do. (*d*).
– 18	...	46	...	9	...	...	...	...	36	60	...	Gotha	H.R.H. the Duke of Saxe-Coburg and Gotha.
15	...	46	...	...	...	...	5¾	32	39½	50½	...	Hungary	Viscount Powerscourt.
– 13	...	46	...	...	...	...	7¼	...	29½	37	...	Carpathians	Prince Altenburg.
– 18	...	46	10	...	...	...	...	...	35	54½	...	Bukowina, Hungary	Count Erbach.

−20	17·05	45·27	10·04	8·07	7·28†	7·48	...	...	...	...	...	Do. .	Count George Erdödy.
−12	20·46	45·27	9·84	6·49	6·69	7·48	...	...	...	...	...	Do. .	Count Belà Szechenyi.
−15	...	45¼	9⅞	...	...	...	...	23⅝	34¼	...	...	Roumania .	Prince Demeter Ghika.
−22	...	45⅛	12	9⅝	7	14 9/16	8¾	29 3/16	34¼	...	...	Hungary .	Prince Henry of Liechtenstein.
19	...	45	...	...	...	...	6½	23	37	...	...	Germany .	Viscount Powerscourt (*b*).
15	...	45	...	...	...	...	5½	23½	36½	43	...	Do. .	Do.
−11	...	45	...	9	...	...	...	38	33	...	...	Gotha	H.R.H. the Duke of Saxe Coburg and Gotha.
−11	...	45	...	...	...	...	6	...	39	46·5	...	Galicia .	E. N. Buxton.
20	...	44½	...	...	...	...	7¼	14⅓	28¾	...	...	Carpathians	Viscount Powerscourt (*g*).
17	...	44½	...	...	...	...	7½	17	32	...	...	Hungary .	Major-Gen. Sir Arthur Ellis K.C.V.O.
−20	15·73	44·49	9·05	7·87	9·05	12·21	...	...	...	...	...	Do. .	Count Tassilo Festetics.
−14	16·17	44·49	10·63	9·45	6·49†	8·07	...	...	...	...	...	Do.	Count Belà Szechenyi.
−8	17·38	44·09	11·41	9·84	7·68†	7·68	...	...	...	...	...	Do. .	Count Michael Esterhazy.
−14	18·37	44·09	11·41	10·24	7·28	6·89	...	...	..	...	...	Do. .	Jeno Kund.
17	...	44	...	...	...	...	7¾	31	39¼	55¼	...	Germany .	Viscount Powerscourt.
16	...	44	...	...	...	...	6¾	23¼	33	...	...	Do. .	Do. (*h*).
8	...	44	...	...	...	...	5¾	24½	39	...	...	Hungary .	A. von André.
−18	19·14	43·7	10·04	8·46	7·09†	9·64	...	...	...	...	...	Do. .	Count Rudolph Erdödy.
−14	20·24	43·7	10·43	8·27	7·09†	7·28	...	...	...	...	...	Do. .	F. Pausinger.
−20	18	43·6	10·02	8·03	...	12·23	7·64	36·06	25·12	...	...	Do.	Count Tassilo Festetics.
12	...	43½	11	...	6¼	5¾	6¼	15	29½	36	...	Do.	A. von André.
−20	17·6	43·31	10·04	8·07	7·28	8·27	...	...	...	...	...	Do. .	Count Tassilo Festetics.
−14	15·95	43·31	10·43	8·66	7·09	7·28	...	...	...	...	...	Do.	Prince Philip of Saxe-Coburg and Gotha.
21	...	43	...	...	..	...	6½	37½	38¼	...	...	Germany .	Viscount Powerscourt (*j*).

OTHER CONTINENTAL RED DEER—*continued.*

Number of Points.	Weight in lbs. Avoirdupois.	Length along Curve.	Circumference of Burr.	Circumference above Burr.	Circumference above Middle Point.	Circumference below Crown.	Circumference between Bez and Trez.	Tip to Tip.	Widest inside.	Spread.	Weight of Stag.	Locality.	Owner.
– 16	18·92	42·91	10·04	8·66	7·48	8·27	...	...	...	...	...	Germany	Prince Philip of Saxe-Coburg and Gotha.
– 20	...	42 15/16	9¼	8½	7 1/16	9⅜	...	47 5/16	29¾	36⅝	257 kilos	Do.	Count Henry Fünfkirchen.
– 16	16·06	42·91	9·84	8·27	6·69	7·09	...	...	...	...	...	Do.	G. Jankovich.
– 14	20·06	42·91	9·64	8·66	7·68	7·28	...	...	...	...	...	Do.	Count B. Keglevich.
– 20	...	42·3	9·1	8·5	...	...	...	...	...	...	...	Do.	Count Szechenyi.
– 18	19·1	42·7	...	8·5	...	...	...	...	...	...	...	Szilvás	Count Bombelles.
– 16	17·6	42·13	11·61	10·24	7·09†	7·68	...	...	...	...	265 kilos	Do.	Count Fery Nádasdy.
– 14	18·85	42·13	9·64	9·05	7·09	7·87	...	...	...	...	...	Do.	Prince Philip of Saxe-Coburg and Gotha.
– 20	18·8	42·1	..	9 1/16	...	...	...	...	...	...	...	Munkacs	Count Jose Hoyos.
18	...	42	..	...	...	...	5¾	26¼	37¾	43	...	Austria	Viscount Powerscourt (*k*).
16	...	42	...	...	...	...	6	21	31½	...	...	Germany	Do.
12	...	42	...		...	...	...	...	35½	40	...	Galicia	E. N. Buxton.
– ...	...	42	...	...	...	...	5½	...	30	...	...	Styria	Sir Clement Hill, Bart.
– 15	...	42	10	...	..	...	...	...	...	43	45	Gotha	H.R.H. the Duke of Saxe Coburg and Gotha.
12	...	41⅞	..	...	...	...	5¼	...	25¼	...	...	Germany	British Museum.
– 18	18·26	41·73	10·24	9·25	7·09†	8·07	...	...	...	...	...	Hungary	Count Fery Nádasdy.
16	...	41½	...	...	...	...	6	28	36	...	...	Do.	Viscount Powerscourt.
14	...	41½	...	...	...	...	6¼	26½	34	...	...	Germany	Do.
14		41	...	...	...	...	6½	26	34	...	...	Hungary	Do.
15	...	41	...	...	...	...	5¾	27½	32¼	...	...	Germany	Do.

– 14	20	40 9/16	...	9½	7⅛	7½	...	...	26	...	...	Hungary .	Prince Philip of Saxe-Coburg and Gotha.
– 13	...	40¼	...	...	...	...	5	20¾	27⅜	...	...	Tyrol	H. R. H. the Duke of Saxe Coburg and Gotha.
– 20	18·50	40·10	...	8·10 (?)	...	...	...	...	...	...	...	Agarév .	Count Tassilo Festetics.
18	...	40	...	...	...	...	5½	34	31¾	40	...	Hungary	Viscount Powerscourt.
– 12	...	40	10	...	...	36	...	31	36	...	...	Tyrol	H.R.H. the Duke of Saxe Coburg and Gotha.
– 18	...	40	10	...	...	...	...	...	28	49	...	Gotha .	Do.
15	...	39½	10	9¼	6½	7½	7½	21¼	30¼	37½	...	Hungary .	A. von André.
8	...	38⅝	9½	8⅜	...	5½	...	27¾	33	36½	...	Do. .	Do.
– 14	26½	37 13/16	13	...	...	8 11/16	...	...	23⅝	...	...	Do. .	Prince August Leopold of Saxe-Coburg and Gotha.
– 14	...	37	...	...	...	...	5¼	21½	30	...	...	Macedonia	H. J. Elwes.
– 20	...	36⅝	10⅝	7⅛	...	7⅞	...	...	12⅝	...	...	Hungary .	Prince Philip of Saxe-Coburg and Gotha.
10	...	31½	...	...	...	...	4¼	12	18½	...	...	Tenuta la Mandria	H. R. H. le Duc d'Orléans.
– 44	19¼	30	...	...	...	...	...	...	...	44½	st. lbs. 24 6 (clean)	Rominten .	H. I. M. the German Emperor.

NOTES AND EXPLANATIONS.

– Many specimens marked thus are uneven pointers.

a. Length of brow tine, 22¾ in. Bez, 23 in.

b. " " " 21¼ in. On papier-mache head. A very large 8 pointer.

c. Palmated tops 6 in. across. Length of brow tine, 17½ in.

d. Length of brow tine, 21 in. Left trez tine, 21 in.

e. Shot by a peasant in a drive in Buckowina, in 1896.

f. Bought in Munich.

g. Length of left trez tine, 25 in. Bought in Vienna in 1863.

h. Right antler is forked at trez tine, and carries three points on this third tine, forming almost a cup. Mounted on a papier-mache head.

i. Tops palmated 6 in. across.

j. Right trez tine forked, tops palmated.

k. Killed in 1809. Bought at Linz, Austria, in 1898.

l. A remarkable specimen of a palmated head.

o. Trez tine on right antler forked.

p. From the Hildesheim Collection, near Hanover.

† The circumference of these antlers is taken above middle tine.

Viscount Powerscourt informs me that the 18 stag heads in the entrance hall at Powerscourt, mounted on papier-mache heads, were bought at Munich in 1863, by the advice of the late Count Arco-Zinneberg, the owner of the famous collection in the Wittelsbacher Platz at Munich. The hall where they hang contains upwards of 2500 heads of German Red-deer and Roe-deer of extraordinary weight and size, forming with the one exception of the King of Saxony's collection at Moritzburg, near Dresden, the finest in the world. Count Arco became so well known as a collector that every fine specimen was brought to him for purchase

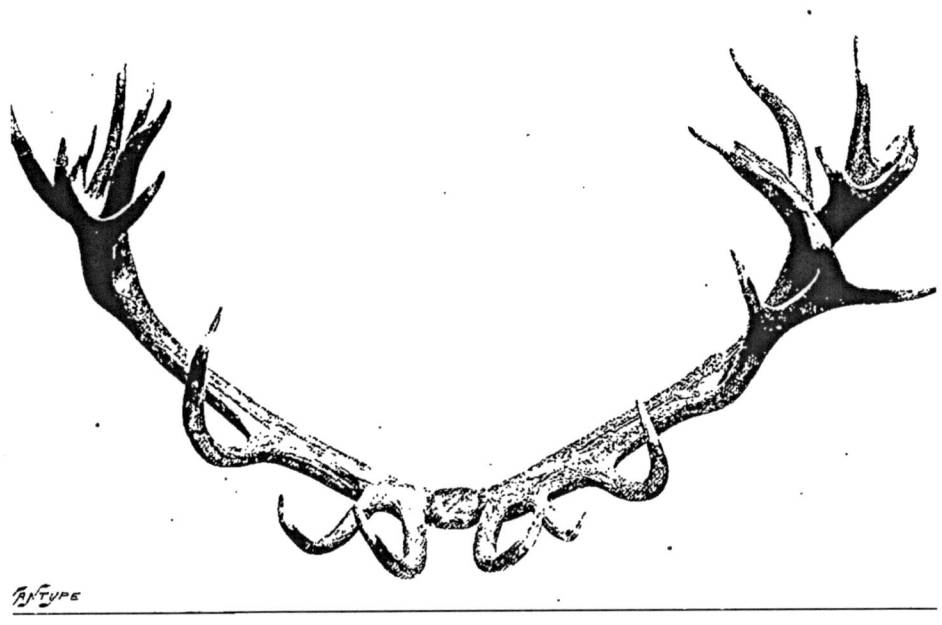

Antlers of Red Deer.   From a specimen in the Castle at Moritzburg.
After Dr. A. B. Meyer.

i.—ANCIENT CONTINENTAL RED DEER.

Length (straight).	Circumference.	Tip to Tip.	Spread.	Points.	Locality.	Owner.
...	...	...	...	33 + 29	?	H.M. the King of Saxony, Moritzburg.
[1]–4S	14 of burr	...	6 ft. 3$\frac{6}{10}$	12 + 11	?	Do.
...	...	..	...	25 + 12	?	Do.
...	...	...	...	2S	?	H.R.H. the Duke of Saxe-Coburg and Gotha.
–46$\frac{1}{2}$	8$\frac{3}{4}$ above trez	5 ft. 2$\frac{1}{4}$	...	22	Alpine Stag?	Count Erbach-Erbach.
...	9$\frac{3}{4}$	...	...	2S	Do.	Do.
... (on curve)	...	...	...	22	Switzerland	Do.
39$\frac{3}{4}$	5$\frac{3}{4}$	16	22$\frac{1}{2}$ inside	9 + 9	?	Viscount Powerscourt.
39$\frac{1}{2}$	6$\frac{1}{2}$	22	31$\frac{1}{2}$ 39 outside	6 + 6	Germany .	Do.

[1] Weight, 41$\frac{1}{2}$ lbs.

j.—NEW ZEALAND RED DEER (*introduced*).

Average height at shoulder, 47 inches.

Length on outside curve.	Circumference between bez and trez.	Tip to Tip.	Widest inside.	Spread.	Points.	Weight.	Locality.	Owner.
-42	5½	...	...	37½	9+7	...	Otago . .	W. Allen.
-41½	6	16	...	28½	6+5	...	Do. . .	Do.
-41	6¼	...	...	31½	6+5	...	Do. . .	J. S. Handyside.
-41	5¼	...	...	37	7+6	...	Do. . .	C. R. Westmacott.
-39	5½	...	...	31	6+6	...	Do. .	H. McLean.
-38	5	...		33	6+6	...	Do. . .	E. C. Studholm.
37½	5¼	19¼	28½	...	6+6 { 400 lb. esti-mated }		Do. . .	C. R. Westmacott.
-37	5	...	...	34	6+5	...	Do. . .	W. Telford.
-36½	6⅜	...	32½	...	9+9	...	Wairarapa .	J. S. Handyside.
-36	4¾	...	...	33¼	5+5	...	Otago . .	W. Telford.
31½	5¾	10½	18	...	6+7		North Island .	Rupert Wilkin.

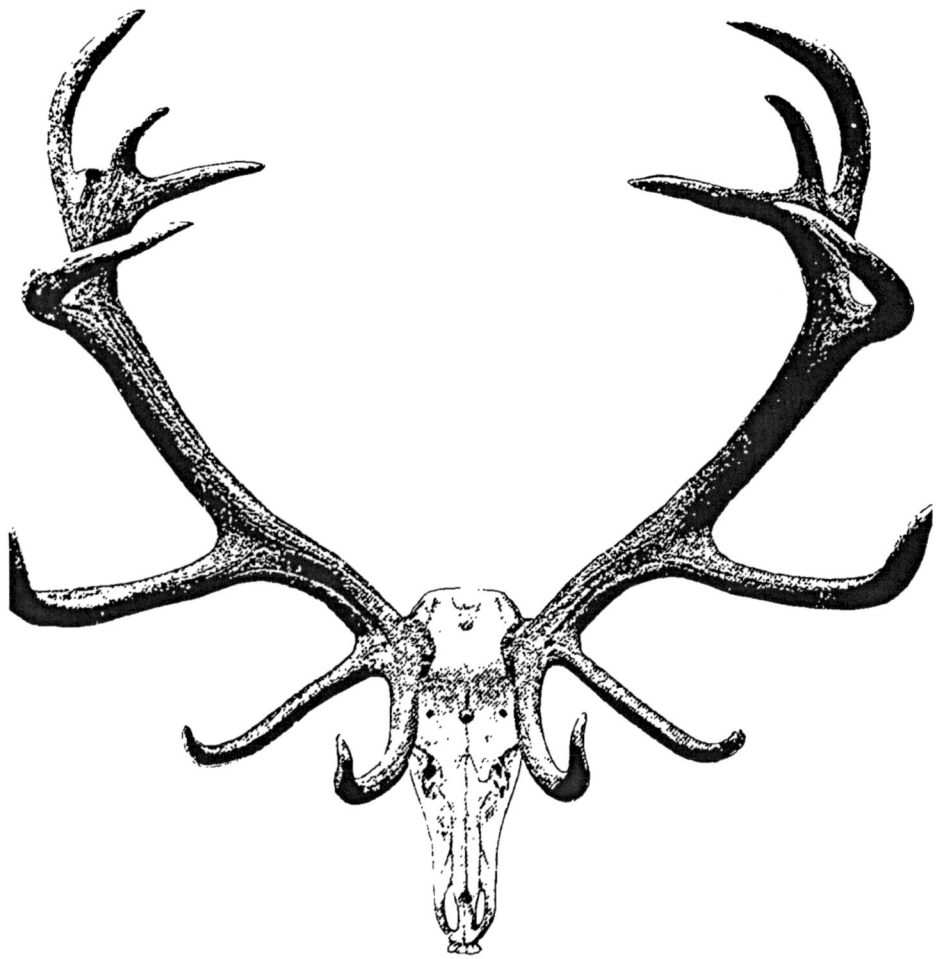

Skull and Antlers of Caspian Red Deer shot in the Western Caucasus by St. George Littledale.

CASPIAN RED DEER or MARAL (Cervus elaphus maral).

In this variety of the red deer, which probably intergrades with the typical race in the western Carpathians, the height at the shoulder reaches to about $4\frac{1}{2}$ feet, and the build is stouter, the neck thicker, and the head longer and more pointed than in the true red deer. The reddish summer coat of immature animals is very generally marked with numerous yellowish spots; and the colour of the winter coat is dark slaty gray on the back, with the tail-patch of a very bright yellow, and a large amount of black on the shoulders, thighs, and under parts. The large and massive antlers are generally less complex than those of the typical race, the number of points being seldom more than eight on a side, and frequently only six; while the bez tine, which may be wanting, is often shorter than the long and upwardly curved brow tine, and the fourth tine is generally more distinct from the crown. The average weight is given as about 40 stone.

The typical locality of this race of red deer is the Caspian provinces of Northern Persia, whence it extends into the Crimea, and probably Asia Minor, and so on into Transcaucasia, the Caucasus, probably Circassia, and the Galician Carpathians. The exact limits between the range of this and the typical race are not yet determined; and it is noteworthy that specimens from the Caucasus have shorter faces than those from Northern Persia, and thus approximate to the true red deer. In Asia the term "maral" is applied not only to this animal, but also to Bedford's Deer and the Altai Wapiti.

Length on outside curve.	Circumference.	Tip to Tip.	Widest inside.	Spread.	Points.	Estimated Weight. st.	lbs.	Locality.	Owner.
48½	6	30	41½	...	5+6	...		Ichater Dagh, Crimea	H.R.H. the Duke of Saxe-Coburg and Gotha.
48½	7¼	(single antler)		...	12	...		Asia Minor .	Lord A. Hay, British Museum.
48	7¼	...	...	...		...		Caucasus .	St. George Littledale.
47⅝	5½	38	...	...	6+5	...		Do. . .	Do.
47	7⅛	36	37¾	...	6+7	...		Do. .	Do.
46¾	5⅜	18	33	...	8+8	...		Do.	Do. British Museum.
45¾	7¾	25⅛	35⅜	...	8+8	...		Do. .	St. George Littledale.
-45½	8⅛	65¼	...	...	14	...		Do.	Grand Duke Mikhaelovitch.
45½	7¼	32¾	40½	46	8+8	...		Do. .	Prince Demidoff.
45⅜	5¾	42	35⅜	...	6+7	...		Ak Dagh, Asia Minor	F. C. Selous.
45⅛	7¾	...	...	...	9+6	...		Asia Minor .	Sir Edmund G. Loder, Bart.
-45	8	36	42	...	11+10	53	4	Caucasus .	Prince Demidoff.
44¾	6½	33¾	35⅛	...	7+5	...		Do. .	St. George Littledale.
44¼	6⅞	(single antler)		...	9	...		Asia Minor .	C. G. Danford, British Museum.
43½	6	...	40	...	8+6	...		Asia Minor .	M. Le C. Findlay.
43½	6¾	21¼	35	...	7+7	...		Caucasus .	St. George Littledale.
43½	5¾	16	28	...	6+6	...		Crimea. .	Earl of Dunmore.

CASPIAN RED DEER or MARAL (Cervus elaphus maral)—*continued.*

Length on outside curve.	Circumference.	Tip to Tip.	Widest inside.	Spread.	Points.	Estimated Weight.	Locality.	Owner.
−42½	6½	25	...	34	10 + 11	...	Crimea (?) .	H. J. Elwes.
42½	7	27	31½	34½	8 + 7	...	Caucasus .	Prince Demidoff.
−42	6	42	...	50	10 + 9	...	Crimea (?) .	H. J. Elwes.
41⅛	5¾	15½	28½	...	6 + 5	...	Caucasus .	H.R.H. le Duc d'Orléa
40½	5⅜	22¼	32½	...	6 + 6	...	Ak Dagh .	H. O. Whittall.
40½	5¾	28½	34½	...	8 + 7	...	?	Duke of Bedford.
40	5½	21¼	27½	...	6 + 6	...	Ak Dagh .	H. O. Whittall.
39¾	5¾	33	36¼	...	8 + 7	...	Do. .	F. C. Selous.

Head of Caspian Red Deer shot in Asia Minor by F. C. Selous.

BARBARY RED DEER (Cervus elaphus barbarus).

For characters, see under heading of *Cervus elaphus.*

Length on outside curve.	Circumference between bez and trez.	Tip to Tip.	Widest inside.	Spread.	Points.	Locality.	Owner.
38⅞	5⅜	...	...	...	6+5	North Africa .	Sir Edmund G. Loder, Bart.
36½	4¾	22⅞	28¾	...	4+4	Do. .	British Museum.
36⅜	4½	17½	25⅝	...	4+4	Do. .	Do.

DUKE OF BEDFORD'S DEER (Cervus xanthopygus).

Apparently allied to the red deer, but the antlers probably with not more than seven points each, and the coat rather more wapiti-like. Tail comparatively short, and limbs relatively long, as is the face. In summer the head and neck are dark slaty, as are the inner sides of the limbs, while the rest of the upper parts is bright foxy red (occasionally browner), with the tail-patch sometimes totally wanting, or rather indistinct, and little or no black on the under parts and inner surfaces of the thighs; in winter the upper parts brownish gray with a very large and conspicuous bright orange tail-patch and a blackish mane, the tips of the hairs showing a large amount of black.

This deer inhabits Manchuria, and probably some of the other districts of North-Eastern Asia, but the western limits of its range are still undetermined. It is regarded by Monsieur E. de Pousargues as inseparable from the Manchurian wapiti; but this is not borne out by the specimens now living in England. If they survive, the question can be decided in a year or two.

Length on outside curve.	Circumference.	Tip to Tip.	Widest inside.	Points.	Locality.	Owner.
-20⅞	4⅜	14¼	16⅛	4+3	Manchuria . .	Paris Museum (Type Specimen).

Head of Hangul. From a specimen shot by J. G. Apcar in Kashmir.

HANGUL or KASHMIR STAG (Cervus cashmirianus).

In this very distinct species the first or brow tine arises at a con-siderable distance above the burr, or coronet, of the antlers, instead of close to it, as in the red deer; the bez tine is usually longer than the brow; the total number of points is generally only five aside, although a third tine may occasionally be added to the normal terminal pair, thus forming an imperfect cup; and the beam of each antler is much curved in towards the middle line of the head. The tail is short, and not included in the light patch on the buttocks, which, at least frequently, is very small; and the tuft on the hind cannon-bone is situated lower down than in the red deer. In winter the general colour of the coat is brown, brownish ash, or liver-colour, with the hairs speckled; the light area on the inner side of the buttocks being dirty white, with a blackish line on the inner sides of the thighs, the upper side of the tail black, and the lips, chin, and inner surface of the ears white or whitish. In the fawns the spotting is stated to remain much longer than in the red deer. In the pairing season the old stags squeal like a wapiti, instead of roaring in the red deer fashion.

The typical hangul inhabits the forest districts of the north side of the vale of Kashmir and some of the neighbouring valleys, at elevations ranging from 9000 to 12,000 feet in summer, but descending to about 5000 feet in winter. In this race (*C. cashmirianus typicus*) the terminal or fifth tines of the antlers are so much bent inwards as to be separated by a comparatively small interval. In the forests of the Yarkand river the species is represented by a second local race (*C. cashmirianus yarcandensis*), in which the antlers are less spreading, with their terminal tines less inclined inwards, and therefore more widely separated. The trez tine in this race is typically larger and longer than either of the lower ones, the brow and bez, in this respect and in the closer proximity of the brow and bez tines more resembling the Caspian than the Kashmir Stag. The height at the shoulder varies from about 4 feet to 4 feet 4 inches; the average weight being about 450 lbs.

This deer, although first discovered by the late Dr. H. Falconer in the Kashmir valley, was named by Dr. G. R. Gray of the British Museum. The finest pair of antlers of which Mr. A. O. Hume has any record were given by Raja Gulab Sing to Colonel King, then commanding the 14th Dragoons. On his death they passed to Captain, afterwards, I think, Colonel, Prettyjohn of the same regiment. What became of these antlers Mr. Hume was never able to ascertain, but he measured them at Meerut in 1852 or 1853, and the record stands, R. 52 L. 53$\frac{1}{2}$, measured along the curve inside. Girth 10 inches at burr, and 7 half-way between bez and trez tines. They were a very wide-branching, symmetrical pair.

Length on outside curve.	Circumference between bez and trez.	Tip to Tip.	Widest inside.	Points.	Locality.	Owner.
-48	...	...	...	...	Kashmir	The late Dr. Leith Adams.
-47	7$\frac{5}{8}$	21	36	7+5	Do.	Bombay Natural History Society's Museum.
47	6$\frac{3}{4}$	21$\frac{1}{4}$	36$\frac{3}{4}$	5+5	Do.	Sir Edmund G. Loder, Bart.
47	6$\frac{1}{4}$	30	35$\frac{1}{2}$	8+8	Do.	Duke of Wellington.
-47	...	...	...	...	?	Major A. E. Ward.
45$\frac{7}{8}$	8	35	41	6+6	Kashmir	Hume Collection, British Museum.
45$\frac{1}{8}$	6	25$\frac{3}{4}$	36	8+8	Do.	Sir Victor Brooke's Collection.
45	6$\frac{3}{4}$	19	34	6+6	Do.	Col. R. Pole-Carew, C.B.

HANGUL or KASHMIR STAG (Cervus cashmirianus)—*continued.*

Length on outside curve.	Circumference between bez and trez.	Tip to Tip.	Widest inside.	Points.	Locality.	Owner.
−44¾	6	20	43	5 + 5	Lidar Valley . .	Officers' Mess, Q.O. C Guides.
−44⅝	6½	31½	44¾	5 + 5	Kishenganga Valley	Do.
−44½	6	21¼	36½	5 + 5	Do. .	The late Capt. E. W. Codr
44	7¼	30¾	40⅞	5 + 5	Sind Valley .	P. H. G. Powell-Cotton.
44	6¾	23¼	36½	5 + 5	Do. .	Naval and Military Club.
44	6	27	36	5 × 5	Kashmir . .	Hon. Walter Rothschild.
43⅞	5⅞	15⅞	32	5 + 5	Do. .	Hon. Charles Ellis.
43⅜	6½	25⅜	36½	...	Do. . .	Do.
43	6	20	35	6 + 5	Sind Valley .	A. O. Hume, C.B.
43	5⅞	26⅛	37⅞	6 + 5	Kashmir . . .	Martyn Kennard.
42	4½	13¼	29¼	5 + 5	?	Duke of Bedford.
42	5¾	13½	26½	5 + 5	Kashmir . . .	E. L. Phelps.
41¾	5¾	23½	35	5 + 5	Do. .	Major Kingsley Foster.
41⅜	5¾	23¾	33	5 + 5	Do. . . .	R. Lydekker, British Mus
41¼	6	15⅝	29	7 + 6	Tral Preserve . .	P. W. Cobbold.
41¼	5¼	34	49	6 + 5	?	C. H. Seely.
−41	...	...	...	13	Tral Preserve	The Maharaja of Travanc G.C.S.I.
−41	...	...	...	12	Do.	
−41	6	23	37½	...	Kashmir . .	The late Major W. D. B.
40½	5⅜	31½	39½	6 + 5	Do. . .	F. W. H. Walshe.
40½	6½	15½	28	5 + 5	Do. . .	Sir Robert Harvey, Bart.
40¼	7⅜	24½	3	5 + 5	Do. . .	Capt. H. W. Codrington.
39½	5¾	21½	33	5 + 5	Do. .	H. Maude.
39	5¼	26	35½	5 + 5	?	Major A. Nugent.
38½	5	14½	29	5 + 5	Rewa Nalla . .	The late Major A. Burton.
37½	5	17	28½	5 + 5	Kashmir . . .	Reginald Beech.
37½	5⅝	26¾	34½	6 + 6	Do. . .	Major C. S. Cumberland.
37	5⅞	22⅜	31¾	6 + 6	Do. . . .	W. R. Bindloss.
37	5	20	29	5 + 5	Do. . .	H. Z. Darrah.
37	5¾	19½	31½	5 + 5	Do. . .	J. G. Apcar (see Illustrati

Skull and Antlers of Yarkand Stag. From A. O. Hume's specimen.

YARKAND STAG (Cervus cashmirianus yarcandensis).

For characters, see Hangul, p. 37.

Length on outside curve.	Circumference.	Tip to Tip.	Widest inside.	Spread.	Points.	Locality.	Owner.
40¼	5½	23¾	31¾	...	5 + 5	Near Maralbashi .	A. O. Hume, C.B. (See illustration.)
40	5½	25	31	...	6 + 5	Maralbashi . .	E. L. Phelps.
39½	6	24½	25	...	7 + 6	Do. . .	A. O. Hume, C.B.
39¼	5¾	16½	28¾	...	6 + 6	Do. . .	David T. Hanbury.

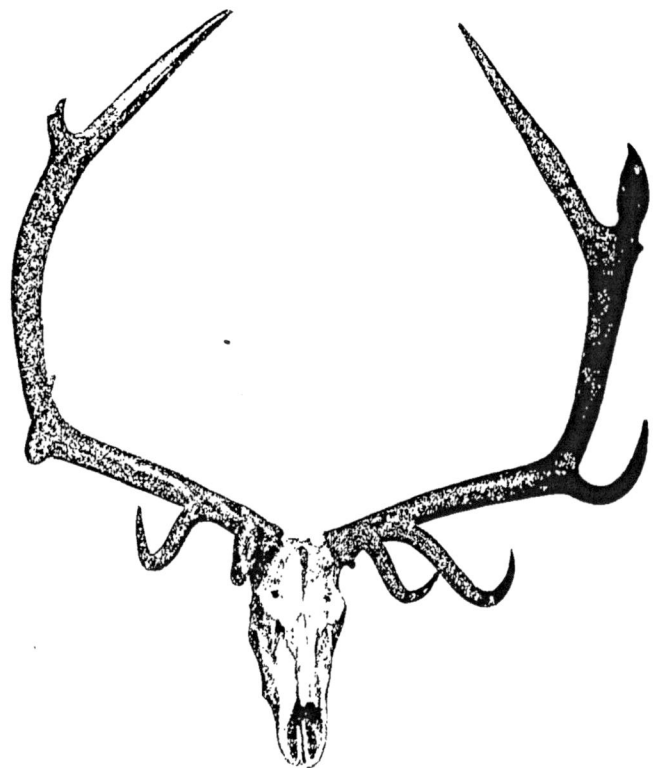

Skull and Antlers of Shou.   From A. O. Hume's specimen.

THE SHOU (Cervus affinis).

A very large stag with antlers of the general type of those of the hangul, but larger, and with the beam bent suddenly forward at the trez tine, so that the upper half overhangs the face, the number of points being usually five ; the brow tine is less constantly longer than the bez.   General colour probably rufous brown, with a light tail-patch in winter.

The habitat of this imperfectly known deer appears to be the districts immediately north of Bhutan, and probably the valley east-wards of Chumbi, which drains northwards into the Sangpo.   An apparently allied, although smaller, deer is found in Russian Turkestan (Bokhara or Khiva).

Length on outside curve.	Circumference.	Tip to Tip.	Widest inside.	Points.	Locality.	Owner.
55¾	6½	17¼	40⅜	7+6	?	A. O. Hume, C.B. (See illustration.)
54⅜	6⅝	21⅝	37¼	5+5	?	Dr. Campbell, British Museum.
55¾	6⅞	26⅛ (see illustration, p. 55)	44	5+5	?	The late B. H. Hodgson, British Museum.
53¼	6⅞	30	45¾	4+5	?	Hume Collection, British Museum.
53	9	...	40	5+5	?	The late Col. H. C. B. Tanner.
52	8	...	...	...	?	Hon. Walter Rothschild.
49½	7½	38	45½	5+5	?	Col. J. Biddulph.
48⅞	6½	19⅜	38⅛	7+5	?	Sir Edmund G. Loder, Bart.
48	6¾	30¾	[1] 39	5+5	Tibetan Frontier	H. J. Elwes.
48	6⅜	17	34½	6+5	?	H.R.H. le Duc d'Orléans.
47⅞	5⅝	30⅜	40½	5+5	?	British Museum.
43	...	...	...	...	Chumbi Valley	The late Sir Ashley Eden, G.C.S.I., Indian Museum.
42¾	5⅞	23⅝	31¼	5+5	?	British Museum.
41	6¼	...	...	6+4	?	Duke of Bedford.
39¾	5⅜	20	31¼	5+5	?	Edward P. Tennant.

[1] Spread.

THOROLD'S DEER (Cervus albirostris).

Thorold's deer is of the same approximate dimensions as the hangul, from which it is readily distinguished by the more flattened antlers, which have no bez tine, and do not curve inwards, but are suddenly bent backwards at the point of origin of the trez; the total number of points being either five or four. Equally distinctive is the pure white muzzle and chin, the white inner surface of the ears, the reversal of the hair on the middle of the back, so as to form a kind of hump on the withers with the points of the hairs directed towards the neck, the low position and large size of the gland-tuft on the hind cannon-bone, and the shortness of the tail, which is included in the very large straw-coloured area of the buttocks. The general colour of the coat is uniformly dark brown, with the hairs, which are remarkable for their coarse and brittle nature, minutely speckled.

The Tibetan plateau, with perhaps some of the neighbouring parts of Central Asia, is the home of this fine species of deer, which was originally described by the late Colonel Przewalski under the name given above. Subsequently two examples were obtained by Dr. W. G. Thorold, to the north-east of Lhasa, at an elevation of between 13,000 and 14,000 feet, which, under the impression that they indicated a new species, were named *C. thoroldi* by Mr. W. T. Blanford.

Length on out-side curve.	Circum-ference.	Tip to Tip.	Widest inside.	Points.	Locality.	Owner.
38½	4⅝	37	27	5+4	Central Tibet .	Hon. Walter Rothschild.
38	5¼	...	...	5+5	Do. . . .	British Museum.
-36	4½	32	32	5+5	?[1]	Indian Museum.

[1] Bought at Darjiling, thither brought by Tibetans.

TRUE WAPITI (Cervus canadensis).

Wapiti are very large deer of the red deer group, easy of recognition by the form of their antlers, which are of great size, carrying more than five tines, curving backwards, and much flattened in the upper half. They always have the bez tine developed, but their most characteristic feature is the great size of the fourth tine, which is larger than either of the others, and with the fifth, which is also long, forms a nearly straight fork ; the fourth, fifth, and sixth tines being situated almost in the plane of the portion of the beam immediately below them, so that they more or less completely hide one another when viewed from the front aspect. The brow tine rises close to the burr, and is nearly as long as the bez. The tail is extremely short, the light tail-patch very large ; and the neck and under parts are blackish, the general colour of the summer coat being yellowish brown on the upper-parts.

Wapiti (known in America as Elk) range from North America to North-Eastern and Central Asia ; the typical form being the East American wapiti (*C. canadensis typicus*), in which the legs are comparatively short, and the portion of the antlers above the fourth tine is fully developed, the height at the shoulder reaching to about 5 feet 4 inches, and the weight from 700 to 1000 lbs. On the other hand, the West American wapiti (*C. canadensis occidentalis*) differs by the abortion of the upper part of the antlers, the darker colour, and lighter build.

Head of East American or true Wapiti.
Shot by W. Moncreiffe.   For measurements see next page.

TRUE WAPITI (Cervus canadensis)—*continued.*

Length on outside curve.	Circumference between bez and trez.	Circumference of burr.	Tip to Tip.	Widest inside.	Widest outside.	Points.	Locality.	Owner.
-70	...	14⅛ above burr.	...	...	68	6+6	Olympic Mts., Washington	W. F. Sheard.
-66	...	...	...	...	60	6+6	Wyoming .	J. Darley.
-65	7⅝	...	...	...	40	7+7	Laramie Plains, Wyoming	Schoverling, Daly, and Gales.
-64¾	...	9¾	41½	49	...	6+7	Wyoming .	James J. Harrison.
64½	8	...	31½	45	52	7+6	?	Viscount Powerscourt.
-64¼	8	...	...	48	...	7+7	N.W. Wyoming	A. Rogers.
-63¾	8¼	...	49¼	48½	...	7+9	North Prong .	Frank Cooper.
62	7⅜	...	33¼	50⅝	...	7+7	Snake River, Colorado	Ernest Farquhar.
61½	7½	...	...	45	...	6+6	Bighorn Mts., Wyoming	,, ,,
-61	8	...	...	52	...	6+6	Do. .	H. Seton-Karr.
61	8.	...	36½	46½	55	8×8	?	Viscount Powerscourt.
[1] -60¾	7⅞	...	...	52	...	6+6	?	W. A. Baillie Grohman.
60½	8¼	...	...	55	...	7+6	Wyoming .	E. Grant.
60⅜	7¼	...	43	46¼	...	6+6	Do. .	Major C. C. Ellis.
60	6¾	...	31½	41¼	44	9+7	?	Viscount Powerscourt.
-59¾	...	13	...	...	...	...	Wyoming .	The late Sir Samuel Baker.
59½	8½	3	37¼	47	...	8+8	S.E. Do. . .	Lieut.-General B. Hankey.
59½	7½	...	...	[1] 45	...	6+6	?	H. Seton-Karr.
58½	8¾	...	39¾	43½	53½	7+6	?	Viscount Powerscourt.
58½	...	9 between brow and bez.	...	46½	50½	10+7	Wyoming	Hon. T. A. Brassey.
-58½	8½	...	...	44½	...	6+6	Do. .	J. D. Cobbold.
-58½	8¼	...	48	...	50	6+6	?	F. B. Tolhurst.
58	9$\frac{1}{16}$	42	47¼	7+6	...	7+6	Wyoming .	A. H. Straker.
58	7⅜	...	43½	49	...	9+8	Do. . .	W. Moncreiffe. (See illustration.)
58	7	...	46	49	51½	6+6	?	Viscount Powerscourt.
57½	6⅞	...	24¼	35⅝	...	6+6	Montana . .	Capt. Abdy.
57⅜	7	...	47	48⅝	...	6+6	Wyoming	Hon. Charles Ellis.
57¼	...	9⅝	32	42¼	...	7+7	Do. . .	Sir Humphrey de Trafford, Bart.

1 Measured by American Exhibition Committee.

TRUE WAPITI (Cervus canadensis)—*continued.*

Length on outside curve.	Circumference between bez and trez.	Circumference of burr.	Tip to Tip.	Widest inside.	Widest outside.	Points.	Locality.	Owner.
57	8⅛	...	35½	34	43	6+6	Wyoming .	Viscount Powerscourt.
−57	7¼	...	...	...	...	7+7	Do. . .	Count F. Trauttmansdorff.
57	7⅛	..	53	49½	61	8+9	Wyoming .	Sir Edmund G. Loder, Bart.
57	7⅛	...	35⅛	41⅛	...	6+6	Yellowstone Park	British Museum.
−56½	6⅞	...	...	...	46⅜	6+6	Two Ocean Pass	Theodore Roosevelt.
56	8	...	39¾	40¾	44	8+6	?	Viscount Powerscourt.
−56	7¾	...	...	...	...	6+6	Wyoming	Count F. Trauttmansdorff.
56	7¼	...	35	43½	...	8+7	Saskatchewan District, Canada	Earl of Ava.
55⅝	7⅝	...	43¼	48⅓	...	7+7	Wyoming .	Hon. Charles Ellis.
55⅝	7	...	43½	47⅝	...	6+5	Saskatchewan District, Canada	Capt. G. Dalrymple White.
−55½	8	...	38	43	..	6+6	Wyoming .	James J. Harrison.
−55½	7½	..	...	48¾	...	8+7	?	Otho Shaw.
55½	6½	...	44	45½	...	6+6	?	A. H. Pollen.
55⅜	7⅛	...	46¼	...	...	7+6	?	St. George Littledale.
55	8¼	...	...	41¼	...	6+6	Wyoming .	Major Maitland Kirwan.
55	8	...	...	45½	...	7+6	Do. .	Do.
55	7⅛	...	...	47½	...	6+5	Do. . .	E. N. Buxton.
−55	8½	...	53	54½	...	17	?	Sir H. B. Meux, Bart.
−55	8⅛	...	...	41¼	...	6+6	?	A. Pendarves Vivian.
[1] 55	7¾	...	21½	35½	43	7+6	?	Viscount Powerscourt.
[2] 55	6⅝	...	...	...	...	14	America . .	Duke of Bedford.
55	6½	...	...	...	...	6+6	Colorado . .	Crawford G. Logan.
−54¾	6¾	...	39⅜	43½	...	6+6	Montana . .	Count Scheibler.
54½	8	...	37	45½	...	6+6	Wyoming .	Sylvester Browne.
54½	...	...	...	...	...	14	Colorado .	Sir Peter Walker, Bart.
54½	8	...	34¼	45½	...	6+5	Wyoming	Lieut.-Col. Hon. W. Coke.
54½	9	...	...	palmated		11+7	Montana (?) .	G. Wrey.
54½	6¾	...	28	37	46	6+6	?	F. J. Mitchell.

[1] Shot by the Earl of Dunmore.

[2] Shed antlers weighed 20 lbs.

TRUE WAPITI (Cervus canadensis)—*continued.*

Length on outside curve.	Circumference between bez and trez.	Circumference of burr.	Tip to Tip.	Widest inside.	Widest outside.	Points.	Locality.	Owner.
54⅜	6½	...	38⅜	44¼	...	7+6	Wyoming .	E. N. Buxton.
-54¼	8	...	...	43½	...	10+10	Montana . .	W. A. Tulloch.
54¼	7⅝	...	49⅞	...	...	9+7	Wyoming .	Hon. Walter Rothschild.
-54	8¼	...	...	...	...	13	Teton Mountains	H. Lennard.
[1] 54	7¼	...	...	48	...	8+7	Wyoming .	Moreton Frewen.
54	7½	...	32¾	39½	47	11+8	Do. .	Viscount Powerscourt.
54	7⅝	...	30¾	37⅜	...	6+6	Do. . .	Capt. E. G. Verschoyle.
54	7¼	...	...	48	...	7+8	Do. . .	Moreton Frewen.
54	7	...	29½	35½	44	7+6	Do. .	H. Seton-Karr.
54	7¾	...	48	44	...	12	?	M. P. Grace.
-53½	8	...	43	44½	...	8+7	Wyoming	Count E. Hoyos.
-53½	6½	...	39	42	...	6+6	Do. .	Captain G. Dalrymple White.
53½	7	...	41½	42	...	7+7	Colorado .	E. T. Logan.
53⅛	7⅜	...	47	49¾	...	8+7 palmated	Wyoming	Ford G. Barclay.
-53	...	12½	...	...	...	...	Do. .	The late Sir Samuel Baker.
53	8¼	...	29½	36	38	7+6	Do.	Duke of Westminster.
53	7¼	...	41	43½	...	6+6	Do. .	Major H. J. Ferguson.
53	7⅝	13	37½	41½	51	7+7	?	Hon. Walter Rothschild.
-52¾	7¾	...	38½	41¾	...	6+5	Wyoming	Charles Makin.
52½	7	...	32	43	49	7+6	Do. . .	J. B. Gilliat.
52½	6½	...	...	34¾	...	7+6	Do. .	Ford G. Barclay.
52½	6½	...	39	42	...	6+6	Do. .	Captain G. Dalrymple White.
52⅜	5¾	...	49⅜	...	...	6+5	Colorado .	Colonel Ralph Vivian.
52	8½	...	...	...	...	6+6	Wyoming	Hon. F. Thellusson.
52	6¾	...	29¼	36¼	...	6+5	Colorado .	T. C. E. Goff.
-52	7½	...	46½	...	...	6+6	Do. . .	Dublin Museum.
52	7½	...	30	33	...	6+6	Wyoming .	Captain G. Dalrymple White.
52	8	...	48½	49½	...	8+7	Do. . .	Major H. C. Morland.

[1] Shot by Sir G. Gore, Bart.

TRUE WAPITI (Cervus canadensis)—*continued.*

Length on outside curve.	Circumference between bez and trez.	Circumference of burr.	Tip to Tip.	Widest inside.	Widest outside.	Points.	Locality.	Owner.
52	8	...	38½	44	...	8+8	Wyoming .	Lord Rodney.
52	8½	...	37	40	...	6+6	Vancouver[1] .	Barclay Bonthron.
52	6½	..	36	36¼	41	6+4	Manitoba . .	Earl of Dunmore.
-52	8½	...	...	42	...	14	Do. . .	Prince Henry of Liechtenstein.
-52	7	...	30½	39	...	6+5	Washington Territory	P. B. Vander-Byl.
51½	7¼	...	42	46½	...	6+6	Colorado . .	Captain E. G. Verschoyle.
51½	6½	...	41	44½	...	7+7	Idaho .	H. C. Nelson.
-51⅜	8¼	...	...	...	50	...	Wyoming .	G. O. Shields.
51	7¼	...	30	35	...	7+7	Do. . .	J. Turner-Turner.
51	6¼	...	39	45	...	6+6	Do. .	Captain E. G. Verschoyle.
-51	8¾	...	...	41	...	7+6	?	Captain Joscelin Bagot.
50⅝	7⅜	...	42	48¼	...	7+7	Colorado . .	Colonel Ralph Vivian.
50½	7	...	36	47	...	7+6	Wyoming .	Major C. F. Blane
-50½	7½	...	...	56½	58½	7+6	Do. .	Hugh Peel.
50½	6¾	...	50	43	...	6+6	Do. .	Major Maitland Kirwan.
50½	7	...	43½	43½	...	6+5	Do. . .	W. Moncreiffe.
50½	6¼	...	41½	47½	...	7+6	Do.	Lieutenant-Colonel Hon. W. Coke.
50½	7½	...	35	41	...	6+6	Do. .	Hon. H. S. Somerset.
50	...	...	49	...	...	8+7	Do. .	Otho Shaw.
50	6½	...	44	44¼	47	6+6	Do. . .	V. Cholmondeley.
-50	...	11	..	...	...	13	Montana . .	T. W. H. Clarke.
50	7½	...	39½	40	...	6+7	Wyoming .	Prince Demidoff.
50	7⅛	...	...	47½	...	6+6	?	J. M. Hanbury.
50	8¼	...	39	40	...	6+6	?	Duke of Bedford.
50	7⅞		43	40¾	...	6+6	?	Duke of Portland.
50	7	...	30½	39	...	6+5	Washington .	P. B. Vander-Byl.
50	6¼	...	40½	36¾	40	7+6	Manitoba .	Major C. S. Cumberland.
-49⅞	6¾		...	33⅝	45	6+6	?	H.R.H. the Duke of Saxe-Coburg and Gotha.

[1] West American race.

TRUE WAPITI (Cervus canadensis)—*continued.*

Length on outside curve.	Circumference between bez and trez.	Circumference of burr.	Tip to Tip.	Widest inside.	Widest outside.	Points.	Locality.	Owner.
–49½	7⅜	...	45¼	45¼	...	7+7	?	H.R.H. le Duc d'Orléans.
49½	8	...	...	43	...	11+8	Wyoming .	Otho Shaw.
49½	6¼	...	34½	37¾	...	6+6	Do.	J. Kenneth Foster.
49⅜	7⅝	...	38⅞	...	...	15+10	Do. . .	Moreton Frewen.
–49¼	...	9¾	28	36¼	...	7+7	Canada . .	Paris Museum.
49¼	8¾	.	38½	41½	...	6+6	Montana .	L. B. Lee.
–49¼	6½	...	38	46¼	...	10+7	Vancouver[1]	A. E. Leatham.
49⅛	6¼	...	...	45	...	13	Montana .	W. A. Fordham.
49	7½	..	26¾	34	41	7+6	Wyoming	J. L. Scarlett.
49	6½	...	48½	51	...	8+7	Do. . .	Hon. Gathorne Hardy.
49	7¾	...	33	41	...	8+5	Do. .	H. Seton-Karr.
–48¾	...	11	27⅝	32¾	...	7+7	Canada . .	Paris Museum.
–48	...	11½	...	...	...	17	Montana .	T. W. H. Clarke.
48	7½	...	41	40¾	...	8+7	?	Duke of Bedford.
48	6¼	...	41	43	...	7+7	Wyoming	F. C. Selous.
48	6	...	40½	39	...	5+6	Do. .	Captain G. J. Fitzgerald.
47¼	5¾	...	48	42	...	8+6	Colorado .	E. T. Logan.
47⅛	7¼	...	40	41	...	7+7	Wyoming .	Sir Victor Brooke's Collection.
47	6½	...	40	42	...	6+6	Do. .	W. W. Ashley.
–45	7¼	...	37	37	...	7+8	Vancouver[1]	Clive Phillipps-Wolley.

[1] West American race.

ALTAI WAPITI (Cervus canadensis asiaticus).

From the typical wapiti this well-marked local variety differs by its inferior size, relatively longer body and shorter limbs, and absolutely larger antlers ; the general colour of the coat being yellowish tawny at all times of year. This wapiti inhabits the forest-clad portions of the Altai and Thian-Shan ranges ; it was first described by Dr. Severtzoff under the name of *C. maral,* var. *asiatica,* and subsequently by Mr. Blanford, on the evidence of detached antlers obtained by the Second Yarkand Mission, as *C. eustephanus.*

Length on outside curve.	Circumference.	Tip to Tip.	Widest inside.	Spread.	Points.	Locality.	Owner.
[1]-55	8	...	...	...	6 + 7	Bought at Kashgar .	Earl of Northbrook.
-51	$10\frac{0}{10}$	...	...	...	...	?	W. T. Blanford.
$50\frac{3}{4}$	6	$29\frac{1}{2}$	$38\frac{1}{2}$	...	8 + 7	Altai . .	Duke of Bedford.
$-49\frac{5}{8}$	8	41	$42\frac{1}{2}$	...	7 + 7	East Thian Shan .	Paris Museum.
$48\frac{1}{2}$	$6\frac{1}{4}$	36	33	...	6 + 6	Altai . .	Duke of Bedford.
$45\frac{1}{2}$	$6\frac{1}{4}$	$34\frac{1}{4}$	$39\frac{1}{2}$	47	5 + 5	Do. .	H. J. Elwes.
$43\frac{3}{4}$	$5\frac{7}{8}$	$20\frac{1}{2}$	35	...	6 + 5	?	A. O. Hume, C.P.
$41\frac{3}{4}$	$6\frac{1}{2}$	$37\frac{1}{2}$	$40\frac{1}{2}$	44	5 + 5	Altai .	H. J. Elwes.
39	$4\frac{7}{8}$	32	36	$37\frac{1}{2}$	6 + 6	Thian Shan .	H. J. Elwes.

[1] Shed antlers bought by Sir Douglas Forsyth.

MANCHURIAN WAPITI (Cervus canadensis luehdorfi).

Antlers of a much shorter and stouter type than in the Altai wapiti, with the portion above the fourth tine (which is also relatively smaller) generally only slightly developed, and sometimes aborted. Not unfrequently "sports" in the neighbourhood of the fourth and fifth tines; and in one instance the fourth tine itself split into a regular fork. Build and colour very similar to that of the typical wapiti, but the height apparently lower. General colour in winter brownish gray, in summer light brown, with the dark winter mane and under parts of the true wapiti.

Although the antlers of this race (known in this country by the under-mentioned and other specimens in the collection of the Duke of Bedford) are at first sight very unlike those of either the Altai or the true wapiti, yet they present the essential wapiti characters. These are shown in their flatness, the preponderating size of the fourth tine, and the position of the fifth tine in the same plane as the latter. They are much more like the antlers of the West American wapiti (a fine pair of which are exhibited in the British Museum); these being relatively short and stout, with a tendency to the abortion of all the tines above the fifth, and also to the production of "sports."

As mentioned above, this deer is identified by Monsieur E. de Pousargues with *C. xanthopygus*; but there is no evidence that the coat is red in summer, and the antlers of immature specimens of the latter now living in England do not display decided wapiti characters. Moreover, these animals roar somewhat like a red deer, instead of squealing or whistling like a wapiti.

Distribution.—Northern Manchuria and Amurland.

Length on outside curve.	Circumference.	Tip to Tip.	Widest inside.	Spread.	Points.	Locality.	Owner.
33¼	5¾	18½	21½	...	6+6	?	H. J. Elwes.
32¼	5¼	26⅞	26⅜	29⅞	7+6	?	Do.
31¾	6	17	25¾	29	8+7	?	Duke of Bedford.
31½	5	23¼	24	26	6+6	?	Do.
31	4¾	26½	25¾	30½	6+5	?	Do.

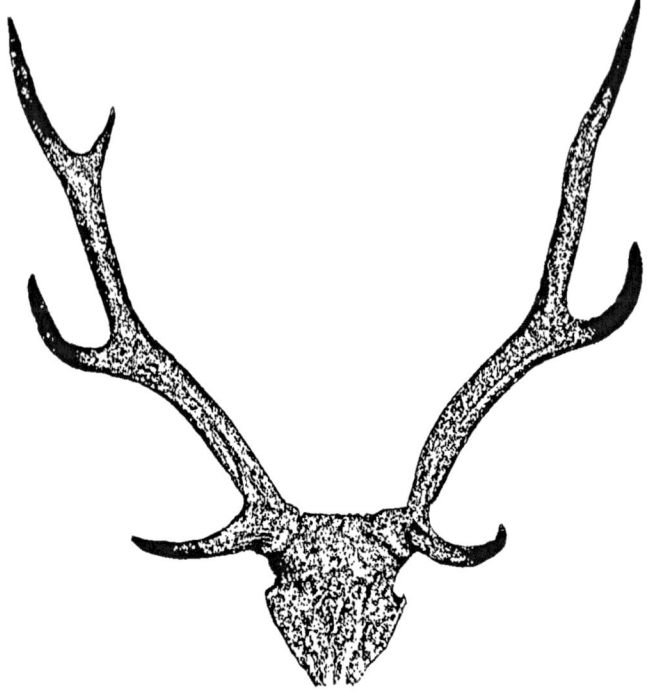

Antlers of Japanese Sika.
From a specimen presented to the British Museum by Viscount Powerscourt.

JAPANESE SIKA (Cervus sica).

This species is the typical representative of a small group of deer in which the antlers are shorter and simpler than is usually the case in the red deer group, and have generally four tines, including a trez, but lacking a bez. The coat is spotted, at least in summer, and there is a black-bordered white area in the region of the tail, which is relatively long. In the Japanese sika the white area on the buttocks is large, and extends on to their lateral surfaces ; while the coat is chestnut red with numerous white spots in summer, and browner, with no, or only indistinct traces of, spots in winter. These deer are distributed over Northern China, Manchuria, and Japan, and are represented by two closely allied races differing chiefly in size. In the true Japanese sika (*C. sica typicus*), which inhabits Japan and Northern China, the height at the shoulder varies from about 2 feet 8 inches to 2 feet 10 inches, whereas in the Manchurian sika (*C. sica manchuricus*) it reaches

3 feet 3 inches. Both races have been acclimatised in English and Irish parks.

Length on outside curve.	Circumference.	Tip to Tip.	Points.	Locality.	Owner.
31¼	5¼	27⅛	4+4	Japan . .	Sir Edmund G. Loder, Bart.
25⅜	4⅛	20¼	4+4	Do. .	Do.
22	4	16¾	5+4	Bred in Ireland . .	Sir Victor Brooke's Collection.
21⅝	3⅜	16½	10+6	Island of Yezzo .	Do.
18½	3¾	...	9	Bred in Ireland . .	Do.
-18½	3⅛	11	4+4	Kobe, Japan	Dr. Percy Rendall.
16¾	3⅛	...	4+3	Japan . . .	British Museum.
16⅝	3	9⅝	4+3	Bred in Ireland . .	Hon. John Ward.
15½	2¾	9¾	4+4	Bred in England .	Duke of Bedford.
[1] 15½	2¾	14¼	4+4	Bred in Ireland . .	Marquis of Hamilton.
[2] -15½	...	...	6+5	Do. .	Viscount Powerscourt.
15¼	3⅜	12¼	4+4	Do. . .	Hon. R. A. Ward.

[1] Weight 10 stones 3 lbs. as it fell.
This stag when killed was estimated to be fifteen or sixteen years old, and had no teeth left.

The following specimens belong to the Manchurian race.

Length on outside curve.	Circumference.	Tip to Tip.	Points.	Locality.	Owner.
-26	4¼	13⅜	4+4	Manchuria	Paris Museum.
15½	3	...	4+4	Woburn	Duke of Bedford.

HYBRID JAPANESE and RED DEER.

Length on outside curve.	Circumference.	Tip to Tip.	Widest inside.	Points.	Weight.	Locality.	Owner.
29¼	4½	17¾	21	5+4	14 st.	?	Viscount Powerscourt.
28¼	4¼	14¼	18	5+4	14 st. clean	?	Do.
26½	4	21½	21	4+4	...	?	Do.

FORMOSAN SIKA (Cervus taëvanus).

Nearly allied to the Japanese and Manchurian sikas, but distinctly spotted in winter, when the coat retains more or less of the rufous summer tinge. The dark line down the middle of the back is very strongly marked, there is a more distinct black bar above the white tail-patch, and the limbs are shorter, and the body proportionately longer. The height at the shoulder is about 2 feet 11 inches. This species is confined to the mountains of the island of Formosa.

Length.	Circumference.	Tip to Tip.	Widest inside.	Points.	Locality.	Owner.
19¾	3⅞	13	16⅝	4 + 4	Island of Formosa .	. British Museum.
19	3¼	...	...	4 + 4	Do. .	. Duke of Bedford.

Head of Pekin Sika, from a specimen in the Museum at Woburn Abbey.

PEKIN or DYBOWSKI'S SIKA (Cervus hortulorum).

In addition to its larger size (at least 3 feet 7 inches at the shoulder), this species is distinguished from the Manchurian sika by the smaller size of the white tail-patch, which in fully adult individuals does not extend on to the sides of the buttocks, although it does so in younger animals. The head and neck are bluish gray, and in immature animals spots persist in the winter coat, although, except on the hind-quarters, they may disappear more or less completely at this season in fully adult bucks, whose coats become very long and shaggy, especially on the throat and neck. Hinds are more brightly coloured in winter than the stags, and retain more distinct spotting. This deer was first named by the late Consul Swinhoe from an immature buck and doe taken at the sack of the Summer Palace, Pekin, and was afterwards obtained in the wild state in the Ussuri district of North-Eastern Manchuria, when it received the name of *C. dybowskii.*

Length on out-side curve.	Circum-ference.	Tip to Tip.	Widest inside.	Points.	Locality.	Owner.
27	$4\frac{1}{8}$	$23\frac{1}{2}$	20	4 + 4	Manchuria . .	Hon. Walter Rothschild.
26	$3\frac{3}{4}$	18	$15\frac{1}{2}$	4 + 4	Do. . . .	Edward P. Tennant.
24	4	$22\frac{1}{2}$	19	4 + 4	Do. . . .	Hon. Walter Rothschild.
$23\frac{1}{2}$	$3\frac{1}{2}$	$18\frac{1}{4}$	$16\frac{1}{2}$	4 + 4	Do. . .	Duke of Bedford.
$15\frac{3}{8}$	3	20	...	4 + 4	Ussuri, South Man-churia	British Museum.

Skull and Antlers of Shou.   From a specimen in the British Museum.

Head of Common Fallow Deer.

FALLOW DEER (Cervus dama).

Antlers normally without a bez, but with a trez tine, above which the beam is palmated, with numerous snags on the hinder edge. Coat spotted with white in summer (except in the black breed), with a black-bordered white area in the neighbourhood of the long tail. Height at shoulder about 3 feet ; weight about 140 lbs. clean. The original distribution includes Greece, Spain, Portugal, Anatolia, Rhodes, Sardinia, Asia Minor, Northern Palestine, and North-Western Africa, but the species has been introduced into Great Britain and some other countries.

Length on out-side curve.	Circum-ference.	Tip to Tip.	Spread inside.	Points.	Width of Palm.	Locality.	Owner.
[1]-31	5	...	...	30	7	?	Sir Victor Brooke's Collection.
[2]-30	4⅞	23½	26½	10+9	4½	Drummond Castle, Perth	J. G. Millais.

[1] Recorded by J. G. Millais (*British Deer and their Horns*).
[2] Weight of antlers, 8 lbs. 1 oz. on skull, no lower jaw (Millais, *British Deer*).

FALLOW DEER (Cervus dama)—*continued.*

Length on outside curve.	Circumference.	Tip to Tip.	Spread inside.	Points.	Width of Palm.	Locality.	Owner.
-30	4½	22	37 outside	16+10	7	Drummond Castle, Perth	J. G. Millais.
-29½	5	17	28½	14+13	7¼	Petworth Park, Sussex	Do.
[1]-28½	4	14½	26	10+11	6	Woburn . .	Duke of Bedford.
[2]28½	4	(Span 34) outside		19	6	Colebrooke .	Sir Victor Brooke's Collection.
[3]28	4	(26)		18	5	Do. .	Do.
[4]-27¾	5	20½	21½	13+7	5¾	Do. . .	A. Basil Brooke.
27¾	4¼	32½	25	11+10	...	Woburn .	Duke of Bedford.
27¼	4	23	...	10+8	...	England .	J. Carr Saunders.
-27	...	...	...	...	...	Nr. Blair Castle .	Dowager Duchess of Atholl.
26⅞	3¾	12	17½	10+7	...	?	British Museum.
-26½	4¼	23½	20½	9+7	5⅞	Perthshire .	A. Basil Brooke.
-26	5	20¾	23¾	10+10	4½	Tasmania .	T. W. H. Clarke.
-26	5¼	20	22½	11+13	7	Ashton Park, Lancashire	J. Whitaker.
25⅜	4¼	26	...	8+8	5⅛	Ireland . .	Sir Victor Brooke's Collection.
-25	4	24¾	25¾	11+10	5¾	Tasmania .	T. W. H. Clarke.
-25	4½	21½	24	11+10	7	England	Sir Edmund G. Loder, Bart.
23½	3¾	14	19½	10+9	4½	?	G. O. M. Herron.
-23	4½	15	18½	10+9	5	?	Dublin Museum.
21⅜	4⅜	...	...	11+10	5	Colebrooke, Ireland	Sir Victor Brooke's Collection.

[1] Weight dressed, 165 lbs. [2] Seven years old, as he fell 237½ lbs., 198 lbs. cleaned.
[3] Seven years old, as he fell 224 lbs. (Millais, *British Deer*). [4] Seven years old.

Head of Mesopotamian Fallow Deer, from a specimen in the British Museum.

MESOPOTAMIAN FALLOW DEER (Cervus mesopotamicus).

Larger and brighter coloured than the common fallow deer, with the spots near the middle of the back tending to form longitudinal stripes, and less black on the tail. Antlers of a totally different type, being somewhat expanded at the origin of the trez tine (which is large, and situated some distance above the short brow tine), but at the summit only moderately flattened, and breaking up on the hinder border into several snags.

Distribution.—The mountains of Luristan in Mesopotamian Persia.

Length on out-side curve.	Circum-ference.	Tip to Tip.	Spread inside.	Points.	Width of Palm.	Locality.	Owner.
−29	4¼	30½	24¼	10 + 11	5½	Asia Minor . .	F. E. Whittall.
−21¼	3⅚	14½	...	9 + 7	...	Do. . .	Paris Museum (Père A. David).
20¼	5	14	..	6 + 5	...	Luristan Mountains	Sir Edmund G. Loder, Bart.

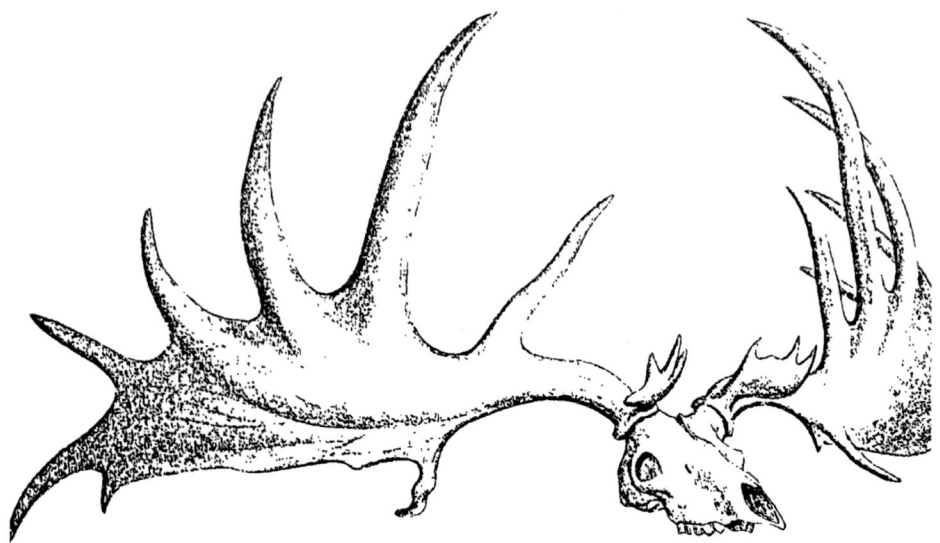

Skull and Antlers of extinct Giant Fallow Deer (Irish Elk).

EXTINCT GIANT FALLOW DEER (Cervus giganteus).

(Commonly called " Irish Elk.")

A huge deer, probably standing at least 6 feet at the shoulder, with the antlers enormously expanded, and carrying several large tines on the front border, of which the one above the trez is the longest ; the brow tine being often flattened and forked. In its typical form this magnificent deer occurs in the prehistoric deposits of Ireland, England, and probably some of the western districts of the Continent.

Spread Tip to Tip.	Length round inside of antler.	Length of both antlers across skull.	Circumference above burr.	Width of Palm.	Points.	Owner.
ft. in.	ft. in.	ft. in.				
-11 3	7 5½	...	12¼	19¼	17	Mrs. Donaldson-Hudson.
-10 4½	6 9	13 10	12	20	...	Earl of Bessborough.
10 2	5 8½	...	9⅞	19¼	19	British Museum.
-10 2	...	...		...	.	Thomas Bate.
9 8	...	..	. .		.	Hon. Walter Rothschild.
9 5	6 2	12 5	11	21¼	11+11	Viscount Powerscourt.
9 5	6 0	12 10	13½	21¼	15+13	Sir Edmund G. Loder, Bart.

EXTINCT GIANT FALLOW DEER (Cervus giganteus)—*continued.*

Spread Tip to Tip.	Length round inside of antler.	Length of both antlers across skull.	Circumference above burr.	Width of Palm.	Points.	Owner.
9 3	6 2	13 5	10	24	12 + 10	Duke of Westminster.
9 2	...	13 6	...	15½	...	Mrs. Graham Lloyd.
-9 2	...	11 10	10¼	22¼	9 + 9	Dublin Museum.
-9 2	...	...	...	...	20	Thomas Bate.
8 11¾	6 1¾	...	8¾	17¾	10 + 13	Hon. Charles Ellis.
8 11	5 10	...	11¼	17	9 + 9	Viscount Powerscourt.
8 10	5 9	11 9½	9¼	17	12 + 11	Duke of Westminster.
-8 10	...	12 10	...	13½	...	Mrs. Graham Lloyd.
-8 9	...	..	...	18¾	9 + 8	H. J. Elwes.
8 7	5 9½	..	10	20	12 + 12	Viscount Powerscourt.
7 6	5 3½	...	8⅛	...	10 + 11	Sir Victor Brooke's Collec

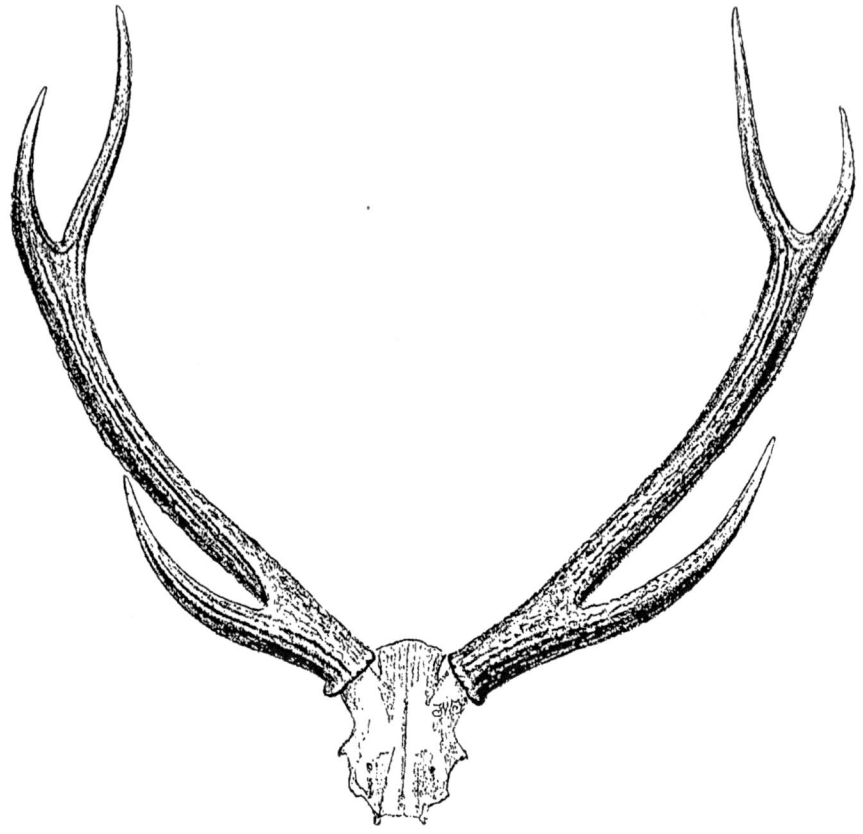

Antlers of Indian Sambar.
From a specimen in the British Museum.

INDIAN SAMBAR (Cervus unicolor).

The typical representative of the Rusine group of deer, in which the antlers are rounded and three-tined, both the bez and trez being wanting, and the summit of the beam simply forked. Height reaching to 5 feet 4 inches at the shoulder. Antlers large and rough, with the brow tine given off at an acute angle to the beam, and the two terminal tines of nearly equal length. Hair coarse and shaggy, uniformly dark umber-brown, with some chestnut on the buttocks, at all ages. Face-glands very large, and capable of being turned inside out. Ears large, and the tail relatively long and bushy. Young uniformly coloured. Weight about 600 lbs., when cleaned about

410 lbs. The wooded hilly districts of India and Ceylon form the habitat of the true sambar, which probably extends into Assam.

The largest, or rather longest, pair of antlers Mr. A. O. Hume ever met with were from the Central Provinces, and measured 48 inches along the curve inside (must have been nearly 50 inches on outside curve). Both brow tines were broken off. They were sent him by Mr. R. Blewitt.

Length on outside curve.	Circumference above brow tine.	Tip to Tip.	Widest inside.	Points.	Locality.	Owner.
48	7	Single dropped horn		3	Khandesh . .	R. H. Madan.
-46⅞	...	49	...	3+3	Cent. Provinces	R. Wordsworth.
46½	6⅜	24⅛	30⅞	3+3	Do.	A. O. Hume, C.B.
-46½	9 below brow tine	45	...	...	Gurhwal	R. M. Nash.
45⅛	6⅝	17¾	32⅛	3+3	?	The late Dr. H. Falconer, British Museum.
45	7⅜	22½	33¾	3+3	Mayoghur, Cent. Provinces	Sir John Morris, K.C.S.I.
45	7¼	44⅞	...	3+3	Western Ghats .	Major-Gen. Sir Arthur Ellis, K.C.V.O.
[1] -45	...	...	...	...	Cent. Provinces .	Bombay Natural History Society's Museum.
-45	9	...	...	...	Orissa .	H.H. The Maharaja of Travancore, G.C.S.I.
-45	8	Picked up by Dr. G. Jones			Cent. Provinces (?)	Heighway Jones.
44⅛	7⅞	44⅜	45⅞	3+3	Rangeer, Do.	Col. W. J. Morris.
-44	...	34	...	3+3	Central Do. .	J. D. Inverarity.
[2] -44	9	...	. .	...	Rewa .	Major A. E. Ward.
44	6	9¼	24⅜	3+3	Do.	Capt. C. F. Pinney.
44	6⅞	19¼	31¾	3+3	Do. .	H. E. M. Davies.
43⅝	5⅝	Single horn		3+3	Do.	Hume Collection, British Museum.
43½	5¼	17	28	3+3	Do.	Sir E. P. Bates.
43½	6¾	25¼	34	3+3	Cent. Provinces	Viscount Powerscourt.
43⅜	6¼	20⅜	29⅛	3+3	Do.	Sir Robert Harvey, Bart.
-43¼	10	...	...	3+3	Do.	Capt. C. Hutton Dowson.
-43	10½	...	...	...	Cuttack	Indian Museum.

[1] This is only the measurement of a portion of a Sambar antler, and was recorded in the *Journal of the Bombay Natural History Society*, iii. p. 228. The animal was shot by Mr. R. Gilbert in the Central Provinces, but got away minus this piece of his antler.

[2] Height at shoulder, 35¼ inches.

INDIAN SAMBAR (Cervus unicolor)—*continued.*

Length on outside curve.	Circumference above brow tine.	Tip to Tip.	Widest inside.	Points.	Locality.	Owner.
43	$7\frac{1}{2}$	$35\frac{1}{2}$	38	3 + 3	Gwalior . . .	Sir Greville Smyth, Bart.
43	6	$24\frac{1}{2}$	30	3 + 3	Khandesh . .	A. Cumine.
-43	$9\frac{1}{2}$	26	23	3 + 3	Cent. Provinces . .	Capt. J. H. Gwynne.
$42\frac{3}{4}$	$5\frac{3}{8}$	26	$32\frac{1}{4}$	3 + 3	Do. .	A. H. Pollen.
$42\frac{1}{2}$	$6\frac{1}{4}$	15	$27\frac{3}{4}$	4 + 4	Ghats of Simrol .	Col. J. Evans, British Museum
-42	$6\frac{1}{4}$	Single antler		...	?	Sir Edmund G. Loder, Bart.
42	6	$26\frac{1}{4}$	$35\frac{1}{2}$	3 + 3	Khandesh . .	A. Cumine.
$41\frac{7}{8}$	$6\frac{1}{4}$	$33\frac{3}{8}$	$35\frac{1}{4}$	3 + 3	Western Ghats .	Major-Gen. Sir Arthur Ellis. K.C.V.O.
$41\frac{3}{4}$	7	$28\frac{1}{4}$	$34\frac{3}{4}$	3 + 3	?	Hon. Walter Rothschild.
$41\frac{1}{8}$	$7\frac{1}{8}$	$31\frac{1}{4}$	$36\frac{3}{4}$	4 + 3	Nepal . .	The late B. H. Hodgson, British Museum.
$41\frac{1}{2}$	$6\frac{1}{4}$	$30\frac{1}{2}$	$36\frac{1}{2}$	4 + 4	Cent. Provinces .	P. Jay.
41	$6\frac{3}{8}$	$18\frac{1}{2}$	29	3 + 3	Do.	Duke of Bedford.
[1] 41	$8\frac{1}{2}$	...	...	3 + 3	N. Gujerat .	S. C. Law.
$40\frac{5}{8}$	6	22	$27\frac{1}{2}$	3 + 3	?	Sir Edmund G. Loder, Bart.
$40\frac{1}{2}$	$7\frac{1}{2}$	$24\frac{1}{2}$	...	3 I 3	?	Major James Grant.
$40\frac{1}{2}$	$5\frac{5}{8}$	33	$37\frac{1}{4}$	3 + 3	?	Hume Collection, British Museum.
$40\frac{1}{4}$	$6\frac{1}{4}$	$28\frac{1}{8}$	32	3 + 3	Nilgiris .	Sir Victor Brooke's Collection
-40	...	$20\frac{1}{2}$	...	3 + 3	Asirghur . .	J. D. Inverarity.
40	6	$31\frac{1}{2}$	$33\frac{3}{4}$	4 + 4	Cent. Provinces . .	H. P. Whitney.
40	$5\frac{7}{8}$	$32\frac{1}{4}$	36	3 + 3	Ghats of Simrol . .	Col. J. Evans, British Museum
$-39\frac{1}{2}$	8	$26\frac{1}{2}$	...	...	Nimar . .	Captain J. N. MacLeod.
$39\frac{1}{4}$	6	$16\frac{1}{2}$	$20\frac{1}{2}$	2 + 2	Nepal . .	H.R.H. the Duke of Saxe-Coburg and Gotha.
-39	6	18	28	...	Satpura Range .	Col. J. Biddulph.
-39	...	$28\frac{1}{4}$	$30\frac{1}{4}$	3 + 3	Asirghur . . .	J. D. Inverarity.
$38\frac{1}{2}$	6	26	$31\frac{1}{2}$	3 + 3	?	Viscount Powerscourt.
$-38\frac{1}{2}$	$5\frac{1}{4}$	38	$29\frac{1}{2}$	3 + 3	Girnar Hill, Kathiawar	Lieut.-Col. L. L. Fenton.
$38\frac{1}{2}$	$6\frac{3}{4}$	$23\frac{1}{4}$	$28\frac{7}{8}$	3 + 3	?	Sir Robert Harvey, Bart.
$38\frac{1}{8}$	$6\frac{7}{8}$	$30\frac{3}{8}$	35	3 + 3	Nilgiris . .	Sir Victor Brooke's Collection.

[1] Malformed.

INDIAN SAMBAR (Cervus unicolor)—*continued.*

Length on outside curve.	Circumference above brow tine.	Tip to Tip.	Widest inside.	Points.	Locality.	Owner.
[1] -38	...	32⅜	...	...	Mandla District, Cent. Provinces	Capt. B. H. Boucher.
-38	6½	...	...	3+3	Cent. Provinces . .	H. Lennard.
38	6½	29¾	41⅜	3+3	Chanda District, Cent. Provinces	Sir John Morris, K.C.S.I.
38	5¾	28	28	3+3	?	Capt. E. H. R. Hibbert.
37¾	6	29¼	31¾	3+3	Cent. Provinces .	Lieut.-Col. M. Cust.
37½	6¾	21⅜	25⅜	4+3	Do. . .	Major C. S. Cumberland.
37½	5½	43	31	3+3	Chanda District, Cent. Provinces	L. Gisborne Smith.
37½	5⅞	29	31½	3+3	Do. . .	C. D. Twopeny.
37½	7½	23	29	3+3	Do. . .	Col. M..M. Bowie.
37½	5¾	23½	31	3+3	Do. . .	C. F. Egerton.
37⅜	5½	19	23¾	3+3	Nimar, Cent. Provinces	Lieut.-Col. H. Wade-Dalton.
37¼	5⅜	19⅝	30¾	3+3	Central Provinces .	Major C. S. Cumberland.
37	5½	20¼	28½	3+3	?	M. Loam.
37	6⅛	27⅛	28¾	3+3	?	H. C. V. Hunter.
-37	6 7/10	21¼	24	3+3	Mount Aboo .	Viscount Edmond de Poncins.
37	9	13	31	3+3	Mounar Valley . .	A. H. Sharp.
36¾	6¼	23½	22	3+3	Rajputana . .	Col. J. Biddulph.
36½	5¾	24¾	27	3+3	Benares . . .	Sir Comer Petheram.
36½	5	23¾	24½	3+3	?	A. M. Caccia.
36½	5¾	29	34	3+3	Nimar, Cent. Provinces	Lieut.-Col. H. Wade-Dalton.
-36	7	19	...	3+3	?	Count J. Potocki.

Ceylon Specimens.

32½	6¼	24	26¼	3+3	Ceylon .	A. R. Hay.
31½	5	20	17	4+3	Do. .	Surgeon-Major G. E. Hale, D.S.O.
-30	8?	21½	19⅝	3+3	Do. .	J. Ryan.
29	4½	25	22¼	3+3	Do. . .	Earl Cairns.
27¼	4¼	16¾	20	3+3	Do.	A. M. Naylor.
-20¾	5⅝	15	15	3+3	Do. . . .	Dr. Percy Kendall.

[1] Height at shoulder, 52 inches.

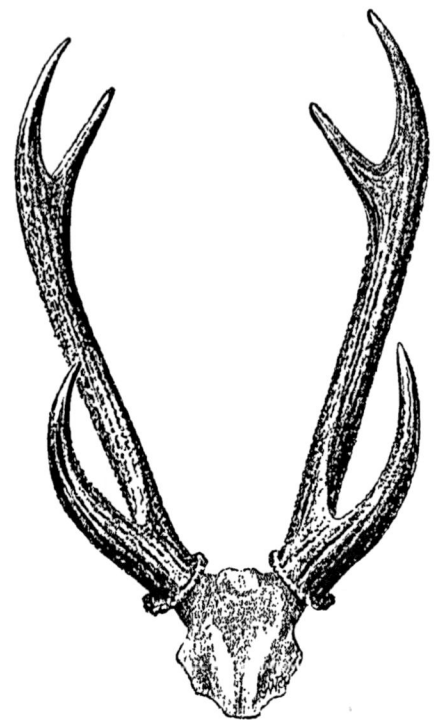

Frontlet and Antlers of Malayan Sambar.
Drawn from a Burmese specimen in the British Museum.

MALAYAN SAMBAR or EQUINE DEER (Cervus unicolor equinus).

This local race is nearly as large as the Indian sambar, but the antlers are generally shorter and thicker, with the hinder or inner tine of the terminal fork much shorter than the front one, and arising as a spur from the inner hind margin of the beam, of which the front tine forms the direct continuation ; the brow tine also generally longer. General colour of coat of adult darker, usually a light ring round the eyes, the ears smaller, often with a white margin, and the tail very bushy. Young spotted. The distributional area extends from Assam and Cachar through Burma and the Malay Peninsula to Siam, Hainan, Borneo, and perhaps Sumatra.

F

MALAYAN SAMBAR or EQUINE DEER (Cervus unicolor equinus)—*continued.*

Length on outside curve.	Circumference.	Tip to Tip.	Widest inside.	Points.	Locality.	Owner.
30⅞	6½	17¼	19⅝	7+7	Borneo .	Sir Edmund G. Loder, Ba
-30½	5⅛	27¾	[1] 30	3+3	Burma	Vet.-Capt. G. H. Evans.
30⅛	4⅜	20¾	21¼	3+3	Do. .	British Museum.
29⅜	6	16⅝	20¾	3+3	Garro Hills, Assam .	Hume Collection, Brit Museum.
-29¼	5½	22½	[1] 23½	3+3	Burma . .	Vet.-Capt. G. H. Evans.
-28½	5	26½	[1] 29½	3+3	Do. . .	Do.
26¾	6	12	13.3	3+3	Garro Hills, Assam .	Hume Collection, Brit Museum.
26½	6¾	11	...	3+3	Borneo . .	Sir Edmund G. Loder, Ba
-26½	6¾	24½	...	3+3	Perak . .	Perak Museum.
23⅛	7	15⅜	...	3+3	Borneo	H. B. Low, British Museu
19⅝	4¼	16⅞	16⅞	4+3	Assam . .	Hume Collection, Brit Museum.
16¼	4¼	5⅝	...	3+2	Borneo .	W. B. Pryer, British Muse

[1] Outside.

FORMOSAN SAMBAR (Cervus unicolor swinhoei).

This race is very closely related to the preceding, from which it distinguished by its shorter head, concave profile, longer limbs, a certain differences in colour; the lower part of the legs being browni or whitish yellow, and the bushy tail black all round. It is confin to the island of Formosa.

Length on outside curve.	Circumference.	Tip to Tip.	Points.	Locality.	Owner.
19¾	...	9	3+3	Island of Formosa . . .	British Museum.
16⅛	3⅝	16	3+3	Do. . .	Do.
13⅝	4¾	13⅛	4+4	Do.	Do.
5⅞	2⅛	6¼	3+2	Do. . . .	Do.

LUZON SAMBAR (Cervus unicolor philippinus).

Nearly allied to the two last, the height at the shoulder being about 28 inches, the build stout and massive, with the hind-quarters specially elevated, and the form that of a small Malayan sambar. On the head is a blackish streak starting from over each eye to form a line down the middle of the face separated by a band of pale fawn from a moustache-like dark mark in the muzzle.

Distribution.—The island of Luzon, in the Philippines; introduced into the Marianne islands, and described as a separate species under the name of *C. mariannus.*

Length on outside curve.	Circumference.	Tip to Tip.	Points.	Locality.	Owner.
21	$4\frac{3}{4}$	$5\frac{1}{2}$	3+3	Island of Luzon . .	Sir Edmund G. Loder, Bart.
$19\frac{5}{8}$	$5\frac{1}{4}$	$7\frac{1}{2}$	4+4	Do. . .	Capt. Belcher, British Museum.
$18\frac{7}{8}$	$5\frac{1}{4}$	$9\frac{3}{4}$	3+5	Do. . .	Do.
$18\frac{3}{8}$	$5\frac{1}{8}$	$14\frac{3}{4}$	4+3	Do. . .	Do.
18	$4\frac{5}{8}$	13	4+4	Do. . .	Do.
16	4	$10\frac{1}{2}$	3+3	Do. . . .	Sir Edmund G. Loder, Bart.
$15\frac{1}{8}$	$5\frac{1}{2}$	$11\frac{1}{4}$	3+3	Do. . . .	Capt. Belcher, British Museum.

BASILAN SAMBAR (Cervus unicolor nigricans).

Length on outside curve.	Circumference.	Tip to Tip.	Points.	Locality.	Owner.
$13\frac{1}{2}$	$4\frac{3}{8}$	$12\frac{1}{8}$	3+3	Basilan Island . .	A. H. Everett, British Museum.
$13\frac{1}{8}$	$4\frac{1}{2}$	$11\frac{5}{8}$	3+3	Do. .	Do.

SZECHUAN SAMBAR (Cervus unicolor dejeani).

Length on outside curve.	Circumference.	Tip to Tip.	Widest inside.	Points.	Locality.	Owner.
$30\frac{3}{8}$	$5\frac{1}{2}$	$15\frac{3}{8}$	$18\frac{1}{2}$	3+3	Ta-tsien-lou Szechuan	Paris Museum (type specimen).

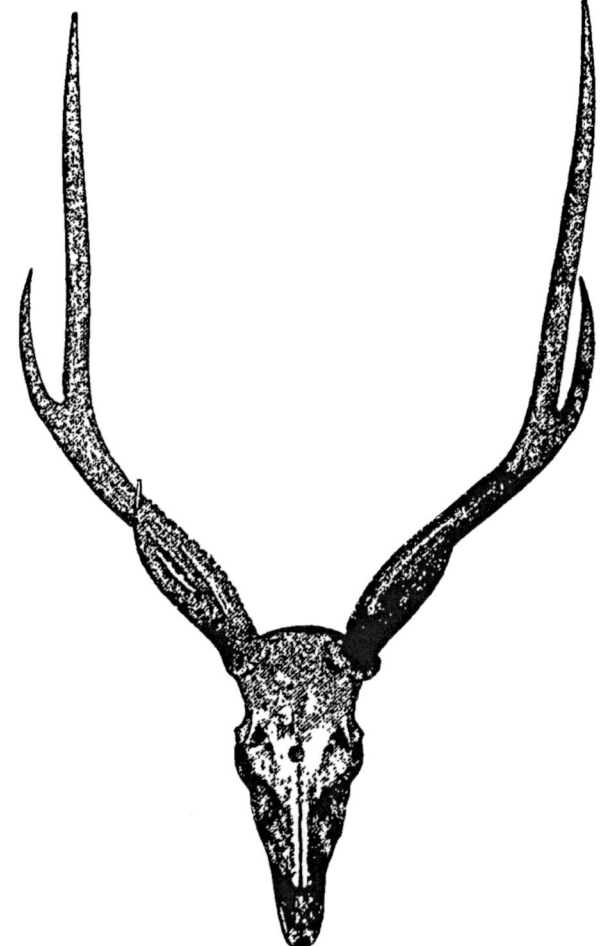

Skull and Antlers of Javan Rusa.
From a specimen in the British Museum.

JAVAN RUSA (Cervus hippelaphus).

General form, coat, and colour sambar-like ; but the ears smaller
the tail thin, the hairs on the back banded with coloured rings, and the
under parts, chin, and inner sides of buttocks whitish.   Antlers comparatively slender and only moderately rough, with the brow tine
medium or short, and making a large acute angle with the beam ; the
hinder or inner tine of the terminal fork much longer than the front
or outer one, and forming the continuation of the beam, from the

front or front outer surface of which the front tine arises as an offshoot; the two antlers enclosing a lyrate space. Young, uniformly coloured. There are two races of this species—one the Javan rusa (*C. hippelaphus typicus*) of the approximate size of a red deer, and the other the Moluccan rusa (*C. hippelaphus moluccensis*), from Celebes and the Moluccas, said to be smaller, and without a distinct mane on the neck or tuft to the tail.

Length on outside curve.	Circumference.	Tip to Tip.	Widest inside.	Points.	Locality.	Owner.
-36	...	11½	...	3+3	Mauritius (introduced)	V.-Admiral Sir William Kennedy.
35½	4⅜	22¾	...	3+3	Java . .	Sir Victor Brooke's Collection.
34½	4⅞	17¼	22¼	3+3	Do. . . .	Commander C. Keppel, C.B., R.N.
[1] 34	...	...	...	...	Rodriguez (introduced)	V.-Admiral Sir William Kennedy.
33¼	4⅞	19½	25	3+3	Java . . .	Commander C. Keppel, C.B., R.N.
33	4½	25½	...	3+3	Do. . . .	Duke of Bedford.
32	4½	19	16¼	3+3	Do. . .	The late H. J. H. Platt.
28¼	4½	11½	12½	3+3	Do. . .	Sir Edmund G. Loder, Bart.

[1] Weight 19 stone 3 lbs.

MOLUCCAN RUSA (Cervus hippelaphus moluccensis).

See Javan rusa above.

Length on outside curve.	Circumference.	Tip to Tip.	Points.	Locality.	Owner.
36⅛	4⅝	18½	3+3	?	Sir Edmund G. Loder, Bart.
27½	4¾	14½	3+3	?	Duke of Bedford.
14¾	3¼	...	3+3	?	Do.
8¾	4	5⅛	...	Batchian . . .	A. R. Wallace, British Museum.
6¼	3⅜	5⅜	...	?	British Museum.

BAVIAN DEER (Cervus kuhli).

A small deer allied to the Javan rusa (*C. hippelaphus*), standing about 27 inches at the shoulder, of light build, and of a uniform brown colour, without a dark stripe down the back.

Distribution.—The Bavian Islands, between Borneo and Java.

Length on outside curve.	Circumference.	Tip to Tip.	Widest inside.	Points.	Locality.	Owner.
9¾	2⅞	10⅞	10⅞	3+3	Bavian Islands	British Museum.

Head of Male Hog-Deer.

HOG-DEER or PARA (Cervus porcinus).

Allied to the Bavian deer, but the antlers larger, the build longer and lower, and the summer coat of the adult, as well as that of the young, spotted with yellowish white. General colour in winter rufous or yellowish brown, somewhat speckled above, and much darker beneath ; in summer, upper parts paler and more or less spotted. Antlers on long pedicles, with the hinder tine of the terminal fork the shorter. Height at shoulder from about 25 to 29 inches. Weight about 90 to 100 lbs. The largest pair ever seen by Mr. A. O. Hume belonged to a specimen he shot in the Ganges Khadir, near Meerut. It measured 20 along the beam inside, and had a mid-beam girth of 3.5. It was destroyed in the Mutiny, the house in which it was hung, with several hundred others, having been burnt down.

Distribution.—India, throughout the Indo-Gangetic plain from Sind and the Punjab to Assam, thence through Sylhet to Burma and Tenasserim.

Length on outside curve.	Circumference above brow tine.	Tip to Tip.	Locality.	Owner.
–23¼	3⅞	12⅞	Burma	Vet.-Capt. G. H. Evans.
–21¾	3½	7¼	Do.	Do.
–21	3½	18¾	Do.	Do.

HOG-DEER or PARA (Cervus porcinus)—*continued.*

Length on outside curve.	Circumference above brow tine.	Tip to Tip.	Locality.	Owner.
–21	3¼	15¼	Pegu . . .	Major-Gen. E. M. Norie.
–20½	3¼	12½	Burma . .	Vet.-Capt. G. H. Evans.
–20⅜	3⅛	...	Nepal . . .	Bombay Natural History Society's Museum.
–20¼	4½	17¼	?	J. Whitaker.
–20⅛	3	9½	N.W. Provinces .	J. Nugent.
–20	...	...	Burma . .	The late Capt. R. C. Beavan, Indian Museum.
–19⅝	3⅛	16	Meerut, N.W.P. .	W. Q. Winwood.
19½	3⅛	13⅝	Dudla Swamp, N.W. Provinces	Capt. W. E. Stobart.
–19½	3⅜	...	Nepal . . .	Bombay Natural History Society's Museum.
–19⅜	...	...	Ganges Khadir .	H. S. King.
19¼	3⅛	9½	Do. .	A. O. Hume, C.B.
19⅛	3¼	16½	Burma . .	Sir Victor Brooke's Collection.
19⅛	3⅜	18¾	?	H. C. V. Hunter.
–19	4¼	5 1/16	Upper Burma .	C. W. A. Bruce.
–18⅜	4 7/16	15	Do. . .	Do.
[1]–18	6½	19	Ganges Khadir .	Col. R. Pole-Carew, C.B.
–18	...	...	?	W. Gillman.
17¾	3½	9¼	Nepal . . .	The late B. H. Hodgson, British Museum.
–17½	...	...	Ganges Khadir .	Major F. D. V. Wing.
17⅛	...	9¼	India . . .	J. Carr Saunders.
–17	3⅛	...	Naini Tal Terai .	Major-General Alexander A. A. Kinloch.
16⅞	3	10⅜	?	British Museum.
–16½	3⅜	14⅛	Nepal . . .	A. E. Leatham.
16⅛	2⅞	8⅝	India . . .	The late Gen. Hardwicke, British Museum.
15½	2⅝	7¼	Do . .	Sir Edmund G. Loder, Bart.
15	2½	...	Laos States, Cambodia	A. Waley.

[1] Ten points.

Head of Chital, shot by Lieut.-Col. F. H. Whitby.

CHITAL or AXIS (Cervus axis).

This beautiful species is distinguished from all the other members of the Rusine group, except the Philippine spotted deer (*C. alfredi*), by the body being profusely spotted with white at all seasons and all ages; the general colour of the upper parts being light rufous fawn, with a dark stripe from the nape to the tip of the tail and a black band on the muzzle. Height at shoulder from 36 to 38 inches; live-weight estimated at about 250 lbs. Antlers supported on short pedicles, long, slender, and moderately rough; the brow tine making nearly a right angle with the beam, and the front tine of the terminal fork, which forms the continuation of the beam, much the longer.

Distribution.—India and Ceylon.

CHITAL or AXIS (Cervus axis)—*continued.*

Length on outside curve.	Circumference above the first point.	Tip to Tip.	Points.	Locality.	Owner.
-38¼	4¾	19½	3+3	Asirgarh Jungle, Central Provinces	Lieut.-Col. M. Cust.
38	4¾	18	3+3	East Berar . .	Lieut.-Col. F. H. Whitby. See Illustration.
-38	...	...	...	Narbada Valley	The late Capt. J. Forsyth.
37½	3¾	19	3+3	Siwalik Hills . .	B. R. M. Glossop.
37½	4¼	24⅜	4+4	Bassim, C.P. .	A. O. Hume, C.B.
37⅜	4	24½	3+3	Déhra Dún .	Do.
37¼	4¼	16⅞	4+5	?	Sir Victor Brooke's Collection.
36¾	4⅜	19⅛	4+4	?	The late W. C. Oswell.
36½	4½	25	4+3	Berar .	C. H. Seely.
-36½	4½	15⅝	4+3	Nepal . . .	A. E. Leatham.
-36½	5¾	19¾	3+3	Central Provinces .	Capt. M. McNeill.
-36½	...	16¾	4+4	Do. . .	Capt. J. H. Gwynne.
36	4¼	25¼	3+4	?	British Museum.
-36	5	15	4+3	Mysore . .	Vet.-Capt. G. H. Evans.
-36	4⅝	21	4+3	?	Major James Grant.
35½	4¼	18⅛	4+4	?	Sir Edmund G. Loder, Bart.
35½	4	12¼	5+5	?	G. W. Hatch.
35¼	4⅛	22⅞	3+3	Western Ghats .	Major-Gen. Sir Arthur Ellis, K.C.V.O.
-35¼	4	21	4+4	?	James J. Harrison.
-35	4½	...	...	N. Kanara . .	Bombay Natural History Society's Museum.
35	4½	20¼	4+3	Kota, Rajputana .	Major H. C. Morland.
-35	...	16½	...	Mandla, Central Provinces	Capt. B. H. Boucher.
35	4	24¼	3+3	Nepal . . .	Capt. G. Roos Keppel.
-35	3½	18	...	?	W. S. Murray.
-34¾	5¾	12⅜	4+4	N.W. Provinces .	Surgeon-Capt. E. M'K. Williams.
34¾	4½	17¾	...	?	H.R.H. the Duke of Saxe-Coburg and Gotha.
-34½	...	...	...	Mirzapore . .	Indian Museum.
-34½	...	22½	3+3	Tapti Valley . .	J. D. Inverarity.
-34¼	3⅞	...	...	North Kanara .	Lieut.-Col. L. L. Fenton.

CHITAL or AXIS (Cervus axis)—*continued*.

Length on outside curve.	Circumference above the first point.	Tip to Tip.	Points.	Locality.	Owner.
34	$4\frac{3}{4}$	$16\frac{1}{2}$	3 + 3	?	Col. R. Pole Carew, C.B.
-34	...	...	...	?	Otho Shaw.
-34	...	29	3 + 3	Narbada Valley .	J. D. Inverarity.
34	$3\frac{1}{2}$	24	4 + 3	?	W. H. Cobb.
$33\frac{1}{2}$	$4\frac{5}{8}$	$16\frac{1}{2}$	3 + 3	Central Provinces .	H. Douglas Taylor.
$33\frac{1}{2}$	$4\frac{3}{8}$	$23\frac{5}{8}$	4 + 5	Do.	Major C. S. Cumberland.
$33\frac{1}{2}$	...	..	...	Ahree District, Central Provinces	Colonel F. C. Lister-Kay.
$33\frac{1}{2}$	$4\frac{5}{8}$	$19\frac{5}{8}$	3 + 3	?	J. Carr Saunders.
$-33\frac{1}{2}$	...	18	3 + 3	Central Provinces .	H. St. Lennard.
$33\frac{1}{2}$	$3\frac{7}{4}$	$18\frac{1}{4}$	3 + 3	?	Col. Scott Chisholme.
$33\frac{1}{4}$	$3\frac{7}{8}$	13	2 + 3	Yeddacurra . .	Sir Victor Brooke's Collection.
$33\frac{1}{8}$	$3\frac{7}{8}$	$14\frac{3}{8}$	3 + 4	?	Sir James Anderson, Bart.
-33	$4\frac{1}{4}$	$16\frac{1}{2}$	5 + 4	?	Dublin Museum.
-33	$6\frac{1}{8}$	22	4 + 4	Déhra Dún . .	Major-General Alexander A. A. Kinloch.
33	$3\frac{3}{4}$	$19\frac{3}{4}$	3 + 3	N.W. Provinces .	Capt. Chambers Didham.
$32\frac{7}{8}$	$4\frac{3}{8}$	$21\frac{1}{2}$	3 + 3	?	Hon. Walter Rothschild.
$32\frac{3}{4}$	$3\frac{7}{8}$	14	3 + 3	?	Sir James Anderson, Bart.
$32\frac{1}{4}$	$4\frac{1}{4}$	$23\frac{3}{8}$	5 + 4	South India . .	Sir Victor Brooke's Collection.
$-32\frac{1}{4}$	$4\frac{1}{4}$	$14\frac{1}{2}$	5 + 4	North Oudh . .	Major J. W. M. Cotton.
32	4	$16\frac{1}{2}$	4 + 4	Jabalpur . . .	A. Leslie Renton.
$-31\frac{1}{2}$	$3\frac{3}{4}$	$17\frac{1}{2}$	3 + 3	Ceylon . . .	Count Scheibler.
$31\frac{1}{4}$	3	$10\frac{1}{2}$	3 + 3	Do. . .	A. R. Hay.
$30\frac{3}{4}$	$3\frac{1}{4}$	$20\frac{1}{2}$	3 + 3	Do. . .	Washington Singer.
30	$3\frac{1}{2}$	15	4 + 3	Do. . .	Lieut.-Col. H. Wade-Dalton.
$29\frac{7}{8}$	$4\frac{1}{8}$	$20\frac{1}{4}$	3 + 3	Do. . .	British Museum.
$28\frac{3}{4}$	$3\frac{1}{4}$	$11\frac{1}{2}$	3 + 3	Do. . .	Capt. G. O. Bigge.
$28\frac{1}{4}$	$4\frac{1}{4}$	$17\frac{1}{2}$	3 + 3	Do. .	Surgeon-Major G. E. Hale, D.S.O.
27	$3\frac{1}{2}$	$8\frac{1}{2}$	3 + 3	Do. . .	Capt. Lewis Jones.
$-25\frac{1}{2}$	3	18	3 + 3	Do. . .	Dr. Percy Rendall.

Side view of Antlers of Swamp-Deer.   From a specimen in the British Museum.

SWAMP-DEER (Cervus duvauceli).

This species belongs to the Rucervine group, in which the antlers resemble those of the Rusine section in the absence of the bez and trez tines, but have the beam regularly forked, and each branch again dividing, so that there are at least four tines.   In the swamp-deer the antlers are smooth and flattened, with a long brow tine rising almost at right angles to the beam, which is undivided for about half the total length of the antler, and then splits into a fork, each branch of which is usually simply forked, but sometimes divided in a more complicated manner.   General colour bright rufous brown, often speckled near the back.   Height at shoulder from 3 feet 8 inches to 3 feet 10 inches ; weight about 51 stone 3 lbs.

Distribution.—India, exclusive of Ceylon.

SWAMP-DEER (Cervus duvauceli)—*continued.*

Length on outside curve.	Circumference.	Tip to Tip.	Widest inside.	Points.	Locality.	Owner.
41	6½	35½	38	8+5	Central Provinces .	Capt. W. W. Hancock.
41	5½	(one antler) broken		6+6	Do.	Do.
39¼	5	35½	37½	5+6	Do.	Major C. S. Cumberland.
38¼	5½	(shed antlers)		6+5	Do.	C. F. Egerton.
–38	...	43	...	6+6	Do.	J. D. Inverarity.
–38	...	...	...	6+6	Do.	Capt. B. H. Boucher.
37⅜	5¼	23⅝	28½	7+6	?	Sir Edmund G. Loder, Bart.
36½	5	...	20 (outside)	23	Mavella District	Measured by Major A. E. Ward.
36	5	29¾	33⅜	6+5	Nepal .	The late B. H. Hodgson, British Museum.
–36	...	29	...	6+6	Do. .	J. D. Inverarity.
–35½	...	...	...	...	Chutia Nagpur .	Indian Museum.
35⅜	4⅞	27	29¾*	...	?	Sir Victor Brooke's Collection.
35¼	5¾	22¼	...	7+6	Nepal . . .	H. C. V. Hunter.
–34¾	...	33	...	12+8	Mymensing .	F. B. Simson.
–34½	5½	24⅞	28⅞	6+5	Nepal	A. E. Leatham.
34½	4⅞	10¾	28	9+6	Mandla, Cent. Provinces	Major A. G. W. Malet.
33½	4⅜	28½	32¼	5+5	N.W. Provinces . .	Capt. Chambers Didham.
32⅞	5¼	22⅜	26⅜	6+5	Gowhatti, Assam	A. O. Hume, C.B.
32⅝	5	33¼	35	6+6	?	Sir Robert Harvey, Bart.
32¾	5	27½	...	7+6	Kuch Behar . . .	Major Henry Streatfeild.
32½	4¼	32	33½	5+5	Central Provinces	Capt. E. D. White.
32⅛	5⅛	19⅝	24½	7+7	Nepal .	H.R.H. the Duke of Saxe-Coburg and Gotha.
32	4	29	19	4+4	?	Sir H. D. Tichborne, Bart.
31	4¾	...	...	...	Herkapur .	Capt. J. H. Purvis.
–30⅝	5	31⅝	...	7+6	Raipur, Central Provinces	Capt. M. M'Neill.
30½	5¾	28½	32¾	8+8	Central Provinces . .	H. Douglas Taylor.
30½	4¼	24¾	27	5+5	?	A. M. Caccia.

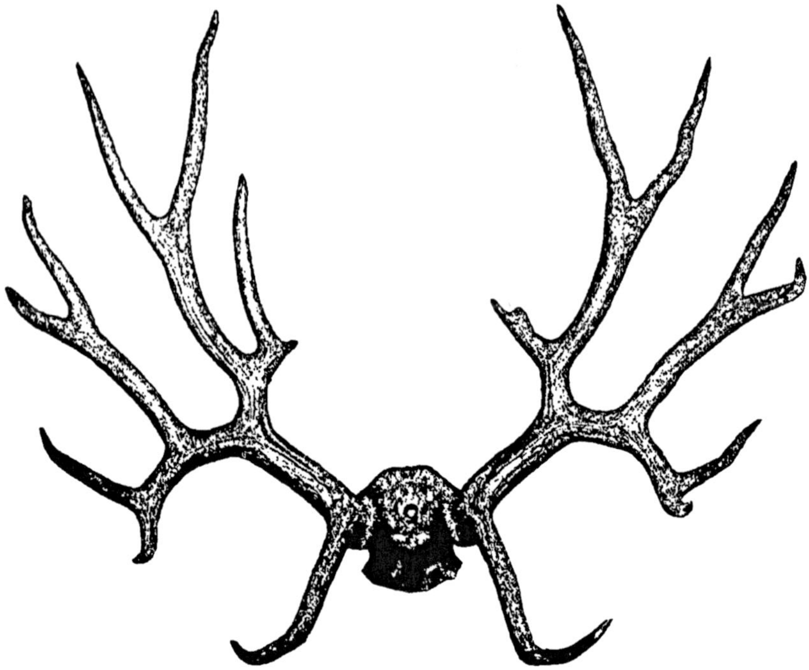

Antlers of Schomburgk's Deer. From a specimen in the British Museum.

SCHOMBURGK'S DEER (Cervus schomburgki).

Allied to the preceding, but the antlers smooth, rounded, and more complex; the brow tine very long, frequently forked, and arising nearly at right angles to the beam, which is very short, compressed, and regularly forked, with each of the main branches about equally developed and again forking in a similar manner to terminate in long cylindrical tines. General colour uniform dark brown. Height at shoulder about 3 feet 5 inches.

Distribution.—The northern districts of Siam.

Length on outside curve.	Circumference.	Tip to Tip.	Widest inside.	Points.	Locality.	Owner.
–$32\frac{1}{8}$	$5\frac{1}{8}$	...	...	12 + 11	Siam	Sir Edmund G. Loder, Bart.
$30\frac{1}{8}$	5	$15\frac{5}{8}$	33	10 + 10	Do.	British Museum.
$29\frac{7}{8}$	$5\frac{1}{8}$	$23\frac{5}{8}$	$26\frac{7}{8}$	9 + 8	Do.	Do.
$29\frac{3}{4}$	$4\frac{3}{4}$	$28\frac{3}{8}$	$31\frac{5}{8}$	10 + 11	Do.	Do.
$29\frac{1}{2}$	6	$19\frac{1}{2}$	27	6 + 7	Do.	J. Carr Saunders.
$28\frac{1}{3}$	$5\frac{1}{4}$	11	$29\frac{3}{8}$	11 + 9	?	Sir Victor Brooke's Collection.
–28.5	5.25	9.5	28.5	10 + 9	Siam	Indian Museum.
$27\frac{7}{8}$	$5\frac{3}{8}$	14	$24\frac{1}{2}$	9 + 8	Do.	British Museum.
$27\frac{3}{4}$	$4\frac{3}{8}$	$18\frac{1}{2}$	$24\frac{7}{8}$	8 + 7	Do.	Do.

Skull and Antlers of Thameng.   From a Burmese specimen.

THAMENG or ELD'S DEER (Cervus eldi).

Although belonging to the same group as the two preceding species, this deer is readily distinguished by the peculiar form of the antlers.   These are rounded and rough, with a long curved brow tine, forming a continuation of the curve of the beam, which is set at right angles to the pedicle ; the beam unbranched for some distance, much curved, and finally forked, with the outer prong more subdivided than the inner.   Height at shoulder about 3 feet 9 inches ; weight from 210 lbs. to 245 lbs.   There are two races of this species.   First, the Burmese thameng (*C. eldi typicus*), ranging from Manipur through Burma to the Malay Peninsula, in which the antlers are rounded throughout, and the coat is uniformly umber-brown.   And, secondly, the Siamese thameng (*C. eldi platyceros*), from Siam and Hainan, in which the tips of the antlers are flattened with a number of small snags, and the coat is redder, with yellowish spots.

Length on outside curve, not including brow tine.	Circum- ference.	Tip to Tip.	Widest inside.	Points.	Length of brow tine.	Locality.	Owner.
42	5	29	24	3 + 2	...	Burma .	A. H. Collins.
41	$5\frac{1}{2}$	$27\frac{5}{8}$	36	5 + 5	...	Upper Burma .	Surgeon - Major O. E. P. Lloyd.
[1] $39\frac{5}{8}$	5	$31\frac{3}{8}$	$36\frac{5}{8}$	20 (small points)	$15\frac{3}{4}$	Siam .	Sir Edmund G. Loder, Bart.
$38\frac{7}{8}$	$6\frac{1}{4}$	$25\frac{1}{2}$	$30\frac{3}{8}$	16 + 19	...	?	British Museum.

[1] Measured on front of antler from highest tip to tip of frontal tine $56\frac{1}{2}$ inches.

THAMENG or ELD'S DEER (Cervus eldi)—*continued.*

Length on outside curve, not including brow tine.	Circumference.	Tip to Tip.	Widest inside.	Points.	Length of brow tine.	Locality.	Owner.
38¼	6¼	24	30¾	6+5	...	Manipur . .	A. O. Hume, C.B.
38	4⅝	29¼	36¾	5+5	...	Pegu . .	G. R. Radmore.
37½	5⅜	20¼	30½	5+5	...	?	British Museum.
37	4½	24¾	32¼	5+5	...	Burma . .	A. H. Collins.
36⅛	5½	28¾	31¾	4+3	...	Manipur .	A. O. Hume, C.B.
35¾	4⅝	19¾	26¼	4+3	...	Do. . .	Viscount Powerscourt.
35½	4½	22¼	31¼	6+6	...	Kyaikto, Lower Burma	J. W. Clough.
35¼	6¼	24	30¾	6+3	18½	Manipur . .	A. O. Hume, C.B.
35	4½	30¼	36	5+5	...	Lower Burma .	G. R. Radmore.
34⅞	5½	27½	32	6+6	...	Burma . .	A. O. Hume, C.B., British Museum.
34½	4	21¼	27	6+6	...	Do. . .	Viscount Powerscourt.
34⅛	5	24	32¼	6+6	...	Do. . .	Hon. Walter Rothschild.
34	5⅞	23½	29¾	10+10	...	Do. . .	J. Carr Saunders.
33¾	4¾	17⅜	24⅜	5+4	...	Do. .	Capt. G. H. Mockler.
33½	...	...	40	...	15	Pegu . .	Col. R. Pole-Carew, C.B.
33⅛	5⅛	33⅛	37¼	5+5	14	Burma . .	Sir Edmund G. Loder, Bart.
33	4⅝	28⅞	32⅛	3+3	...	Do. .	Sir Victor Brooke's Collection.
32⅛	5⅜	20¼	20½	4+3	...	Do. . .	Gen. Sir Henry Collett, K.C.B.
32	4½	18¼	24¼	6+5	...	Do. . .	Col. J. Biddulph.
-32	...	...	...	...	...	?	Maharaja of Travancore, G.C.S.I.
31⅛	5	25⅞	29⅛	7+6	...	?	The late B. H. Hodgson, British Museum.
24¾	3¼	19½	21⅜	5+5	...	Burma . .	Dr. W. P. Y. Bainbrigge.
-24	4½	18	18½	5+5	..	Do. . .	Dublin Museum.
18½	3⅝	12½	13½	6+5	...	?	The late R. Swinhoe, British Museum.
13⅝	3¼	...	12⅜	6+5	...	Siam .	British Museum.

THAMENG or ELD'S DEER (Cervus eldi)—*continued.*

Extreme length of right antler round the outside curve, highest point, to tip of brow tine.	Circumference.	Tip to Tip.	Widest span.	Number of points.	Locality.	Owner.
-56¼	5⅝	28	37	13	Burma . .	W. F. Loftus-Tottenham.
-55¼	4½	34½	42¼	12	Do. . .	Do.
-55	7	28½	38½	12	Do. . .	Vet.-Capt. G. H. Evans.
-55	5¾	30	37	15	Do. . .	Do.
-55	5	...	42	13	Do. . .	Do.
-53½	5½	...	38	16	Do. . .	W. F. Loftus-Tottenham.
-52¾	4½	24⅝	36¾	12	Do. . .	Do.
-51⅛	5	...	33½	7	Do. . .	Do.
-51	5½	27	37½	10	Do. . .	Vet.-Capt. G. H. Evans.
-50½	7¼	36	39½	14	Do. . .	Do.
-50½	5½	...	29½	14	Do. .	Do.
-50½	5	30½	37	8	Do. . .	Do.
-50	5¼	25½	33	12	Do. . .	W. F. Loftus-Tottenham.
-49½	6½	27	37½	9	Do. . .	Vet.-Capt. G. H. Evans.
-49½	5¼	27½	36	10	Do. . .	W. F. Loftus-Tottenham.
-48½	5¼	23¾	36	13	Do. . .	Do.
-47½	5	...	34⅝	13	Do. . .	Vet.-Capt. G. H. Evans.
-46½	6	16	...	9+6	Do. . .	S. E. F. Jenkins.
-46	5¼	20	30	10	Do. .	Vet.-Capt. G. H. Evans.
-44½	5	...	23	10	Do. . .	Do.
-44	5	22	36	14	Do. .	Do.
-43½	5½	30	33	10	Do. . .	W. F. Loftus-Tottenham.
-43½	5½	16½	27½	14	Do. . .	Vet.-Capt. G. H. Evans.
-43	4¾	...	34½	12	Do. . .	Do.
-40½	4¾	28	33½	9	Do. . .	Do.
-40	5½	...	40¼	10	Do . .	W. F. Loftus-Tottenham.

Frontlet and Antlers of Indian Muntjac.

INDIAN MUNTJAC or BARKING DEER (Cervulus muntjac).

This species is the typical representative of a genus of small Oriental deer differing widely from all those included in *Cervus*. The antlers, which do not exceed half the length of the head, have a short brow tine and an unbranched beam, and are supported on long skin-covered pedicles, continued downwards as convergent ridges on the forehead, whence the name of rib-faced deer. Tufts of bristly hair occupy the position of the antlers in the females. The muzzle has a large naked portion, and although there is generally a pair of glands on the face, there are none either on the hock or the cannon-bone. The young are spotted, but the adults uniformly coloured. In the Indian muntjac, which is one of the reddish-coloured species, and whose range extends from Ceylon and India through Burma to China, the Malay Peninsula, Sumatra, and Java, the height at the shoulder varies from 20 to 22 inches. The Chinese muntjac (*C. reevesi*), from Southern China and Formosa, is a much smaller species, also reddish in colour; but in the rare Tenasserim muntjac (*C. feæ*), and the larger but equally scarce hairy-fronted muntjac (*C. crinifrons*) of Eastern China, the general hue of the body is dark purplish sepia-brown, with white on the buttocks and under surface of the tail. The average height at the shoulder is about 26 inches, and weight about 28 lbs.; a female stands about 23 inches and weighs about 32 lbs. In 1852 Mr. Wilson ("Mountaineer") had a specimen of which Mr. A. O. Hume recorded the measurements as follows: antlers round the curve outside, 9.5 and 9.0 long. In those days he did not collect horns, and only noted them.

G

INDIAN MUNTJAC or BARKING DEER (Cervulus muntjac)—*continued.*

Length on outside curve of antler from burr to tip.	Circumference above burr.	Tip to Tip.	Locality.	Owner.
$-10\frac{3}{8}$	...	...	Java .	H. Van Son.
$7\frac{5}{8}$	$4\frac{1}{2}$	$3\frac{1}{2}$	Lombok .	Hon. Walter Rothschild.
$^1-7\frac{1}{2}$	...	...	Near Mussuri .	Major A. E. Ward.
$7\frac{1}{4}$	$3\frac{1}{4}$	$3\frac{7}{8}$	Lombok	Hon. Walter Rothschild.
$-6\frac{3}{4}$	$2\frac{3}{4}$	$2\frac{1}{2}$	Perak .	Perak Museum.
$6\frac{3}{4}$	$2\frac{1}{4}$	3	Ranikhet	Surgeon - Major B. W. Deeble.
$-6\frac{3}{4}$	...	...	Dugshai, Punjab	J. Johnston-Stewart.
$6\frac{5}{8}$	$2\frac{1}{4}$	$3\frac{1}{8}$	Java . . .	J. C. Van Son.
$-6\frac{1}{2}$	..	...	Do. .	H. Van Son.
$6\frac{1}{2}$	$2\frac{5}{8}$	$3\frac{1}{2}$	Nepal .	The late B. H. Hodgson, British Museum.
$6\frac{1}{2}$	3	$3\frac{3}{8}$	?	A. O. Hume, C.B.
$-6\frac{1}{2}$	$2\frac{1}{2}$	$3\frac{1}{8}$	Namba Forest, Assam	Surgeon-Capt. H. S. Wood.
$-6\frac{1}{2}$	$2\frac{3}{4}$	...	North of Mussuri	Capt. Harry V. Brooke.
6	$2\frac{5}{8}$	$4\frac{3}{4}$	Taroy, Burma .	Vet.-Capt. G. H. Evans.
$-5\frac{1}{2}$	...	...	?	Indian Museum.
$5\frac{1}{2}$	$3\frac{1}{2}$	$2\frac{1}{2}$	Assam . .	A. H. Straker.
$5\frac{1}{2}$	2	2	Laos States, Cambodia	A. Waley.
$5\frac{3}{8}$	3	...	?	Col. R. J. Heber-Percy.
$5\frac{1}{4}$	2	$3\frac{1}{2}$	S. India .	Sir Victor Brooke's Collection
$5\frac{1}{4}$	$3\frac{1}{4}$	$3\frac{1}{8}$	Assam	P. Russel.
$-5\frac{1}{4}$	...	...	Mandla Dist., C.P.	Capt. B. H. Boucher.
5	3	3	Assam	Major C. S. Cumberland.
-5	$3\frac{1}{2}$	$3\frac{5}{8}$	North Kanara .	Lieut.-Col. L. L. Fenton.

¹ Weight 37 lbs.

TIBETAN MUNTJAC (Cervulus lachrymans).

Nearly allied to the last, but smaller.

Length on outside curve of longest antler.	Circumference.	Tip to Tip.	Locality.	Owner.
$2\frac{1}{2}$	$1\frac{5}{8}$	3	Ningpo . . .	The late R. Swinhoe, British Museum.
$-2\frac{1}{2}$	$1\frac{1}{2}$	$3\frac{1}{4}$	Do.	Dublin Museum.

Head of Hairy-fronted Muntjac.

THE HAIRY-FRONTED MUNTJAC (Cervulus crinifrons).

Length on outside curve of longest antler.	Circumference.	Tip to Tip.	Locality.	Owner.
1½	...	4½	Ningpo	British Museum.

TENASSERIM MUNTJAC (Cervulus feæ).

Antlers about two inches long.

EUROPEAN ROE (Capreolus vulgaris).

Roe may be recognised by the rudimentary tail, and the medium-sized antlers rising close together and almost vertically from the head, without a brow tine, and regularly forking at a point about two-thirds the total length, with the posterior prong again subdividing, so that the number of points is usually three. There is no gland and tuft on the hock, but one on the upper part of the hinder cannon-bone. In the European roe the height at the shoulder is about 26 inches. In winter the coat is dark speckly brown with a large white rump-patch, but in summer foxy red, with little or no white behind. The range embraces the greater part of Europe as far as the Caucasus, and probably Asia Minor.

EUROPEAN ROE (Capreolus vulgaris)—*continued.*

Length on outside curve.	Circumference.	Tip to Tip.	Locality.	Owner.
13	4	14½	Germany . .	Viscount Powerscourt.
13	4	14½	Do. .	Do.
13	3½	10¼	Do.	Do.
-13	6½	8½	Do. . .	H.R.H. the Duke of Saxe-Coburg and Gotha.
-13	7	10	Do.	Do.
-13	6½	8	Do.	Do.
12¾	3	8½	Do. .	Viscount Powerscourt.
12½	4	9½	Do. .	Do.
12¼	4¾	9	Servia .	Do.
-12⅛	3¾	4½	Austria .	Capt. John Marriott.
[1] -12⅛	...	...	Perthshire .	R. Moncrieff.
11⅝	...	6	Monymusk, N.B.	Sir Arthur Grant, Bart.
[2] 11½	...	...	Orton, Speyside	Sir G. Macpherson Grant, Bart.
11½	3	8¾	Germany	Viscount Powerscourt.
-11¼	6	6	Perth	J. G. Millais.
11¼	4½	8¾	Servia . . .	Viscount Powerscourt.
-11⅛	4¾	...	Scotland	Duke of Bedford.
-11⅛	4½	...	(Single antler dug up)	J. G. Millais.
11	7¼	...	Ross-shire . . .	H. M. Warrand.
-11	...	7¼	Aberdeenshire	Col. Gordon Cumming.
11	5 1/16	7½	Ross-shire .	H. M. Warrand.
11	[3] 8	8¾	Germany .	Viscount Powerscourt.
11	7⅛	6⅞	Sligo, Ireland . .	Sir Henry Gore Booth, Bart.
10½	...	...	Beaufort, Ross-shire	J. G. Millais.
10½	6½	6	Ballindalloch . .	Sir G. Macpherson Grant, Bart. .
10½	3½	5¾	Inverness . .	C. Macpherson Grant.
10¼	3½	8¼	?	Major James Grant.
-10¼	...	...	?	J. G. Millais.

[1] and [2] Recorded by J. G. Millais (*British Deer and their Horns*). [3] Abnormal (Peraque).

EUROPEAN ROE (Capreolus vulgaris)—*continued.*

Length on outside curve.	Circumference.	Tip to Tip.	Locality.	Owner.
-10¼	3⅛	Single antler	Dorset . .	A. Du Cane.
10	2¼	4½	Ross .	Sir Edmund G. Loder, Bart.
9¾	2¾	3½	Austria . .	H.R.H. le Duc d'Orléans.
9¾	8⅛	12 points	Sligo, Ireland . .	Sir Henry Gore Booth, Bart.
9⅞	5	5	Dorset . . .	J. E. Harting.
9⅞	3¾	5¾	Moray . .	Sir Victor Brooke's Collection.
9½	3¾	4½	?	Col. Ralph Vivian.
9½	3¼	7¾	New Forest . .	Hon. Gerald Lascelles.
-9¼	5½	5	Beaufort, Ross-shire .	J. G. Millais.
-9¼	4	5 1/16	Ross-shire . . .	Col. A. J. Warrand.
-9¼	3½	7 1/16	Do. .	Do.
9	3	6½	Banff . .	H. Brinsley Brooke.
8¾	2¾	5½	Glenrinnes . .	J. G. Williams.
8⅝	3	4	Scotland . . .	Col. Ralph Vivian.
8½	6¼	3 antlers 4⅞	Lissadell, Ireland .	Sir Henry Gore Booth, Bart.
8½	3	4½	Scotland	C. C. Branch.
8½	3	4½	France	British Museum.
8½	2¾	...	Islay . .	Capt. M. M'Neill.
-8½	4⅛	3	Scotland .	C. V. A. Peel.
8¼	3⅝	27⅛	Lissadell .	J. Kenneth Foster.

Head of Siberian Roe.

SIBERIAN ROE (Capreolus pygargus).

Larger than the last, the height at the shoulder varying from 28 to 34 inches ; the ears shorter and more hairy, the white rump-patch larger, and the antlers longer and more rugose with numerous nodose snags.

Mr. St. George Littledale says the specimens he observed barked like a " barking deer."

Distribution.—From the Altai and mountains of Turkestan to Siberia, and probably the Caspian provinces of Persia.

SIBERIAN ROE (Capreolus pygargus)—*continued.*

Length on outside curve.	Circumference.	Tip to Tip.	Locality.	Owner.
$-18\frac{9}{16}$	$^1 6\frac{3}{4}$	...	?	Carl Hagenbeck.
16	$4\frac{1}{2}$	12	?	Viscount Powerscourt.
$15\frac{1}{2}$	$4\frac{1}{4}$	$8\frac{1}{2}$	?	Do.
15	$4\frac{3}{4}$	...	Siberia	Sir Edmund G. Loder, Bart.
$-14\frac{3}{16}$	$3\frac{15}{16}$	...	Do. . .	Paris Museum.
14	$3\frac{1}{2}$	$13\frac{3}{4}$	Altai, Mongolia .	St. George Littledale. (See illustration.)
$13\frac{7}{8}$	$2\frac{7}{8}$	$13\frac{5}{8}$	Semirechensk Altai .	H. J. Elwes.
$13\frac{3}{4}$	3	6	Asia ? .	British Museum.
$13\frac{1}{4}$	$3\frac{3}{4}$	$11\frac{1}{2}$	?	H.R.H. le Duc d'Orléans.
$13\frac{5}{8}$	4	9	Upper Yenisei Valley	
$13\frac{1}{2}$	$3\frac{3}{4}$	$8\frac{3}{4}$	Semirechensk Altai .	
$13\frac{1}{2}$	$3\frac{3}{4}$	$9\frac{5}{8}$	Upper Venisei Valley .	H. J. Elwes.
$13\frac{1}{2}$	$4\frac{7}{8}$	$12\frac{3}{4}$	Do. . .	
$13\frac{1}{2}$	$3\frac{1}{2}$	$11\frac{1}{4}$	S. Siberia .	W. A. L. Fletcher.
$13\frac{3}{8}$	$3\frac{15}{16}$	$9\frac{1}{2}$	Siberia .	Paris Museum.
$13\frac{1}{4}$	4	$9\frac{1}{2}$	Do. . .	Duke of Bedford.
$13\frac{1}{4}$	4	$8\frac{7}{8}$	S. Manchuria[2] .	H. E. M. James, British Museum.
$13\frac{1}{4}$	$3\frac{7}{8}$	$9\frac{1}{2}$	Upper Yenisei Valley .	H. J. Elwes.
$13\frac{1}{4}$	$4\frac{7}{8}$	14	Do. . .	Do.
$12\frac{3}{4}$	3	$7\frac{3}{4}$	Semirechensk Altai	Do.
$12\frac{1}{2}$	3	$6\frac{3}{4}$	?	H.R.H. le Duc d'Orléans.
$12\frac{3}{8}$	$3\frac{1}{2}$	$7\frac{1}{4}$	Caucasus . .	H. J. Elwes.
$12\frac{1}{4}$	$3\frac{1}{2}$	3	?	Duke of Bedford.
$11\frac{3}{8}$	4	$8\frac{1}{8}$	Manchuria[2] . .	British Museum.

[1] Circumference of burr.

[2] These probably belong to the somewhat smaller Manchurian Roe.

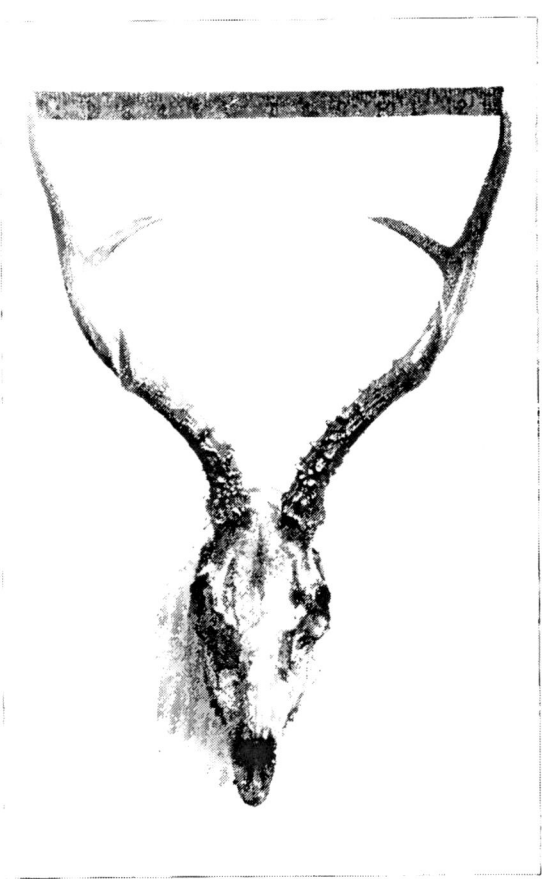

Skull and Antlers of Siberian Roe shot by St. George Littledale.

Antlers of Père David's Milou Deer at Different Ages.
From specimens at Woburn Abbey.

PÈRE DAVID'S MILOU DEER (Elaphurus davidianus).

This remarkable deer differs from all the preceding, except the roes, by the absence of a brow tine to the antlers, which are large and branching, the beam forking at a comparatively short distance above the burr, and the front prong of the fork again dividing, while the hind prong is long and straight. The bushy tail is longer than in any other deer, and the neck of the male is maned. There is a gland-tuft on the upper half of the hind cannon-bone, but none on the hock. In the adult the colour is uniformly tawny, but spotted in the young. Height at shoulder about 3 feet 9 inches.

Distribution.—Northern China ; probably unknown in the wild state.

PÈRE DAVID'S MILOU DEER (Elaphurus davidianus)—*continued.*

Length on outside curve.	Circumference.	Tip to Tip.	Widest inside.	Points.	Locality.	Owner.
$32\frac{7}{8}$	$6\frac{3}{8}$	$13\frac{5}{8}$	$18\frac{1}{2}$	8 + 8	Near Pekin . .	Sir Edmund G. Loder, Bart.
$-30\frac{3}{4}$	5	$35\frac{1}{16}$	$35\frac{1}{16}$	11 + 10	Imperial Park, Pekin	Paris Museum (Type Specimen), Père A. David.
$28\frac{1}{4}$	$5\frac{3}{8}$	$26\frac{1}{2}$	...	3 ÷ 3	?	Hon. Walter Rothschild.
27	$5\frac{7}{8}$	$20\frac{1}{4}$	...	6 + 5	?	British Museum.
[1] 25	5	...	...	6 + 4	Bred in England .	Duke of Bedford.
22	$4\frac{5}{8}$	...	...	4 + 3	Do. .	Do.

[1] Back point of this head measured 28 inches from beam of antler.

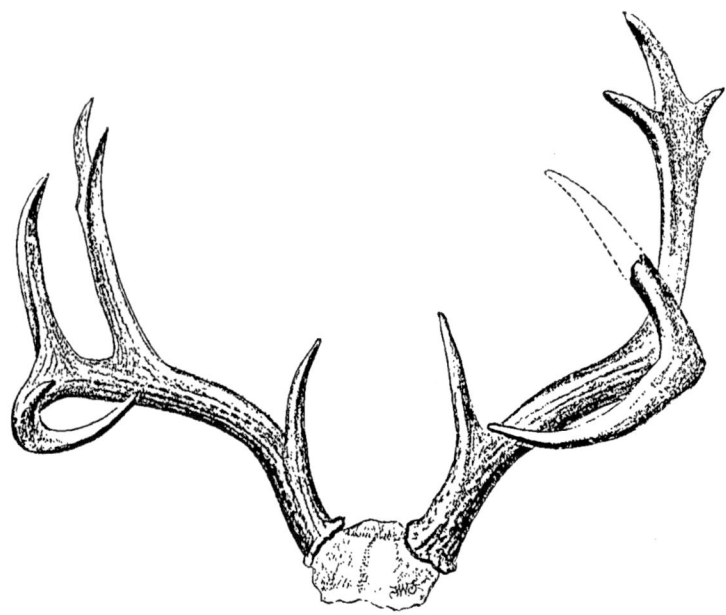

Antlers of Virginian Deer. From a specimen in the British Museum.

COMMON AMERICAN or VIRGINIAN DEER (Mazama americana).

With the exception of the wapiti and elk, all the deer of America are distinguished from those of the Old World, save the roe and milou deer, by the absence of a brow tine to the antlers, which are either regularly forked or spike-like, and quite different from those of either the roe or milou deer. In the Virginian deer they are large and complex, with a long sub-basal snag, and the front prong of the main fork developed at the expense of the hinder, and carrying a number of snags on its upper surface. Tail long. A gland-tuft on the hock, and a small cylindrical white one with a black centre near the lower end of the hind cannon-bone. Colour of upper parts chestnut in summer and bluish gray in winter, with the under surface of the tail and the buttocks pure white. Typically from Eastern North America, where the height at the shoulder reaches to 3 feet 1 inch, but represented by numerous races in other parts of the Continent, which gradually decrease in size and complexity of antlers towards the south, where they extend to Peru, Bolivia, and Guiana. Weight, 12 st. 7 lbs. (F. C. Selous). Commonly called white-tailed deer.

COMMON AMERICAN or VIRGINIAN DEER (Mazama americana)—*continued.*

Length on outside curve.	Circumference.	Tip to Tip.	Widest inside.	Points.	Locality.	Owner.
$27\frac{5}{8}$	$5\frac{3}{8}$	Single antler	...	16	N. America	British Museum.
$27\frac{1}{8}$	$4\frac{3}{8}$	$14\frac{1}{4}$	19	6 + 6	Do.	Do.
$26\frac{3}{4}$	$4\frac{3}{4}$	$9\frac{1}{8}$	20	20	Do.	Major James Grant.
$25\frac{3}{4}$	$4\frac{1}{2}$	9	19	11	Maine	H. S. Wellcome.
$25\frac{3}{8}$	$4\frac{5}{8}$	$10\frac{3}{8}$	19	15 + 13	Texas	Capt. F. Cookson.
$25\frac{1}{4}$	$4\frac{3}{4}$	$12\frac{7}{8}$	$17\frac{1}{8}$	11 + 9	N. America	British Museum.
$24\frac{1}{2}$	$4\frac{1}{2}$	$12\frac{3}{8}$	$18\frac{1}{2}$	6 + 6	Do.	J. Carr Saunders.
$24\frac{1}{2}$	$4\frac{1}{8}$	$11\frac{1}{8}$	$19\frac{1}{2}$	6 + 6	Do.	British Museum.
24	$4\frac{5}{8}$	[1] $19\frac{1}{2}$	...	18	Nebraska	G. B. Grinnell.
$23\frac{3}{4}$	6	12	$16\frac{3}{4}$	5 + 4	Wyoming	James J. Harrison.
23	5	5	16	6 + 6	B. Columbia	J. Turner-Turner.
$22\frac{1}{2}$	4	[1] $15\frac{3}{4}$	...	12	Medora, N.D.	Theodore Roosevelt.
$21\frac{1}{2}$	$3\frac{3}{4}$	$3\frac{1}{4}$	$13\frac{1}{2}$	4 + 4	New York State	Sir Edmund G. L Bart.
21	5	$18\frac{3}{4}$	19	4 + 4	?	L. C. R. Messel.
$19\frac{1}{2}$	$4\frac{1}{4}$	12	15	5 + 5	Wyoming	F. C. Selous.
$19\frac{1}{2}$	$3\frac{1}{2}$	$12\frac{1}{2}$	$15\frac{1}{2}$	5 + 5	B. Columbia	T. P. Kempson.
$17\frac{3}{4}$	$4\frac{3}{4}$	...	...	27 + 25	Do.	Moreton Frewen.
[1] ♀ $12\frac{1}{4}$	4	8	...	3 + 3	Do.	J Turner-Turner.

[1] Spread.

MEXICAN DEER (Mazama americana mexicana).

One of the smaller races of the preceding, the height at the shou being about 2 feet 9 inches, and the antlers smaller and simpler.

Distribution.—South Mexico.

Length on outside curve.	Circumference.	Tip to Tip.	Widest inside.	Points.	Locality.	Owner.
$13\frac{5}{8}$	$3\frac{3}{8}$	$6\frac{7}{8}$	$11\frac{3}{4}$	3 + 3	Mexico	British Museum.
$8\frac{1}{4}$	$3\frac{1}{2}$	6	$6\frac{1}{2}$	3 + 3	Do.	Sir Edmund G. Loder, Bart
$8\frac{1}{4}$	$2\frac{1}{8}$	$4\frac{3}{4}$	$6\frac{5}{8}$	3 + 4	Do.	Sir Victor Brooke's Collectic

Head of Mule-Deer.   From a specimen in the possession of E. S. Cameron.

MULE-DEER (Mazama hemionus).

Antlers with a much shorter sub-basal snag than in the Virginian deer, beyond which the beam is directed outwards for a short distance, and then curves upwards to form a regular fork, both prongs of which are usually equal, and generally subdivide so as to form five points on each side.   Ears very large and heavy ; tail moderate, terminating in a bush-like tuft.   Gland-tufts on hock and cannon-bone coloured like the leg ; the latter of these elongated and situated in the upper half of the cannon-bone.   General colour of upper parts reddish tawny in summer, brownish or rufous speckled gray in winter, with a brown horse-shoe mark on the forehead. Height at the shoulder, 3 feet 3 or 4 inches in the typical form. Weight, 17 stone 2 lbs. (F. C. Selous).

Distribution.—The greater part of North America westward of the Missouri, extending from British Columbia to California. There are several local races, among which the South Californian (*M. hemionus peninsulæ*) is one of the smallest.

Length on outside curve.	Circumference.	Tip to Tip.	Widest inside.	Points.	Locality.	Owner.
30	5¾	...	41	17	White River, Colorado	H. A. James.
28⅝	4½	13¼	17¾	5+5	Wyoming .	Ford G. Barclay.
28½	5	18¾	21	6+4	British Columbia	J. McI. M'Iver Campbell.
28½	...	...	24½	...	White River, Colorado	Major Maitland Kirwan.
27	5¼	19½	21⅝	6+5	North America	Sir Edmund G. Loder, Bart.
27	5¼	19½	22¾	5+5	British Columbia .	D. H. Crake.
–26⅞	5	...	...	35	North Dakota .	Theodore Roosevelt.
–26¾	...	...	...	26	?	W. A. Baillie-Grohman.
26¾	4¾	19⅝	20⅛	5+5	Wyoming .	Ernest Farquhar.
26½	5	15½	18½	6+5	British Columbia	T. P. Kempson.
26½	5¾	...	17½	12	Wyoming	Hon. F. Thellusson.
26⅛	4⅛	15⅞	22⅞	6+6	Do. . .	Capt. F. Cookson.
26	4½	20	21¾	7+5	Do. . .	The Maclaine of Lochbuie.
26	5	15¼	19½	4+4	British Columbia	J. V. Colby.
–25⅝	5½	14¾	28	11+8	Frazer River, B.C.	A. E. Leatham.
25½	5½	...	21½	8	Do. . .	Sir Peter Walker, Bart.
–25½	4¾	...	...	28	Montana . .	P. Liebinger.
25½	4¾	18	24¼	5+5	Colorado .	E. T. Logan.
25½	4¼	27	29	5+5	Wyoming	Capt. G. J. Fitzgerald.
25⅜	4⅛	19	20	5+5	Do. . .	A. H. Pollen.
25	5¼	27⅜	27⅜	16+13	Montana	Moreton Frewen.
25	5	20¾	24	5+5	Wyoming . .	J. L. Scarlett.
25	5	10	16¾	5+4	Do.	F. C. Selous.
–25	5¾	17½	21½	7+5	Do.	James J. Harrison.
24½	5¼	...	23½	10	Maine . .	H. S. Wellcome.

MULE-DEER (Mazama hemionus)—*continued.*

Length on outside curve.	Circumference.	Tip to Tip.	Widest inside.		Locality.	Owner.
24½	5½	...	25	10	Wyoming . .	T. W. H. Clarke.
24½	5	19	24	5 + 5	Do. . . .	F. C. Selous.
24	5	13¾	17	10	British Columbia .	T. P. Kempson.
24	4½	20¼	20	6 + 5	Do. . .	R. Rankin.
24	4¼	19¼	25½	5 + 5	Wyoming . .	Capt. J. M'Call Maxwell.
24	4½	15¾	19½	5 + 5	Do. . . .	Count E. Hoyos.
23½	7	18	21	26	British Columbia .	J. Turner-Turner.

Head of Mule-Deer. From a specimen shot by J. McI. M'Iver Campbell.

BLACK-TAILED DEER (Mazama columbiana).

Nearly allied to the mule-deer, but of inferior size, with relatively smaller ears and finer hair ; but specially characterised by the shorter gland and tuft on the hind cannon-bone, and the larger amount of black on the tail, of which only the basal third of the lower surface is white.

Distribution.—Western North America, from British Columbia to California.

Length on out-side curve.	Circum-ference.	Tip to Tip.	Widest inside.	Points.	Locality.	Owner.
27¾	6	15¼	19¼	9 + 6	British Columbia .	G. Wrey.
−22	4¼	...	¹ 22	...	Vancouver .	Clive Phillipps-Wolley.
−20¼	5	17	17	5 + 7	Do. .	A. E. Leatham.
19¼	4¼	14	16½	3 + 3	S. California . .	Sir Victor Brooke's Collection.

¹ Outside.

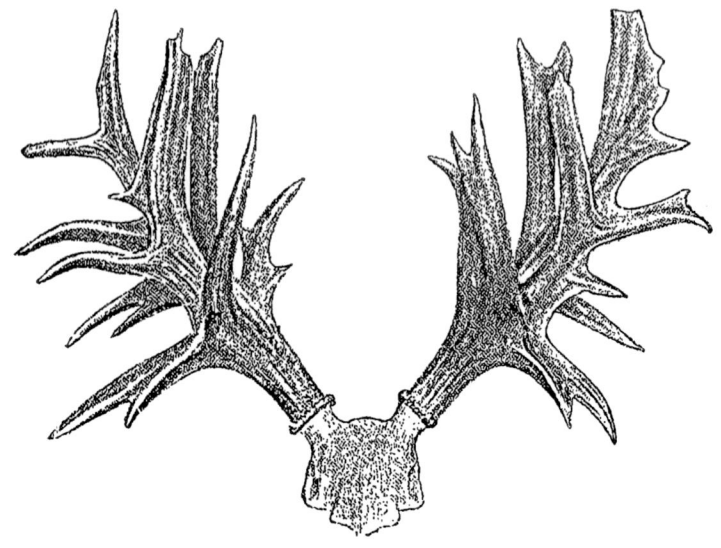

Malformed Marsh-Deer Antlers.

MARSH-DEER (Mazama dichotoma).

Antlers without a sub-basal snag, forking regularly, with both prongs again dividing, and the upper one usually more complex than the lower. Ears large, with white hair internally. Hair long and coarse, reversed on the withers for a short distance. General colour of upper parts bright rufous chestnut in summer, browner in winter ; legs black from the knees and hocks downward. No tuft on cannon-bone. Size, approximately that of a red deer. Although ten is the usual number of points, sports are common.

Distribution.—From Brazil to the inner wooded districts of Argentina.

Length on outside curve.	Circumference.	Tip to Tip.	Widest inside.	Points.	Locality.	Owner.
24½	5	16	18	5+5	Chaco of Paraguay .	Vice-Admiral Sir William Kennedy.
23½	6¾	26	25	5+5	?	Sir Edmund G. Loder, Bart.
23¾	5½	15¾	16½	5+4	S. America . .	British Museum.
23¼	6	...	19½	12	Do. . . .	G. R. Stuart.
22⅝	6¼	20	20½	5+5	Brazil . . .	Sir Victor Brooke's Collection.
−22½	7½	...	15½	6+6	Argentina . .	Kenyon Slaney.

H

MARSH-DEER (Mazama dichotoma)—*continued.*

Length on outside curve.	Circumference.	Tip to Tip.	Widest inside.	Points.	Locality.	Owner.
$22\frac{3}{8}$	$5\frac{1}{2}$	25	...	28	Argentina . .	A. Vans-Agnew.
$21\frac{1}{2}$	$5\frac{1}{2}$	22	$16\frac{1}{2}$	6+6	Paraguay . .	S. Pulley.
$21\frac{1}{2}$	5	$12\frac{3}{4}$	16	5+5	Do. . . .	Vice-Admiral Sir William Kennedy.
$-21\frac{1}{2}$	...	$19\frac{3}{4}$	...	6+5	Entre Rios . .	T. Taylor.
20	$5\frac{1}{4}$	20	...	4+4	Paraguay . .	Count Henry Coudenhove.
-20	$6\frac{3}{4}$	$19\frac{1}{4}$	$18\frac{3}{4}$	4+4	Uruguay . . .	Staff-Surgeon J. Dowson, R.N.
$17\frac{1}{2}$	$4\frac{1}{4}$	11	...	10	Paraguay . .	Hon. Walter Rothschild.

Side view of Antlers of Marsh-Deer. From a specimen in the British Museum.

PAMPAS DEER (Mazama bezoartica).

A small deer nearly allied to the last, but with the front prong of the antlers simple, and the hinder one divided. A whorl in the hair on the middle of the back and another at the base of the neck, so that the fur of the withers is directed forwards for a considerable distance. Colour of upper parts light reddish brown, under parts and lower surface of tail white ; upper surface of latter black.

Vice-Admiral Sir William Kennedy, in his *Sporting Sketches of South America*, thus describes it :—" The gama is of a light buff colour, carries a pretty symmetrical pair of horns, generally six points, but emits so strong an odour as to be called the stinking deer. Height at shoulder, 2 ft. 6 in."

Distribution.—Brazil to Northern Patagonia, in open districts.

Length on outside curve.	Circumference.	Tip to Tip.	Points.	Locality.	Owner.
14⅝	2⅝	13¼	3 + 3	Argentina .	British Museum.
14¼	3	11	3 + 3	South America .	Sir Edmund G. Loder, Bart.
14	4¼	11¼	3 + 3	Paraguay .	Vice-Admiral Sir William Kennedy.
13	2½	12⅜	3 + 3	?	W. Livingstone Learmonth.
-12½	3½	7	12 + 11	Uruguay . .	J. Burnett.
12½	2⅛	8½	3 + 3	?	Sir Victor Brooke's Collection.
11⅛	3⅞	13¼	3 + 3	?	The late Charles Darwin, British Museum.
10⅜	2½	13⅛	3 + 3	North Patagonia	British Museum.
10	2¼	12⅛	3 + 3	Argentina .	Count Henry Coudenhove.
7½	2¼	5½	3 + 3	?	Duke of Bedford.

PERUVIAN GUEMAL (Mazama antisiensis).

Together with the closely allied Chilian guemal (*M. chilensis*), this species constitutes a group characterised by the antlers forming a single fork, of which the front prong is the smaller, and curves upwards towards the hinder one. There is no gland-tuft on the hind cannon-bone, the short tail is rather bushy, and the hair coarse and brittle.

Distribution.—The high Andes, from Peru to Northern Chili.

Length on outside curve.	Circumference.	Tip to Tip.	Locality.	Owner.
9½	7⅝	4⅝	Tinta, South Peru . .	H. Whitely, British Museum.
9⅜	2½	8⅛	Ceuchepate, Peru (11,000 ft.)	Do.

WOOD BROCKET (Mazama nemorivaga).

The brockets are some of the smallest deer included in the genus *Mazama*, of which they are the typical representatives. They are recognisable by their simple spike-like antlers, the tufted crown of the head, and the radiation of the hair of the face from two whorls, which causes that on the nose to be directed downwards. The present species is distinguished by its small size (height at shoulder about 19 inches), its pale pepper-and-salt brownish or gray colour, the streak on the forehead, and the absence of a gland and tuft on the hock.

Distribution.—Guiana, Colombia, Bolivia, Brazil, and Trinidad.

Length on front of horn.	Girth.	Tip to Tip	Locality.	Owner.
-4⅝	3¾	4	Trinidad .	Dr. Percy Rendall.

MUSK-DEER (Moschus moschiferus).

From all living deer except the Chinese water-deer this species is distinguished by the absence of antlers, whose function as weapons is discharged in the male by long upper tusks. The tail is rudimentary, the fur coarse and brittle, and the lateral hoofs are very large. The males have a glandular pouch which secretes the musk from which the species takes its name. Height at shoulder about 20 inches, at rump 22 inches.

Distribution.—The forest districts of the Himalaya as far west as Gilgit, at elevations of 8000 feet or more in summer, to Tibet, Siberia, and Western China.

Length of Tusk.	Locality.	Owner.
-3¼	Himalaya . . .	. J. Johnston-Stewart.
3	Gurhwal . . .	. A. O. Hume, C.B.
3	Amurland .	British Museum.
2¾	Himalaya . .	. Rowland Ward.
2¹¹⁄₁₆	Do.	. Dr. Percy Rendall.
2¼	Kashmir . .	. Sir Edmund G. Loder, Bart.
2⅛	Do. . .	. Major A. Nugent.

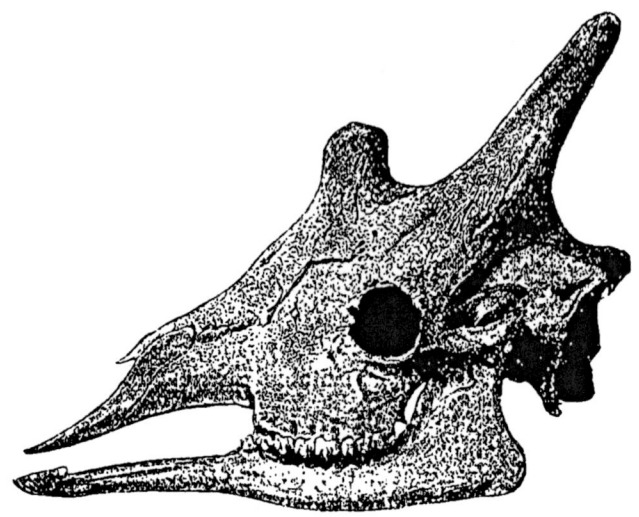

A. H. Neumann's Northern Giraffe Skull.   From De Winton, *P.Z.S.* February 1897.

NORTHERN GIRAFFE (Giraffa camelopardalis).

Ihuhla of the Swazis.   *Ngabe* of the Masawaras.
Indhlulamiti of the Zulus.   *Giri* or *Halgiri* of the Somalis.
Tuthla of the Basutos.   *Kameel* of the Boers.

The long and stilted limbs, the peculiarly-formed head, and the dappled hide, render giraffes distinguishable at a glance from all other living ruminants; with none of which they have, indeed, any very close affinity, although their nearest relatives are the deer. So great are their distinctions, that they constitute a family by themselves—the *Giraffidæ*. For many years it was supposed that this family was represented only by a single species; but it is now ascertained that the North and South African giraffes are markedly distinct from one another; the difference being apparently sufficient to admit of their being regarded as species. As a family characteristic, one of the most marked peculiarities of the giraffes is to be found in the horns. These consist of a pair of bony processes arising from the head between the ears, and covered during life with skin. They are never shed; and in the adult are immovably united to the bones of the skull, although separate in young animals. In addition to these, there is a more or less distinct third horn, or boss, situated on the forehead between the eyes. Giraffes have a long, extensile tongue, hairy lips, and broad, low-crowned molar teeth.   There are no tusks in the upper jaw ; and the false hoofs are likewise wanting.

In the present species the third horn is well developed, measuring from three to five inches in height in old bulls.   The ground-colour of the coat varies from white to fawn ; the orange-red or reddish chocolate dark blotches having sharply defined edges, with the spaces between them generally narrow and distinctly demarcated, even in old individuals.   Beneath the knees and hocks the legs are white in typical examples.

Distribution.—From the Tana river northwards through the Galla country and Somaliland to Abyssinia, Kordofan, and thence probably across Africa, in suitable districts to Senegambia from about Lat. 15° N. to the Equator.   An unusual tall female giraffe from Nigeria has been regarded as indicating a western race of this species, under the name of *G. camelopardalis peralta.* The giraffes of Nyasaland and the Kilimanjaro districts have been described by Dr. P. Matschie as distinct species, but their right to separation stands in need of confirmation.

SOUTHERN GIRAFFE (Giraffa capensis).

In the southern giraffe the third horn, even in old bulls, is so reduced in size as scarcely to merit that name at all.   The ground-colour of the coat varies from white to dull fawn ; and the dark blotches, which may be either dun or deep coffee colour, always have the centre darker than the edges, and the latter irregular and not sharply defined, so that in the adult the intervening light spaces are broad.   In young individuals, however, the skin shows very clearly defined white lines between the dark blotches, forming a conspicuous network pattern ; the margin of the blotches receding with age.   In size, the species appears very similar to the last ; and in both kinds the old bulls become much darker than the cows or immature males.

Distribution.—Within the last half century this species has ranged from the Orange to the Zambesi rivers.   Northward of this latter river on the eastern half of the continent, at least, no giraffe is found for about 12 degrees ; but north of the Rufizi river they again appear and continue through German East Africa, reaching westward to Lake Tanganyika, and occurring east of the Mari escarpment and south of the Tana river in British East Africa (De Winton).

SOUTHERN GIRAFFE (Giraffa capensis)—*continued.*

Total height.	At shoulder.	Locality.	Owner.
ft. ins. −18 7	ft. ins. ...	South-East Africa .	F. Vaughan Kirby.
¹−18 0	12 0	South Africa	The late Sir W. Cornwallis Harris.
−17 6	Average height	South-East Africa	F. Vaughan Kirby.
♂ 17 0	...	W. Matabeleland	F. C. Selous.
♀ 16 6	...	N. Kalahari .	Do.
− ♀ 15 6 to 16 0	Average height	South-East Africa .	F. Vaughan Kirby.

NORTHERN GIRAFFE (Giraffa camelopardalis).

Total height.	At shoulder.	Locality.	Owner.
ft. ins. −16 0	ft. ins. ...	Central East Africa	A. H. Neumann.

¹ *Portraits of the Game and Wild Animals of Southern Africa.*

Head of Male Prong-horn.

PRONG-HORN (Antilocapra americana).

Although commonly termed an antelope, this animal differs from all the members of the *Bovidæ* by the forking of the horns. These are annually shed from their bony sheaths and replaced by a new pair, which commence to grow up beneath the old ones before they are cast off. In consequence of this difference the species represents a family (*Antilocapridæ*) by itself. Horns generally absent in the female. Ears long and pointed, tail short, and neck maned. General colour chestnut, with a white rump-patch, and white bars on the neck. Height at shoulder, 36 inches; weight, 70 to 80 lbs. clean.

Distribution.—Western United States, from British Columbia to Mexico.

Length on outside curve.	Circumference.	Tip to Tip.	Widest inside.	Locality.	Owner.
−17¼	6½	.	9	N.W. Canada	J. Whitaker.
−17	...		20 outside	?	Otho Shaw.
−16	6½	...	...	N. Dakota	Theodore Roosevelt.
15¾	6¼	5⅞	...	Wyoming	St. George Littledale.

PRONG-HORN (Antilocapra americana)—*continued.*

Length on outside curve.	Circumference.	Tip to Tip.	Widest inside.	Locality.	Owner.
−15¾	5⅛	...	20 outside	?	Otho Shaw.
−15⅝	6	2⅞	...	Teton Mountains .	H. Lennard.
15½	4½	9½	...	Wyoming . . .	W. R. Cookson.
−15¼	5¾	6¼	...	Do. . . .	Count E. Hoyos.
15⅛	6¼	7⅝	...	?	Col. Ralph Vivian.
15	5⅝	5¾	10¼	Wyoming .	St. George Littledale.
14⅞	5	5¼	...	New Mexico . . .	Capt. F. Cookson.
14½	5¾	12	...	?	C. F. Bengough.
−14½	...	...	12½	Wyoming	T. W. H. Clarke.
14½	6	...	9½	Laramie Plains, Wyoming .	Ford G. Barclay.
14½	6⅝	5¼	...	Wyoming .	Lieut.-Col. Hon. W. Coke.
14¼	5⅜	6¼	10	Do. . .	Count Scheibler.
14¼	6	2⅝	...	?	Sir Victor Brooke's Collection.
14¼	7	4¼	...	?	J. McI. M'Iver Campbell.
14	5½	10¼	...	Wyoming . .	F. C. Selous.
14	5¾	13¾	...	Colorado . .	E. T. Logan.
14	6	6⅝	...	Wyoming . .	Sir Peter Walker, Bart.
14	6	3¼	...	Do. . .	J. B. Gilliat.
14	5½	9¼	...	?	J. Carr Saunders.
13⅝	5¼	4⅝	...	Wyoming . . .	W. W. Ashley.
13½	5½	7¾	...	Do.	Capt. Hugh Fraser.
13½	5½	7	...	Do. .	Capt. G. J. Fitzgerald.
13	5½	4⅞	...	Do. . .	Capt. J. M'Call Maxwell.
13	5½	...	5½	Do. .	Crawford G. Logan.
13	6½	5½	5½	Colorado . . .	Sir Edmund G. Loder, Bart.
13	6½	8½	9	Wyoming .	Dublin Museum.

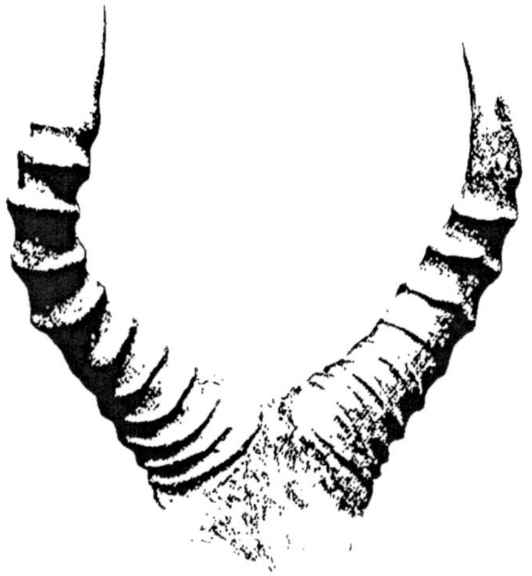

Horns of Bubaline Hartebeest. From Julius Jeppe's specimen.

BUBALINE HARTEBEEST (Bubalis boselaphus).

This species brings us to the great family of hollow-horned ruminants, or *Bovidæ*, in which the horns are in the form of unbranched hollow sheaths, which are never shed, and are supported on bony cores. The hartebeests are large antelopes with naked muzzles, abnormally long faces, doubly curved horns, small face-glands, large valvular nostrils (of which the lower lids are covered with short hairs), long, tufted tails, and large lateral hoofs. The present species is the smallest of the group, standing only 43 inches at the shoulder. It has a short pedicle supporting the horns, which are in the form of the letter W, and the colour is uniform tawny, with the tail-tuft black.

Distribution.—Northern Africa (interior of Morocco, Algeria, and Tunisia) and Arabia.

Length on front curve.	Circumference.	Tip to Tip.	Locality.	Owner.
$14\frac{1}{2}$	$8\frac{5}{8}$	$9\frac{3}{8}$	North Africa	British Museum.
$14\frac{1}{8}$	$6\frac{3}{4}$	$9\frac{3}{4}$	?	Col. Ralph Vivian.
$13\frac{3}{4}$	$9\frac{1}{4}$	$9\frac{1}{4}$	Tunisia	Julius Jeppe.
$13\frac{1}{3}$	7	$5\frac{1}{4}$	North Africa	British Museum.

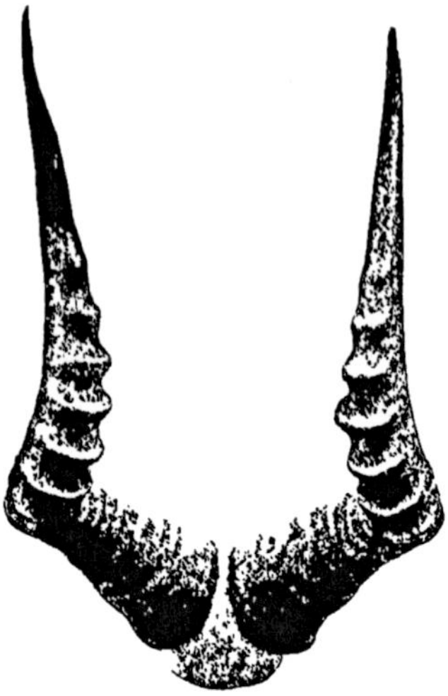

Horns of West African Hartebeest. Shot by J. W. Carroll.

WEST AFRICAN HARTEBEEST (Bubalis major).

Closely related to the preceding animal, of which, when fully known, it may turn out to be merely a local race with more massive horns. Body said to be of a uniform grayish brown, face deep brown, the fore-legs streaked with dark brown or blackish from the knees downwards, and the tail-tuft black.

Distribution.—Gambia, Lower Nigeria, and the interior of the Cameroons.

Length on front curve.	Circumference.	Tip to Tip.	Locality.	Owner.
$25\frac{1}{2}$	$11\frac{3}{4}$	$12\frac{1}{2}$	Nigeria . . .	P. A. Clive.
$25\frac{3}{8}$	$12\frac{1}{4}$	$11\frac{1}{4}$	Yauri, Hausa States	J. W. Carroll. (See illustration.)
$25\frac{1}{4}$	$12\frac{3}{4}$	$13\frac{3}{8}$	Near Borgu . .	Capt. N. C. Welch.
25	$11\frac{3}{4}$	$10\frac{1}{4}$	Benue River . .	Julius Jeppe.
$23\frac{1}{4}$	$11\frac{1}{2}$	$22\frac{1}{2}$ malformed	Yauri, Hausa States	J. W. Carroll.
-23·5	12·5	6	Togoland . .	Berlin Museum.
23	$12\frac{1}{4}$	$9\frac{1}{4}$	Niger Sudan . .	Hon. Walter Rothschild.
22	11	$19\frac{3}{4}$ malformed	Ibi, Nigeria . .	Capt. A. H. Festing.
$21\frac{3}{4}$	$12\frac{1}{4}$	$8\frac{3}{4}$	Near Borgu . .	Capt. N. C. Welch.

WEST AFRICAN HARTEBEEST (Bubalis major)—*continued.*

Length on front curve.	Circumference.	Tip to Tip.	Locality.	Owner.
¹21½	12¼	...	Lokoja .	. Capt. C. A. Wilding.
21½	10½	13¾	Do. .	Capt. A. H. Festing.
21¼	12	12¼	Gambia .	H. L. Stephen.
−21¼	11	9⅛	Do.	Paris Museum.
21	11	9¼	Lokoja .	Col. F. D. Lugard, C.B., D.S.O.
21	12	11	Do. .	F. H. Barber.
21	11½	10¾	Do.	. A. Ohlsson.
20⅜	10¼	7	Nigeria	. British Museum.
20	11	10¼	Do.	Mr. Justice Hopley.
♀ 20	9⅝	6	Lokoja	A. W. M. Brodie.
−19⅞	11½	10⅜	Gambia	Dr. Percy Rendall.
♀ 19¾	9	6½	Lokoja .	F. H. Barber.
♀ 19	8¼	13	Nigeria	. Major A. J. Arnold, D.S.O.
♀ 18	8¼	14	Do. .	Hon. Walter Rothschild.
♀ 18	9	7	Lokoja .	. The late Dr. Higgs.
♀ 17½	8¾	7½	Benue River	. Julius Jeppe.
♀ 17¼	9	5½	Lokoja . .	. Col. F. D. Lugard, C.B., D.S.O.

¹ Height at shoulder, 54 inches.

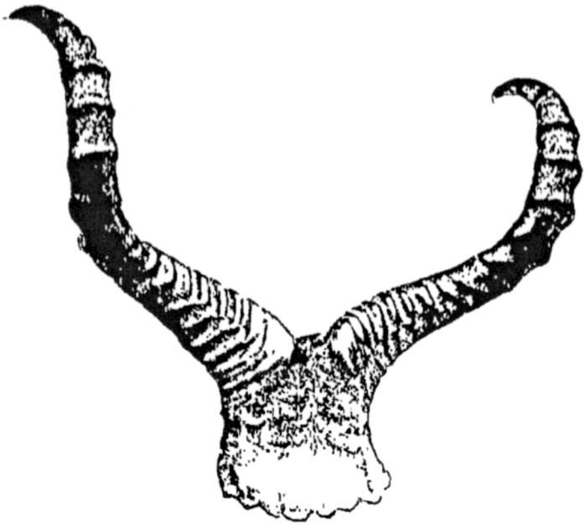

Frontlet and Horns of Tora Hartebeest. Shot by Lieut.-Col. Hon. W. Coke.

TORA or TETEL HARTEBEEST (Bubalis tora).

Horn-pedicle of medium length, the horns themselves in the form of an inverted bracket (⏝). Height at shoulder about 48 inches. Colour uniformly pale tawny fulvous, with the exception of the tail-tuft and chin, which are black. Although of the same uniform colour, this species is easily distinguished from *B. boselaphus* by its superior size, higher gait, and differently shaped horns.

Distribution.—Upper Nubia, Northern Abyssinia and Kordofan.

Length on front curve.	Circumference.	Tip to Tip	Locality.	Owner.
21	9	19[illegible]	Sudan	Lieut.-Col. Hon. W. Coke. (See illustration.)
20⅞	9¼	14½	Do.	Hon. Walter Rothschild.
20	9⅝	15⅝	Do.	British Museum.
20	9½	14¾	Lake Zuay, Abyssinia .	Prince de Lucinge.
19¾	9	16⅛	Dombelas, Abyssinia .	British Museum.
19¼	9	13¾	Do. . .	Sir Victor Brooke's Collection.
18½	8¾	15¼	Sudan	Col. Ralph Vivian.
18½	...	$16\frac{3}{16}$	Upper Basalam River, Abyssinia	J. Menges.
18¼	8½	11¼	Nubia	Julius Jeppe.
18	8½	14½	Settite River	W. D. James.
17½	9¾	18	Bogos-land, Abyssinia .	British Museum.

TORA or TETEL HARTEBEEST (Bubalis tora)—*continued.*

Length on front curve.	Circumference.	Tip to Tip.	Locality.	Owner.
17	$9\frac{1}{2}$	$13\frac{1}{2}$	Settite River . . .	W. D. James.
♀ $14\frac{1}{2}$	$6\frac{7}{8}$	$5\frac{5}{8}$	Sudan	Hon. Walter Rothschild.
♀ $14\frac{1}{4}$	$6\frac{1}{4}$	18	Upper Nubia . . .	Julius Jeppe.
♀ $13\frac{7}{8}$	$6\frac{3}{4}$	14	Do. . . .	Sir Edmund G. Loder, Bart.
♀ $13\frac{5}{8}$	..	$14\frac{5}{8}$	Abyssinia	J. Menges.

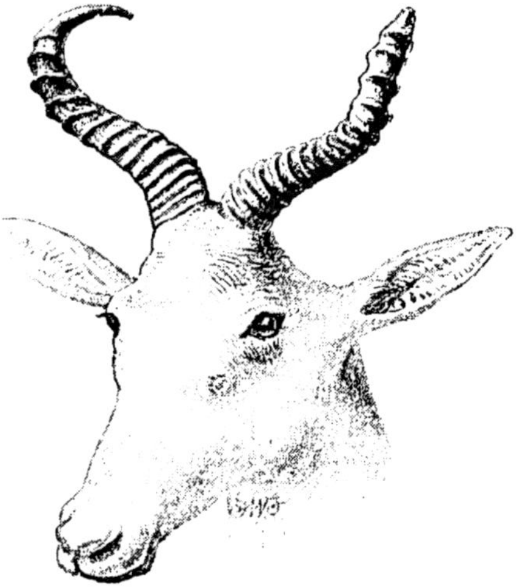

Head of Tora Hartebeest.

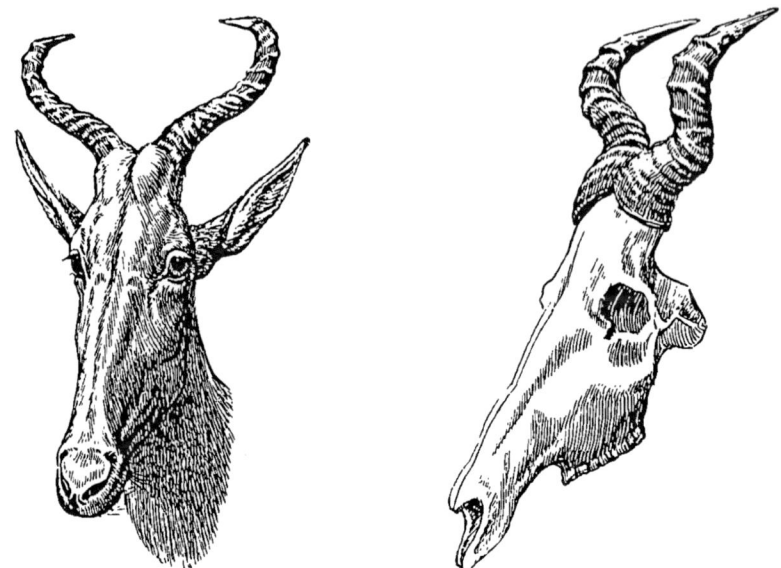

Head of Female and Skull of Male Neumann's Hartebeest.

NEUMANN'S HARTEBEEST (Bubalis tora neumanni).

Nearly allied to the typical tora, but distinguished by the stouter horns, on which the rings are less distinct and do not extend so far round, and the generally richer coloration. The horns are also less divergent. Mr. Walter Rothschild, the describer of this form, gives the following particulars :—

Colour of hair fulvous fawn, much richer on the back, where there are also some darker spots, which may be stains or natural ; below very much paler. Chin blackish, tip of tail black. The male is brighter and darker in colour than the female. There are also on the back some patches with longer, thicker, almost whitish-buff hair, perhaps remains of the winter fur.

Description.—East Africa, in the neighbourhood of Lake Rudolph. Discovered by A. H. Neumann.

Length on outside curve.	Circumference.	Tip to Tip.	Locality.	Owner.
16½	10¾	8½	N.E. of Lake Rudolph . . .	A. H. Neumann.
♀ 13½	7¼	9⅞	E. shore of Lake Rudolph . .	Do.
♀ 13¾	7½	10	?	Lord Delamere.

Head of Swayne's Hartebeest.   Shot by Major H. G. C. Swayne.

SIG or **SWAYNE'S HARTEBEEST** (Bubalis swaynei).

Sig of the Somalis.   *Korkci* of the Gallas.

Horn-pedicle and horns of the same general type as in the last species.   Height at shoulder about 47 inches ; weight about 300 lbs. General colour pale chocolate-brown, with white tips to the hairs ; face black, except the muzzle and a line between the eyes ; shoulders and upper part of fore-legs, a well as a patch on upper part of hind-legs, also black.

Distribution.—Interior of Northern Somaliland and Shoa ; in Somaliland it is found on the dry plateau known as the *haud.*

Length on front curve.	Circumference.	Tip to Tip.	Locality.		Owner.
20¼	8⅞	26¾	Somaliland	.	Major H. G. C. Swayne.
19½	9½	22½	Do. . .		G. H. Cheetham.
−19¼	...	24⅓	N. Somaliland .		J. Menges.
−19	9¼	18¼	Do. .	.	Capt. M. M'Neill.

SIG or SWAYNE'S HARTEBEEST (Bubalis swaynei)—*continued.*

Length on front curve.	Circumference.	Tip to Tip.	Locality.	Owner.
18¾	9¼	16	N. Somaliland .	Ford G. Barclay.
18½	9¼	19¼	Do.	T. W. Greenfield.
18⅜	8¾	18	Do.	Major H. G. C. Swayne.
-18	8¾	10¾	Do. .	Count J. Potocki.
18	9	22	Do.	B. R. M. Glossop.
17¾	11	17	Galla Country	Viscount Edmond de Poncins.
17¾	8¾	21	Somaliland .	Count J. de Bylands.
17¾	10	21½	Do. .	E. Lee Townshend.
17¾	10	20	Do. .	Digby Davies.
17½	8⅛	19½	Do.	T. W. H. Clarke.
17½	9¼	19	Do.	Sir Edmund G. Loder, Bart.
17½	9	21¾	Do. .	J. J. Richardson.
17½	10	21¾	Do. .	Capt. J. M'Call Maxwell.
17½	9¾	21	Do.	H. A. Bryden.
-17½	9	19½	Do.	C. V. A. Peel.
17¼	8½	21	Do. .	Major C. F. Blane.
-17¼	8½	19⅛	Do. .	J. Johnston-Stewart.
--17¼	...	...	Do.	Major George Douglas.
-17⅛	10¹⁄₁₀	18⅛	Abyssinia .	Prince A. de Lucinge.
17	9	10	Somaliland	W. W. Ashley.
17	9	20¾	Do. . .	J. Byng Paget.
17	9½	19	Do. .	Sir H. D. Tichborne, Bart.
17 .	8¾	15½	Do. .	Capt. George Campbell.
17	9½	18½	Do. .	R. M'D. Hawker.
-17	9 .	17	Do. .	A. E. Pease.
17	8¾	17½	Do. .	Capt. F. C. Quicke.
16½	9	12¼	Do. .	W. R. Bindloss.
-16½	9½	15¾	Do. .	Paris Museum.
16½	10	16	Do. .	J. Kenneth Foster.
16½	9¾	12¾	Do.	Hon. Walter Rothschild.

I

SIG or SWAYNE'S HARTEBEEST (Bubalis swaynei)—*continued.*

Length on front curve.	Circumference.	Tip to Tip.	Locality.	Owner
16½	10¼	16	Somaliland	E. T. Marshall.
16⅜	9	17⅛	Do.	W. D. James.
16¼	8½	20½	Do.	Lord Delamere.
16	8⅛	18	Do.	H.R.H. le Duc d'Orléans.
16	9¾	17½	Do.	Prince Nicolas Ghika.
16	8½	15	Do.	Capt. C. S. Timins.
16	9	18½	Do.	R. Wahrmann.
16	10	16¾	Do.	J. Benett-Stanford.
♀ 15½	6¾	19	Do.	Count J. de Bylands.
♀ 15½	7	11⅛	Galla Country .	Viscount Edmond de Poncins.
- ♀ 15⅜		...	N. Somaliland .	J. Menges.
- ♀ 13¼	7	19	Somaliland .	C. V. A. Peel.

KONGONI or COKE'S HARTEBEEST (Bubalis cokei).

Horn-pedicle moderate, horns bracket-shaped, very short and thick. Height at shoulder about 45 inches. General colour uniform bright fawn, with the lower lip somewhat browner, and the lower part of the rump paler; tail long, with the black tuft ascending some way up the hinder surface.

Distribution.—Eastern Africa, from Usagara northwards to Kilimanjaro and Masailand. This hartebeest is named after Lieut.-Col. Hon. W. Coke, by whom it was first killed. A bull shot by Capt. R. A. J. Montgomerie, C.B., R.N., in Masailand weighed 312 lbs.

Mr. F. J. Jackson says: "This hartebeest ranges as far north as L. Naivasha, south into German territory and east to within a few miles of the coast at the back of the Shimba hills."

Length on front curve.	Circumference.	Tip to Tip.	Locality.	Owner.
−20¼	...	...	East Africa .	Julius Jeppe.
19¼	10	18¾	Do.	J. Gardiner Muir.
19	9¾	16	Do.	Sir Robert Harvey, Bart.
−19	10¾	14	Do.	Berlin Museum.
18⅝	8¼	16¼	Do.	F. J. Jackson, C.B.
−18½	10½	18	West of Mombasa .	C. W. Hobley.

KONGONI or COKE'S HARTEBEEST (Bubalis cokei)—*continued.*

Length on front curve.	Circumference.	Tip to Tip.	Locality.	Owner.
18¼	9½	13⅛	East Africa .	H. C. V. Hunter.
–18	7½	12½	Masailand .	Count Scheibler.
–17½	8⅛	15¾	East Africa . . .	Do.
17⅜	9½	11	Do. . . .	J. Carr Saunders.
17	9½	12	Do. . . .	Lord Delamere.
17	9⅜	13¼	Machakos . .	Col. F. D. Lugard, C.B., D.S.O.
17	8¾	14¼	East Africa . .	S. L. Hinde.
16⅜	8	12⅜	Do. . .	British Museum.
16¼	9	17¼	Do. .	Sir Victor Brooke's Collection.
16⅛	8⅝	13¼	Kilimanjaro .	Sir John Kirk, K.C.B.
16⅛	10¼	13¾	?	C. Steuart Betton.
16⅛	10	15	?	Julius Jeppe.
16	9¾	12	East Africa . .	E. Gedge.
15¾	8¾	10⅛	Taita . .	J. Wray, British Musuem.
15½	10¼	11½	?	Sir Edmund G. Loder, Bart.
♀ 15¼	7¼	12½	East Africa . .	S. L. Hinde.
♀ 13	6¾	13	?	Lord Delamere.

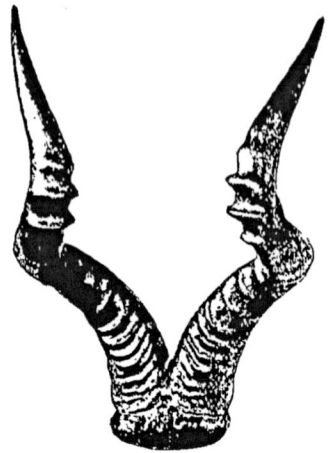

Horns of Cape Hartebeest. F. H. Barber's specimen.

CAPE HARTEBEEST (Bubalis cama).

Khama of the Bechuanas.   *Ingama* of the Makalakas.

Horn-pedicle greatly elongated, horns forming a letter V when viewed from the front.   Height at shoulder about 48 inches.   General colour brownish fulvous, darker than in any of the preceding ; face (except between the eyes), back of neck, chin, shoulders, thighs, and tail, black or blackish ; lower portion of buttocks with a conspicuous whitish or yellowish blaze, forming a marked contrast to the other colours.

Distribution.—South Africa southwards of the Limpopo, but extending farther northwards along the confines of the Kalahari desert.   This fleet and handsome species (the roi hartebeest) is now nearly exterminated in the Cape, although still found in the Transvaal.   A few still linger in the old Bushman country in the north-west of Cape Colony.   Although practically exterminated in the Orange Free State and in most of the Transvaal (except to the north-west), numbers of hartebeest are to be found in the pleasant country—partly plains, partly open forest—of British Bechuanaland and the Bechuanaland Protectorate.   In the North Kalahari and the desert regions about the Botletli River big troops are to be met with.   This hartebeest is an extremely good sporting animal, remarkably fleet and enduring, and not by any means easy to bring to bag.   Its flesh is very palatable, and its brilliant coat is much sought after by the native tribes.

CAPE HARTEBEEST (Bubalis cama)—*continued.*

Length on front curve.	Circum-ference.	Tip to Tip.	Locality.	Owner.
-25	...	...	Orange Free State .	F. H. Barber. (See illustration.)
25	11	10	?	C. Rube.
-24 7/8	11	7	Nata River	H. M. Barber.
24 1/2	12	9 1/2	South Africa	C. D. Rudd.
-24 3/8	10 1/4	9 13/16	Damaraland	Th. Rehbock.
-24 1/4	11	7 7/8	South Africa	Julius Jeppe.
23 3/4	10	8 3/8	Do.	The late Sir Andrew Smith, British Museum.
-23 1/2	11 1/2	11 7/8	Do.	Julius Jeppe.
23 1/2	11 1/2	9 1/8	Do.	Hon. Walter Rothschild.
23 1/2	11 1/2	10 1/2	Khama's Country .	F. C. Selous.
23 1/4	10 3/8	8 1/8	Makari Kari Salt Pan	The late J. S. Jameson.
23	12	5 1/2	South Africa .	G. Richards.
23	11 1/4	6	Do.	F. C. Selous.
23	11	11	Do.	A. Beit.
-22 1/2	11	8 1/2	Do.	A. Ohlsson.
22 1/2	10 3/4	10 1/8	Do.	Sir Edmund G. Loder, Bart.
22 1/4	11 1/2	8	Do.	A. Moseley.
22 1/4	12 1/4	6 1/8	Do.	Major R. Hayes Sadler.
-22 1/16	13	11	Do. .	Paris Museum.
-22	11 1/2	10 1/2	Do.	Dublin Museum.
22	10 5/8	8 1/8	Do. .	Sir Victor Brooke's Collection.
-♀ 20	...	...	Orange Free State .	Cape Town Museum.
-♀ 19 7/8	7 11/16	11 11/16	Damaraland	Th. Rehbock.
♀ 19 3/4	7 1/2	9	South Africa . .	The late J. S. Jameson.
♀ 19 1/2	8 3/8	8 1/4	Do.	G. Richards.
♀ 19	8 1/2	6 1/2	Kalahari .	H. A. Bryden.

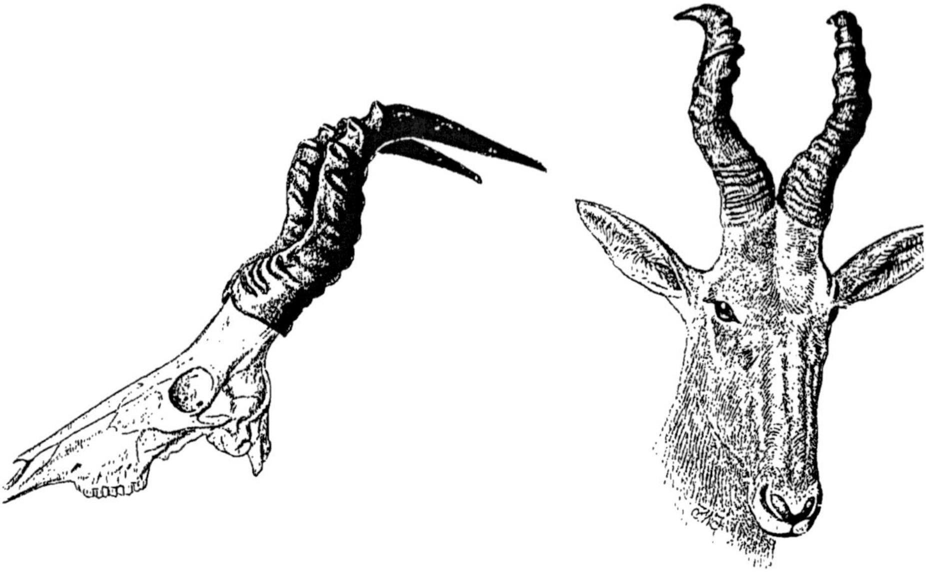

Skull and Head of Jackson's Hartebeest.

JACKSON'S HARTEBEEST (Bubalis jacksoni).

Generally similar to the preceding, but without the black blaze on the face, and with the horns less abruptly bent backwards from above. Other differences may be found to exist when the coloration of the body becomes fully known.

Distribution.—The interior of British Central Africa, north of Lake Baringo, Uganda, and probably northwards to the White Nile and westwards to Congoland.

Length on front curve.	Circumference.	Tip to Tip.	Locality.	Owner.
$24\frac{1}{2}$	$10\frac{1}{2}$	$11\frac{1}{4}$	East Central Africa . .	F. J. Jackson, C.B.
24	$10\frac{3}{8}$	$6\frac{7}{8}$	Do. . .	Do.
$23\frac{1}{2}$	12	9	Do. . .	E. Gedge.
$23\frac{1}{2}$	$11\frac{1}{2}$	$6\frac{1}{2}$	North End of Lake Albert	Col. Trevor Ternan.
$23\frac{1}{4}$	$11\frac{5}{8}$	$10\frac{1}{2}$	Rangata Nyuki . . .	Major A. E. Smith.
23	$11\frac{3}{4}$	$8\frac{1}{4}$	E. C. Africa . . .	Sir Edmund G. Loder, Bart.
-$22\frac{7}{8}$	$10\frac{1}{8}$	$11\frac{3}{4}$	E. of Victoria Nyanza .	Paris Museum.

JACKSON'S HARTEBEEST (Bubalis jacksoni)—*continued.*

Length on front curve.	Circumference.	Tip to Tip.	Locality.	Owner.
22½	10¼	10¾	E. C. Africa	Capt. E. J. Tickell.
22⅜	10¼	11	E. of Victoria Nyanza	Col. F. D. Lugard, C.B., D.S.O.
22	11	11	E. C. Africa	T. E. Buckley.
21	10½	9½	Do.	Julius Jeppe.
20¼	11½	7¾	Do.	Capt. E. J. Tickell.
19½	11½	7½	Do.	Lord Delamere.
♀ 18¼	8	5¾	Uganda	Col. Trevor Ternan.
♀ 16½	8	9½	E. C. Africa	F. J. Jackson, C.B.
♀ 16¼	8½	9½	Do.	Julius Jeppe.
♀ 16½	7⅜	4½	Do.	Mr. Justice Hopley.

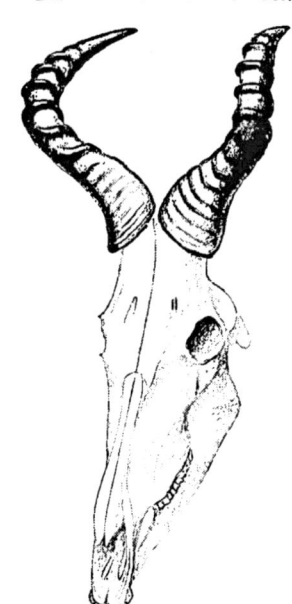

Skull and Horns of Hybrid Hartebeest.   Shot by Major C. H. Villiers.

HYBRID HARTEBEEST (presumed between Bubalis cokei and jacksoni).

Length on front curve.	Circumference.	Tip to Tip.	Locality.	Owner.
19½	10½	9½	Lake Naraku	J. Ponsonby.
18¾	10	9	Mau Plateau	Major C. H. Villiers.
17½	9½	6½	West of Eldoma Ravine	G. E. Smith.

Head of Lichtenstein's Hartebeest.

LICHTENSTEIN'S HARTEBEEST (Bubalis lichtensteini).

Horn-pedicle very short and broad, and the horns themselves much curved inwards towards one another below the terminal backward inclination. Height at shoulder about 50 inches, weight about 300 lbs. General colour tawny fulvous, becoming more rufous along the back, with the chin, tail-tuft, and front of cannon-bones black.

Distribution.—East Africa north of the Sabi River, throughout Nyasa-land and Mozambique to Usagara.

Godonko of Zambesia.   *Konze* in the Chilala and Chibisa
Inkulando of the Mashonas.   countries.
Kokotombwi in Barotseland.   *Ngondo* in the Chinyanja.

LICHTENSTEIN'S HARTEBEEST (Bubalis lichtensteini)—*continued.*

Length on front curve.	Circumference.	Tip to Tip.	Locality.	Owner.
–22 7/8	11	7 7/8	?	Mr. Justice Hopley.
–22 3/4	...	...	Nyasaland	F. Watkinson.
–21 3/4	10 3/4	9	?	Mr. Justice Hopley.
21 1/2	12 1/2	9	Batoka Plateau .	F. Smitheman.
–21 1/2	...	...	Batokaland .	R. T. Coryndon.
21	12 1/4	8 3/4	Barotseland	H. Timmins.
–21	...	...	?	O. R. Dunell.
–20 3/4	12 3/8	7 3/8	Portuguese East Africa .	F. Vaughan Kirby.
–20 3/4	...	...	?	Julius Jeppe.
20 5/8	13	6	Fort Johnstone, B.C.A.	C. C. Bowring.
–20 9/16	11 15/16	7 5/16	British Central Africa . .	A. S. Hamilton.
20 1/8	12 1/4	10 1/4	Congo Free State .	Julius Jeppe.
20	12 1/8	8	Wami River, East Africa	Sir John Kirk, K.C.B.
20	13 1/4	8	Fort Hill, B.C.A. .	John Yule.
19 1/2	11 1/2	8 1/8	S.E. Africa . . .	Hon. Walter Rothschild.
–19 1/2	11 3/4	8 1/2	British Central Africa .	F. Vaughan Kirby.
19 1/4	10 3/8	6 5/8	East Africa	Sir John Kirk, K.C.B.
19	12	4 1/4	Liwondes, B.C.A.	C. C. Bowring.
19	11 3/4	5 1/4	Pungwe .	J. W. Allen.
19	11 1/2	4 7/8	East Africa .	British Museum.
–18 7/8	11 1/2	7 3/4	Barotseland . .	F. Aitkens.
18 3/4	12	5 3/4	Batoka Plateau, Northern Rhodesia	F. Smitheman.
18 3/4	12	8 1/4	Barotseland .	Major H. J. Goold-Adams, C.M.G.
18 5/8	11 3/8	3 1/8	Manica Plateau	F. C. Selous.
18 1/2	12 3/4	4 3/4	Pungwe .	Hon. T. Thynne.
18 1/2	10 1/4	5	S.E. Africa	F. C. Selous, British Museu
18 1/2	13 1/2	6	E. Mashonaland .	A. Neilson.
18 1/2	13	2 1/2	Songwe, Nyasaland .	James Yule.
18 1/4	12	8	Pangani, East Africa	General Sir Lloyd W. Mattl

LICHTENSTEIN'S HARTEBEEST (Bubalis lichtensteini)—*continued.*

Length on front curve.	Circumference.	Tip to Tip.	Locality.	Owner.
18¼	11¼	5⅝	Wami River, East Africa .	F. J. Jackson.
18¼	12	6½	Pungwe . .	R. K. Micklethwait.
−18¼	12	6½	Beira . . .	Dr. Percy Rendall.
18	12	3¾	British Central Africa . .	J. E. Gough.
−18	12¾	8¾	Nyasaland . . .	Major P. W. Forbes.
−18	...	...	Beira . .	Cape Town Museum.
−18	12½	6	East Central Africa	James J. Harrison.
17½	11¾	5¼	Pungwe .	C. C. Gouldsmith.
17½	12	6½	Do. .	H. R. Holden.
−17½	11	3⅞	Do. . .	A. M. Naylor.
−17⅞	11⅞	9¹⁰⁄₁₆	East Africa . .	Paris Museum.
17¼	12¼	3⅞	Maskanala	Hon. K. Campbell.
17	12¾	5⅝	Pungwe .	Capt. F. H. Lehmann.
17	11	4¾	Lower Shiré .	Staff-Surgeon J. Dowson, R.N.
17	10	4¾	East Africa . .	Dublin Museum.
−17	11½	5½	Pungwe	Julius Jeppe.
−17	8½	2½	Do. . .	A. Ohlsson.
16⅝	11⅛	6¼	River Sabi, Mashonaland .	F. C. Selous, British Museum.
♀ 15	8⅞	4¾	Do. .	Do.
− ♀ 15	7¾	5¾	Portuguese East Africa .	F. Vaughan Kirby.
♀ 12¼	7	5½	?	Julius Jeppe.

Head of Hunter's Hartebeest.   From a specimen shot by H. C. V. Hunter.

HUNTER'S HARTEBEEST (Damaliscus hunteri).

With this species we come to a group of antelopes closely allied to the true hartebeests, but in which the frontal region is not elevated into a horn-pedicle, while the horns themselves form in most cases a lyrate or simple curve, and the face is of medium length. In the present species the slender horns are indeed doubly curved, although without the sudden angulation of the true hartebeests. They slant upwards and outwards, then bend downwards, while their long points are directed upwards. Colour uniform rufous, with a chevron on the face, the inner surface of the ears, and the tail-tuft white. Height at shoulders about 4 feet, and the build light and graceful.

Distribution.—Southern Somaliland to north bank of Tana River. Discovered by H. C. V. Hunter in 1888.

Length.		Circumference.	Tip to Tip.	Locality.	Owner.
On front curve.	Straight.				
26¼	22	8⅛	12½	Bank of the Tana River, East Africa	Sir Robert Harvey, Bart.
24⅞	...	8⅛	15½	Do.	H. C. V. Hunter.
24⅝	21¼	8⅜	9¾	Do.	Sir Robert Harvey, Bart.
♀ 21	...	5¾	7	Do.	F. H. Barber.
20⅛	...	5⅝	8⅞	Do.	Hon. Walter Rothschild.

Head of Korrigum.

KORRIGUM or SENEGAL HARTEBEEST (Damaliscus corrigum).

Horns with a single slightly lyrate curve. Size medium. General colour reddish, with patches on the face, shoulders, upper part of fore-legs, hips, and thighs, and the tail-tuft black ; no dark markings on back and feet.

Distribution.—Senegambia and the interior of West Africa. Discovered by Col. Denham and Capt. Clapperton in 1822-24.

Length on front curve.	Circumference.	Tip to Tip.	Locality.	Owner.
$22\frac{1}{2}$	$8\frac{3}{4}$	$11\frac{3}{4}$	Gambia . . .	Julius Jeppe.
$-21\frac{5}{8}$	$9\frac{7}{8}$	$15\frac{5}{8}$	Do. . . .	Paris Museum.
$-21\frac{3}{8}$	$9\frac{1}{4}$	$11\frac{3}{4}$	Do. . . .	Dr. P. Rendall, British Museum.
19	$6\frac{3}{4}$	10	Do. . . .	Late Earl of Derby, British Museum.
$18\frac{3}{4}$	$9\frac{1}{8}$	11	Do. . . .	Do.
$-15\frac{1}{2}$	7	8	Do. . . .	Dublin Museum.

TIANG (Damaliscus corrigum tiang).

Apparently only a local race of the korrigum, from which it is distinguished, so far as at present known, by its slightly inferior dimensions, and certain differences in the black markings on the face and limbs.

Distribution.—Sennar, Kordofan, and Bahr-el-Ghazal.

Length on front curve.	Circumference.	Tip to Tip.	Locality.	Owner.
♀ $20\frac{1}{4}$	$6\frac{3}{4}$	$6\frac{7}{8}$	Bahr-el-Ghazal .	The late Consul Petherick, British Museum.
$10\frac{1}{8}$	$6\frac{3}{4}$	$7\frac{7}{8}$	Do. .	Do.

Head of Topi. From a specimen shot by A. H. Neumann.

TOPI (Damaliscus corrigum jimela).

The southern representation of the last, distinguished by its still smaller size (height at shoulder, 43-44 inches), shorter and more slender horns, and the somewhat brindled appearance of the coat, due to patches of longer hairs on the otherwise short fur. General colour a peculiar purple-brown, with the dark markings less defined and less black than in *D. corrigum typicus*. Weight about 250 lbs.

Distribution.—British East Africa from the Juba to the Sabuki River, and thence to Uganda and Uniamwezi.

Length on front curve.	Circumference.	Tip to Tip.	Locality.	Owner.
21	8	6½	North End of Lake Rudolph .	H. Andrew.
19¼	6⅝	3⅜	East Africa	H. C. V. Hunter.
19	7½	8	Do.	Rowland Ward.
18¾	8¼	6¼	North End of Lake Rudolph .	A. H. Neumann.

TOPI (Damaliscus corrigum jimela)—*continued.*

Length on front curve.	Circumference.	Tip to Tip.	Locality.	Owner.
18½	8¾	8½	East Africa	Sir Edmund G. Loder, Bart.
18½	8⅜	5¼	Do.	J. Carr Saunders.
18½	7⅝	6	North End of Lake Rudolph	Julius Jeppe.
18⅛	6⅜	5⅞	East Africa	Sir Robert Harvey, Bart.
18	8⅛	5⅜	Do. . .	F. J. Jackson, C.B.
17½	8	7¼	Uganda . .	Hon. Walter Rothschild.
17⅛	7¾	5	East Africa	H. C. V. Hunter.
17	8	7	Do.	Sir Robert Harvey, Bart.
♀ 17	5¾	4½	North End of Lake Rudolph	A. H. Neumann.
16⅞	7	5½	Do.	F. J. Jackson, C.B.
16⅞	7¾	4½	East Africa	Capt. R. A. J. Montgomerie, C.B., R.N.
16⅜	6⅛	5½	Coast Region between Lamu and River Juba	Sir John Kirk, K.C.B.
16⅜	5⅞	5	River Juba	Do.
15⅝	7⅝	5¾	Coast Region between Lamu and River Juba	Hon. Walter Rothschild.
15½	8½	7	Do.	E. Gedge.
15½	7⅝	5⅝	East Africa	F. H. Barber.
-14½	6¾	6¾	Coast Region between Lamu and River Juba	Mr. Justice Hopley.
-14¼	5	9¾	?	Berlin Museum.

Head of Bontebok.

BONTEBOK (Damaliscus pygargus).

Distinguished from the preceding species of the genus by the white blaze on the face, which is continuous from the horns to the nose. Height at shoulder about 40 inches. Weight about 200 lbs. Colour of fore part of back rufous fawn darkening into blackish on the rump, flanks, shoulders, front of limbs, and tail-tuft; rump, upper half of tail, under parts, and much of hinder surface of limbs white.

The curious pied marking of the bontebok, its snow-white face, belly, legs, and rump, and the glaze-like, purplish-lilac gloss of the upper part of the coat—which may be described as chestnut upon the neck and warm purplish-brown upon the body—are very remarkable. The horns very nearly resemble those of the blesbok in shape, but the colour is much darker. The blesbok and bontebok formerly gave great sport to the Boers and European hunters. Both of these blaze-faced antelopes run steadily up-wind, "carrying their broad white noses close to the ground like a pack of harriers in full cry."

Distribution.—Cape Colony, south of the Vaal River; now nearly ex-terminated. Although formerly abounding in tens of thousands on the Karoos of Cape Colony and the plains of the Orange Free State, bontebok are now reduced to a single herd carefully preserved on some flats on the estate of Mr. Vander-Byl, near Swellendam, in the south of Cape Colony.

K

BONTEBOK (Damaliscus pygargus)—*continued.*

Length on front curve.	Circumference.	Tip to Tip.	Locality.	Owner.
$16\frac{3}{8}$	$6\frac{3}{4}$	$9\frac{1}{8}$	?	British Museum.
$16\frac{1}{4}$	$6\frac{5}{8}$	$8\frac{3}{4}$	Bredasdorp .	A. C. Campbell.
[1] $15\frac{7}{8}$	$6\frac{7}{8}$	8	Do. .	F. C. Selous, British Museum
$15\frac{1}{2}$	$6\frac{1}{2}$	$8\frac{1}{2}$	Do. .	Hon. Walter Rothschild.
$-15\frac{1}{2}$	$6\frac{1}{2}$	$8\frac{1}{4}$	Do. .	Dr. W. P. Y. Bainbrigge.
$-15\frac{1}{2}$	$6\frac{1}{2}$	5	Do. .	A. Ohlsson.
$15\frac{1}{2}$	$6\frac{1}{2}$	$9\frac{3}{8}$	Do. .	A. C. Humbert.
$-15\frac{1}{2}$	$6\frac{3}{8}$	$9\frac{3}{4}$	Do.	Mr. Justice Hopley.
$15\frac{3}{8}$	$6\frac{1}{8}$	$8\frac{1}{8}$	Cape Colony	Sir Victor Brooke's Collection.
$-15\frac{5}{16}$	$6\frac{1}{8}$	$7\frac{1}{4}$	Bredasdorp	Dr. Percy Rendall.
15	$6\frac{1}{4}$	$8\frac{1}{2}$	Cape Colony	F. C. Selous.
15	$6\frac{3}{8}$	$7\frac{5}{8}$	Do.	Capt. F. Cookson.
15	$6\frac{1}{4}$	$6\frac{3}{4}$	Bredasdorp . .	W. S. Curtis.
-15	$6\frac{1}{4}$	$7\frac{5}{8}$	?	Julius Jeppe.
-15	...	...	?	C. T. Jones.
$-14\frac{1}{2}$	...	...	Bredasdorp .	Cape Town Museum.
$-14\frac{1}{2}$	$6\frac{1}{2}$	$8\frac{3}{8}$	Do.	Julius Jeppe.
15	$6\frac{3}{4}$	$8\frac{1}{2}$	Cape Colony	F. C. Selous.
$14\frac{1}{2}$	$6\frac{1}{4}$	$8\frac{1}{4}$	Bredasdorp .	Hon. Walter Rothschild.
$-\,♀\,14\frac{1}{4}$	$5\frac{3}{8}$	$7\frac{5}{8}$	Do. .	Julius Jeppe.
$14\frac{1}{8}$	$5\frac{3}{8}$	$7\frac{3}{8}$	Cape Colony . . .	F. C. Selous.
$♀\,13\frac{1}{2}$	$5\frac{1}{4}$	$7\frac{5}{8}$	Bredasdorp . . .	Julius Jeppe.
[2] $♀\,13\frac{1}{2}$	$5\frac{1}{4}$	$7\frac{1}{2}$	Do. . . .	F. C. Selous, British Museum.

[1] Weight, 200 lbs.; height, $41\frac{1}{2}$ at shoulder.   [2] Height at shoulder, $36\frac{3}{4}$.

BLESBOK (Damaliscus albifrons).

Nunni of the Bechuanas.

Closely allied to the last (of which it may be only a local race), but with less black on the body and limbs, the blaze divided by a white line between the eyes, and the rings on the horns yellowish.

Formerly to be numbered by hundreds of thousands, the beautiful blesbok has in the last twenty years grown very scarce indeed. It can now scarcely be reckoned as a South African beast of chase, being only met with in small numbers on a few Boer farms in the Transvaal and the Orange Free State. Yet, thirty or forty years ago, blesboks often literally darkened the face of the land with their innumerable legions. The north of the Cape Colony, Griqualand West, the Free State, and the plains of the Western and Southern Transvaal may be described as the true home of this charming antelope in the old days. In 1848 Gordon Cumming speaks of a sight he beheld in the blesbok country. "The plains," he says, "exhibited one purple mass of graceful blesboks, which extended without a break as far as my eyes could strain; the depth of their vast legions covered a breadth of about six hundred yards." What a contrast with the scarcity of the present day!

Distribution.—Northern plains of Cape Colony, Orange Free State, Transvaal, and Bechuanaland; now nearly exterminated.

Length on front curve.	Circumference.	Tip to Tip.	Locality.	Owner.
18¼	5¾	12¼	South Africa . . .	Sir Edmund G. Loder, Bart.
–18	6½	10⅝	Orange Free State . .	F. R. N. Findlay.
17¼	6¾	7	Transvaal	Abe Bailey.
–17⅛	7	7½	Do. . .	Dr. W. P. Y. Bainbrigge.
–16⅞	7	7½	Orange Free State . .	Count E. Hoyos.
–16⅝	6⅝	9½	Do. .	Julius Jeppe.
– ♀ 16½	6¼	8¾	Do. .	Do.
–16½	...	...	?	O. R. Dunell.
16½	7	8	Orange Free State .	Capt. H. D. Livingstone.
16¼	6⅜	7¼	?	Capt. G. F. Henry.
16⅛	6¼	8⅛	South Africa . .	Sir Edmund G. Loder, Bart.
16	6¾	8⅜	?	Capt. Lord Douglas Compton.

BLESBOK (Damaliscus albifrons)—*continued.*

Length on front curve.	Circumference.	Tip to Tip.	Locality.	Owner
-16	...	...	?	Cape Town Museum.
-15⅞	6½	5½	?	Mr. Justice Hopley.
-15¾	...	...	?	C. T. Jones.
15⅝	6¾	5½	?	A. Beit.
15½	6⅞	8¼	?	Capt. F. H. Lehmann.
15½	5⅛	7½	?	C. H. Akroyd.
15¼	6½	[1] 10	Driefontein, O.F.S.	F. C. Selous, British Museum.
15¼	6⅛	5¾	South Africa . . .	Hon. Walter Rothschild.
15¼	6⅛	6½	Zululand .	Major-Gen. Sir Arthur Ellis, K.C.V.O.
15⅛	6½	7¾	South Africa . .	Hon. Walter Rothschild.
-15	6¼	8½	?	Julius Jeppe.
♀ 15	5¼	...	Orange Free State . .	Capt. H. D. Livingstone.
14¼	6⅛	8¾	Cape Colony . .	H.R.H. the Duke of Saxe-Coburg and Gotha.
-14⅛	5⅛	7	Transvaal .	F. Vaughan Kirby.
14	6⅜	7½	Do. .	Sir Victor Brooke's Collection.
14	6½	7½	Heidelberg	R. H. Sawyer.
-14	8¾	6¼	Transvaal . .	T. E. Buckley.
-14	6	7½	?	A. Ohlsson.
-14	7¾	12⅞	?	Mr. Justice Hopley.
14	4⅞	6½	?	Dr. W. P. Y. Bainbrigge.
13½	5	5¾	?	F. C. Selous.
12¾	4⅝	7½	Driefontein, O.F.S. .	F. C. Selous, British Museum.

[1] Weight, 180 lbs. Height at shoulder, 39½ inches.

Head of Sassaby.   From a specimen shot in Mashonaland by F. C. Selous.

SASSABY or BASTARD HARTEBEEST (Damaliscus lunatus).

Incolomo of the Matabele.

Ingalowana of the Basutos.

Inkwcko of the Masubias.

Inyundo of the Makalakas.

Kaboli in the Barotse country and Lake Ngami country.

Luchu of the Masaras.

M'tengo in the Chilala and Chibisa countries.

Mzanci of the Swazis.

Mzanzi of all Zulu tribes

Unchuru of the Makubas.

Horns starting obliquely outwards, with a single upward and backward lunate curve.   Height at shoulder nearly 4 feet.   General colour dark chestnut rufous, with the face, shoulders, hips, upper portions of limbs, and tail-tuft black, and the region of the groin and margin of the ears white.

The sassaby has the reputation—in the opinion of all hunters who have tested its speed—of being the fleetest and most enduring animal in South Africa.   Were it not that this handsome antelope, in common with its near relative the Cape hartebeest, happens to be lacking in presence of mind, it would very seldom fall to the sportsman's rifle.   The sassaby is not difficult to circumvent.   A troop can be often turned from its course, or brought to a halt, by firing a bullet or two over the heads of the fleeing animals. Or if the leader of the troop can be wounded and turned out, the rest of the herd become confused and now and again offer easy shots. Like the Cape hartebeest the sassaby has extremely drooping quarters. The skin of one of these antelopes, freshly killed, is very beautiful, the wonderful smoothness and the brilliant purplish bloom of the coat being specially noticeable.

Distribution.—South-East Africa, from north of the Orange River to the Zambesi, and westward to Lake Ngami, and northwards to British Central Africa (see below).

Length on front curve.	Circumference.	Tip to Tip.	Locality.	Owner.
15¾	7½	15½	Mashonaland . .	Sir John Willoughby, Bart.
15⅝	7½	11¾	?	Sir Edmund G. Loder, Bart.
15¼	8⅛	12½	Daka, S. of Victoria Falls	F. C. Selous.
15¼	8	12¼	S.E. Africa .	The late Sir Andrew Smith, British Museum.
-15¼	7⅛	12¾	Do. .	Julius Jeppe.
15⅛	7⅛	12	Do. . .	Sir Victor Brooke's Collection.
15	8⅜	11⅝	Do. . .	G. Richards.
15	7	11	Do.	A. Moseley.
14⅞	8	10	Lebombo Mountains	F. Vaughan Kirby.
14¾	7⅜	11⅝	Pungwe . . .	J. W. Allen.
14¾	7½	12	North of Delagoa Bay	A. Cameron.
-14½	8	15¼	Matabeleland . .	J. Brander Dunbar.
-14½	8	15	S.E. Africa .	James J. Harrison.
14½	7⅝	11	Mashonaland .	F. C. Selous, British Museum.
14½	7⅞	11¼	Do. .	Do.
14½	7	10	Pungwe . .	Capt. G. F. Henry.
14½	7	10	Matabeleland .	Rev. Dr. R. J. Nevin.
-♀ 14½	6	9	Do.	Dr. W. P. Y. Bainbrigge.
14½	7⅜	13	Do. . . .	W. Van Ness.
[1] 14½	7½	12½	Bangweolo Flats, British Central Africa	F. Smitheman.
-14½	8¼	11	Pungwe	Count E. Hoyos.

[1] The locality noted is of great interest, as indicating the existence of this species north of the Zambesi.

SASSABY or BASTARD HARTEBEEST (Damaliscus lunatus)—*continued.*

ength on front curve.	Circumference.	Tip to Tip.	Locality.			Owner.
14¼	7½	10¼	Mashonaland			Hon. Walter Rothschild.
-14¼	7½	13	S.E. Africa	.		Dr. W. P. Y. Bainbrigge.
14¼	8	14	Matabeleland	.		Hon. R. A. Ward.
-14¼	...	...	Do.	.		C. T. Jones.
14⅛	6¾	9⅝	Pungwe			C. M. Swire.
14	7¼	10	Do.	.	.	Marquis of Hamilton.
-14	6¾	12⅞	Do.	.		A. Beit.
-14	8	12½	Do.	.	.	T. E. Buckley.
14	7¼	10¾	Do.	.		Hon. T. Thynne.
14	7	11½	Do.	.	.	R. K. Micklethwait.
♀ 13⅞	6⅝	11½	Mashonaland	.	.	F. C. Selous, British Museum.
♀ 13⅞	6¼	12¾	Do.	.	.	H. and C. Beddington.
♀ 13½	...	...	Lebombo Mts.	.	.	F. Vaughan Kirby.
♀ 13½	...	11⅞	Mabonga River	.	.	H. M. Barber.
♀ 13	6	13¾	Matabeleland	.		Lord Brackley.

Horns of Brindled Gnu.   From Julius Jeppe's specimen.

BRINDLED GNU (Connochœtes taurinus).

Ec-vumba of the Makalakas.   *Inkongone* of the Swazis and Zulus.
Ikokoni of the Basutos.   *Minyumbzve* of the Batongas.
Inkonc-kone of the Amandebele.   *Numbo* of the Masubias.
                    Unzozo of the Makubas.

From their near relatives the hartebeests the gnus, or wildebeests, are distinguishable at a glance by their grotesque shape and smooth horns, as they also are by their habits.   The short, broad, and massive head has a blunt and bristly muzzle, and tufts of coarse hair on the forehead and chin ; the chin-tuft also extending on to the throat. The horns, which are placed on the crown of the head, are approximated at their bases, especially in old bulls, and are nearly smooth, more or less flattened at the bases, but almost cylindrical at the tips ; the curvature being at first outwards, or outwards and downwards, and then bending upwards at the tips.   An abundant mane of stiff, upright hair clothes the back of the neck ; and the tail is covered with longer and softer hairs, reaching considerably below the hocks.   It is from the equine form of the tail that these animals were long popularly known by the name of " horned horse."   The hoofs are characterised by their narrow form.

The blue wildebeest, as this species is called at the Cape, is a large animal, standing about 4 feet 3 inches at the shoulder.   Its most characteristic features are the outward direction of the horns, which are but little expanded at the base, and not unlike those of a buffalo, the uniformly black tail, and the absence of long hair on the lower part of the chest and belly.   The general colour varies from grizzled roan to blackish slaty brown, with more or less distinct vertical dark stripes on the sides of the neck and fore-quarters ; these stripes being most conspicuous in the lighter-coloured specimens.   Typically, the fringe of hair on the throat, like the mane and tuft on the forehead, is black.

Distribution.—Formerly ranging from the north of the Orange River for a long distance up East Africa, the brindled gnu is now practically exterminated in the Orange Free State and the adjacent districts south of the Limpopo. It is, however, still to be met with in parts of Griqualand West and of the Kalahari, as well as in British Bechuanaland ; while in Khama's country and Rhodesia, and thence north-

Head of Bull Nyasaland Gnu.
From Sir H. H. Johnston's *British Central Africa*, published by Messrs. Methuen.

wards through Central and East Africa, it is comparatively abundant, or, at all events, was so before the ravages of the rinderpest, and it also occurs in Mozambique. In spite of its clumsy and ungainly appearance, the brindled gnu is a rapid mover ; and even when severely wounded will not unfrequently succeed in making good its escape from the mounted hunter.

It is generally distributed in South-East Central Africa, and north of the Zambesi is represented by the Nyasaland gnu (*C. taurinus johnstoni*), which Mr. F. Vaughan Kirby found also in the Mozambique province.

Widest outside.	Widest inside.	Length on front curve.	Breadth of palm.	Tip to Tip.	Locality.	Owner.
...	29	31	[1] 13¼	15¼	Sabi Flats .	Dr. R. P. Mitchell.
-33½	28¾	...	6½	24	Do. .	B. Secretan.
32½	29	20	4	26½	P. E. Africa .	F. Vaughan Kirby.
...	28½	21⅝	5¼	17⅜	Matabeleland	G. H. M. Banks.
...	28½	20¾	5	16	Pungwe . .	C. C. Gouldsmith.
[2] 31½	28	...	8	18⅛	P. E. Africa	F. Vaughan Kirby.
31	...	23	[1] 11½	19½	S.E. Africa	The late J. A. Nicolls.
30½	...	...	...	...	Do.	F. C. Selous.
30½	...	...	...	17	Do. .	F. H. Barber.
...	27½	23½	4¾	16¾	?	Julius Jeppe.
...	-27	21	4½	20½	?	Mr. Justice Hopley.
...	-26¾	29	5	16¾	?	Julius Jeppe.
...	26½	21¼	4⅝	20½	Matabeleland .	Major R. Hayes-Sadler.
...	26½	19½	4¾	17	Do.	F. G. Shaw.
...	-26½	31¼	...	17	Delagoa Bay	H. T. and A. H. Glynn.
30½	26½	22	4½	20½	Beira .	Rowland Ward.
...	-26	31	4¾	21	Lydenburg .	F. H. Barber.
...	26	22¼	6	18⅛	Mababe Plain	F. C. Selous.
...	26	21½	7	17½	Pungwe . .	Frank Harris.
	25½	22	4¼	17	S. Africa . .	G. Richards.
...	♀ 25	22¼	4½	10	P. E. Africa .	F. Vaughan Kirby.
29	25¼	21	4½	18¾	Zululand . .	Lieut.-Col. Hon. W. Coke.
-28¼	25	...	11	13	?	F. J. Newnham.
...	24¾	20¾	4¾	16¾	Pungwe . .	Capt. F. H. Lehmann.
...	-24½	31¾	[1] 14	16½	Sabi Flats .	James J. Harrison.
...	24½	20½	5	17¾	Matabeleland .	Rev. Dr. R. J. Nevin.

[1] Circumference. [2] Height at shoulder, 53½.

BRINDLED GNU (Connochœtes taurinus)—*continued.*

Widest outside.	Widest inside.	Length on front curve.	Breadth of Palm.	Tip to Tip.	Locality.	Owner.
...	24½	20	4	17⅝	Pungwe . .	P. B. Vander-Byl.
...	24½	21	4½	15½	Do. . .	Marquis of Hamilton.
28⅝	24¼	22	5½	19¼	S. Africa . .	Sir Edmund G. Loder, Bart.
...	24¼	15¼	4⅛	19½	Pungwe . .	Ford G. Barclay.
...	24¼	20¾	4½	17½	Barotseland .	H. Timmins.
	23¾	19½	4½	16½	Pungwe . .	H. R. Holden.
	23¾	20	5½	13¾	S. Africa . .	C. D. Rudd.
...	23½	19¼	[1] 11⅛	17⅛	?	H. Atkinson.
...	23½	21½	.	18½	S. Africa . .	T. E. Buckley.
...	23½	24⅝	7	15¼	Beira . .	A. M. Naylor.
...	23½	20½	4⅝	16¼	Mashonaland .	J. A. Jameson.

Head of Brindled Gnu.

[1] Circumference.

BRINDLED GNU (Connochœtes taurinus)—*continued.*

Widest outside.	Widest inside.	Length on outside curve.	Breadth of Palm.	Tip to Tip.	Locality.	Owner.
...	$23\frac{1}{2}$	$20\frac{1}{2}$	^{1} 12	$14\frac{5}{8}$	Botletli River .	H. A. Bryden.
...	-23	$22\frac{7}{8}$	$4\frac{11}{16}$	$17\frac{7}{16}$	North of Great Namaqualand	Th. Rehbock.
...	-23	...	^{1} $13\frac{1}{2}$	14	?	A. Ohlsson.
...	-23	20	^{1} $14\frac{1}{2}$	$16\frac{1}{2}$	S. Africa .	Dr. W. P. Y. Bainbrigge.
...	$-22\frac{5}{8}$	$21\frac{7}{8}$	$6\frac{1}{4}$	...	Pungwe . .	Count E. Hoyos.
...	20	$18\frac{3}{4}$	4	$13\frac{1}{8}$	Benguela, Angola	G. W. Penrice.
...	...	21	...	...	Damaraland .	Cape Town Museum.
...	♀ $17\frac{1}{2}$	$18\frac{1}{4}$	^{1} 8	8	?	Dr. W. P. Y. Bainbrigge.
...	27	$19\frac{1}{4}$	$4\frac{1}{2}$	$15\frac{1}{2}$	Tushila Plains, B.C.A.	G. N. Barclay.
...	$24\frac{1}{2}$	19	4	$16\frac{3}{4}$	B.C.A. .	J. E. Gough.
...	$22\frac{3}{4}$	$18\frac{1}{2}$	$4\frac{1}{2}$	15	Tushila Plains, B.C.A.	C. C. Bowring.
...	$16\frac{1}{2}$	$12\frac{1}{2}$	^{1} 10	12	E.C.A. .	James J. Harrison.

^{1} Circumference.

Head of White-Bearded Gnu.

WHITE-BEARDED GNU (Connochœtes taurinus albojubatus).

Swahili name *Nyumbu.*

Apparently a local race of the brindled gnu, distinguished by its slightly paler coloration, and the yellowish white throat-fringe, a few whitish hairs being also mingled with the mane.

The widest part of the front of the horns is somewhat different from the corresponding portion of the typical variety, as will be seen by reference to the illustrations.

Distribution.—East Africa, Athi plains, Ukambani, north of Kilimanjaro.

Widest inside.	Length on front curve.	Breadth of Palm.	Tip to Tip.	Locality.	Owner.
[2] 27½	22	6	15½	East Africa . .	Lord Delamere.
[2] 28	...	...	16	Do. . . .	Sir John Willoughby, Bart.
[2] 27	20	[1] 12	17	Do. . . .	R. P. Carroll.
26¼	22⅝	...	18¾	Do. . . .	H. C. V. Hunter.
25⅜	22⅞	...	16½	Do. . . .	F. J. Jackson, C.B.
25	20½	[1] 12½	12½	Do. . . .	Rowland Ward.
24	20⅝	...	15⅛	Do. . . .	Sir Robert Harvey, Bart.
23½	18¼	4½	12	?	S. L. Hinde.

1 Circumference. 2 Outside.

WHITE-BEARDED GNU (Connochœtes taurinus albojubatus)—*continued.*

Widest inside.	Length on front curve.	Breadth of Palm.	Tip to Tip.	Locality.	Owner.
[2] 24	17		15	East Africa . .	W. Astor Chanler.
22⅛	20	5¼	16¾	Athi Plains . .	E. Gedge.
21⅜	19¾	5	13½	East Africa . .	Capt. R. A. J. Montgomer C.B., R.N.
21⅜	18¼	4	17¼	Athi Plains . .	Col. F. D. Lugard, C.B., D.S.
21½	21	5¼	15½	East Africa . .	Capt. J. W. Pringle.
21¾	21 13/16	[1] 12¾	17¾	Do. . .	Lionel Decle, Paris Museum.
21½	19	4¾	15	Do. . .	E. J. L. Berkeley.
22	19	4	15½	Do. . .	Henry Charrington.
♀ 19½	15	3	13½	Do. . .	Lord Delamere.
21¼	19⅝	5⅜	12½	?	Hon. Walter Rothschild.
20½	16½	4	15½	East Africa . .	Do.

[1] Circumference. [2] Outside.

Skull and Horns of White-Bearded Gnu.

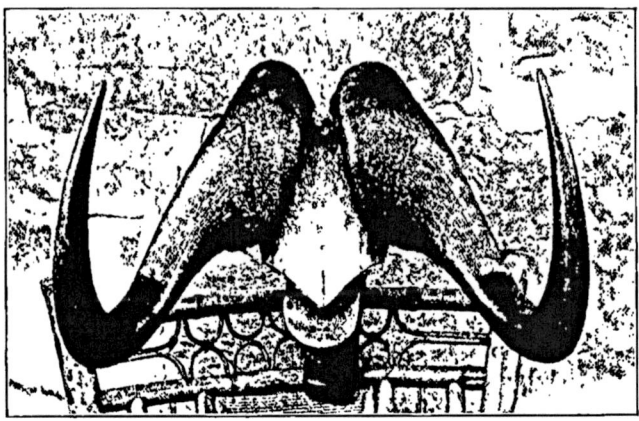

Horns of White-Tailed Gnu.   From F. H. Barber's specimen.

WHITE-TAILED GNU (Connochœtes gnu).

This southern species is the true gnu, being formerly known to the Hottentots by that name, while, by the colonists, it is termed the black wildebeest.   Its inferior size (height at shoulder about 3 ft. 10 ins.), the downward curvature of the horns at starting and their great expansion at the base, the pure white tail, and the abundant fringe of long hair on the chest and fore part of the belly, serve at once to distinguish it from the brindled gnu.   The general colour is uniform deep amber-brown, passing into black.   Females are much smaller than males ; and have the horns more slender and less expanded at the base.

Distribution.—The northern range of this species was approximately limited by the Vaal, or northern branch of the Orange River. Like most of the large animals of the Cape it is now rapidly approaching extermination, being apparently at present represented by herds of a few hundred head preserved by the Boers of the Orange Free State.   On the plains of the latter country, as well as on the Karoos of Cape Colony, it was formerly found in vast herds, generally in company with quaggas.   Fierce and treacherous in disposition, it was especially characterised by its habit of indulging in grotesque capers and frolics on the approach of strangers ; a practice totally unknown to its cousin on the farther side of the Vaal River.

WHITE-TAILED GNU (Connochœtes gnu)—*continued.*

Head of White-Tailed Gnu.

Length on front curve.	Breadth of Palm.	Tip to Tip.	Locality.	Owner.
-30⅞	[1] 22½	14	Kalahari . . .	Dr. F. H. H. Guillemard.
-30	10½	17⅛	?	Mr. Justice Hopley.
-28	...	...	Colesburg . .	F. H. Barber. (See illustration.)
-27⅞	7	11	Orange Free State .	Count E. Hoyos.
-27½	...	...	Wynburg . .	F. H. Barber. (See illustration.)
-27½	...	...	Victoria W., Cape Colony	Cape Town Museum.
-27½	8½	13	?	Mr. Justice Hopley.
26½	8	14½	South Africa . .	Sir Edmund G. Loder, Bart.
-26½	7½	7⅛	Orange Free State .	Julius Jeppe.
-26¼	[1] 20¼	12¾	Do. . .	Dr. W. P. Y. Bainbrigge.
-26	11⅜	16¼	Do. . .	The Maclaine of Lochbuie.
25	6¾	15¼	Do. . .	A. Payne-Gallwey.
-24½	8½	8	Do. . .	Julius Jeppe.

[1] Circumference.

WHITE-TAILED GNU (Connochœtes gnu)—*continued.*

Length on front curve.	Breadth of Palm.	Tip to Tip.	Locality.	Owner.
24½	6¾	15½	Orange Free State .	Julius Jeppe.
24	8½	15	Do. . .	Hon. Walter Rothschild.
24	8¼	13¼	Do. . .	C. D. Rudd.
23	7¾	17¼	Do. . .	A. H. Neumann.
23	7½	15	Do. . .	Bloemfontein Museum.
22¾	7¼	15	Do. . .	F. C. Selous.
22⅜	8½	15¼	Do. . .	F. C. Selous.
–22¼	9½	11¾	Do. . .	Julius Jeppe.
–22$\frac{3}{16}$	8	14¾	Do. . .	Dr. Percy Rendall.
22	9	17⅛	Do. . .	Hon. Walter Rothschild.
–22	9	11¾	Do. .	Julius Jeppe.
21¾	10⅝	18⅝	Do. . .	British Museum.
–21½	[1] 20	12½	Do. .	A. Ohlsson.
21	10	18½	Do. .	Dublin Museum.
20	5¼	11¾	Do. . .	Julius Jeppe.
♀ 19¾	[1] 13½	10¾	Do. . .	Dr. W. P. Y. Bainbrigge.
♀ 16	4¾	11½	Do. .	Bloemfontein Museum.
-♀ 15½	5	14¾	Do. .	Julius Jeppe.
♀ 14	5	11	Do. . .	Rowland Ward.

[1] Circumference.

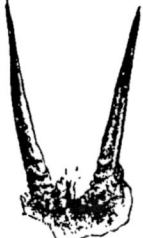

Horns of Common Duiker.   From a specimen shot by F. C. Selous.

COMMON DUIKER (Cephalophus grimmi).

Puti of the Bechuanas.   *Impungi* of the Swazis and Zulus.
Impunzi of the Matabele.   *Imputi* of the Basutos.
                     Gwapi of the Chinyanjas.

The common duiker, or " diver," is the southern representative of an
extensive group of small or medium-sized antelopes, mostly confined
to Africa, but also containing one genus and species from India.   In
all of these the muzzle is naked ; face-glands of a more or less elongated form are present, as are false hoofs ; the tail is of medium
length, the knees have no tufts of long hair, and the females are pro-
vided with four teats.   The horns, which are short and straight, are
generally present in both sexes, but are smoother and more slender in
the does than in the bucks ; and the upper molar teeth have low
crowns, with square grinding surfaces.   The African duikers have a
single pair of horns, generally present in both sexes, and more or less
hidden by a tuft of long hairs growing from the crown of the head ;
and the face-glands are arranged to form a bare line of pores on each
side of the muzzle.   The present species—the true duikerbok—is the
largest member of a group of three duikers, characterised by the horns
(usually absent in the females) inclining upwards at a sharp angle
above the plane of the profile of the nose.   Other features of the sub-
group are the long and pointed ears, the general yellowish or grayish
colour, devoid of dark markings, save for a brown nose-spot.   Although
essentially a southern form, the common duiker, which measures
about 23 inches at the shoulder, ranges on the west coast as far north
as Angola, and on the eastern side of the continent to British East
Africa and Somaliland.   Weight about 25 lbs.   Throughout its habitat
the timid duiker is to be met with wherever sufficient covert exists ;
and its furtive, squatting, dodging habits are most aptly indicated by

its name. Met with either singly or in pairs, it is never found far away from covert, strictly avoiding both open plains and steep, rocky mountains. Absence of water is, however, no bar to its existence, as it thrives in the heart of the Kalahari. It is occasionally hunted with foxhounds ; its flesh is but moderately good.

Length on front.	Circumference.	Tip to Tip.	Locality.	Owner.
–6	$2\frac{5}{8}$	$3\frac{1}{4}$	S. Africa . . .	James J. Harrison.
$–5\frac{5}{8}$	$2\frac{1}{2}$	$2\frac{1}{2}$	Do. . .	Julius Jeppe.
$–5\frac{1}{2}$	$2\frac{1}{8}$	$2\frac{7}{8}$	Selinya, Khama's country	F. C. Selous.
$5\frac{1}{2}$	$2\frac{1}{4}$	$2\frac{3}{8}$	Cape Colony .	Mr. Justice Hopley.
$–5\frac{1}{2}$	...	...	S. Africa	Lionel Phillips.
$– ? 5\frac{1}{2}$	$1\frac{1}{2}$	3	Do. .	Dr. W. P. Y. Bainbrigge.
$5\frac{1}{4}$	$2\frac{1}{4}$	$1\frac{1}{2}$	Zululand . . .	Capt. L. O. Williams.
$–5\frac{1}{4}$	...	...	?	O. R. Dunell.
$–5\frac{1}{4}$	$2\frac{1}{4}$	$1\frac{1}{2}$	?	Julius Jeppe.
$–5\frac{1}{4}$	$2\frac{1}{8}$	2	Inyamonga, P. E. Africa	F. Vaughan Kirby.
$–5\frac{1}{8}$	$2\frac{1}{8}$	$1\frac{7}{8}$	Bredasdorp, C. Colony	Mr. Justice Hopley.
$5\frac{1}{8}$	2	$2\frac{3}{8}$	Transvaal . .	H. T. and A. H. Glynn.
5	$2\frac{1}{4}$	$2\frac{1}{4}$	S. Africa	G. Richards.
5	$2\frac{1}{4}$	$2\frac{1}{2}$	Do. .	F. C. Selous.
–5	$2\frac{1}{2}$	$\frac{3}{8}$	Transvaal . .	F. Vaughan Kirby.
–5	...	...	Natal .	T. E. Buckley.
5	$2\frac{1}{4}$	$3\frac{1}{4}$	Northern Rhodesia .	F. Smitheman.
$4\frac{1}{2}$	...	$2\frac{7}{8}$	Algoa Bay . . .	F. C. Selous, British Museum.
$4\frac{1}{4}$	$2\frac{1}{4}$	$1\frac{3}{4}$	South Africa . .	G. H. M. Banks.
$4\frac{1}{2}$	$2\frac{1}{8}$	$2\frac{1}{4}$	Do. .	'R. A. Cooper.
$–4\frac{1}{2}$	$2\frac{1}{4}$	$2\frac{1}{2}$	Mashonaland .	A. Ohlsson.
$4\frac{1}{2}$	2	$2\frac{3}{4}$	South Africa .	Dr. W. P. Y. Bainbrigge.
$–4\frac{1}{2}$	...	...	?	Cape Town Museum.
$–4\frac{1}{2}$	...	...	?	C. T. Jones.
$4\frac{3}{8}$	2	$1\frac{5}{8}$	Matabeleland . .	Lord Brackley.
$4\frac{3}{8}$	$2\frac{1}{8}$	$2\frac{1}{4}$	Chanda . . .	C. C. Bowring.

COMMON DUIKER (Cephalophus grimmi)—*continued.*

Length on front.	Circumference.	Tip to Tip.	Locality.	Owner.
$4\frac{3}{8}$	2	$2\frac{5}{8}$	Zululand . .	A. Cameron.
$4\frac{1}{4}$	$1\frac{7}{8}$	$2\frac{3}{4}$	E. Africa . .	Sir Robert Harvey, Bart.
$-4\frac{1}{4}$	$2\frac{1}{4}$	$2\frac{15}{16}$	Barberton .	Dr. Percy Rendall.
$4\frac{1}{8}$	2	$1\frac{1}{2}$	Benguela, Angola .	G. W. Penrice.
$4\frac{1}{8}$	$1\frac{7}{8}$	$2\frac{5}{8}$	Natal . . .	J. Wahlberg, British Museum.
$4\frac{1}{8}$	$2\frac{5}{16}$	$2\frac{1}{4}$	Near Borgu, West Africa	Capt. N. C. Welch.
4	2	$2\frac{3}{4}$	Barotseland . .	R. T. Coryndon.
4	2	$1\frac{7}{8}$	East Africa .	F. J. Jackson, C.B.
♀ 4	$1\frac{3}{8}$	$1\frac{1}{4}$	North of Great Namaqualand	Th. Rehbock.
4	$1\frac{7}{8}$	$1\frac{1}{2}$	South Africa . .	H. and C. Beddington.
4	2	$1\frac{3}{4}$	Matabeleland .	W. W. Ashley.
♀ $3\frac{3}{4}$	$1\frac{1}{2}$	$1\frac{3}{8}$	Transvaal . .	Julius Jeppe.

ABYSSINIAN DUIKER (Cephalophus abyssinicus).

Abyssinian name *Midaku.*

Belonging to the same sub-group as the common duiker, and agreeing with the crowned duiker (*C. coronatus*) in size, this species differs from the latter by the general colour of the fur being grayish brown, instead of bright yellow. It was discovered by the traveller Rüppell, and its habits have been well described by Mr. W. T. Blanford in his *Geology and Zoology of Abyssinia.*

Distribution.—The highlands of Abyssinia.

Length on front.	Circumference.	Tip to Tip.	Locality.	Owner.
$-3\frac{9}{16}$	$2\frac{3}{16}$	$2\frac{1}{8}$	Abyssinia . .	Prince A. de Lucinge.
$-3\frac{1}{2}$	$1\frac{7}{8}$	$1\frac{3}{8}$	Do. .	Sir Victor Brooke's Collection.
$-3\frac{1}{16}$	2	$1\frac{13}{16}$	Galla country . .	Viscount Edmond de Poncins.
$2\frac{3}{4}$	$1\frac{7}{8}$	$1\frac{1}{4}$	Abyssinia . .	British Museum.

Head of Blue Duiker.

BLUE DUIKER (Cephalophus monticola).

Ipiti of all the Zulu tribes.

In the great majority of the duikers, that is to say all except the three included in the group mentioned above, the horns, which are generally present in both sexes, slope backwards either in or just below the line of the profile of the nose. The present species is included in a sub-group characterised by the smoky-brown or blackish coloration; and is especially distinguished by the rufous legs and uniformly coloured rump, the height at the shoulder being 13 inches. Weight about 26 lbs.

Distribution.—Southern Africa, from the wooded districts of Cape Colony northwards to Benguela on the west, and Nyasaland on the east.

Length on front.	Circumference.	Tip to Tip.	Locality.	Owner.
$-2\frac{1}{2}$	...	$1\frac{1}{2}$	Cape Colony . .	F. Vaughan Kirby.
$2\frac{1}{2}$	$1\frac{3}{4}$	$1\frac{1}{2}$	Tushila Plain, B.C.A.	Hon. Walter Rothschild.
$-2\frac{1}{4}$	...	...	Knysna, Cape Colony	Cape Town Museum.
$-2\frac{1}{8}$	$1\frac{1}{2}$	$1\frac{5}{8}$	Do. . .	Mr. Justice Hopley.
$-2\frac{1}{16}$	$1\frac{5}{8}$	$\frac{1}{2}$	Natal . . .	Dr. Percy Rendall.
2	...	$1\frac{3}{4}$	Do. . . .	F. C. Selous.
2	$1\frac{5}{8}$	$1\frac{3}{4}$	Benguela . . .	G. W. Penrice.
-2	...	...	?	O. R. Dunell.
$1\frac{3}{4}$	$1\frac{5}{8}$	$1\frac{3}{8}$	Benguela . . .	Hon. Walter Rothschild.
$-1\frac{3}{4}$	$1\frac{1}{4}$	$1\frac{3}{4}$	?	A. Ohlsson.
$-1\frac{3}{4}$	...	...	?	C. T. Jones.
♀ $1\frac{11}{16}$	$1\frac{11}{16}$	$1\frac{15}{16}$	Natal . . .	Dr. Percy Rendall.
$-1\frac{5}{8}$	$1\frac{5}{8}$	$1\frac{7}{8}$	?	Julius Jeppe.
$1\frac{9}{16}$	$1\frac{5}{16}$	$1\frac{3}{8}$	?	Major H. J. Goold-Adams, C.B., C.M.G.
$-1\frac{3}{8}$	$1\frac{7}{8}$	$1\frac{1}{4}$	?	Julius Jeppe.

MAXWELL'S DUIKER (Cephalophus maxwelli).

This species belongs to the sub-group characterised by the smoky-brown or blackish colour. In size it is small (height at shoulder about 14 inches). The face is coloured like the back; the limbs, like the body, are grayish brown; and the rump is not parti-coloured. It was first brought to England by Col. C. Maxwell, and described by Major Hamilton Smith in 1827.

Distribution.—West Africa, from Gambia to the Gold Coast.

Length on front.	Circumference.	Tip to Tip.	Locality.	Owner.
1⅝	2⅛	2	Fanti . . .	Hon. Walter Rothschild.

RED or NATAL DUIKER (Cephalophus natalensis).

Rooi-Bosch-bokje of the Boers. *Msumbi* of the Swazis and Malonga.
Mkumbi of the Zulus. *Izikupu* of the Basutos.
Chisimbi of the Lower Zambesi natives.

This duiker is classed in another sub-group of small or medium-sized species characterised by the fulvous, rufous, or chestnut ground-colour; and is specially distinguished by its small size (height at shoulder, 17 inches) and completely uniform coloration, having no dark markings on either the face or body.

Distribution.—Natal, Transvaal, and Mashonaland (including all the forest and bush country of the East Coast), also seen by F. Vaughan Kirby and James J. Harrison near the Lualwa River, Mozambique Province.

Length on front.	Circumference.	Tip to Tip.	Locality.	Owner.
-3⅞	2¾	2	?	Julius Jeppe.
-3⅜	2⅞	2¼	Shupanga Forest .	F. Vaughan Kirby.
3⅜	2½	2⅛	Sabi Flats .	James J. Harrison.
-3⅜	2⅜	2	Makongwa Mountains, Barberton (about 6000 ft.)	Dr. Percy Rendall.
-3¼	3	2	Foothills of Kahlamba .	F. Vaughan Kirby.
-3¼	2⅞	2⅜	?	Julius Jeppe.
-3½	2⅝	2¼	Spitzkop . .	H. T. and A. H. Glynn.

RED or NATAL DUIKER (Cephalophus natalensis)—*continued.*

Length on front.	Circumference.	Tip to Tip.	Locality.	Owner.
$3\frac{1}{8}$	...	$2\frac{1}{8}$	Natal	Dr. A. Kraus, British Museum.
$-3\frac{1}{8}$	$2\frac{1}{2}$	$1\frac{7}{8}$	Do. . .	Mr. Justice Hopley.
-3	...	...	?	C. T. Jones.
-3	...	2	?	F. J. Newnham.
3	$2\frac{3}{8}$	$1\frac{3}{8}$	Natal .	Major H. J. Goold-Adams, C.B., C.M.G.
♀ $2\frac{3}{4}$	$1\frac{7}{8}$	1	Foothills of Kahlamba .	F. Vaughan Kirby.
$2\frac{3}{4}$	2	...	?	Sir Edmund G. Loder, Bart.
$2\frac{3}{4}$	$2\frac{5}{8}$	$2\frac{1}{4}$	South Africa . .	Dr. Oakshott.
$-2\frac{3}{4}$	...	...	Lydenburg	Cape Town Museum.
$2\frac{5}{8}$	$2\frac{1}{2}$	$1\frac{7}{8}$	?	F. E. Potter.
$-2\frac{5}{8}$	...	...	?	O. R. Dunell.
$-2\frac{1}{2}$	$2\frac{3}{4}$	2	Natal . . .	Dr. W. P. Y. Bainbrigge.
$2\frac{1}{2}$	$2\frac{1}{2}$	$1\frac{3}{4}$	S.E. Africa . .	G. Richards.
$-2\frac{1}{2}$	$1\frac{3}{4}$	...	?	A. Ohlsson.
$2\frac{5}{16}$	...	$2\frac{1}{16}$	Near Durban .	F. C. Selous.
♀ $1\frac{7}{8}$	$1\frac{3}{4}$	1	Barberton . . .	Dr. Percy Rendall.
♀ $1\frac{5}{8}$	...	1	Near Durban . .	F. C. Selous.
♀ $1\frac{5}{8}$	$1\frac{7}{8}$	2	?	Hon. Walter Rothschild.

BAY DUIKER (Cephalophus dorsalis).

From the last species the bay duiker, together with some allied [W]est African forms, differs by the presence of a black stripe running [al]ong the back and continued to the tail. As a species, its special [ch]aracters are the dark colour of the hams, and the evenly haired tail, [w]hich shows no sign of a tuft, and is parti-coloured.

[D]*istribution.*—West Africa, from Sierra Leone to the Cameroons; there being a northern and a southern race.

[L]ength on front.	Girth.	Tip to Tip.	Locality.	Owner.
$3\frac{1}{16}$	$2\frac{1}{8}$	2	West Africa . . .	Hon. Walter Rothschild.

BANDED DUIKER (Cephalophus doriæ).

The tiger-like transverse black bands on the orange ground of the back suffice to distinguish at a glance this pretty little duiker from all its kindred.

Distribution.—The interior of the West Coast of Africa from Liberia to Sierra Leone, where it is commonly known as the mountain deer.

Length on front.	Circum-ference.	Tip to Tip.	Locality.	Owner.
$-1\frac{7}{8}$	...	I	Liberia . . .	Dr. J. Büttikofer, British Museum.
$1\frac{5}{8}$	$1\frac{1}{4}$	$1\frac{1}{4}$	Do. . . .	Hon. Walter Rothschild.

YELLOW-BACKED DUIKER (Cephalophus sylvicultor).

This species is distinguished from all the other members of the genus by its large size, coupled with its blackish coloration, and the presence of a yellowish crest and similarly coloured longitudinal patch on the rump. Height at shoulder, 34 inches.

Distribution.—The West Coast of Africa from Liberia to Angola.

Length on front.	Circum-ference.	Tip to Tip.	Locality.	Owner.
$6\frac{3}{4}$	...	$4\frac{1}{2}$	Fanti . . .	British Museum.
$6\frac{5}{8}$	$3\frac{5}{8}$	$4\frac{3}{8}$	Do. .	Do.
$6\frac{1}{4}$	4	$3\frac{1}{4}$	Liberia . .	Dr. J. Büttikofer, British Museum.
$5\frac{1}{2}$	$3\frac{3}{8}$	$4\frac{1}{8}$	Gaboon .	Sir Edmund G. Loder, Bart.
$4\frac{5}{8}$	...	$2\frac{1}{4}$	Fanti	British Museum.

Head of Male Four-horned Antelope.

FOUR-HORNED ANTELOPE or **CHOUSINGHA** (**Tetraceros quadricornis**).

This antelope is the Oriental representative of the African duikers, from which it is distinguished by the following features. Typically there are two pairs of horns, and the face-glands form deep slits on the sides of the muzzle instead of a long naked line; the females being hornless. Height at shoulder about 25 inches, and weight about 40 lbs. General colour dull rufous brown, becoming whitish beneath, with the muzzle, the outer surface of the ears, and a line down the front of each leg blackish brown, and some white on the outer side of the pasterns. The front horns are not unfrequently mere knobs, and may even be wanting, as in most of the Kathiawar specimens.

Distribution.—Peninsular India south of the Himalayas.

Length of horns on front.		Circumference.		Tip to Tip.		Locality.	Owner.
Rear.	Fore.	Rear.	Fore.	Rear.	Fore.		
-5	...	...	...	...	...	Jhalawar . .	H.H. Maharaja Rana Bahadur of Jhalawar.
-4½	2½	2¼	1⅞	2⅛	1	Lulitpur . .	Surg.-Gen. Walker.
-4½	2½	...	...	...	...	Gurhwal . . .	Capt. Ging.
4⅜	2½	2¼	2⅜	1⅝	2⅞	India . . .	Sir Edmund G. Loder, Bart.
-4⅛	1½	...	..	...	...	Do.	J. D. Inverarity.

FOUR-HORNED ANTELOPE or CHOUSINGHA (Tetraceros quadricornis)—*continued.*

Length of horns on front.		Circumference.		Tip to Tip.		Locality.	Owner.
Rear.	Fore.	Rear.	Fore.	Rear.	Fore.		
4	$2\frac{1}{2}$	$1\frac{7}{8}$	$1\frac{7}{8}$	3	$1\frac{1}{8}$	Indore . .	Col. J. Evans, British Museum.
4	2	3	$1\frac{7}{8}$	$1\frac{3}{4}$	$2\frac{1}{2}$	Karkote Jungle, near Mhow	Lieut.-Col. G. D. F. Sulivan.
$-3\frac{3}{4}$	...	...	...	...	...	India . . .	Indian Museum.
$3\frac{5}{8}$	$1\frac{3}{4}$	$1\frac{7}{8}$	2	$1\frac{1}{8}$	$2\frac{1}{2}$	Do. . .	Sir Robert Harvey, Bart.
$-3\frac{5}{8}$	$1\frac{7}{8}$	...	...	...	...	Do. .	J. D. Inverarity.
$3\frac{1}{2}$	2	$3\frac{1}{8}$	$1\frac{7}{8}$	$1\frac{7}{8}$	$1\frac{5}{8}$	Central Provinces .	C. F. Egerton.
$3\frac{1}{2}$	2	$1\frac{5}{8}$	$1\frac{5}{8}$	$1\frac{1}{4}$	$2\frac{1}{2}$	India .	H.R.H. the Duke of Saxe-Coburg and Gotha.
$-3\frac{1}{2}$	$2\frac{1}{4}$	...	...	...	...	Do. . . .	Indian Museum.
$-3\frac{1}{2}$	$3\frac{3}{4}$	...	...	...	...	Mandla, C.P. .	Capt. B. H. Boucher.
$3\frac{3}{8}$	$1\frac{5}{8}$	2	$1\frac{3}{4}$	...	...	Central Provinces	Hon. Walter Rothschild.
$3\frac{1}{4}$	$1\frac{3}{8}$	2	$1\frac{3}{4}$	...	...	Jhalawar	Mr. Justice Hopley.
$3\frac{3}{8}$	$2\frac{1}{4}$	$2\frac{5}{8}$	$1\frac{3}{4}$	2	$\frac{1}{4}$	Central Provinces	C. D. Twopeny.
$-3\frac{3}{8}$	...	...	...	...	...	Kathiawar .	Lieut.-Col. L. L. Fenton.
$-3\frac{1}{4}$	2	$2\frac{1}{4}$	$2\frac{1}{8}$	$2\frac{3}{4}$	$1\frac{7}{8}$	Central Provinces .	Bombay Natural History Society's Museum.
$3\frac{1}{8}$	$1\frac{7}{8}$	$1\frac{3}{4}$	$1\frac{1}{2}$	$2\frac{5}{8}$	$1\frac{1}{8}$	N.W. Provinces .	Capt. R. B. Fell.
$3\frac{1}{8}$	$1\frac{11}{16}$	2	...	$2\frac{1}{4}$	$1\frac{1}{4}$	India	A. M. Caccia.

Head of Salt's Dik-dik.

SALT'S DIK-DIK (Madoqua saltiana).

This species, the Beni Israel of the Arabs, is the typical representative of a group of tiny, slenderly-built antelopes characterised by the elongated, trunk-like nose, of which the tip is almost entirely hairy, the tuft of hair on the crown of the head, the short and almost rudimentary tail, and the minute size of the lateral hoofs. In the present species the last tooth in the lower jaw lacks the third lobe found in almost all ruminants, the trunk is but moderately developed, and the general colour fulvous or rufous fawn, scarcely more rufous on the sides than on the back. Height at the shoulder, 14 or 15 inches.

Distribution.—The Coast Range of Eastern Abyssinia, and adjacent districts of Somaliland.

Length on front.	Circum- ference.	Tip to Tip.	Locality.	Owner.
3	1	1	Abyssinia . . .	Sir Edmund G. Loder, Bart.
2¾	1	1	Do. . . .	Rowland Ward.
2⅝	...	1¾	Do. . . .	Sir Victor Brooke's Collection.
2½	1½	...	North Kassala . .	Col. Ralph Vivian.
2¾	...	1⅝	?	British Museum.

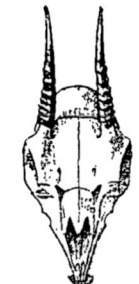

Skull of Phillips's Dik-dik.   Head of Swayne's Dik-dik.

SOMALI DIK-DIKS (Madoqua swaynei, M. phillipsi, and M. guentheri).

General native name, *Sakáro*.

Different districts of Somaliland are inhabited by the three species of dik-diks above named. The first of these is allied to Salt's dik-dik, but is of smaller size; it inhabits the northern half of Somaliland. Phillips's dik-dik, which also occurs in Northern Somaliland, is intermediate in size between Salt's and Swayne's dik-dik, from both of which it is distinguished by having the back gray and the sides and shoulders rich rufous or cinnamon. On the other hand, Günther's dik-dik is widely different from both, being nearly allied to the under-mentioned Kirk's dik-dik, from which it is distinguished by the form of the nasal bones in the skull.

Height at shoulder about 14 inches. Weight, ♂ 6 lbs. ;
♀ 5 lbs. (T. W. H. Clarke).

Sakáro Guyu (Madoqua swaynei).　　*Distribution.*—Berbera District.

Sakáro Gol-Ass (Madoqua phillipsi).　　„　Northern half of Somaliland.

Sakáro Gussuli (Madoqua guentheri).　　„　Plateau of Central Somaliland.

Length on front.	Girth.	Tip to Tip.	Locality.		Owner.
3½	1¼	1⅝	Somaliland	. .	J. Kenneth Foster.
-3½	...	...	Do.	. .	Capt. F. A. Wilson.
3¼	1¼	1⅜	Do.	. .	W. W. Ashley.
3¼	1¼	1½	Do.	. .	Major C. F. Blane.

SOMALI DIK-DIKS (Madoqua swaynei, M. phillipsi, and M. guentheri)— *continued.*

Length on front.	Girth.	Tip to Tip.	Locality.	Owner.
[1]–$3\frac{1}{8}$	$1\frac{1}{2}$	$1\frac{3}{4}$	Somaliland . .	A. E. Pease.
–$3\frac{1}{8}$	...	...	Do. .	J. Brander Dunbar.
3	...	1	Do. . .	Sir Edmund G. Loder, Bart.
3	$1\frac{1}{2}$	...	Do. . .	Col. Arthur Paget.
–3	...	$1\frac{3}{4}$	Do. .	Viscount Edmond de Poncins.
–$2\frac{15}{16}$	$1\frac{1}{2}$	$1\frac{1}{8}$	Do.	Do.
–$2\frac{7}{8}$	$1\frac{1}{4}$	$1\frac{1}{8}$	Do. . .	J. Johnston-Stewart.
$2\frac{7}{8}$	$1\frac{3}{8}$	$1\frac{5}{8}$	Do. . .	Lord Delamere.
$2\frac{3}{4}$	1	1	Do. . .	T. W. H. Clarke.
$2\frac{3}{4}$	$1\frac{1}{2}$	...	Do. . .	C. Liddell.
–$2\frac{5}{8}$	...	...	Do. .	J. Brander Dunbar.
[1]–$2\frac{1}{2}$	1	...	Do. .	C. V. A. Peel.
$2\frac{1}{2}$	...	...	Do. .	Rowland Ward.
$2\frac{1}{2}$	1	$1\frac{3}{8}$	Do. . .	Major H. G. C. Swayne.
$2\frac{1}{2}$	...	$1\frac{3}{8}$	Do. .	Sir Edmund G. Loder, Bart.
$2\frac{3}{8}$	$1\frac{1}{2}$	...	Do. . .	C. Liddell.
–$2\frac{1}{4}$	$1\frac{3}{8}$	$1\frac{1}{4}$	Do. . .	Dr. Percy Rendall.
[1]–$2\frac{1}{8}$	$1\frac{1}{8}$	$1\frac{3}{4}$	Do. . .	Julius Jeppe.
–$1\frac{3}{4}$	$1\frac{1}{8}$	$1\frac{7}{8}$	Do. .	Do.
[2]–$3\frac{1}{4}$	...	$1\frac{1}{4}$	Do. . .	C. V. A. Peel.
[2]–$2\frac{1}{2}$	...	...	Njemps . . .	F. J. Jackson, C.B.

[1] M. phillipsi. [2] M. guentheri.

The following are the dimensions of a specimen of *M. guentheri*:— Length, $23\frac{1}{4}$. Height, $15\frac{1}{4}$. Horns, $2\frac{1}{2}$. Weight, $8\frac{1}{4}$ lbs. Shot at Njemps, 26 : 9 : 96, by F. J. Jackson, C.B.

Kirk's Dik-dik.

KIRK'S DIK-DIK (Madoqua kirki).

This dik-dik belongs to a small group of species differing from the one containing *M. saltiana* by the presence of three lobes to the last tooth of the lower jaw, and likewise by the more decidedly trunk-like character of the muzzle. Of the other members of the group, *M. damarensis* differs by its superior size, and *M. guentheri* by the still greater development of the trunk.

Distribution.—East Africa, from Southern Somaliland to Ugogo, most numerous on the coast.

Length on front.	Circumference.	Tip to Tip.	Locality.	Owner.
3	...	$1\frac{1}{2}$	East Africa . .	F. J. Jackson, C.B.
$2\frac{3}{4}$	...	$1\frac{5}{8}$	Do. . . .	British Museum.
$2\frac{5}{8}$	$1\frac{1}{2}$	$1\frac{3}{8}$	Do. . . .	Col. Trevor Ternan.
$2\frac{5}{8}$	...	$1\frac{1}{2}$	Do. . . .	Sir Robert Harvey, Bart.
$2\frac{5}{8}$	$1\frac{1}{2}$	$1\frac{5}{8}$	Kilimanjaro . .	H. C. V. Hunter, British Museum.
$2\frac{5}{8}$	...	$1\frac{3}{4}$	East Africa . .	Sir Robert Harvey, Bart.
$2\frac{5}{8}$	$1\frac{1}{2}$	$1\frac{3}{8}$	East African Coast .	Col. Trevor Ternan.
$2\frac{1}{2}$	...	$1\frac{5}{8}$	East Africa . .	Hon. Walter Rothschild.
$2\frac{1}{2}$	...	$1\frac{3}{8}$	Do. . . .	Rowland Ward.
$2\frac{3}{8}$	...	$1\frac{3}{8}$	Manda Island . .	Sir John Kirk, K.C.B.

DAMARALAND DUIKER (Madoqua damarensis).

Character mentioned under heading of the preceding species.
Distribution.—Damaraland.

Length on front.	Circum-ference.	Tip to Tip.	Locality.	Owner.
$-2\frac{1}{2}$	...	...	Damaraland	Cape Town Museum (type specimen).
$-2\frac{1}{2}$	$1\frac{1}{2}$	$1\frac{1}{2}$	Do.	. A. Ohlsson.

HEMPRICH'S DIK-DIK (Madoqua hemprichiana).

Further information is desirable as to the right of this form to specific distinction.

Length on front.	Circum-ference.	Tip to Tip	Locality.	Owner.
$2\frac{5}{16}$	$1\frac{3}{8}$	$1\frac{1}{16}$	Abyssinia .	. Hon. Walter Rothschild.

Head of Male Oribi from Pungwe, South-East Africa.

CAPE ORIBI (Oribia scoparia).

Inla of the Swazis and Zulus.   *Pulukudukamani* of the Basutos.

The oribis, grysbuck, klipspringer, and their allies constitute a group of comparatively small African antelopes presenting the following characters in common.   The muzzle has a naked tip, the head is devoid of a tuft of hair, large face-glands open beneath the eyes by a small aperture on each side, the tail is short or moderate, and false hoofs may or may not be retained.   Horns are present only in the bucks, and are short, almost, or quite, straight, with smoothed tips and ridged bases.   The upper molar teeth have tall and narrow crowns.   The dik-diks are nearly allied, but differ by their tufted heads, and elongated hairy muzzles. The oribis, which are the largest members of the group, have normal hoofs and hair, and are specially distinguished by the presence of a bare glandular spot beneath each ear, and of a large opening in the skull beneath each eye-socket.   In the Cape species the horns of the bucks are comparatively smooth and slender, with only their basal two inches slightly ridged ; the tail being tufted and moderately bushy, with its terminal two-thirds black.   Height at shoulders, 24 inches.

Distribution.—Typically, Africa south of the Zambesi.   On grassy plains this graceful little antelope is still plentiful in many districts ; and the gunner in search of bustard or francolin will often see one of them start up from its form before his pointer, to scud away at a great rate, occasionally making springs from side to side.   At close quarters a charge of shot will suffice to bowl over this diminutive little buck, and thus add some capital venison to the larder. Formerly oribi afforded excellent sport with greyhounds in the eastern districts of Cape Colony.

Length on front.	Circumference.	Tip to Tip.	Locality.	Owner.
−7½	2¾	2⅝	Zomba, B.C.A. . . .	D. MacAlpine.
6¼	2¼	...	E. Griqualand . .	Jff. Darling, British Museum.
6	2⅛	2¼	Spitzkop .	H. T. and A. H. Glynn.
−6	...	...	Natal . .	Cape Town Museum.
−5 15/16	2	2½	?	Mr. Justice Hopley.
−5⅞	2	3¼	?	Do.
5¾	2	3¼	Barotseland . . .	H. Timmins.
5⅝	2	2¾	Bangueolo . .	F. Smitheman.
5⅝	2⅛	1⅞	Transvaal . .	F. R. N. Findlay.
5½	1⅞	3	Pungwe . .	G. L. Bonham.
−5½	1⅞	3¼	?	Julius Jeppe.
−5½	2	2½	Gorongoza, P. E. Africa .	F. Vaughan Kirby.
−5½	1⅞	3½	?	A. Ohlsson.
5½	2	2¾	M'peta Island, Upper Zambesi	R. T. Coryndon.
−5⅜	2	2½	Do.	Do.
−5¼	...	...	?	O. R. Dunell.
5⅛	1	2¼	S.E. of Lake Bangueolo .	Poulett-Weatherley.
5	2	1⅞	Pungwe . . .	Col. G. A. Percy.
5	1¾	1⅞	?	F. Vaughan Kirby.
−5	1⅞	2½	M'peta Island . . .	F. Aitkens.
−5	2	2 5/16	Barberton . . .	Dr. Percy Rendall.
−4⅞	...	...	Transvaal	C. T. Jones.
−4¾	2⅛	2⅜	M'peta Island . . .	F. V. Worthington.
4 13/16	1¾	1⅞	Pungwe . . .	A. C. Humbert.
4¾	2	2½	Cape Colony . . .	British Museum.
4¾	2⅛	2⅝	British Central Africa .	J. E. Gough.
4¾	1¾	2	Manica Plateau . . .	F. C. Selous.

CAPE ORIBI (Oribia scoparia)—*continued.*

Length on front.	Circumference.	Tip to Tip.	Locality.	Owner.
$4\frac{3}{4}$	$1\frac{5}{8}$	$1\frac{7}{8}$	?	Julius Jeppe.
$4\frac{1}{2}$	$1\frac{5}{8}$	$1\frac{7}{8}$	Pungwe . . .	R. K. Micklethwait.
$4\frac{1}{2}$	$1\frac{3}{4}$	$1\frac{3}{8}$	?	G. Richards.
$-4\frac{1}{2}$	$1\frac{7}{8}$	$2\frac{1}{2}$	?	Count E. Hoyos.
$-4\frac{3}{8}$	$2\frac{7}{16}$	$2\frac{5}{16}$	Upper Shiré Valley .	Dr. Percy Rendall.
$-4\frac{3}{8}$	$1\frac{3}{4}$	$2\frac{1}{4}$	?	Dr. W. P. Y. Bainbrigge.
$4\frac{1}{4}$	$1\frac{5}{8}$	$2\frac{1}{2}$	Pungwe .	A. Cameron.
$4\frac{5}{16}$	$1\frac{3}{4}$	$2\frac{1}{4}$	Tuchila Plain, B.C.A.	Hon. Walter Rothschild.
4	$1\frac{3}{4}$	$2\frac{1}{8}$	Pungwe . . .	G. Micklethwait.

ABYSSINIAN ORIBI (Oribia montana).

Miwaka of the Abyssinians.

Very similar in most characters to the Cape species, but with a shorter and less bushy tail, the tip of which has only a few sparse black hairs. Height at shoulder, $22\frac{1}{2}$ inches. These antelopes are shy and rarely seen in the open, preferring the thick bush and long grass. If disturbed they go at a great pace with their heads quite close to the ground. Their flesh is very good.

Viscount Edmond de Poncins states that a fine male weighed 30 lbs. 13 oz., and stood $19\frac{1}{2}$ inches at the shoulder.

Distribution.—Abyssinia and Bongoland.

Length on front.	Circumference.	Tip to Tip.	Locality.	Owner.
5	...	$2\frac{1}{2}$	Abyssinia .	Sir Edmund G. Loder, Bart.
$-4\frac{7}{8}$	$2\frac{3}{8}$	2	Hawash, Abyssinia .	Prince A. de Lucinge.
$-4\frac{1}{2}$	2	2	Do. .	Viscount Edmond de Poncins.
$4\frac{3}{8}$	$1\frac{3}{4}$	$2\frac{1}{2}$	Dombelas, Abyssinia .	British Museum.
4.12	2.2	2.3	Sudan . . .	Prince Henry of Liechtenstein.
4	2	2.6	Do. .	Do.
$3\frac{1}{4}$	2	$2\frac{1}{4}$	Do. . . .	Lieut.-Col. Hon. W. Coke.

WEST AFRICAN ORIBI (Oribia nigricaudata).

The present species is very close to the Abyssinian oribi, but of smaller size, grayer, and with a distinct black tip to the tail, as in the Cape species.   Height at shoulder, 20 inches.

Distribution.—The open country of Senegal and Gambia.

Length on front.	Circumference.	Tip to Tip.	Locality.	Owner.
$3\frac{11}{16}$	$1\frac{7}{8}$	$1\frac{3}{4}$	Nigeria . .	Capt. A. H. Festing.
$3\frac{3}{4}$	$1\frac{1}{2}$	...	Kiama .	A. W. M. Brodie.
3	$1\frac{5}{8}$	$2\frac{3}{4}$	Gambia . .	Charles B. Mosse, British Museum.

HAGGARD'S ORIBI (Oribia haggardi).

Swahili name, *Taya*.

Still imperfectly known, but distinguished from all the other oribis by the stouter horns, which are strongly ridged for rather more than the basal half of their length.   Height at shoulder about 24 inches.
Distribution.—The coast districts of East Africa in the neighbourhood of Lamu.   Discovered in 1887 by Mr. J. G. Haggard.

Length on front.	Circumference.	Tip to Tip.	Locality.	Owner.
[1] $5\frac{1}{8}$	$2\frac{1}{4}$	2	East Central Africa . .	Hon. Walter Rothschild.
[1] $5\frac{1}{8}$	$1\frac{13}{16}$	$2\frac{3}{8}$	North end of Lake Albert .	Col. Trevor Ternan.
$4\frac{5}{8}$	2	$2\frac{1}{4}$	East Africa . . .	F. J. Jackson, C.B.
[1] $4\frac{9}{16}$	2	$2\frac{1}{4}$	Lake Albert .	Col. Trevor Ternan.
[1] $4\frac{7}{16}$	?	$2\frac{5}{8}$	Do. . . .	Do.
$4\frac{1}{8}$	$1\frac{3}{4}$	$2\frac{1}{2}$	East Africa . . .	F. J. Jackson, C.B.

[1] Determination provisional.

ZANZIBAR ANTELOPE (Nesotragus moschatus).

The two elegant little antelopes included in the genus *Nesotragus* are near relatives of the oribis, from which they are distinguished by the absence of a naked glandular patch below each ear and the want of lateral hoofs. They are further characterised by the horns being directed backwards nearly or quite in the plane of the face, and extending at least as far as the back of the head, as also by the large size of the empty spaces in the skull below the sockets of the eyes, and by the nasal bones. In the present species the horns are short and slender, and the colour, inclusive of the tail-tip, fawn gray. Height at shoulder about 13 inches.

Distribution.—Islets near Zanzibar and adjacent coast from Kilimanjaro to Mozambique.

Length on front.	Circumference.	Tip to Tip.	Locality.	Owner.
3¼	1½	2	Coral Islands, Zanzibar .	Sir John Kirk, K.C.B.
3¼	1⅞	1½	Zanzibar . . .	The late Capt. Speke, British Museum.
3¼	1¼	1½	Do. . .	Sir John Kirk, K.C.B., British Museum.
2⅝	1¼	1¾	Do. . .	Sir Victor Brooke's Collection.

Skull and Horns of Livingstone's Antelope, from a specimen shot by F. Vaughan Kirby.

LIVINGSTONE'S ANTELOPE (Nesotragus livingstonianus).

Lumswi of the Shupanga.　　　　*Intilengana* of the Amatonga.

Distinguished from the preceding species by its slightly superior dimensions (height at shoulder, 15 inches), the longer and thicker horns, more rufous coloration, and the blackish upper surface of the tail.

Two specimens killed by F. Vaughan Kirby measured—

	Male.	Female.
Extreme length over all, tip of nose to end of tail	$27\frac{1}{5}$ ins.	$25\frac{3}{4}$ ins.
Length of tail	$3\frac{1}{2}$,,	3 ,,
Perpendicular shoulder-height . . .	$14\frac{1}{4}$,,	$13\frac{1}{8}$,,
,,　　　height at croup . . .	$14\frac{3}{4}$,,	$14\frac{1}{4}$,,
Girth of neck	$6\frac{1}{2}$,,	6 ,,
,, behind the shoulder	$14\frac{1}{8}$,,	$13\frac{5}{8}$,,

Distribution.—South-East Africa, from Mozambique to Zululand ; the form from Zululand being distinguished as *N. livingstonianus zuluensis.*

Length on front.	Circumference.	Tip to Tip.	Locality.	Owner.
$4\frac{1}{2}$	$1\frac{3}{4}$	$1\frac{3}{4}$	Shupanga Forest .	F. Vaughan Kirby.
$-4\frac{1}{2}$	...	$1\frac{3}{4}$	?	F. J. Newnham.
$4\frac{3}{8}$	$2\frac{1}{8}$	...	Gungunyana's country	H. T. Glynn, British Museum.
$-4\frac{3}{8}$	...	...	Delagoa Bay . .	F. H. Barber.

LIVINGSTONE'S ANTELOPE (Nesotragus livingstonianus)—*continued.*

Length on front.	Circumference.	Tip to Tip.	Locality.	Owner.
−4¼	...	...	?	O. R. Dunell.
−4⅛	...	...	?	C. T. Jones.
−4⅛	...	1	Delagoa Bay . .	F. C. Selous.
−4	1¾	1⅜	?	Julius Jeppe.
−4	...	...	?	C. T. Jones.
−4	1¾	1⅜	?	Julius Jeppe.
3¾	1¾	2	?	C. D. Rudd.
−3¾	1½	1¾	Zambesi . . .	Sir Edmund Loder, Bart.
$3\frac{11}{16}$	1¾	$2\frac{5}{16}$	Delagoa Bay .	Hon. Walter Rothschild.
3⅜	1½	2⅛	Do.	G. Richards.
−3⅜	1⅝	1⅝	Do. . .	Julius Jeppe.
−3⅜	1¾	1⅝	Do. .	Mr. Justice Hopley.
$3\frac{5}{16}$	...	...	Do. .	Dr. Percy Rendall.
3¼	1⅝	1⅝	?	Major H. J. Goold-Adams, C.B., C.M.G.
$3\frac{3}{16}$	1¾	1⅜	?	F. E. Potter.
−3⅛	1⅞	1¾	?	A. Ohlsson.
$3\frac{1}{16}$	2	...	Northern Zululand .	A. H. Neumann, British Museum.
3	1⅝	2⅛	Zululand . .	A. Cameron.

Head of Grysbuck, from a specimen shot by F. C. Selous.

GRYSBUCK (Rhaphiceros melanotis).

Isikupi of the Basutos.

From the other members of the oribi group the grysbuck and its cousin the steinbuck are readily distinguished by the horns rising nearly vertically from the skull, in which the open spaces below the eye-sockets are unusually small. Curiously enough, the grysbuck retains the lateral hoofs, which have disappeared in the steinbuck. In addition to this feature, the former is distinguished by the fur showing a large admixture of white, instead of being uniformly coloured. Height at shoulder, 22 inches.

Distribution.—South Africa, extending as far north as the Zambesi and Mozambique.

Length on front.	Circumference.	Tip to Tip.	Locality.	Owner.
$4\frac{7}{8}$	$1\frac{1}{2}$	$1\frac{7}{8}$	?	R. A. Cooper.
-4	...	...	Caledon, C.C. . .	Cape Town Museum.
$3\frac{9}{16}$	$1\frac{3}{4}$	$1\frac{7}{8}$	Cape Colony . . .	F. C. Selous. (See illustration.)
·$3\frac{1}{4}$	...	...	Limpopo . . .	C. T. Jones.
$3\frac{1}{4}$	$1\frac{1}{2}$	$2\frac{3}{8}$	Knysna, C.C. . .	Mr. Justice Hopley.
$3\frac{1}{4}$	$1\frac{1}{2}$	$1\frac{3}{4}$	?	Major H. J. Goold-Adams, C.B., C.M.G.
·$3\frac{1}{8}$	$1\frac{1}{2}$	$1\frac{1}{2}$	Knysna, C.C. . .	Mr. Justice Hopley.
-$3\frac{1}{8}$	$1\frac{3}{4}$	$2\frac{1}{2}$	Komati Poort . .	F. Vaughan Kirby.
-3	$1\frac{1}{2}$	2	?	A. Ohlsson.
$2\frac{7}{8}$	$1\frac{1}{2}$	$1\frac{1}{2}$	?	G. Richards.
-$2\frac{3}{4}$	$1\frac{1}{4}$	$1\frac{1}{4}$	?	Julius Jeppe.

Head of Steinbuck.

STEINBUCK (Rhaphiceros campestris).

Ishah of the Swahilis.   *Impulupudi* of the Basutos.
Ingaina of the Swazis.   *Phuduhudu* of the Bechuanas.
                    Umgwena of the Matabele.

As mentioned before, this species is at once distinguished from the grysbuck by the absence of the lateral hoofs and the uniform colour of the fur. The general tint of the latter is bright sandy rufous, becoming richer on the head, and frequently with the tip of the muzzle and a horseshoe-mark on the crown brown. Height at withers about $19\frac{1}{2}$ inches.

Distribution.—Africa south of the Zambesi on the east, and the Cunene on the west ; northwards of the Tana to Nyasaland represented by Neumann's steinbok (*R. campestris neumanni*), distinguished by the absence of dark markings on the head. Probably owing to its small size, the steinbuck has managed to escape the fate that has befallen so many of the South African antelopes. Wherever the traveller journeys on the veldt, he is almost certain to meet this species, which may be regarded as the most familiar game animal of the plains. Like many of its kindred, it is independent of water, and can thus exist in the heart of the Kalahari, where water may not occur for a distance of fully fifty miles. The excellence of its flesh renders it a welcome addition to the bag of the hungry hunter; and in addition to affording sport with the shot-gun, or, more rarely, the rifle, steinbuck may either be hunted with foxhounds or coursed with greyhounds.

Length in front.	Circumference.	Tip to Tip.	Locality.	Owner.
–$6\frac{7}{8}$	...	...	Graffreinett	F. H. Barber.
–$5\frac{7}{8}$	...	...	Kikumbulin	W. Russell Bowker.
–$5\frac{7}{8}$	$1\frac{7}{8}$	3	?	Mr. Justice Hopley.
–$5\frac{3}{4}$	$1\frac{3}{4}$	$1\frac{7}{8}$	?	J. Whitaker.
–$5\frac{5}{8}$	2	$1\frac{1}{4}$	?	Julius Jeppe.
[1] $5\frac{1}{2}$	..	$1\frac{9}{16}$	Kimberley	F. C. Selous.
–$5\frac{1}{2}$	...	...	?	O. R. Dunell.
$5\frac{3}{8}$	?	$1\frac{3}{4}$	E. Africa	E. Gedge.
–$5\frac{1}{4}$	...	...	?	Cape Town Museum.
–$5\frac{1}{4}$	$1\frac{3}{8}$	$2\frac{7}{8}$	Cape Colony	F. R. N. Findlay.
$5\frac{1}{8}$	$1\frac{3}{4}$	2	?	Julius Jeppe.
5	...	$2\frac{1}{2}$	E. Africa	Sir John Willoughby, Bart.
5	$1\frac{7}{8}$	$2\frac{7}{8}$	S.E. Africa	Dr. W. P. Y. Bainbrigge.
–$4\frac{3}{4}$	$1\frac{3}{4}$	$1\frac{5}{8}$	Do.	James J. Harrison.
$4\frac{5}{8}$	$1\frac{1}{2}$	$2\frac{3}{4}$	Portuguese E. Africa	F. Vaughan Kirby.
$4\frac{5}{8}$	$1\frac{1}{4}$	$2\frac{1}{2}$	S. Africa	G. Richards.
$4\frac{1}{2}$	$1\frac{3}{4}$	$2\frac{1}{4}$	Mashonaland	Jff. Darling, British Museum.
$4\frac{1}{2}$	$1\frac{1}{2}$	$2\frac{1}{8}$	?	Major H. J. Goold-Adams, C.B., C.M.G.
$4\frac{1}{2}$	$1\frac{3}{4}$	$1\frac{5}{8}$	S. Africa	H. and C. Beddington.
$4\frac{1}{2}$	$1\frac{5}{8}$	$2\frac{5}{8}$	Do.	F. C. Selous.
–$4\frac{1}{2}$	...	...	Matabeleland	T. E. Buckley.
–$4\frac{1}{2}$	$1\frac{7}{8}$	$3\frac{1}{2}$	Barberton	Dr. Percy Rendall.
$4\frac{3}{8}$	$1\frac{5}{8}$	$2\frac{3}{8}$	Tana Valley	Sir Robert Harvey, Bart.
–$4\frac{3}{8}$	...	...	Matabeleland	Major A. St. H. Gibbons.
$4\frac{1}{8}$	$1\frac{1}{2}$	2	Do.	Rev. Dr. R. J. Nevin.
$4\frac{1}{4}$	$1\frac{1}{2}$	$2\frac{3}{4}$	E. Africa	Lord Delamere.
$4\frac{1}{4}$	$1\frac{1}{2}$	2	Matabeleland	Major James Grant.
$4\frac{1}{8}$	$1\frac{7}{8}$	$2\frac{1}{4}$	Sudan	Col. Ralph Vivian.
$4\frac{1}{8}$	$1\frac{5}{8}$	$2\frac{3}{8}$	Kaokoland	Capt. F. Cookson.
–$4\frac{1}{8}$	...	...	?	C. T. Jones.
$4\frac{3}{8}$	$1\frac{5}{8}$	$1\frac{3}{4}$	Zululand	Lieut.-Col. Hon. W. Coke.
4	$1\frac{5}{8}$	$2\frac{3}{4}$	Matabeleland	Duke of Roxburghe.
–$3\frac{7}{8}$	2	2	Komati Valley, S.A.	Count E. Hoyos.

[1] Killed with hounds.

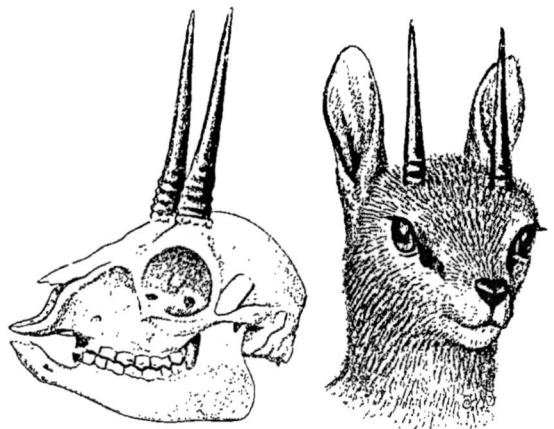

Skull and Head of Male Klipspringer, from specimens shot in Somaliland by Major H. G. C. Swayne.

KLIPSPRINGER (Oreotragus saltator).

Alakud of the Somalis.

Chibila in the Chilala and Chibisa countries.

Ingululu of the Makalakas.

Ikumi of the Basutos.

Klipbok of the Boers.

Ligoka of the Zulus and Swazis.

Njerere in the Batoka country.

Sass of the Abyssinians.

Not only from the other members of the oribi group, but from antelopes of all kinds, the agile little klipspringer, or "rock-jumper," is distinguished by the peculiar conformation of its hoofs and the structure of its hair. The former are large, cylindrical, blunt, and so situated in regard to the rest of the limb, that the animal walks on what corresponds to their tips in other antelopes, the whole hoof thus rising vertically from the ground. As regards the hair, this may best be compared with that of the musk-deer, having the same brittle, pithy structure. Lateral hoofs are retained ; the tail is reduced to a mere rudimentary stump ; and the horns of the bucks rise nearly vertically from the head, with a slight forward curvature, and are ringed for their basal third. The speckly olive-gray hue of the fur is too well known to need description. Height at shoulder from about 20 to 22 inches.

Distribution.—Mountainous and rocky districts in South and East Africa, from the Cape northwards to Abyssinia. Klipspringer-shooting is the best mountain sport to be obtained in Africa ; and a pair of these active little animals bounding, as if made of indiarubber, from rock to rock is a sight never to be forgotten. To bag these exceedingly active and shy little antelopes, the sportsman, especially in the steep mountain ranges of Cape Colony, must, however, be prepared for a long and difficult stalk under a blazing sun. Except when they require its hair for stuffing saddles, the Boers leave the klipspringer alone ; which is doubtless one reason that it is still comparatively abundant. Its venison is of excellent quality.

Length on front.	Circumference.	Tip to Tip.	Locality.	Owner.
$5\frac{3}{8}$	$2\frac{1}{8}$	$2\frac{7}{8}$	Mashonaland	The late H. H. Eyre.
$5\frac{1}{8}$	$2\frac{1}{8}$	$2\frac{5}{8}$	Transvaal . . .	F. Vaughan Kirby.
$4\frac{1}{2}$	$2\frac{3}{16}$	$2\frac{11}{16}$	Wittberg, Cape Colony	H. A. Bryden.
$4\frac{1}{2}$	2	$3\frac{1}{4}$	East Africa	E. Gedge.
$-4\frac{1}{2}$	...	...	Barberton .	Dr. Percy Rendall.
$4\frac{3}{8}$	$1\frac{3}{4}$	$2\frac{1}{4}$	Matabeleland	Hon. R. A. Ward.
$4\frac{3}{8}$	2	$3\frac{1}{4}$	S.E. Africa	F. C. Selous.
$4\frac{1}{4}$	2	$3\frac{5}{8}$	Near Lake Rudolph .	H. S. H. Cavendish.
$-4\frac{1}{4}$	$2\frac{1}{2}$	3	Somaliland .	C. V. A. Peel.
$-4\frac{1}{4}$	$3\frac{1}{8}$	$2\frac{1}{2}$	South Africa	A. Ohlsson.
$-4\frac{1}{4}$	$1\frac{5}{8}$	$2\frac{7}{8}$	Do.	Mr. Justice Hopley.
$-4\frac{1}{8}$	2	$2\frac{1}{2}$	Somaliland	Sir Edmund G. Loder, Bart.
$4\frac{1}{8}$	$2\frac{1}{2}$	$1\frac{3}{4}$	North Nyasaland	James Yule.
4	$1\frac{1}{2}$	2	East Africa	Lord Delamere.
4	$1\frac{7}{8}$	$2\frac{1}{8}$	?	Mr. Justice Hopley.
4	$2\frac{1}{8}$	$1\frac{1}{4}$	Matabeleland	W. W. Ashley.
4	$2\frac{1}{2}$	$1\frac{7}{8}$	South Africa	H. and C. Beddington.
$3\frac{7}{8}$	$2\frac{1}{8}$	2	Do.	A. Beit.
$3\frac{3}{4}$	2	$2\frac{1}{4}$	East Africa	J. Gardiner Muir.
$3\frac{3}{4}$	$1\frac{3}{4}$	$2\frac{3}{8}$	Somaliland	Prince Boris Czetwertynski.
$3\frac{3}{4}$	2	2	Do.	T. W. H. Clarke.
$3\frac{3}{4}$	...	$1\frac{7}{8}$	Abyssinia .	British Museum.
$-3\frac{3}{4}$	$2\frac{3}{8}$	$3\frac{1}{8}$	South Africa	Dr. W. P. Y. Bainbrigge.
$-3\frac{3}{4}$	2	2	Do.	Julius Jeppe.

KLIPSPRINGER (Oreotragus saltator)—*continued.*

Length on front.	Circumference.	Tip to Tip.	Locality.	Owner.
$-3\frac{3}{4}$	...	...	Matabeleland . .	J. Brander Dunbar.
$3\frac{1}{2}$	$2\frac{1}{2}$	$1\frac{7}{8}$	Somaliland .	The late W. Babington.
$3\frac{1}{2}$	$1\frac{3}{4}$	$2\frac{1}{8}$	Matabeleland .	Hon. John Ward.
$3\frac{1}{2}$	2	$2\frac{3}{4}$	Do. . .	R. A. Cooper.
$-♀3\frac{1}{2}$	...	...	East Africa .	F. J. Jackson, C.B.
$3\frac{3}{8}$	$1\frac{7}{8}$	2	Abyssinia . . .	Viscount Edmond de Poncins.
$3\frac{1}{4}$	$1\frac{7}{8}$	2	South Africa .	G. Richards.
$3\frac{1}{4}$	...	...	Somaliland	Major H. G. C. Swayne.
$-3\frac{1}{4}$	$1\frac{3}{4}$	4	?	Dublin Museum.
$3\frac{1}{16}$	$1\frac{7}{8}$	2	Abyssinia . .	Viscount Edmond de Poncins.
3	$1\frac{7}{8}$	$2\frac{3}{4}$	Somaliland .	G. D. E. Chapman.
3	$1\frac{5}{8}$	$1\frac{3}{4}$	Do. . .	W. W. Ashley.
3	...	...	?	Cape Town Museum.

Horns of Waterbuck, F. H. Barber's specimen.

COMMON WATERBUCK (Cobus ellipsiprymnus).

Kooli in the Chilala and Chibisa countries.

Kring-gaat of the Dutch.

Li Tumogha of the Matabele.

M'dongoma or *Matutwi* in the Barotse country.

Swahili name *Koru.*

Tumoga of the Bechuanas.

The waterbucks and their near allies the kobs, together with the reedbucks and vaal rhebok, constitute a well-defined group of large or medium African antelopes presenting the following characteristics. They have the muzzle naked, no face-glands, a moderately long tail, well-developed lateral hoofs, and the horns confined to the bucks. In shape and size the horns are variable, being either long or medium, but never spirally twisted, and always with smooth tips, below which they are ridged ; usually they are at first inclined somewhat backwards, after which they are curved upwards and more or less forwards, although they may have a sinuous curvature, and in the vaal rhebok are straight. The upper molar teeth are tall and narrow. In the waterbucks and kobs, which include the largest representatives of the group, there are no naked patches on the head below the ears, the tail is comparatively long, with a slight terminal tuft, and the lateral hoofs are large. A characteristic feature of the skull is the presence of a deep hollow in the forehead. From its allies the true or common waterbuck is recognisable at a glance by the elliptical white ring on the buttocks, which extends downwards to the thighs. Height at shoulder about 43 inches to 53.

Distribution.—Africa north of the Limpopo along the eastern coast region as far as the Shebeyli River in Somaliland; thus including Nyasaland and British and German East Africa. Never, apparently, very abundant, this handsome antelope, whose head and horns form one of the chief prizes of the South African hunter, has had its range much curtailed of late years. Its present strongholds are the unhealthy districts between the Sabi and Zambesi, the affluents of the latter river, and the Chobi, Okavango, and other rivers above Lake Ngami. Although the flesh is uneatable by Europeans, the excellence of the hide for shoe-leather causes the kring-gaat, as it is called by the Boers, to be persistently hunted.

Length on front.	Circumference.	Tip to Tip.	Locality.	Owner.
–36½	...	...	Delagoa Bay	F. H. Barber. (See illustration.)
–36¼	...	...	South Africa	O. R. Dunell.
–35¼	9	14	?	Mr. Justice Hopley.
–34½	...	...	Limpopo Valley	H. T. and A. H. Glynn.
–33½	10⅛	21⅜	S.E. Africa	F. Vaughan Kirby.
33½	9¼	21½	Do.	Hon. Walter Rothschild.
33	9⅜	11½	Mashonaland	F. C. Selous, British Museum.
33	8¾	24	Do.	J. G. Millais.
–33	8¾	17¼	Do.	A. Ohlsson.
–33	...	...	Lake Ngami	Cape Town Museum.
32¾	9¾	21⅜	South Africa	Sir Victor Brooke's Collection.
31¾	9¼	24	Zululand	Capt. L. O. Williams.
–31¾	8¼	21⅞	North of Pungwe	Count E. Hoyos.
–31½	9	17	?	Julius Jeppe.
31⅜	8½	21⅞	?	British Museum.
31¼	10⅛	13⅝	Pungwe	Earl of Dunmore.

COMMON WATERBUCK (Cobus ellipsiprymnus)—*continued.*

Length on front.	Circumference.	Tip to Tip.	Locality.	Owner.
31¼	9⅝	19¼	?	Sir Edmund G. Loder, Bart.
–31¼	.	...	Transvaal . .	C. T. Jones.
31	...	...	Mashonaland . . .	F. C. Selous.
–31	9¾	17	E. C. Africa . .	James J. Harrison.
30¾	8	23¼	Pungwe	Capt. Lord Douglas Compton.
30½	8¾	25	Do. . . .	R. Hughes.
–30½	9½	16½	E. C. Africa . .	James J. Harrison.
–30½	9	26	Do. . .	Julius Jeppe.
30⅜	9⅛	23½	Zululand . . .	A. J. Brandon.
–30⅛	...	...	Macloutsie . .	Capt. G. F. T. Leather.
30⅛	8½	13⅞	Mashonaland . . .	F. C. Selous.
–30	9½	11¼	Komati River, S. Africa .	Count E. Hoyos.
29⅞	9⅛	12⅞	Zululand . . .	Hon. Charles Ellis.
29¾	9½	21⅞	Mashonaland . . .	F. C. Selous.
–29¾	...	...	Somaliland . . .	Dr. Donaldson Smith.
–29 9/16	9 7/16	19 11/16	Danakil . .	Prince A. de Lucinge.
29⅜	9⅜	...	Zululand . .	A. H. Neumann.
29	9¼	5½ malformed	Do. . .	A. W. Davis.
29	10¾	16	Sabi River . .	Sir Thomas Fowler, Bart.
29	9½	26	East Africa . . .	E. Gedge.
29	9½	16½	Do. .	Major W. H. Williams.
–29	8½	19	Do. . .	T. E. Buckley.
29	9	16	South Africa . . .	Lieut.-Col. Hon. W. Coke.
29	9	14⅝	Pungwe . .	Capt. F. H. Lehmann.
29	9	12¾	Do. . .	R. A. Cooper.
29	8⅝	19¾	Do. .	Frank Harris.
–29	8	22¼	Do. . .	C. C. Gouldsmith.
28¾	9⅛	21⅜	?	H.R.H. the Duke of Saxe-Coburg and Gotha.
28¾	8	27	Shiré Valley . . .	H. H. Williams.
28¾	8	15¼	South Africa . . .	G. H. M. Banks.

COMMON WATERBUCK (Cobus ellipsiprymnus)—*continued.*

Length on front.	Circumference.	Tip to Tip.	Locality.	Owner.
28½	8¾	15¼	Pungwe . . .	Viscount Ennismore.
−28½	8¼	...	Shiré Valley . .	Staff-Surgeon J. Dowson, R.N.
−28	10¾	8	S.E. Africa .	T. E. Buckley.
−28	...	18	East Africa .	Sir John Willoughby, Bart.
28	9	18	Matabeleland . .	Major James Grant.
28	8½	13½	Pungwe .	Durban Museum.
28½	8	22½	Do. .	H. R. Holden.
27¾	9¼	14¾	East Africa . .	F. J. Jackson, C.B.
−27¾	8¾	10½	Barberton . .	Dr. Percy Rendall.
27⅝	8	9⅞	Zululand	Major-Gen. Sir Arthur Ellis, K.C.V.O.
27½	8¾	22	South Africa	D. Norman Ritchie.
27½	8½	18	Pungwe . .	G. L. Bonham.
27¼	8¾	16¾	Barotseland .	H. Timmins.
27¼	9¼	13½	East Africa	J. Gardiner Muir.
27	9½	13	Zululand . . .	A. Cameron.
27	8	15¾	Pungwe . . .	Lord Edward Manners.
27	8⅜	17½	Danakil . . .	Viscount Edmond de Poncins.
27	8	17¾	Pungwe . . .	Ford G. Barclay.
27	7¼	34½	Zambesia . . .	Comdr. A. T. Hunt.
27	9	4¾	Matabeleland . .	W. Crosley.
26¾	9	18½	Pungwe . .	Capt. G. F. Henry.
26¾	8¼	14	Do.	Col. G. A. Percy.
26¾	6½	18¼	E. C. Africa .	Lord Delamere.
26½	8	11¼	Do. . .	Lord Edward Manners.
−26½	8½	15½	Masailand . .	Count Scheibler.
−26	8	17½	South Africa . . .	Dublin Museum.
−26	8¼	18	Do. .	James J. Harrison.
−26	7½	20¼	Do. . .	Dr. W. P. Y. Bainbrigge.
25⅞	8⅜	17½	Sudan	Col. Ralph Vivian.
25⅝	8¼	11	East Africa	The late Capt. Speke, British Museum.

COMMON WATERBUCK (Cobus ellipsiprymnus)—*continued.*

Length on front.	Circumference.	Tip to Tip.	Locality.	Owner.
25½	8½	19½	British Central Africa .	J. E. Gough.
25⅜	7¾	18½	?	Lord Delamere.
25¼	8¾	13⅞	East Africa . . .	Sir Robert Harvey, Bart.
25⅛	8	13¾	Do. . . .	H. C. V. Hunter.
24¼	7½	9¾	Somaliland . . .	W. D. James.
23.6	8.13	10.1	British East Africa .	Prince Henry of Liechtenstein.
22¾	6⅝	15¼	Somaliland . . .	Major H. G. C. Swayne.
22¼	7½	12⅞	Do.	A. H. Straker.
22	7¼	9¼	Do.	Prince Demeter Ghika.
21¾	7¼	9⅞	Do.	Count E. Hoyos.

Head of Common Waterbuck, from a specimen shot in Somaliland.

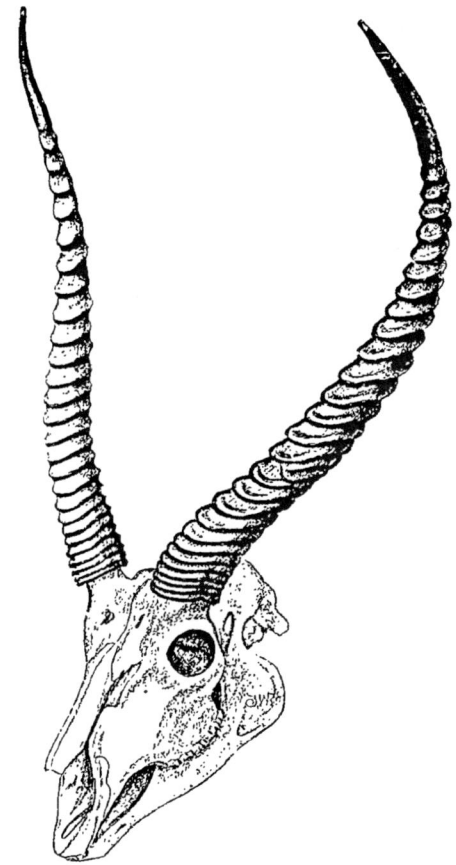

Skull of Male Sing-sing Waterbuck, from a specimen in the British Museum.

SING-SING WATERBUCK (Cobus defassa).

Distinguished from the common water-buck (*C. ellipsiprymnus*) by the presence of a large white patch on the lower part of the buttocks, instead of a white elliptical ring extending higher up.   Four more or less distinct local races of this species may be recognised.   First, the West African sing-sing (*C. defassa unctuosus*), of Senegal and Gambia, characterised by its rufous colour and the small amount of white in the region of the eye.   Second, Crawshay's sing-sing (*C. defassa crawshayi*), from British Central Africa, with a dusky coloration. Third, Penrice's sing-sing (*C. defassa penricei*), from the interior of Benguela, Angola, in which the colour is so dark as to be almost black.

And, fourth, the defassa sing-sing (*C. defassa typicus*), extending from Western Abyssinia through Sennar, Kordofan, and the valley of the White Nile to Uganda and British and German East Africa, in which the ears are longer and more pointed, and there is more white in the region of the eye than in the other races; the general colour being rufous. The four races are frequently regarded as distinct species, but they are so evidently local modifications of a single somewhat variable form that it appears far preferable to include them all under a single specific heading.

Length on front.	Circumference.	Tip to Tip.	Locality.	Owner.
[1] -35½	...	...	Near Toru	Major C. G. H. Sitwell.
-29⅜	8⅝	29⅜	Sudan . .	Count T. Palffy.
-29	9½	17½	?	Dublin Museum.
-29	8⅛	28 3/10	Upper Basaland, Abyssinia	J. Menges.
-29	8	6½	?	Julius Jeppe.
-27⅞	8⅛	9⅞	Sudan . . .	Count T. Palffy.
27⅜	8⅛	13½	?	British Museum.
27¼	7½	18¼	Atbara Valley, Abyssinia .	Do.
-27¼	9	12	East Africa . .	Lord Delamere.
27¼	7½	18¼	Atbara Valley, Abyssinia	British Museum.
27	8	15¼	Kavalli, Lake Albert . .	Col. Trevor Ternan.
26⅞	7¾	15⅛	Uganda .	The late Captain Speke, British Museum.
26¾	8⅝	15¼	East Africa	E. Gedge.
-26	7⅞	13¾	Borders of Lake Tchad	Paris Museum.
25¾	9	15¾	Bahr-el-Salam, Sudan	Lieut.-Col. Hon. W. Coke.
25¼	8¼	16¼	Kikuyu .	E. Russell.
25⅛	8⅝	13⅜	British East Africa	Hon. Walter Rothschild.
24⅛	8¾	16¼	Molo River .	G. E. Smith.
23½	8	8¾	?	Lord Delamere.

[1] Mr. F. R. Hicks favours me with this measurement.

DEFASSA SING-SING (Cobus defassa unctuosus).

See page 178.

Height at shoulder, 47 to 48 ins.—Major A. J. Arnold, D.S.O.

Length front.	Circum- ference.	Tip to Tip.	Locality.	Owner.
24¾	8½	...	Gambia . . .	Julius Jeppe.
24½	9	12	Nigeria	Dr. Percy Rendall.
24	7¼	15¾	Do.	P. A. Clive.
23¾	7¼	14½	Do.	F. Swanzy.
23¾	7½	13¼	Do.	Major A. J. Arnold, D.S.O.
23	7	16	Do. .	Do.
23	7	13¾	Boussa, Nigeria	A. W. M. Brodie.
22⅞	8½	10¾	Nigeria . .	Sir Edmund G. Loder, Bart.
22	7	17¼	Do.	Major G. S. C. Jenkinson.

PENRICE'S SING-SING (Cobus defassa penricei).

See page 178.

Length front.	Circum- ference.	Tip to Tip.	Locality.	Owner.
29	8¾	18½	Benguela	G. W. Penrice.
28¼	8¼	11½	Do. . .	A. Ohlsson.
28	8	22½	Do. .	G. W. Penrice.
24½	8	9⅛	Do. . .	Hon. Walter Rothschild.
20¼	6⅞	12¼	Do.	Julius Jeppe.

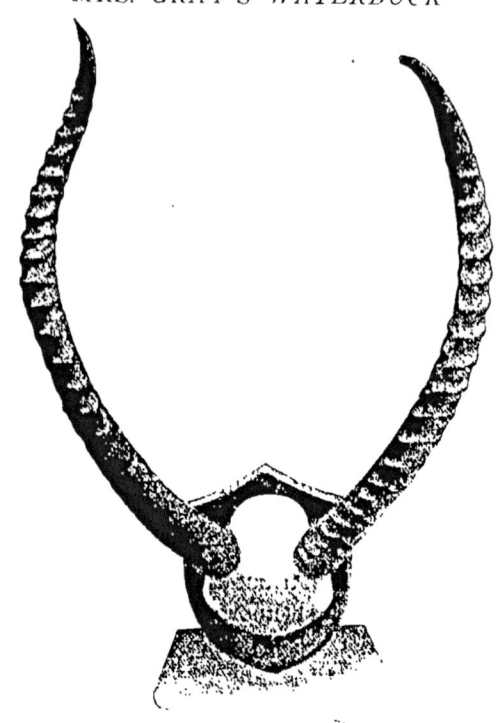

Horns of Mrs. Gray's Waterbuck, from Lieut.-Col. Hon. W. Coke's specimen.

MRS. GRAY'S WATERBUCK (Cobus maria).

This species is the last of the typical group of *Cobus*, in all the members of which the size is large, the fur grizzled, and the neck maned. From the preceding species Mrs. Gray's waterbuck differs by the presence of an hour-glass-shaped white area on the back of the neck, and the form of the horns, which are highly sinuous and inclined backwards ; the general colour of the fur being dark reddish brown. Height at shoulder apparently from 35 to 40 inches.

Distribution.—The swamps bordering the White Nile and its tributaries.

Very rare in collections, being represented by complete specimens only in the museums of Vienna and Berlin. It was discovered by Heuglin, but has been confounded with the very different white-eared kob.

Length on front.	Circumference.	Tip to Tip.	Locality.	Owner.
-30¼	6½	17	?	Berlin Museum.
29¾	6¼	12	?	Hon. Walter Rothschild.
26¾	6¾	13⅜	Arwan, Bahr-el-Ghazal	The late Consul J. Petherick, Brit. Mus.
26½	6½	12	White Nile.	Lieut.-Col. Hon. W. Coke.

WHITE-EARED KOB (Cobus leucotis).

The smaller antelopes included in the genus *Cobus* may be popularly termed kobs, and differ from the water-bucks not only by their inferior size, but by the uniformly rufous hue of the upper parts, and the absence of a mane on the neck. From its allies the present species is sufficiently distinguished by the white outer surface of the ears and upper part of the head, including the region of the eyes. Height at shoulder about 34 or 35 inches.

Distribution.—The region of the Upper Nile, including the Sobat, Bahr-el-Ghazal, and their tributaries, and extending to the Niam-Niam country. The first known example was sent to Berlin by the German artist and traveller Werne, who obtained it in Sennar.

Length on front.	Circumference.	Tip to Tip.	Locality.	Owner.
–21⅝	7⅞	13 13/16	White Nile	Paris Museum.
–20	7	7½	Do.	Berlin Museum.
19⅞	6⅜	7¼	Bahr-el-Ghazal	British Museum.
19⅛	5⅞	9½	Do.	The late Consul J. Petherick, British Museum.
17¼	6	7¼	?	Sir Victor Brooke's Collection.

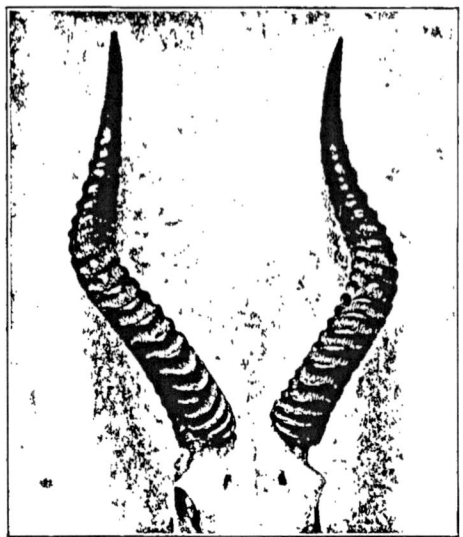

Frontlet and Horns of Buffon's Kob.

BUFFON'S KOB (Cobus cob).

In common with the Uganda kob and the puku (*C. vardoni*), this species has the back of the ears rufous like the body; and it agrees with the latter of these in having the horns less than twice the length of the head, the hair short, and the front of the fore-legs black; its peculiar distinctive features being the presence of a white line over each eye and its comparatively small size, the approximate height at the shoulder being from 32 to 33 inches.

Although this species was known to the French naturalist Buffon, it is only of late years that its affinities have been fully worked out. The puku differs from both this species and the under-mentioned sunu by its much longer hair and the absence of the black down the front of the legs.

Distribution.—West Africa, from the Gambia to Nigeria.

Length on front.	Circumference.	Tip to Tip.	Locality.	Owner.
19¾	6⅞	7¼	Nigeria . . .	Captain A. H. Festing.
18¾	5½	7½	Do. . .	Captain J. S. Brogden.
‑17¼	...	...	Do. . . .	Major A. F. Mockler-Ferryman.
16¾	6	7	Do. . . .	Major A. J. Arnold, D.S.O.

BUFFON'S KOB (Cobus cob)—*continued.*

Length on front.	Circumference.	Tip to Tip.	Locality.	Owner.
16¾	5½	8	Ibi District . .	Carl Jeppe.
16½	6	7⅜	Do. . .	Mr. Justice Hopley.
16	5¾	7¾	?	Sir Edmund G. Loder, Bart.
15¼	5⅞	7	Ibi District . .	Julius Jeppe.
15¼	6¼	8	Gando, Western Sudan	J. W. Carroll.
13½	6	7¼	Gaboon . . .	Hon. Walter Rothschild.
9½	5	3	Gambia . . .	A former Earl of Derby, British Museum.
8	4⅝	4⅞	Do. . . .	Do.

Head of Lichi.

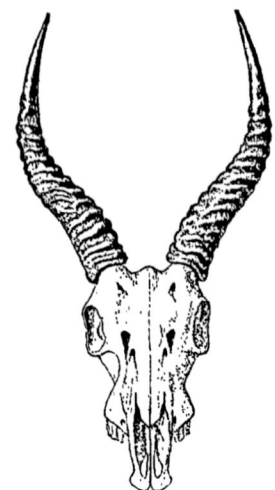

Skull of Uganda Kob, from a specimen shot by F. J. Jackson.

UGANDA KOB (Cobus thomasi).

The East African representative of Buffon's kob, from which it is distinguished mainly by its superior size, and the presence of a complete white ring round each eye, instead of having only a white line above the same. General colour rich fulvous, with the muzzle, lips, chin, under parts, and inner surfaces of upper portion of fore-legs and thighs white ; front of fore-legs with a black line, and hind-legs with a similar line, which does not, however, ascend within some distance of the hocks. Height at shoulder about $35\frac{1}{2}$ inches.

Distribution.—East Africa, from Kavirondo to Uganda.

Native name, *Sunu* or *N'Sunu*.

Length on front.	Circumference.	Tip to Tip.	Locality.	Owner.
$20\frac{1}{8}$	7	$9\frac{3}{4}$	North end of Lake Albert	Col. Trevor Ternan.
$19\frac{3}{4}$	7	$9\frac{5}{8}$	Victoria Nyanza .	E. Gedge.
$18\frac{1}{2}$	$6\frac{5}{8}$	$8\frac{5}{8}$	Lake Albert .	Col. F. D. Lugard, C.B., D.S.O.
$18\frac{1}{4}$	...	...	Lake Victoria .	Major W. H. Williams.
18	$7\frac{1}{4}$	$11\frac{1}{2}$	Uganda .	E. Gedge.
$17\frac{1}{2}$	$6\frac{3}{4}$	$11\frac{1}{2}$	Do. . .	M. F. Gage.
$17\frac{3}{4}$	$6\frac{1}{4}$	$7\frac{3}{4}$	Kavirondo .	F. J. Jackson, C.B.
$17\frac{1}{4}$	$7\frac{1}{2}$	$5\frac{1}{4}$	Do. .	Rowland Ward.
$17\frac{1}{8}$	7	5	Do. .	F. J. Jackson, C.B., British Museum.
−17	$5\frac{15}{16}$	$9\frac{1}{4}$	East Africa .	Paris Museum.
$16\frac{3}{4}$	$6\frac{1}{4}$	$6\frac{1}{4}$	Uganda .	Sir Edmund G. Loder, Bart.
16	$6\frac{3}{4}$	10	East Africa .	F. H. Barber.
$15\frac{3}{4}$	$5\frac{7}{8}$	$10\frac{1}{2}$	Do. .	Julius Jeppe.
$14\frac{3}{4}$	6	$9\frac{3}{4}$	Victoria Nyanza	C. F. S. Vandeleur, D.S.O.

F. H. Barber's Lichi Horns.

LICHI or LECHWE (Cobus lichi).

Lechwi in the Barotse and Lake Ngami countries.

Njha in the Chilala and Chibisa countries.

Leché, Lee-gwee of the Makololo.

Inya of the Masubias.

Oonya of the Makubas.

In this handsome antelope the horns are longer than in its allies, considerably exceeding twice the length of the head, while the front of the fore-legs is black, and the hair long.   Height at shoulder, 40 or 41 inches.

Like the puku, this kob was discovered by Livingstone and his companions Oswell and Murray during their journey to Lake Ngami in 1849.   In point of size it approximates to the true water-bucks, from which, however, in addition to the features already mentioned, it may always be distinguished by its lighter and more graceful build.   The general colour is fulvous, of a lighter tint than in the Uganda kob.

The lichi affords excellent and often exciting sport for the gunner. Seldom found very far from water, this antelope is most abundant in the lagoons and swamps created by the annual rising of the Upper

Zambesi, the Botletli, Chobe, Tamulakan, and other rivers of the interior, in localities where the surrounding flats are inundated for some part of the year. The lichi seldom ventures into the deep rivers from fear of the crocodiles, but among the reed beds, the shallow lagoons, and flooded flats it is a familiar figure. It is often to be found, in the less accessible regions, in vast herds. An excellent swimmer, it can progress by a succession of splashing bounds at great speed through the lagoons and shallows. It is extremely tenacious of life, and requires very straight powder. The thick rufous-yellow coat of the lichi is extremely handsome, and the skin is greatly prized by the natives.

Distribution.—Zambesia, reaching northwards to Lake Mweru, and to Lake Ngami towards the south-west.

Length on front.	Circumference.	Tip to Tip.	Locality.	Owner.
-33½	7	26¾	Lake Bangweolo	Poulett-Weatherley.
-28½	...	...	Zambesia . .	F. H. Barber. (See illustration.)
-28	...	...	?	T. Poole.
27¾	8	14	Okavango Valley .	Major H. J. Goold-Adams, C.B., C.M.G.
27½	10¾	19⅛	Chobe Valley . .	F. C. Selous, British Museum.
27¼	8	14¾	Do. .	F. C. Selous.
-27	7¼	14	Okavango Valley	Sir Edmund G. Loder, Bart.
-26½	9	20¼	?	Julius Jeppe.
26¼	8⅜	21	South Africa .	A. Beit.
-26¼	6⅝	16	?	Mr. Justice Hopley.
26⅛	8	15 (about)	Linyanti, Chobe Valley	F. C. Selous.
25¾	7¼	12¾	?	G. Richards.
-25¾	7½	18	Zambesia . .	T. E. Buckley.
-25⅝	7½	13⅜	Do. . .	Dr. Holub, Paris Museum.
-25½	7¼	16½	?	Julius Jeppe.
-25⅜	7¼	14½	Lake Ngami	Dr. Percy Rendall.
25¼	7¾	11¼	?	Mr. Justice Hopley.
24¾	7	19¼	?	R. A. Cooper.
24½	7½	11½	South Africa . .	Hon. Walter Rothschild.
24⅜	7⅝	13⅝	Zambesia .	The late J. S. Jameson.
-24¼	...	...	Do. . .	C. T. Jones.
24	7¼	12¼	?	A. Ohlsson.
23½	7½	14½	Chobe Valley	F. C. Selous.
-23	...	...	Do.	O. R. Dunell.
23	9	9	Do.	E. Gedge.
22⅜	6⅜	12⅜	Barotseland	R. T. Coryndon.

Head of Puku, from a specimen in the British Museum.

PUKU (Cobus vardoni).

Impookoo of the Masubias.　　　　*Pookoo* in the Lake Ngami country.
Muntinya in the Barotse country.　*Seūla* in the Chilala and Chibisa
　　　　　　　　　　　　　　　countries.

From the other small kobs with the back of the ears rufous, the puku is distinguishable at once by the uniformly foxy colour of the fore-legs, as well as by the greater length of the hair, especially in the region of the back and loins, where it has a tendency to curl. General colour reddish-yellow. Height at shoulder about 39 or 40 inches.

Distribution.—Mainly confined to a narrow belt of country extending along the southern bank of the Chobe for about sixty miles from its junction with the Zambesi. The herds are small, seldom including more than ten or a dozen individuals.

PUKU (Cobus vardoni)—*continued.*

Length on front curve.	Circumference.	Tip to Tip.	Locality.	Owner.
20¼	8½	12¼	Luswesi Valley . .	F. Smitheman.
19⅛	6¾	8½	South Africa	J. Carr Saunders.
–18⅝	...	...	Njoko Valley .	Major A. St. H. Gibbons.
18⅜	6⅜	9¼	Barotseland .	R. T. Coryndon.
–18	6½	9	Luwulé Valley, Congo Free State	Poulett-Weatherley.
18	6¼	8¾	Luapulu Valley .	F. Smitheman.
17½	6½	7	Bangweolo . .	Do.
17½	6¾	5½	Barotseland .	R. T. Coryndon.
–17½	7	6⅝	Choma Valley, B.C.A.	R. H. Ferrers Stranack.
17⅜	6¼	18 malformed	Kabampo Valley .	Major H. J. Goold-Adams, C.B., C.M.G.
16¾	6½	8¾	Do. .	Do.
–16¾	6¼	7½	Luwulé, B.C.A. . .	Poulett-Weatherley.
–16¼	7	6½	Choma Valley, B.C.A.	Julius Jeppe.
16¼	6⅝	7½	South Africa . .	British Museum.
16	6½	6¾	South bank of Chobe Valley	F. C. Selous.
16⅜	6¾	5⅞	Choma Valley, B.C.A.	Mr. Justice Hopley.
16	5½	4¾	West Nyasaland . .	C. C. Bowring.
–16	6½	8	?	A. Ohlsson.
[1]–15¾	...	...	Njoko Valley . .	R. T. Coryndon.
15⅜	6⅛	5⅛	British Central Africa	Rowland Ward.
15⅜	6½	6⅝	Chobe Valley . .	F. C. Selous.
15⅛	6	10	South Africa . .	J. Carr Saunders.
[2]–15⅛	...	...	Njoko Valley	R. T. Coryndon.
–15	6¼	6¼	Zambesia . . .	T. E. Buckley.
[3]–15	...	...	Njoko Valley . .	R. T. Coryndon.
14⅝	6¼	7½	Lofu Valley, B.C.A. .	John Yule.
14½	6¼	3½	British Central Africa	Julius Jeppe.
14⅛	6⅝	5⅛	Chobe Valley . .	F. C. Selous, British Museum.

[1] Weight as he fell, 177 lbs. [2] Weight as he fell, 185 lbs. [3] Weight as he fell, 196 lbs.

Head of Vaal Rhebok.

GRAY or VAAL RHEBOK (Pelea capreolus).

Iliza of the Swazis.　　　　　　　*Pshiatla* of the Basutos.
Peeli of the Bechuanas.

The short, upright, straight, and slender horns, together with the somewhat woolly nature of the hair, serve to differentiate the vaal rhebok from the antelopes of the kindred genera. The tail, like that of the reedbucks, is short and bushy ; the ears are tall and narrow ; the build is slight and graceful ; and the general colour is uniformly pale gray, tending somewhat to fawn on the head and limbs. Height at shoulder about 29 or 30 inches. The chief essential distinctions between this antelope and the reedbucks are the form of the horns and the absence of the bare patches below the eyes.

Distribution.—The open hilly districts of Africa south of the Zambesi.

In the mountain ranges of the eastern and northern districts of Cape Colony, and thence onwards to the Zambesi, the vaal rhebok affords good and exciting sport. And although its somewhat stiff and stilty appearance is not at first suggestive of unusual activity, yet the pace and regularity with which a party of six or eight of these antelopes will race up the steep flank of a mountain are calculated to remove any doubts on this point. The most peculiar feature of the vaal rhebok is the soft and woolly nature of the gray coat; the horns afford but insignificant trophies, and the flesh is of decidedly poor quality for the table.

Length on front.	Circumference.	Tip to Tip.	Locality.	Owner.
–11½	...	...	Spitzkop .	F. H. Barber.
–11½	...	...	Cape Colony .	Cape Town Museum.
–11	...	...	?	M. E. Bowker.
10¾	2	2½	Basutoland .	Julius Jeppe.
–10½	2⅛	4⅝	Transvaal . .	H. T. and A. H. Glynn.
–10¼	...	...	Cape Colony .	Cape Town Museum.
–9½	2⅜	2⅝	?	Julius Jeppe.
–9½	...	...	Transvaal . .	C. T. Jones.
–9⅜	2	4¼	Basutoland .	Sir A. Milner.
9¼	2½	2¾	?	Dr. Oakshott.
9	2⅝	2⅜	?	Mr. Justice Hopley.
–8 13/16	2¾	Single horn	Barberton .	Dr. Percy Rendall.
–8¾	2⅝	3⅝	?	A. Ohlsson.
8⅜	2½	2¾	Cape Colony	R. H. Venables-Kyrke.
8⅝	2½	2⅝	South Africa .	The late Dr. Burchell, British Museum.
8½	2½	2	?	G. Richards.
8⅜	2	3¼	?	Sir Edmund G. Loder, Bart.
8¼	2	2⅞	?	F. C. Selous.
–8¼	2⅛	3¾	?	Dr. W. P. Y. Bainbrigge.
–8	2	3	Mauchberg . .	F. Vaughan Kirby.
7¾	...	...	?	O. R. Dunell.
7¾	2½	3¾	?	Hon. Walter Rothschild.
7½	2⅜	3	?	H. Atkinson.
7¼	2¼	3½	Basutoland . .	A. Beit.
7	2	2½	?	Capt. H. A. Livingstone.

Head of Common Reedbuck.

COMMON REEDBUCK (Cervicapra arundinum).

Bemba of the Masaras.

Inzeegee of the Amandebele.

Im-vwee of the Masubias.

Um-vwee of the Makubas.

Iuhlango of the Swazis.

Iklabu of the Basutos.

Impoyo of the Lower Zambesi tribes.

Mziki of the Zulus and Matabele.

Natafwi in the Mashukulumbwi country.

Mutobo in the Barotse country.

Sibughat in the Lake Ngami country.

Mpoyo in the Chilala and Chibisa country.

All the reedbucks, as the members of the genus *Cervicapra* may be collectively termed, differ from the waterbucks and kobs by their inferior size, lighter build, and the presence of a completely bare or very short-haired patch on each side of the head immediately beneath the ear. The tail, too, is more bushy and shorter, the lateral hoofs are relatively smaller, and the horns, which are of medium length and stoutness, curve regularly upwards, and in some cases also forwards. The present species, the true reitbok of the Boers, is the largest of the genus, standing about 36 or 37 inches at the shoulder; and has the ear-patch completely bare, and the horns inclining markedly forwards. Length from nose to tail 37 inches in a specimen shot by Dr. Percy Rendall.

Distribution.—South Africa, extending as far north as Angola on the west, and to Mozambique on the east coast. Although formerly numerous in the eastern districts of Cape Colony and Natal, reedbuck have now become scarce in South Africa, and it is not till Khama's country is reached that they are met with in any numbers. As their name implies, reedbuck frequent the reed-brakes fringing so many African rivers; and some of the rivers where they are still fairly abundant are the Lotsani in Bamangwato and those of Ngamiland and the country between Mashonaland and the east coast. They are generally met with in small family parties; and when excited or alarmed utter a characteristic shrill whistle. As their flesh is of fair quality, and their shooting by no means difficult, they are much sought after by sportsmen.

Length on front curve.	Circumference.	Tip to Tip.	Locality.	Owner.
[1]-18	...	...	S. Africa	F. Vaughan Kirby.
-17½	6½	17½	Barotseland . . .	Percy C. Reid.
-16⅝	6¾	19½	Mpimbi, B.C.A. .	Major F. Trollope.
-16	5½	11½	S. Africa . .	A. Ohlsson.
15⅞	6¼	10½	Do.	C. D. Rudd.
15⅞	6¼	14¼	Do.	British Museum.
-15⅞	6⅞	10⅛	Zululand	F. R. N. Findlay.
[2]15¾	6⅛	13½	Transvaal	Julius Jeppe.
15¾	6⅛	...	South Africa . . .	The late J. S. Jameson.
-15½	...	...	Nyoko Valley, B.C.A. .	Major A. St. H. Gibbons.
-15½	6⅝	15½	Transvaal	F. Vaughan Kirby.

1 This was seen and measured by Mr. Kirby. It had one horn only; the other was shot off.

2 Abnormal head.

COMMON REEDBUCK (Cervicapra arundinum)—*continued.*

Length on front curve.	Circumference.	Tip to Tip.	Locality.	Owner.
-15½	...	16	?	Lord David Kennedy.
-15½	...	...	Damaraland . . .	Cape Town Museum.
-15¼	...	...	?	F. H. Barber.
15⅛	6⅝	11¼	Manica Plateau, N. of Zambesi	F. C. Selous.
15	6½	9¾	Mashonaland . .	Sir John Willoughby, B
15	6	12½	Barotseland . .	H. Timmins.
-15	...	...	?	H. T. and A. H. Glynn
-15	6½	9⅜	?	T. E. Buckley.
-15	...	...	?	O. R. Dunell.
14¾	6	15⅛	Zomba, B.C.A. . .	C. C. Bowring.
-14¾	6¾	10½	Sabi Flats . . .	Dr. Percy Rendall.
14⅝	7⅜	9⅛	?	Hon. Walter Rothschild
14½	6⅜	7⅝	?	Sir Edmund G. Loder,
14½	6¼	12⅜	Mashonaland . . .	A. Eyre.
14⅜	5½	16¾	S. Africa . . .	Lieut.-Col. Hon. W. C
14¼	5½	11¼	British Central Africa .	J. E. Gough.
-14¼	...	...	Transvaal	C. T. Jones.
14	6½	11¼	Barotseland . . .	R. T. Coryndon.
13¾	5¾	11¼	S. Africa	W. A. Edmonds.
13¾	6	10¾	Do.	R. A. Cooper.
13¾	6	8¾	Pungwe	H. R. Holden.
13⅝	6	12	Northern Rhodesia . .	F. Smitheman.
13½	6	9¼	?	Hon. Walter Rothschild
13½	6¼	6	Pungwe . . .	Viscount Ennismore.
13½	6¾	6⅞	S. Africa	Major-General Sir F. C ton, K.C.B., K.C.M.
-13½	5¾	12½	Matabeleland . .	J. Brander Dunbar.
13¼	7¼	11¼	Zululand . . .	A. Cameron.
13¼	6¼	9¼	S. Africa	G. Richards.
-13	7	7½	Do.	James J. Harrison.

COMMON REEDBUCK (Cervicapra arundinum)—*continued*.

Length on front curve.	Circumference.	Tip to Tip.	Locality.	Owner.
-13	6½	10¾	?	Mr. Justice Hopley.
12⅞	5⅝	8	Zululand	Capt. L. O. Williams.
12¾	5¾	8½	Busi Valley . . .	E. S. Grogan.
-12¾	4¾	11	Nyasaland . . .	Major P. W. Forbes.
12¾	6⅛	8⅜	Near Bubye River . .	A. M. Sagar-Musgrave.
12¾	5¼	9¼	Zambesia	Comdr. A. T. Hunt.
12½	6	6½	S. Africa . . .	F. E. Potter.
12½	6	9⅝	Pungwe . . .	Capt. G. F. Henry.
12½	5¾	13¾	Do.	R. K. Micklethwait.
12	6¾	8¾	Do.	Capt. F. H. Lehmann.
12	5¼	9¾	Do.	Hon. T. Thynne.
12	6	7	Do.	Col. G. A. Percy.
12	5⅝	9½	?	Julius Jeppe.
12	5½	10¾	S. Africa	Montrose Cloete.
11¾	5¾	10¼	Benguela . .	G. W. Penrice.
11¾	5	9	Pungwe . . .	C. C. Gouldsmith.
11½	6	13	Do.	Count E. Hoyos.
11¼	7	9¼	Do.	P. B. Vander-Byl.
-11¼	6¾	9⅛	?	Dr. W. P. Y. Bainbrigge.
11	6¼	11¼	Zululand	A. J. Brandon.
10⅞	6	8½	Pungwe	Lord Edward Manners.
10½	5	6	Do. . . .	G. L. Bonham.
10½	4⅝	6	Do. . . .	G. Micklethwait.

BOHOR REEDBUCK (Cervicapra bohor).

Boroufa of the Gallas.　　　*Porhé* of the Swahilis.

From the common reedbuck (*C. arundinum*) the present species is chiefly distinguished by its smaller size (height at shoulder about 31 inches), while it is considerably larger than either of the other three members of its genus. Young animals have the horns more hooked at their tips than is the case with the common reedbuck, but with advancing age even this point of distinction becomes little apparent, owing to the wearing away of the tips of the horns. Both the head and body are more uniformly fawn-coloured than in the common species.

Viscount Edmond de Poncins says :—" These antelopes are very numerous in the Galla country near Mount Yokoila ; they like open grassy plains more or less dotted with the small mimosa bushes and are found in small herds of from four to eight, sometimes even fifteen or twenty. They are not very wild and may easily be stalked at less than 200 yards in the middle of the day. Old males frequently are found in the long grass quite alone, when if disturbed they gallop through the grass, jumping very high ; on the plains they go easy and fast without jumping. The flesh is not bad eating, and the Gallas are very keen about getting the skins. Weight about 80 lbs."

A female shot by him measured from nose to root of tail $51\frac{1}{4}$ inches ; height at shoulder, $31\frac{1}{2}$ inches ; round the body, 30 inches.

A good male shot in the Galla country south of the Shoa, by the same sportsman, measured from nose to root of tail $57\frac{1}{2}$ inches ; tail, $6\frac{1}{4}$ inches ; height at shoulder, $34\frac{1}{4}$ inches ; round the body, $34\frac{3}{4}$.

Distribution.—From Abyssinia through East Africa as far south as Kilimanjaro. Discovered by Rüppell in Abyssinia.

Length on front curve.	Circumference.	Tip to Tip.	Locality.	Owner.
$13\frac{3}{8}$	$5\frac{1}{8}$	$8\frac{1}{8}$	East Africa . . .	British Museum.
$13\frac{1}{2}$	$5\frac{1}{2}$	$4\frac{1}{2}$	Do. . . .	Major J. R. Macdonald.
$12\frac{1}{2}$	$5\frac{6}{8}$	$5\frac{3}{8}$	Do. . . .	Sir John Kirk, K.C.B., British Museum.
$10\frac{6}{8}$	$4\frac{1}{2}$	$5\frac{1}{2}$	Do. . . .	Sir Robert Harvey, Bart.
$-9\frac{7}{8}$	$4\frac{6}{8}$	$3\frac{3}{4}$	Galla country . . .	Viscount Edmond de Poncins.
$-9\frac{1}{16}$	$5\frac{1}{2}$	$6\frac{1}{4}$	Do.	Do.
$9\frac{1}{4}$	$4\frac{7}{8}$	$5\frac{1}{8}$	Usongola . . .	Col. F. D. Lugard, C.B., D.S.O.

BOHOR REEDBUCK (Cervicapra bohor)—*continued.*

Length on front curve.	Circumference.	Tip to Tip.	Locality.	Owner.
9⅛	5⅜	8½	Sudan	The late Dr. Burchell, British Museum.
9⅛	4⅞	4⅝	Masailand . .	H. C. V. Hunter.
-9 1/16	5⅛	5⅞	Galla country . . .	Prince de Lucinge.
9	5¼	3⅛	Zanzibar	Sir John Kirk, K.C.B.
9	5	3¾	Ganda, Nigeria . .	J. W. Carroll.
-9	6	5	Shoa, Abyssina . .	Prince de Lucinge.
8¾	5	3⅞	East Africa	Sir Robert Harvey, Bart.
8¾	4⅞	3¾	Masailand . .	H. C. V. Hunter.
8¼	5¾	5	East Africa . . .	R. P. Carroll.
8¼	4½	5¼	Do.	Sir Edmund G. Loder, Bart.
8¼	4¾	4⅜	Unyoro	Col. Trevor Ternan.
8⅛	4¾	2½	Masailand . . .	H. C. V. Hunter, British Museum.
7¾	4⅞	2¾	East Africa . . .	F. J. Jackson, C.B.
-7¾	5⅛	6	Do.	Julius Jeppe.

Head of Mountain Reedbuck.

MOUNTAIN REEDBUCK or ROOI RHEBOK (Cervicapra fulvorufula).

Inhlang-amatshe of the Swazis and Zulus.

This and the nagor are the two smallest representatives of the reed-bucks, both measuring about 28 inches at the shoulder. The present one is specially distinguished by the absence of a distinct forward hook to the tips of the horns, and the general grayish fawn colour of the fur, which has, however, in some cases a more or less distinctly rufous tinge.

Distribution.—Eastern Africa to the south of the Zambesi, particularly Natal, Zululand, and Bechuanaland ; represented farther north by the under-mentioned form. The rooi (red) rhebok differs from the typical representative of its genus in being an inhabitant of the basal slopes of mountains, at a lower level than the tract frequented by the vaal rhebok. They are generally found in small troops of a dozen head or less ; and from their active habits and the difficult nature of the ground they frequent, afford excellent stalking. Although rare in most of the Transvaal, good bags of this antelope have been made in the western districts of that country. In the neighbourhood of the tributaries of the Limpopo, on the Mabube, Tamulikan, Machabe, Sunta, and Chobe rivers, as well as the tributaries of the Zambesi east of the Victoria Falls, and throughout Mashonaland and Matabeleland, rooi rhebok are still very abundant. Those reported from the Manica plateau, north of the Zambesi, may be the so-called Chanler's reedbuck.

Length on front curve.	Circumference.	Tip to Tip.	Locality.	Owner.
−8¼	3¾	4¼	Transvaal . .	F. R. N. Findlay.
7¾	4¾	4¾	S. Africa . .	Hon. Walter Rothschild. (Shot by F. C. Selous.)
−7¾	4⅝	4	Transvaal . .	F. Vaughan Kirby.
−7½	4	3½	Lebombo Range, S.A.	Count E. Hoyos.
−7½	...	...	?	H. T. and A. H. Glynn.
7⅜	4¼	3	Zululand . .	A. H. Neumann.
−7¼	...	...	?	O. R. Dunell.
−7¼	4⅛	2½	?	Mr. Justice Hopley.
−7⅛	4¼	5¾	?	Julius Jeppe.
7	3½	4¼	Zululand .	A. Cameron.
6¾	4¾	4¾	?	Bloemfontein Museum.
6¾	4⅝	4¾	?	F. E. Potter.
−6⅝	3¾	3⅜	?	Mr. Justice Hopley.
6½	4	3¼	Zululand . .	Lieut.-Col. Hon. W. Coke.
−6½	3¾	4¾	Barberton .	Dr. Percy Rendall.
−6½	4	3½	?	Dr. W. P. Y. Bainbrigge.
6⅜	4¼	3⅞	Zululand	A. J. Brandon.
−6¼	...	...	?	C. T. Jones.
−6¼	4½	4	?	A. Ohlsson.
−6	3⅞	2⅞	Swaziland .	T. E. Buckley.
6	4	3⅜	Zululand . .	Captain L. O. Williams.

LYDENBURG REEDBUCK (Cervicapra fulvorufula subalpina).

The reedbuck discovered by Mr. Vaughan Kirby in the Lydenburg ange of the Transvaal departs from the ordinary type of the mountain eedbuck in exhibiting a tendency to partial albinism. Whether this eculiarity entitles it to be regarded as a distinct race must, for the resent, remain a moot point.

Head of Chanler's Reedbuck.   From a specimen shot by W. Astor Chanler.

CHANLER'S REEDBUCK (Cervicapra fulvorufula chanleri).

A reedbuck from East Africa described by the Hon. Walter Rothschild from a single skin, as a distinct species, appears to be nothing more than a local race of the rooi rhebok, from which it is even doubtful whether it should be separated as a sub-species.   In the type specimen the nose shows a dark streak like the one often seen in the rooi rhebok and common reedbuck.   Other skins have been obtained by Mr. F. J. Jackson, C.B.

Distribution.—The mountainous districts of British East Africa to the east of Mount Kenia and adjacent regions.   By Mr. H. S. H. Cavendish these antelopes were seen in the Boran country.

Length on front curve.	Circumference.	Tip to Tip.	Locality.	Owner.
5⅝	4	4	?	Lord Delamere.
5⅝	3½	4⅞	?	Major A. E. Smith.
5¼	3½	3⅞	Zombènè Range .	W. Astor Chanler.

NAGOR REEDBUCK (Cervicapra redunca).

Distinguished from the mountain reedbuck (with which it agrees approximately in size) by the distinct forward curvature of the tips of the horns, so as to form a hook. General colour uniformly bright fawn, without darker markings on the limbs; tail only slightly bushy, fawn-coloured above and white beneath.

Distribution.—Senegal and Gambia.

Length on front curve.	Circumference.	Tip to Tip.	Locality.	Owner.
9½	5	3⅛	Ganda, Nigeria	J. W. Carroll.
8	5¼	3½	Ibi, Benue River, West Africa	Julius Jeppe.
8	6	7¾	West Africa . .	Hon. Walter Rothschild.
8	5	5⅜	Gambia . .	Guy H. Sangster.
7½	5½	2	?	Sir Edmund G. Loder, Bart.
6¾	4¾	2⅛	Ibi . . .	Capt. A. H. Festing.

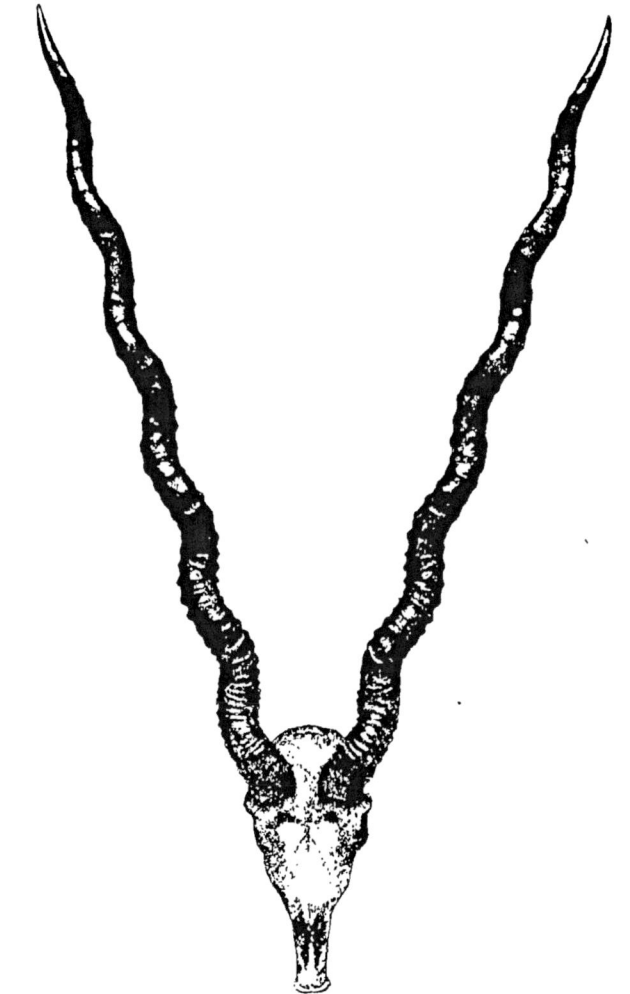

Skull and Horns of Blackbuck.   From Mr. A. O. Hume's specimen.

BLACKBUCK or INDIAN ANTELOPE (Antilope bezoartica).

Although in former days almost or quite all of the then known species of antelope was included in the genus *Antilope*, the extent of the latter has been gradually whittled down until it comprises the Indian blackbuck alone.   In addition to being the sole representative of the genus, this animal is also the type of a sub-family or group of antelopes, embracing among others the saiga, the gazelles, the impala, and springbuck. All these are small or medium-sized antelopes, with hairy muzzles, generally short tails, and tall, narrow-crowned cheek-teeth, like those of sheep. With the exception of the springbuck and the majority of the gazelles, horns are confined to the males. From all the other members of this assemblage the blackbuck is distinguished by the beautiful spiral formed by its horns. It has large face-glands, a short and compressed tail, and well-developed lateral hoofs. Height at shoulder about 32 inches; average weight, 85 lbs. It is only in adult males that the characteristic dark tint from which the species takes its name is developed; young males being uniformly brownish fawn above like the does.

Distribution.—India, from the foot of the Himalaya to Cape Comorin, and from the Punjab to Lower Assam; unknown in Ceylon and the countries to the eastward of the Bay of Bengal.

Length straight.	Circumference.	Tip to Tip.	Locality.	Owner.
[1]–28¾	...	...	Jeypore . . .	Major-Gen. Sir B. Blood, K.C.B.
28¼	5	17¾	Near Delhi . .	A. O. Hume, C.B. (See illustration.)
–28	...	20	Do. . .	Major P. Dunell Pank.
–28	5	15	38 miles north of Ahmedabad	T. Le Mesurier.
–27⅞	...	...	Jeypore . . .	Major-Gen. Sir B. Blood, K.C.B.
–27	5	19½	Bikanir . .	Capt. Harry V. Brooke,
26¾	4¾	25¼	Bhurtpore, N.W.P.	Col. E. T. H. Hutton.
–26¾	5	19½	Bikanir . . .	Capt. Harry V. Brooke.
–26¾	4¾	...	Do. . . .	Major-Gen. Alexander A. A. Kinloch.
–26⅓	...	...	N.W.P. . . .	C. B. Oldfield.
26⅜	5	17⅞	Sirsa, Punjab . .	A. O. Hume, C.B.
–26$\frac{5}{16}$	5¼	22	Bikanir . .	Lieut.-Col. G. D. F. Sulivan.
26¼	5	23⅛	Oudh . . .	E. St. J. Lawson.
26	5	21⅞	Bikanir . . .	Capt. H. W. Codrington.
–26	...	...	Jeypore . . .	Capt. G. L. Holdsworth.
25½	...	15	?	Col. Martin.
25⅓	4⅞	18	Punjab . . .	Major R. H. Rattray.
25⅜	5½	14½	Sirsa, Punjab . .	Hume Collection, British Museum.

[1] Measured and recorded by A. O. Hume, but not now in the possession of General Sir B. Blood, K.C.B.

BLACKBUCK or INDIAN ANTELOPE (Antilope bezoartica)—*continued.*

Length straight.	Circumference.	Tip to Tip.	Locality.	Owner.
–25⅜	5	19	?	Count E. Hoyos.
25¼	4¾	19	Jeypore . .	A. B. Graves.
25⅛	5⅛	15	Kathiawar . .	Lieut.-Col. L. L. Fenton.
25	4⅞	19	Sirsa, Punjab . .	Hume Collection, British Museum.
–25	5¼	13½	?	Bombay Natural History Society's Museum.
–25	...	...	?	Lucknow Museum.
24¾	5	20	Jeypore . . .	Surgeon-Major J. B. Buchanan.
24¾	4½	17¼	Dholpur . . .	A. J. Coppinger.
24½	5⅜	20¼	Bikanir . . .	H.H. Maharaja of Bikanir.
24⅜	4⅞	18¼	Do. . .	Lieut.-Col. G. D. F. Sulivan.
24¼	4¾	19½	?	A. Leslie Renton.
24¼	5	18½	?	Marquis of Ailsa.
–24¼	4.33	20.85	Udepur . . .	Viscount Edmond de Poncins.
–24¼	5	19¼	Punjab .	Capt. A. Hicks-Beach.
24	5	18⅞	Aligahr .	St. George Littledale.
24	4 6/8	16¾	Rajpura . .	The late J. E. Ubsdell.
–24	4⅞	...	Punjab . . .	J. Johnston-Stewart.
24	...	20	?	Duke of Bedford.
–24	...	...	?	Otho Shaw.
23¾	5⅜	21	?	H.R.H. the Duke of Saxe-Coburg and Gotha.
23¾	4¾	13¼	?	Capt. F. C. Quicke.
–23¾	...	...	Central Provinces .	Capt. H. M. Biddulph.
23¾	5	16¼	Punjab	Major J. W. M. Cotton.
23⅝	4⅞	19¼	Patiala .	Lieut.-Col. E. E. Carr.
23⅝	5⅛	14¾	?	Hon. Walter Rothschild.
23⅝	4¾	16⅜	Central Provinces .	C. D. Twopeny.
[1] 23½	3¼	20¼	?	A. O. Hume, C.B.
23½	5⅛	16¾	Bikanir . . .	Capt. F. E. S. Adair.
23½	4½	17¼	Do. .	Major H. C. Morland.

[1] Malformed, curving backwards like an ibex.

BLACKBUCK or INDIAN ANTELOPE (Antilope bezoartica)—*continued.*

Length straight.	Circumference.	Tip to Tip.	Locality.	Owner.
-23½	5	17½	?	James J. Harrison.
23½	5	24½	Bikanir . .	U. O. Thynne.
23½	5½	18	Gaziabad . .	Major G. Douglas.
23¼	5½	18½	Do. . . .	Hume Collection, British Museum.
23¼	4¾	17¾	Sirhind . . .	Col. R. J. Heber-Percy.
23	5⅛	13⅜	North India . .	Sir Victor Brooke's Collection.
23	5¼	15¼	Indore . . .	Col. Cunliffe Martin.
23	5¼	15½	?	H. G. Buxton.

Head of Blackbuck.

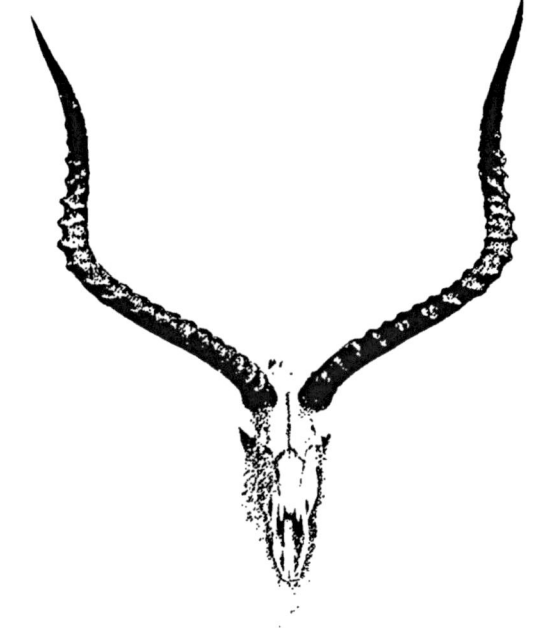

Skull and Horns of Impala, from a specimen shot by A. H. Neumann.

IMPALA (Æpyceros melampus).

Inzero of the Masubias.   *Mpala* in the Barotse, Lake Ngami,
Swalah of the Swahilis.   and the Chilala and Chibisa.

This beautiful impala, or pala, differs from all the members of the gazelle group by the absence of the lateral hoofs; its specific name (black-footed) being taken from the pair of tufts of black hair on each hind foot. The horns of the bucks, which are of considerable length in proportion to the size of the animal, show a characteristic and graceful double curvature; and the bright foxy red hue of the shining fur of the upper parts aids in the easy identification of the species. Height at shoulder about 33 inches. The Boer name of rooibok (red buck) is happily chosen. Weight about 110 lbs.

Distribution.—Southern and South-Eastern Africa, extending as far north as Lower Kordofan. In Angola replaced by a closely allied form (*Æ. petersi*), usually regarded as a distinct species, but which may be merely a local race; it is distinguished by the presence of a purplish black streak down the middle of the face and another through each eye. In the days of their abundance impala were to be found in big troops; and such are still to be met with on the Upper Zambesi, in East Mashonaland, and parts of British East and Central Africa. Half a century ago, or even less, they were to be found in similar numbers among the covert on the banks of every river in the Transvaal and Bechuanaland; but now it is not till the northern borders of the former country that they are to be met with, and even then only in small parties here and there. Impala are some of the fleetest of all antelopes, and are also in the habit of leaping high in the air; their presence always implies the neighbourhood of water.

Length.					
·ont ve.	Straight.	Circumference.	Tip to Tip.	Locality.	Owner.
ɔ	24	6¼	17½	E. C. Africa . .	Lord Delamere.
9	22¼	5⅝	11	Do. . .	Do.
3	23	5¾	22¾	Do. .	A. H. Neumann. (See illustration.)
.	22⅞	...	...	Masailand . .	F. J. Jackson, C.B.
3	21	5⅞	12¼	E. Africa . .	G. E. Smith.
7½	21	5⅞	14¼	South Africa . .	The late Dr. Burchell, British Museum.
7	23	6	23¼	Between Lakes Baringo and Rudolph	H. Andrew.
7	22½	...	15⅛	Between Lakes Naivasha and Baringo	F. J. Jackson, C.B.
7	22¼	6	10¾	E. Africa . .	Major A. E. Smith.
7	21½	6	9	Do. .	E. Gedge.
5½	20¾	...	...	South Africa . .	Grahamstown Museum.
5⅜	21	5⅝	16	Do. . .	Hon. Walter Rothschild.
5¼	22¾	5¾	15	Uganda . . .	Col. F. D. Lugard, C.B., D.S.O.
5¼	19¾	5¾	22¼	E. Africa . .	C. W. Hobley.
5½	21¼	6¼	12⅞	Do. . .	G. E. Smith.
.	20½	5¾	15	Do. . .	W. Astor Chanler.
.	20½	5⅝	11½	Do. . .	H. C. V. Hunter.
5½	20	6	14	Matamiri Bush .	F. Vaughan Kirby.
5½	20	6	13¾	E. Africa .	Henry Charrington.
5¼	20½	5	12⅝	Do. . .	F. J. Jackson, C.B.
.13	20	5.12	15.7	Do. . .	Prince Henry of Liechtenstein.

IMPALA (Æpyceros melampus)—*continued.*

Length.		Circumference.	Tip to Tip.	Locality.	Owner.
On front curve.	Straight.				
-25⅛	20¼	...	10¾	?	F. J. Newnham.
25	21⅛	5⅞	17⅝	East Africa .	F. J. Jackson, C.B.
24⅞	19¾	5⅞	11⅝	Do.	Sir Edmund G. Loder, Bart.
24½	19⅛	5⅝	12⅜	S. Africa . .	British Museum.
..	20	...	...	Chobe Valley .	F. C. Selous.
...	20	...	...	E. Africa . .	Sir John Willoughby, Bart.
24	20	5½	16	Do. .	J. Gardiner Muir.
24	20	6	11¾	Do. .	E. J. L. Berkeley.
-24	20½	5½	13½	S. Africa	Dublin Museum.
-24	19	5½	10	Do.	Mr. Justice Hopley.
-24	...	6½	16¼	E. Africa .	T. E. Buckley.
23⅝	19¼	5⅜	16⅜	Do.	Capt. R. A. J. Montgomerie, C.B., R.N.
23⅝	...	5½	9⅜	Do. .	Hon. Walter Rothschild.
-23½	19	...	12⅝	Lydenburg . .	F. H. Barber.
23½	19	5	8	E. Africa .	C. F. S. Vandeleur, D.S.O.
23⅜	20⅜	6	14½	Do. .	Sir Robert Harvey, Bart.
23⅛	19⅜	5⅜	12¾	Ndi, E. Africa	C. Steuart Betton.
-23	18¼	5	10	S. Africa . .	A. Ohlsson.
22¾	18¾	6	14¾	E. Africa . .	Major W. H. Williams.
22½	18½	5½	14⅜	Matabeleland . .	Hon. R. A. Ward.
-22½	18	...	...	?	O. R. Dunell.
-22	19	...	...	S. Africa . .	Cape Town Museum.
-...	19	...	...	Njoko River .	R. T. Coryndon.
22	18	6	10½	S. Africa . .	James J. Harrison.
21¾	18	5	9¼	Pungwe . . .	Hon. T. Thynne.
21½	17¼	5½	12¾	S.E. Africa . .	E. Lort-Phillips.
21¼	18¾	5¼	10	Do. . . .	Col. G. A. Percy.
21¼	17½	5¼	11¼	Do. . . .	G. L. Bonham.
21¼	17	5	8¼	Do. . . .	Viscount Ennismore.

The following specimens belong to the small form described as *Æ. johnstoni*, now regarded as inseparable from the ordinary impala :—

Length. On front curve.	Length. Straight.	Circumference.	Tip to Tip.	Locality.	Owner.
$19\frac{3}{8}$	$15\frac{3}{4}$	$4\frac{7}{8}$	$5\frac{5}{8}$	Choma River, B.C.A.	R. H. Ferrers Stranach.
19	$14\frac{3}{4}$	$5\frac{1}{4}$	7	B.C.A.	John Yule.
$17\frac{1}{2}$	$14\frac{3}{4}$	$4\frac{3}{4}$	$9\frac{3}{4}$	Do.	C. C. Bowring.
17	$14\frac{1}{2}$	$5\frac{1}{4}$	8	Do.	Hon. Walter Rothschild.

ANGOLAN IMPALA (Æpyceros petersi).

See page 206.

$23\frac{1}{4}$	$18\frac{3}{4}$	6	$12\frac{1}{4}$	Kaokoland . .	Capt. F. Cookson.
21	$17\frac{7}{8}$	$5\frac{7}{8}$	$11\frac{3}{4}$	Angola	Hon. Walter Rothschild.
21	$17\frac{7}{8}$	6	$9\frac{3}{4}$	?	Count E. Hoyos.

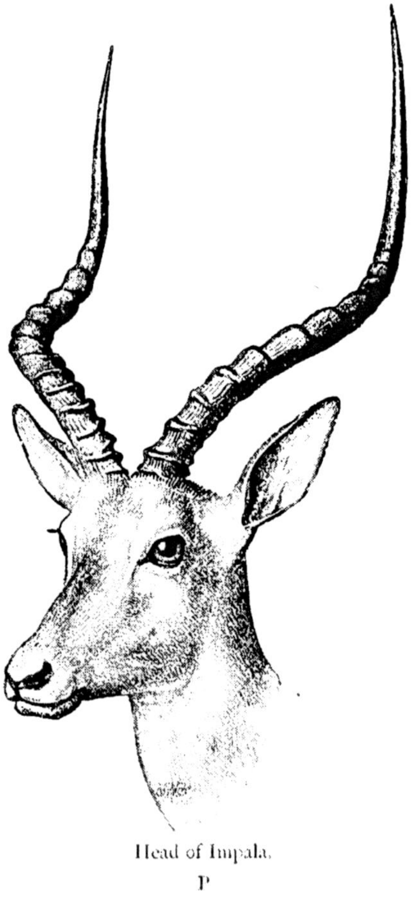

Head of Impala.

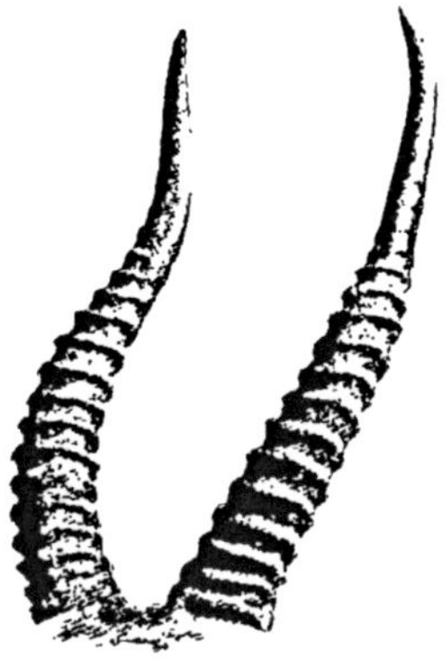

Horns of Saiga, from the Hon. Walter Rothschild's specimen.

SAIGA (Saiga tatarica).

One of the most remarkable of all antelopes is the Central Asian saiga, which, although belonging to the same group as the blackbuck, differs from most of its kindred by the extraordinary inflated and puffy shape of the nose. This forms a kind of trunk, comparable to that of the dik-diks, with the nostrils directed downwards. The tail is short, and lateral hoofs, which are wanting in the impala, are present. In summer the colour is dull yellowish above and whitish beneath, but in winter the whole fur is uniformly whitish. The short and blunt ears are very thickly covered with hair, and the horns of the males pale amber colour. Height at shoulder about 30 inches.

Distribution.—The open steppes of Southern Russia and South-Eastern Siberia. Formerly the range of this animal was much more extensive in Europe, reaching to the confines of Poland, but nowadays it is restricted to the Kalmuk Steppes between the rivers Don and Volga.

Length on front curve.	Circumference.	Tip to Tip.	Locality.	Owner.
14 3/8	5 1/4	3 1/2	Siberia	Hon. Walter Rothschild. (See illustration.)
13 3/4	5	...	Volga	Sir Edmund G. Loder, Bart.
13 3/4	4 3/8	3 1/2	?	Sir Victor Brooke's Collection.
13 5/8	5	5 1/2	Sarepta, South Russia . .	British Museum.
13 1/8	5 3/8	4 3/8	Russia	Hon. Walter Rothschild.

SAIGA (Saiga tatarica)—*continued.*

Length on front curve.	Circumference.	Tip to Tip.	Locality.	Owner.
$12\frac{7}{8}$	$5\frac{3}{8}$	single horn	Russia	British Museum.
$12\frac{7}{8}$	$4\frac{5}{8}$	$5\frac{5}{8}$	Sarepta, South Russia . . .	Do.
$-12\frac{1}{2}$	5	$4\frac{1}{4}$	Siberia	Dublin Museum.
11	$4\frac{7}{8}$	$4\frac{1}{2}$	Do.	British Museum.

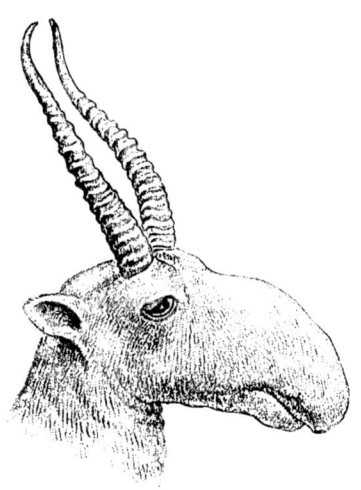

Head of Male Saiga.

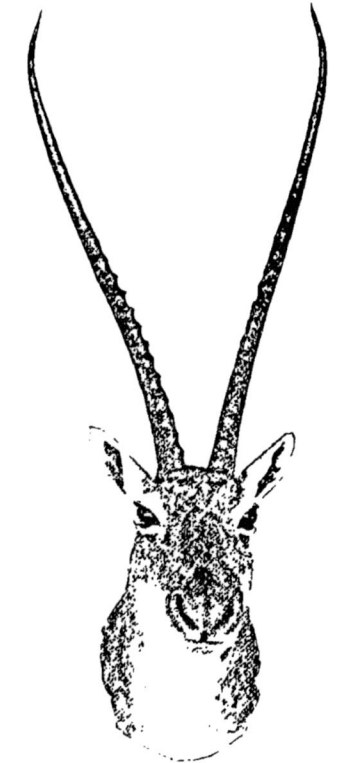

Head of Chiru, from H. Z. Darrah's specimen.

CHIRU or TIBETAN ANTELOPE (Pantholops hodgsoni).

Among several animals peculiar to the Tibetan plateau none is more interesting than the so-called chiru, whose beautiful horns form some of the most cherished trophies of the sportsman. Although very unlike in general appearance, the chiru is evidently a near ally of the saiga, having the nose even more swollen at the sides, at least in the male, but less bent downwards at the tip. The long black horns, which are somewhat compressed, rise almost vertically from the head, and are slightly divergent, nearly straight below, but evenly curving forwards above, and ridged in front. General colour of fur, which is very dense and short, pale fawn above, with a pinkish suffusion, but the face of the male black. Height at shoulder about 31 or 32 inches; weight from 90 to 120 lbs.

Distribution.—The plateau of Tibet, at elevations of from 13,000 to

16,000 feet, or even more; the animal associates in pairs or small parties.

Length on front curve.	Circumference.	Tip to Tip.	Locality.	Owner.
27¾	6⅛	13½	From the Darma Side across the Beansi Pass	A. O. Hume, C.B.
27⅝	5½	11¼	Tibet	Sir Robert Harvey, Bart.
27⅛	5⅞	15⅛	Hills N. of the Beansi Pass	A. O. Hume, C.B.
–27	...	12	?	J. D. Inverarity.
–26½	...	...	Chang Chenmo . .	Major A. E. Ward.
26⅜	5⅞	13⅝	Ladak .	Hon. Charles Ellis.
26	4⅞	12⅞	Tibet . .	Captain G. Campbell.
25⅝	5½	12¾	?	Arnold Pike.
25½	5¾	11½	Tibet	Captain C. B. Vandeleur.
25⅜	5⅝	12½	Hills north of Leh .	Hume Collection, British Museum.
25¼	5¾	12¾	Hills north of Kumaon	Do.
25	5¾	11½	Chang Chenmo . .	H. Z. Darrah. (See illustration.)
–25¼	5	10¾	Tibet . .	P. H. G. Powell Cotton.
24¾	5⅝	11½	?	Sir Edmund G. Loder, Bart.
24¾	5	11	?	E. L. Phelps.
24⅝	5⅝	11¾	Tibet .	Sir Robert Harvey, Bart.
–24½	4¾	...	Do. . .	Major-General Alexander A. A. Kinloch.
24⅜	5¼	16½	?	British Museum.
–24	...	...	Changchingris .	Otho Shaw.
–24	5½	12	?	T. E. Buckley.
–24	...	...	Chang Chenmo .	Captain H. Trevor.
–24	...	...	?	Indian Museum.
–24	...	...	?	H.H. the Maharaja of Travancore, G.C.S.I.
–24	5¼	12½	Tibet . . .	Captain C. B. Vandeleur.
–23⅝	5¼	11⅝	Do.	H. C. V. Hunter.
–23⅝	5⅛	13⅞	Chang Chenmo .	Paris Museum.
–23½	5½	8¼	Do. .	P. Church.
23½	5	15¼	Do.	Major H. C. Morland.
23½	5	14¾	Do.	Reginald Beech.
23½	5¼	12⅞	Do.	Captain H. Trevor.
23⅜	5¼	11⅜	Ladak	Major C. S. Cumberland.
23¼	5⅜	14⅝	Do.	Hon. Walter Rothschild.
23¼	5⅛	13¾	Do. . .	Captain H. M. Biddulph.
23¼	...	11¼	Do. .	Colonel R. J. Heber-Percy.
23¼	5	8¼	Do.	G. B. Milne.
23⅛	5½	...	Do. . . .	Dr. W. P. Y. Bainbrigge.
23	4⅞	11¾	Do. .	Captain H. Trevor.
23	5	15	Do. .	H.R.H. le Duc d'Orléans.

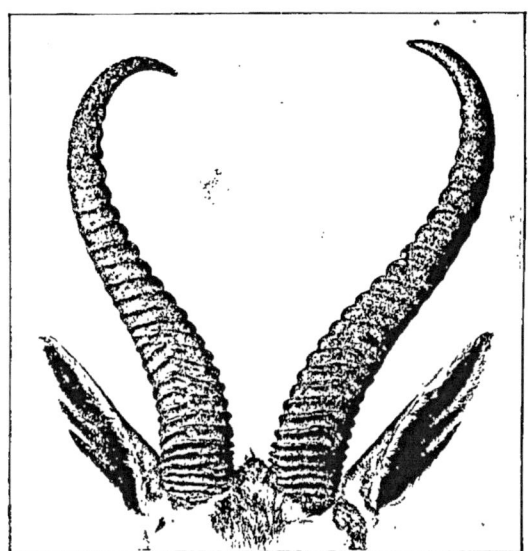

Head of Springbuck, from F. H. Barber's specimen.

SPRINGBUCK (Antidorcas euchore).

Although nearly allied to the gazelles, both in bodily form, coloration, and the shape of the horns, the springbuck presents a peculiarity
entitling it to be regarded as the representative of a genus by itself.   This
peculiarity is the presence of a fold, or narrow pouch, running down the
middle of the hinder part of the back, and lined with long pure white hairs.
In periods of excitement this pouch is capable of being turned partially
inside out, when the long white hairs are erected, and give a totally
different appearance to this region of the animal.   Owing to the dark
nose-streak stopping short at the level of the eyes, the springbuck has
more white on the face than is the case with the majority of gazelles ; and
the white on the rump, which includes the tail and joins that of the
middle of the back, also occupies a larger area.   Height at shoulder,
30 inches.

Distribution.—The plains of Southern Africa, extending in the central
districts of the continent to about latitude 20° S., where its limits
are defined by the forests to the south of the Mabebe River ; in the
west ranging as far north as Mossamedes and Benguela in Southern
Angola, and in the east at least up to the Limpopo.   Although now
never found in the countless thousands which formerly swarmed over
the plains of the Transvaal and Bechuanaland, springbuck are still

abundant in many districts. Protected to a certain degree by law, they are to be met with in parts of Cape Colony and the Orange Free State; while on the plains bordering the Botletli and the neighbouring salt-pans, as well as in Great Namaqualand, Damaraland, and the Ovampo Flats, they occur in large numbers. Springbuck-stalking on the open veldt affords excellent rifle practice; zest being added to the sport from the fact that the venison is most excellent for the table.

Length on front curve.	Circumference.	Tip to Tip.	Locality.	Owner.
[1] 19	5	20¼	Kalahari .	The late W. F. Webb.
–17	...	...	Middleburg Flats .	F. H. Barber. (See illustration.)
–16½	...	...	Bechuanaland .	Vryburg Club.
15½	6½	7¼	?	Hon. T. Thynne.
–15½	6½	...	?	Dr. Maloney.
15½	6⅛	3½	Cape Colony . . .	C. D. Rudd.
–15½	6	2¾	S. of Great Namaqualand	Th. Rehbock.
–15¼	5½	4⅛	?	Dr. W. P. Y. Bainbrigge.
15⅛	6¼	5⅞	Ovampo Flats . . .	Capt. F. Cookson.
15⅛	5¾	10⅞	?	The late W. C. Oswell.
15	5½	8¼	?	Capt. E. J. Lugard.
–15	6	6¼	?	A. Ohlsson.
–15	...	...	Langberg, Kimberley .	Cape Town Museum.
–14½	...	...	?	Alfred Ebden.
14¼	7	2½	South Africa .	A. W. Davis.
14¼	6¼	5	Do. . .	C. Ansell.
14	5¾	4¼	?	British Museum.
14	5½	5	?	F. E. Potter.
13⅞	6	5⅜	Griqualand . .	F. C. Selous.
13⅝	5¼	5⅝	Benguela . .	G. W. Penrice.
13⅝	5½	7⅛	?	Sir Victor Brooke's Collection
13½	5½	5	Botletli River, Ngamiland	H. A. Bryden.
13½	5⅜	3¾	?	Sir Edmund G. Loder, Bart.

[1] A malformed specimen.

SPRINGBUCK (Antidorcas euchore)—*continued.*

Length on front curve.	Circumference.	Tip to Tip.	Locality.	Owner.
$-13\frac{1}{2}$	...	...	?	O. R. Dunell.
$13\frac{3}{8}$	$5\frac{7}{8}$	$4\frac{3}{8}$	South Africa	F. C. Selous.
$13\frac{1}{4}$	$8\frac{1}{4}$	$4\frac{1}{2}$	Do.	R. A. Cooper.
$13\frac{1}{4}$	6	4	Do.	Hon. John Ward.
♀ 13	...	...	Middleburg Flats	F. H. Barber.
$-$ ♀ 13	...	...	South Africa	Alfred Ebden.
13	$5\frac{1}{4}$	6	Britstown, South Africa	W. S. Curtis.
$12\frac{3}{4}$	$5\frac{1}{4}$	$3\frac{1}{4}$	Cape Colony	Rowland Ward.
$12\frac{5}{8}$	$5\frac{5}{8}$	$7\frac{1}{8}$	Orange Free State	Julius Jeppe.
$-12\frac{1}{2}$	5	4	Do.	Do.
$12\frac{1}{2}$	$5\frac{1}{2}$	$4\frac{1}{2}$	South Africa	P. H. Illingworth.
$-12\frac{3}{8}$	$4\frac{13}{16}$	$7\frac{13}{16}$	Transvaal	Dr. Percy Rendall.
$-12\frac{3}{8}$	$5\frac{1}{2}$	$4\frac{3}{8}$	Orange Free State	Count E. Hoyos.
♀ $12\frac{1}{8}$	$2\frac{7}{8}$	...	S. of Great Namaqualand	Th. Rehbock.
$-$ ♀ 12	...	...	Damaraland	F. H. Barber.
-12	...	...	?	C. T. Jones.
$-$ ♀ $11\frac{1}{4}$	3	3	?	Dr. W. P. Y. Bainbrigge.
♀ $10\frac{3}{4}$	$3\frac{1}{4}$	$5\frac{3}{4}$	South Africa	F. C. Selous.
♀ $10\frac{1}{8}$	$3\frac{3}{8}$	$2\frac{1}{2}$	Ovampoland	Capt. F. Cookson.
♀ $9\frac{1}{4}$	$3\frac{3}{8}$	$4\frac{1}{4}$	Benguela	G. W. Penrice.
$8\frac{5}{8}$	$2\frac{1}{2}$	4	Natal	British Museum.
$-$ ♀ $8\frac{1}{8}$	$2\frac{11}{16}$	$3\frac{13}{16}$	Transvaal	Dr. Percy Rendall.
♀ 8	$3\frac{1}{8}$	$2\frac{1}{2}$	South Africa	A. Beit.
♀ $7\frac{1}{2}$	$2\frac{5}{8}$	$2\frac{7}{8}$	Do.	F. C. Selous.

GOA or TIBETAN GAZELLE (Gazella picticaudata).

The true gazelles, from which the springbuck is now separated as a genus by itself (*Antidorcas*), form a very extensive group of delicately built antelopes of easy definition. They are of medium or rather small size, with the muzzle of ordinary shape, the neck not unduly elongated, and no fold containing a crest of long erectile hairs down the middle of the back. To suit the nature of their haunts, their coloration is generally of a sandy hue, with the under parts white, and the face in most cases marked with parallel dark and light longitudinal streaks ; dark bands being also frequently present on the rump and on the flanks to separate the tawny of the back from the white beneath. The knees are very generally furnished with brush-like tufts of long, stiff hairs ; and the tail is either short or of medium length. With the exception of four species, horns are present in both sexes ; those of the males being stout, distinctly ridged, and generally of about the same length as the head, although occasionally much longer. Except at the tips, they curve backwards, so as to present an anteriorly convex lower portion, above which they are generally more or less curved forwards and upwards. Gazelles have a wider geographical distribution than any other genus of antelopes, and are, for the most part, inhabitants of more or less desert regions, or their confines.

The Tibetan goa belongs to a small and aberrant group of the genus in which the tail is very short, the usual dark and light streaks on the face are wanting, and the females are hornless. As a species, it is distinguished by its comparatively small size, and the strongly marked backward curvature of the horns, which are not hooked at the tips. Height at shoulder about 25 inches. Weight about 45 lbs.

Distribution.—The plateau of Tibet and some of the adjacent parts of Central Asia.

Length on front curve.	Circumference.	Tip to Tip.	Locality.	Owner.
14⅛	3⅝	2	Hanle, Spiti	Hon. Walter Rothschild.
-13½	...	...	?	Lieut.-Col. T. Greenaway.
13½	3⅝	5¼	Hills N. of Sikim	Hume Collection, British Museum.
-13¼	4	...	Tibet . .	Major-General Alexander A. A. Kinloch.
-13¼	3½	3	Ladak	Capt. H. W. Codrington.
-13⅛	4	2¼	Do.	Do.
13⅛	4	3⅝	Tibet	H. C. V. Hunter.
-13⅛	3⅝	6¼	S.E. of Hanle	P. H. G. Powell-Cotton.
-13	3¾	5¾	Tibet .	Bombay Natural History Society's Museum.
13	4⅛	4½	East Ladak .	Col. J. Biddulph.
13	3¾	1½	?	Captain C. B. Vandeleur.
13	...	...	?	Indian Museum.
13	3¾	5⅜	N. Sikim .	Surgeon-Captain A. Pearse.
12⅞	3⅞	4¾	Hills N. of Kumaon	A. O. Hume, C.B.
12⅞	3⅞	4⅜	?	The late B. H. Hodgson, British Museum.
12¾	3⅞	2½	Hills N. of Kumaon	Hume Collection, British Museum.
12⅝	4¾	5⅛	Near Hanle .	H. Z. Darrah.
12½	3⅜	7	?	Arnold Pike.
12⅜	3½	5½	South of Hanle	Col. F. C. Lister-Kay.
12¼	3½	6¼	Ladak . .	David T. Hanbury.
-12¼	3½	3 3/16	Tibet . . .	Prince Henri d'Orléans, Paris Museum.
-12⅛	3½	6½	Do.	Sir Edmund G. Loder, Bart.
12⅛	3⅝	5	Ladak	Capt. F. E. S. Adair.
-12	3¾	5	Tibet .	Capt. H. M. Biddulph.
12	3⅝	2½	Do.	H. C. V. Hunter.
12	4	5½	Do.	Rowland Ward.
11¾	3¼	3½	?	R. Johnstone.
11⅝	3⅜	5⅞	Tibet	The late B. H. Hodgson, British Museum.
11½	3⅝	4⅛	Do.	Hon. Walter Rothschild.
11¼	3½	4¼	Hanle	F. W. H. Walshe.
11¼	3¾	4¼	?	J. V. Phelps.
11	3⅝	3⅜	Ladak .	R. Lydekker, British Museum.

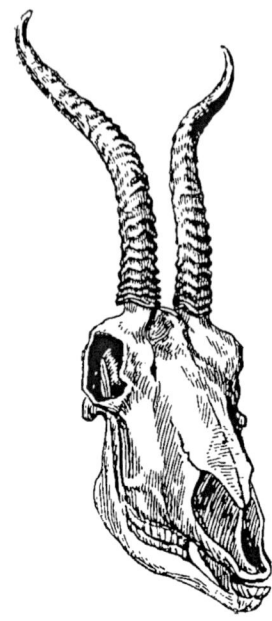

Skull and Horns of Przewalski's Gazelle, from a specimen shot by Prince Demidoff.

PRZEWALSKI'S GAZELLE (Gazella przewalskii).

Nearly allied to the goa, from which it differs by its rather larger size, and the distinct hooks formed by the tips of the horns of the bucks. General colour in summer, deep fawn ; in winter, pale finely grizzled fawn ; white of buttocks running up in an angle on each side of the tail, which is very sharp, and almost concealed by the fur. Front of limbs more or less brown ; no tufts of hair on the knees.

Distribution.—Mongolia.

Length on front curve.	Circumference.	Tip to Tip.	Locality.	Owner.
11	$4\frac{3}{8}$	$4\frac{3}{8}$	Altai . . .	St. George Littledale.
$10\frac{1}{4}$	$4\frac{3}{4}$	$2\frac{3}{4}$	?	British Museum.
10	4	$4\frac{5}{8}$	?	Henri de Bourbon, Comte de Bardi.
10	$4\frac{7}{16}$	6	Altai . . .	Prince Demidoff.
$9\frac{3}{4}$	$4\frac{1}{8}$	$4\frac{3}{8}$	North of Pekin .	The late R. Swinhoe, British Museum.
$-8\frac{11}{16}$	$3\frac{3}{4}$	$4\frac{3}{8}$	North China . .	Père A. David, Paris Museum.

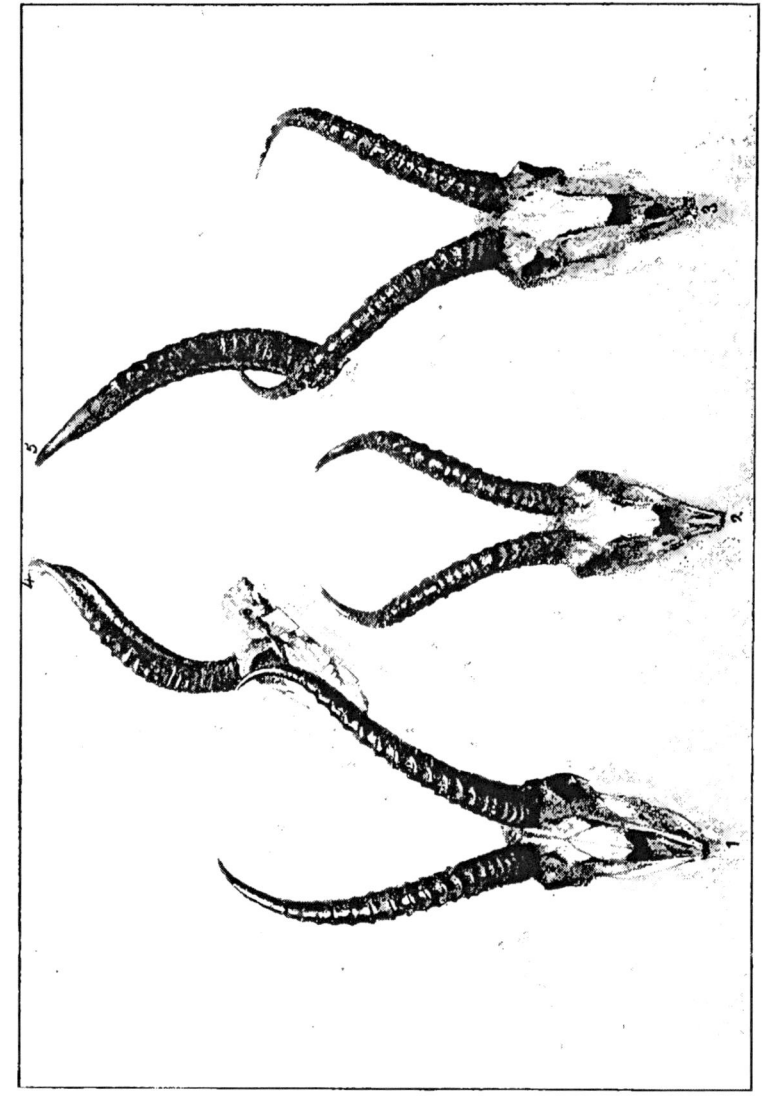

Skulls and Horns of Mongolian (1, 3, 5) and Persian (2, 4) Gazelle.   From specimens in the Collection of A. O. Hume.

MONGOLIAN GAZELLE (Gazella gutturosa).

Jaeisw or *Sava-keek* in Turkestan. *Hwang-yang* in Mongolia.

Belonging to the same group of the genus as the goa, this larger species takes its scientific title from the peculiar swollen condition of the throat of the male during the pairing season. In addition to its size (height at shoulder about 30 inches), the species is characterised by the comparatively slight backward curvature of the horns, which are not hooked at the tips; the general colour being pale fawn, with the rump, flanks, and the whole of the limbs white.

Distribution.—Northern and Eastern Mongolia and the southern borders of Russian Transbaikalia. This gazelle was discovered by the Russian traveller Pallas, who described it as long ago as the year 1777.

Length on front curve.	Circumference.	Tip to Tip.	Locality.	Owner.
15¾	5	6.34	Lob Nor . .	A. O. Hume, C.B.
14¾	4⅞	3	Chinese Turkestan .	Major C. S. Cumberland.
–14⅝	3 9/16	4¾	Lob Nor . .	Prince Henri d'Orléans, Paris Museum.
14¼	4¼	3	Wana Plain, Waziristan	A. J. Grant.
13¾	4⅞	4½	Chinese Turkestan .	E. L. Phelps.
13¾	4½ .	6	Saissan, West Siberia .	Dr. O. Finsch, British Museum.
13⅜	4¾	5½	?	Hume Collection, British Museum.
–13¼	3¾	3⅛	?	Capt. P. J. Gordon.
13⅛	4⅝	6¼	Mongolia	Sir Edmund G. Loder, Bart.
11½	4⅞	3	Chinese Turkestan	Reginald Beech.

PERSIAN GAZELLE (Gazella subgutturosa).

A near relation of the Mongolian species, but distinguished by the longer tail, of which the upper surface is crested with black, and the presence of dark and light markings on the face. These face-markings differ, however, from those of all other species save the Marica gazelle (*G. marica*) of Arabia, in that the upper portion of the face, at least in aged individuals, is pure white, so that the central dark band is interrupted on the forehead. From the Marica the Persian gazelle may be distinguished by its superior size (height at shoulder from 26 to 27 inches), and the absence of horns in the female. The larynx is swollen, forming a peculiar prominence on the front of the upper part of the throat.

There are two distinct local races of this gazelle, the ordinary Caspian and Persian *G. subgutturosa typica*, and the Yarkand *G. subgutturosa yarcandensis ;* the latter being distinguished by its superior dimensions and darker face-markings, as well as by the much smaller degree of divergence of the horns of the males, which are also relatively shorter.

Distribution.—Western Asia from Asia Minor and Caucasia in the west to Turkestan, Yarkand, and Mongolia in the east.

Length on front curve.	Circumference.	Tip to Tip.	Locality.	Owner.
–14¼	5¼	6	Near Tiflis .	Clive Phillipps-Wolley.
13¼	4¼	4	Khelat	A. O. Hume, C.B.
12⅜	4	5¼	Syria . .	Hon. Walter Rothschild.
12	4	5	Asia Minor	Do.
12	4	2¾	Khelat . .	A. O. Hume C.B.

The undermentioned belong to the Yarkand race.

16	5	3¼	Yarkand .	A. O. Hume, C.B.
15⅞	5	3¼	Do.	Do.
–15¼	...	5	Maralbashi	H. Lennard.
14	4¾	5.75	Yarkand . . .	A. O. Hume, C.B.
14	5	5¾	Eastern Turkestan .	Col. J. Biddulph.
13½	4¾	6⅛	Maralbashi . .	David T. Hanbury.

PERSIAN GAZELLE (Gazella subgutturosa)—*continued.*

Length on front curve.	Circumference.	Tip to Tip.	Locality.	Owner.
$-13\frac{3}{8}$	$5\frac{3}{16}$	$7\frac{1}{8}$	Altai .	Prince Henri d'Orléans, Paris Museum.
13	$4\frac{5}{8}$	$7\frac{1}{8}$	Maralbashi	P. Church.
$12\frac{5}{8}$	$4\frac{3}{8}$	$3\frac{3}{8}$	Altai .	St. George Littledale.
12	...	2	Maralbashi	H. Lennard.

Head of Springbuck.

Head of Dorcas Gazelle.

DORCAS GAZELLE (Gazella dorcas).

This well-known species brings us to the more typical group of gazelles, in the members of which the central dark face-band is continued uninterruptedly up the forehead, and horns are developed in both sexes. Among the special characteristics of the present species may be noted the circumstance that the white area of the rump does not invade the fawn of the back, the indistinctness of the dark lateral band dividing the fawn of the upper parts from the white beneath, and the perfectly lyrate form of the horns, which are of medium length, with the middle portion twisted outwardly, and the tips converging towards one another. Height at shoulder, 21 to 22 inches ; total length about 42 inches. General colour pale fawn, of rather variable tint, with the face-markings distinct.

Distribution.—Morocco, Algeria, and thence eastwards through Egypt into Palestine and Syria. By the Arabs of Algeria this gazelle is known as rhozal or hemar.

DORCAS GAZELLE (Gazella dorcas)—*continued.*

Length on front curve.	Circumference.	Tip to Tip.	Locality.	Owner.
13⅛	4¼	2½	Algeria	Sir Edmund G. Loder, Bart.
–12½	3⅝	5⅛	Do.	Viscount Edmond de Poncins.
12½	3⅝	3¾	Southern Sahara .	J. J. S. Whitaker.
12⅜	3¾	2¾	Algeria . .	Sir Edmund G. Loder, Bart.
12⅜	3⅜	...	Do. . .	British Museum.
12¼	4	2¼	Do.	Rowland Ward.
–12¼	3½	3¾	Do. . .	A. E. Pease.
12	4	3¾	Do.	J. H. Thomas.
11⅞	3⅝	4½	Do. . . .	Sir Victor Brooke's Collection.
–11¾	3¾	5⅛	Do.	Julius Jeppe.
11¼	3½	3⅞	Do. . .	E. N. Buxton.
–11¼	3⅝	3⅛	Do. . .	W. E. Pease.
–10⅞	4	4¼	Do.	Count E. Hoyos.
10⅛	4	2¼	Shores of Red Sea . .	British Museum.
10⅛	3⅝	2¾	Nubia . . .	Sir Victor Brooke's Collection.
♀ 9⅞	...	...	Algeria . . .	A. E. Pease.
–9¾	4	3¾	Do.	Dr. Percy Rendall.
♀ 9¼	1¾	5½	Do. . . .	A. E. Pease.
–8¾	4	3½	Do. . . .	Count Scheibler.
♀ 6	...	...	Do. .	Viscount Edmond de Poncins.

EDMI or ATLAS GAZELLE (Gazella cuvieri).

From the dorcas the present species may be readily distinguished by its superior size, the imperfectly lyrate form of the horns, which diverge more or less regularly upwards, the presence of a black spot on the tip of the muzzle, and the rough character of the hair. General colour dull fawn, with a very indistinct lateral band, well-defined face-markings, the lower portion of the tail crested with black, and the under parts, buttocks, and inner surfaces of fore-legs pure white. Height at shoulder from 26 to 27 inches.

Distribution.—The mountains of Morocco, Algeria, and Tunisia, where it is known by the name of edmi or admi.

Length on front curve.	Circumference.	Tip to Tip.	Locality.	Owner.
14⅞	5	3⅝	Algeria	Sir Edmund G. Loder, Bart.
-14½	3⅞	3½	Do.	A. E. Pease.
14¼	3¾	5¼	Southern Sahara	J. J. S. Whitaker.
-14⅛	...	...	Algeria	A. E. Pease.
♀ 13⅞	3½	7⅛	Do.	E. N. Buxton.
-13⅝	4¼	5½	Do.	Viscount Edmond de Poncins.
-13½	4	½	Do.	A. E. Pease.
12¾	4⅜	3⅝	Do.	E. N. Buxton.
12⅜	3¾	5½	Do.	Rowland Ward.
12⅜	3½	5¼	Do.	Hon. R. A. Ward.
♀ 11	2½	5⅞	Do.	J. J. S. Whitaker.
- ♀ 9½	2¾	4	Do.	A. E. Pease.
♀ 8	2⅓	5½	Do.	Capt. G. J. Cuthbert.

ARABIAN GAZELLE (Gazella arabica).

Belonging to the same sub-group of the genus as the edmi, this elegant gazelle may be differentiated from that species by its smaller size, smoother hair, and darker coloration, the general tint of the upper parts being dark smoky fawn, with the central face-band rufous fawn, and a black spot on the tip of the muzzle. Height at shoulder, 24 or 25 inches.

Distribution.—Western Arabia, where it is known as ghasal, its Syrian title being ariel or aiel. In spite of its being one of the commonest of the gazelles, and also one which can easily be obtained in captivity, very little authentic information is forthcoming as to its habits, and even its range is not yet fully determined.

Length on front curve.	Circum- ference.	Tip to Tip.	Locality.	Owner.
8½	4	2	Mocha, South Arabia	W. T. Blanford, British Museum.
- ♀ 7½	2	4¾	?	Dr. Percy Rendall.
4⅞	3⅛	3⅝	South Arabia	Sir Victor Brooke's Collection.
♀ 4½	1¾	2½	?	Major H. G. C. Swayne.

Head of Indian Gazelle, from a specimen shot by Loftus M. le Champion.

INDIAN GAZELLE (Gazella bennetti).

Closely allied to the Arabian species, this gazelle (the chikara of the natives and the ravine-deer of many Anglo-Indian sportsmen) is of smaller dimensions and much lighter colour ; the height at the shoulder varying from 23 to 24 inches, and the general colour of the upper parts being dull fawn.

Distribution.—Peninsular India, thence extending westward through Baluchistan to the shores of the Persian Gulf. In the *Book of Antelopes* Messrs. Sclater and Thomas remark that, like the lion and the hunting-leopard, this gazelle belongs to an African type, and appears to have been originally a migrant from the west into India, whence it has spread over the greater part of the peninsula. It should, however, be remembered that extinct gazelles and hunting-leopards occur in the north of India.

Length on front curve.	Circumference.	Tip to Tip.	Locality.		Owner.
-15	5	...	Rajputana .	.	H.H. Maharaj Rana Bahadur of Jhalawar.
14½	4½	8⅝	?		L. M. le Champion. (See illustration.)
-14¼	...	...	Ferozepore District	.	Captain Harry V. Brooke.

INDIAN GAZELLE (Gazella bennetti)—*continued.*

Length on front curve.	Circumference.	Tip to Tip.	Locality.	Owner.
-14⅛	...	...	Sirsa District, Punjab	Captain H. Trevor.
14	4⅜	5¾	Ferozepore District .	Captain Harry V. Brooke.
-14	...	...	Near Lahore . .	Major-General Alexander A. A. Kinloch (measured by).
-13⅞	4¼	6½	Do. . .	C. P. Down.
13¾	4½	7	?	Sir Victor Brooke's Collection.
13¾	4⅜	8½	Sind	L. Napier.
13⅝	4⅜	7½	Bikanir . . .	C. F. Vander-Byl.
13¼	4	4¼	?	Sir Edmund G. Loder, Bart.
13¼	4	6¼	?	Major O. A. Chambers.
-13¼	4¼	...	Delhi . . .	Major-General Alexander A. A. Kinloch.
-13⅛	4½	4	Hissar . .	Captain P. J. Gordon.
13	3½	6	Bikanir . .	Major H. C. Morland.
-13	3$\frac{15}{16}$	3$\frac{15}{16}$	Gwalior . .	Viscount Edmond de Poncins.
-13	4¼	5	?	Major Colvin Stewart.
13	3¾	6	?	Major R. H. Rattray.
12¾	4¼	5	Goorgaon, Punjab .	A. O. Hume, C.B.
12¾	4⅜	7½	?	H. C. V. Hunter.
12¾	4¼	5⅞	North Punjab .	Colonel J. Biddulph.
12¾	4¼	7	?	Captain L. I. B. Hulke.
-12¾	4¾	6¾	Bikanir . . .	Captain H. W. Codrington.
-12¾	4	6	Jodhpore . .	H.H. Maharaja of Bikanir.
12½	4¼	5¼	Bikanir . . .	Lieut.-Col. G. D. F. Sulivan.
-12½	...	...	?	H.H. the Maharaja of Travancore, C.C.S.I.
12⅜	4	5½	Simrol, Bengal . .	Colonel John Evans, British Museum.
12⅜	4⅞	5⅝	Bikanir . . .	Lieut.-Col. G. D. F. Sulivan.
12⅜	4⅛	6	Do. . .	P. B. Vander-Byl.
-12⅜	4⅝	6⅜	Kythal, Punjab .	Captain M. M'Neill.
12¼	4⅜	5¼	Dholpur . .	A. J. Coppinger.
-12¼	4	7	Bikanir . .	Captain C. B. Vandeleur.
12	4	7½	Punjab . .	Captain A. Hicks-Beach.

INDIAN GAZELLE (Gazella bennetti)—*continued.*

Length on front curve.	Circumference.	Tip to Tip.	Locality.	Owner.
−12	...	...	Kathiawar	Lieut.-Col. L. L. Fenton.
12	...	...	Banda District	Indian Museum.
12	$4\frac{1}{2}$	...	Meerut, N.W. Provinces	C. Hastings-Wood.
12	$3\frac{5}{8}$	6	Khandesh	A. Cumine.
−12	$4\frac{1}{4}$	$6\frac{3}{8}$	Deccan	Vety.-Capt. G. H. Evans.
−12	$3\frac{3}{4}$	$7\frac{1}{4}$	Bikanir	H.H. Maharaja of Bikanir.
$11\frac{5}{8}$	4	$4\frac{3}{4}$	?	Do.
$11\frac{5}{8}$	4	$4\frac{1}{2}$	?	Sir Robert Harvey, Bart.
$11\frac{1}{2}$	$4\frac{1}{2}$	$5\frac{1}{4}$	Bikanir	Captain F. E. S. Adair.
$11\frac{3}{8}$	$3\frac{5}{8}$	$4\frac{8}{8}$	?	Captain N. C. Taylor.
$11\frac{1}{4}$	$4\frac{1}{4}$	5	Nagaon, Central Provinces	Colonel R. J. Heber-Percy.
$11\frac{1}{8}$	$4\frac{5}{8}$	$5\frac{3}{8}$	Etawah	Hume Collection, British Museum.
$11\frac{1}{8}$	$4\frac{1}{4}$	5	Jodhpore	Captain G. J. Fitzgerald.
11	4	$5\frac{1}{4}$	Bikanir	Captain C. F. Pinney.
11	$3\frac{3}{4}$	6	Berar	C. H. Seely.
♀ $7\frac{1}{8}$	$\frac{5}{8}$	$2\frac{1}{4}$	?	Sir Victor Brooke's Collection.
− ♀ $5\frac{1}{2}$	...	...	Banda District	Indian Museum.

Head of Female Speke's Gazelle.

SPEKE'S GAZELLE (Gazella spekei).

Dhero of the Somalis.

From the edmi and its allies, with which it agrees in its leading characteristics, this very peculiar gazelle is readily distinguished by the development of a flabby corrugated elevation on the skin of the nose ; the general colour of the upper parts being pale brownish fawn, with the lateral band darker than in the other members of the sub-group. Height at shoulder from 23 to 24 inches.

The protuberance on the nose is probably connected with the sexual function ; in dead specimens it exhibits a slight cavity beneath the skin which can be inflated by blowing air into the nostrils, and it is therefore probably capable of distension during life.

Distribution.—The plateau in the interior of Somaliland,

SPEKE'S GAZELLE (Gazella spekei)—*continued.*

Length on front curve.	Circum-ference.	Tip to Tip.	Locality.	Owner.
-12	$3\frac{3}{4}$	$5\frac{1}{4}$	Somaliland	Viscount Edmond de Poncins.
-12	...	...	Northern Somaliland	J. Menges.
$11\frac{3}{4}$	$3\frac{3}{4}$	$4\frac{5}{8}$	The Haud	Major H. G. C. Swayne.
$11\frac{5}{8}$	$3\frac{3}{4}$	$2\frac{1}{2}$	Do.	Col. A. Paget.
$11\frac{1}{2}$	$4\frac{3}{8}$	$2\frac{3}{4}$	Somaliland	T. W. H. Clarke.
$11\frac{1}{4}$	$3\frac{7}{8}$	$4\frac{5}{8}$	Do.	Viscount Edmond de Poncins.
$11\frac{1}{4}$	4	4	Do.	W. H. Cobb.
$11\frac{1}{8}$	4	$5\frac{1}{4}$	Do.	C. Liddell.
11	4	4	Do.	A. H. Straker.
11	$3\frac{7}{8}$	5	Do.	Major H. C. Morland.
11	$4\frac{1}{8}$	$3\frac{5}{8}$	Do.	Lord Delamere.
$10\frac{3}{4}$	$3\frac{1}{4}$	$3\frac{3}{4}$	Do.	Sir Edmund G. Loder, Bart.
$10\frac{3}{4}$	$4\frac{5}{8}$	$5\frac{1}{4}$	Do.	B. R. M. Glossop.
$10\frac{3}{4}$	4	4	Do.	R. M'D. Hawker.
$10\frac{3}{4}$	$3\frac{7}{8}$	3	Do.	C. N. Welsh.
$10\frac{3}{4}$	$3\frac{3}{4}$	$3\frac{3}{4}$	Do.	E. Lort-Phillips.
$10\frac{3}{4}$	4	$3\frac{3}{4}$	Do.	B. Vincent.
$10\frac{5}{8}$	$3\frac{7}{8}$	$4\frac{1}{4}$	Do.	Capt. G. F. T. Leather.
$-10\frac{1}{2}$	$4\frac{1}{8}$	$3\frac{1}{2}$	Do.	Count Scheibler.
$10\frac{1}{2}$	$3\frac{3}{4}$	$2\frac{1}{2}$	Do.	The late W. Babington.
$-10\frac{1}{2}$	$4\frac{5}{8}$	$3\frac{3}{4}$	Do.	J. Brander Dunbar.
$10\frac{1}{2}$	$3\frac{3}{4}$	4	Do.	Capt. G. Campbell.
$-10\frac{3}{8}$	$3\frac{7}{8}$	$4\frac{1}{2}$	Do.	Count E. Hoyos.
$10\frac{3}{8}$	$3\frac{7}{8}$	$4\frac{1}{8}$	Do.	Sir H. D. Tichborne, Bart.
$-10\frac{3}{8}$	$3\frac{3}{8}$	$3\frac{3}{4}$	Do.	P. H. G. Powell Cotton.
$10\frac{1}{4}$	4	$4\frac{1}{4}$	Do.	F. G. Gunnis.
$10\frac{1}{4}$	$3\frac{3}{4}$	$3\frac{3}{4}$	Do.	P. B. Vander-Byl.
$10\frac{1}{4}$	$3\frac{7}{8}$	4	Do.	H.R.H. le Duc d'Orléans.
$-10\frac{1}{4}$	...	...	Do.	C. V. A. Peel.
$-10\frac{1}{4}$	4	$4\frac{1}{4}$	Do.	J. Johnston-Stewart.

SPEKE'S GAZELLE (Gazella spekei)—*continued.*

Length on front curve.	Circumference.	Tip to Tip.	Locality.	Owner.
$10\frac{1}{8}$	$3\frac{7}{8}$	$4\frac{1}{2}$	Somaliland	Hon. Walter Rothschild.
$10\frac{1}{8}$	$3\frac{5}{8}$	$3\frac{1}{2}$	Do.	W. D. James.
10	$3\frac{1}{2}$	$4\frac{3}{8}$	Do.	Count J. de Bylands.
10	4	$4\frac{1}{4}$	Do.	A. E. Pease.
10	4	$5\frac{1}{4}$	Do.	Julius Jeppe.
10	$3\frac{3}{4}$	$2\frac{1}{4}$	Do.	Dr. Percy Rendall.
♀ $9\frac{7}{8}$	...	...	Do.	J. Menges.
♀ $9\frac{1}{2}$	$2\frac{7}{8}$	$3\frac{1}{4}$	Do.	T. W. H. Clarke.
♀ 9	$2\frac{1}{2}$	$5\frac{1}{4}$	Do.	Capt. G. F. T. Leather.
♀ 8	$2\frac{1}{2}$	4	Do.	B. R. M. Glossop.
♀ 8	$2\frac{1}{4}$	$3\frac{1}{4}$	Do.	J. Benett-Stanford.
♀ $7\frac{3}{4}$	2	$2\frac{1}{4}$	Do.	A. E. Pease.
♀ $7\frac{3}{4}$	...	..	Do.	C. V. A. Peel.

Head of Male Speke's Gazelle.

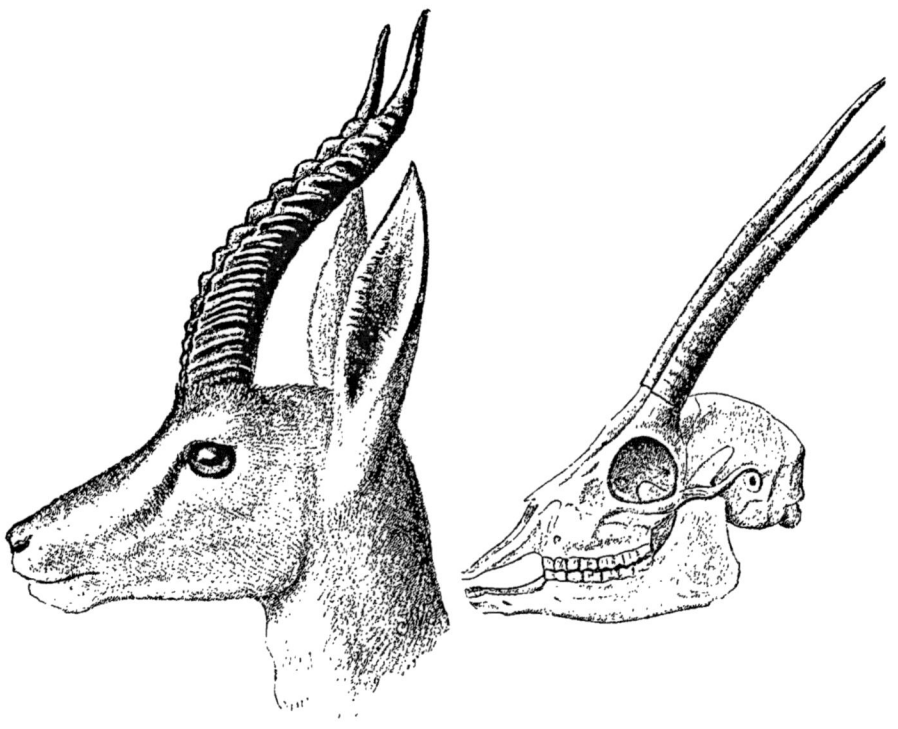

Head of Male and Skull of Female Pelzeln's Gazelle.

PELZELN'S GAZELLE (Gazella pelzelni).

This species, the lowland gazelle of Somaliland, is nearly related to the last, from which it differs by the absence both of the corrugated elevation on the nose and of the black spot on the muzzle. It is also slightly larger than Speke's gazelle, the height at the shoulder being about 25 inches ; and its colour is somewhat more rufous, the light lateral band being distinct, and the dark band rufous brown only somewhat darker than the back, without any tendency to blackness. The dark and light bands on the cheeks are relatively short and indistinct.

Distribution.—The plains of Northern Somaliland, bordering the sea. Within fifty miles of the shore this gazelle is exceedingly numerous, and may often be seen in large herds. It is termed by the natives dhero, in common with Speke's gazelle.

PELZELN'S GAZELLE (Gazella pelzelni)—*continued.*

Length on front curve.	Circumference.	Tip to Tip.	Locality.	Owner.
$-13\frac{3}{16}$	...	...	Northern Somaliland	J. Menges.
$12\frac{1}{4}$	$3\frac{3}{4}$	$4\frac{1}{4}$	Somaliland	Major H. G. C. Swayne.
$12\frac{1}{4}$	$4\frac{1}{8}$	$5\frac{1}{2}$	Do.	Lord Delamere.
$12\frac{1}{8}$	$3\frac{5}{8}$	$4\frac{1}{4}$	Do.	The late W. Babington.
-12	$3\frac{1}{8}$	$4\frac{3}{4}$	Do.	Count E. Hoyos.
12	$3\frac{3}{4}$	$4\frac{1}{8}$	Do.	Capt. G. Campbell.
12	$3\frac{3}{4}$	$5\frac{1}{4}$	Do.	Viscount Edmond de Poncins.
$11\frac{1}{2}$	$3\frac{1}{2}$	$5\frac{1}{2}$	Do.	T. W. H. Clarke.
$11\frac{1}{2}$	$3\frac{1}{2}$	$4\frac{1}{4}$	Do.	Major H. C. Morland.
$11\frac{1}{2}$	$3\frac{1}{2}$	5	Do.	Capt. W. H. Williamson.
$11\frac{1}{4}$	$4\frac{1}{8}$	$5\frac{1}{2}$	Do.	A. H. Straker.
$11\frac{1}{4}$	$3\frac{7}{8}$	$4\frac{3}{8}$	Do.	Rowland Ward.
$-11\frac{1}{4}$	$4\frac{1}{2}$	$5\frac{1}{2}$	Do.	S. Payne-Gallwey.
$-11\frac{1}{4}$	$3\frac{1}{4}$	$4\frac{1}{4}$	Do.	A. E. Pease.
$-11\frac{1}{4}$	4	$3\frac{1}{2}$	Do.	Sir Edmund G. Loder, Bart.
$-11\frac{1}{4}$	$3\frac{5}{8}$	5	Do.	J. Johnston-Stewart.
$11\frac{1}{8}$	$3\frac{5}{8}$	$4\frac{1}{4}$	Do.	Capt. G. F. T. Leather.
$11\frac{1}{8}$	$3\frac{3}{4}$	$3\frac{3}{4}$	Do.	Col. A. Paget.
$-11\frac{1}{8}$	4	5	Do.	J. Brander Dunbar.
11	$3\frac{3}{4}$	$4\frac{1}{8}$	Do.	A. S. Trevor.
11	$3\frac{3}{4}$	$3\frac{3}{8}$	Do.	Prince Boris Czetwertynski.
11	$3\frac{3}{4}$	$3\frac{3}{4}$	Do.	R. M'D. Hawker.
$10\frac{3}{4}$	$3\frac{3}{4}$	$4\frac{1}{8}$	Do.	Sir Edmund G. Loder, Bart.
$10\frac{5}{8}$	$3\frac{3}{4}$	$4\frac{1}{4}$	Do.	F. G. Gunnis.
$-10\frac{1}{2}$	$3\frac{1}{4}$	...	Do.	C. V. A. Peel.
$10\frac{3}{8}$	$3\frac{5}{8}$	$2\frac{7}{8}$	Do.	Julius Jeppe.
♀ $8\frac{5}{8}$	...	...	Do.	J. Menges.
$-$♀ $8\frac{1}{4}$	$2\frac{1}{2}$	...	Do.	C. V. A. Peel.
$-$♀ $8\frac{1}{8}$	...	...	Do.	J. Brander Dunbar.
♀ 8	$1\frac{7}{8}$	$3\frac{3}{4}$	Do.	Julius Jeppe.
♀ $7\frac{5}{8}$	$1\frac{3}{4}$	$2\frac{3}{4}$	Do.	T. W. H. Clarke.

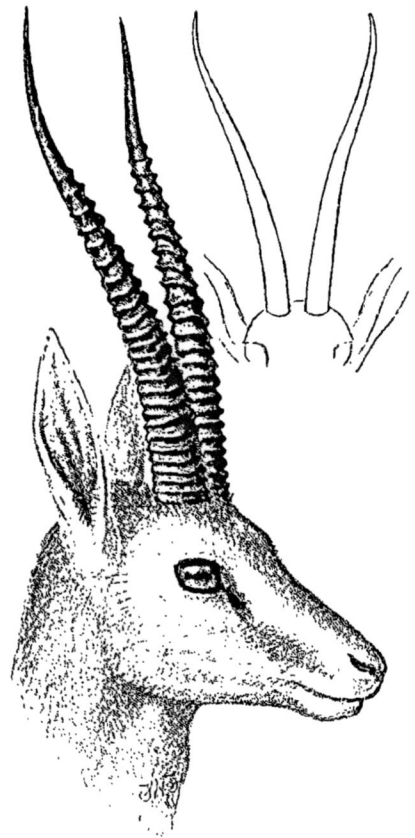

Head of Loder's Gazelle.

LODER'S GAZELLE (Gazella leptoceros).

Arab name, *Rhim.*

Although originally described as long ago as the year 1842, very little was known of this gazelle till specimens were procured by Sir E. G. Loder, and described as a new species under the name of *G. loderi.* Further investigation proved them to be inseparable from the species named by F. Cuvier. Agreeing with the preceding members of the group in the white of the rump not invading the haunches, the species is easily recognisable by the long and slender form of the horns, and the very pale tone of the coloration of the upper parts, which may be described as pale sandy fawn, with the characteristic gazelline markings only indistinctly defined. On the face the dark streaks are sandy instead of rufous; and the light bands on the flanks are almost imperceptible, while the dark ones below them are pale sandy with the very slightest tinge of brown; the tail being sandy at the base and gradually darkening to brownish-black towards the tip. In the male the horns are about twice the length of the head, very slender, and closely and heavily ridged almost to the tips. Height at shoulder about 28 inches. Weight, 34 lbs.

Distribution.—The sandy tracts of the interior of Algeria, Tunisia, and Western Egypt, thence extending southwards into Nubia and Sennar. The native name is rhem or rhim (reem).

Length on front curve.	Circumference.	Tip to Tip.	Locality.	Owner.
15 7/8	3 1/2	6 1/4	South of Biskra	Dr. Dawtrey Drewitt.
14 1/2	3 1/2	5 1/2	Do.	F. H. Barber.
14 7/10	3 7/8	4 3/4	Algeria	Julius Jeppe.
14 1/4	3 1/2	10 1/4	Do.	Sir Edmund G. Loder, Bart.
14 1/4	3 3/4	6 3/8	Southern Tunisia	J. J. S. Whitaker.
14	3 7/8	3	Algeria	Hon. R. A. Ward.
–14	3 5/8	5 1/4	Tue Erg	A. E. Pease.
14	3 3/4	4 3/4	Algeria	Mr. Justice Hopley.
13 5/8	3 5/8	5 1/2	Do.	W. E. Pease.
13 1/2	3 3/4	8 3/4	Southern Tunisia	Sir Edmund G. Loder, Bart.
–13 3/8	...	...	Do.	A. E. Pease.
–13 3/8	...	...	Do.	J. Menges.
–13 1/4	3 3/4	3 3/4	Sahara	Viscount Edmond de Poncins.
13 1/4	3 1/2	4 3/4	Do.	Rowland Ward.
13 1/4	3 1/2	5 3/4	Southern Tunisia	J. J. S. Whitaker.
13 1/8	3 3/4	4 1/8	Algeria	J. H. Thomas.
–12 1/2	3 3/4	6 1/2	Do.	Julius Jeppe.
–12 1/4	3 1/2	5 1/2	Tue Erg	A. E. Pease.
12 1/8	3 7/8	4 3/4	Algeria	Hon. Walter Rothschild.
♀ –11 5/8	...	...	Southern Tunisia	J. Menges.
♀ 10 1/4	2 1/8	3 1/2	South of Atlas Mts.	Lord Grantley.
♀ 9 5/8	2 1/8	3 7/8	Algeria	F. H. Barber.
♀ 9 1/8	1 7/8	3 1/4	Do.	Hon. Walter Rothschild.
♀ 9 1/8	2 1/8	2 3/4	Tunisia	Do.
♀ 9	2 1/4	1 3/4	Southern Tunisia	J. J. S. Whitaker.

ISABELLA GAZELLE (Gazella isabella).

In all the foregoing gazelles with horns in both sexes, the horns themselves have their tips slightly curved either inwards or upwards, and never bent back so as to form a right angle with the basal portion. On the other hand, the present species and the Muscat gazelle (*G. muscatensis*), while resembling the foregoing in the shape of the white rump-patch and the comparatively light tint of the flank-band, differ by the tips of the horns being hooked inwards or upwards so as to form nearly or completely a right angle. From its ally the present species differs by the pale fawn colour of the upper parts ; the lateral bands and other markings being also fawn, instead of blackish. Height at shoulder about 25 inches.

Distribution.—The Red Sea littoral from Suakin to Massowa, and through the interior to Bogosland, Barca, and Taka.

Length on front curve.	Circumference.	Tip to Tip.	Locality.	Owner.
10¼	3¾	2¾	Anseba River, Abyssinia	Sir Victor Brooke's Collection.
10⅛	3¾	4	Komayli, Abyssinia .	W. T. Blanford, British Museum.
9¾	3¾	2⅜	Bogosland . .	Sir Victor Brooke's Collection.
–9.14	4	3	Between Suakin and Kassala	Prince Henry of Liechtenstein.
9.11	...	...	Do.	Do.
–8.14	4.2	3.12	Do.	Do.
♀ 7	2	3	Do.	Sir Victor Brooke's Collection.
♀ 7	1⅞	2⅜	Kordofan .	British Museum.

HEUGLIN'S GAZELLE (Gazella tilonura).

This well-marked species brings us to a small sub-group in which the dark band on the flanks is very strongly defined, and black in colour; the present species being distinguished from its allies by the abrupt inward hooking of the tips of the horns. The general colour is deep sandy, with the central face-band but little darker than the back, no black nose-spot, and the tail sandy at the base but black elsewhere. Height at shoulder about 27 inches.

Distribution.—Bogosland, in North-Eastern Africa. Very little is known of this rare species.

Length on front curve.	Circumference.	Tip to Tip.	Locality.	Owner.
11 1/4	4	2 1/3	Sudan . . .	Lieut.-Col. Hon. W. Coke.
10 3/4	3 3/4	4 1/2	?	E. Lort-Phillips.
10 3/4	4	2 1/8	Bogosland, Abyssinia	British Museum.
10 1/4	4 1/8	3 3/4	Do.	Do.
10 1/4	4 1/8	2 7/8	North Africa .	Col. Ralph Vivian.
9 7/8	4 3/8	1 7/8	Bogosland, Abyssinia	Sir Victor Brooke's Collection.
-9 1/16	...	...	Eastern Sudan .	J. Menges.
9 7/8	...	1 1/2	Anseba River, Abyssinia	Sir Victor Brooke's Collection.
9 3/4	3 3/4	3 1/2	North Africa	Col. Ralph Vivian.
9 1/2	4 1/4	1 3/4	Do. .	Do.
8 1/4	3 3/8	2 1/2	?	Lieut. E. Lacy, R.N.
7 3/4	3 7/8	1 5/8	Bogosland, Abyssinia	British Museum.
♀ -6 1/2	...	...	Eastern Sudan .	J. Menges.
♀ 5 1/8	1 3/4	1 3/4	Abyssinia .	Sir Victor Brooke's Collection.

SENEGAL or RED-FRONTED GAZELLE (Gazella rufifrons).

This medium-sized and rather stoutly built species agrees with Heuglin's gazelle in the black flank-stripe, but differs by the absence of a distinct inward hooking of the tips of the horns; the general colour being deep sandy rufous, brightening into rich rufous on the forehead and muzzle, without a black nose-spot. The knee-tufts so generally present in gazelles are wanting; and the tail, with the exception of the sandy upper surface of the basal portion, is black. Horns relatively small, regularly divergent, curving at first slightly backwards and then forwards, heavily ridged till the terminal two or three inches.

Distribution.—Senegal and Gambia.

Length on front curve.	Circumference.	Tip to Tip.	Locality.	Owner.
10½	4⅝	6⅞	Senegal . . .	Sir Victor Brooke's Collection.
♀ 6¼	2⅛	2¾	Do. . . .	British Museum.

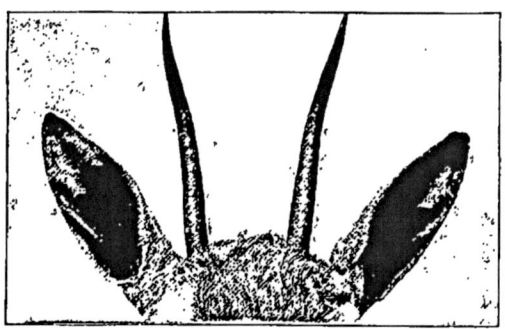

Horns and Ears of Female Thomson's Gazelle.

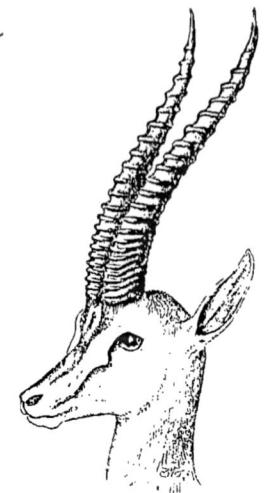

Head of Male Thomson's Gazelle

THOMSON'S GAZELLE (Gazella thomsoni).

Swahili name, *Swallah.*

The distinct black nose-patch and the great width of the black flank-band serve at once to distinguish this handsome species from *G. rufifrons*, with which it agrees in the general form of the horns. The general colour of the upper parts is deep sandy rufous, with all the markings well developed and sharply defined ; the central face-streak being a deeper rufous, and the light lateral band present, although only slightly paler than the back. There is also a narrow black band bordering the white on the sides of the rump; and knee-tufts are developed. The horns are long, and rather like those of the Indian gazelle on an enlarged scale. Height at shoulder about 25 inches.

Distribution.—The interior districts of British and German East Africa, from Lake Rudolph southwards to Irangi. Discovered by Joseph Thomson during his expedition to the Victoria Nyanza in 1883-84, and named by Dr. Günther in the latter year.

Measurements of 4 males and 1 female shot by F. J. Jackson, C.B.

	ft.	in.	ft.	in.	ft.	in.	ft.	in.	ft.	in.
Length	3	10	4	1	3	11½	4	4	3	8½
Height	2	1	2	3	2	1½	2	2	1	11½
Weight	52 lbs.		54 lbs.		56 lbs.		62 lbs.		32 lbs.	

R

THOMSON'S GAZELLE (Gazella thomsoni)—*continued.*

Length on front curve.	Circumference.	Tip to Tip.	Locality.	Owner.
15½	4¾	3¾	Masailand	F. J. Jackson, C.B.
15½	4½	8½	Do.	E. Gedge.
15¼	4¾	4⅜	Do.	F. J. Jackson, C.B., British Museum
15¼	4½	4⅛	East Africa	Major A. E. Smith.
15⅛	4⅞	5⅞	Do.	Lord Basil Blackwood.
–14⅞	3⅞	3¾	Do.	Julius Jeppe.
14⅞	4½	4½	Do.	Col. Trevor Ternan.
14¾	4¾	4½	Do.	Lord Delamere.
14½	4	3¼	Do.	Sir Edmund G. Loder, Bart.
–14½	4½	2½	Do.	Count Scheibler.
–14½	4¾	5¾	Do.	T. E. Buckley.
14½	4½	4¾	Masailand	J. Gardiner Muir.
14⅜	4¼	3⅛	East Africa	Sir Robert Harvey, Bart.
14¼	4¼	5⅞	Masailand	H. C. V. Hunter, British Museum.
14¼	4½	5	East Africa	Col. Trevor Ternan.
14	4½	4¾	Do.	Henry Charrington.
14	4¼	3	Do.	S. L. Hinde.
13¾	4½	4¾	Do.	Col. F. D. Lugard, C.B., D.S.O.
–13¾	4⅜	3⅝	Do.	Mr. Justice Hopley.
13½	4½	5	Lake Naivasha	J. Ponsonby.
13⅜	4⅝	4¼	Do.	Sir Robert Harvey, Bart.
13⅜	4½	5⅜	Do.	Hon. Walter Rothschild.
–13¼	3¾	7⅛	East Africa	Julius Jeppe.
–13¼	3½	5½	Do.	A. Ohlsson.
13¼	4¾	4¾	Lorogi District	A. H. Neumann.
13¼	4	5	East Africa	E. J. L. Berkeley.
13⅛	4¾	5½	Do.	Capt. J. W. Pringle.
13	4½	4	Do.	W. Astor Chanler.
13	4½	6	Do.	J. Gardiner Muir.
13	4⅛	4½	Do.	G. E. Smith.
–12·12	4	3·13	Do.	Prince Henry of Liechtenstein.
♀ 5½	1⅝	3⅛	Lake Naivasha	F. J. Jackson, C.B.

Skulls and Horns of Grant's Gazelle (male and female), from A. H. Neumann's specimens.

GRANT'S GAZELLE (Gazella granti).

With this handsome species we reach the last group of the genus *Gazella*, which includes species, for the most part of large size, characterised by the fawn colour of the back being invaded to a greater or less degree by the white of the rump. In the present animal the fawn of the back is cut off from the tail, which is included in the white rump-patch, and there is a dark streak on the hinder border of each side of this patch. On the neck and back the hair has a peculiar wavy appearance recalling that of watered silk. Height at shoulder about 38 inches; weight of male from 150 to 170 lbs., when cleaned about 115 lbs.

Distribution.—East Africa, throughout Masailand, and round Kilimanjaro, north of Baringo, and around Mount Elgon and the Suk country; generally on open grass-lands. Two well-defined local races of this species may be recognised. First, the typical race (*G. granti typica*), of the interior of East Africa, in which the dark flank-bands are either wanting, or are present in young specimens below the light flank-band. Secondly, the northern race (*G. granti notata*), of Northern British East Africa, in which dark bands are present both above and below the light band, behind which they unite with each other. Although described by O. Thomas in 1897 as a local race, the latter form was raised by him to the rank of a distinct species in the following year.

F. J. Jackson says they are found "throughout the Masai country, up in Turkwel and Suk country. Those from Njemps, Turkwel and Suk are smaller than those from Kilimanjaro, Naivasha, Athi plains, etc. In the Njemp district a 20-inch head is good."

Measurements of 4 male specimens shot by the last-named sportsman.

		ft.	in.	ft.	in.	ft.	in.	ft.	in.
Length	. .	5	8	5	7	5	7	5	3^1
Height		3	$1\frac{1}{2}$	3	$2\frac{1}{2}$	3	$6\frac{1}{2}$	2	11
Horns			$28\frac{1}{4}$		27		24		20
Weight	.		158 lbs.		167 lbs.		166 lbs.		135 lbs.
Habitat	.		Lake Naivasha,		Lake Naivasha,		Lake Naivasha,		Njemp.

Length on front curve.	Circumference.	Tip to Tip.	Locality.	Owner.
$28\frac{1}{4}$	$6\frac{5}{8}$	$15\frac{1}{4}$	East Africa .	F. J. Jackson, C.B.
$27\frac{7}{8}$	$6\frac{5}{8}$	$18\frac{3}{8}$	Do.	H. C. V. Hunter.
$27\frac{1}{2}$	$6\frac{1}{2}$	16	Do. .	F. J. Jackson, C.B.
$27\frac{1}{4}$	$6\frac{1}{2}$	$18\frac{7}{8}$	Do. . .	Sir Robert Harvey, Bart.
27	...	16	Do. . . .	Sir John Willoughby, Bart.
$26\frac{3}{4}$	$6\frac{1}{4}$	$13\frac{1}{2}$	Shores of Lake Naivasha . .	A. H. Neumann.
$26\frac{1}{2}$	$7\frac{1}{4}$	18	East Africa .	Major A. E. Smith.
$26\frac{1}{4}$	$6\frac{3}{8}$	$16\frac{3}{4}$	Do. .	Sir Victor Brooke's Collection.
26	$6\frac{1}{2}$	$10\frac{3}{4}$	N.E. of Lake Rudolph	A. H. Neumann.
$25\frac{3}{4}$	$6\frac{3}{4}$	15	E. Africa	Lord Delamere.
$25\frac{3}{4}$	6	17	Do. . .	J. Gardiner Muir.
$25\frac{1}{2}$	$6\frac{1}{4}$	15	Do. . . .	Lord Delamere.

[1] This was the old buck of a herd in which there were three or four other bucks. It was in good condition. I saw a lot of other bucks, but none had horns more than 20 inches.

GRANT'S GAZELLE (Gazella granti)—*continued.*

Length on front curve.	Circumference.	Tip to Tip.	Locality.	Owner.
25⅛	6½	15⅜	E. Africa . .	Capt. R. A. J. Montgomerie, C.B., R.N.
-25.11	6.8	13.14	Do. . . .	Prince Henry of Liechtenstein.
-25.10	6.1	15.14	Do. . . .	Do.
25	6⅝	12¾	Nakuru Lake, E. Africa .	G. E. Smith.
25	6½	14	Kilimanjaro . .	T. W. Greenfield.
24¾	6¾	12½	East Africa . .	S. L. Hinde.
24.13	6.14	14.10	Do. . .	Prince Henry of Liechtenstein.
24½	6¾	13½	Do. .	E. J. L. Berkeley.
24½	7⅜	14	Do. . .	Sir Edmund G. Loder, Bart.
24¼	6½	11¾	N.E. of Lake Rudolph .	Hon. Walter Rothschild.
24	7¼	8¼	East Africa	Henry Charrington.
23¼	6⅝	13⅝	Do. .	Capt. E. J. Tickell.
23¼	6½	13	Do. . .	Major W. H. Williams.
23	6½	13⅜	Do. . . .	Col. F. D. Lugard, C.B., D.S.O.
23	7¼	9	Do. . .	E. Gedge.
-23	6¼	9⅓	Do. . . .	Julius Jeppe.
♀ 17½	3¾	9	Do. . .	H. C. V. Hunter.
♀ 17	...	6	Lake Jipé . .	Sir John Willoughby, Bart.
♀ 16½	3½	4⅝	E. Africa . . .	Lord Delamere.
♀ 15	4	6¾	Do. . .	E. Gedge.

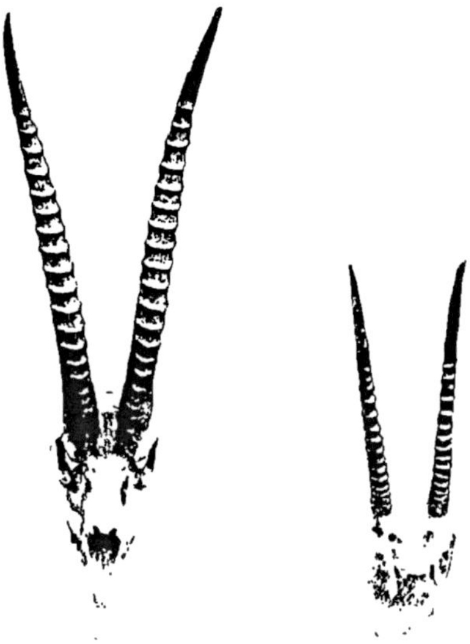

Skulls and Horns of Peters's Gazelle (male and female), from A. H. Neumann's specimens.

PETERS'S GAZELLE (Gazella petersi).

This species belongs to the same group as Grant's gazelle and the aoul, showing the same extension of the white of the rump on to the back. It has a dark band separating the white of the rump from the fawn of the back, and differs from the other species showing the same feature by the fawn colour of the back being continued in the middle line on to the base of the tail, which is otherwise black. Height at shoulder about 26 inches.

Distribution.—Coast districts of East Africa.

Length on front curve.	Circumference.	Tip to Tip.	Locality.	Owner.
22⅛	6⅜	5⅞	Shererini	F. J. Jackson, C.B., British Museum.
21¾	5½	8¼	Pica Pica, B.E.A. . .	L. E. Caine, British Museum.
20¼	6⅛	8⅞	Ndura	C. Steuart Betton.
19	6	5¼	Taru Desert . . .	Lieut. G. H. Welch, R.N.
17¾	5¼	7⅝	Near Pica Pica . .	A. H. Neumann.
♀ 10⅝	3	4¼	Do. . .	Do.

Head of Sœmmerring's Gazelle, from a specimen shot by G. H. Cheetham.

SŒMMERRING'S GAZELLE (Gazella sœmmerringi).

Somali name, *Aoul.*　　　　　Abyssinian name, *Meidafihel.*
Abyssinian (Danakil) name, *Maëdedo.*

In addition to the forward extent of the white rump-patch, the leading characteristics of this splendid species are to be found in the absence of a black streak dividing the sides of the rump-patch from the fawn of the body, the black-tipped tail, and the very distinct inward hooking of the horns. The ears are long and bordered with black externally, and the face markings well-defined and nearly black. Height at shoulder about 30 to 36 inches. Weight clean about 70 to 90 lbs.

Distribution.—The Abyssinian coast of the Red Sea, Berber, East Sennar, Danakil, and Somaliland; in the latter country occurring all over the Haud and Ogaden.

a. Gazella sœmmerringi berberana.

Length on front curve.	Circumference.	Tip to Tip.	Locality.	Owner.
20¾	5¾	3⅝	Somaliland	G. H. Cheetham.
-20¼	...	...	Do.	Norman B. Smith.
20	5¾	4	Do.	Lieut.-Col. J. W. H. Flanagan.
20	5¼	5½	Danakil	Viscount Edmond de Poncins.
♀ -20	...	5¾	Somaliland	A. E. Pease.
-20	5⅞	6½	Do.	Capt. M. M'Neill.
19¾	5⅝	5¼	Do.	Count J. de Bylands.
-19¾	5⅛	5⅜	The Haud	P. H. G. Powell-Cotton.
-19$\frac{11}{16}$	...	...	N. Somaliland	J. Menges.
19½	5½	5⅝	Somaliland	T. W. H. Clarke.
19½	5$\frac{9}{10}$	2	Do.	Sir Edmund G. Loder, Bart.
19½	5½	4¾	Do.	J. J. Richardson.
-19½	6¼	3	Do.	S. Payne-Gallwey.
-19½	5½	4⅝	Do.	Count J. Potocki.
19¼	6½	4¾	Do.	R. McD. Hawker.
19¼	5½	6½	Do.	T. W. H. Clarke.
19¼	5¼	4½	Do.	Capt. B. L. Carew.
19¼	5½	...	Do.	Surgeon-Major J. S. Edye.
19	5	4	Do.	Col. A. Paget.
19	5¼	4¾	Do.	J. Benett-Stanford.
19	5	7½	Do.	B. R. M. Glossop.
19	5½	5½	Do.	Ford G. Barclay.
19	5	4	Do.	Capt. F. C. Quicke.
-19	4	3¼	Do.	Prince Nicolas Ghika.
-19	5¾	8	Do.	J. Brander Dunbar.
-19	...	4¾	Do.	J. D. Inverarity.
-19	5¾	5⅜	Do.	Mr. Justice Hopley.

SŒMMERRING'S GAZELLE (Gazella sœmmerringi berberana)—*continued.*

Length on front curve.	Circumference.	Tip to Tip.	Locality.	Owner.
18¾	5½	6	Somaliland	F. H. Barber.
18⅝	5⅛	5½	Do.	Capt. G. R. Cuningham.
18½	5½	7⅝	Do.	Capt. G. Campbell.
18½	5½	4½	Do.	A. H. Straker.
18½	5½	5	Do.	P. B. Vander-Byl.
18½	5	5¾	Do.	A. Leslie Renton.
18⅜	5⅛	5	Do.	Sir H. Tichborne, Bart.
–18⅜	5	5½	Do.	J. Johnston-Stewart.
♀ 18¼	...	6	Do.	T. W. H. Clarke.
18⅛	5⅜	4½	Do.	W. D. James.
18	5½	4¾	Do.	J. Kenneth Foster.
18	5	7⅜	Do.	Major H. C. Morland.
18	5½	4	Do.	T. W. Greenfield.
18	5¼	5¾	Do.	R. Wahrmann.
18	5	6½	Do.	P. R. Denny.
–18	...	4½	Do.	A. E. Pease.
18	5⅜	7¼	Do.	W. W. Ashley.
♀ 18	3½	8½	Danakil	Viscount Edmond de Poncins.
17⅞	5	5¼	Somaliland	W. W. Ashley.
–17¾	5½	1⅝	Do.	Count Scheibler.
17¾	5⅝	4	Do.	Major C. C. Ellis.
–17¾	4⅞	3¼	Do.	Julius Jeppe.
–17¾	6	...	Do.	C. V. A. Peel.
17⅝	5	4⅞	Do.	Prince Boris Czetwertynski.
–17⅝	5	3¾	Do.	A. E. Leatham.
17½	5½	6	Do.	Capt. C. S. Timins.
17½	5½	5¾	Do.	J. Byng Paget.
17½	5¼	6¾	Do.	W. R. Bindloss.
17½	5¼	7¾	Do.	Digby Davies.
–17½	5¾	4¾	Do.	A. Ohlsson.

SŒMMERRING'S GAZELLE (Gazella sœmmerringi berberana)—*continued.*

Length on front curve.	Circumference.	Tip to Tip.	Locality.	Owner.
$17\frac{3}{8}$	6	4	Somaliland	Lord Wolverton.
$-17\frac{3}{8}$	$4\frac{5}{8}$	$4\frac{3}{8}$	Do.	Count E. Hoyos.
− ♀ $17\frac{1}{4}$	...	...	Danakil	Prince de Lucinge.
♀ $16\frac{3}{4}$	$3\frac{1}{2}$	$6\frac{1}{4}$	Somaliland	H.R.H. le Duc d'Orléans.
♀ 16	$3\frac{1}{8}$	6	Do.	Major H. G. C. Swayne.
♀ 16	$3\frac{1}{4}$	$10\frac{1}{2}$	Do.	R. Wahrmann.
		b. **Gazella sœmmerringi typica.**		
$15\frac{1}{2}$	$5\frac{3}{8}$	5	Sudan	Col. Ralph Vivian.
♀ $15\frac{1}{4}$	$2\frac{7}{8}$	$7\frac{3}{8}$	Do.	Lieut.-Col. Hon. W. Coke.
$14\frac{3}{4}$	$5\frac{1}{2}$	$4\frac{1}{4}$	Near Suakin	B. Cotton.
$14\frac{1}{2}$	$5\frac{1}{8}$	$5\frac{1}{2}$	Eastern Sudan	Major W. H. Besant.
14	$5\frac{1}{8}$	$5\frac{3}{4}$	Sudan	Lieut.-Col. Hon. W. Coke.
14	$5\frac{1}{2}$	$5\frac{1}{2}$	Do.	Col. A. Paget.
−14	5.12	3.13	?	Prince Henry of Liechtenstein.
−14	5.2	3.1	?	Do.
$13\frac{3}{4}$	$5\frac{1}{2}$	6	Sudan	W. D. James.
$13\frac{1}{2}$	$5\frac{1}{2}$	4	Do.	Sir Victor Brooke's Collection.
$13\frac{1}{2}$	$5\frac{3}{8}$	$5\frac{5}{8}$	Suakin	Hon. Walter Rothschild.
$12\frac{3}{4}$	5	5	Abyssinia	Sir Edmund G. Loder, Bart.
♀ $12\frac{5}{8}$	$3\frac{1}{2}$	$8\frac{1}{4}$	Sudan	Col. Ralph Vivian.
♀ 12	$3\frac{1}{4}$	$5\frac{1}{8}$	Abyssinia	Sir Victor Brooke's Collection.
♀ $8\frac{1}{2}$	$3\frac{3}{4}$	5	Sudan	Hon. Walter Rothschild.

ADDRA GAZELLE (Gazella ruficollis).

The last three representatives of the genus *Gazella* are not only th largest of the tribe, but are distinguished from all their relatives by th white of the rump extending on to the tail (which is either whol white or merely tipped with fawn) coupled with the complete absen of a black band between the white of the rump-patch and the fawn the body; the horns being hooked upwards and forwards, and n distinctly inwards. In the present species, which measures about 36 inches at the shoulder, the neck and front portion of the back alone display a distinctly rufous tint, the lines of division between the fawn of the upper parts and the white beneath being obscure.

Distribution.—Kordofan and Sennar.

Length on front curve.	Circumference.	Tip to Tip.	Locality.	Owner.
12¼	4	5⅝	Sennar . .	British Museum.
11⅞	5⅝	⅝	Kordofan .	Do.

DAMA GAZELLE (Gazella dama).

Together with its northern representative the mhorr of Morocco, the dama differs from the aoul by the rufous tint extending completely over the body and flanks, and being well defined from the white of the under parts. In the present form, which is from Senegal, the sides of the thighs are white, so that the rufous of the body is cut off from that of the hind-legs. The height is at least 35 inches.

Length on front curve.	Circumference.	Tip to Tip.	Locality.	Owner.
–12⅝	5⅛	5½	?	Paris Museum.
12½	5½	6	?	Mr. Justice Hopley.
–12¼	5 15/16	3 9/16	Senegambia .	Paris Museum.
8½	3½	5⅜	?	Hon. Walter Rothschild.

MHORR or SWIFT GAZELLE (Gazella dama mhorr).

Although commonly regarded as a distinct species, this fine but somewhat leggy gazelle seems to be only a northern race of the dama gazelle of Senegal, which is the largest member of the genus. The mhorr, as it is called by the Arabs, differs from the dama by the sides of the thighs and legs being of the same rufous hue as the body, instead of white. Height at shoulder at least 34½ inches.

Distribution.—The desert districts of South-West Morocco.

Length on front curve.	Circumference.	Tip to Tip.	Locality.	Owner.
11¾	6	3¾	Wednoon, Mogador	W. Willshire, British Museum.
–4 13/16	3 11/16	2½	Morocco . .	Dr. Percy Rendall.

Skull and Horns of Dibatag, from a specimen shot by T. W. H. Clarke in Somaliland.

DIBATAG or CLARKE'S GAZELLE (Ammodorcas clarkei).

Although resembling the true gazelles in the face-markings, the dibatag, as it is called by the Somalis, is so different from these animals as to be entitled to constitute a genus by itself; being in many respects intermediate between the former and the gerenuk. The horns, which are present only in the males, are rather short, and have a regular upward and forward curvature, somewhat like those of a reed-buck; they are ridged on the front for a considerable portion of their length. The neck is considerably elongated, and the tail long and thin. The general colour of the upper parts is a deep cinnamon. Height at shoulder about 33 inches; weight from 65 to 70 lbs. When running, the long neck is thrown back towards the tail, which is elevated, so that the two look as though they would touch. Discovered by T. W. H. Clarke.

Distribution.—Central Somaliland, in the eastern districts of the Haud.

DIBATAG or CLARKE'S GAZELLE (Ammodorcas clarkei)—*continued.*

ıgth front rve.	Circumference.	Tip to Tip.	Locality.	Owner.
13	...	...	Somaliland . .	J. D. Inverarity.
13	...	...	Do. .	J. Menges.
12 5/8	5 1/4	4 5/8	Do. . .	Hon. Walter Rothschild.
11 3/4	4 7/8	3 5/8	Do.	Col. Arthur Paget.
11 3/4	4 3/4	3 5/8	Do. . .	T. W. H. Clarke.
11 3/4	4 1/4	5	Do.	J. Brander Dunbar.
11 1/4	4 1/4	6	Do. .	R. McD. Hawker.
11	4 1/2	5 5/8	Do. . . .	Capt. F. C. Quicke.
11	5 1/2	2 1/4	Do. . .	B. R. M. Glossop.
11	5	5 1/2	Do. . .	S. Payne-Gallwey.
10 3/4	4 1/4	4 3/4	Do, . . .	Mr. Justice Hopley.
10 3/4	5 1/2	4	Do. . . .	Sir Edmund G. Loder, Bart.
10 1/2	4 1/2	4 1/2	Do. . . .	A. E. Pease.
10 1/4	4 1/4	4 7/8	Eidegalla, Haud .	J. Johnston-Stewart.
10 1/4	4 1/2	4 1/2	Somaliland .	C. V. A. Peel.
10 1/8	4 1/4	4 7/8	Somaliland . .	Rowland Ward.
10 1/8	4 1/8	4 1/2	West of Hargeisa . .	P. H. G. Powell-Cotton.
10	4 1/3	4 1/2	Somaliland . .	C. V. A. Peel.
10	4 1/2	4	Do. . .	Count J. de Bylands.
10	4 1/4	4 1/8	?	Julius Jeppe.
9 3/4	4 1/2	5 1/8	Somaliland . .	T. W. H. Clarke, British Museum.
9 3/4	4 1/2	4 3/4	Do. . .	Major H. G. C. Swayne.
9 1/2	4 1/3	4 3/4	Do.	B. Vincent.
-9 5/16	4 1/8	4 15/16	Dalbahanta Country .	Dr. Percy Rendall.
-9 1/4	4 1/2	4 1/3	?	A. Ohlsson.
9	3 1/2	3 3/8	Dalbahanta Country .	A. S. Trevor.
9	4 1/2	4 5/8	Do. . . .	Lord Delamere.
8 3/8	4 5/8	4 1/2	Do. . .	W. H. Cobb.
8 5/8	4	4 3/4	Do. .	T. W. Greenfield.

DIBATAG or CLARKE'S GAZELLE (Ammodorcas clarkei)—*continued.*

Length on front curve.	Circumference.	Tip to Tip.	Locality.	Owner.
8½	4	3	Dalbahanta Country .	Count Grudzinski.
8	4	3¾	Do. . . .	H. R. H. le Duc d'Orléans.
7¾	4	4½	Do. . .	Ford G. Barclay.

Head of Male Dibatag.

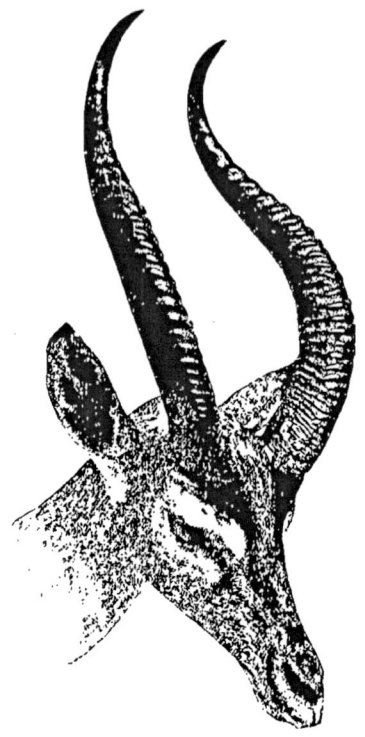

Head of Male Gerenuk, from a specimen shot by H.R.H. le Duc d'Orléans.

GERENUK or WALLER'S GAZELLE (Lithocranius walleri).

Somali name, *Gerenuk*.   Danakil name, *Gudan Godu*.

Even more aberrant than the last is the gerenuk, in which the elongation of the neck attains its supreme development, while the slender legs are lengthened in proportion.   Horns are wanting in the females, and those of the males curve forwards at the tips, where the ridges stop, in a peculiarly characteristic manner.   The general colour of the upper parts is a deep rufous fawn, but down the middle of the back runs a broad dark-brown band, nearly eight inches in width. The skull is characterised by its dense and solid structure, as well as by its straightness, the shortness of the facial portion, and the very small size of the cheek-teeth. ↖ Height at shoulder, 41 inches ; weight, 115 lbs. (T. W. H. Clarke).

This curious antelope, which was first described by the late Sir V.

Brooke on the evidence of a flat skin, is reported to rear itself on its hind-legs when browsing, and is thus enabled to reach boughs at a very considerable distance above the ground.

The horns of the specimens from Somaliland are, as a rule, very much longer than those from British East Africa, as will be seen by reference to the list below.

Length on front curve.	Circumference.	Tip to Tip.	Locality.	Owner.
17	5¼	3¾	Somaliland	H.R.H. le Duc d'Orléans. (See illustration.)
–16¾	...	...	Do.	Lieut.-Col. H. G. Mainwaring.
–16½	5¾	3⅝	Do.	E. L. Cappel.
16½	5½	1⅝	Do.	Mr. Justice Hopley.
–16¼	5½	2⅞	Do.	The late J. Rose.
–16⅛	...	...	Northern Somaliland	J. Menges.
16	5¾	6	Do.	Sir Edmund G. Loder, Bart.
15¾	6	4¾	Do.	Rowland Ward.
–15¾	6	2¾	Do.	A. E. Pease.
15½	5½	3	Do.	J. Kenneth Foster.
–15½	5⅞	4⅞	Do.	F. H. Barber.
15⅜	5⅝	4	Do.	Major H. G. C. Swayne.
15⅜	5⅜	4⅛	Do.	C. Liddell.
15⅜	5⅜	4¾	Do.	Lord Wolverton.
–15¼	5½	1⅝	Do.	J. Johnston-Stewart.
15	5⅜	6⅜	Do.	F. G. Gunnis.
15	5	4¾	Do.	Capt. J. M'Call Maxwell.
–15	6	...	Do.	Lieut.-Col. J. W. H. Flanagan.
–15	5	4	Do.	Sir H. B. Meux, Bart.
–14 15/16	5½	7¼	Do.	H.R.H. le Duc d'Orléans, Paris Museum.
14¾	5⅛	4¾	Do.	Lord Delamere.
14¾	5¼	3¾	Do.	J. J. Richardson.
14½	5	5	Do.	Count J. de Bylands.
–14½	5¼	7⅛	Do.	Count Scheibler.
–14½	4¾	4	Do.	Count E. Hoyos.
14⅜	6½	4½	Do.	Capt. F. C. Quicke.

GERENUK or WALLER'S GAZELLE (Lithocranius walleri)—*continued.*

Length on front curve.	Circumference.	Tip to Tip.	Locality.	Owner.
14¼	5¾	4½	Northern Somaliland	A. Leslie Renton.
14¼	5¼	3½	Do.	W. W. Ashley.
14	...	3	East Africa	Sir John Willoughby, Bart.
14	6¾	4½	Somaliland	W. H. Cobb.
14	5	3⅛	Do.	Col. A. Paget.
14	5¾	6¼	Do.	P. B. Vander-Byl.
14	5½	4¾	Do.	Ford G. Barclay.
14	5¼	5½	Do.	Viscount Edmond de Poncins.
−14	6	5	Do.	S. Payne-Gallwey.
−14	5¼	4	Do.	P. H. G. Powell-Cotton.
−14	5½	3¾	Do.	J. D. Inverarity.
13⅞	4⅝	5⅛	East Africa	H. C. V. Hunter.
13¾	4⅞	4⅛	Do.	E. Lort-Phillips.
13¾	5⅝	2⅞	Northern Somaliland	J. Menges, British Museum.
13¾	5⅜	3⅞	Somaliland	Hon. Walter Rothschild.
13¾	5½	3	Do.	Capt. G. F. T. Leather.
13¾	5¼	5	Do.	Digby Davies.
−13¾	5¼	7½	Do.	C. V. A. Peel.
−13¾	5⅝	5	Do.	J. Johnston-Stewart.
−13⅝	5¾	5⅝	East Africa	T. E. Buckley.
12½	5⅜	4¾	Do.	F. J. Jackson, C.B.

Skulls of Beira, from specimens shot by Lord Delamere.

BEIRA (Dorcatragus melanotis).

In spite of its presenting a certain superficial resemblance to the members of the oribi group and its allies, this peculiar little antelope is considered to be best placed in the neighbourhood of the gazelles. From all the members of the group in which the latter are included, the beira is at once distinguished by the short and spike-like horns of the bucks.　Perhaps its most striking peculiarity is the great size of its ears, which led its discoverer, Herr Menges, to describe it as a species of klipspringer.　Another noticeable feature is the large size of the rounded hoofs.　In colour, the upper parts and legs are pinkish fawn ; a darker band defining the fawn from the white of the under parts, which (the white) is continued down the inner surfaces of the limbs as far as the knees and hocks.　The head, from the ears to the nose, is bright rufous.　Height at shoulder about 23 inches.

Viscount Edmond de Poncins writes that "they are good hill-climbers, and keep on rocky ground.　The general shape is slender, legs are long, the head is kept erect, the ears are very big and broad, shaped like the dik-dik's, eyes big and dark, nostrils black.

"Colour a sort of grayish blue, a bit like what we call in French *gorge de pigeon,* and exactly matching the colour of the ground, so, unless they are on the move, it is difficult to distinguish them.　Unlike a gazelle, its tail is generally kept down.　Horns resemble those of the klipspringer, but curve forward slightly more."　From nose to root of tail $32\frac{5}{16}$, height at shoulder 21 inches, horns 4 inches ; weight about 20 lbs.

Distribution.—The interior of Somaliland, where it appears to be rare
and local, going about either singly or in pairs, and inhabiting
the open desert. The beira was first made known to science in ·
1894: its habits have lately been well described by Captain P. Z.
Cox in the eleventh volume of the *Journal* of the Bombay Natural
History Society.

Length on front.	Circumference.	Tip to Tip.	Locality.	Owner.
$4\frac{16}{16}$ [1]	$1\frac{7}{8}$	...	?	Lord Delamere. (See illustration.)
$4\frac{3}{4}$	...	...	Northern Somaliland	J. Menges.
4	2	$2\frac{1}{16}$	French Somaliland	Viscount Edmond de Poncins.
4	$2\frac{1}{8}$	$2\frac{3}{4}$	Somaliland	Sir Edmund G. Loder, Bart.
$3\frac{7}{8}$	$1\frac{3}{4}$	$3\frac{1}{8}$	?	Lord Delamere.
$3\frac{3}{4}$	$1\frac{5}{8}$	...	French Somaliland	Viscount Edmond de Poncins.
$3\frac{1}{2}$	$1\frac{11}{16}$	$2\frac{1}{4}$	?	Lord Delamere.
$2\frac{5}{8}$	$1\frac{3}{4}$	$1\frac{1}{4}$	French Somaliland	Viscount Edmond de Poncins.

[1] Length straight $32\frac{7}{8}$ inches, along curves $35\frac{3}{4}$ inches; height at shoulder, $25\frac{1}{4}$ inches; girth, $19\frac{1}{4}$ inches; weight, 23 lbs. as he fell.

Head of Grant's Gazelle.

Skull and Horns of Sable Antelope, from R. T. Coryndon's specimen.

SABLE ANTELOPE (Hippotragus niger).

Impengo of the Masubias.

Impalampala of the Swazis and Zulus.

Ookwa of the Makubas.

Potoquane of the Southern Bechuanas.

Pala-hala of the Swahilis.

Pala-pala of the Makalakas.

Qualata inchu of the Bamangwatos and Makololos.

Solupe of the Masaras.

Utjiele of the Amandebele.

Qualata and *T'choo* in the Barotse country.

Qualata and *Tshumu* in the Lake Ngami country.

Nkwalandi in the Chilala and Chibisa countries.

The group of antelopes which includes the present species, the roan antelope, the gemsbuck, addax, etc., differs very markedly from all those before mentioned. Among the leading features are the scimitar-shaped, conical, or spiral horns, which are placed just over the eyes, and are present in both sexes, the hairy muzzle, the absence of face-glands, and the long, tufted tail. Even more remarkable are the upper molar teeth, which have square grinding-surfaces and tall crowns, like those of oxen.

From the other members of the group the beautiful sable antelope and its near ally the roan antelope are well distinguished by the scimitar-shaped horns, which arise at an angle with the plane of the face, as well as by the maned neck, the tufts of long hair below the eyes, and the large size of the ears. By far the handsomer of the two is the present species, whose sable coat and great length of horn render the buck the most striking of its tribe. Other distinctive features are the continuance of the white eye-stripe to the muzzle, the length of the mane, and the relatively moderate size of the ears. Height at shoulder about 4½ feet. A single horn in the Florence Museum measured by Mr. F. C. Selous is 61 inches on the front curve.

Distribution.—From about the centre of the Transvaal northwards to Nyasaland and the adjacent districts of South-East and East Africa. Still abundant in parts of Eastern Mashonaland, and thence towards the coast, as well as on the Manica plateau to the north of the Zambesi. Scarcer in Central East Africa and Mozambique. Admired by all who have seen it in its native haunts, the sable antelope when wounded is a dangerous antagonist, to be approached with extreme caution. It runs with considerable speed, and possesses much staying power.

Length on front curve.	Circumference.	Tip to Tip.	Locality.	Owner.
-47⅞	...	...	Rhodesia	Measured by F. C. Selous (Fielden's specimen).
47¼	9½	26½	?	R. T. Coryndon. (See illustration.)
-46	...	...	Eastern Border of Transvaal	W. Russell Bowker.
45½	9¼	15½	Mashonaland . . .	Major G. A. L. Carew, D.S.O.
45⅜	10	14¾	Lebombo Mountains . .	F. Vaughan Kirby.
45¼	9½	12¼	S.E. Mashonaland . .	J. G. Millais.
-45¼	...	12¼	Pandamatenka . . .	R. T. Coryndon.
-45¼	9½	20½	?	Mr. Justice Hopley.
-45	...	...	Batoka Country . .	R. T. Coryndon.
-45	10½	...	South Africa . . .	Earl of Dartmouth.
-45	...	...	Angwa River . . .	Capt. J. A. Spreckley.
44¾	10⅝	13½	Barotseland . . .	H. Timmins.
44½	9¼	16	?	R. T. Coryndon.
44½	9	17	Transvaal	J. P. Fitzpatrick.
-44½	...	...	?	H. T. and A. H. A. Glynn.
-44½	(single horn)		Batoka Country . .	F. V. Worthington.

SABLE ANTELOPE (Hippotragus niger)—*continued.*

Length on front curve.	Circumference.	Tip to Tip.	Locality.	Owner.
44⅜	9½	14	Eastern Transvaal . .	F. Vaughan Kirby.
44⅛	9½	8¼	Eastern Mashonaland .	F. C. Selous.
-44	...	...	Batoka Country . .	F. V. Worthington.
-44	...	...	Lydenburg . . .	F. H. Barber.
-44	10	32½	?	Berlin Museum.
-43¾	9⅞	8	Matabeleland . . .	Count E. Hoyos.
43½	9½	9½	?	Sir Edmund G. Loder, Bart.
43½	9¾	15	Matabeleland . . .	The late J. S. Jameson.
43¼	9½	10½	Mashonaland . .	S. Chillingworth.
43	10⅜	16⅛	Chobe Valley . . .	F. C. Selous.
43	9¾	6½	Do. . .	F. C. Selous, British Museum.
43	...	...	Do. . . .	Major Hon. R. T. Lawley.
43	10¼	13	Mashonaland . . .	Major H. J. Goold-Adams, C.B., C.M.G.
42⅞	9¾	4⅞	Eastern Transvaal . .	F. Vaughan Kirby.
42¾	9⅜	12½	Mashonaland . . .	J. A. Jameson.
42⅝	9⅞	9½	South Africa . . .	Bethnal Green Museum
42½	9¾	6	Mashonaland . . .	G. H. M. Banks.
-42½	...	...	?	Cape Town Museum.
42¼	9½	5	Rhodesia	W. W. Ashley.
-42	10	3½	South Africa . . .	Dublin Museum.
-42	...	...	Transvaal	Cape Town Museum.
-42	...	...	S.E. Mashonaland . .	J. G. Millais.
41¾	9⅝	12	Do. . .	A. Beit.
41¾	...	9½	Do. . .	A. C. Fountaine.
41¾	9½	9	Muchinga Plateau, Northern Rhodesia	F. Smitheman.
41½	9	5¼	Do. . .	C. D. Rudd.
41½	9¾	16½	?	Col. F. Rhodes, D.S.O.
41¼	10	12⅞	S.E. Mashonaland . .	Hon. Walter Rothschild.
41¼	10⅜	11½	Sabi River . . .	Earl of Dunmore.

SABLE ANTELOPE (Hippotragus niger)—*continued.*

Length on front curve.	Circumference.	Tip to Tip.	Locality.	Owner.
41¼	9	10½	South Africa . . .	R. A. Cooper.
-41¼	8½	17¾	Do. . . .	Julius Jeppe.
41	9¼	10¾	Matabeleland .	W. Van Ness.
41	10	12	Do. .	Hon. R. A. Ward.
41	9½	12¾	Do. . . .	Capt. Sir K. Fraser, Bart.
41	9½	12	Do. . . .	Major James Grant.
-41	9¼	9	Pungwe . .	James J. Harrison.
40½	8	13	N.E. Transvaal . .	A. M. Naylor.
-40⅜	9½	15	Sabi Flats	Dr. Percy Rendall.
40⅜	9⅜	16	Upper Zambesi . . .	M. C. Greaves-Bagshawe.
40¼	10	13	?	F. Struben.
40¼	9½	13	Matabeleland . . .	Hon. R. A. Ward.
-40⅛	9¼	15¼	South Africa . . .	Dr. W. P. Y. Bainbrigge.
40	10	22	Matabeleland . . .	Abe Bailey.
40	9¼	10½	Near Ruo River, S.E. Africa	C. C. Bowring.
-40	...	...	Nyasaland . . .	S. Pulley.
-40	10	13½	South Africa .	A. Ohlsson.
-39½	...	...	?	O. R. Dunell.
-39¼	...	...	Mashonaland . . .	J. Vaughan.
♀ 39⅛	6¼	6⅝	Do. . .	F. C. Selous.
39	10	7¾	Do. .	F. B. Dunsford.
39	9	10⅜	?	Sir Victor Brooke's Collection.
38¾	9¾	2½	Matabeleland .	Rev. Dr. R. J. Nevin.
38½	8⅞	13	Pungwe . . .	Capt. F. H. Lehmann.
38½	9¼	9	Matabeleland . .	Duke of Roxburghe.
38¼	9	15½	Do. .	Hon. C. Greville.
38	9¾	14⅞	Mashonaland . .	D. Norman Ritchie.
37	9	14	Matabeleland . . .	Hon. John Ward.
-37	...	...	?	C. T. Jones.

SABLE ANTELOPE (Hippotragus niger)—*continued.*

Length on front curve.	Circumference.	Tip to Tip.	Locality.	Owner.
32½	9	15½	British Central Africa . .	J. E. Gough.
♀ 35¾	6¾	...	Lebombo Mountains . .	F. Vaughan Kirby.
♀ 34¼	6½	10	Matabeleland . . .	Hon. R. A. Ward.
♀ 33¾	6⅞	12½	?	G. Richards.
♀ 33¼	6⅝	3¾	Sabi Flats	Dr. Percy Rendall.
♀ 32	...	...	Mashonaland . . .	F. C. Selous.
~♀ 32		...	?	H. T. and A. H. A. Glynn.
♀ 31½	7	12⅝	Algoa Bay	British Museum.
♀ 31	7	7½	Matabeleland . . .	J. A. Pease.
♀ 30	6½	11½	Do. . . .	Lord Brackley.

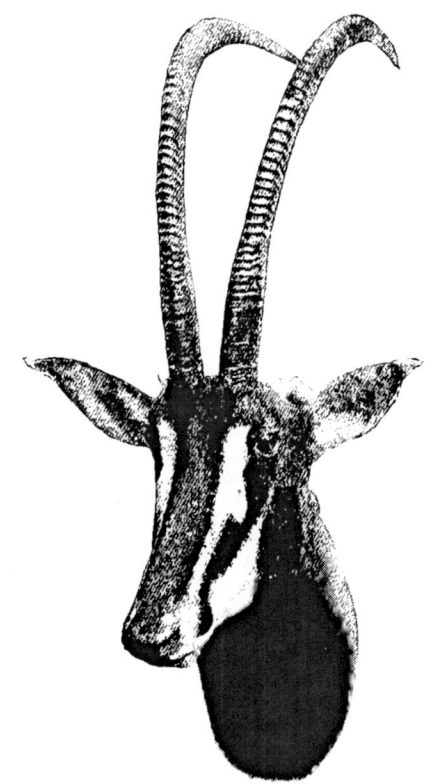

Head of Sable Antelope, from a specimen shot by F. C. Selous.

Head of Roan Antelope, from a specimen shot by F. C. Selous.

ROAN ANTELOPE (Hippotragus equinus).

Ee-taka of the Amandebele.

Ee-pala-pala chena of the Maka-lakas.

Impengo cetuba of the Masubias.

Kwar of the Masaras.

Klabakila of the Basuto.

M'pelembe in the Chilala and Chibisa countries.

Mtagaisi of the Swazis and Zulus.

Oo-ka-mooh-we of the Makubas.

Qualata of the Northern Bech-uanas.

Qualata and *Etsetla* in the Lake Ngami country.

Qualata and *Tseu* in the Barotse country.

Tai-hait-sa of the Southern Bechuanas.

In spite of its larger size (height at shoulder about 4 feet 9 inches), the shorter horns and mane, the larger ears and eye-tufts, and, above all, the grizzled roan coat, render the present species a much less striking animal than its sable cousin. A marked character of the face of the roan antelope is the cutting-off of the white eye-stripe from the muzzle by a transverse dark bar connecting the dark nose-streak with the brown of the cheeks ; while the dark nose-streak itself likewise stops short of the muzzle, which is thus wholly white.

Distribution.—From north of the Vaal and Orange Rivers through East and East Central Africa to the Sudan and Abyssinia, and westward to Angola, Nigeria, Gambia, and Senegambia. Recently the name *H. rufopallidus* has been applied to an antelope from East Africa, but it would seem unlikely that this can be anything more than a local race of the present species. Gordon Cumming shot the roan antelope just north of the Orange River in Griqualand West, where it has for many years been exterminated. Nowhere abundant, the species is most plentiful in Mashonaland and neighbouring districts; in the Transvaal it is only sparsely distributed. South of the Orange River this group of antelopes was formerly represented by the much smaller blaubok, or blue antelope (*H. leucophæus*), long since exterminated.

Length on front curve.	Circumference.	Tip to Tip.	Locality.	Owner.
-35	9½	8½	South Africa . .	A. Ohlsson.
34¼	9	7	Okavango Valley .	Major H. J. Goold-Adams, C.B., C.M.G.
33	...	...	Northern Matabeleland	A. C. Fountaine.
32¾	8⅝	9½	Mashonaland . .	Julius Jeppe.
32	9½	12	Hanyani Valley . .	F. C. Selous.
-32	10	13⅜	Mashonaland . .	Major A. St. H. Gibbons.
31¾	9½	5½	South Africa . .	Sir Edmund G. Loder, Bart.
31½	9½	11⅞	Mashonaland . .	F. C. Selous.
-31½	8½	12½	Nyasaland . .	Major P. W. Forbes.
31	8¾	13	Mashonaland . .	J. A. Jameson.
-31	10	6¾	?	Mr. Justice Hopley.
-30¾	10	14⅜	Sudan . . .	Count T. Palffy.
♀ 30½	7	7⅜	Mashonaland . .	F. C. Selous.
30½	9	13¼	South Africa . .	G. Richards.
-30½	10	11½	Portuguese East Africa	F. Vaughan Kirby.
-30½	8⅞	9	Matabeleland . .	Count E. Hoyos.
-30½	...	...	?	O. R. Dunell.
29⅞	10⅛	14⅝	Matabeleland . .	W. Van Ness.
29⅞	9⅝	11¼	Mashonaland . .	Hon. Walter Rothschild.
29¾	9⅞	10	Do. . .	Sir John Willoughby, Bart.
29½	9¼	4	Bahr-el-Salam, Sudan .	Lieut.-Col. Hon. W. Coke.
-29	...	...	?	Cape Town Museum.
-29	...	...	Batoka Country . .	F. V. Worthington.
-28¾	8⅝	12⅛	Gambia . .	Dr. Percy Rendall.

ROAN ANTELOPE (Hippotragus equinus)—*continued.*

Length on front curve.	Circumference.	Tip to Tip.	Locality.	Owner.
28⅝	9¾	9⅝	Mashonaland .	F. C. Selous, British Museum.
28½	8½	...	Sudan . . .	Col. Ralph Vivian.
28½	8⅝	9½	Mashonaland . .	S. Chillingworth.
28¼	9¼	12¾	Matabeleland . .	Hon. R. A. Ward.
– ♀ 28¼	6½	10½	?	Dr. W. P. Y. Bainbrigge.
28	9½	11½	Upper Zambesia. .	M. C. Greaves-Bagshawe.
28	9	11⅛	Lo Magondi's Country	Earl of Dunmore.
28	9⅜	5	Nigeria . . .	A. W. M. Brodie.
27⅞	8¾	8¼	?	Sir Edmund G. Loder, Bart.
27¾	8⅞	6¼	Karonga, B.C.A. .	C. C. Bowring.
27¾	9¾	8¾	Sudan . . .	Hon. Walter Rothschild.
27⅝	9⅛	9	?	J. Carr Saunders.
27½	9	11½	Matabeleland .	G. H. M. Banks.
27⅜	9	10	Barotseland . .	H. Timmins.
27⅜	9¾	8½	South Africa . .	A. Beit.
27¼	10¼	6¾	Matabeleland . .	Rev. Dr. R. J. Nevin.
27¼	9	10½	Dahomey . . .	F. C. Fuller.
–27¼	9½	10⅝	Noggara, Abyssinia .	J. Menges.
27	9	...	?	Dr. W. P. Y. Bainbrigge.
♀ 27	7	8¾	British Central Africa.	J. E. Gough.
26⅞	8⅝	10½	Gambia . .	Dr. Percy Rendall, British Museum.
26¾	8¾	5¾	Mashonaland .	J. G. Millais.
26½	9¾	14¾	Matabeleland . .	Hon. John Ward.
26½	9⅞	12	Muchinga Plateau, Northern Rhodesia	F. Smitheman.
–26.3	8.14	13.8	North of Kassala .	Prince Henry of Liechtenstein.
26	8⅞	7⅛	Gambia . . .	The late Earl of Derby.
♀ 25⅞	6¾	7	Mashonaland . .	F. C. Selous.
25¼	9½	10½	Nigeria . . .	Major A. J. Arnold, D.S.O.
♀ 25¼	6⅞	...	Do.	J. W. Carroll.
25⅛	9¾	5⅜	Sudan .	Sir Edmund G. Loder, Bart.

ROAN ANTELOPE (Hippotragus equinus)—*continued.*

Length on front curve.	Circumference.	Tip to Tip.	Locality.	Owner.
25	$8\frac{1}{2}$	$20\frac{3}{4}$	Gambia . .	H. C. Goddard.
♀ $24\frac{1}{2}$	$6\frac{1}{2}$	$10\frac{1}{8}$	Nigeria . .	A. W. M. Brodie.
24	$9\frac{1}{2}$	$14\frac{1}{4}$	Benguela . . .	G. W. Penrice.
♀ 24	$6\frac{3}{8}$	$6\frac{1}{2}$	Gambia .	H. C. Goddard.
♀ $22\frac{1}{4}$	7	$8\frac{1}{2}$	Songwe, B.C.A.	C. C. Bowring.
♀ $22\frac{1}{4}$	$6\frac{3}{4}$	$8\frac{1}{2}$	Sudan	Hon. Walter Rothschild.
$22\frac{1}{8}$	$7\frac{1}{8}$	8	Do.	W. D. James.
-22	9	$9\frac{1}{4}$	Nigeria . .	B. R. M. Glossop.
$21\frac{7}{8}$	7	$9\frac{1}{8}$	Abyssinia . .	E. Lort-Phillips.
$-♀ 21\frac{1}{2}$	...	...	Nigeria . . .	B. R. M. Glossop.
$-♀ 20$	$6\frac{1}{4}$	$10\frac{3}{4}$	?	T. E. Buckley.
$19\frac{1}{4}$	8	$8\frac{3}{4}$	Nigeria . .	Lieutenant-Colonel T. D. Pilcher.
$17\frac{3}{4}$	$6\frac{1}{8}$	$9\frac{1}{4}$	Abyssinia . .	British Museum.
$12\frac{3}{4}$	7	$7\frac{1}{4}$	British East Africa .	S. L. Hinde.

Skull and Horns of Gemsbuck, from F. H. Barber's specimen.

GEMSBUCK (Oryx gazella).

The long, straight, spear-like horns, of which even the lion fights shy, render the gemsbuck and its more immediate allies an easily recognised sub-group. And even when, as in the white oryx, the horns are scimitar-shaped, they differ from those of the sable antelope by starting in the plane of the face. It is also a noteworthy fact that in the present species the horns of the females are longer and finer, and therefore more prized, than those of the bulls. An adult gemsbuck stands about 3 feet 9 inches at the shoulder. In addition to the length of its horns, the species is sufficiently characterised by the presence of a tuft of hair on the throat, and the cutting-off of the white eye-stripe from the muzzle by the union of the dark central nose-streak with the black of the cheeks.

Distribution.—The desert regions of South-Western Africa, from the northern Karoos of Cape Colony through the Kalahari and Damaraland to Southern Angola in Mossamedes and perhaps Benguela. North of the Chobe and eastwards of Khama's country the species appears to be unknown. So late as 1846 Gordon Cumming found gemsbuck abundant on the northern Karoos of Cape Colony; and even now a few linger on the plains to the south of the lower reaches of the Orange River. In the northern Kalahari, where they exist for months without water, they are still abundant. The splendid horns of the gemsbuck are always regarded as prime trophies of the hunter's skill; the finding, riding-down, and shooting of one of these wary and enduring desert-bred antelopes being a feat of which any man, however well mounted, may be deservedly proud.

Length on front.	Circumference.	Tip to Tip.	Locality.	Owner.
$47\frac{1}{2}$	$6\frac{3}{4}$	$17\frac{1}{2}$	South Africa . .	The late J. S. Jameson.
-♀ $45\frac{1}{2}$	...	...	Bechuanaland . .	F. H. Barber. (See illustration.)
♀ $45\frac{1}{4}$	$6\frac{1}{4}$	$33\frac{3}{4}$	Lake Ngami . .	Major H. J. Goold-Adams, C.B., C.M.G.
45	$8\frac{1}{8}$	$18\frac{1}{2}$	Do. . .	Hon. Walter Rothschild.
$-44\frac{15}{16}$	...	...	South Africa .	Dr. A. Schopf.
-44	$6\frac{1}{2}$	17	?	A. Ohlsson.
$-43\frac{3}{4}$	7	21	?	Dr. W. P. Y. Bainbrigge.
$43\frac{3}{8}$	$6\frac{3}{8}$	$18\frac{1}{2}$	Nata River . .	F. C. Selous.
$43\frac{1}{4}$	$6\frac{5}{8}$	$20\frac{7}{8}$	?	Sir Victor Brooke's Collection.
$-43\frac{1}{4}$	8	16	?	James J. Harrison.
$43\frac{1}{8}$	$6\frac{7}{8}$	...	Botletli River . .	F. C. Selous.
43	7	$18\frac{3}{4}$	South Africa .	Rowland Ward.
-43	$7\frac{1}{2}$	...	?	Earl of Dartmouth.
43	$6\frac{1}{2}$	22	?	W. Y. Campbell.

GEMSBUCK (Oryx gazella)—*continued.*

Length on front curve.	Circumference.	Tip to Tip.	Locality.	Owner.
42⅞	7	14	?	A. Beit.
42½	7	20½	Bechuanaland . .	A. Neilson.
42½	7	...	Do. . .	Major H. J. Goold-Adams, C.B., C.M.G.
42⅜	6¼	19½	Do. . .	Capt. F. H. Lehmann.
–42¼	7	23½	?	A. Ohlsson.
–42	6⅝	22	?	Julius Jeppe.
42	6⅛	20¾	?	A. Ryley.
–41 7/16	8	15⅝	Great Namaqualand . .	Th. Rehbock.
41¼	7	22¾	?	C. D. Rudd.
♀ 41¼	6½	22¾	?	Mr. Justice Hopley.
♀ 41⅛	5 13/16	29⅞	Great Namaqualand . .	Th. Rehbock.
♀ 41	7	19	?	Major R. Hayes-Sadler.
♀ 40¾	6⅝	17⅛	Cunene River . .	Capt. F. Cookson.
–40¾	...	...	?	O. R. Dunell.
40⅜	6¾	16½	?	Lewis Atkinson.
–40¼	6½	18½	South Africa . . .	R. C. Peake.
-♀ 40¼	...	...	?	O. R. Dunell.
40	6⅞	18¼	South Africa . . .	Sir Edmund G. Loder, Bart.
-♀ 40	...	...	Do. . . .	Cape Town Museum.
-♀ 39¾	6½	15¼	Do. .	Julius Jeppe.
39¼	6¾	18	Bechuanaland . .	Lieut.-Col. W. Sitwell.
39	7¼	22	?	R. A. Cooper.
39	6½	16	South Africa . . .	A. J. Forbes.
♀ 38¼	6⅝	15⅞	Kalahari . . .	H. A. Bryden.
38	...	18¾	Bechuanaland . . .	A. C. Fountaine.
38	8½	8½	South Africa . . .	F. E. Potter.
–38	7	18	Do.	A. E. Pease.
–38	...	...	?	C. T. Jones.
♀ 37	6¼	17½	South Africa . . .	Dr. W. P. Y. Bainbrigge.
♀ 36¾	6⅝	...	North Bechuanaland . .	F. C. Selous; British Museum.

Head of Beisa.

BEISA (Oryx beisa).

Bcida of the Somalis.   *Sala* of the Abyssinians of Danakil.

The beisa may be regarded as the north-eastern representative of the gemsbuck, from which it may be distinguished at a glance not only by the absence of a tuft of hair on the throat, but also by the separation of the black nose-stripe from the eye-stripes.   There is also no black on the haunches or thighs, and the horns are considerably shorter and less divergent.   Height at shoulder reaching to about 4 feet.   Weight 458 lbs. (F. J. Jackson, C.B.).

Distribution.—North-East Africa, from Suakin through Abyssinia to Berbera in Somaliland, and south to Lake Baringo and the Equator.

Length on front curve.	Circumference.	Tip to Tip.	Locality.	Owner.
40	...	...	?	Measured by A. O. Hume, C.B., at Aden.
♀ 39	5½	8	Near Hargeisa, Somaliland	E. P. Hare.
37¼	7	11¼	Somaliland . .	G. D. E. Chapman.
36¼	6½	6⁷	Do. . .	Prince Boris Czetwertynski.
– ♀ 36½	...	...	Northern Somaliland .	J. Menges.
36	7	6¼	Somaliland . .	G. D. E. Chapman.
36	6¾	7¾	East of Lake Rudolph	A. H. Neumann.

BEISA (Oryx beisa)—*continued.*

Length on front.	Circum-ference.	Tip to Tip.	Locality.	Owner.
36	6½	10½	50 miles from coast of Somaliland	Capt. J. T. Brinkley.
36	6	8½	Somaliland .	Count J. Potocki.
-♀ 36	...	...	Do. . .	Dr. Donaldson Smith.
35¾	6¾	9⅛	Do. .	Lord Delamere.
♀ 35¾	5¾	8	Do. .	R. Wahrmann.
35½	6½	8¾	Do. .	Prince Nicolas Ghika.
♀ 35¼	6	10½	East of Lake Rudolph	A. H. Neumann.
35	6	9	Somaliland . .	Col. Arthur Paget.
♀ 35	5½	7¾	Danakil	Viscount Edmond de Poncins.
35	5¾	7⅝	Somaliland	A. S. Trevor.
-35	6⅝	6¼	Do. .	J. Johnston-Stewart.
♀ 34¾	5½	8½	Do. .	G. M. Norrie.
♀ 34½	6	10½	Do. . .	Capt. J. M'Call Maxwell.
34½	6¾	8¾	Do.	Alex. R. Alston.
34½	7	6	Do.	Ford G. Barclay.
♀ 34½	5¾	8¾	Do. .	R. McD. Hawker.
♀ 34½	5⅛	13	Do. .	T. W. H. Clarke.
34½	6¾	8½	Do.	E. Lee Townshend.
34½	5¼	8	Do. .	Sir H. D. Tichborne, Bart.
-34⅜	6	10¾	Do. .	Count Scheibler.
-34⅜	8⅞	11⅝	Do. .	T. W. H. Clarke.
-34¼	7½	10½	S.E. Somaliland .	S. Payne-Gallwey.
-♀ 34⅛	5¼	7½	Burgo	P. H. G. Powell-Cotton.
34	6¼	7¾	Somaliland .	E. N. Buxton.
34	5	9	Do. . .	Lord Wolverton.
-♀ 34	6	11	Do.	S. Payne-Gallwey.
-♀ 34	5	10	Do. .	A. E. Pease.
-33⅞	6½	8	Do. .	Sir Edmund G. Loder, Bart.
33¾	6	9	Do. .	Capt. C. S. Timins.
33¾	6	9	Do. . .	Digby Davies.

T

BEISA (Oryx beisa)—*continued.*

Length on front.	Circumference.	Tip to Tip.	Locality.	Owner.
♀ 33¾	4¾	8	Somaliland . . .	J. Arkcoll.
-33¾	6¼	8⅜	Do.	A. E. Leatham.
33⅝	6¾	9⅜	Do. .	A. H. Straker.
33⅝	5¾	8¼	Do.	Major H. G. C. Swayne.
33½	5½	7⅝	Do. .	Col. Arthur Paget.
33½	6½	10½	Do.	G. M. Norrie.
-33½	6⅛	8⅝	Do. . .	Count E. Hoyos.
- ♀ 33½	5½	7½	Do.	Capt. M. M'Neill.
-33½	...	...	Do.	J. Menges.
33⅜	4⅞	7⅝	Do.	W. D. James.
33¼	6⅛	9	Do.	Major C. C. Ellis.
-33¼	5¾	5¾	Do.	C. V. A. Peel.
33	6⅝	7¼	Do. .	Capt. B. L. Carew.
♀ 33	5	6¾	Do. .	Capt. G. Campbell.
-33	...	...	Njemps, E. Africa .	F. J. Jackson, C.B.
-33	7	11¼.	Somaliland . . .	Lieut.-Col. J. W. H. Flanagan.
32¾	6¾	12¼	?	Lord Delamere.
32¾	7½	8⅜	Somaliland . .	Capt. F. C. Quicke.
32¾	6½	8¼	Do. . .	J. Byng-Paget.
32¾	6½	11¼	Danakil . . .	Viscount Edmond de Poncins.
♀ 32⅝	5	8	Somaliland . . .	Capt. C. H. Villiers.
32½	6	8	Do.	P. B. Vander-Byl.
32½	6	7	Do.	Count J. de Bylands.
32½	6½	8¾	Do. . .	Major H. C. Morland.
-32½	6¾	8½	Do. . .	W. W. Ashley.
32½	5¼	7½	Do. . .	A. Leslie Renton.
-32½	6½	10½	Do. . . .	Major G. Douglas.
32⅜	6¼	6¼	Do. .	Lord Delamere.
♀ 32⅜	5½	11	Do. .	Julius Jeppe.
32¼	6½	8¼	Do. . .	B. Vincent.
32¼	6½	9	Do.	J. J. Richardson.
32	6¾	6	Do. . .	T. W. Greenfield.
♀ 32	5½	6	Do. .	E. T. Marshall.
32	6¼	8¾	Do.	G. H. Cheetham.
-31½	4⅞	11¼	Do. . . .	Dr. Percy Rendall.
31¼	5⅛	8½	East Central Africa .	A. H. Neumann.
♀ 31	5¼	7	Somaliland . . .	Major W. L. H. Paget.
31	5¾	7½	Do. . . .	B. R. M. Glossop.

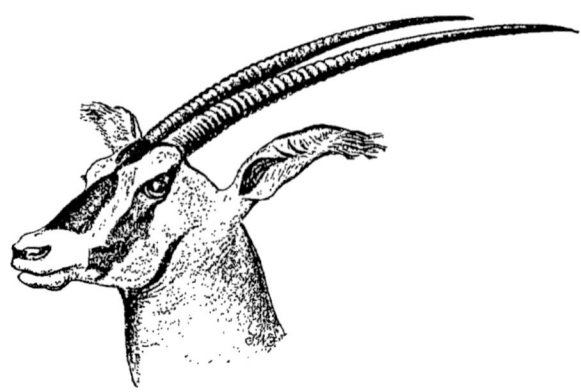

Head of Fringe-eared Beisa.

FRINGE-EARED BEISA (Oryx callotis).

Distinguished from the ordinary beisa by the fringe of long hairs surmounting the ears, by the extension of the eye-stripe to the lower jaw, along which it runs to join the throat-stripe, by the absence of any black on the front of the legs below the knees, and by the rich fawn of the ground-colour of the upper part of the face. Height at shoulder, 48 inches.

Distribution.—East Africa, from Kilimanjaro and the Galla country to Masailand and the adjacent territory, probably not so far north as the Athi plains. Although considered a distinct species, it might perhaps be better to regard this animal as a well-marked local race of the ordinary beisa. It is generally found in bush-covered country, either singly or in small herds, and is of a remarkably shy disposition. The Swahili name is cheroa.

Length on front.	Circumference.	Tip to Tip.	Locality.	Owner.
-32	...	...	Athi River . . .	R. Cator. "
30½	5¼	10½	East Africa . .	F. J. Jackson, C.B.
30¼	...	6	Sabaki River District .	T. W. Greenfield.
-30	...	10	East Africa . .	Sir John Willoughby, Bart.
29½	5⅝	7¾	Do. . . .	Sir Robert Harvey, Bart.
29	6	6½	Masailand . . .	Lieut.-Col. Hon. W. Coke.
29	5¼	11½	Do. . . .	Sir Edmund G. Loder, Bart.
28¾	5⅝	6	Do. . . .	H. C. V. Hunter.

FRINGE-EARED BEISA (Oryx callotis)—*continued.*

Length on front.	Circumference.	Tip to Tip.	Locality.	Owner.
♀ 28⅝	4¾	12¼	Masailand	Henry Charrington.
27¾	6⅞	10¼	Do.	F. J. Jackson, C.B.
27⅛	6⅞	8½	Do.	Sir Robert Harvey, Bart.
27	6	9	Do.	E. Gedge.
27	7⅛	7⅜	Do.	H. C. V. Hunter.
26¾	7	9	Do.	J. Gardiner Muir.
♀ 26¾	5½	10	Do.	Capt. R. A. J. Montgomerie, C.B., R.N.
26⅝	7	13	Do.	Sir Robert Harvey, Bart.
26½	6½	9¼	Do.	C. Steuart Betton.
-24	7	8½	Do.	Count Scheibler.
21	6¾	10	Do.	British Museum.

BEATRIX ORYX (Oryx beatrix).

This oryx is a much smaller animal than the beisa, measuring about 2 feet 8 inches at the shoulder, and is of a whitish colour, with a dark spot on the face, and a large dark patch on each cheek, which meets its fellow beneath the throat; the knees and the front of the lower portion of the legs being blackish brown, and the tail-tuft black.

Distribution.—The interior of Arabia, especially the Nejd districts and the confines of the great desert south of Orman, and, it is said, the Bushire district at the head of the Persian Gulf. This antelope has very rarely been killed by British sportsmen.

Length on front.	Circumference.	Tip to Tip.	Locality.	Owner.
-26 13/16	4¾	10¼	Arabia	Paris Museum.
23¾	5	9¼	Do.	Sir Edmund G. Loder, Bart.
♀ 15	3⅜	4½	Head of Persian Gulf	B. T. Ffinch, British Museum.

Head of White Oryx.

WHITE ORYX (Oryx leucoryx).

A very distinct species of the genus, agreeing approximately in size with the beisa, but with long recurving scimitar-shaped horns and a generally whitish coloration, showing a more or less distinct chestnut tinge. The chestnut shows itself chiefly on the neck, shoulders, under parts, and upper portions of the limbs; and in addition to this there are six brownish patches or streaks on the face, two of which are situated in the middle line, while two form eye-stripes, the other pair being between the horns and the eyes.

Distribution.—North-Western Central Africa, from Sennar and Kordofan to parts of Nubia and the Sudan. Rare in collections and menageries.

Length on front.	Circumference.	Tip to Tip.	Locality.	Owner.
39⅝	4⅞	14⅛	?	British Museum.
[1] 39	5¼	...	N. of Sokoto . . .	Capt. P. S. Wilkinson.
37⅝	5¼	7¼	?	British Museum.
35⅝	5½	11⅞	?	J. Carr Saunders.
35	5⅛	12	?	Sir Edmund G. Loder, Bart.
33⅞	5½	8	?	Hon. Walter Rothschild.
33¼	5	8¼	?	Duke of Bedford.
24¾	4¼	8¾	?	Sir Edmund G. Loder, Bart.

[1] Single horn.

Skull and Horns of mounted specimen of Addax presented to
the British Museum by J. J. S. Whitaker.

ADDAX (Addax nasomaculatus).

This antelope is another member of the oryx group, but is referred
to a genus apart, of which it is the sole representative. Its most
distinctive features are the spirally twisted and closely ringed horns,
which recall those of the Indian blackbuck, and the heavy mass of
long hair clothing the neck and shoulders and forming a forelock on
the forehead. The general colour is yellowish white in summer and
grayish in winter, but the head, neck, and mane are brown, although a
streak across the face below the eyes, the lips, and a spot on the outer
surface of each ear are white. Hoofs very wide and shallow, almost
like those of the reindeer. Height at shoulder about 3 feet 6 inches.

Distribution.—North Africa and Arabia.

ADDAX (Addax nasomaculatus)—*continued.*

Length. On front curve.	Length. Straight line.	Circumference.	Tip to Tip.	Locality.	Owner.
38½	30½	6½	12½	South Tunisia . .	J. J. S. Whitaker, British Museum. (See illustration.)
37¾	31¾	5¾	23½	Sahara . .	W. Barry.
35¾	28	6⅜	13⅝	North Africa .	Hon. Walter Rothschild.
35	29	6½	14	Do. .	W. Barry.
34½	27	6½	17¼	South Tunisia . .	J. J. S. Whitaker.
-34¼	27¾	6½	17	Do. .	A. E. Pease.
33⅞	28⅜	5⅞	22	Do. .	Sir Edmund G. Loder, Bart.
33½	27¼	6½	17¼	Do. .	J. J. S. Whitaker.
33½	26	5½	12¼	Do.	Hon. R. A. Ward.
32¼	26⅛	6⅛	13½	Do.	Rowland Ward.
31⅝	26¼	6⅜	17⅜	Do. .	F. H. Barber.
31	25½	5¼	13	Do.	J. H. Thomas.
-31	28	...	...	Do. . .	Sir H. H. Johnston, K.C.B.
♀ 30¾	27¼	4¾	17¼	South Algeria .	Hon. Walter Rothschild.
-♀ 30½	27½	...	...	South Tunisia .	Sir H. H. Johnston, K.C.B.
29½	24¾	6¼	14	Sahara . .	Hon. Walter Rothschild.
29¼	25⅝	5¼	19½	South Algeria .	Julius Jeppe.
28¾	24⅞	5½	12⅝	Do.	British Museum.

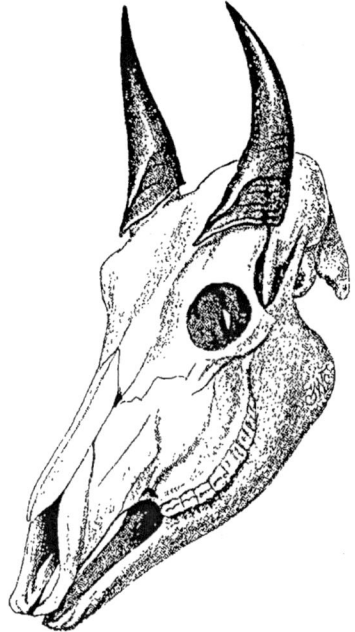

Skull of Male Nilgai.

NILGAI (Boselaphus tragocamelus).

This somewhat ungainly and decidedly small-horned antelope is the single Oriental representative of an important group whose other members are African.   Most are of large size, and, with the exception of the elands, lack horns in the females.   In the males the horns are angulated in front and generally spirally twisted, but in no case ridged. There are small face-glands, the muzzle is naked, and the tail is long and tufted.   Except in the nilgai, the cheek-teeth have short and broad crowns.

From the other members of the group the nilgai is readily distinguished by its short, upright horns, which, although angulated in front, show no distinct spiral twist.   With a long and pointed head, this antelope has the fore-legs considerably longer than the hinder pair ; and it is chiefly to this peculiarity that its ungainly appearance is due.   Both sexes have a mane on the neck, but the bulls alone possess a tuft of long hair on the middle of the throat.   The general colour of the adult bull is dark gray, tinged with blue or brown ; but the mane and tufts of long hair are black, and streaks and patches on the face, ears, and throat, as well as the under parts, the lower surface of the tail, and a ring above and below each fetlock, are white. Height at shoulder from 4 feet 4 inches to 4 feet 8 inches. Mr. A. O. Hume shot a specimen in the Aligurh district in 1855 whose horns measured 11¾ along the front curve, and had a circumference of 9.5. They were unfortunately destroyed in the Mutiny.

Distribution.—The peninsula of India, from the foot of the Himalaya to the south of Mysore; common in parts of the Eastern Punjab, the North-West Provinces, Guzerat, and the Central Provinces.

Length on front.	Circumference.	Tip to Tip.	Locality.	Owner.
9⅞	7¾	5½	?	Sir Edmund G. Loder, Bart.
9½	7½	6¼	?	J. Whitaker.
-9½	8½	...	Bhurtpur . .	Capt. E. R. Gordon.
9¼	6¾	4⅞	?	British Museum.
9	7	9	?	J. Whitaker.
9	6⅝	3½	?	A. O. Hume, C.B.
8⅞	6½	5¼	Central Provinces .	C. D. Twopeny.
8¾	6¼	5¾	Bhurtpur .	Major J. M. Fawcett.
-8¾	...	...	Jumna Valley .	Indian Museum.
8½	7½	4¾	Central Provinces .	Capt. E. H. R. Hibbert.
8½	5½	4¼	Do. . .	Marquis of Dufferin and Ava.
-8½	6½	6	Do.	Dublin Museum.
8½	7½	5¼	Do. .	Dr. W. P. Y. Bainbrigge.
-8½	6	5½	Do. .	Count J. Potocki.
-8⅜	7¾	6½	Do. .	Dr. Percy Rendall.
8¼	7⅛	7¾	North India .	Sir Victor Brooke's Collection.
-8.25	7·80	6·70	Ulwar . .	Viscount Edmond de Poncins.
8¼	...	...	Kathiawar . .	Lieut.-Col. L. L. Fenton.
-8¼	...	...	Kota .	H.H. Maharaja of Bikanir.
8⅛	6⅛	5	?	Hume Collection, British Museum.
8	6¾	6¼	Nimar, Cent. Prov. .	Lieut.-Col. H. Wade-Dalton.
7¾	7½	5¾	?	H. G. Buxton.
7¾	7	6	Central Provinces .	Major A. Colville.
7⅝	6	7¼	?	L. M. Le Champion.

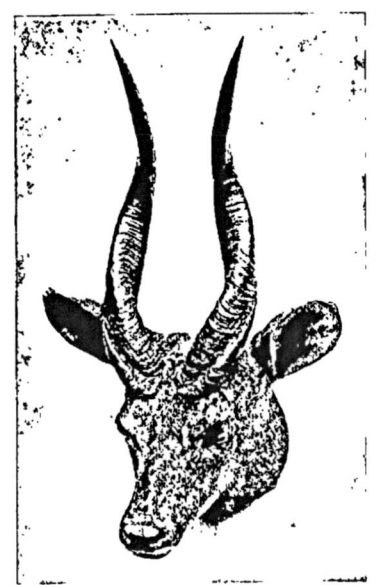

Head of Bushbuck shot by A. M. Naylor.

BUSHBUCK (Tragelaphus scriptus).

Assali, Danakil name.

Bawala in the Chilala and Chibisa countries.

Boschbok of the Dutch.

Dol of the Somalis.

Ibawara of the Lower Zambesi natives.

Imbabala of the Swazis and Matonga.

Inkonka (male), *Imbabala* (female) of the Zulus.

M'babala in the Barotse country.

M'babala and *Serolo buchuhu* in the Lake Ngami country.

Mbawara of the Swahilis.

Serolobutuku of the Bamangwatos.

Ungurungu of the Makubas.

The bushbucks and harnessed antelopes form an extensive group of species nearly allied to the kudus, but usually displaying great sexual differences in the colour of the coat, and generally having a simpler spiral to the horns. The females are nearly always striped with white on a chestnut ground, but the bucks may be darker and more uniformly coloured. As in the kudus, the females are hornless. The true or lesser bushbuck is the smallest and at the same time the most widely spread member of the group, having several local races. The height at the shoulder ranges from $2\frac{1}{2}$ to 3 feet, and the weight from 100 lbs. to 170 lbs. In the Abyssinian bushbuck (*T. scriptus decula*), which ranges into the dense forests bordering the Webbe River in Somaliland, and is locally known as *dol*, the build is low and stout, and the general colour yellowish, the light stripes being nearly obsolete. In the West African bushbuck (*T. scriptus typicus*), from West, Central, and South-Central Africa, the ground-colour is bright rufous, and the spots and stripes are very conspicuous. On the other hand, in the East African race (*T. scriptus roualeyni*) the bucks are dark brown, with only faint indications of white markings. Finally, in the Cape bushbuck (*T. scriptus sylvaticus*) the colour is dark brown without transverse white stripes, and the spots reduced to a few indistinct ones on the haunches.

In the southern districts of Cape Colony bushbuck are still to be found in abundance, even in the neighbourhood of large towns like Port Elizabeth. Recourse is, however, had to preserving for the greater part of the year, by which means the well-known Easter Hunts, when driving is practised and large bags are made, are still kept up. In more inland districts either the does or both sexes are periodically protected. A wounded bushbuck will often make a desperate and dangerous charge.

Length on front curve.	Circumference.	Tip to Tip.	Locality.	Owner.
$-19\frac{7}{10}$	$5\frac{3}{4}$	11	Lower Zambesia	Surgeon W. H. S. Stalkartt, R. N.
$17\frac{7}{8}$	$6\frac{1}{4}$	$5\frac{7}{8}$	East Africa	Sir John Kirk, K.C.B.
$-17\frac{1}{2}$	$6\frac{1}{4}$	$7\frac{5}{8}$	Mount Zomba, B.C.A.	D. MacAlpine.
$17\frac{1}{4}$	6	$5\frac{1}{4}$	N.E. Gazaland	A. M. Naylor. (See illustration.)
17	$5\frac{1}{2}$	$8\frac{1}{8}$	Mount Zomba, B.C.A.	C. C. Bowring.
$16\frac{5}{8}$	$5\frac{7}{8}$	$6\frac{1}{4}$	Manda Island, B.E.A.	British Museum.
$16\frac{1}{2}$	$5\frac{3}{4}$	(one horn)	Pungwe	Col. G. A. Percy.
$-16\frac{1}{2}$	$5\frac{1}{2}$	$5\frac{1}{2}$	?	Julius Jeppe.
$-16\frac{1}{2}$	...	...	South Africa	A. Bowker, Grahamstown Museum.
$-16\frac{1}{2}$	...	...	?	O. R. Dunell.
$-16\frac{1}{2}$	$6\frac{1}{2}$	$7\frac{1}{2}$	Natal	General A. W. Drayson.
-16	$6\frac{1}{2}$	...	Kalamba Hills	F. Vaughan Kirby.
$15\frac{3}{4}$	6	$5\frac{3}{8}$	Okavango River	Major H. J. Goold-Adams, C.B., C.M.G.
$15\frac{3}{4}$	6	$8\frac{1}{8}$	Zululand	A. H. Neumann.
$15\frac{3}{4}$	5	$3\frac{3}{4}$	Do.	Capt. L. O. Williams.
$-15\frac{3}{4}$	...	...	South Africa	F. H. Barber.
$15\frac{5}{8}$	$5\frac{1}{2}$	3	British East Africa	G. E. Smith.

BUSHBUCK (Tragelaphus scriptus)—*continued.*

Length on front curve.	Circumference.	Tip to Tip.	Locality.	Owner.
15⅝	5¼	5	Pungwe	Hon. T. Thynne.
15½	5½	3⅝	Transvaal .	C. F. Eustace.
15½	5⅜	4½	South Africa .	F. C. Selous.
-15½	...	...	Do.	H. T. and A. H. Glynn.
15⅜	6⅜	7½	Do.	Major-General Sir Arthur Ellis, K.C.V.O.
15⅜	5½	7⅛	Zululand	Hon. Charles Ellis.
15¼	6	6¾	Pungwe	H. R. Holden.
-15¼	7¼	6½	Nyasaland .	Alex. R. Alston.
15⅛	5½	8½	?	Mr. Justice Hopley.
14¾	5⅜	6¾	Shiré River, B.C.A. .	H. H. Williams.
14¾	5¼	6½	Zululand	Lieut.-Col. Hon. W. Coke.
14¾	5	6½	South Africa	R. A. Cooper.
-14¾	5¾	3¾	Nyasaland.	Alex. R. Alston.
14⅝	5¾	2¾	Matabeleland .	G. H. M. Banks.
14⅜	5½	7	Zambesia . . .	G. Richards.
-14½	...	...	Cape Colony	F. H. Barber.
-14¼	...	...	Transvaal . .	C. T. Jones.
-14⅛	5	7	Pungwe .	Julius Jeppe.
14	...	...	East Africa .	F. J. Jackson, C.B.
14	5⅞	5¾	Matabeleland	H. and C. Beddington.
14	5⅞	6⅛	South Africa	C. D. Rudd.
14	5½	10¼	Pungwe .	G. Micklethwait.
14	5¼	7	Ngamiland	Capt. E. J. Lugard.
-14	6	7½	South Africa	James J. Harrison.
13⅞	5¾	5½	Do.	H.R.H. the Duke of Saxe-Coburg and Gotha.
13¾	5¾	6½	Do.	Hon. Walter Rothschild.
13¾	5½	5⅜	Do.	Sir Edmund G. Loder, Bart.
-13¾	6¼	6	Natal	T. E. Buckley.
13⅝	5½	5½	East Africa . .	H. C. V. Hunter.
13⅝	5⅜	4⅛	?	Sir Victor Brooke's Collection.

BUSHBUCK (Tragelaphus scriptus)—*continued.*

Length on front curve.	Circumference.	Tip to Tip.	Locality.	Owner.
13½	5½	7	South Africa	F. C. Selous.
13½	5¼	5⅜	Do.	British Museum.
13½	5⅛	4⅜	Do.	Sir John Willoughby, Bart.
-13⅜	5⅞	7¼	North of Pungwe	Count E. Hoyos.
-13¼	...	...	Cape Colony	C. T. Jones.
13	6¼	5⅛	East Africa .	F. J. Jackson, C.B.
13	5½	7	Benguela	G. W. Penrice.
13	5¼	5	Pungwe .	G. L. Bonham.
13	5¼	5½	British Central Africa .	J. E. Gough.
-13	...	...	Zambesia	C. T. Jones.
12¾	5	4½	South Africa	A. E. Capell.
-12¾	5¾	8¼	Barberton . .	Dr. Percy Rendall.
12¾	4⅞	5½	?	Dr. W. P. Y. Bainbrigge.
12⅜	5⅛	4⅝	Chobe Valley . .	F. C. Selous, British Museum.
12¼	6½	7½	South Africa	E. G. Christian.
-12¼	5	5¼	Matabeleland	J. Brander Dunbar.
11¾	5⅝	4¾	Pungwe	Hon. T. Thynne.
11¾	5⅛	4½	Uganda	The late Capt. Speke, British Museum.
11¾	5	6⅜	East Africa . .	Sir Robert Harvey, Bart.
-11¾	...	...	Adda Bush .	Cape Town Museum.
10¾	4½	5	Nigeria . . .	Major A. J. Arnold, D.S.O.
10½	4½	2¼	Gambia . . .	A late Earl of Derby, British Museum.
-9⅜	4½	6⅛	Songwe, Nyasaland .	John Yule.

Head of Abyssinian Bushbuck shot in the Webbe Shebayle River District, Somaliland,
by Major H. G. C. Swayne.

The following specimens belong to the Abyssinian race (*T. scriptus
decula*); the body measurements being those of one shot by Viscount
Edmond de Poncins on the Hawash River, 1898 :—

From nose to root of tail	.	$48\frac{3}{8}$ ins.
Tail (hair included)	. .	$10\frac{3}{4}$,,
Height at withers .	. .	$26\frac{3}{4}$,,
Round the body .	. .	$30\frac{3}{8}$,,

Length on front curve.	Circumference.	Tip to Tip.	Locality.	Owner.
-17	...	...	Somaliland . . .	Major H. G. C. Swayne.
$-16\frac{1}{2}$	$6\frac{1}{4}$	5	Do. . . .	A. H. Straker.
16	6	$7\frac{1}{4}$	Do. . . .	Major H. G. Swayne.
$14\frac{1}{4}$	$6\frac{7}{8}$	5	Do. . . .	A. H. Straker.
$-13\frac{3}{4}$	$5\frac{1}{2}$	$5\frac{1}{4}$	Harar, Abyssinia . .	Prince de Lucinge.
-13	$5\frac{1}{2}$	$6\frac{5}{16}$	Do. . .	Do.
$-12\frac{7}{8}$	$5\frac{1}{4}$	$3\frac{1}{4}$	Near Hawash River, Abyssinia	Viscount Edmond de Poncins.
$12\frac{5}{8}$	5	$5\frac{1}{4}$	Abyssinia . . .	W. D. James.
12	$5\frac{1}{8}$	$5\frac{1}{8}$	Do. . . .	British Museum.
11	$5\frac{1}{8}$	5	Settite River, Abyssinia .	Col. Ralph Vivian.
11	$4\frac{3}{8}$	$2\frac{5}{8}$	Northern Abyssinia . .	British Museum.

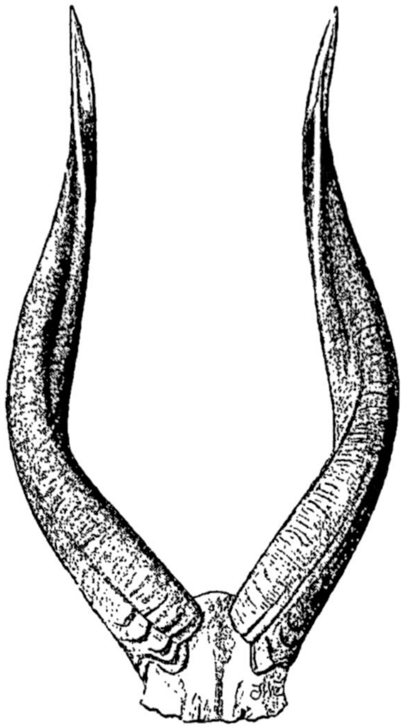

Horns of Male Bongo, from the type specimen in the British Museum.

BONGO or BROAD-HORNED ANTELOPE (Tragelaphus euryceros).

This West African species is the largest of the harnessed antelopes. In addition to its large size, it is characterised by the bright chestnut colour of the males, marked with a number of narrow transverse white stripes, the shortness of the hair, the absence of a throat-fringe, and the smooth and stout horns, of which the tips become yellow by wear. The markings on the face take the form of a pair of white spots below the eyes, and there is a white crescent on the breast. Height at the shoulder probably about 4 feet.

Distribution.—West Africa, from Liberia, through Fanti to the Ashkankolu Mountains and the Gaboon. It is doubtful if this rare and beautiful antelope has ever been killed by British sportsmen. The original specimens were obtained by P. Du Chaillu, and are in the British Museum.

Length.					
On front curve.	Straight.	Circumference.	Tip to Tip.	Locality.	Owner.
32¾	27¼	9⅛	16⅛	Gaboon . . .	Sir Edmund G. Loder, Bart.
31¾	26⅓	9¾	12⅜	West Africa . .	Sir Victor Brooke's Collection.
30¾	24⅞	10⅞	12¾	Do. . .	Do.
30	24⅛	9⅝	11¼	Ashkankolu Mountains	British Museum.
29½	25⅛	9¾	10⅛	Gaboon . . .	P. Du Chaillu, British Museum.
27⅝	23¾	10⅛	10⅝	Fanti	Do.

Horns of Nyala, from a specimen in the possession of F. H. Barber.

NYALA (Tragelaphus angasi).

The next African representative of the larger harnessed antelopes is a smaller and more delicately built animal than the bongo, standing about 3 feet 6 inches at the shoulder.   Weight about 250 lbs. to 300 lbs.   In both sexes the hair is very long and coarse, but in the male its colour is dark grayish brown with a small number of indistinct white stripes, while in the female it is bright reddish chestnut with clearly defined stripes.   The males have a fringe of long hair on the neck and the under parts of the body, their horns being much rougher than those of the bongo.   As in the latter, the hoofs are short.

Distribution.— South-East Africa, including Zululand, Delagoa Bay, and Nyasaland ; on the West Coast it has been reported from Angola, although this form may indicate a distinct local race.

Length.		Circum-ference.	Tip to Tip.	Locality.	Owner.
On front curve.	Straight.				
31⅛	24½	8¼	3½	Shiré River, B. C. A.	Fergus Maclagan.
−29¼	24	...	11½	?	F. J. Newnham.
−29⅛	...	...	...	Delagoa Bay . .	F. H. Barber. (See illustration.)

NYALA (Tragelaphus angasi)—*continued.*

Length. On front curve.	Length. Straight.	Circumference.	Tip to Tip.	Locality.	Owner.
–29⅛	...	...	...	?	O. R. Dunell.
28½	23¾	8	12¾	Zululand . .	Hon. Walter Rothschild.
–28½	...	...	...	?	W. Russell Bowker.
–28½	...	...	...	Delagoa Bay . .	F. H. Barber.
–28½	...	...	...	Do. . .	Prince Boris Czetwertynski.
28	24	8	15	Katanga, B.C.A. .	John Yule.
28	23	7¼	13¼	Near Chiromo, B.C.A.	Staff-Surgeon J. Dowson, R.N.
28	...	8⅛	10⅛	South Africa . .	British Museum.
–28	24¼	7½	11¾	Delagoa Bay .	C. T. Jones.
–28	23¾	8	11	?	Dr. W. P. Y. Bainbrigge.
27⅝	22½	7⅞	9½	South Africa .	Sir Victor Brooke's Collection.
27⅝	23	7⅞	8¼	Do. . .	Earl of Dunmore.
–27½	23	8½	13	Do. . .	E. D. Scott.
27½	22¼	7⅝	8½	?	C. D. Rudd.
27½	23½	7½	15⅜	Delagoa Bay . .	Major H. J. Goold-Adams, C.B., C.M.G.
27⅜	...	8⅛	10⅛	South Africa .	Sir Edmund G. Loder, Bart.
–27¼	...	7¼	10⅝	?	Julius Jeppe.
–27⅛	23½	...	14	Delagoa Bay . .	H. T. and A. H. Glynn.
27	...	8	9⅛	Shiré River, B.C.A.	F. Vaughan Kirby.
27	22⅝	7¾	11¼	?	J. R. Buckler.
26¾	22¼	7½	11	?	F. E. Potter.
26¾	22⅜	7	11¾	Amatongaland .	H. A. Bryden.
26½	22	7¼	7	Delagoa Bay	Frank Harris.
–26½	22½	7⅝	6⅛	Do. .	Dr. Percy Rendall.
26¼	22	6⅞	11⅝	Do. .	F. C. Selous.
26	...	7⅜	8⅞	Zululand . .	Hon. Charles Ellis.
25	21	8	9⅜	?	Capt. A. M'Lean Wait.
–25	22½	8	12¼	?	A. Ohlsson.
24½	20½	...	...	Amatongaland .	Cape Town Museum.
23⅜	20	7⅝	11⅝	Zululand . . .	Durban Museum.
23¼	20¼	7¼	7½	Do. .	G. Richards.
23⅛	19	6⅞	7	Do. .	A. H. Neumann.
23	...	7	5⅝	Do. . . .	British Museum.
–22¼	19½	7	9⅞	Delagoa Bay . .	Count E. Hoyos.
–22	...	...	...	St. Lucia Bay .	G. F. Angas.
21	19	9	...	Do. . .	Lieut.-Col. Hon. W. Coke.

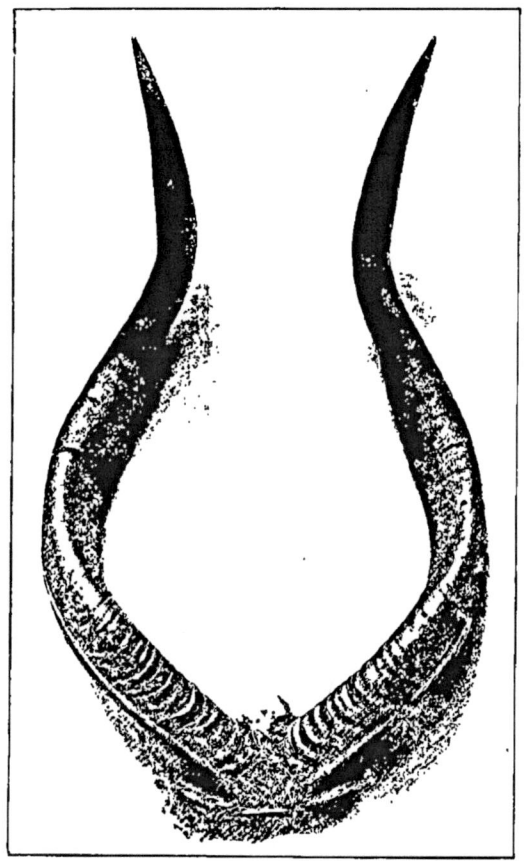

Horns of West African Harnessed Antelope, from the Gambia.

WEST AFRICAN HARNESSED ANTELOPE (Tragelaphus gratus).

Together with its near ally the situtunga, this species differs from all the other members of the group by the extreme elongation of the hoofs, which are thus adapted for supporting the weight of the body on the spongy soil of the marshes in which these antelopes dwell. The lateral hoofs, too, are much more developed than in other harnessed antelopes. The general coloration of the West African species is very similar to that of the nyala, the ground-colour of the coat of the male being olive, and that of the female bright rufous, marked in both sexes with white stripes on the body and spots on the face. There is, however, no fringe of long hair on the throat. Height at shoulder about 3 feet 7 inches. Both in this species and the situtunga the horns of the males are longer and more twisted than in the other members of the genus, and thus come very close to those of the kudus. In the situtunga the coloration of the adult is uniform grayish brown. The West African species ranges from the Congo to the Gaboon and Cameroon districts. It has but seldom been collected by sportsmen, so that very little is known of its habits in the wild state. Several specimens have been bred in captivity at the Zoological Gardens, Amsterdam.

Length. On front curve.	Length. Straight line.	Circumference.	Tip to Tip.	Locality.	Owner.
30	$26\frac{1}{4}$	$7\frac{3}{4}$	$14\frac{7}{8}$	?	Rowland Ward.
$29\frac{1}{2}$	$24\frac{1}{2}$	$8\frac{1}{8}$	14	Gaboon . . .	Sir Edmund G. Loder, Bart.
$28\frac{1}{2}$	23	8	8	Gambia	Rowland Ward. (See illustration.)
$25\frac{3}{4}$	$21\frac{1}{4}$	$6\frac{3}{4}$	$12\frac{1}{4}$	Do. .	Guy H. Sangster.
$25\frac{1}{2}$	22	8	...	French Congo .	Hon. Walter Rothschild.
$-24\frac{11}{16}$	$21\frac{1}{4}$	$7\frac{3}{8}$	$6\frac{1}{2}$	West Africa .	Dr. Percy Rendall.
$-23\frac{1}{2}$	$20\frac{1}{8}$	$8\frac{1}{8}$	$9\frac{1}{16}$	Do. .	Do.
...	19	...	...	Gaboon .	British Museum.
$23\frac{1}{2}$	18	$7\frac{7}{8}$	$11\frac{3}{4}$	Do. .	Sir Victor Brooke's Collection.
23	$20\frac{1}{2}$	$6\frac{7}{8}$	$9\frac{1}{2}$	West Africa	Hon. Walter Rothschild.
$22\frac{3}{4}$	$19\frac{1}{2}$	7	$10\frac{3}{8}$	Nigeria .	J. A. Burdon.
$22\frac{3}{8}$	$19\frac{3}{4}$	7	$11\frac{1}{4}$	Gambia	Rowland Ward.
-21.5	...	7.8	...	?	Berlin Museum.
-17	$14\frac{3}{16}$	$6\frac{3}{8}$	...	Ogooné . .	Paris Museum.

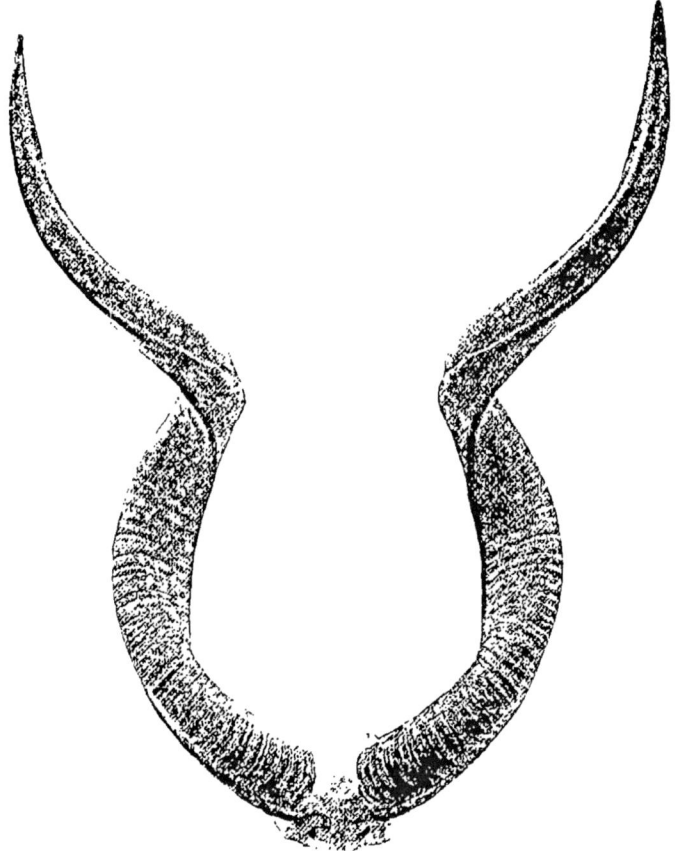

Frontlet and Horns of Situtunga, from John Yule's specimen.

SITUTUNGA (Tragelaphus spekei).

Situtunga in the Barotse country.
Zowè in the Chilala and Chibisa countries.
Nakong of the Batauwani at Lake Ngami.

Situtunga, Puvula, Unzuzu of the tribes on the Chobe and Central Zambesi.
N'zoé of the natives of Lakanga River north of the Zambesi.

This species, also known as the nakong, has the same habits and make as the West African harnessed antelope, from which it differs by its uniformly grayish-brown colour ; the young alone being faintly barred and spotted.   Another peculiarity is to be found in the length and silkiness of the hair. The horns, which are nearly smooth and strongly keeled, form nearly two complete turns, and thus approximate to those of the kudu.

Distribution.—The situtunga is an inhabitant of the dense reed-swamps bordering the rivers of Central, South-Central and East Africa; and is semi-aquatic in its habits, frequently burying itself up to the eyes in the water. Consequently it is one of the most difficult of all antelopes to kill; and has even baffled the energy of Mr. Selous. By firing the reed-beds in the dry season, the natives are able to spear the situtunga as they cross open water. At night these antelopes leave the reed-brakes for the islands in the rivers, but before dawn return to their impenetrable covert. Mr. A. B. Phipps, in a letter dated October 1895, states that they have become very rare in the swamps bordering the Okavango River, owing to that river having changed its course and ceased to flow into the Botletli. Consequently they go down to the latter for water, and are shot. A few are found on a bush-clad rocky island far out in the Victoria Nyanza; in which neighbourhood the species was first discovered by the late Captain Speke.

Length.					
On front curve.	Straight line.	Circumference.	Tip to Tip.	Locality.	Owner.
35	28	7½	15½	South end of Lake Tanganyika	John Yule. (See illustration.)
-33½	27⅝	7⅞	19	?	Julius Jeppe.
33¼	26¼	8	16⅝	Okavango Valley .	Major H. J. Goold-Adams, C.B., C.M.G.
-33	...	...	...	?	Alfred Ebden.
32⅝	27	7½	16⅜	Chobe Valley . .	F. C. Selous.
-32½	...	...	...	?	C. T. Jones.
31⅞	25¾	8⅛	17¼	Near Linyanti . .	F. C. Selous.
31½	24⅜	7	16⅛	Chobe Valley	F. C. Selous, British Museum.
-31½	25¾	7½	13¼	Bangweolo . . .	F. Smitheman.
-31⅛	25 9/10	7⅞	14⅝	Congoland .	S. de Brazza, Paris Museum.
31	23¾	8	9½	?	G. Richards.
-30½	...	...	...	?	O. R. Dunell.
-30½	23½	8½	15½	?	Julius Jeppe.
-30	25	7⅞	18	?	Mr. Justice Hopley.
29¾	25	8¾	17	?	R. A. Cooper.

SITUTUNGA (Tragelaphus spekei)—*continued.*

Length. On front curve.	Length. Straight line.	Circumference.	Tip to Tip.	Locality.	Owner.
–29½	26	7¾	16	?	A. Ohlsson.
–28¾	26¼	7⅝	14⅞	Lake Mweru, B.C.A.	R. H. Ferrers Stranack.
27½	23⅛	7⅛	10	B.C.A. . .	Rowland Ward.
27¼	21½	8	6	Barotseland	H. Timmins.
27⅛	22⅜	7⅝	14⅞	Lake Mweru, B.C.A.	Rowland Ward.
26¾	21¾	7¼	11⅜	?	W. Van Ness.
26½	21¾	7½	17	Chobe Valley . .	Frank Harris.
26	22⅝	7	17½	?	Sir Victor Brooke's Collection.
...	25	...	...	Okavango Valley .	A. B. Phipps.
25⅞	22¼	7¼	19⅜	Chobe Valley .	F. C. Selous, British Museum.
25½	21¾	7	13⅜	Bangweolo .	F. Smitheman.
25	21	8	16¼	Botletli Valley	Hon. Walter Rothschild.
24	20	7½	11¼	Barotseland	E. D. Scott.
23⅝	...	7¼	10	?	Major H. J. Goold-Adams, C.B., C.M.G.
23	20¼	...	5⅞	?	F. H. Barber.
22¾	19½	10	7½	?	Hon. Walter Rothschild.
20¾	18¼	6¼	10	Benguela .	G. W. Penrice.
20¾	17¼	6¼	5	Do. .	Do.
19⅜	16⅞	6⅜	9¼	Barotseland . .	R. T. Coryndon.
·17¼	...	5¾	7	Victoria Nyanza .	E. Gedge.
15⅜	14⅛	5⅜	8¾	Do. .	Hon. Walter Rothschild.

Head of Male Greater Kudu.

GREATER KUDU (Strepsiceros kudu).

Eebala-bala of the Amandebele.

Ee-zilarwa of the Makalakas.

Dwar of the Masaras.

Godir of the Somalis.

Itolo of the Basutos.

Itshongonons of the Swazis.

Muzeeloua of the Batongas.

Ngoma in the Chilala and Chibisa countries.

Noro of the Mashonas.

Tolo of the Bechuanas.

Tolo in the Barotse and Lake Ngami countries.

Unza of the Mazubias.

Unzwa of the Makubas.

A male shot by Dr. Percy Rendall, in Nyasaland, measured :

	inches.			inches.
Nose to tail . . .	91½	Girth of barrel .	.	72
Height at shoulder .	55	„ before hips		54
Point of shoulder to nose	32	„ of fore-leg .	.	14¾
Length of tail .	. 17½	„ „ thigh .	.	19½
Girth of neck (min.) .	30	„ „ neck (max.)	.	43

Although rather less brilliantly coloured than some of the harnessed antelopes, the kudus are among the handsomest of all antelopes, their spiral horns, striped coat, and noble carriage rendering them really magnificent creatures. Their chief difference from the bushbucks is to be found in the fuller spiral formed by the horns : both sexes being nearly similar in colour. The special characteristics of the greater or true kudu are the large size (height at shoulder reaching to 4 feet 10 inches or 5 feet), the presence of a thick fringe of long hair on the throat, and the open spiral of the horns of the bull. The colour is too well known to require description.

Distribution.—The kudu, in suitable localities, ranges over the greater part of Africa south of the Sahara, extending from Abyssinia and Somaliland through East and Central Africa to the Cape, and westward across the continent to Angola, where the Congo apparently forms its northern limits. In spite of its bulk, it is an adept at concealment ; and this trait, coupled with its general wariness and acute sense of smell and hearing, has largely contributed to its survival in districts where it is much hunted. Except in the Uitenhage jungles, where it is preserved by English farmers, the kudu has, however, been exterminated from Cape Colony. In Eastern Mashonaland it is still abundant, as it is in the highlands of Somaliland, in which country it is rarely met with on the plains.

Although an adept at getting across rocky hills, this animal is by no means a good performer on the flat (where it seldom allows itself to be surprised), and can be ridden down without much difficulty by a fairly well-mounted hunter.

Horned females occur very rarely; but three specimens with horns are recorded on p. 302.

Length. On outside curve.	Length. Straight line.	Circumference.	Tip to Tip.	Locality.	Owner.
-...	48⅞	...	...	Ngamiland	F. H. Barber. (See illustration.)
63	48½	12½	49	Macloutsie River	E. W. Tompson.
-63	44½	...	42¾	Nr. Tete, Zambesi	Major P. W. Forbes.
-63	39	10½	12	?	Mr. Justice Hopley.
-...	45½	...	...	Delagoa Bay	F. H. Barber.
61½	-45¼	...	...	South Africa	O. R. Dunell.
60¾	44½	12	29	Do.	Frank Harris.
60⅝	45⅜	11½	33	Macloutsie River	F. C. Selous.
-60⅝	44	...	31	South Africa	H. T. and A. H. Glynn.
-60½	47	10½	44¾	Do.	A. Ohlsson.
-60	39	10	7⅝	Lebombo Mountains	F. Vaughan Kirby.
-59¾	45 1/16	...	39⅜	Pungwe Valley	Major A. St. H. Gibbons.
59¼	42¼	11⅝	19	?	G. Richards.
-58¾	46½	11½	41¾	Transvaal	F. Van Zeller.
-58½	45	...	46	?	O. R. Dunell.
-58½	45	11½	44¾	?	Mr. Justice Hopley.
-58¼	46	10	39¾	South Africa	Julius Jeppe.
58	46	11⅝	39	S.E. Mashonaland	J. G. Millais.
-58	46	...	...	Zomba, B.C.A.	D. MacAlpine.
58	43½	10¼	32½	Okavango River	Major H. J. Goold-Adams, C.B., C.M.G.
-58	44	11	44	Lebombo Mountains	F. Vaughan Kirby.
-58	41	...	...	South Africa	Cape Town Museum.
57½	41	11⅛	21½	N.E. Transvaal	A. M. Naylor.
-57½	39¾	11⅞	15	South Africa	Julius Jeppe.
-57⅜	39	9⅝	32	Somaliland	J. Johnston-Stewart.
57¼	45⅜	10¾	35	B. C. Africa	H. C. Macdonald.

GREATER KUDU (Strepsiceros kudu)—*continued.*

Length. On outside curve.	Length. Straight line.	Circumference.	Tip to Tip.	Locality.	Owner.
57¼	44⅞	11¾	34⅜	South Africa	Sir Edmund G. Loder, Bart.
57⅛	43	11⅝	34¾	Mashonaland . .	H. and C. Beddington.
57	43	14	32	South Africa .	A. Moseley.
57	42¼	11	31	Do. .	Capt. M. D. Graham.
57	39½	9⅝	36½	Somaliland .	H.R.H. le Duc d'Orléans.
56½	43½	11½	26½	Matabeleland .	W. Van Ness.
56½	42⅝	10⅜	38¾	?	Sir Victor Brooke's Collection.
56½	41½	10½	23¾	Matabeleland	Hon. C. Greville.
56½	38¾	9½	28¾	Somaliland . .	J. Benett-Stanford.
56½	35	10⅛	30	Do.	Sir Edmund G. Loder, Bart.
56¼	44¼	11⅜	33¼	South Africa .	Hon. Walter Rothschild.
56	43	10¾	43	Mashonaland	F. C. Selous.
56	44	10¾	39	South Africa . .	F. B. Dunsford.
55¾	41	10¾	36	Do. . .	F. Struben.
55½	39½	10¾	26½	Mashonaland .	A. Neilson.
55½	42½	11½	37	Matabeleland .	Lord Brackley.
55½	42½	10½	38	Do. .	Major James Grant.
55¼	40¼	11	27¾	E. C. Africa . .	H. S. H. Cavendish.
55	41¼	11¾	28	Matabeleland	Major R. Hayes-Sadler.
55	40½	12½	32½	Zululand	C. D. Rudd.
55	41	10	41	?	The Maclaine of Lochbuie.
54½	39¼	10½	27½	Upper Shiré, B.C.A.	C. C. Bowring.
54½	40½	11	21½	Mashonaland .	S. Chillingworth.
54½	39	11	27½	South Africa . .	Dublin Museum.
54½	38¼	11	26	Do. . .	Durban Museum.
54½	32½	...	...	N. Somaliland	J. Menges.
54¼	40¾	10½	39½	Zululand .	C. H. Akroyd.
54⅛	38⅞	10¼	22⅝	Somaliland . .	P. H. G. Powell-Cotton.
54	40	10¼	32	Do. .	Captain C. S. Timins.

GREATER KUDU (Strepsiceros kudu)—*continued.*

Length. ide s.	Straight line.	Circumference.	Tip to Tip.	Locality.	Owner.
	41	11	37¾	?	Sir Edmund G. Loder, Bart.
	42	10¾	35¼	Zululand . . .	A. Cameron.

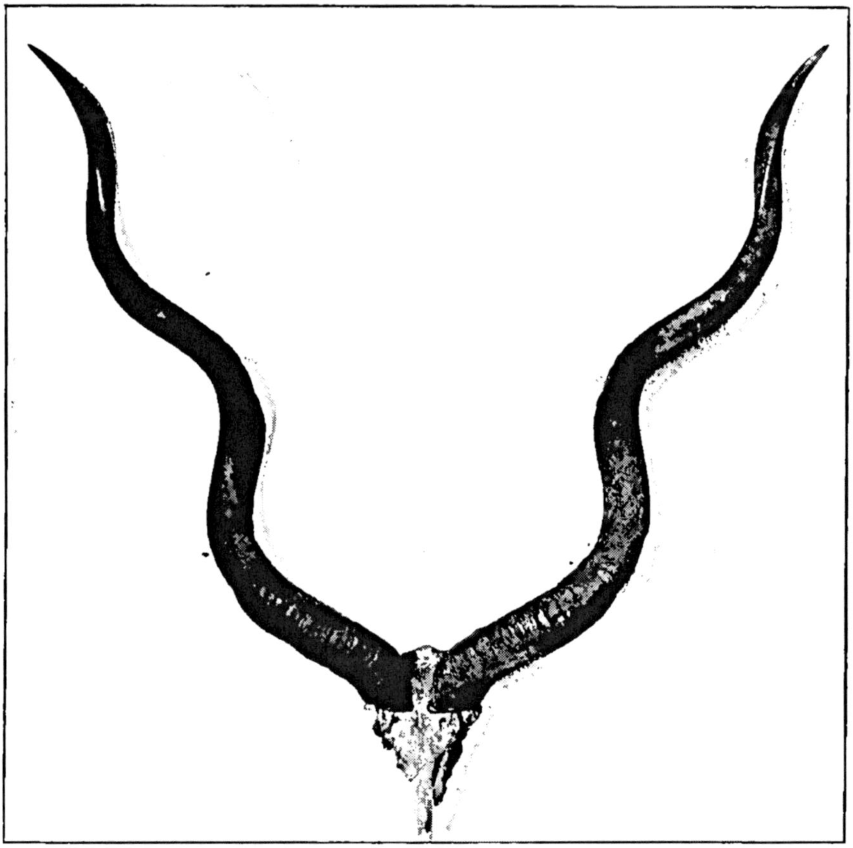

Frontlet and Horns of Greater Kudu, from F. H. Barber's specimen.

	42	11¾	39¾	Mashonaland . .	Earl of Dunmore.
	40½	10½	31¼	South Africa . .	Dr. W. P. Y. Bainbrigge.
	40	11¼	24	Do. .	Lieut.-Col. W. Sitwell.
	39	10¼	32	Somaliland . . .	Norman B. Smith.
	41¼	10¼	32½	S.W. Somaliland . .	C. V. A. Peel.

GREATER KUDU (Strepsiceros kudu)—*continued.*

Length. On outside curve.	Length. Straight line.	Circumference.	Tip to Tip.	Locality.	Owner.
53⅝	41	10	25	Mashonaland	J. A. Jameson.
-53½	36½	9½	23½	Somaliland	J. Brander Dunbar.
53½	39	10½	31¼	Zululand	Lieut.-Col. Hon. W. Coke.
-53½	40½	11½	40½	Lebombo Mountains	Count E. Hoyos.
53½	37	9⅝	23	Somaliland	E. Lort-Phillips.
53	41¼	10¼	28¾	South Africa	W. Y. Campbell.
...	40.7	8.8	30.9	Bahr Setit	Prince Henry of Liechtenstein.
52⅞	40	10⅛	37	Delagoa Bay	Sir John Kirk, K.C.B.
52¾	39¾	9¾	25⅝	Mashonaland	Sir John Willoughby, Bart.
-53½	36½	9½	23½	Do.	J. Brander Dunbar.
52½	35½	9¾	22	Somaliland	The late W. Babington.
52½	37¼	...	...	Do.	Major H. G. C. Swayne.
52⅜	40¼	10	36½	Zululand	Major-Gen. Sir Arthur Ellis, K.C.V.O.
52¼	42	11½	35	Natwani River	R. J. Cuninghame.
-52½	44	11	43¾	Lebombo Mountains	Count E. Hoyos.
52⅛	41⅞	10¾	39⅝	Zululand	Hon. Charles Ellis.
52⅛	37½	9¼	23½	Somaliland	T. W. H. Clarke.
52	42	10⅜	33	South Africa	The late W. F. Webb.
52	36½	10	39½	Somaliland	E. N. Buxton.
-52	43 5/16	10	39⅜	Damaraland	Th. Rehbock.
-52	38¾	10½	35	South Africa	James J. Harrison.
-52	38½	...	...	Do.	C. T. Jones.
51½	36½	11	29	Zululand	A. J. Brandon.
51½	39½	10	31½	Somaliland	W. H. Cobb.
51½	39¾	10¼	28⅝	South Africa	W. P. Rylands.
51½	38½	10	26½	British Central Africa	John Yule.
51½	36½	11	29	Zululand	A. J. Brandon.
51¼	40½	10¾	28¾	Mashonaland	Col. F. Rhodes, D.S.O.
50¾	38	9¼	34	Somaliland	J. Benett-Stanford.

GREATER KUDU (Strepsiceros kudu)—*continued.*

Length. On outside curve.	Length. Straight line.	Circumference.	Tip to Tip.	Locality.	Owner.
50½	38½	10	36⅝	Somaliland . .	Digby Davies.
50½	38	9½	30¾	Do. .	Captain G. Campbell.
50½	38	10¾	22¼	South Africa . . .	R. A. Cooper.
...	38	12	36	?	Earl of Dartmouth.
50¼	38½	8½	29½	Somaliland .	W. D. James.
50¼	35	9¼	24½	Do. . . .	B. R. M. Glossop.
-50	39	10½	48½	Khama's Country	H. A. Bryden.
50	35	9½	13½	Somaliland . .	Captain J. M'Call Maxwell.
-50	45	11	37	Abyssinia . .	Prince de Lucinge.
50	37¼	10	28¾	South Africa . .	E. D. Scott.
49⅞	39⅞	10⅞	40½	Limpopo River .	R. M. Sagar-Musgrave.
49¾	40¼	9½	33¾	Zomba, B.C.A. . .	C. C. Bowring.
-49½	37¾	10½	19½	Somaliland . .	C. V. A. Peel.
49½	36	9½	31¼	Do. . .	Major C. F. Blane.
49½	40½	11¾	47	Matabeleland	Hon. John Ward.
49	38	8⅞	29⅝	Somaliland . .	C. Liddell.
-49	39	11¾	25	Nyasaland . .	Alex. R. Alston.
48¼	38	10	32	Sabi River . .	Sir Thomas Fowler, Bart.
48	37	10½	27¾	British Central Africa .	Commander A. T. Hunt.
48	35½	10	31	Somaliland . . .	R. McD. Hawker.
48	35	10½	30	Do. .	W. W. Ashley.
-48	...	10	33½	Do. . .	A. E. Pease.
47⅞	35¾	9⅞	24⅝	Do. .	A. H. Straker.
47½	36½	10¼	27⅝	South Africa . .	British Museum.
47½	35½	9½	26½	Somaliland . .	Prince Nicolas Ghika.
47½	35	8¾	38⅝	Sudan . .	Col. Ralph Vivian.
47¼	37⅛	10¼	35½	South Africa . .	H.R.H. the Duke of Saxe-Coburg and Gotha.
47¼	34¾	9¼	25	Somaliland . .	Lord Delamere.
47⅛	34¼	10	21	Do. . .	Major C. C. Ellis.

GREATER KUDU (Strepsiceros kudu)—*continued.*

Length. On outside curve.	Length. Straight line.	Circumference.	Tip to Tip.	Locality.	Owner.
47	35¾	10½	33½	Somaliland .	J. Kenneth Foster.
47	35¾	10	31	Do. . .	T. W. Greenfield.
47	35½	10½	31¼	Do.	P. B. Vander-Byl.
47	35	8¾	23¼	Do. .	Captain B. L. Carew.
46¾	37½	9¾	39¼	Do.	F. G. Gunnis.
46½	34¾	10	25¼	Sudan . .	Lieut.-Col. Hon. W. Coke.
46½	34½	9½	...	Abyssinia .	British Museum.
46½	33¾	9½	24½	Somaliland .	Major H. G. C. Swayne.
46½	34½	10	31	Do. . .	P. R. Denny.
46½	38	10¾	41¼	Do. . . .	A. J. Forbes.
46	36	9¾	27⅜	Do.	G. H. Cheetham.
46	36	9½	16	Do.	Count Scheibler.
45⅞	33⅝	9⅛	25⅝	Sudan .	Count T. Palffy.
45½	31⅛	9½	18½	Somaliland	Lord Delamere.
45⅜	34¼	9½	11⅒	Do.	Paris Museum.
45	35	9⅜	32⅛	Kaokoland .	Captain F. Cookson.
43½	34½	9¾	29	Benguela .	G. W. Penrice.
♀ 37	10	...	...	South Africa .	F. C. Selous.
♀ 27½	...	3¾	8¾	Do. .	Julius Jeppe.
♀ See *Field*, 4th February 1893				Do. . . .	F. C. Selous.
♀ 26¾	...	...	36	?	C. T. Jones.

Head of Lesser Kudu, from a specimen shot by Mr. Norman B. Smith.

LESSER KUDU (Strepsiceros imberbis).

Godir of the Somalis.   *Sara* of the Abyssinians of Danakil.
Kungu of the Swahilis.

An old male shot by Viscount Edmond de Poncins, 18th Nov. 1897, Digago, Somaliland, measured as follows :—

	inches.
From nose to root of tail	67
Tail	$11\frac{7}{8}$
Height at withers	$41\frac{3}{5}$
Round the body	41
„ neck	$20\frac{1}{2}$

Except for its brighter colour, the closer spiral and smaller diverence of the horns, and the absence of a fringe of long hair on the throat (whence the name *imberbis*), this beautiful little antelope might almost pass for a miniature of its larger relation. Height at shoulder about 3 feet 5 inches.

Distribution.—North-East Africa, from Somaliland to German and British East Africa. This antelope generally goes in pairs or threes, and is partial to the cover of thick bush, from which it seldom emerges except for the purpose of feeding. Till the opening up of its habitat, it was very rare in collections.

Length. On outside curve.	Length. Straight line.	Circumference.	Tip to Tip.	Locality.	Owner.
35¼	26¼	7½	16½	N. Somaliland	Norman B. Smith. (See illustration.)
34	26½	...	...	Do.	Major H. G. C. Swayne.
34	26	6¾	14¼	Do.	W. W. Ashley.
34	27	6¾	11	Do.	R. McD. Hawker, British Museum.
33	26	7½	9½	Do.	Norman B. Smith.
32½	25⅛	7	8	Somaliland	Capt. T. R. Harkness.
32¼	25¾	7	17	Do.	Sir Edmund G. Loder, Bart.
-32	26	6½	10½	Hawash, Abyssinia	Prince de Lucinge.
-31⅞	25⅝	...	11⅞	N. Somaliland	J. Menges.
31¾	24¼	6¼	14½	Do.	Lord Delamere.
31½	25¼	6⅜	11⅝	Do.	Sir John Kirk, K.C.B.
-31½	24	6½	12	Do.	T. W. H. Clarke.
31½	24	6¾	...	Do.	Major C. C. Ellis.
31¼	25	7	10	Do.	Capt. G. F. T. Leather.
31¼	24½	6¾	14½	Do.	Major H. G. C. Swayne.
31	25	7¼	9½	Do.	W. H. Cobb.
31	24	6¾	9½	Do.	G. H. Cheetham.
-30¾	25	6½	9¾	Do.	Viscount Edmond de Poncins.
30¾	24⅜	6⅝	11⅞	Do.	W. D. James.
30¾	24	6⅞	9	Do.	E. P. Hare.
30⅝	25½	6⅜	11⅛	Do.	A. H. Straker.
-30½	23	6½	8½	Teita, East Africa	E. Gedge.
-30½	24	6	12½	Somaliland	T. W. H. Clarke.
30½	24¾	6⅝	10¼	Do.	Lord Delamere.
-...	24	...	...	Do.	Bombay Natural History Society's Museum.

LESSER KUDU (Strepsiceros imberbis)—*continued.*

Length. On outside curve.	Length. Straight line.	Circumference.	Tip to Tip.	Locality.	Owner.
30¼	24	6⅝	11⅞	Somaliland	H.R.H. le Duc d'Orléans.
-30	25½	7	14	Do.	Capt. M. M'Neill.
29¾	22½	6¾	13¼	Do.	R. Wahrmann.
-29¾	21½	6½	10½	Do.	Count J. de Bylands.
29½	23	6½	13¾	Do.	Prince Demeter Ghika.
29⅜	22½	6¾	13⅞	Do.	E. Lort-Phillips.
-29¼	25	7	12¾	Do.	A. H. Straker.
29	23½	6¾	13½	Do.	J. Kenneth Foster.
29	23½	6½	11⅛	East Africa	Sir Robert Harvey, Bart.
-29	22	6½	12	Somaliland	A. Ohlsson.
29	23½	6	12½	Do.	R. McD. Hawker.
28⅞	21⅞	6½	9	East Africa	H. C. V. Hunter.
28¾	22½	6¾	11	Somaliland	Sir H. D. Tichborne, Bart.
28¾	21½	5	9	East Africa	Sir Edmund G. Loder, Bart.
28¾	22	6¼	13	Somaliland	R. McD. Hawker.
-28⅝	23	7	11	Do.	Dr. Percy Rendall.
28¼	23¼	7⅛	10	Do.	T. W. Greenfield.
-28¼	20½	7	13½	Do.	Count E. Hoyos.
28⅛	23	5½	11⅝	Do.	Sir John Kirk, K.C.B., British Museum.
...	23	6¾	10¾	Do.	Col. Arthur Paget.
28	23	...	15	Do.	Lieut.-Col. J. W. H. Flanagan.
28	23	6¼	11¼	Do.	P. B. Vander-Byl.
28	22	6¾	9½	Do.	Captain C. H. Villiers.
28	22	6¾	13½	Do.	Dr. Donaldson Smith.
27¾	24	6½	11	Do.	Ford G. Barclay.
...	-24	6¾	13½	Do.	C. V. A. Peel.
27¼	21⅝	6½	12¾	South Somaliland	Sir John Kirk, K.C.B.
27¼	22	6¼	7	Somaliland	Hon. Walter Rothschild.
-27	...	6½	13	Do.	A. E. Pease.

LESSER KUDU (Strepsiceros imberbis)—*continued.*

Length.		Circumference.	Tip to Tip.	Locality.		Owner.
On outside curve.	Straight line.					
−26$\frac{15}{16}$	24	6$\frac{3}{4}$	13	Somaliland	.	Prince Demeter Ghika.
26$\frac{3}{4}$	19$\frac{3}{4}$	6$\frac{1}{4}$	10$\frac{1}{4}$	Do.		Edinburgh Museum.
26$\frac{1}{2}$	22	6	14	Do.		Captain C. S. Timins.
26$\frac{1}{4}$	21$\frac{3}{4}$	6$\frac{1}{2}$	12$\frac{5}{8}$	Do.		Major H. C. Morland.
26$\frac{1}{8}$	21$\frac{1}{2}$	6$\frac{1}{2}$	12$\frac{3}{4}$	Do.		F. G. Gunnis.
−25$\frac{3}{4}$	21$\frac{1}{4}$	6$\frac{1}{2}$	12$\frac{3}{4}$	Do.	.	Count Scheibler.
−...	21	...	...	Do.	.	J. D. Inverarity.
−25$\frac{5}{8}$	20$\frac{6}{c}$	6$\frac{3}{8}$	11	Do.		Paris Museum.
−25	21$\frac{3}{4}$	6$\frac{1}{2}$	10$\frac{1}{2}$	Do.	.	Digby Davies.
24$\frac{3}{4}$	19$\frac{1}{4}$	5$\frac{3}{4}$	9$\frac{3}{4}$	Do.	.	.	Captain W. H. Williamson.
24	20	6	14	East Africa	.	.	W. Astor Chanler.
−24	19	6	14$\frac{1}{2}$	Somaliland	.	.	J. Brander-Dunbar.
−24	20$\frac{3}{4}$	5$\frac{1}{2}$	9$\frac{1}{2}$	Do.	.	.	Julius Jeppe.

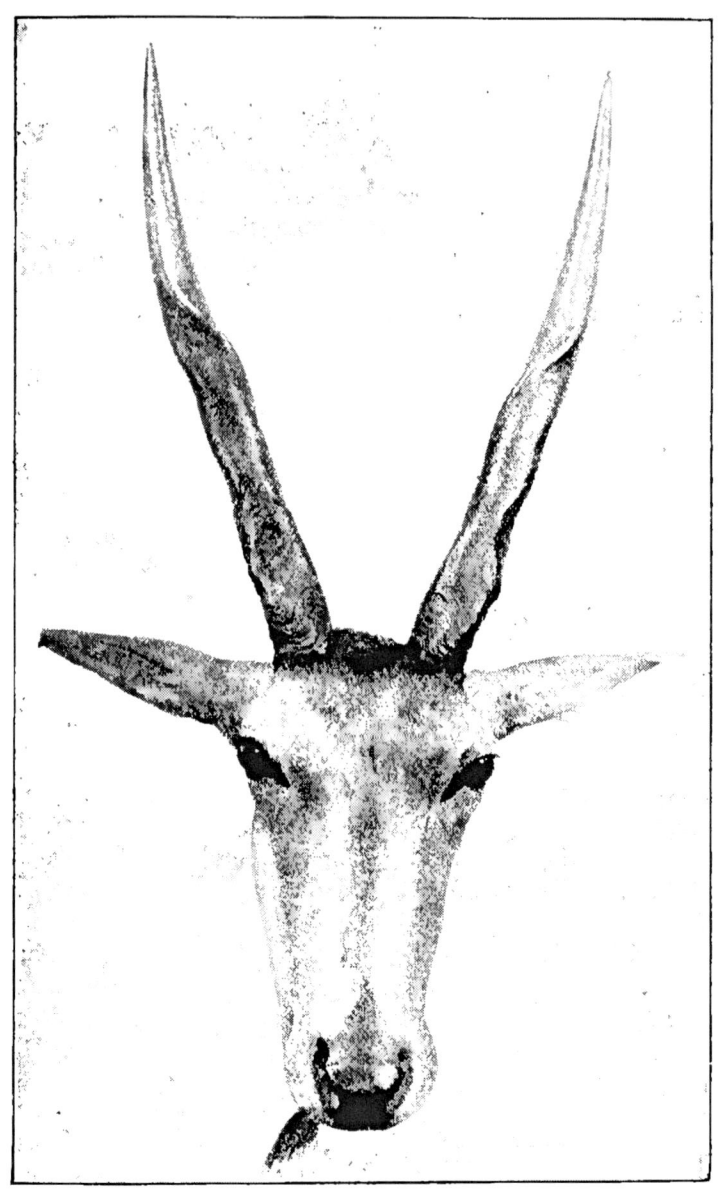

Head of Cow Eland shot by F. C. Selous.

ELAND (Taurotragus oryx).

Doo of the Masaras.
Ee-pofo of the Makalakas.
Eland of the Dutch and English.
Impofo of the Amandebele.
Insefo of the Masubias and Batongas.

Mofo of the Mashonas.
Mpofu of Swahili.
Mpofu in the Barotse country.
Mpofu in the Lake Ngami country.
Oo-schefo of the Macubas.
Pofo of the Bechuanas.

Tsefu in the Chilala and Chibisa countries.

In addition to being the largest of all antelopes, eland are distinguished from their immediate relatives by the presence of horns in both sexes; these forming a close spiral like a screw, with an upward and outward direction. Female horns are more slender than those of the bulls. Other distinctive features of the genus are to be found in the large dewlap and the long, tufted, ox-like tail.

Bulls of the common eland stand from 5 feet 9 inches to as much as $6\frac{1}{2}$ feet at the shoulder. They have a large tuft of brown hair on the forehead, and the horns are of moderate length and stoutness. The typical race (*T. oryx typicus*), which formerly extended from the Cape nearly to the Zambesi, has a uniformly tawny skin, without transverse white stripes or a dark brown band above the knees; and appears to be the largest form. Apparently somewhere in Rhodesia a dark brown band is assumed by immature bulls. And as we go northward towards the Zambesi, and thence north and east into the heart of the continent, the bulls have not only this dark leg-band, but the body in both sexes is marked by fine vertical white lines. As this striped variety was discovered by Livingstone and his companions, it has been appropriately named *T. oryx livingstonianus.* Westward the species ranges into Angola.

Throughout Southern Africa, largely owing to the skin-hunters, eland are now becoming exceedingly scarce; and they have already more or less completely disappeared from Cape Colony, Natal, the Orange Free State, Griqualand West, and the Transvaal. In the northern Kalahari, where they subsist for a great part of the year without water, large herds are still to be met with. No species of large game is more easily approached than eland, and, as a rule, none succumbs more speedily to the bullet. Occasionally female eland develop horns in which the spiral is almost obsolete and the length exaggerated; these have been supposed to indicate a distinct species (*Antilope triangularis*).

Head of Bull Eland.

ELAND (Taurotragus oryx)—*continued.*

Length straight line.	Circumference.	Tip to Tip.	Locality.	Owner.
– ♀ 35$\frac{3}{16}$	8$\frac{9}{16}$	20$\frac{1}{16}$	Zomba Plain, B.C.A. .	Dr. Percy Rendall.
– ♀ 33$\frac{1}{2}$	...	...	?	F. H. Barber.
♀ 32$\frac{1}{4}$	6$\frac{3}{4}$	...	Near Chobe River	M. C. Greaves-Bagshawe.
[1] ♀ 32$\frac{1}{4}$	6$\frac{3}{4}$	5$\frac{3}{4}$	South Africa .	Julius Jeppe.
–32$\frac{1}{4}$	...	...	?	Carl Hagenbeck.
[1] ♀ 32$\frac{5}{8}$	7$\frac{1}{8}$	8$\frac{3}{4}$	?	Mr. Justice Hopley.
–32	...	...	?	J. Benett-Stanford.
31$\frac{3}{4}$	12$\frac{1}{4}$	22$\frac{3}{4}$	?	Hon. Walter Rothschild.
♀ 31$\frac{3}{4}$	7$\frac{3}{4}$	17	Matabeleland .	Major R. Hayes-Sadler.
♀ 31$\frac{3}{4}$	7$\frac{1}{2}$	15$\frac{1}{2}$	?	F. Struben.
♀ 31$\frac{3}{4}$	7$\frac{1}{2}$	18$\frac{1}{2}$	Mashonaland	S. Chillingworth.
31$\frac{5}{8}$	10$\frac{1}{4}$	25$\frac{1}{2}$	East Africa. .	F. J. Jackson, C.B.
31$\frac{1}{2}$	12$\frac{3}{4}$	12$\frac{1}{2}$	Near where Salisbury now stands	F. C. Selous, British Museum.
♀ 31$\frac{1}{2}$	8$\frac{1}{4}$	20$\frac{3}{8}$	Mashonaland . .	' Do.
– ♀ 31$\frac{1}{4}$	7	17$\frac{1}{4}$	?	Julius Jeppe.
31	13	12	Mashonaland . .	F. C. Selous.
–31	9$\frac{1}{2}$	21	Nyasaland . .	F. Vaughan Kirby.
– ♀ 31	...	...	?	J. Benett-Stanford.
–30$\frac{3}{4}$	11$\frac{1}{2}$	28$\frac{3}{4}$	Nyasaland . .	Major P. W. Forbes.
30$\frac{3}{4}$	8$\frac{1}{4}$	25	?	R. A. Cooper.
♀ 30$\frac{5}{8}$	7$\frac{1}{2}$	21$\frac{3}{4}$	Lake Ngami . .	Major H. J. Goold-Adams, C.B., C.M.G.
–30$\frac{1}{2}$	...	...	?	O. R. Dunell.
♀ 30	7$\frac{1}{4}$	20$\frac{1}{4}$	Hanyani River . .	Capt. M. D. Graham.
–29$\frac{3}{4}$	9$\frac{1}{2}$	9	British Central Africa .	H. C. Macdonald.
–29$\frac{3}{4}$	9$\frac{1}{2}$	9	Do.	Dr. Percy Rendall.
29$\frac{1}{2}$	8	22	Do.	Commander A. T. Hunt.
29$\frac{1}{2}$	7$\frac{1}{2}$	8	S. Africa .	C. D. Rudd.
–29$\frac{1}{4}$	15$\frac{1}{2}$	12$\frac{3}{4}$	Do. .	A. Ohlsson.
– ♀ 29$\frac{1}{4}$	8$\frac{1}{2}$	17	Do.	Mr. Justice Hopley.

[1] The so-called *A. triangularis.*

ELAND (Taurotragus oryx)—*continued.*

Length straight line.	Circumference.	Tip to Tip.	Locality.	Owner.
29	10	17	Near Lake Ngami	Major H. J. Goold-Adams, C.B., C.M.G.
♀ 29	7⅛	18½	Matabeleland . .	Hon. C. Greville.
29	12½	14	Do.	Abe Bailey.
29	8¼	13¾	Benguela . .	G. W. Penrice.
–29	...	...	Pungwe .	Count E. Hoyos.
28¾	13½	4½	Matabeleland .	W. Van Ness.
28¾	11½	24	?	F. Struben.
♀ 28½	7¾	6½	Kalahari . . .	H. A. Bryden.
28½	11½	8⅜	British Central Africa .	Rowland Ward.
28½	11	18¾	Barotseland . .	R. T. Coryndon.
28⅛	10⅞	12½	?	Sir Edmund G. Loder, Bart.
28	10½	19½	British Central Africa .	J. E. Gough.
28	12	19	Upper Shiré, B.C.A. .	C. C. Bowring.
–28	8½	15¼	E. C. Africa . .	James J. Harrison.
– ♀ 28	...	...	?	Cape Town Museum.
♀ 28	8¼	19½	Barotseland . .	R. T. Coryndon.
27⅞	11	16	Mashonaland . .	Sir John Willoughby, Bart.
27½	10½	18	B. E. Africa . .	Lord Delamere.
27½	11¾	12½	?	R. A. Cooper.
– ♀ 27½	7½	16	?	James J. Harrison.
♀ 27½	8¼	5	Rhodesia . .	W. W. Ashley.
27½	8⅜	10	Matabeleland	Capt. Sir K. Fraser, Bart.
27¼	11	15¼	Pungwe	P. B. Vander-Byl.
♀ 27¼	13	20	Matabeleland .	Major James Grant.
– ♀ 27	...	10	East Africa	Sir John Willoughby, Bart.
27	11	10¾	Pungwe .	Marquis of Hamilton.
27	11½	13	Do.	F. J. Mitchell.
♀ 26	7¾	13¼	East Africa .	Lord Delamere.
26	8¼	10⅛	Kaokaland . .	Capt. F. Cookson.

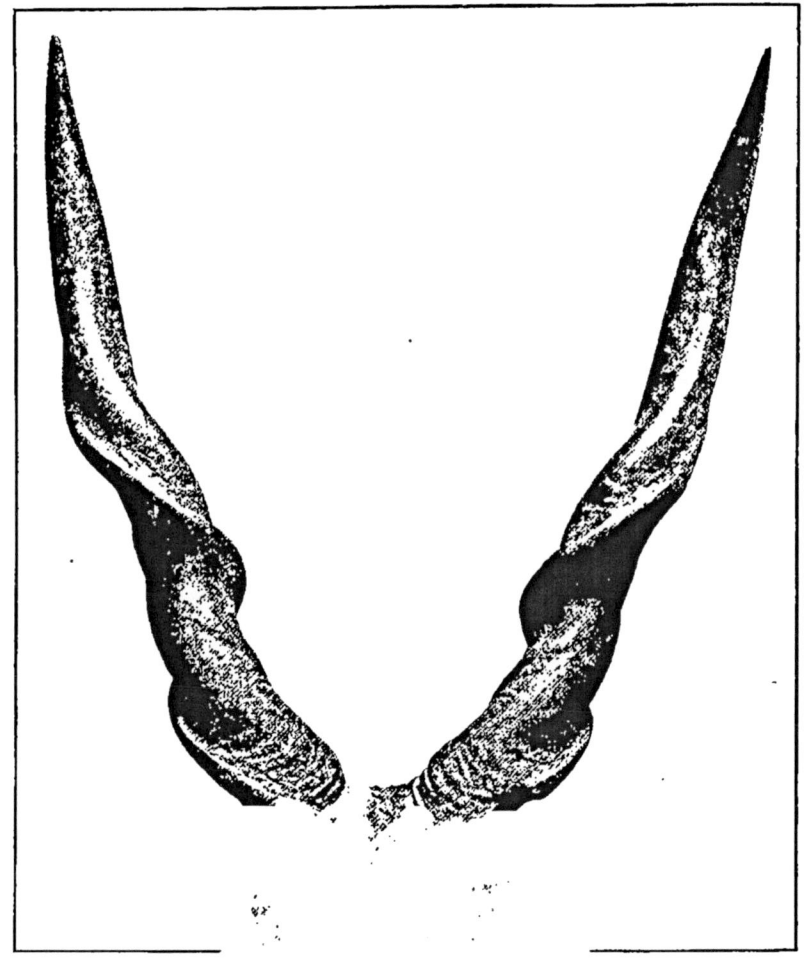

Frontlet and Horns of Senegambian Eland, from the Gambia.

SENEGAMBIAN ELAND (Taurotragus derbianus).

Although living specimens appear formerly to have been in the collection at Knowsley, this magnificent species is chiefly known in England by the horns. These are longer and stouter than those of the common species, and thus confirm the statements as to the larger size of the western animal. The bulls are reported to have no dark fore-lock, but a dark-brown mane. Horns of cows are relatively small.

Distribution.—The open districts of the interior of Senegambia and Gambia.

SENEGAMBIAN ELAND (Taurotragus derbianus)—*continued.*

Length straight line.	Circumference.	Tip to Tip.	Locality.	Owner.
-40	13½	Single horn	?	Berlin Museum.
-39⅜	...	...	?	Paris Museum.
34¼	14⅛	22¾	Gambia	Sir Edmund G. Loder, Bart.
-34	13½	...	?	F. Coburn.
34	12¾	...	?	J. Carr Saunders.
-34	11½	17	Gambia	Dublin Museum.
32½	12½	29⅞	Do.	A late Earl of Derby, British Museum.
32½	9¼	12¾	?	Sir Edmund G. Loder, Bart.
32¼	13	23¼	Gambia	H.R.H. le Duc d'Orléans.
32	13	24¼	?	Hon. Walter Rothschild.
31⅞	11⅝	28⅝	Gambia	A late Earl of Derby, British Museum.
31¼	12½	15¼	Do.	H. C. Goddard.
31⅛	12	18⅝	?	Sir Victor Brooke's Collection.
-31	11½	...	Gambia	Sir R. B. Llewelyn, K.C.M.G.
30⅞	10¾	26¾	?	F. W. Reade, British Museum.
-27⁹⁄₁₆	13⅜	23⅝	Senegambia	Paris Museum.
24¼	9	6¼	Do.	F. W. Reade, British Museum.

Frontlet and Horns of Count Arpad Teleki's Chamois.

CHAMOIS (Rupicapra tragus).

With the chamois we take leave of the antelopes properly so-called, and come to a group connecting the former to a considerable extent with the true goats, one member of the group being indeed commonly designated the Rocky Mountain goat.   Most of these ruminants are more or less goat-like in general appearance, having narrow goat-like teeth and short or moderately long tails.   Their horns, which are black in colour, are, however, quite distinct from those of the goats, being for the most part cylindrical in section, and curving backwards. From the other members of the group the chamois is at once distinguished by the sharp hook formed by the backward curvature of the horns, which rise almost vertically from the head.   The coloration is too well known to need description, although attention may be directed to the dark streak running from the eye to the sides of the muzzle.   Height at shoulder reaching 32 inches; weight of male generally about 65 lbs. (although 125 lbs. has been recorded in one case), that of female from 45 to 50 lbs.

Distribution.—The mountains of Central and Southern Europe, from the Pyrenees to the Caucasus.   Probably three distinct races may be recognised, namely, the comparatively small izard of the

Pyrenees, the true chamois, or gems, of the Alps, and a third form in the Caucasus.

Length on front curve.	Circumference.	Tip to Tip.	Weight.	Locality.	Owner.
[1]–12¼	4⅛	...	123⅛ lbs. not clean	Retyezat, Carpathians	Count Arpad Teleki. (See illustration.)
–12	...	9½	103 lhs. clean	Tyrol . . .	W. A. Baillie-Grohman.
–12	4	...	...	Hinter Riss . .	H.R.H. the Duke of Saxe-Coburg and Gotha.
–12	...	...	...	Tyrol . . .	Count Arco.
–11½	3⅝	6⅞	...	Albreis Morteratch, Engadine	A. E. Pease.
11¼	3½	6½	...	?	Col. Howard.
–11¼	...	$4\frac{15}{16}$	...	Retzezah, Transylvania	Baron A. Nopcsa.
–11	4	...	...	Tyrol . .	W. A. Baillie-Grohman.
–11	3¾	5½	...	?	Count John of Meran.
10¾	3½	$4\frac{3}{10}$	...	Tyrol . . .	Sir Edmund G. Loder, Bart.
10¾	3½	$4\frac{3}{10}$	...	Do. . .	Do.
–10¾	3¾	7½	...	?	Eberhard Hollinek.
–10½	3½	5⅜	...	Austria .	H.R.H. the Duke of Braganza.
–10½	2¾	5	...	?	Count John of Meran.
–10⅜	3	4⅛	...	?	Marquis Ivrea.
10¼	3½	5¼	...	?	E. N. Buxton.
10¼	4⅛	3⅞	...	Tyrol .	Sir Edmund G. Loder, Bart.
–10¼	3	5⅜	...	?	Count Palffy.
–10¼	...	...	...	Transylvania .	C. G. Danford.
♀ 10¼	...	...	...	Grindelwald .	F. A. Labouchere.
10⅛	3¼	4⅛	...	Austrian Tyrol	G. A. Goldschmidt.
10	3⅝	4¾	...	Transylvania	J. G. K. Young.
–10	...	...	...	Grindelwald .	F. A. Labouchere.
9⅞	3¼	4¼	...	Tyrol . .	H.R.H. the Duke of Saxe-Coburg and Gotha.
9¾	3¼	3⅞	...	Transylvania .	C. G. Danford, British Museum.
9¾	3¾	3	...	W. Caucasus .	St. George Littledale.

1 Greatest width, 7½ inches.

CHAMOIS (Rupicapra tragus)—*continued.*

Length on front curve.	Circumference.	Tip to Tip.	Locality.	Owner.
$9\frac{5}{8}$	$3\frac{1}{4}$	$4\frac{1}{2}$	Caucasus	St. George Littledale.
$9\frac{5}{8}$	$3\frac{1}{2}$	4	Austrian Tyrol	Capt. R. A. J. Montgomerie, C.B., R.N.
$9\frac{5}{8}$	3	$3\frac{5}{8}$	?	Hon. Walter Rothschild.
$-9\frac{5}{8}$	$3\frac{1}{2}$	$3\frac{1}{2}$	Valtelline Alps	Major C. C. Ellis.
$-9\frac{1}{2}$	3	$3\frac{1}{2}$	Alps	Dublin Museum.
9·05	3·15	4·75	Savoy	Viscount Edmond de Poncins.
$9\frac{1}{4}$	$3\frac{1}{4}$	$3\frac{1}{2}$	W. Caucasus	St. George Littledale.
$-9\frac{1}{4}$	$2\frac{3}{8}$	$3\frac{1}{2}$	Austria	H. Brinsley Brooke.
9	3	$5\frac{1}{4}$	Pyrenees	Sir Victor Brooke's Collection.
9	$3\frac{1}{4}$	4	Tyrol	Julius Jeppe.
♀ 9	$2\frac{3}{4}$	$4\frac{1}{2}$	Styria	Major-Gen. Sir Arthur Ellis, K.C.V.O.
−9	$3\frac{1}{2}$	$2\frac{3}{4}$	Valtelline Alps	Count Scheibler.
9	3	$3\frac{3}{4}$	Zillerthall	Noel Fenwick.
$8\frac{3}{4}$	$3\frac{3}{8}$	$4\frac{1}{8}$	Austrian Tyrol	Major-Gen. Sir Arthur Ellis, K.C.V.O.
$8\frac{3}{4}$	$3\frac{3}{8}$	3	Caucasus	St. George Littledale.
$8\frac{3}{4}$	$3\frac{1}{2}$	$3\frac{3}{4}$	Austria	P. B. Vander-Byl.
$8\frac{3}{4}$	3	$4\frac{1}{4}$	Caucasus	Prince Demidoff.
$8\frac{5}{8}$	$3\frac{1}{2}$	$2\frac{3}{8}$	Do.	St. George Littledale.
♀ $8\frac{5}{8}$	...	$3\frac{1}{8}$	Bavaria 1870	F. C. Selous.
$8\frac{1}{2}$	$2\frac{5}{8}$	4	Alps	The late J. Gould, British Museum.
♀ $8\frac{3}{8}$	$2\frac{1}{4}$	$4\frac{3}{8}$	Pyrenees	Sir Victor Brooke's Collection.
$8\frac{1}{4}$	$3\frac{1}{8}$	$3\frac{3}{8}$	?	Sir Clement Hill, Bart.
♀ $8\frac{1}{8}$	3	2	Caucasus	St. George Littledale.
8	$2\frac{5}{8}$	...	Asturias	H. Brinsley Brooke.
8	$2\frac{1}{2}$	$1\frac{1}{2}$	Caucasus	Prince Demidoff.
♀ $7\frac{1}{2}$	$2\frac{1}{2}$	$7\frac{7}{8}$	Do.	Do.

Head of Himalayan Goral.   From a specimen shot in Nepal, in the British Museum.

HIMALAYAN GORAL (Cemas goral).

Goral of the W. Himalaya.   *Pÿ, Pÿar, Rai, Rom* of Kashmir.
Sáhare, Sarr of the Sutlej valley.

The gorals are near relatives of the serows, from which they may be distinguished by their inferior size, shorter horns, and absence of face-glands, as well as by certain differences in the conformation of the skull.   The horns curve regularly backwards, are conical in form, and marked by small irregular ridges for the greater part of their length. The hair is somewhat rough and shaggy, and the tail considerably longer than in the chamois.   In general colour the Himalayan goral is brown, tending more or less to rufous or grayish, with the face paler and rufescent, a black line from the nape down the back to the tail (which is also black), and a dark stripe down the front of each leg. Height at shoulder from 26 to 28 inches ; weight from 58 to 63 lbs.

By English sportsmen the goral is commonly termed the Himalayan chamois, its habits being very similar to those of the true chamois.

Distribution.—The Himalaya, from Bhutan and Sikim to Kashmir, at elevations from 3000 to 6000 feet.

HIMALAYAN GORAL (Cemas goral)—*continued.*

Length on front curve.	Girth.	Tip to Tip.	Locality.	Owner.
$-8\frac{1}{2}$	...	...	Bissahir .	Major A. E. Ward.
♀ $-8\frac{1}{2}$	...	...	Dalhousie	J. Johnston-Stewart.
-8	...	...	Kumaon	Major A. E. Ward.
-8	...	...	Chamba	Capt. C. B. Vandeleur.
8	$3\frac{3}{4}$	$3\frac{1}{8}$	Do.	Capt. Cecil Levita.
$7\frac{5}{8}$	$3\frac{3}{4}$	$3\frac{1}{2}$	?	Hume Collection, British Museum.
$7\frac{1}{2}$	3	$2\frac{3}{4}$	Near Musuri	A. O. Hume, C.B.
$-7\frac{1}{2}$	...	...	Mountains near Dalhousie .	Capt. F. E. S. Adair.
$7\frac{7}{16}$	$3\frac{1}{2}$	$2\frac{3}{4}$	Chamba	A. H. Ogilvy Spence.
$7\frac{1}{4}$	3	3	Do.	F. W. H. Walshe.
$7\frac{1}{8}$	$3\frac{1}{4}$	$2\frac{1}{2}$	Do.	Sir Edmund G. Loder, Bart.
$-7\frac{1}{8}$	$3\frac{3}{4}$	$3\frac{5}{8}$	Jhelam Valley, Kashmir	P. H. G. Powell-Cotton.
7	$2\frac{3}{4}$	$3\frac{3}{4}$	?	Major J. A. Orr-Ewing.
-7	$3\frac{1}{4}$	$3\frac{1}{8}$	?	Capt. H. W. Codrington.
-7	...	...	Near Almora, N.W.P.	Capt. B. H. Boucher.
-7	...	...	?	Indian Museum.
-7	...	...	Punjab	Capt. A. Hicks-Beach.
$6\frac{7}{8}$	$4\frac{1}{8}$	3	Kumaon	A. S. Crum.
$6\frac{7}{8}$	$3\frac{1}{2}$	$2\frac{7}{8}$	?	Owen Bevan.
$-6\frac{3}{4}$	...	...	?	Major R. H. Rattray.
$6\frac{3}{4}$	$3\frac{3}{4}$	$3\frac{1}{8}$	?	Capt. H. C. Copeman.
$-6\frac{3}{4}$	$3\frac{1}{2}$	2	Dalhousie . .	J. Johnston-Stewart.
$6\frac{5}{8}$	$3\frac{3}{8}$	$2\frac{3}{8}$	?	Dr. W. P. Y. Bainbrigge.
$6\frac{1}{2}$	$3\frac{3}{8}$	$3\frac{1}{4}$	West of Musuri . .	B. R. M. Glossop.
$6\frac{1}{4}$	3	$4\frac{1}{8}$	?	Capt. L. I. B. Hulke.
6	4	$2\frac{3}{4}$	?	J. E. Vaughan.
$-$ ♀ $5\frac{1}{2}$	$2\frac{1}{2}$	$1\frac{3}{4}$	Jhelam Valley, Kashmir	P. H. G. Powell-Cotton.
♀ $4\frac{3}{4}$	$2\frac{1}{4}$	$2\frac{1}{2}$	?	E. L. Phelps.

OTHER GORALS.

Species.	Collected by	Length on front curve.	Girth.	Tip to Tip.	Locality.	Owner.
Cemas edwardsi .	Père A. David	$8\frac{11}{16}$ $8\frac{6}{16}$	$7\frac{1}{2}$ $7\frac{1}{4}$	4 2	Moupin, Tibet	Paris Museum.
,, argyrochœtus	Do.	$9\frac{1}{2}$	$7\frac{1}{8}$	4	Ta - tsien - lou, Szechuan	Do.
,, caudatus	Do.	$6\frac{6}{16}$ $6\frac{1}{4}$	$3\frac{9}{16}$ 4	$3\frac{1}{8}$ $3\frac{1}{3}$	North of Pekin ?	Do. British Museum.
,, cinereus	Do.	$7\frac{1}{2}$	$3\frac{1}{8}$	$3\frac{6}{16}$	Tibet .	Paris Museum.
,, griseus .	Do.	$4\frac{3}{4}$	$3\frac{1}{8}$	$2\frac{3}{8}$	Do.	Do.

JAPANESE SEROW or GORAL (Nemorhædus crispus).

A small species serving in some degree to connect the gorals with the serows, since it agrees approximately in size with the former, but in other characters with the latter.

Distribution.—The southern islands of Japan ; an allied species . (*N. swinhoei*) inhabiting the island of Formosa.

Length on front curve.	Circum-ference.	Tip to Tip.	Locality.	Owner.
$5\frac{1}{4}$	$3\frac{5}{8}$	$3\frac{1}{8}$	Japan .	British Museum.

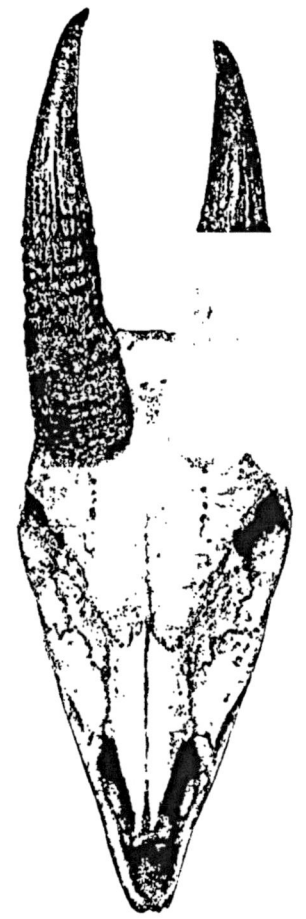

Skull and Horns of Himalayan Serow (A. O. Hume's record specimen).

HIMALAYAN SEROW (Nemorhædus bubalinus).

Serow, serowa of Gurhwal and many parts of the Himalaya.

Ramu-Halj, Sálábheer.   *Jungal*, Kangra.
Yamu, Kulu.   *Goa*, Chamba.
Aimu, Kumaon.

A large and clumsily built ruminant, with the ears long, the hair coarse, rather thin, and elongated into a crest from the nape to the withers ; the under-fur found in the gorals being absent.   The general colour of the upper parts is black or dark gray, with a grizzled appearance, owing to the whitish bases of the hairs ; the under parts, shoulders, and thighs being rusty red. Although by no means large, the shining black, somewhat rugose horns form decidedly handsome trophies. Height at shoulder from 33 to 37 or 38 inches ; weight from 120 to 190 lbs.

Distribution.—Throughout the Himalaya from Kashmir to the Mishmi Hills, at elevations of from 6000 to 12,000 feet ; also recorded from Yunnan.

Head of Male Himalayan Serow.
From a specimen shot by W. T. Blanford in Sikim, now in the British Museum.

Length on front curve.	Circumference.	Tip to Tip.	Locality.	Owner.
-12.25	6.5	2.75	Gurhwal . . .	A. O. Hume, C.B. (See Illustration on page 320.)
-12	...	...	Himalaya . . .	Major A. E. Ward.
-11	...	...	?	Major R. H. Rattray.
10½	5¾	3½	?	Hon. Charles Ellis.
-10½	5⅝	3½	Gurhwal . . .	A. P. Davis.
-10⅛	...	...	North of Musuri . .	Capt. Harry V. Brooke.
-10	5¾	5½	Mishmi Hills . .	A. O. Hume, C.B.
10	...	...	Kumaon . . .	Major A. E. Ward.

Y

HIMALAYAN SEROW (Nemorhædus bubalinus)—*continued.*

Length on front curve.	Circumference.	Tip to Tip.	Locality.	Owner.
$9\frac{7}{8}$	$5\frac{5}{8}$	$4\frac{1}{2}$	?	Sir Victor Brooke's Collection.
$9\frac{3}{4}$	$5\frac{1}{8}$	6	Pir Panjal . . .	R. Lydekker, British Museum.
$9\frac{1}{2}$	$5\frac{5}{8}$	$4\frac{3}{4}$	Kashmir .	St. George Littledale.
$9\frac{1}{2}$	$4\frac{7}{8}$	$3\frac{1}{4}$	Nepal . . .	The late B. H. Hodgson, British Museum.
$9\frac{1}{2}$	$5\frac{5}{8}$	$3\frac{3}{4}$	?	Sir Edmund G. Loder, Bart.
$- ♀ 9\frac{3}{8}$	$5\frac{1}{8}$	4	Sind Valley . .	P. H. G. Powell-Cotton.
9	$4\frac{1}{2}$	$2\frac{1}{2}$	North of Musuri .	B. R. M. Glossop.
$-8\frac{9}{10}$	$5\frac{3}{10}$	3	Gurhwal . . .	Lieut.-Col. L. L. Fenton.
$8\frac{1}{2}$	$4\frac{3}{4}$	4	Pir Panjal . .	Capt. N. C. Taylor.
$8\frac{1}{2}$	$5\frac{1}{4}$	$4\frac{1}{2}$	Kashmir . .	Col. R. Pole Carew, C.B.
$8\frac{1}{2}$	$4\frac{1}{2}$	$5\frac{1}{4}$	Ranikhet . .	D. R. Napier.
8	$4\frac{3}{4}$	$4\frac{3}{4}$	Near Darjiling .	R. Lydekker, British Museum.
$♀ 7\frac{1}{2}$	5	$2\frac{1}{2}$	Gangutri . .	Col. R. J. Heber-Percy.
$7\frac{1}{2}$	$4\frac{5}{8}$	3	?	Dr. W. P. Y. Bainbrigge.

BURMESE SEROW (Nemorhædus bubalinus sumatrensis).

Although commonly regarded as a distinct species, there can be little hesitation in classing this animal as a local race of the last, more especially as intermediate forms appear to occur in the neighbourhood of Darjiling. The chief distinction is the more decidedly rufous tint of the hair of the eastern race. Height at shoulder about $34\frac{1}{2}$ inches.

Distribution.—From the Eastern Himalaya, Moupin in Tibet, and Yunnan, to Sumatra, occurring throughout the Assam Hills, Burma, Siam, and the elevated tracts of the Malay Peninsula.

Length on front curve.	Circumference.	Tip to Tip.	Locality.	Owner.
9.25	5	2.75	Garro Hills . .	A. O. Hume, C.B.
-9.5	5	5.5	Arakan Hills .	Do.
9	$5\frac{1}{2}$	5	Burma . .	The late A. G. Trapmann.
9	5	2	Sumatra . . .	Hume Collection, British Museum.
-9	5	5	Burma . .	Vet.-Capt. G. H. Evans.
-9	...	...	Arakan Hills	Indian Museum.
$8\frac{3}{4}$	$5\frac{1}{4}$	$4\frac{1}{2}$	?	Hume Collection, British Museum.
$8\frac{3}{4}$	5.5	$4\frac{3}{4}$	Muleyit . . .	A. O. Hume, C.B.
$-8\frac{3}{4}$	$4\frac{7}{8}$	$2\frac{1}{8}$	Perak .	Perak Museum.
$-8\frac{1}{2}$	$5\frac{7}{8}$	6	Burma . . .	Vet.-Capt. G. H. Evans.
$8\frac{1}{4}$	5	$3\frac{1}{2}$	Upper Burma . .	Hon. Walter Rothschild.
$-8\frac{1}{8}$	$5\frac{1}{8}$	$5\frac{1}{4}$	Perak . . .	Perak Museum.
$7\frac{3}{4}$	$4\frac{5}{8}$	$4\frac{1}{4}$	Assam . .	A. M. Long.
$7\frac{1}{2}$	$4\frac{3}{4}$	5	?	Duke of Bedford.
$-7\frac{1}{8}$	$4\frac{7}{8}$	$3\frac{3}{8}$	Garro Hills . .	Dr. Percy Rendall.
$5\frac{7}{8}$	$3\frac{3}{4}$	$3\frac{5}{8}$	Moulmein, Tenasserim	The late Capt. R. C. Beavan, British Museum.

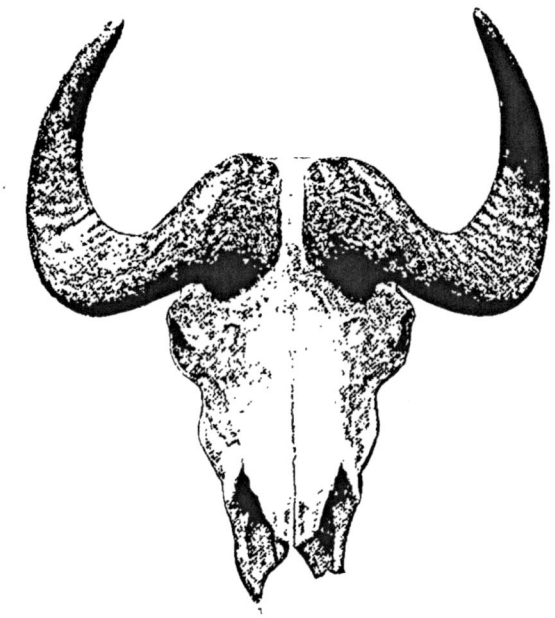

Skull and Horns of Male Takin.   From Col. J. Biddulph's record specimen.

TAKIN (Budorcas taxicolor).

Although recently suggested to be related to the musk-ox, this strange ruminant is more generally regarded as an aberrant relative of the serows.   It is heavily built, with stout limbs, large lateral hoofs, a short tail, a convex profile, and an almost completely hairy muzzle. But its most remarkable feature is to be found in the horns, which are large, massive, and bent somewhat after the fashion of those of a gnu, curving at first outwards and somewhat downwards, and then bending abruptly upwards about the middle of their length.   Height at shoulder about $3\frac{1}{2}$ feet.   Horns are present in both sexes, as in the serows and gorals, those of the female measuring about a foot in length, and lacking the curvature of those of the males.

Distribution.—Typically the Mishmi Hills on the northern frontier of Assam, but represented by a variety or allied species in Tibet, and perhaps a third in China.   Although living within sight of Indian territory, it does not appear that takin have ever been killed by English sportsmen ; and specimens are very rare in collections.

TAKIN (Budorcas taxicolor)—*continued.*

Length on front curve.	Circumference.	Tip to Tip.	Locality.	Owner.
–$24\frac{1}{4}$	...	...	Mishmi Hills . .	Col. J. Biddulph. (See illustration.)
–24.25	12.75	12.75	Do. . .	Indian Museum.
$22\frac{3}{8}$	$10\frac{5}{8}$	$14\frac{3}{4}$	Assam . . .	British Museum.
–22.5	13.5	10.75	Mishmi Hills . .	Indian Museum.
–22	$12\frac{3}{4}$	$12\frac{1}{4}$	Do. . .	Bombay Natural History Society's Museum.
$21\frac{11}{16}$	$11\frac{15}{16}$	$11\frac{3}{4}$	Do. . .	Dr. Percy Rendall.
21	12	$13\frac{1}{2}$	Do. . .	A. J. Walter.
$20\frac{7}{8}$	$11\frac{3}{8}$	$11\frac{7}{8}$	Assam . . .	Hume Collection, British Museum.
$20\frac{3}{4}$	$11\frac{7}{8}$	$12\frac{1}{2}$	Mishmi Hills . .	A. O. Hume, C.B.
$20\frac{3}{4}$	10	$12\frac{1}{8}$	Do. . .	Hon. Walter Rothschild.
$20\frac{1}{2}$	$10\frac{7}{8}$	$12\frac{3}{8}$	?	The late B. H. Hodgson, British Museum.
$19\frac{3}{4}$	11	$11\frac{1}{2}$	Mishmi Hills . .	Col. J. Biddulph.
$19\frac{3}{8}$	11	15	?	Sir Edmund G. Loder, Bart.
–19	...	...	?	Capt. E. T. Dalton, Indian Museum.
18	$10\frac{1}{4}$	8	?	British Museum.
$15\frac{1}{4}$	$9\frac{3}{8}$	$5\frac{3}{4}$	Mishmi Hills . .	The late B. H. Hodgson, British Museum.
$14\frac{3}{8}$	$8\frac{3}{4}$	$8\frac{7}{8}$	Upper Assam . .	Lieut.-Col. Graham.
♀ $10\frac{1}{4}$	8	13	Mishmi Hills . .	A. O. Hume, C.B. (See illustration.)

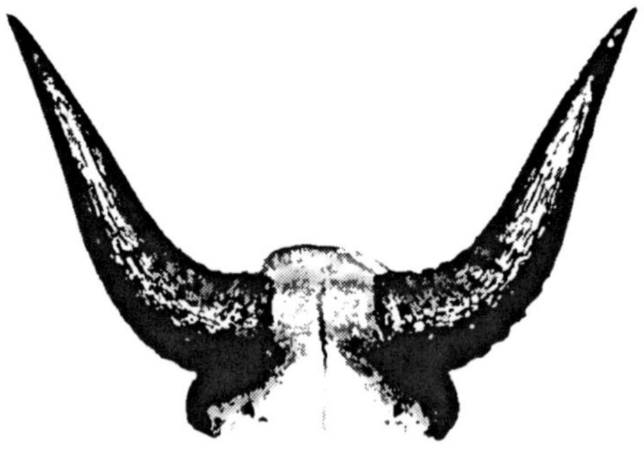

Frontlet and Horns of Female Takin. From A. O. Hume's specimen.

TIBETAN TAKIN (Budorcas taxicolor tibetanus).

Length on front curve.	Circumference.	Tip to Tip.	Locality.	Owner.
–19⅜	11½	13⅜	Tibet . .	Père A. David, Paris Museum.

KANSU TAKIN (Budorcas taxicolor sinensis).

20½	11½	11¾	Kansu, China . .	Hon. Walter Rothschild.

ROCKY MOUNTAIN GOAT (Haploceros montanus).

This is one of the very few mammals that are permanently white or whitish at all seasons; and although commonly termed a goat, it really belongs to the same group as the serows, which it closely resembles in the form and colour of the horns. In winter the hair is very long and pure white in colour; along the back it is erect, and much elongated on the withers and haunches, so as to give to the animal the appearance of possessing a pair of humps. The summer coat is comparatively short, and has a yellowish tinge. Height at shoulder just short of 3 feet; weight from 180 to 300 lbs.

Distribution.—North America; throughout the Rocky Mountains, from about lat. 36° in California at least as far north as lat. 60°. By American naturalists the proper generic name of the animal is considered to be *Oreamnos* instead of *Haploceros*.

Length on front curve.	Circumference.	Tip to Tip.	Locality.	Owner.
–11½	...	...	British Columbia .	Clive Phillipps-Wolley.
–11	...	...	Kutenay, B.C. . .	John T. Fannin (measured by).
–10½	5¾	...	Montana . . .	Walter James.
10¼	5¼	5½	British Columbia .	R. Rankin.
–10⅛	6½	...	Similkameen River, British Columbia	Arthur Pearse.
10⅛	5	6⅛	?	E. N. Buxton.
– ♀ 10⅛	4¾	...	British Columbia .	Capt. A. Egerton.
10	5⅜	6⅜	Do. . .	J. V. Colby.
–9¾	5	...	Montana . . .	Theodore Roosevelt.
9¾	5½	6¼	N.W. Territories .	S. Ratcliff.
9¾	5¼	6	Do. . .	H.R.H. le Duc d'Orleans.
9⅝	5¼	6⅛	Do. . .	Sir Edmund G. Loder, Bart.

ROCKY MOUNTAIN GOAT (Haploceros montanus)—*continued.*

Length on front curve.	Circumference.	Tip to Tip.	Locality.	Owner.
9½	5½	6¼	Alaska . . .	St. George Littledale.
9½	4½	...	North America . .	J. D. Cobbold.
♀ 9½	4¼	5½	British Columbia .	P. B. Vander-Byl.
9½	5¼	6⅜	East Kutenay, British Columbia	A. E. Butter.
9½	5¼	6⅛	Bitter Root Mts., U.S.A.	James J. Harrison.
♀ 9⅜	4½	5⅝	British Columbia .	A. E. Leatham.
9⅜	5⅜	6¾	Do. . .	T. W. H. Clarke.
9¼	5½	5¼	Do. . .	J. Turner-Turner.
9¼	5½	...	North America . .	Earl of Lonsdale.
9¼	5½	5¾	British Columbia .	G. Lloyd Graeme.
9⅛	...	6	Montana . . .	Thomas Bate, British Museum.
9⅛	5¼	5	British Columbia .	Sir Peter Walker, Bart.
9	4¾	6	Do. . .	T. P. Kempson.
8⅞	5½	4⅛	Do. . .	Count E. Hoyos.
8¼	4⅜	5¼	Do. . .	Count Scheibler.

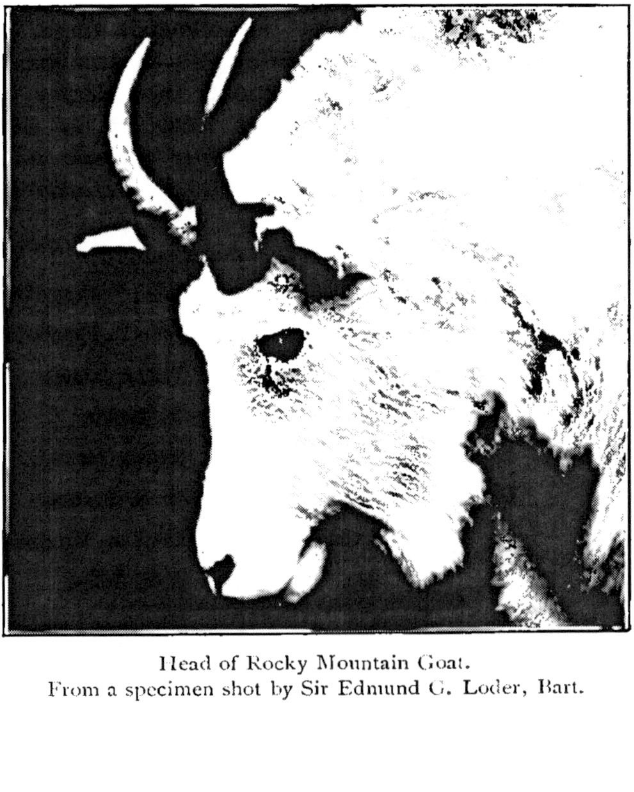

Head of Rocky Mountain Goat.
From a specimen shot by Sir Edmund G. Loder, Bart.

Head of Male Himalayan Tahr.

HIMALAYAN TAHR (Hemitragus jemlaicus).

The three species of tahr are the first representatives of that great group of ruminants which also includes the true goats and sheep.   In all these animals horns are, as a rule, present in both sexes, and are generally more or less distinctly angulated ; while the cheek-teeth have tall and narrow crowns like those of the serows, which the tahr serve to connect with the true goats.   From the latter tahr are readily distinguished by the small size of their horns, which exceed but little in length the head, as well as by the absence of a beard on the chin of the males.   The Himalayan tahr is easily recognised by the great length of the hair of the body, which, although in museum specimens generally combed straight, is very shaggy in nature ; and likewise by the form of the horns, which have a knotted sharp keel in front.   Height at shoulder from 36 to 40 inches ; weight about 200 lbs.   Mr. Wilson, " Mountaineer," had a pair of horns, length 16.5 and girth 10.5, which Mr. A. O. Hume measured.

Distribution.—The Himalaya, from Bhutan to Kashmir.

HIMALAYAN TAHR (Hemitragus jemlaicus)—*continued.*

Length on front curve.	Circumference.	Tip to Tip.	Locality.	Owner.
–14¾	...	...	Chamba . . .	A. H. Ogilvy Spence.
–14⅝	...	...	?	H. Vansittart.
14$\frac{9}{10}$	8¾	...	Chamba	J. S. Rivett-Carnac.
–14½	9¾	6¾	Do. . .	A. H. Ogilvy Spence.
14¼	8⅞	4⅜	?	A. Cadell.
14⅛	8⅞	6⅝	Kumaon . . .	A. O. Hume, C.B.
–14⅛	...	...	?	A. B. Lindsay.
14	...	...	?	Capt. R. L. Tottenham.
–14	...	...	?	Major A. E. Ward.
13⅞	9	8⅜	Chamba	Hugo de Burgh.
13⅞	...	...	Do.	Col. R. J. Heber-Percy.
13¾	9	11¼	?	Hume Collection, British Museum.
13¾	8⅜	6⅞	Danpur, Kumaon .	A. O. Hume, C.B.
13¾	8¼	7¾	?	I. Morse.
13⅝	8	6¼	?	Hume Collection, British Museum.
–13½	10	...	?	Major C. F. Blane.
13⅜	9⅛	5¾	?	Hon. Walter Rothschild.
13¼	8⅞	5¾	?	Sir Victor Brooke's Collection.
13¼	8¼	6⅞	Nepal (?) . .	Sir Edmund G. Loder, Bart.
13¼	8½	...	?	E. L. Phelps.
–13¼	9	5	?	P. H. G. Powell-Cotton.
–13	9	...	?	Indian Museum.
–13	9¾	...	Chamba	Capt. A. Hicks-Beach.
–13	9¼	...	Himalaya	Major-General Alexander A. A. Kinloch.
–12¾	...	...	Chamba . .	Col. R. J. Heber-Percy.
–12¾	9	7¾	Do. . . .	H. L. S. MacLean, Officers' Mess, Queen's Own Corps of Guides.
12½	8½	10	?	The late J. E. Ubsdell.
12¼	8⅞	4¾	?	Sir Robert Harvey, Bart.
12¼	8¼	6½	?	H.R.H. the Duke of Saxe-Coburg and Gotha.

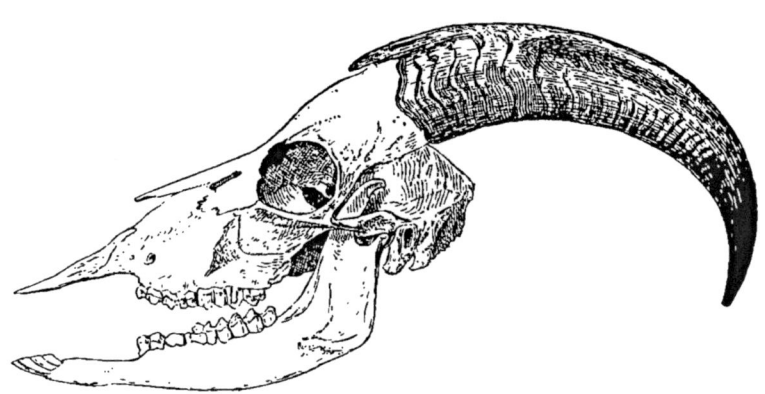

Skull and Horns of Male Arabian Tahr. (From Thomas, *P.Z.S.* 1894.)

ARABIAN TAHR (Hemitragus jayakeri).

A much smaller and rather shorter-haired species than the last, of a generally tawny brown colour, with relatively longer and more slender horns, which are less boldly knotted on the front edge. Height at shoulder about $24\frac{1}{2}$ inches.

This species, of which the type specimen is in the British Museum, was first obtained by Dr. A. S. G. Jayakar, in honour of whom it was named by Mr. O. Thomas in 1894.

Distribution.—Jebel Taw, and probably some of the other ranges of Oman, in South-East Arabia.

Length on front curve.	Locality.	Owner.
$-11\frac{5}{8}$	Oman Mountains . .	Surgeon Lieut.-Col. A. S. G. Jayaker.

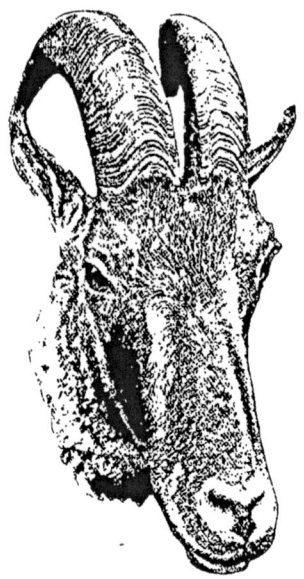

Head of Male Nilgiri Tahr.

NILGIRI TAHR (Hemitragus hylocrius).

Although commonly designated by British sportsmen the " Nilgiri ibex," this species (the warriattu of the native shikaris) is really a member of the same genus as the Himalayan tahr. From that species it is at once distinguished by its short hair and the form of the horns ; the latter having the outer surface convex instead of flat, and lacking the knotted front keel. The general colour is dark blackish-brown, old males developing a light saddle-like patch on the back. Height at shoulder from 39 to 42 inches in the males, and up to 35 inches in the females.

Distribution.—The hill-ranges of Southern India, including the Nilgiris, Anamalais, and the Western Ghats nearly to Cape Comorin ; usually at elevations of from 4000 to 6000 feet, but occasionally descending to lower levels. This interesting species has been greatly reduced in numbers by constant persecution, but as the herds have now been placed under Government protection, and a special permit is necessary for shooting, there is hope that it may shortly increase.

NILGIRI TAHR (Hemitragus hylocrius)—*continued.*

Length on front curve.	Circumference.	Tip to Tip.	Locality.	Owner.
-17.5	9.9	6	Nilgiris	Rhodes Morgan.
-17	$9\frac{3}{4}$	...	Do. .	Measured by General MacMaster, 1869.
$16\frac{1}{4}$	$8\frac{7}{8}$	$5\frac{5}{8}$	?	A. O. Hume, C.B.
-$16\frac{1}{2}$	...	...	Nilgiris .	St. George Littledale.
$16\frac{1}{2}$	$8\frac{1}{4}$	6	Do. .	S. G. Bird.
-16	9.5	5	Do. . .	Rhodes Morgan.
$15\frac{1}{2}$	$8\frac{3}{8}$	$7\frac{7}{8}$	Do. .	Sir Edmund G. Loder, Bart.
$15\frac{3}{8}$	$8\frac{3}{4}$	$6\frac{3}{4}$	Do. . .	Martyn Kennard.
$15\frac{7}{8}$	$8\frac{1}{4}$	6	Do. . . .	St. George Littledale.
$15\frac{1}{8}$	$8\frac{5}{8}$	$4\frac{3}{4}$	Do. . .	Martyn Kennard.
$15\frac{1}{8}$	$8\frac{5}{8}$	$4\frac{3}{4}$	Do. .	St. George Littledale.
-15	$8\frac{1}{4}$	$5\frac{1}{8}$	Do. . .	Sir H. D. Tichborne, Bart.
$14\frac{3}{4}$	$8\frac{1}{2}$	$5\frac{1}{2}$	Do. .	Capt. C. S. Timins.
$14\frac{3}{4}$	$8\frac{7}{8}$	$5\frac{1}{2}$	Do. . .	R. A. Sterndale.
$14\frac{3}{4}$	$8\frac{1}{4}$	$7\frac{1}{4}$	Do. .	M. Loam.
$14\frac{1}{2}$	$8\frac{3}{4}$	$6\frac{1}{4}$	Do.	British Museum.
$14\frac{1}{2}$	$8\frac{5}{8}$	$5\frac{5}{8}$	Do. .	Sir Victor Brooke's Collection.
$14\frac{5}{8}$	8	$4\frac{5}{8}$	Anamalai Hills .	T. W. Greenfield.
-$14\frac{1}{4}$	$8\frac{1}{4}$	4	Travancore . .	J. D. Inverarity.
-$14\frac{1}{4}$	8	$4\frac{1}{2}$	Do. .	A. E. Leatham.
14	$7\frac{3}{4}$	5	Do. .	Capt. Hon. E. Baring.
14	$7\frac{3}{4}$	$6\frac{1}{2}$	Do. .	Major G. S. Rodon.
14	$7\frac{5}{8}$	$6\frac{3}{8}$	Do. . .	Col. J. Biddulph.
♀ $12\frac{3}{8}$	$5\frac{1}{2}$	$2\frac{3}{8}$	Anamalai Hills .	M. Loam.
♀ $11\frac{3}{4}$	$5\frac{3}{4}$	$4\frac{1}{8}$	Do. . .	Hon. Walter Rothschild.
♀ 11.25	5.25	4	Do. .	A. O. Hume, C.B.
♀ $11\frac{1}{8}$	$5\frac{3}{4}$	...	Travancore .	Col. Hon. Francis C. Bridgeman.
♀ 10	$5\frac{3}{4}$	4	Nilgiris . .	St. George Littledale.
♀ $9\frac{3}{4}$	...	...	Do.	Indian Museum.
♀ $9\frac{1}{4}$	$5\frac{1}{2}$	$3\frac{1}{2}$	Do. .	Lieut.-Col. Hon. W. Coke.

Horns of Pir Panjal Markhor.
Shot by Major J. C. Shirres, in the Kajnag, April 22, 1884.

ASTOR and the PIR PANJAL MARKHOR

(Capra falconeri typica, and C. falconeri cashmiriensis).

The markhor, of which there are four local races, probably passing more or less completely into one another, introduces us to the true goats (*Capra*). The males differ from the tahr by their much larger horns, whose length greatly exceeds that of the head, and likewise by the presence of a more or less distinct beard on the chin. In all the varieties of the markhor the beard is extended so as to form a fringe on the throat and chest; the hair on the body being also elongated. Moreover, the horns form a spiral, quite unlike the scimitar-shape characteristic of the ibex and common goat. In the Astor (*C. falconeri typica*) and Pir Panjal (*C. falconeri cashmiriensis*) races of the markhor the horns take the form of an open corkscrew-like spiral, with comparatively few turns, recalling those of the kudu; the spiral being most open, the spread widest, and the turns fewest in the Astor variety. Height at shoulder of a Gilgit specimen, $38\frac{1}{2}$ inches; of Kashmir specimens, from 38 to 41 inches; weight from about 200 to 240 lbs.   The Astor race is found in Astor and Baltistan, while the Pir Panjal variety inhabits the Pir Panjal and Kajnag ranges of Kashmir, and extends to the north-west into Hazara and Gilgit, where it probably intergrades with the former.

Horns of Astor Markhor.   From A. O. Hume's specimen.

Length.		Circum-ference.	Tip to Tip.	Locality.	Owner.
On outside curve.	Straight line.				
63	...	...	...	?	Major - General Alexander A. A. Kinloch.[1]
60	...	...	...	Astor . .	Lucknow Museum.
59	...	12	36	Kajnag . .	Major J. C. Shirres, D.S.O. (See illustration on p. 333.)
59	...	...	...	Pir Panjal . .	Lucknow Museum.
58½	40½	10	38½	Gilgit . .	Marquis of Lansdowne, K.G., K.C.M.G.
56½	38	11	38	Kashmir . .	J. Benett-Stanford.
56	...	...	...	Astor . .	Capt. H. Trevor.
56	36⅔	13¾	34¾	Do. . .	Viscount Edmond de Poncins.
55	44½	11	47	?	East India Club.

[1] Picked up either on the Pir Panjal or Kajnag Ranges by the late Col. Cuppage, and measured by Major-General Alexander A. A. Kinloch.

ASTOR and the PIR PANJAL MARKHOR
(Capra falconeri typica and C. falconeri cashmiriensis)—*continued.*

Length. On outside curve.	Length. Straight line.	Circumference.	Tip to Tip.	Locality.	Owner.
-55	...	...	...	Astor	Otho Shaw.
54¼	...	10½	26½	?	A. O. Hume, C.B.
54	...	10⅝	33¾	Astor	Martyn Kennard.
53¼	42½	11½	52 about	Do.	Sir Victor Brooke's Collection.[1]
53	36¼	10¼	30¼	?	A. O. Hume, C.B. (See illustration on page 337.)
-53	...	9⅛	26	?	Major A. E. Ward.
53	38¾	9¾	35½	Gilgit	Hon. Walter Rothschild.
52¾	39¾	12⅛	33¾	Astor	Martyn Kennard.
52	35	9½	42½	Gilgit	Major F. H. Taylor.
51⅜	37⅛	10	33	Pir Panjal	Sir Edmund G. Loder, Bart
51⅛	...	11⅜	49⅜	Astor	Martyn Kennard.
-51⅛	...	12	44¼	Haramosh	P. H. G. Powell-Cotton.
50	38	11¾	36	Astor	Sir Edmund G. Loder, Bart
50	36	10	33	Chitral	R. H. Macdonald.
50	36½	12	36	Chilas	Capt. W. Hayes-Sadler.
50	...	11⅝	35¼	Astor	Martyn Kennard.
-50	...	...	...	Do.	Capt. H. V. Oliver.
-50	29	11½	31	Haramosh	E. L. Phelps.
-49¾	...	11½	40	Astor	H. Lennard.
-49½	32¼	10¼	43	Gilgit	Col. J. Biddulph.
-49½	35	10	37¼	Kajnag	P. H. G. Powell-Cotton.
49¼	36	11¼	32	Chilas	L. W. S. Oldham.
-49	39¼	11⅛	...	Chitral	C. R. Johnson.
-49	...	11	35	Haramosh	Capt. H. W. Codrington, Officers' Mess, Q.C. Corps of Guides.
49	35	14	44	?	A. O. Hume, C.B. (See illustration on page 334.)
-49	...	...	42	Astor	Otho Shaw.
48½	...	11½	45	Do.	Capt. M. Murphy.

[1] Shot by Capt. Harry V. Brooke.

ASTOR and the PIR PANJAL MARKHOR
(Capra falconeri typica and C. falconeri cashmiriensis)—*continued.*

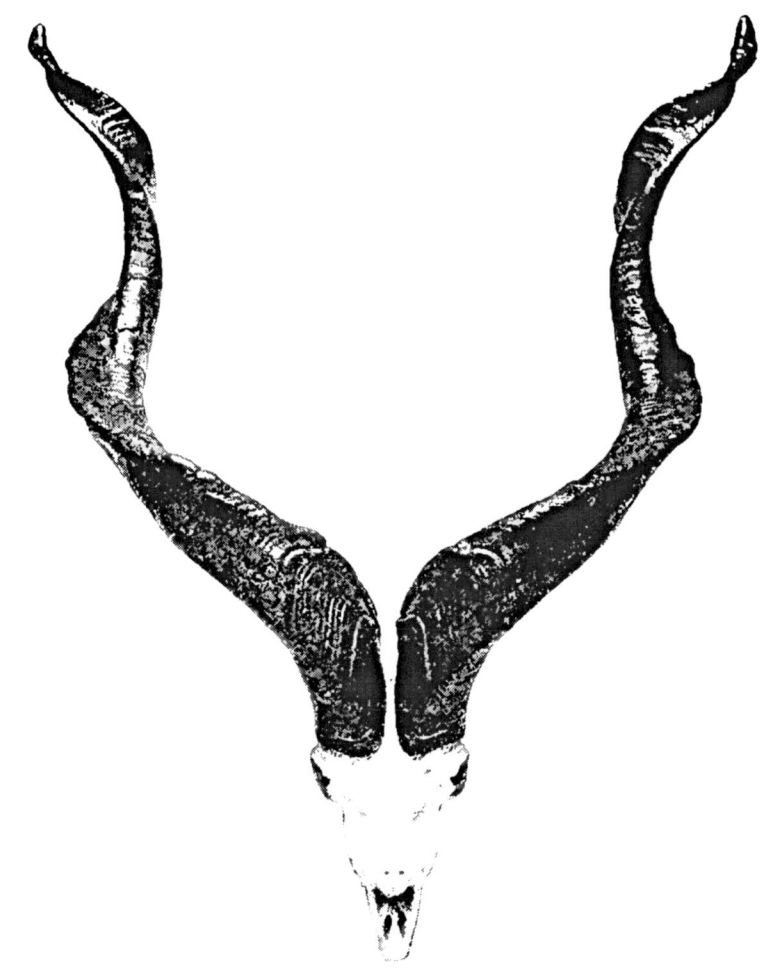

Skull and Horns of Pir Panjal Markhor.　From A. O. Hume's specimen.

Length.		Circum-ference.	Tip to Tip.	Locality.	Owner.
On outside curve.	Straight line.				
48½	31½	11¾	26½	Baltistan . .	H. Z. Darrah.
48	37¾	12¾	29	Pir Panjal . .	A. O. Hume, C.B. above illustration.)
48	31½	12	38	Haramosh . .	J. V. Phelps.

ASTOR and the PIR PANJAL MARKHOR
(Capra falconeri typica and C. falconeri cashmiriensis)—*continued.*

| Length. | | Circum-ference. | Tip to Tip. | Locality. | Owner. |
On outside curve.	Straight line.				
47½	..	11	...	Kashmir .	Major-Gen. Alexander A. A. Kinloch.
47¼	37	12½	38	Chilas . .	L. W. S. Oldham.
47	36	11⅝	39	Do. . . .	Sir Victor Brooke's Collection.

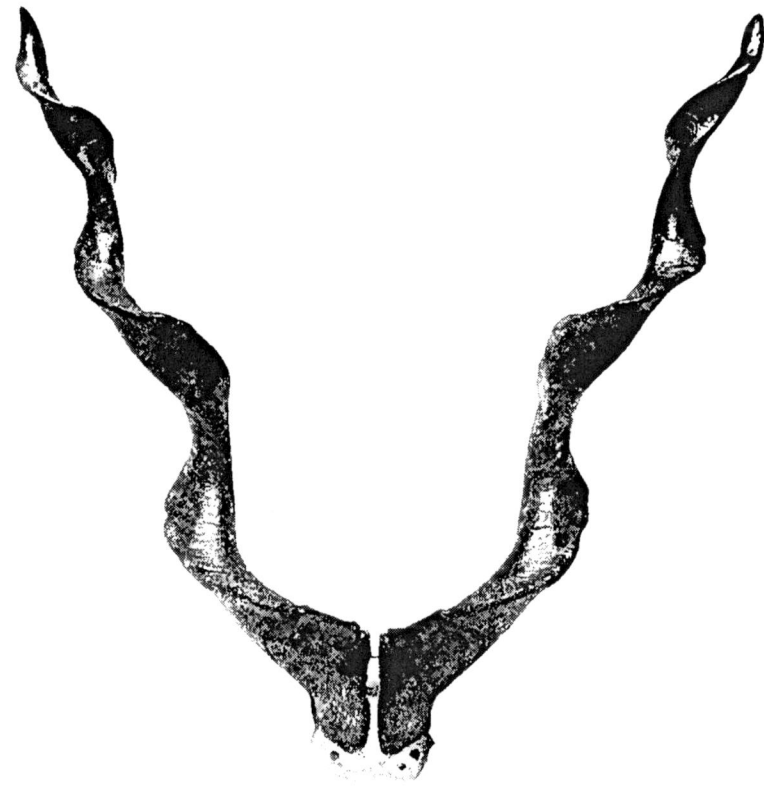

Horns of Variety of Pir Panjal Markhor. From A. O. Hume's specimen.

47	34¼	12	40	Pir Panjal . .	Dr. W. P. Y. Bainbrigge.
47		11	32	Rondu, Baltistan .	F. W. H. Walshe.
47		11½	...	Indus Valley .	Captain H. M. Biddulph.
46½		11½	Odd horn	Astor Valley . .	British Museum.

Z

Skull and Horns of (1) Cabul, and (2) Suleman Markhor.   From A. O. Hume's specimens.

ASTOR and the PIR PANJAL MARKHOR

(Capra falconeri typica and C. falconeri cashmiriensis)—*continued.*

Length. On outside curve.	Length. Straight line.	Circumference.	Tip to Tip.	Locality.	Owner.
–...	34	..	...	?	Maharaja of Travancore, G.C.S.I.
46	31½	10	35	Bunji . .	Col. F. C. Lister-Kay.
46	33½	10	34½	Kajnag .	Sir Edward Ion Grogan, Bart.
45½	...	11⅜	37½	Chilas .	Major C. S. Cumberland.
–45		...	...	Kajnag . . .	Otho Shaw.
45	35¾	11	36	Haramosh . .	P. Church.
43¾	...	10½	32⅞	Kashmir . . .	Hon. Charles Ellis.
43½	32½	12	38½	Do. . . .	I. Morse.
43	31	9½	28	Baltistan .	Major C. H. Hayes.
–43	...	9⅝	30	Do. . .	Capt. T. A. Salt.
–43	20½	13	35	Astor .	E. L. Phelps.
42¾	...	12	32½	Kashmir . .	Sir Robert Harvey, Bart.
42½	32½	11¼	32⅝	Astor . .	Hon. Walter Rothschild.
42	31	11½	32	Pir Panjal . .	W. R. Lawrence.
–42	36	11¾	...	Chitral . .	C. R. Johnson.
41¼	...	10	30⅞	Gilgit .	St. George Littledale.
41	...	12¼	42⅜	Indus Valley	Capt. M. Murphy, British Museum.
41	...	10	27⅜	Pir Panjal	R. Lydekker, British Museum.
39¾	31¾	11	37	?	P. W. Cobbold.
39½	29	11	27½	Baltistan . .	Major H. C. Morland.
–37½	...	12	33	Kashmir . . .	Dublin Museum.
37½	27½	11	35½	Do. . .	Major A. Nugent.
♀ 16¼	13⅜	5⅜	13	Astor . .	Martyn Kennard.

Head of Suleman Markhor.   From A. J. Grant's Waziristan specimen.

CABUL and SULEMAN MARKHOR

(Capra falconeri megaceros and C. falconeri jerdoni).

In the Cabul race of the markhor (*C. falconeri megaceros*), from the trans-Indus districts near Cabul, the horns are nearly straight, but show a slightly open spiral, being intermediate between those of the Pir Panjal and Suleman races.   On the other hand, in the latter (*C. falconeri jerdoni*) the relatively small horns form a perfectly straight cone, upon which the spiral ridges run like the "worm" of a screw. The distributional area of the latter race includes the trans-Indus hill-ranges on the frontier of the Punjab, Afghanistan, and Baluchistan, extending in the Suleman range as far as Mithankot, and also to the Quetta district.

Length in straight line.	Circumference.	Tip to Tip.	Locality.	Owner.
48½	7¾	Odd horn Suleman race	?	British Museum.
39⅜	10¼	24¼	Afghanistan	The late Col. Grant, British Museum.
39¼	12¼	38	Mountain range 25 miles N.W. of Wana	A. J. Grant. (See illustration, page 340.)
38½	10½	23⅞	Afghanistan .	H.R.H. the Duke of Saxe-Coburg and Gotha.
37	10	32	?	Capt. G. Roos Keppel.
[1] 35½	10	25	Baluchistan	Col. J. Biddulph.
–35	...	...	Afghanistan	Major A. E. Ward.
34¾	10⅜	28	Baluchistan	The late Capt. E. W. Codrington.
33	9¼	19¾	Afghanistan	Sir Edmund G. Loder, Bart.
32½	10	22½	Bunu	Officers' Mess, Queen's Own Corps of Guides.
32¼	9¾	28	?	A. O. Hume, C.B.
32	10	27½	Cabul .	A. O. Hume, C.B. (See illustration on page 338.)
31½	9½	27	Suleman Range	Hon. Walter Rothschild.
30¾	8¾	21½	?	Sir Victor Brooke's Collection.
29¾	8¼	23¾	Baluchistan	Major R. H. Rattray.
29	9	21	Do.	The late Capt. E. W. Codrington.
–28	..	...	?	Otho Shaw.
27⅛	8¾	21	Sheik Budin	Sir Edmund G. Loder, Bart.
27	9	18	Do.	Col. J. Biddulph.
26.75	11.25	22.5	Suleman Range	A. O. Hume, C.B. (See illustration on page 338.)
26¼	...	18	Bunu . .	Capt. H. W. Codrington.
26	8¾	18½	Sheikh Budin	Gen. Sir H. Collett, K.C.B.
26	9	16½	Bunu	Capt. H. W. Codrington.
24	9¾	20	?	G. Blois Johnson.
–24	...	...	Sheikh Budin	Major-General Alexander A. A. Kinloch.
22½	10¼	15¾	East Afghanistan	J. E. Penton.

[1] Straight line 30¾.

Head of Himalayan Ibex.   From H. Z. Darrah's specimen.

ASIATIC IBEX (Capra sibirica).

The first of the true ibexes, in all of which the long scimitar-shaped horns carry bold transverse knots on the front surface.   In the present species the horns are characterised by their large size and well-developed front surface ; the second distinctive feature being the long beard of the males.   Height at shoulder from 40 to 42 inches ; weight about 206 lbs., when cleaned from 128 to 153 lbs.

Distribution.—The mountains of Central Asia, from the Altai to the Himalaya (exclusive of the Pir Panjal), and from the neighbourhood of Herat to Kumaon.   Apparently two races of this species, distinguished by the coloration of the lower part of the legs, may be recognised ; namely, the Thian Shan ibex (*C. sibirica typica*), from the Thian Shan, Altai, Baltistan, etc. ; and the Himalayan ibex (*C. sibirica sacin*), from the mountains to the northward of Kashmir and adjacent districts as far east as the source of the Ganges.

ASIATIC IBEX (Capra sibirica)—*continued.*

Length on front curve.	Circumference.	Tip to Tip.	Locality.	Owner.
-56	...	...	Tagdumbash . .	Major A. E. Ward.
-54⅜	10¼	25	Gilgit . . .	Officers' Mess, Queen's Own Corps of Guides.[1]
53¼	10½	20¼	Do. . .	Col. J. Biddulph.
-52	11½	...	Do. . . .	Major A. E. Ward.
-52	10	...	Baltistan	Maharaja of Travancore, G.C.S.I.
-52	...	...	?	The late E. Blyth, *P.Z.S.* 1840, p. 80.
-51½	...	...	Kashmir . .	Martyn Kennard.
-51¼	10½	16	?	The late E. Blyth, *P.Z.S.* 1840, p. 80.
51	9⅜	28½	?	Sir Victor Brooke's Collection.
-50	11	30½	?	Marquis of Lansdowne, K.G., K.C.M.G.
-50	10¼	21	?	Capt. H. Newton.
-50	...	...	?	Capt. H. Trevor.
-50	...	...	?	Officers' Mess, 7th Hussars.
49¾	10⅝	25¼	?	Sir Edmund G. Loder, Bart.
49½	10⅓	42	Kashmir .	Martyn Kennard.
-49½	11¼	27½	Baltistan . .	Major James Grant.
49	10¼	9½	Skardo .	Major George Douglas.
-48½	9¾	34½	Gilgit. .	Officers' Mess, Queen's Own Corps of Guides.
48½	9⅝	30½	Nubra valley, north of Leh	A. O. Hume, C.B.
-48	...	...	Skardo	J. L. Wood.
48	10½	24½	Tilel Valley, Kashmir	J. Campbell of Kilberry.
-47¼	...	...	Thian Shan .	F. A. Labouchere.
-47.5	9.5	20.5	Mushral, Nr. Khoga .	A. O. Hume, C.B.
47	11¾	...	?	Carl Hagenbeck.
-47	...	...	Baltistan . .	Major E. Guinness.
47	10½	29¾	Kashmir . . .	Martyn Kennard.
47	10	...	?	Capt. J. Manners Smith, V.C.
-47	...	...	Baltistan . .	A. R. Oldfield.
46½	11	24¾	Kashmir . . .	Hon. Charles Ellis.

[1] Picked up by Lieut.-Col. R. E. Hutchinson.

ASIATIC IBEX (Capra sibirica)—continued.

Length on front curve.	Circumference.	Tip to Tip.	Locality.	Owner.
-46½	...	...	?	Indian Museum.
46	9¾	25	?	Sir Victor Brooke's Collection.
-46	11¼	27	Sind Valley	A. O. Hume, C.B.
-46	..	...	Kashmir	Capt. Hon. J. G. Beresford.
-45¼	9⅝	24¾	Baltistan	Capt. H. W. Codrington, Officers' Mess, Queen's Own Corps of Guides.
45	10½	29	Ladak	P. H. G. Powell-Cotton.
45	10½	26	Astor .	Capt. F. C. Quicke.
-45	10	20¼	Gilgit .	Col. J. Biddulph.
-45	...	...	Kashmir	Major R. L. Walter.
45	9	12½	Baltistan	Capt. C. B. Vandeleur.
-44¾	...	...	Do.	Hon. C. B. Fulke-Greville.
44⅝	10¾	30	Upper Shyok Valley	A. O. Hume, C.B.
44½	11¾	26	?	Major J. A. Orr-Ewing.
44½	11	19	?	J. Benett-Stanford.
-44½	...	...	Kashmir	Major G. A. L. Carew, D.S.O.
44½	9½	27½	Astor .	The late Capt. E. W. Codrington.
44¼	10	34	Ladak	Lieut.-Col. H. Wade-Dalton.
-44	...	...	Baltistan	E. Ezra.
-44	...	..	Do.	C. H. Rankin.
43¾	9½	16½	Kashmir	S. V. Occleston.
43⅝	10¼	24¾	?	Sir. Robert Harvey, Bart.
-43½	9¾	19	?	Hume Collection, British Museum.
-43½	...	...	Astor .	Otho Shaw.
-43½	11½	...	Himalaya	Major-General Alexander A. A. Kinloch.
-43½	10	31¼	Altai .	H. J. Elwes.
43½	9¾	18¾	Kashmir	Capt. M. S. Wellby.
43½	9½	23	Do.	Dr. W. P. Y. Bainbrigge.
43½	...	...	Baltistan	J. Vaughan.
-43½	11	...	?	Maharaja of Travancore, G.C.S.I.

ASIATIC IBEX (Capra sibirica)—*continued.*

Length on front curve.	Circumference.	Tip to Tip.	Locality.	Owner.
-43½	...	...	Haramosh	A. R. Oldfield.
-43¼	10¾	22½	Do.	J. V. Phelps.
43⅛	9⅝	...	Mustagh Range	Capt. F. E. S. Adair.
43	12⅓	35½	Basha Nalla, Baltistan	T. W. Greenfield.
43	11	10	?	Major J. Harden.
43	10	9	?	E. F. Holden.
43	9¾	28½	?	R. Rankin.
-43	...	...	?	Lucknow Museum.
42¾	10	25½	Baltistan	P. S. Allan.
-42¾	10¾	24	Haramosh	J. V. Phelps.
42⅝	8¾	21	Baltistan	H. Z. Darrah.
42½	10½	22	Kashmir	Col. R. J. Heber-Percy.
42½	9½	21½	?	Arnold Pike.
-42½	10½	27	Astor	E. L. Phelps.
-42½	9½	...	Mongolia	J. D. Cobbold.
42	9¼	26	Ladak	Lieut.-Col. H. Wade-Dalton.
-42	...	...	Kashmir	The late Major W. D. B. Fenton.
-42	...	...	Baltistan	F. W. Wormold.
-41¾	10	...	Do.	Capt. H. M. Biddulph.
-41¾	9¾	19½	Haramosh	E. L. Phelps.
-41⅝	10⅛	20½	Skardo	Major G. Douglas.
41½	9	21	Chitral	Capt. R. L. Tottenham.
41	10½	26¾	?	Capt. J. H. Purvis.
-41	10¼	14	Baltistan	Major H. R. Kelham.
41	9¼	26½	Shyok Valley	Capt. F. E. S. Adair.
41	11¼	25½	Baltistan	V. F. A. Keith-Falconer.
41	9¾	24	Do.	Major A. Nugent.
41	9½	12	Do.	W. J. M'Lachlan.
40¾	10½	22½	Do.	Major C. H. Hayes.
40⅝	10¾	33¾	?	Sir Edmund G. Loder, Bart.

ASIATIC IBEX (Capra sibirica)—*continued.*

Length on front curve.	Circumference.	Tip to Tip.	Locality.	Owner.
40½	10	20½	?	A. C. Hall.
40½	11¼	21½	?	Hon. Charles Ellis.
40½	10½	19	Altai .	Prince Demidoff.
40	10½	29¼	Baltistan	Major C. S. Cumberland.
40	10	30	Chilas . .	L. W. S. Oldham.
−40	9½	20	?	Dublin Museum.
−40	9¾	20¾	Kandgut .	Viscount Edmond de Poncins.
40	9¾	22¼	?	Viscount Fincastle, V.C.
40	10	9¾	?	H. De Prée.
40	9¾	23	Kashgar . .	R. P. Cobbold.
40	9	29½	Kashmir . .	B. Vincent.
39⅝	9	21⅛ ·	Mongolia . .	St. George Littledale.
39½	10½	29¾	Kashmir . .	Capt. N. C. Taylor.
39½	10	21¾	Ladak . . .	W. R. Codrington.
39½	9½	22½	Do. . .	Col. Strachey, British Museum.
39½	9½	14¾	Thian Shan .	Col. J. Biddulph.
39½	9¾	23	Baltistan . . .	Capt. W. E. Gordon.
39½	9¾	13	?	J. R. Carden.
−39½	12	28	Kashmir . . .	J. Benett-Stanford.
39	10½	27½	?	Capt. L. I. B. Hulke.
39	9¾	20	Kashmir .	Earl of Dunmore.
39	9¼	17	Do.	A. Leslie Renton.
38½	10	21½	Do. .	S. Melville.
38¼	10½	19	Do. . .	E. Langworthy.
38¼	10⅝	22½	Do. .	Hon. Walter Rothschild.
38	9½	16	?	David T. Hanbury.
38	10	27	Altai	Prince Demidoff.
37½	10½	21	?	Duke of Portland.
35⅛	9	11	Saiar Mountains, Altai	St. George Littledale, British Museum.
33½	9	21	Altai	St. George Littledale.

ASIATIC IBEX (Capra sibirica)—*continued.*

Length on front curve.	Circumference.	Tip to Tip.	Locality.	Owner.
-27⅞	8¾	9⅞	Russian Turkestan .	Viscount Edmond de Poncins.
- ♀ 13⅛	5	8	Tilel Valley .	J. Campbell of Kilberry.
♀ 11⅝	4	5	Kashmir	Sir Edmund G. Loder, Bart.
♀ 11¼	4	8¼	Do. . . .	Capt. Cecil Levita.

ALPINE IBEX (Capra ibex).

This species, which only survives in a protected state, differs from the Asiatic ibex by the much smaller size of the beard of the male, as well as by a slight variation in the horns; the height at the shoulder reaching to about 40 inches. Weight from 85 to 106 lbs., clean. Formerly distributed throughout the higher Alps of Switzerland, Savoy, and the Tyrol, but now surviving only in a few valleys on the Italian side of Monte Rosa. Most of the few specimens now obtainable are comparatively small, and good horns are very scarce in English collections.

Length on front curve.	Circumference.	Tip to Tip.	Locality.	Owner.
-44⅝	10¼	[1]...	Valley of Aosta . .	H.M. the King of Italy.
-38⅝	...	...	Do.	Do.
-37¾	...	...	Do. .	Do.
35⅜	9	26¾	Do.	Do.
34½	9¾	...	Styria . .	Sir Edmund G. Loder, Bart.
-34¼	9	26	Valley of Aosta .	H.M. the King of Italy.
-33⅛	9	39⅜	Do.	Shot by H.M. the late Victor Emanuel, King of Italy.
-31¾	9⅛	18¾	Alps of Savoy . . .	Sir Edmund G. Loder, Bart.
-30	9	21	?	Dublin Museum.
-28¼	9⅜	18	Valley of Aosta .	C. H. Wilczek.
26¾	8⅜	22⅛	Do. . .	British Museum.
23½	8¾	17½	?	Do.
21½	8⅝	14⅞	Valley of Aosta . .	Do.
-17½	8½	13	Do. .	Count E. Hoyos.

[1] Height at shoulder, 33⅝; weight, 170 lbs.

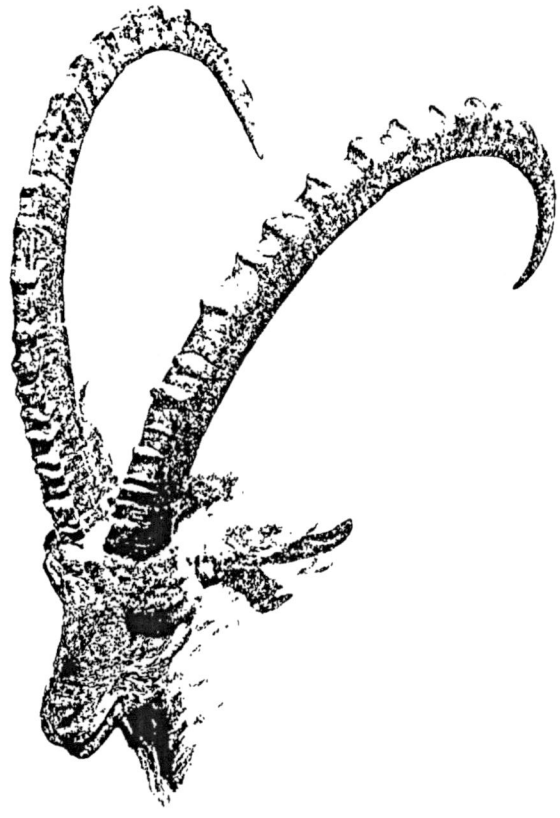

Head of Arabian Ibex, from the Sinaitic Peninsula.

ARABIAN IBEX (Capra nubiana).

This species may be easily distinguished from both the Asiatic and the Alpine species by the form of the horns, which are very long, rather slender, and with the outer front angle much bevelled off, so that the proper front surface is very narrow, and its transverse knots proportionately short.

Distribution.—The mountains of Southern Arabia, Palestine, the Sinaitic Peninsula, Upper Egypt, and probably also those of Morocco and the interior of Senegambia. Arabian name, *beden.* Comparatively few European sportsmen have killed this handsome ibex, but it has been shot by E. N. Buxton.

ARABIAN IBEX (Capra nubiana)—*continued.*

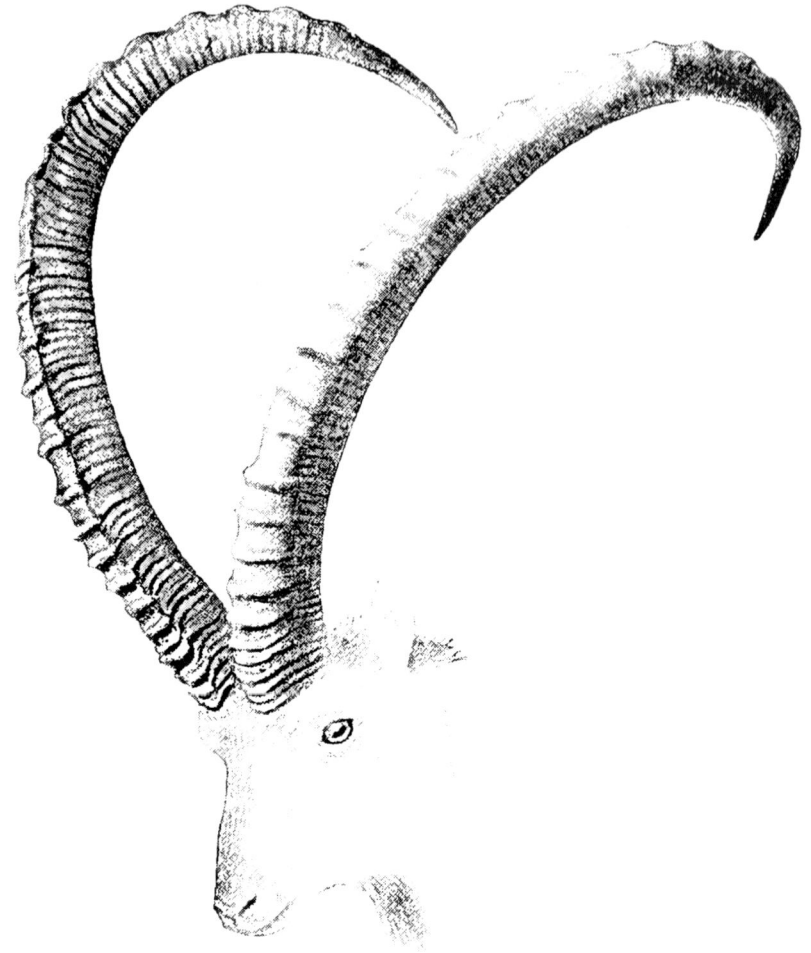

Head of Arabian Ibex, from Arabia ; Sclater, *P.Z.S.* 1897.

Length on front curve.	Circumference.	Tip to Tip.	Locality.	Owner.
50	9	...	Southern Arabia .	. Capt. J. T. Brinkley.
42	7¼		Arabia	. East India Club.
41¹⁄₂₀	...		Hadramut, S.E. Arabia .	. J. Menges.
39¾	9⅞	...	Markat	Do.

ARABIAN IBEX (Capra nubiana)—*continued.*

Length on front curve.	Circumference.	Tip to Tip.	Locality.	Owner.
39½	8⅞	19½	South-East Arabia	Hon. Walter Rothschild.
35½	6½	12	Sinaitic Peninsula	W. E. Pease.
35¼	7	15⅜	Do. . . .	J. D. Cobbold.
-32⅞	6½	7	Do.	Captain John Marriott.
32¼	7	18½	Do.	E. H. Pease.
31⅜	8	13¼	Arabia .	Dr. Percy Rendall.
31⅜	6½	13½	Sinaitic Peninsula	W. Moncreiffe.
31¼	6¾	7	Do. . .	W. E. Pease.
29¾	6⅜	9¼	Do.	E. H. Pease.
29	...	13	Do. .	Hon. Walter Rothschild.
28½	7½	6	Do.	E. N. Buxton.
25¼	6	12	Do.	British Museum.
♀ 10⅜	3¼	2½	Do.	W. E. Pease.
♀ 8¾	3⅛	5¾	Do. .	W. Moncreiffe.

The following specimens are of African origin:—

46⅛	8	...	North Africa . .	British Museum.
43	7¼	22	Suakin	Col. G. E. Lloyd, D.S.O.
42¼	9¼	15¼	Mountain Range of Assoutribai, N.W. of Suakin	The late Major E. M. Barttelot.
41¾	7⅝	17⅜	North Africa	Major W. H. Besant.
38⅞	7½	12½	Upper Egypt . .	Sir Edmund G. Loder, Bart.
38½	7½	27¼	Suakin	Col. G. E. Lloyd, D.S.O.
38¼	8	21	Do.	Capt. A. King.
35⅛	7⅛	12	Do. . .	W. P. Gore-Graham.
30½	8	17¼	Do.	Commander A. T. Hunt.

ABYSSINIAN IBEX (Capra vali).

This ibex, which inhabits the mountains of the interior of Abyssinia, is still very imperfectly known. Its most distinctive feature appears to be a prominent boss on the forehead.

25½	7¼	13	Abyssinia . .	Hon. Walter Rothschild.

Skull and Horns of Sind Wild Goat.   From A. O. Hume's specimen.

PERSIAN WILD GOAT (Capra hircus ægagrus).
SIND WILD GOAT (Capra hircus blythi).

The horns of the Persian wild goat, which appears to be the ancestral form of the domestic goat of Europe (*C. hircus*), differ from those of the various species of ibex by having no distinct front surface, but merely a sharp notched keel, representing the inner front angle of the ibex horn.   In old males the beard is very long.   The general colour of the upper parts is brownish gray in winter and reddish brown in summer, with the under parts white, and blackish brown and white markings on the face and limbs.   Height at shoulder reaching to 37 inches.

The so-called Sind ibex (*C. hircus blythi*) appears to be a second local race of the species, inhabiting Sind and parts of Baluchistan, where it probably passes imperceptibly into the Persian race.   It is distinguished mainly by a slight difference in the form of the horns.

Distribution.—The islands of South-Eastern Europe, and the mountains of South-Eastern Europe and South-Western Asia from the Caucasus through Persia to the confines of Baluchistan and Sind. Native Persian name, *pasang* (rock-footed).

Length on front curve.	Circumference.	Tip to Tip.	Locality.	Owner.
55½	...	24	Persia	Carl Hagenbeck.
52⅜	7⅞	8¾	Sind . .	A. O. Hume, C.B. (Shot by Col. F. Marston.) See illustration.
48¼	8¾	13⅞	Caucasus	British Museum.
–48	8	20½	Sind	J. D. Inverarity.
46¾	7⅝	14	Do. .	Sir Edmund G. Loder, Bart.
46½	8⅞	18⅞	Asia Minor .	F. C. Selous.
46	7⅝	11	Sind .	Major C. S. Cumberland.
–45¾	8¾	9¾	Daghestan . .	E. N. Buxton.
45¼	8	11¾	Sind .	Col. J Biddulph.
44½	8⅞	21⅜	Caucasus	British Museum.
44½	8⅝	11	?	Hume Collection, British Museum.
43⅜	8⅜	14⅝	Kurrachi District	A. O. Hume, C.B.
43	9⅛	...	Asia Minor .	F. C. Selous.
43	9	15¾	Taurus Mountains .	Sir Edmund G. Loder, Bart.
43	8⅛	22⅜	?	J. Carr Saunders.
–42	9	...	?	The Maclaine of Lochbuie.
–42	7	12	Sind .	J. D. Inverarity.
–41½	...	...	Do. .	Capt. E. C. Tidswell.
–40¾	...	...	?	Indian Museum.
39⅞	9⅝	1¼	Erzerum	British Museum.
39⅞	7⅞	27	Mekran Coast, near Ormara	A. O. Hume, C.B.
38	9¾	...	?	Major C. S. Cumberland.
–38	10⅛	15	Asia Minor . .	Capt. John Marriott.
–38	...	...	?	Maharaja of Travancore, G.C.S.I.
36	8¼	6¾	Baluchistan .	Hon. Walter Rothschild.
–35¾	8	11½	Do. . .	Lieut.-Col. L. L. Fenton.
–35½	9	16	Daghestan . .	Ford G. Barclay.

WILD GOAT (Capra hircus ægagrus and blythi)—*continued.*

Length on front curve.	Circumference.	Tip to Tip.	Locality.	Owner.
35⅝	9⅛	13⅜	Mount Ararat . .	British Museum.
35	8¼	6¼	Julfa, Persian Frontier	Prince Demidoff.
34½	9½	18	Baluchistan . .	Sir Victor Brooke's Collection. (Shot by Major Hogg.)
32½	8¾	11¾	Julfa	Prince Demidoff.
32½	9	13½	North Persia .	Hon. C. Hardinge, C.B.
-31	7⅞	15¼	Sind . .	Dr. Percy Rendall.
30⅜	8¼	15¾	Julfa .	Prince Demidoft.
29¼	8¾	12	Asia Minor . .	H. O. Whittall.
29⅝	9¼	8⅜	Cilician Taurus, Asia Minor	C. G. Danford, British Museum.
-27	...	...	Antimilo .	H. Toppin.
-26⅜	...	...	Do. .	Marquis of Ivrea.
♀ 10⅞	4⅜	3⅝	Caucasus	Sir Victor Brooke's Collection.

DOMESTIC GOAT (Capra hircus typicus).

Length on front curve.	Circumference.	Tip to Tip.	Locality.	Owner.
52½	10½	40⅝	Daghestan	Sir Edmund G. Loder, Bart.
44¼	6	29¼	Angora . .	Do.
40½	9⅜	...	Daghestan .	Do.
-37	7½	35	Meoble, N.B. .	Walter Jones.
-30½	7½	35	Do.	Do.
25¼	7¾	4	South Wales .	Major G. Palmer.
24	...	...	Joura . . .	Marquis of Ivrea.
-16	6	13½	Loch Ness, N.B.	C. V. A. Peel.

Head of Spanish Tur.   Drawn from Abel Chapman's specimen.

SPANISH TUR or IBEX (Capra pyrenaica).

Although commonly designated an ibex, the Spanish wild goat has horns more like those of one of the Caucasian tur, and is therefore better designated as a species of that group.   The horns, which have a sharp inner edge, are twisted in a very open semi-spiral, with the tips generally turned outwards, and are quite unlike those of the true ibex. In having dark and light markings on the limbs the species is, however, much more like the Persian wild goat than either of the Caucasian tur. The beard of the males varies greatly in size according to age and season.   Height at shoulder from about 27 to 32 inches at the shoulder ; weight, when clean, about 10 stone.

Distribution.—The Pyrenees and the high ranges of Central Spain, Andalusia, and Portugal.   The typical form of the species inhabits the Pyrenees ; those inhabiting the more southern parts may be distinguished as a separate race (*C. pyrenaica hispanica*).

SPANISH TUR or IBEX (Capra pyrenaica)—*continued.*

Length on outside curve.	Circumference.	Tip to Tip.	Locality.	Owner.
31	8¾	...	Pyrenees	Sir Victor Brooke's Collection.
-30¼	9½	23½	Central Spain	Abel Chapman and W. J. Buck.
-29¾	8¼	23¼	Almeira	H. Brinsley Brooke.
29¼	9½	23¼	Sierra Nevada	Abel Chapman.
28	9⅛	23⅜	Spain	British Museum.
27¾	9	25	Do.	Sir Edmund G. Loder, Bart.
27½	10⅜	19½	Pyrenees	British Museum.
25⅝	8½	16⅝	Spain	Hon. Walter Rothschild.
24½	10	14	Val d'Arras	E. N. Buxton.
23⅜	8	16	Southern Spain	Pablo Larios.
22¾	9½	18¾	Val d'Arras	E. N. Buxton.
22	7¾	14	Spain	Pablo Larios.
16	7½	11	Do.	Col. R. J. Heber-Percy.
-♀ 10¾	5⅝	7½	Val d'Arras	A. E. Leatham.
♀ 9½	5⅜	6¼	Do.	E. N. Buxton.

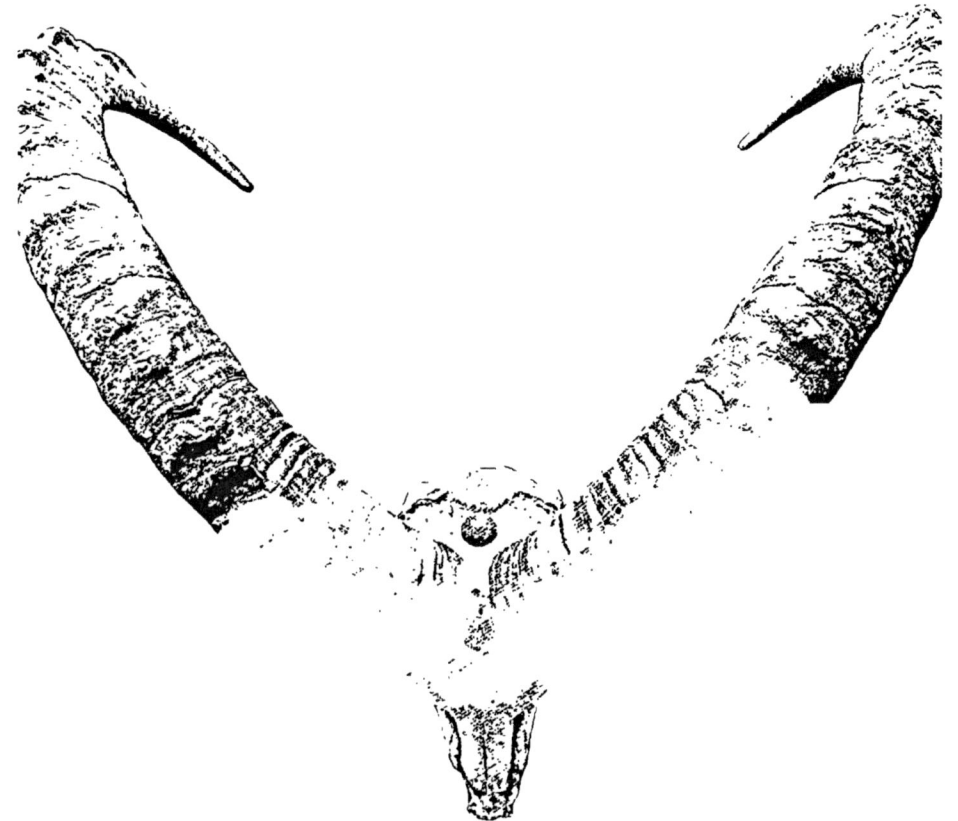

Skull and Horns of West Caucasian Tur.   Shot by St. George Littledale.

WEST CAUCASIAN TUR or IBEX (Capra caucasica).

Of the two peculiar kinds of wild goats inhabiting the Caucasus, and locally known as tur, the present species is easily recognised by the approximation in the form of its horns (especially in immature individuals) to those of true ibex, and the uniform bright chestnut-brown colour of the hair of the adult male in the summer coat ; the chin, beard, and lower parts of the legs being alone black.   Although the horns present a considerable resemblance to those of ibex, they are decidedly thicker, have a different curvature, and show distinct knobs, or knots only in their upper half.   In young males the knots extend the whole length of the front of the horns, and the long winter coat is a pale drab colour.   Height at shoulder about $37\frac{1}{2}$ inches.

Distribution.—The western half of the main chain of the Caucasus. Certain peculiarly-shaped horns appear to indicate the existence of a hybrid race between this species and the East Caucasian tur in the Central Caucasus.

Length on front curve.	Circumference.	Tip to Tip.	Locality.	Owner.
40⅛	12⅝	15¼	Caucasus	St. George Littledale.
36⅞	11⅝	27⅝	Do.	Do.
34¾	11⅝	22⅞	Do.	Do.
34½	12	22	Kouban, Caucasus	Prince Demidoff.
33¼	10⅝	26¾	Do.	St. George Littledale.
32½	11¾	25½	Do.	Do.
32¼	11½	25¼	Do.	Prince Demidoff.
31½	12½	24½	Do.	Do.
30⅝	11⅜	16⅜	Do.	Sir Edmund G. Loder, Bart.
30	11½	19½	Do.	Hon. Walter Rothschild.
26¾	11½	20½	Do.	St. George Littledale.
[1] 22¾	10⅞	22¼	Do.	Do.
19⅞	10⅝	16¼	Caucasus	P. A. Holt, British Museum.

[1] Presumed hybrid between C. caucasica and C. cylindricornis.

Head of East Caucasian Tur.

EAST CAUCASIAN TUR (Capra cylindricornis).

A very different-looking creature from the last is the wild goat commonly designated by sportsmen the "Caucasian bharal"; this name being derived from the resemblance of its horns to those of the true Himalayan bharal. In spite of this point of resemblance, its affinities are, however, evidently with the goats, although it not improbably indicates a step from the more typical members of that group in the direction of the sheep. In addition to the peculiar form of its horns, this tur is characterised by the extreme shortness of the beard, which merely forms a curling fringe on each side of the chin, instead of the long central tuft observable at certain seasons in the West Caucasian species. The general colour of the fur is uniform dull brown, except on the chin, the tip of the tail, and portions of the legs, where it is blackish brown. Height at shoulder about 3 feet.

Distribution.—The Eastern Caucasus, from Kasbek to Daghestan.

It has been killed by few English sportsmen.

EAST CAUCASIAN TUR (Capra cylindricornis)—*continued.*

Length on front curve.	Circumference.	Tip to Tip.	Locality.	Owner.
38¼	12½	...	Eastern Caucasus .	Hon. Walter Rothschild.
36	13	...	Daghestan . . .	J. D. Cobbold.
34½	10⅞	13½	Caucasus .	Major Talbot.
33⅜	12	19¾	Do. .	British Museum.
32½	10½	13½	Kasbek .	Prince Demidoff.
32	13	19	Caucasus	Berthold Smith.
31½	12	7¾	Do. .	Ford G. Barclay.
31	11	28	Northern Caucasus	Capt. H. H. P. Deasy.
30	12	17	Daghestan .	Ford G. Barclay.
29½	12	20	Caucasus	Sir Edmund G. Loder, Bart.
28½	11	16½	Do.	Sir Victor Brooke's Collection.
26½	10⅝	18	Do.	Sir Edmund G. Loder, Bart.
26	11	19	Do.	Major C. S. Cumberland.
—26	13¼	26	Do. .	Clive Phillipps-Wolley.
22¼	10¾	19½	Northern Caucasus	Arnold Pike.
20½	10	11½	Caucasus .	H. R. H. le Duc d'Orléans.

Head of Male Bharal.

BHARAL (Ovis nahura).

Having horns not unlike those of the East Caucasian tur, the bharal, or blue sheep of Tibet, differs from the goats by the absence of a beard and a strong odour in the males, and on account of these and other points of difference from the goats is placed among the sheep, of which group it forms a very aberrant member. The most distinctive external features are the comparatively smooth and olive-coloured horns, which curve at first outwards and then backwards from the sides of the head ; and the bluish gray colour of the thick fur of the back and sides ; the flanks, under parts, and legs being handsomely marked with black and white. Height at shoulder about 33 inches ; weight about 130 lbs. In the complete absence of glands on the face the bharal differs from the more typical sheep and resembles the goats.

Distribution.—Tibet, from Shigar, in Baltistan, and near Sanju, south-east of Yarkand, to Moupin in Eastern Tibet, and from the main axis of the Himalaya, or locally some distance south of the same, to the Kuenlun and Altyn Tag ; in summer usually met with at elevations between 14,000 and 16,000 feet, and apparently never found below about 10,000 feet.

Length on front curve.	Circumference.	Tip to Tip.	Locality.	Owner.
–32	...	...	?	The late B. H. Hodgson, *P.Z.S.* 1840, p. 66.
31½	13½	22½	Ladak	J. Campbell of Kilberry.

BHARAL (Ovis nahura)—*continued.*

Length on front curve.	Circumference.	Tip to Tip.	Locality.	Owner.
30⅞	12¼	21⅞	Gurhwal .	A. O. Hume, C.B.
-30½	11	15½	Ladak . . .	P. H. G. Powell-Cotton.
30	11	24	Hanle, Spiti . .	Capt. B. L. Carew.
29¾	12½	22½	Gurhwal .	A. O. Hume, C.B.
29½	11⅝	25½	?	H.R.H. the Duke of Saxe-Coburg and Gotha.
29½	12	26½	Northern Sikim . .	Surg.-Capt. A. Pearse.
-29	12	...	?	Major A. E. Ward.
-29	...	...	?	Lucknow Museum.
-28½	...	...	?	Capt. H. Trevor.
28½	12¼	26½	Hanle .	F. W. H. Walshe.
-28½	10½	...	?	Indian Museum.
28	11	20¼	?	Hume Collection, British Museum.
28	11	16	Hanle . .	Arnold Pike.
27¾	10¼	10	Ladak .	Capt. G. Campbell.
27¼	11	21½	Do. . .	St. George Littledale.
-27	...	...	Do. . .	Otho Shaw.
27	11½	28	Tibet . . .	Major C. S. Cumberland.
26¾	11½	23	Ladak .	Col. F. C. Lister-Kay.
26½	10½	20	?	A. S. Crum.
26¼	11⅞	23	?	Sir Victor Brooke's Collection.
26¼	10¾	22	?	Sir Edmund G. Loder, Bart.
26	10¾	25½	?	R. Johnstone.
26	10¼	20½	?	Capt. W. H. Williamson.
25⅞	12½	31½	East of Padam, Zanskar	Capt. M. S. Wellby.
25⅞	11¼	18½	?	Capt. C. B. Vandeleur.
-25½	11½	...	Ladak . .	Major-General Alexander A. A. Kinloch.
25⅜	11¼	25¼	Do. . .	St. George Littledale.
-25¼	11½	24½	Do. . .	Capt. H. W. Codrington.
25	10	25¼	?	Major H. C. Morland.
-24½	12¼	26	?	J. Carr Saunders.

BHARAL (Ovis nahura)—*continued.*

Length on front curve.	Circum- ference.	Tip to Tip.	Locality.	Owner.
-24½	...	...	Upper Indus Valley .	Col. J. Biddulph.
24½	11	26½	?	J. R. Carden.
24½	11	18	Shyok Valley .	J. V. Phelps.
-24½	..	...	Do. .	E. L. Phelps.
24⅜	10⅞	27¼	South-east of Leh	Major J. A. Orr-Ewing.
24	11	22¾	Nepal . .	The late B. H. Hodgson, British Museum.
24	11½	25	Ladak .	P. Church.
-24	11½	...	?	Maharaja of Travancore, G.C.S.I.
-23¾	11¾	...	Kumaon .	W. H. Lane.
23½	10	18	Ladak .	Capt. F. E. S. Adair.
23½	9½	17¼	Hanle . . .	Capt. H. W. Codrington.
23½	13	25	?	Dr. W. P. Y. Bainbrigge.
23⅜	11¾	24¼	?	Sir Robert Harvey, Bart.
23	12	26	Ladak .	H.R.H. the Duke of Saxe-Coburg and Gotha.
23	10½	23¾	Do. . .	Reginald Beech.
♀ 7	4¼	8¾	Northern Sikim	Hon. Walter Rothschild.

Head of Male Arui.

ARUI or UDAD (Ovis lervia).

The only wild sheep found throughout the continent of Africa is the arui, or fechstal of the Arabs, the udad or Barbary sheep of naturalists ; a species with horns not very unlike those of the bharal, and also lacking glands on the face, but readily distinguished by its uniformly tawny colour, the fringe of long hair depending from the throat, chest, and the upper portion of the fore-legs, and the unusual length of the tail, which exceeds that of all other wild sheep. In the length of this appendage the arui approaches domesticated sheep, of which, however, it is not likely to be the ancestor. Height at shoulder about 3 feet 3 inches.

Distribution.—The mountains of Northern Africa, from Egypt to Morocco. This sheep is very difficult to find on its own ground.

ARUI or UDAD (Ovis lervia)—*continued.*

Length on outside curve.	Circumference.	Tip to Tip.	Locality.	Owner.
29⅛	12½	19	Algeria	V. Cholmondeley.
28½	11½	18	Do.	Hon. John Ward, British Museum.
28½	11⅝	18½	Algeria	Sir Edmund G. Loder, Bart.
-28	11½	16½	S. Tunisia	J. J. S. Whitaker.
-27¾	11¼	14 9/10	Algeria	Viscount Edmond de Poncins.
26⅜	10¾	15¼	North Africa	British Museum.
26	11	17¾	Do.	Do.
25½	11½	17½	Algeria	Hon. John Ward.
25½	11½	17	Do.	F. de Murietta.
25½	10⅝	16	Do.	Capt. G. J. Cuthbert.
-25½	12⅛	20½	Do.	Capt. John Marriott.
-25½	11	18	Tunisia	A. E. Pease.
25	11¼	13½	North Africa	W. E. Pease.
24½	10½	19½	Do.	Hon. R. A. Ward.
-♀ 20¼	10	16	Algeria	A. E. Pease.
♀ 19	7	17	Tunisia	Capt. John Marriott.
-♀ 17	7½	16⅛	Atlas Mountains	Viscount Edmond de Poncins.

Head of American Bighorn, from W. F. Sheard's specimen.

AMERICAN BIGHORN (Ovis canadensis).

The bighorn of the American continent, inclusive of its local races (frequently regarded as distinct species), is a large sheep, distinguished from the Asiatic argalis, among other features, by the comparative smoothness of the horns, in which the outer front angle is prominent, and the inner one rounded off, and also by the smaller size of the face-glands. There is a well-marked whitish patch on the rump, but the amount of white on the under parts and legs shows considerable local variation. In the typical Rocky Mountain race (*O. canadensis typica*) the ears are long and pointed, with short hair, and the horns, which are very heavy, diverge but little outwards, and generally have the tips broken. The Californian *O. canadensis nelsoni* is a paler southern race. On the other hand, in *O. canadensis stonei* of the North-West Territories the colour of the back is very dark, and the white on the belly and legs sharply defined. And both in this race and the light-coloured *O. canadensis dalli* of Alaska the horns are lighter, more divergent, and sharper pointed, while the ears tend to become shorter, blunter, and more hairy. Height at shoulder about 3 feet 2 inches. Weight about 350 lbs.

The horns of the ewes are very small in comparison to those of the rams, seldom measuring more than 15 inches on the curve from base to tip. Large male horns are now difficult to obtain, and of late years it is seldom that those of fresh-killed specimens are seen exceeding 38 inches on the curve from tip to tip. American sportsmen are keen to obtain horns of large basal girth; but these, as will be seen from the following table, rarely exceed 16 inches. The Maclaine of Lochbuie possesses a specimen whose girth according to his own measurement is 19 inches.

Distribution.—North America, from the Rocky Mountains southwards to Sonora, Northern Mexico, and California, and northwards to Alaska and the shores of Bering Sea. The Alaskan race, for at least some portion of the year, is snow-white.

Length on front curve.	Circumference.	Tip to Tip.	Locality.	Owner.
-52½	18½	...	The Selkirks, B.C., 1885	W. F. Sheard. (See illustration.)
-45	...	...	?	W. Grant Mackay.
-42½	16¼	25¾	Lower California	George H. Gould.
42	16	(tips much worn)	Wyoming .	Picked up by T. W. H. Clarke.
-...	17¼	...	Do.	T. W. H. Clarke.
∓41½	15	...	Kootenay, B.C. .	Measured by John Fannin, Provincial Museum, B.C.
-40¾	16½	...	Yellowstone	British Museum.
40¼	15¼	20¼	?	Sir Edmund G. Loder, Bart.
-40	15¼	...	Rocky Mountains .	Otho Shaw.
40	15	21½	British Columbia .	J. W. R. Young.
39⅝	15⅜	...	Colorado .	St. George Littledale.
39½	16½	24¾	Montana . .	British Museum.
39½	15½	19	?	Sir Edmund G. Loder, Bart.
-39	15¾	...	?	W. A. Baillie-Grohman.
38⅜	15½	22	?	Gerald Buxton.
38¼	16⅜	...	Bighorn Mountains	H. Seton-Karr.
38¼	15¼	19¼	Montana . .	Edmund Littledale.
38¼	16	19	N.W. Territories .	S. Ratcliff.
38	17	...	Alberta, N.W.T. .	Arnold Pike.
38	15	...	British Columbia .	Captain F. Cookson.
-38	16½	...	Do.	Major C. C. Ellis.
37¾	15⅞	23⅜	Mexico . .	J. A. H. Drought.
-37¾	16¼	22½	British Columbia .	J. O. Shields.
37¼	15½	16	Do.	J. Turner-Turner.
-37	16	31	Wyoming . .	T. W. H. Clarke.

AMERICAN BIGHORN (Ovis canadensis)—*continued.*

ngth on it curve.	Circumference.	Tip to Tip.	Locality.	Owner.
37	16¼	...	Montana . .	Major Maitland Kirwan.
37	16⅝	16	British Columbia .	R. H. Venables Kyrke.
37	15½	18½	Wyoming .	Lord Rodney.
36¾	19	15	British Columbia	C. H. Kennard.
36¾	15¼	22½	Wyoming .	Moreton Frewen.
36½	14½	...	Do.	Gerald Buxton.
36½	16	...	?	Thomas Bate.
36½	14	...	?	J. D. Cobbold.
36¼	14⅜	18½	?	Gerald Buxton.
36	14¾	16½	Montana . .	R. H. Sawyer.
36	15½	...	Alberta, N.W.T. . .	Arnold Pike.
36	14¾	16	Wyoming	Captain G. Dalrymple White.
–35⅞	14¾	17½	Do. . .	Count E. Hoyos.
35¾	15¼	18½	British Columbia .	G. Wrey.
35¾	13¾	17½	Do. .	Hon. S. Tollemache.
35½	16	21	Do.	T. P. Kempson.
35¼	12¼	16	California	Sir Victor Brooke's Collection
35¼	15¼	18½	British Columbia . .	Sir Peter Walker, Bart.
35	14	18½	Do. .	Admiral Sir Michael Culme Seymour, Bart.
–35	15	19¾	Wyoming .	Count Scheibler.
35	14	16	Do. .	Gerald Hardy.
34½	14¾	19	S.E. Montana	J. A. Jameson.
34½	14½	...	California . . .	G. P. Fitzgerald.
–34	16	17	N.W. Wyoming . .	A. Rogers.
34	16¼	20	British Columbia Border	Barclay Bonthron.
33½	15¼	...	British Columbia .	Admiral Sir Michael Culme Seymour, Bart.
33	15⅝	18	Do.	Capt. E. G. Verschoyle.
33	14¾	24½	Wyoming . . .	Lieut.-Col. Hon. W. Coke.
33	14½	22	?	F. H. B. Ellis.
33	14	23	British Columbia . .	T. P. Kempson.

AMERICAN BIGHORN (Ovis canadensis)—*continued.*

Length on front curve.	Circumference.	Tip to Tip.	Locality.	Owner.
33	15½	22	British Columbia .	A. E. Butter.
32¾	15½	17½	?	C. G. R. Lee.
32½	14⅝	19½	Fraser River, B.C.	A. E. Leatham.
32½	15	17½	Lower California	G. Barnardiston.
32	15¼	19½	British Columbia .	J. W. Wood, jun.
32	14¾	17¼	Yellowstone River .	British Museum.
31½	14½	17½	N.W. Territory	Major Algernon Heber-Percy.
31	17½	...	Grand Encampment, Wyoming	Frank Cooper.
31	13	22	British Columbia .	T. E. Buckley.
30¾	15	23 about	?	Hon. Walter Rothschild.
30½	15¾	17½	Lower California .	Ely Quilter.
30½	15½	18	Wyoming	J. L. Scarlett.
30½	14	15½	Do.	Hugh Peel.
30	15¼	14	Alberta, N.W.T.	F. C. Williamson.

ALASKAN BIGHORN (Ovis canadensis dalli).

Length on front curve.	Circumference.	Tip to Tip.	Locality.	Owner.
34	12⅝	18⅛	Alaska	Rowland Ward.
33	12¾	15	Do.	Hon. Walter Rothschild.
32½	13¼	20½	Do.	J. T. Studley, British Museum.
♀ 9⅛	4⅞	8	Do. .	Do.

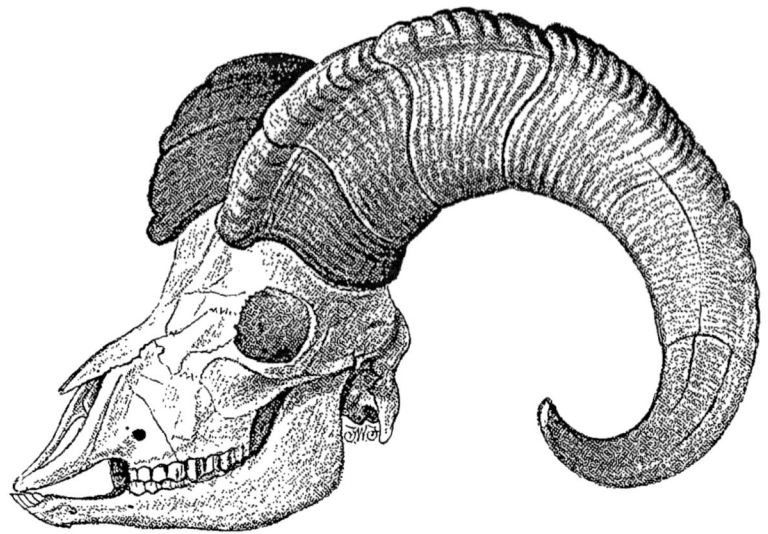

Skull and Horns of Male Kamschatkan Bighorn.

KAMSCHATKAN BIGHORN (Ovis canadensis nivicola).

Although the Kamschatkan wild sheep can be readily distinguished from the Rocky Mountain bighorn (*O. canadensis typica*) by the slenderness of the horns at the points, and their wider tip-to-tip measurement, as well as by shorter, blunter, and more thickly haired ears, the shorter face, the longer hair of the body, and the inferior size of the white patch on the rump, yet there are several varieties of the bighorn from the more northern districts of America which tend more or less completely to bridge over these points of difference. Among these are the Alaskan bighorn (*O. canadensis dalli*) and the N.W. bighorn (*O. canadensis stonei*), in which the horns are of the Kamschatkan type, and the ears are shorter than in the Rocky Mountain race. These transitions indicate that all the bighorns are essentially local modifications of the same animal; the Kamschatkan form being, as might be expected from its isolation, the most aberrant. Like the Alaskan race, the Kamschatkan bighorn appears, at least sometimes, to turn white in winter. Height at shoulder about 37 or 38 inches ; weight about 330 lbs.

Distribution.—Kamschatka, and the Stanovoi Mountains as far south as the sources of the Utschuri River ; perhaps also in parts of Siberia.

2 B

KAMSCHATKAN BIGHORN (Ovis canadensis nivicola)—*continued.*

Length on front curve.	Circumference.	Tip to Tip.	Locality.	Owner.
38	13½	26	Kamschatka	Dr. F. H. H. Guillemard's pa the "Marchesa," *P.Z.S.* p. 675.
35½	14	26½	Do.	Do.
34½	11⅞	17¾	Do.	British Museum.
34	13½	23⅝	Do.	Hon. Walter Rothschild.
32¾	13½	23	Do.	Sir Edmund G. Loder, Bart.
31½	14	26	Do.	Dublin Museum.
31½	13⅝	21	Cape Chepunske	Col. J. Biddulph.
31½	13¾	24	Kamschatka	Dublin Museum.
27½	13⅝	25½	Do.	Rowland Ward.
10¾	5	14½	Do.	Hon. Walter Rothschild.

Ils and Horns of Siberian Argali, from specimens shot in the Altai by Major C. S. Cumbe

Head of Marco Polo's Sheep. From David T. Hanbury's specimen.

MARCO POLO'S SHEEP (Ovis poli).

In common with the following members of the genus *Ovis*, this splendid sheep has the transverse wrinklings of the horns well developed, and small glands are present on the face. The horns of the adult male are characterised by their comparative slenderness and great length, forming a spiral of more than one complete circle, with the front angles typically well developed. The hind-quarters show a large amount of white, extending over the greater part of the thighs; and in winter the throat is furnished with a voluminous ruff of long white hairs, which disappears in summer. Height at shoulder about 4 feet, or perhaps rather less; weight of adult male about 22 stone.

Distribution.—Typically the plateau of the Pamirs in Central Asia, but represented by a closely allied race (*O. poli karelini*) in the Thian Shan range of Turkestan, in which the horns are generally somewhat shorter, and may have the front outer angle rounded off. This sheep was first definitely made known in England by specimens obtained during the Second Yarkand Mission under the late Sir D. Forsyth ; since which date it has been killed by Mr. St. George Littledale, Major C. S. Cumberland, Capt. H. Bower, Viscount de Poncins, and many other sportsmen.

Length on front curve.	Circumference.	Tip to Tip.	Locality.	Owner.
·75	16	54½	Pamir	Field-Marshal Lord Roberts, V.C.
73	15	48	Little Pamir	The late Col. H. C. B. Tanner.
·71	15½	53¾	Great Pamir	Viscount Edmond de Poncins.
70	17	52	Do.	Maharaja of Kuch Behar.
69½	15¼	56	?	Marquis of Lansdowne, K.G., K.C.M.G.
69½	14½	39	Tagdumbash	Sir Edmund G. Loder, Bart.
68½	15	35¾	?	Lewis Flower.
68	17	43	Pamir	Col. R. Pole Carew, C.B.
·68	16	52	?	Indian Museum.
·67⅜	16	53¾	?	Col. J. Biddulph, Indian Museum.
67	16½	42	Pamir	Col. R. Pole Carew, C.B.
·67	16	...	Thian Shan	Maharaja of Travancore, G.C.S.I.
67	15½	42½	?	Duke of Westminster.
66⅞	15⅝	46	?	Sir Edmund G. Loder, Bart.
66⅞	13⅞	46½	Valley between Little and Great Pamir	A. O. Hume, C.B.
66	16¾	47	Do.	Do.
66	15¼	44	Do.	Hume Collection, British Museum.
66	15¾	42	?	A. Leslie Renton.
65½	16	53	Great Pamir (16,000 feet)	Col. T. E. Gordon, British Museum.
·65	16	41	Central Asia	Dublin Museum.
65	16½	49½	?	Major C. F. Blane.
·65	...	...	?	St. George Littledale (presented to the Empress of Russia).
64½	16½	46	Pamir	Major C. C. Ellis.
64¼	16½	41	Do.	W. Lawrence.
64¼	15¼	39	Do.	H. C. V. Hunter.
64	15½	50	Little Pamir	R. P. Cobbold.
64	15	49	?	Duke of Portland.

MARCO POLO'S SHEEP (Ovis poli)—*continued.*

Length on front curve.	Circumference.	Tip to Tip.	Locality.	Owner.
63⅝	16⅛	42½	Pamir . .	Hon. Walter Rothschild.
63½	15¾	57½	Valley between Great and Little Pamir	A. O. Hume, C.B.
63⅜	15⅜	46¼	Tagdumbash .	Earl of Dunmore.
63	16	49½	Little Pamir	R. P. Cobbold (Bachelors' Club).
62¾	16¼	51	Tagdumbash	T. W. Greenfield.
62½	15	57	?	Sir Edmund G. Loder, Bart.
62	15¼	40	?	Hon. Charles Ellis.
61½	15½	46¼	Tagdumbash .	E. L. Phelps.
60¾	15¾	46⅞	Pamir .	St. George Littledale.
60	16	49½	Little Pamir .	R. P. Cobbold.
60	15¾	46¾	Tagdumbash .	T. W. Greenfield.
60	15½	46	Do. .	P. Church.
–60	...	...	?	Capt. H. Bower.
–60	17	...	Tagdumbash	H. Dauvergne.
–60	16	52	Do.	H. Lennard.
59¾	15½	45⅝	Pamir	Earl of Dunmore.
59	16¼	47	?	Viscount Powerscourt.
59	15¾	41	?	Martyn Kennard.
59	14	42¾	Tagdumbash	David T. Hanbury.
58	16	43	Do.	Do.
57¾	15	46¾	?	Major-General Sir Arthur Ellis, K.C.V.O.
57¾	14¾	50	Pamir	Reginald Beech.
57½	16⅛	49¼	?	W. Lawrence.
57½	14¾	48	Pamir	Reginald Beech.
57	15¼	42	Do.	Hon. R. A. Ward.
56⅞	15⅛	35½	Do.	St. George Littledale.
56	17½	42	Do. .	E. L. Phelps.
56	15	44	Do. .	E. P. Tennant.
55¾	15¾	43	?	J. Carr Saunders.

MARCO POLO'S SHEEP (Ovis poli)—*continued.*

Length on front curve.	Circumference.	Tip to Tip.	Locality.	Owner.
$55\frac{5}{8}$	$16\frac{1}{2}$	43	Pamir	Major C. S. Cumberland.
$55\frac{1}{2}$	$16\frac{7}{8}$	44	Do.	Sir Edmund G. Loder, Bart.
$55\frac{1}{2}$	$15\frac{1}{8}$	39	?	The late W. F. Webb.
55	16	44	?	H.R.H. le Duc d'Orléans.
$54\frac{7}{8}$	$15\frac{1}{4}$	$48\frac{3}{8}$	Pamir . .	Sir Victor Brooke's Collection.
$54\frac{1}{4}$	$16\frac{1}{8}$	$34\frac{3}{4}$	West Mongolia .	St. George Littledale.
54	$16\frac{3}{4}$	39	?	Viscount Fincastle, V.C.
$53\frac{7}{8}$	$15\frac{5}{8}$	$43\frac{3}{4}$	Lake Karakol	St. George Littledale.
53	$14\frac{1}{4}$	45	Tagdumbash	Major H. C. Morland.
53	...	...	?	Lucknow Museum.
52	16	41	Tagdumbash	H.M. the King of Italy.
52	$15\frac{1}{2}$	39	Do. .	Capt. J. Manners-Smith, V.C., C.I.E.
$51\frac{1}{4}$	15	48	Do. .	J. G. Millais.
51	$15\frac{1}{4}$	$38\frac{3}{4}$	Do. .	A. Leslie Renton.
$50\frac{1}{2}$	15	$42\frac{3}{4}$	Altai Plateau, Pamir .	Capt. J. Manners-Smith, V.C., C.I.E., British Museum.
♀ 14·7	5·90	15·75	Great Pamir .	Viscount Edmond de Poncins.
♀ $10\frac{1}{2}$	$5\frac{1}{2}$	$13\frac{1}{2}$	Tagdumbash	David T. Hanbury.

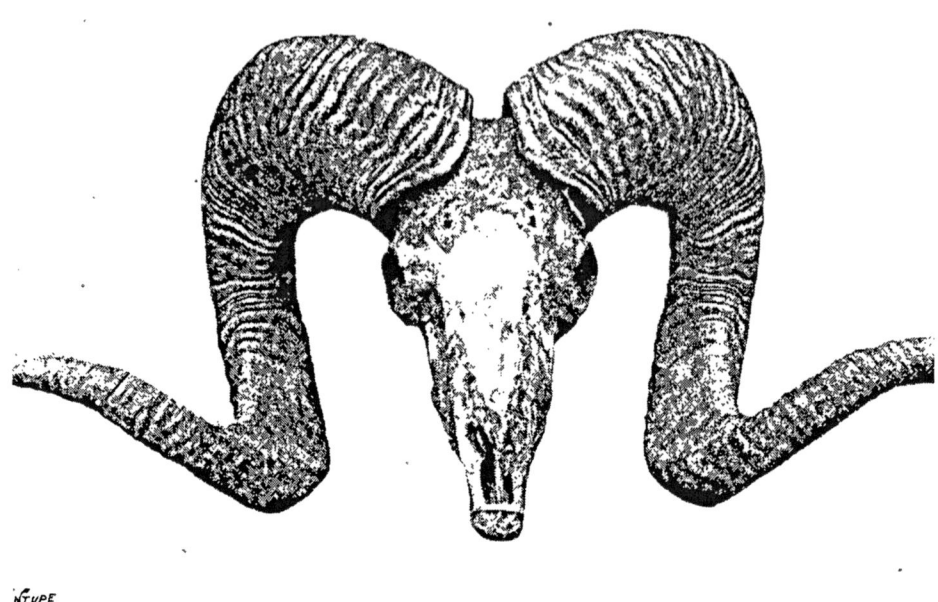

Skull and Horns of Siberian Argali.
From a specimen shot by St. George Littledale in the Altai.

SIBERIAN ARGALI or AMMON SHEEP (Ovis ammon).

Closely allied to Marco Polo's sheep, but distinguished by the thicker and less expanded horns, which often have the outer front angle much rounded off, and the wrinklings very fine. A more or less distinct white patch on the rump, not extending on to the thigh, which is dark-coloured like the back ; no ruff on the throat, even in the long winter coat. In summer the coat of old males, which is very short, tends to become more or less light-coloured all over. Height at shoulder from about 45 inches to 4 feet ; weight from about 250 to 350 lbs.

As in the Tibetan race, considerable individual variation may be noticed in the horns, some having the outer front angle much more developed than usual ; it does not appear that these differences can be accounted for by age.

Distribution.—In former times apparently extending from the Baikal Mountains in the south of Eastern Siberia through Northern Mongolia to the Semipalatinsk Altai ; now chiefly restricted to the two latter localities.

SIBERIAN ARGALI or AMMON SHEEP (Ovis ammon)—*continued.*

Length on front curve.	Circumference.	Tip to Tip.	Locality	Owner.
62¼	19¾	38¼	Altai	St. George Littledale.
62	19	38¾	Do.	H. J. Elwes.
61½	19¼	39¼	Do.	St. George Littledale, Brit Museum.
59⅛	19⅛	38¼	Do.	St. George Littledale.
56½	18½	33½	Do.	Major C. S. Cumberland.
55	18	39	Do.	Prince Demidoff.
54¾	18¾	30	Do.	Major C. S. Cumberland.
54½	19¾	33¾	Do.	Do.
54½	19	35	Do.	Do.
53¼	19	22	Do.	St. George Littledale.
52½	19¾	33	Do.	Prince Demidoff.
52½	18½	38½	Do.	Do.
52	19	37½	Do.	Do.
51½	18⅛	26	Do.	Do.
51¼	19⅜	31	Do.	Do.
51	19¾	33	Do.	Do.
51	19¼	33	Do.	St. George Littledale.
50½	18¼	37¾	Do.	Do.
50	19½	31½	Do.	Major C. S. Cumberland.
50	19¼	36	Do.	St. George Littledale.
50	19¼	27¼	Do.	Sir Edmund G. Loder, Bart
49½	20¼	25	Do.	St. George Littledale.
47¾	19	31½	Siberia	British Museum.
45½	20	27¼	Altai	Prince Demidoff.
40	16	33	Do.	Princess Demidoff.

Head of Tibetan Argali.

TIBETAN ARGALI (Ovis ammon hodgsoni).

Chiefly distinguished from the true ammon sheep by the development of a distinct white ruff on the throat of the males, at least in the winter coat, and also by the less degree of lateral expansion of the horns, which do not form more than a single complete circle, and are generally broken at the tips. The wrinkles on the horns are perhaps somewhat less prominent, and the outer front angle is frequently well developed.

The height at the shoulder is perhaps rather less than in the true ammon, of which this sheep is best regarded as a local race. A specimen measured by Major Greenway was 76 inches from the nose to the tip of the tail, and the weight about 212 lbs. In another male, whose age was estimated at 10 years, the height at the shoulder was 43 inches, the girth 50 inches, and the weight 205 lbs. (P. H. G. Powell-Cotton).

Distribution.—The plateau of Tibet, from Northern Ladak to the districts north of Sikim, and northwards to the Kuenlun ; eastern limits unknown.

Length on front curve.	Circumference.	Tip to Tip.	Locality.		Owner.
57	18¾	29	Ladak	. .	Arnold Pike.
50½	18¼	19	Pangong Lake		Sir Edmund G. Loder, Bart.
−50	17	...	Tibet .		W. H. Lane.
−48½	19	...	Do. .		E. Howard Brooke.
48	16	23	Rudok	.	Major G. A. L. Carew, D.S.O.
48	18½	20	Ladak	. .	Major H. C. Morland.
48	18	31	Do.	.	Major Hon. A. Dalzell.
−47	17	...	Do.	. .	Otho Shaw.
46½	19¾	20	Do.	.	A. O. Hume, C.B.
−46½	16½	21	Ladak		P. H. G. Powell-Cotton.
46½	16¾	...	Do.	. .	Capt. H. M. Biddulph.
−46	19	...	?		Major C. S. Cumberland.
46	16	17	?		Hon. R. A. Ward.
45½	16¼	17	?		Duke of Teck, G.C.B.
45	17	16	Ladak	. .	J. V. Phelps.
−45	...	...	?		Lucknow Museum.
44⅝	17½	22½	Tibet .	.	The late B. H. Hodgson.
−44½	17	21⅞	Ladak		A. E. Leatham.
44	16⅛	19¼	Do.		Major C. S. Cumberland.
44	16	17½	Do.	.	W. R. Lawrence.
−44	18	...	Do.	.	Maharaja of Travancore, G.C.S.I.
−43	...	...	Do.	.	Capt. W. Bailey.
42½	16½	19	?		A. O. Hume, C.B.
42½	17	...	?		Lieut.-Col. T. Greenaway.
−42½	16	15	Ladak	.	Capt. H. M. Biddulph.
42½	16	18	Do.	. .	Hume Collection, Brit. Museum.
42½	15¼	...	?		J. Carr Saunders.
42⅜	16¼	20	Tibet .	. .	H.R.H. the Duke of Saxe-Coburg and Gotha.

TIBETAN ARGALI (Ovis ammon hodgsoni)—*continued.*

Length on front curve.	Circumference.	Tip to Tip.	Locality.	Owner.
42⅛	16¾	14¼	Ladak . . .	Hume Collection, British Museum.
42	15⅛	17	Near Hanle . .	Capt. F. E. S. Adair.
42	...	...	Rudok . .	Major G. A. L. Carew, D.S.O.
41⅞	16	...	Tibet . . .	Hon. Walter Rothschild.
41½	16	15	?	Duke of Westminster.
-41½	...	...	Ladak . . .	G. G. Thatcher.
41⅛	16¾	19	Do. . .	Sir Victor Brooke's Collection.
-41	...	18½	Do. .	Major A. E. Ward.
41	17¼	...	Do.	E. L. Phelps.
41	16½	17	Do. . .	R. Johnstone.
40½	14½	26¼	?	St. George Littledale, Brit. Museum.
40⅜	17⅝	20⅜	Ladak .	Hon. Charles Ellis.
40¼	16¼	19	Do.	Col. R. J. Heber-Percy.
40¼	15¾	18¾	Do. .	A. C. Bailey.
-40	17	...	Do. . .	Major-General Alexander A. A. Kinloch.
-40	...	...	?	Capt. H. Trevor.
40	17	19½	Ladak . .	Sir Edmund G. Loder, Bart.
-40	17	...	?	Indian Museum.
-40	...	...	Ladak .	Otho Shaw.
-40	17¼	...	Hanle .	Capt. H. W. Codrington.
39½	17	14	Ladak	F. W. H. Walshe.
39¼	17	14¾	Do.	Hon. Charles Ellis.
39¼	17½	21½	Do.	Dr. W. P. Y. Bainbrigge.
39	17	19	Do. . .	Sir Robert Harvey, Bart.
♀ 18½	8½	23	Do. .	David T. Hanbury.
♀ 18	7	19¾	Tibet . . .	The late B. H. Hodgson, British Museum.
♀ 14½	7½	17½	Ladak	Sir Victor Brooke's Collection.

MONGOLIAN ARGALI (Ovis ammon jubata).

Nearly allied to the Tibetan race, having a distinct yellowish-white hroat ruff and generally similar horns, but, in some cases at least, the uter front angles of the latter much rounded off. The white on the uttocks and hinder surface more abundant and purer in colour.

Distribution.—Eastern Mongolia to the north of Pekin.

Length on ront curve.	Circumference.	Tip to Tip.	Locality.	Owner.
44¾	16½	23	Manchuria . . .	Henri de Bourbon, Comte de Bardi.

Head of Male Shapu.

SHAPU or URIAL (Ovis vignei).

A much smaller sheep than either of the Asiatic argalis, with comparatively slender and well-wrinkled horns of considerable length,
which when fully developed curve forwards along the sides of the face ;
the males with a more or less strongly developed white ruff on the
throat.   General colour varying from rufous brown to gray in summer,
with the chest, under parts, and portions of the legs white, and sometimes blackish "points." Females with small horns.   Height at
shoulder about 32 inches ; weight about 120 lbs.

Distribution.—From Ladak and Zanskar to Russian Turkestan,
    Afghanistan, Baluchistan, Southern Persia, the North-West Frontier
    of India, and the Punjab Salt-Range.   Two local races, which
    probably intergrade in the Indus valley, may be recognised.
    First, the typical urin of Astor, the sha or shapu of Ladak (*O.
    vignei typica*) ; and secondly, the smaller Punjab urial (*O. vignei*),
    in which the colour is redder, the ruff more developed, and the
    front angles of the horns often show a knotted keel.   There is
    also *O. vignei blanfordi* of Baluchistan ; and it is possible the
    Persian form, in which the ruff is said to be but little developed,
    may form a fourth.

(a) **SHAPU** (Ovis vignei typica).

Length on front curve.	Circumference.	Tip to Tip.	Locality.	Owner.
39	11¾	15½	?	Major Sir H. S. Rawlinson, Bart.
38⅝	12¼	11¼	?	J. Carr Saunders.
38½	11¼	8½	Near Leh	E. L. Phelps.
36¼	11½	4¼	Near Ley	A. O. Hume, C.B.
-36¼	11¾	...	Near Leh	Major A. E. Ward.
-36¼	10⅞	10¼	Baltistan	Capt. T. A. Salt.
34⅜	11	...	?	East India Club.
-33¾	12¼	13	Ladak	P. H. G. Powell-Cotton.
33¼	12	12	Do.	Arnold Pike.
-33⅛	11½	10⅝	Do.	Sir Edmund G. Loder, Bart.
33	10½	15	Do.	F. W. H. Walshe.
32¼	10½	11¾		Sir Victor Brooke's Collection.
-32	11	9¾	Ladak	Col. J. Biddulph.
31¾	10¼	7	Do.	Col. F. C. Lister-Kay.
-31	11	...	Do.	J. D. Cobbold.
30½	8½	19	Do.	K. Dingwall.
30	11¾	16	?	Hon. Walter Rothschild.
-30	...	...	Ladak	Otho Shaw.
-30	11	...	?	Maharaja of Travancore, G.C.S.I.
-30	...	...	?	Lucknow Museum.
29⅞	10¾	...	?	H. C. V. Hunter.
29½	10½	13	Ladak	J. V. Phelps.
29½	10¼	15½	Tochi Valley	J. Johnston-Stewart.
29	11⅛	...	?	Sir Robert Harvey, Bart.
29	11	9¾	Ladak, W. bank of the Indus	A. Leslie Renton.
-28	...	...	Gilgit	Otho Shaw.
28	10¾	13	?	B. Vincent.
27½	11⅛	18¼	?	Martyn Kennard.
-27½	10	...	West Ladak	Capt. F. E. S. Adair.

(*a*) SHAPU (Ovis vignei typica)—*continued.*

Length on front curve.	Circumference.	Tip to Tip.	Locality.	Owner.
-27½	...	...	Skardo	Major George Douglas.
-27½	11¼	19	Astor .	Capt. H. W. Codrington, Officers' Mess Queen's Own Corps of Guides.
-27⅛	10¼	15	Do.	Capt. F. E. S. Adair.
-26¾	10¾	...	Shigar	E. L. Phelps.
26½	10½	13	Ladak	St. George Littledale.
26½	9¾	19½	?	W. J. M'Lachlan.
25½	11¼	15⅝	?	Hon. Charles Ellis.

(*b*) URIAL (Ovis vignei cycloceros).

Strictly speaking, *cycloceros* has no right to stand for this race, as it was given to the typical form, but at present it seems inadvisable to change it.

Length on front curve.	Circumference.	Tip to Tip.	Locality.	Owner.
39½	10¾	18¼	Punjab . . .	Major F. H. Taylor. (See illustration.)
-38½	...	...	Jouaka Land .	Royal Artillery Mess at Attock.
-37	9	...	?	Major J. C. Shirres, D.S.O.
38¾	9.75	9.5	Chita Oapar Range, near Attock	Royal Artillery Mess, Woolwich, Major C. F. Massey.
36¾	9	9	Hills north-west of Peshawur	Mess of 60th Rifles, Lord Walter Fitzgerald.
35½	10½	16	Gulran, Afghanistan .	Dr. J. Aitchison, British Museum.
-35½	10¼	20¾	?	Mess, 21st Punjab Infantry.
35¼	10½	9½	Punjab . . .	Major F. H. Taylor.
-35	11	14	Near Cabul . .	Major J. W. M. Cotton.
34½	8¼	16	Sind . . .	L. Napier.
33½	9¼	12½	Salt-Range .	A. O. Hume, C.B.
33½	9⅝	8¾	?	Capt. R. L. Tottenham.
32½	10	11½	?	Sir Victor Brooke's Collection.
32⅜	7¾	12	Punjab . .	G. Blois Johnson.
32¼	10	11½	?	Hume Collection, British Museum.
31½	9½	16¾	Salt-Range .	Capt. H. W. Codrington.
-31	10¼	...	Punjab . . .	Major-General Alexander A. A. Kinloch.

(*b*) URIAL (Ovis vignei cycloceros)—*continued.*

Length on front curve.	Circumference.	Tip to Tip.	Locality.	Owner.
31	$9\frac{3}{8}$	$14\frac{1}{2}$	Punjab . . .	Major R. H. Rattray.
$30\frac{7}{8}$	$9\frac{7}{8}$	$20\frac{1}{8}$	Salt-Range . .	Sir Victor Brooke's Collection.
$30\frac{3}{4}$	$11\frac{3}{4}$	$11\frac{1}{4}$	Do. . . .	Col. J. Biddulph.
30	$8\frac{1}{2}$	$6\frac{1}{2}$	?	Dublin Museum.
$29\frac{5}{8}$	$10\frac{3}{8}$	...	Salt-Range . .	H. C. V. Hunter.
$29\frac{3}{4}$	$10\frac{1}{2}$	$16\frac{1}{2}$	Sind Hills . . .	Major C. S. Cumberland.
$29\frac{1}{2}$	9	...	Sheik Budin, near Dera Ismail Khan	Capt. Harry V. Brooke.
$28\frac{1}{4}$	9	$15\frac{1}{2}$	Kusan, Afghanistan .	Dr. J. Aitchison, British Museum.
$27\frac{1}{2}$	...	...	Afghan Hills . .	Col. J. Biddulph.
$26\frac{1}{2}$	$9\frac{1}{4}$	12	Salt-Range . .	Capt. B. L. Carew.
26	...	...	Sind	J. D. Inverarity.
26	..	...	Salt-Range . .	Major-General Alexander A. A. Kinloch.
$25\frac{7}{8}$	$8\frac{1}{4}$	$14\frac{1}{2}$	Punjab . . .	Dr. Percy Rendall.
$25\frac{3}{8}$	$9\frac{3}{4}$	$13\frac{3}{4}$	Salt-Range . .	Sir Edmund G. Loder, Bart.

Head of Male Urial. Major F. H. Taylor's specimen.

(*b*) URIAL (Ovis vignei cycloceros)—*continued.*

Length on front curve.	Circumference.	Tip to Tip.	Locality.	Owner.
25⅛	9⅝	17½	Kohrod, Persia .	Sir Victor Brooke's Collection.
-24	8½	13	Salt-Range .	Col. J. Biddulph.
21½	9¾	15	?	Lieut.-Col. H. Wade-Dalton.

(*c*) KELAT RACE (Ovis vignei blanfordi).

Possibly inseparable from the last, in which case the name *blanfordi* should supersede *cycloceros*, which was really given to specimens of *typica.*

Length on front curve.	Circumference.	Tip to Tip.	Locality.	Owner.
37½	10¼	11	Haji Khan, Kelat, 3000 ft.	A. O. Hume, C.B.
36	9¼	17	Kelat .	Do.
31⅜	9⅜	13¾	Do. .	Hume Collection, Brit. Museum.
28½	9	10	Baluchistan .	Col. J. Biddulph.
-25½	9¼	10¾	Do. .	Lieut.-Col. L. L. Fenton.

ARMENIAN MUFLON (Ovis orientalis).

This sheep differs from all the preceding species by the absence of horns in the females; the horns of the males being not unlike those of the urial, but curving backwards, so that their points are situated behind the neck instead of beneath the eyes. General colour of upper parts some shade of yellow or foxy red; the under parts and lower portions of the legs white. Height at shoulder about 2 feet 9 inches.

Distribution.—The mountains of Armenia, Eastern Persia, and Asia Minor.

Length on outside curve.	Circumference.	Tip to Tip.	Locality.	Owner.
40¼	10½	5½	?	W. Burchart Barker, British Museum.
36¼	10⅜	5¾	?	British Museum.
36	10¼	15	Persia	Hon. Walter Rothschild.
30½	10⅝	18	?	Sir Victor Brooke's Collection.
-26$\frac{1}{10}$	8½	12⅛	Cilician Taurus . .	C. G. Danford.
[1] 24½	9¼	11½	Persian Frontier . .	Prince Demidoff.
24	9⅝	17	Asia Minor .	Col. J. Biddulph.
[1] 23¾	9½	13½	Persian Frontier	Prince Demidoff.
23¾	9½	11¾	Persia . .	Major C. S. Cumberland.

[1] Determination provisional.

Head of Male Cyprian Muflon. (From Biddulph, *Proc. Zool. Soc.* 1884.)

CYPRIAN MUFLON (Ovis orientalis ophion).

A small local race of the preceding distinguished by certain differences in coloration, and the complete rounding-off of the front outer angle of the horns of the male. This is the smallest of the wild sheep, and comparatively a rare trophy. Height at shoulder about 28 inches. The horns closely resemble those of the Armenian race in general characters, but are less massive, and curve gradually from the base, instead of diverging nearly straight outwards, as is generally the case in the latter. The type specimen of the species is preserved in the Berlin Museum.

Distribution.—The Tröodos Mountains of Cyprus.

Length on front curve.	Circumference.	Tip to Tip.	Locality.		Owner.
25	8	15¾ (weight 5 stone)	Tröodos Mountains	.	H. Williamson.
-24	8	4⅜	Do.	.	The late Lord Lilford.
23½	8·15	12·20	Do.	.	Col. J. Biddulph.
23	7	5¾	Do.	.	British Museum.
22⅞	7¼	6	Do.	.	Gen. Sir R. Biddulph, British Museum.
22¼	8	12¾	Do.	.	Sir Victor Brooke's Collection.
-17½	8	1½	Do.	.	Dublin Museum.
16	7¼	16½ (weight 4 stone)	Do.	.	Hon. Walter Rothschild.

2 C

Head of Male European Muflon.
From a specimen in the British Museum, shot by Ford G. Barclay.

EUROPEAN MUFLON (Ovis musimon).

The large light-coloured saddle on the otherwise dark summer coat of the rams of this handsome and well-known little sheep is so distinctive of the species that nothing in the way of description need be attempted in this place.   It may be observed, however, that the ewes are generally hornless, and that the horns of the rams curve forwards so as to have their tips below the eyes, and are comparatively massive, with the wrinkles of a type somewhat different from that obtaining in the Armenian sheep.   Height at shoulder about 27 inches.

A good account of muflon-shooting will be found in Mr. E. N. Buxton's *Short Stalks* (first series).

Distribution.—At the present day the islands of Sardinia and Corsica.

Length on front curve.	Circumference.	Tip to Tip.	Locality.	Owner.
34½	8¾	16⅜	Sardinia	W. Moncreiffe.
30½	8⅞	11	Do.	C. Sloane Stanley.
30¼	8⅝	14	Do.	Rhys Williams.

EUROPEAN MUFLON (Ovis musimon)—*continued.*

Length on front curve.	Circumference.	Tip to Tip.	Locality.	Owner.
29¾	8⅝	8⅜	Sardinia . . .	Rhys Williams.
29¾	8	12½	Do. .	C. Sloane Stanley.
29¾	8	...	Do. .	J. D. Cobbold.
29⅝	8¾	11	Do. .	Hon. R. A. Ward.
29	8¾	11	Do. .	W. Moncreiffe.
28⅞	8⅛	21	Do. .	E. N. Buxton.
28¾	9	10	Do. .	Ford G. Barclay.
28¼	9⅝	9⅜	Do. .	Edinburgh Museum.
27⅞	8¾	5¼	Do. .	W. E. Pease.
27	9½	10½	Do. .	Sir Edmund G. Loder, Bart.
27	8½	10	Do. . .	British Museum.
27	8¾	11½	Do. .	Rhys Williams.
–26⅝	8½	9	Do. .	H. Brinsley Brooke.
–26	10⅜	10½	Corsica .	Capt. John Marriott.
25½	8¾	6	Sardinia .	A. Y. Lethbridge.
25	8¼	10	Do. .	Hon. Walter Rothschild.
24½	9⅛	9⅞	South-West Sardinia .	Sir Victor Brooke's Collection.

DOMESTIC SHEEP (Ovis aries).

The history and ancestry of the various breeds of domestic sheep are lost in the mists of antiquity, and naturalists are totally unable to point to the wild stock from which any or all of them are derived. This is the more to be regretted, seeing that the Swedish breed is the type of the genus *Ovis*. Most domesticated breeds differ from wild sheep by the woolly nature of their coat ; but since hairy tame sheep are met with in several uncivilised countries, this point of difference is of comparatively little importance. More weight has been attached to the great length of the tail, which is much longer than even that of the arui ; and, as mentioned above, that species is almost certainly not the father of the domesticated sheep. There is, however, some degree of probability that the long tails of the domestic breeds are due to a kind of degeneration. And if this be really the case, their ancestry might be looked for among the muflons or urial or some allied extinct form, since the horns of most breeds approximate to the muflon type. The presence of horns in the females of many breeds, Dorsetshire, for example, may be either an inherited character, or a redundancy of a nature similar to that which has produced four, or even five, horns in the males of certain oriental breeds. Some eastern sheep, like the Wallachian, have further departed from the muflon type by the development of upright corkscrew horns comparable with those of the markhor or kudu.

Length on outside curve.	Circum- ference.	Tip to Tip.	Locality.	Owner.
39½	8¾	21	?	H. E. Surtees.
37	8¼	20	Loch Awe, N.B.	H. Murray.
35½	8	16⅞	?	Sir Victor Brooke's Collection.
33	11	22¼	Yarkand	Hume Collection, Brit. Museum.
32	8⅝	27¾	Do.	Do.
28¾	8	21½	Scotland	Rowland Ward.
22⅝	9½	20¼	Yarkand	Hume Collection, Brit. Museum.
22⅜	9¼	22½	Do.	Do.
18	8¾	16¼	Fezzan	British Museum.

Abnormally-horned Specimens.

Length on outside curve.	Circum- ference.	Tip to Tip.	Number of Horns.	Owner.
20¼ + 16	6 + 4¾	15½	Four	Sir H. B. Meux, Bart.
19¾ + 14	6½ + 4½	21 + 16	Do.	P. C. Millbank.
17⅞ + 14⅛	7⅝ + 4¾	4½ + 6¾	Do.	Hume Collection, British Museum.
17 + 11¾	6¾ + 5	6 + 8½	Do.	British Museum.
13¼ + 10⅞	5¾ + 4½	...	Five	Hume Collection, British Museum.
13 + 9⅞	7⅝ + 5	14¾	Four	A. O. Hume, C.B.
12 + 9¾	6½ + 4	17¼	Do.	Do.

The following specimens belong to the Wallachian breed :—

Length on the curve.	Length in a straight line	Girth.	Tip to Tip.	Owner.
33	17½	7½	19½	H.R.H. le Duc d'Orléans.
32	24	7¼	38	Do.

Head of Bull Musk-Ox.

MUSK - OX (Ovibos moschatus).

In spite of its name, this Arctic ruminant has no near affinity with the members of the ox tribe, the molar teeth being more like those of the sheep and goats, the muzzle, except for a small strip between the nostrils, hairy, and the tail reduced to a mere stump concealed among the long hair of the hind-quarters. On the other hand, the resemblance to the sheep is not very close, the horns, which in old males nearly meet in the middle line of the forehead, being of a totally different form and structure, and the skull likewise very distinct. In the males the horns are much flattened and expanded at the bases, after which they are bent suddenly down behind the eyes, to curve upwards again at the tips. In the females they are much smaller, less expanded, and not approximated at their bases. In both sexes their texture is coarse and fibrous, and their colour yellow. The long coat of dark brown hair depending from the back and sides like a mantle affords an adequate protection against the rigors of an Arctic winter ; and the broad spreading hoofs, with hair on their under surface, give a firm foothold on snow and ice. Height at shoulder about 4 feet; weight about 8 to 9 cwt.

Distribution.—Arctic America, approximately north and east of a line drawn from the mouth of the Mackenzie River to Fort Churchill on Hudson Bay, Greenland, and Grinnell-land, in lat. 32° 27′; approximate southern limit lat. 40° N.

Length on outside curve.	Breadth of Palm.	Tip to Tip.	Locality.	Owner.
–29¾	13	...	?	W. W. Hart.
27¾	10	27½	Barren Grounds of Northern Canada	David T. Hanbury.
27¼	12½	27	Do.	Earl of Lonsdale.
27	9½	25½	Do.	David T. Hanbury.
26⅞	11	27	Do.	Warburton Pike.
26¾	12⅜	...	North America .	J. Rae, British Museum.
26¼	13⅛	27⅝	Do. . .	British Museum.
24¾	11	25½	Barren Grounds of Northern Canada	Warburton Pike.
24¼	7½	19	Do.	J. Talbot Clifton.
24¼	10½	26	Do.	Hon. Walter Rothschild.
24	20 (circumference)	30	North America . .	Earl of Lonsdale.
24	9¾	23⅛	Do. .	Sir Edmund G. Loder, Bart.
22¾	9¼	19¼	Grinnell-land .	Col. W. H. Fielden, British Museum.
–21½	9	27	?	Dublin Museum.
♀ 18⅝	4¼	...	North America .	A. G. Dallas, British Museum.
♀ 18¼	4⅛	...	Do.	Do.

Horns of Cape Buffalo (F. H. Barber's specimen).

CAPE BUFFALO (Bos caffer).

Inyati of the Swazis and Zulus.
Mbogo and *Nyati* of the Swahilis.
Nari of the Basutos.

Nadi in the Barotse and Lake N'gami countries.
Mboa and *Nyati* in the Chilala and Chibisa countries.

Among the distinctive features of this splendid bovine may be noted the enormous helmet-like mass formed by the closely approximated bases of the horns in old bulls, the backward inclination and comparatively slight angulation of the horns themselves, the shortness of the face, and the great width and size of the heavily fringed and flapping ears. In colour both the skin and the sparse hairs with which it is clothed are for the most part jetty black; the hairs themselves being directed uniformly backwards from the nape to the rump. Height at shoulder about five feet.

Distribution.—Southern Africa from the Cape to the southern bank of the Congo on the west side, and approximately to the neighbourhood of the Victoria Nyanza on the east side of the continent. Northwards of this it not improbably gradually passes into the Abyssinian buffalo. Except on the Zambesi, Chobe, and some neighbouring rivers, buffaloes have now become very scarce in South Africa. But between Umtali and the east coast at Beira, and also from the latter station to the mouth of the Zambesi, they are to be met with in vast herds; and a few years ago existed in countless numbers. Here they are much protected by the unhealthy nature of the country, which is deadly to Europeans, except between the end of May and November. Save for a few protected herds in the Addo bush, the Knysna and Zitzikamma forests, and thickets of the Fish and Sunday rivers, the species has long since been exterminated in the Cape. It is even rare and local in British East Africa, where, as in other districts on the eastern side of the continent, the rinderpest has of late years played sad havoc with the herds.

Greatest Width. Outside.	Greatest Width. Inside.	Tip to Tip.	Width of Palm measured on face of horn.	Locality.	Owner.
-49½	43⅜	30⅞	12	Sabi River . .	F. H. Barber. (See illustration.)
49	44½	40½	11¼	Limpopo . .	Sir Richard Glyn, Bart.
-48⅞	44½	36	10	Chiromo, B.C.A.	H. C. Macdonald.
47	41	28½	12	Limpopo . .	The late W. F. Webb.
47	40⅞	...	12¼	East Africa .	F. J. Jackson, C.B.
...	40½	26	...	Do.	Prince Boris Czetwertynski.
46½	44¼	37½	6½	Pungwe . .	C. M. Swire.
45¾	41¼	37⅛	...	South Africa . .	British Museum.
45¾	40	28¾	12	Nyasaland .	F. Vaughan Kirby.
45½	41	30	...	East Africa . .	W. Astor Chanler.
45½	...	...	11½	Kilimanjaro .	H. C. V. Hunter.
-45	39¾	36½	14	East Africa . .	Count Scheibler.
-45	...	...	...	Nyasaland .	S. Pulley.
44¾	39⅝	27½	11¼	East Africa .	Sir Robert Harvey, Bart.
44½	39¼	29	12	Pungwe . . .	F. S. Staples.
44½	39¼	29	14	Near River Ramokwebani, S. Africa	F. C. Selous.
44½	...	37½	12	East Africa .	F. Charrington.
44	40¼	37¾	12	Do. .	Capt. R. A. J. Montgomerie, C.B., R.N.
-44	40	...	11½	South Africa	J. Lamont.
-44	37½	14	...	Chiringoma, P.E.A.	F. Vaughan Kirby.
43⅝	37¾	26½	12¾	East Africa .	Hon. Walter Rothschild.
43½	38½	25½	9	Pungwe . .	H. R. Holden.
43¼	38¼	24½	13¼	South Africa .	Sir John Willoughby, Bart.
43	37⅝	29¾	14	Do. . . .	C. D. Rudd.
42¾	38	33⅜	9¾	East Africa	E. J. L. Berkeley.

CAPE BUFFALO (Bos caffer)—*continued.*

Greatest Width. Outside.	Greatest Width. Inside.	Tip to Tip.	Width of Palm measured on face of horn.	Locality.	Owner.
—42½	...	...	13	Manicaland	F. Lean.
—42½	36½	29	14½	E. C. Africa . .	James J. Harrison.
42⅜	36¾	29½	12½	?	Sir Victor Brooke's Collection.
42	38	35¼	9	East Africa . .	Lord Delamere.
42	37⅜	26¼	11	Pungwe	Capt. F. H. Lehmann.
42	37	30¼	10¼	Barotseland	E. D. Scott.
—42	36	19	16	?	Mr. Justice Hopley.
41⅓	37¾	34½	10	Pungwe .	R. H. Venables-Kyrke.
41½	36⅞	28	...	South Africa . .	British Museum.
—41½	39	39	14¼	South-east Africa .	James J. Harrison.
41	38	35	8½	East Africa . .	Lord Delamere.
41	36¾	37	11	Zambesia .	Comdr. A. T. Hunt.
41	36	30	11½	?	Rowland Ward.
41	35⅞	28¾	...	Mashonaland	F. C. Selous, British Museum.
41	36½	26½	9½	Pungwe . . .	Capt. Lord Douglas Compton.
—40⅝	35	19⅝	13⅓	Do. .	Count E. Hoyos.
40½	36¾	25½	9½	Do.	Marquis of Hamilton.
—40½	36	35	15	South Africa	A. Ohlsson.
—40¼	36	20⅜	12	Lower Shiré .	Staff-Surgeon J. Dowson, R.N.
—...	36	21	...	East Africa .	Sir John Willoughby, Bart.
40	37	35	...	Do. .	Gen. Sir Lloyd William Mathews.
40	35¾	...	14⅝	Do.	F. J. Jackson.
♀ 40	34⅜	21	8¼	Pungwe . .	J. W. Allen.
40	35	21¼	10	Matabeleland .	Major James Grant.
40	34¾	21¾	8	Pungwe . .	C. C. Gouldsmith.
39¾	34½	9½	14	Do.	G. L. Bonham.
39¼	35	34½	9	Do. .	R. Hughes.
39.12	37	36.11	12	British East Africa .	Prince Henry of Liechtenstein.
39	36	35¼	12	Zululand	A. J. Brandon.

CAPE BUFFALO (Bos caffer)—*continued.*

Greatest Width. Outside.	Inside.	Tip to Tip.	Width of Palm measured on face of horn.	Locality.	Owner.
39	$34\frac{1}{2}$	$22\frac{1}{2}$	10	Mashonaland . .	A. Neilson.
39	$34\frac{1}{4}$	27	$11\frac{1}{2}$	Benguela . .	G. W. Penrice.
39	34	19	$10\frac{1}{2}$	Shiré Valley . .	H. H. Williams.
$38\frac{1}{2}$	$33\frac{3}{4}$	27	$9\frac{1}{3}$	Pungwe . .	R. K. Micklethwait.
$38\frac{1}{4}$	$32\frac{1}{2}$	$19\frac{3}{4}$	13	?	Sir Edmund G. Loder, Bart.
$38\frac{1}{4}$	$33\frac{1}{2}$	$23\frac{1}{4}$	$9\frac{1}{2}$	Shiré Valley . .	C. C. Bowring.
38	$33\frac{1}{4}$ ·	$26\frac{1}{2}$	8	Pungwe . .	A. Cameron.
38	$33\frac{1}{2}$	$31\frac{1}{2}$	$14\frac{3}{4}$	?	Julius Jeppe.
38	$32\frac{1}{2}$	$20\frac{3}{4}$	11	?	Do.
38	$34\frac{1}{4}$	$31\frac{1}{4}$	$10\frac{1}{2}$	?	F. Watkins.
$37\frac{1}{2}$	$33\frac{3}{4}$	30	10	British Central Africa	J. E. Gough.
$-37\frac{1}{2}$	$31\frac{3}{4}$	25	$11\frac{3}{4}$	Shiré Valley . .	Alex. R. Alston.
$37\frac{1}{4}$	$33\frac{1}{2}$	$32\frac{3}{4}$	$12\frac{1}{2}$	East Africa	Sir John Kirk, K.C.B.
$37\frac{1}{8}$	$31\frac{7}{8}$	$23\frac{5}{8}$	13	?	H.R.H. the Duke of Saxe-Coburg and Gotha.
37	32	$16\frac{1}{4}$	$9\frac{1}{2}$ (about)	Pungwe . .	Viscount Ennismore.
37	33	$30\frac{1}{2}$	$10\frac{1}{2}$	Goronza Plain, P.E.A.	Earl of Dunmore.
37	$31\frac{1}{2}$	21	$11\frac{1}{2}$	?	L. Rawstorne.
37	$30\frac{1}{2}$	19	10	South Africa .	R. A. Cooper.
♀ $36\frac{1}{2}$	33	$26\frac{1}{2}$	$5\frac{1}{2}$	Mozambique	F. Vaughan Kirby.

Skull and Horns of Abyssinian Buffalo.

ABYSSINIAN BUFFALO (Bos caffer æquinoctialis).

A smaller animal than the last (height at shoulder about 4 feet), with the general colour blackish or tawny brown, tinged locally with rufous, and tending to grayish on the legs. Horns smaller, much more flattened at the bases, where they are more widely separated, and in some, although not all, cases retreating less markedly behind the plane of the eyes. The fact that in East African specimens of the Cape buffalo the horns are usually less rugged than in more southern examples, tends to confirm the view that the present animal should be regarded as a variety rather than as a species.

Distribution.—From Abyssinia and southern Somaliland through the Egyptian Sudan for a considerable distance up the White Nile; but the southern limits, if definable, not yet determined.

Greatest Width. Outside.	Inside.	Tip to Tip.	Width of Palm.	Locality.	Owner.
40	37	32	$11\frac{7}{8}$	Abyssinia . .	E. Lort-Phillips.
$-37\frac{7}{8}$	$34\frac{3}{4}$	$34\frac{1}{4}$	$8\frac{3}{4}$	Upper Basaland .	J. Menges.
36	29	24	...	Mount Elgon, East Africa	E. Gedge.
32	28	22	$6\frac{3}{8}$	Basé Country . .	The late F. L. James.
$31\frac{3}{4}$	$28\frac{1}{4}$	$25\frac{3}{4}$	$8\frac{1}{2}$	Settite River . .	Col. Ralph Vivian.
$31\frac{1}{2}$	$26\frac{1}{2}$	$21\frac{1}{4}$	$9\frac{1}{4}$	Bogosland . .	G. P. V. Aylmer and W. D. James.
$31\frac{3}{8}$	$26\frac{7}{8}$	$24\frac{3}{4}$	...	Do. . .	British Museum.
31	$28\frac{1}{2}$	$21\frac{3}{4}$	11	Abyssinia . .	Sir Edmund G. Loder, Bart.
$-30\frac{3}{4}$	$26\frac{5}{8}$	$20\frac{1}{4}$	$10\frac{1}{4}$	Settite River . .	Count T. Palffy.
$30\frac{1}{2}$	23	$20\frac{1}{2}$	$8\frac{1}{2}$	Sudan . .	Lieut.-Col. Hon. W. Coke.
$-$ ♀ $23\frac{5}{8}$	$20\frac{1}{4}$	$16\frac{1}{2}$	$5\frac{1}{8}$	Lower Basaland .	J. Menges.

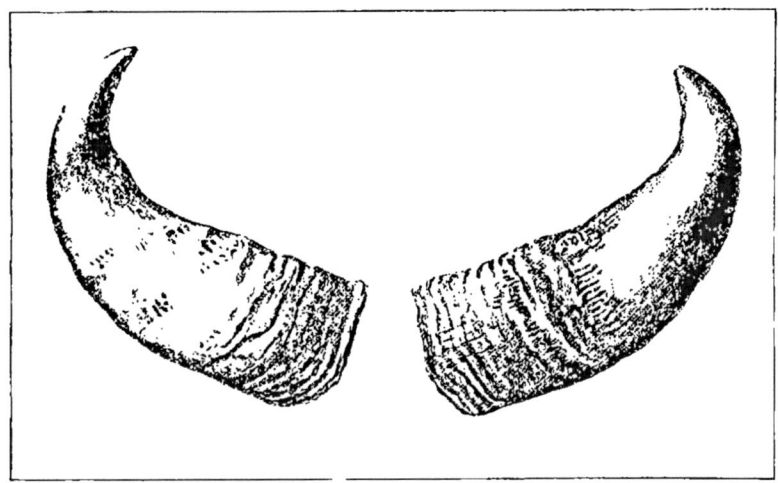

Horns of old Male Senegambian Buffalo, from the type specimen
in the British Museum.

SMALLER AFRICAN BUFFALOES.

Lake Tchad Buffalo (*Bos caffer brachyceros*).
Senegambian Buffalo (*Bos caffer planiceros*).
Dwarf Congo Buffalo (*Bos caffer nanus*).

Despite the enormous differences, alike in size, colour, and the form
of the horns, between the little red buffalo of the Congo and its gigantic
black cousin of the Cape, such a gradual and apparently complete
transition can be traced from the one type to the other, that both
seem local modifications of one very variable animal. In the dwarf
buffalo of the Congo the colour of the hair is red or yellow, the ears
are fringed with very long hair, and the horns are much flattened at
the base, with long smooth tips directed upwards. This type may be
traced, with some modifications, to the Gaboon and Gambia ; but in
the interior of Senegambia it apparently passes into the larger brown
buffalo, with more laterally expanded and recurved horns, known as
B. caffer planiceros. And this latter is, in its turn, very close to the
Abyssinian buffalo (*B. caffer æquinoctialis*) of East Central Africa,
which is nearly allied to the typical Cape form. Another type is
indicated by the Lake Tchad buffalo (*B. caffer brachyceros*), first discovered by Denham and Clapperton. In height the Congo dwarf
buffalo only reaches some 42 inches at the shoulder.

SMALLER AFRICAN BUFFALOES—*continued.*

Length on outside curve.	Circumference.	Tip to Tip.	Locality.	Owner.
23½	15	10	Gold Coast . .	Major G. S. C. Jenkinson.
23	16½	8¼	Nigeria . . .	Julius Jeppe.
21⅜	15¾	4	Do. . . .	Capt. C. A. Wilding.
21⅛	12¾	2¼	West Africa . .	British Museum.
21	15	9¼	Nigeria . . .	A. Ohlsson.
18¼	10¾	5½	Central Africa . .	Capt. Denham and Col. Clapperton, Brit. Museum.
18	16½	17½	Victoria Island, Lower Niger	R. H. Monck-Mason.
17	18½	19½	Nigeria . . .	A. W. M. Brodie.
♀ 17	11⅜	6¾	Central Africa . .	British Museum.
17	12	14½	Nigeria . . .	P. A. Clive.
16¾	10¼	6¼	Jebba, Nigeria . .	Capt. A. H. Festing.
15¾	11	9¼	Nigeria . . .	Sir Edmund G. Loder, Bart.
15	6½ [1]	14	Do. . .	Major A. J. Arnold, D.S.O.
14¾	11¼	8¾	Gaboon . . .	Dr. Percy Rendall.
14⅝	8⅛	7⅛	Sette Cama., W. Africa	British Museum.
14¼	12¼	10⅝	?	Sir Victor Brooke's Collection.
13⅞	10¼	28½	Gambia . . .	Late Earl of Derby, Brit. Museum.
♀ 13	10½	10½	Nigeria . . .	Julius Jeppe.
♀ 11½	9½	...	Lokoja . .	Major A. J. Arnold, D.S.O., Brit. Museum.
♀ 11	8½	10	West Africa . .	Sir Edmund G. Loder, Bart.
♀ 9½	7¾	8½	Do. . . .	Hon. Walter Rothschild.

[1] Width of palm.

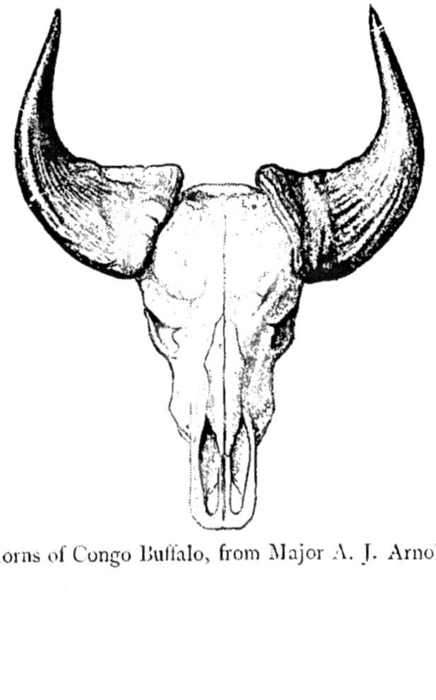

Skull and Horns of Congo Buffalo, from Major A. J. Arnold's specimen.

Head of Indian Buffalo.   Shot by the Maharaja of Kuch Behar.

INDIAN BUFFALO or ARNA (Bos bubalis).

No one is the least likely to confuse this animal with the Cape species.   Both belong, indeed, to the same group of the genus *Bos*, and have the rounded upper portion of the head and angulated horns. In the Indian species, however, the head is much longer, the ears are narrower and less heavily haired, and the horns of the male are widely separated on the forehead, and totally different in form.   Two types of horns may be recognised, one very massive, and curving regularly up from each side of the head in a subcircular manner ; the other much slenderer, though quite as long often, directed for the greater part of their length almost straight out from the head, and always with a wider spread ; these latter horns being those of females. Height at shoulder about 6 feet 2 inches ; girth behind shoulder, 10 feet 8 inches.   In a bull shot by the Maharaja of Kuch Behar the length from the nose to the tip of the tail was 14 feet 2 inches, and to the base of the tail 11 feet ; the maximum girth being 10 feet 8 inches, and the weight of the head when cut off, 158 lbs.

Distribution.—Typically India, where the range includes the plains of the Bramaputra and Ganges from the eastern end of Assam to Tirhut, and the Terai as far west as Rohilcund, the plains near the coast in Midnapore and Orissa, and also the plains in the Eastern

Central Provinces as far south as the Godaveri and Pranhita rivers. A fawn-coloured race occurs in Assam, and smaller varieties in Ceylon and some of the Malayan islands. In a domesticated state, South Europe, Egypt, etc. Native name of male, *arna*; of female, *arni*.

Length on outside curve.	Circumference.	Tip to Tip.	Widest inside.	Widest outside.	Locality.	Owner.
77⅜	17⅞	...	...	...	?	British Museum.
–71	21½	34¾	60	...	Assam . . .	Measured by A. O. Hume, C.B.; shot by A. Forbes.
-♀ 70½	18	...	64	78	Do. . .	The late Sir A. Campbell-Orde.
65¾	20¼	...	...	...	Do. . .	Col. J. Mathie, British Museum.
-♀ 64½	18	42½	60	96	Do. . . .	The late Sir A. Campbell-Orde.
–63	18	...	...	60	Do. . . .	Do.
62	17	101	...	...	Do. . . .	Hon. Walter Rothschild.
♀ 61⅞	15¾	22⅙	45¼	...	Kuch Behar .	H.H. the Maharaja of Kuch Behar.
♀ 61½	16	22	48	...	Assam . . .	Hon. Walter Rothschild.
60	22	...	64	72	Central Provinces .	B. Vincent.
60	20	40	52	...	?	Sir Edmund G. Loder, Bart.
58⅝	12⅜	...	...	...	?	British Museum.
58½	12¾	...	...	...	?	Do.
♀ 58	15	46½	59	...	Assam . . .	Rowland Ward.
–57	18	...	...	...	Central Provinces	J. D. Inverarity.
57	18½	41½	60	...	Do. .	Lieut.-Col. G. D. F. Sulivan.
–57	15	49	52	...	Assam .	A. H. Straker.
-♀ 57	14½	53	61	...	?	Sir Edmund G. Loder, Bart.
–56	18	29½	...	57½	?	J. Whitaker.
56¼	21½	40	52¾	...	Assam . .	A. O. Hume, C.B.
♀ 56	19¼	33⅞	50¼	...	Kuch Behar	H.H. the Maharaja of Kuch Behar.
56	15½	55½	58	...	Do. . .	Eyre Coote.
55½	18½	29	44	...	?	J. Carr Saunders.
-♀ 55	13½	...	...	...	Bhutan Duars . .	Major-Gen. Alexander A. A. Kinloch.
55	22	55½	62	66	Central Provinces .	L. T. Harris.
54½	18⅛	38¼	48⅞	...	?	Hume Collection, British Museum.

INDIAN BUFFALO or ARNA (Bos bubalis)—*continued.*

Length on outside curve.	Circumference.	Tip to Tip.	Widest inside.	Widest outside.	Locality.	Owner.
♀ 54½	12¾	69¾	70	...	Assam	A. O. Hume, C.B.
54½	19	50	59	64	?	Viscount Powerscourt.
54	20	40	47	55	?	Do.
-54	23	39	...	59½	Burma	Pegu Club, Rangoon.
53¼	12⅛	23¼	40⅝	...	?	Hume Collection, British Museum.
53⅙	12½	...	...	...	Nepal	The late B. H. Hodgson, British Museum.
[1] 53⅙	23	30 (6 ft. 2½ ins. at shoulder)	42½	...	Kuch Behar	H.H. the Maharaja of Kuch Behar.
53	...	...	...	...	?	Lucknow Museum.
51¾	18½	22	38¼	...	Assam	Sir Peter Walker, Bart.
-51⅜	19⅜	45⅜	50	...	Central Provinces	P. H. G. Powell-Cotton.
-50¾	18⅜	55¼	...	65	Patna State	Lieut.-Col. F. H. Whitby.
♀ 50½	14¾	40¼	59	...	Central Provinces	Col. M. M. Bowie.
50	18½	48½	60	...	Do.	Capt. C. F. Pinney.
50	13¼	33	38½	...	Assam	Noel Fenwick.
50	17	31¾	50	...	Do.	D. M. Lumsden.
-49¾	17¼	16¼	37	...	Kuch Behar	Count Scheibler.
48½	18½	33	51	...	Central Provinces	Col. F. C. Lister-Kay.
48½	19	27	47	...	Assam	Major E. T. Paul.
-48½	13¾	48¾	57	...	Central Provinces	P. H. G. Powell-Cotton.
48	19	33	50	...	Do.	Major H. C. Morland.
48	11¾	29¾	41½	...	Assam	Surg.-Capt. A. Pearse.
-48	20	...	...	...	Do.	H. Lennard.
♀ 47½	13¾	23	47	...	?	Major C. B. Wood.
47	19	25	50	...	?	H. De Prée.
-46½	20	42¼	55½	...	Kuch Behar	Prince Hans Henry of Pless.
46½	20	42½	54	...	Assam	Col. R. Pole-Carew, C.B.
46½	13¾	32	41	..	Kuch Behar	J. C. O'Donnell.
46½	17½	32	41	...	?	Dublin Museum.

[1] Measured round outside curves across skull, 9 ft. 11⅞ in. Another pair, 10 ft. 5 ins., circumference of horn at bone, 21 inches.

INDIAN BUFFALO or ARNA (Bos bubalis)—*continued*.

Length on outside curve.	Circumference.	Tip to Tip.	Widest inside.	Widest outside.	Locality.	Owner.
46	17½	32	41	...	?	Dublin Museum.
45¼	13	39	49	...	Kuch Behar .	Lord Wolverton.
44½	14½	15½	38	...	Assam .	L. Truninger.
44	19	27¼	46½	...	Do.	Hon. S. Tollemache.
44	20	28½	44	...	Do.	A. J. Walter.
♀ 43¾	12½	38½	...	...	Durbangah .	Duke of Portland.

The following specimens are mostly from Ceylon :—

Length on outside curve.	Circumference.	Tip to Tip.	Widest inside.	Widest outside.	Locality.	Owner.
♀ 35	9½	31¼	37¼	...	Ceylon .	R. Wahrmann.
34¼	15¼	25⅜	35	...	Do.	Earl Cairns.
♀ 33¼	9	31½	37	...	Do. .	Do.
31¾	16	28	...	38½	Do. .	Marquis Camden.
31½	16	...	47¼	...	South Australia (introduced)	H. L. Heber Percy.
♀ 31¼	11¾	34½	...	38½	Ceylon . . .	Surg.-Major G. E. Hale, D.S.O.
30¾	14	28	33¾	...	Do. . .	Count J. Potocki.
30¾	14	22	32	...	Do. . . .	H. E. Lindsay.
30¼	15	22	...	35½	Do. .	A. R. Hay.
29¼	10½	26	32	...	Do. . .	Capt. John Fuller.
26⅜	14¾	28⅜	25	...	Formosa (introduced)	The late R. Swinhoe, British Museum.

2 D

Head of Bull Anoa, from life.

ANOA (Bos depressicornis).

The smallest member of the ox tribe, characterised by its straight, upright horns, and the frequent presence of white spots on the sides of the head or elsewhere. Although so different in the form of the head and horns from the adult Indian buffalo, the anoa is in these respects much more like the young of the latter ; and they are connected to a considerable extent by the tamarau, or Philippine buffalo (*Bos mindorensis*) of the island of Mindoro. As in all the Oriental bovines, the hair of the fore part of the back is directed forwards in the anoa. Height at shoulder about 3 feet 3 inches.

Distribution.—The island of Celebes.

Length on front curve.	Circumference.	Tip to Tip.	Locality.				Owner.
$-15\frac{3}{4}$	$7\frac{1}{8}$	$7\frac{1}{2}$	Celebes	.	.	.	Paris Museum.
$12\frac{3}{4}$	6	$6\frac{1}{2}$	Do.	.	.	.	British Museum.
$12\frac{1}{4}$	$6\frac{1}{4}$	$8\frac{3}{4}$	Do.	.	.	.	Do.
$11\frac{1}{2}$	$5\frac{3}{4}$	$7\frac{1}{4}$	Do.	.	.	.	The late Gen. Hardwicke, British Museum.
10	$5\frac{7}{8}$	$5\frac{5}{8}$	Do.	.	.	.	Sir Victor Brooke's Collection.
$-9\frac{1}{2}$	$8\frac{1}{2}$	$8\frac{1}{2}$	Do.	.	.	.	Dublin Museum.
$8\frac{7}{8}$	$4\frac{3}{4}$	$4\frac{3}{4}$	Do.	.	.	.	Sir Edmund G. Loder, Bart.

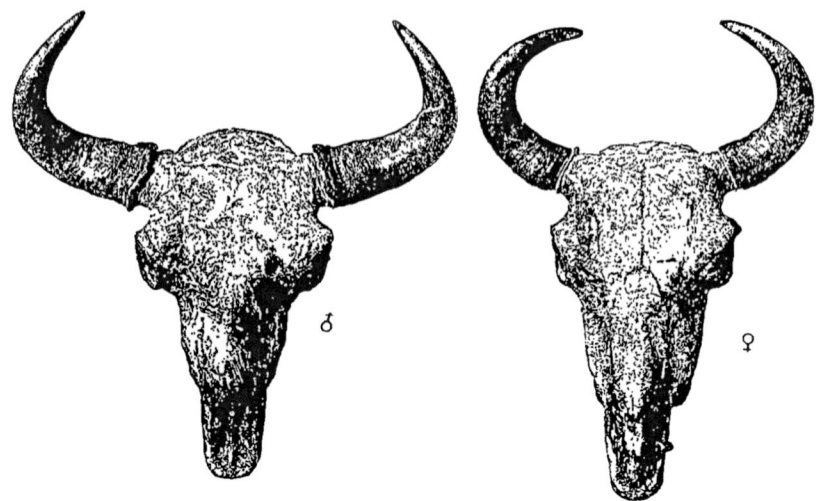

Skull and Horns of Bull and Cow Bison, shot by St. George Littledale.

EUROPEAN BISON or ZUBR (Bos bonasus).

The great elevation of the fore-quarters, the mass of long hair clothing the head, shoulders, and fore-part of the body, together with the peculiar form of the head and horns, the latter of which are cylindrical, serve at once to distinguish the bison from the other members of the ox tribe. There is also a difference in the number of ribs between the bison and the more typical oxen, the number in the former varying from 14 to 15 pairs. In the European species the mass of hair on the fore-quarters is not so long as in its American cousin, the form of the skull is different, and there are marked points of difference in the general appearance which render it easy to distinguish between the two species. Some difference may be noted between Caucasian and Lithuanian specimens, but it is doubtful whether these are sufficient to indicate a racial distinction. Height at shoulder 6 feet 1 or 2 inches. In a bull killed by Mr. St. George Littledale, the length from the nose to the root of the tail measured 10 feet 1 inch, the height at the shoulder 5 feet 11 inches, and the approximate girth of the body 8 feet 4 inches.

Distribution.—At the present day restricted to the Caucasus and the forest of Bielowitzka in Lithuania ; the herds in the latter district existing in a protected state. The name aurochs, so commonly applied to the bison, properly belongs to the extinct wild ox of Europe.

EUROPEAN BISON or ZUBR (Bos bonasus)—*continued.*

Length on outside curve.	Circumference.	Tip to Tip.	Widest inside.	Locality.	Owner.
18¼	12⅛	13¾	19¼	Lithuania	British Museum (presented by the Czar of Russia).
-18.2	10.8	17.5	20.14	Bielowitzka	Prince Henry of Liechtenstein.
-18	12⅛	16	20	Caucasus	St. George Littledale.
17½	10	18½	...	Bielowitzka .	Major Algernon Heber-Percy.
17.4	13.3	13.4	20.10	Do. .	Prince Henry of Liechtenstein.
16¾	12¼	21⅞	24¼	?	Sir Edmund G. Loder, Bart.
♀ 15¼	8	6	...	?	Major Algernon Heber-Percy.
♀ 13	8¼	9¾	14	Caucasus .	St. George Littledale.

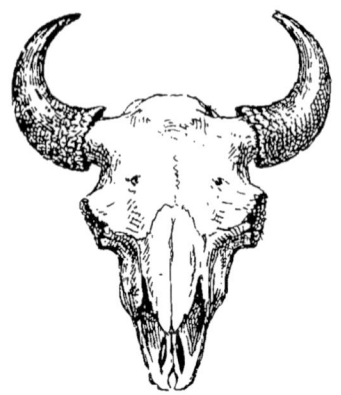

Skull and Horns of American Bison.

AMERICAN BISON (Bos bison).

Some of the points distinguishing this species from the European bison have been mentioned under the head of the latter, but it may be added that in the typical race of the former the horns are shorter, thicker, blunter, and more sharply curved. In the skull of the American animal the sockets of the eyes have a more tubular form. Height at shoulder about 6 feet; weight from 15 to 20 cwt.; an adult bull weighed by W. T. Hornaday scaled 1727 lbs.

Distribution.—The greater portion of Western North America, ascending to the Great Slave Lake, and descending to New Mexico and Texas; now nearly exterminated. American writers recognise two races (or species), the prairie bison (*B. bison typicus*) and the larger wood-bison (*B. bison athabascæ*) of the forest highlands of the North-West.

Length on outside curve.	Circumference.	Tip to Tip.	Widest inside spread.	Locality.	Owner.
$-21\frac{1}{2}$	$15\frac{1}{4}$	...	35 outside	Northern Montana .	W. F. Sheard.
$20\frac{7}{8}$	15	...	$30\frac{1}{2}$	Wyoming . . .	Hon. F. Thellusson.
$-20\frac{1}{4}$	$16\frac{1}{8}$	$33\frac{1}{2}$	...	?	W. H. Root.
-19	$12\frac{1}{2}$	...	...	W. Montana . .	P. Liebinger.
$18\frac{7}{8}$	$14\frac{3}{4}$	...	$16\frac{7}{8}$	Do. . .	The late J. S. Jameson.
$-18\frac{1}{4}$	14	$26\frac{1}{4}$	29	Sioux Country . .	Sir Greville Smyth, Bart.
-18	14	...	...	Montana . . .	F. Sauter.

AMERICAN BISON (Bos bison)—*continued*.

Length on outside curve.	Circum-ference.	Tip to Tip.	Widest inside.	Locality.	Owner.
17¾	12⅜	15⅛	...	?	H.R.H. the Duke of Saxe-Coburg and Gotha.
−17½	12½	...	...	S.-W. Montana	Theodore Roosevelt.
17½	12	...	25½	Wyoming	H.R.H. le Duc d'Orléans.
17½	13½	21	...	?	Viscount Powerscourt.
17⅛	11⅜	10⅜	17⅛	?	British Museum.
−17	14	17½	...	Yellowstone, Montana	Count E. Hoyos.
16⅝	14¼	24	...	Bighorn Mts., Wyoming	Moreton Frewen.
¹ 16½	12½	19⅜	...	Colorado .	Sir Edmund G. Loder, Bart.
16¼	13½	14¼	...	?	Duke of Portland.
16⅛	15⅞	25¾	...	Colorado	Sir Edmund G. Loder, Bart.
15½	14⅜	...	19¾	Wyoming .	St. George Littledale.
−15.8	12.14	15	...	Indian Territory near Texas	Prince Henry of Liechten-stein.
.14	...	12¼	...	North Park, Colorado	Col. Ralph Vivian.
13½	13½	17½	...	?	G. Wrey.
13⅜	12	...	...	?	Hon. Walter Rothschild.

¹ Wood Bison.

Skull of Male Yak. From a specimen in the British Museum,
presented by A. O. Hume, C.B.

YAK (Bos grunniens).

The plateau of Tibet is remarkable for the number of its peculiar
mammals, among which is the yak. Apparently its nearest relatives
are the bisons, but the yak has not the great elevation of the withers
in comparison with the hind-quarters so distinctive of the latter, and
the long hair forms a fringe on each side of the flanks, shoulders, and
thighs, as well as a tuft on the chest, while the tail is clothed with a
huge mass of similar long hair, forming, when cut off and mounted, the
well-known "chowries." Yak horns are much larger than those of
living bison, and have a totally different curvature; while there are
also important differences in the skull. Height at shoulder from about
4 feet 10 inches to at least $5\frac{1}{2}$ feet; girth behind shoulder, 9 feet $1\frac{1}{2}$
inches; length from between horns to base of tail, 8 feet $\frac{1}{2}$ inch;

tail, 3 feet 2½ inches ; from between horns to nose, 1 foot 3½ inches
(Capt. H. M. Biddulph). Weight about 1140 lbs.· Wild yak are
uniformly blackish brown in colour, any trace of white indicating
domestication, and probably cross-breeding.

Distribution.—The plateau of Tibet, part of the Kansu province of
China, and Northern Ladak, at elevations between about 14,000
and 20,000 feet. The peculiar grunting cry from which the animal
takes its name is developed only in the domestic breed.

Length on outside curve.	Circum- ference.	Tip to Tip.	Locality.	Owner.
−39	...	...	?	Lucknow Museum.
−38¾	18½	26¼	Kuenluen Mts.	A. O. Hume, C.B., (shot by late A. Dalgleish).
38¼	17	19	Do.	Hume Collection, Brit. Museum (picked up by Mr. Carey).
35½	15	16	?	E. L. Phelps.
35¼	14½	17	Tibet .	St. George Littledale.
34	12	30½	Ladak	Hon. Walter Rothschild.
−32¾	16¼	18¾	Do.	Capt. H. M. Biddulph.
−32¾	14	17⅛	Do.	P. H. G. Powell-Cotton.
32	13⅞	15¼	Do.	H. C. V. Hunter.
32	14½	9	Do.	I. Morse.
32	16	17	Do.	P. Church.
−31⅞	14¼	18¼	Chang Chenmo	P. H. G. Powell-Cotton.
31¾	16	16¾	Do.	Rowland Ward.
31	14	...	Do.	Col. F. C. Lister-Kay.
31	13½	14	Ladak	Arnold Pike.
30¾	13½	10½	Do.	Sir Robert Harvey, Bart.
30	13	15¼	Chang Chenmo .	H. Z. Darrah.
29¾	14	12	?	Hume Collection, British Museum.
29½	13⅜	11	Chang Chenmo .	Lieut-Col. G. D. F. Sulivan.
29	15	9	Do.	Sir Edmund G. Loder, Bart.
29	13½	13¼	Ladak	Arnold Pike.
28¾	15	13	Do.	G. B. Milne.
28¼	15¾	14½	Do.	P. Church.
−28	16	17⅞	Tibet .	Major-General Alexander A. A. Kinloch.

YAK (Bos grunniens)—*continued.*

Length on outside curve.	Circumference.	Tip to Tip.	Locality.	Owner.
28	13	28	Tibet	J. Benett Stanford.
28	13¼	29½	Near Manasarowar Lake	Capt. B. H. Boucher.
27⅞	11¾	18⅜	?	The late B. H. Hodgson, British Museum.
27½	13½	16½	Tibet	Capt. C. B. Vandeleur.
27	13	15¼	Ladak . . .	Major C. S. Cumberland.
26½	13½	19	Chang Chenmo . .	Col. J. Biddulph.
25¾	12	16¾	Ladak . . .	Major J. A. Orr-Ewing.
25½	13	17	Do. . . .	Capt. H. H. P. Deasy.
24½	11¼	14	Tibet	T. W. Greenfield.
♀ 24½	8½	5¾	Ladak . . .	G. B. Milne.

Head of Bull Yak.

Head of Male Gaur.
(After Forsyth.)

GAUR (Bos gaurus).

This splendid bovine, the miscalled bison of Anglo-Indian sportsmen, is the typical representative of a group of three oriental species
nearly related to the domestic ox, but presenting certain well-marked
points of difference.　Among these may be noted the shorter head and
tail, the frequently elliptical section of the horns, and, above all, the
presence of a more or less distinct ridge running from the withers to
the middle of the back, where it terminates in a sudden step.　In the
gaur this ridge is very strongly developed, but the most distinctive
feature of the animal is the great arch on the crown of the head
between the horns, which bends forward to communicate a concave
profile to the forehead.　With the exception of the white "stockings"

common to all the members of the group, the colour of the gaur is uniform ; but the much flattened horns are of a peculiar yellowish green tint at the base. The height of adult bulls at the shoulder varies from about 6 feet to 6 feet 4 inches, though specimens of not more than 5 feet 5 or 6 inches are killed.

Distribution.—The forest hill-tracts of Peninsular India, Assam, Burma, and the Malay Peninsula, as well as the forests along the outer Himalaya as far west as Nepal. South of the Ganges, where it has not been exterminated, the gaur inhabits suitable districts in Chutia Nagpur, Orissa, the Northern Circars, Central Provinces, Hyderabad territories, and all the Western Ghats.

Length on outside curve of longest horn.	Circumference at base.	Tip to Tip.	Widest inside.	Widest outside.	Locality.	Owner.
–39¼	20¼	18¾	...	43	Salwin, Burma	Bombay Natural History Society's Museum.
–39	19¼	18¼	32	...	N. Travancore .	Arthur W. Turner.
–35	18	...	...	...	S. India . .	The late General Douglas Hamilton.
34¾	20	25	...	40½	Vardi Mullay .	Baron von Massow.
–34	19¼	33¼	...	...	?	Measured by Colonel J. Biddulph.
33¾	18	24	...	41	Pulny Hills, Madura District	J. D. Goldingham, Bethnal Green Museum.
...	17¾	28¾	...	43½	Travancore	H.H. the Maharaja of Travancore, G.C.S.I.
–...	17¾	25	...	...	Do. .	Do.
33½	18½	25	33¼	42½	Do. .	T. W. Greenfield.
–33½	21	...	32½	38¾	Mysore . .	Surgeon-Captain C. W. H. Whitestone.
33⅛	18	23½	34½	...	Kuch Behar	Maharaja of Kuch Behar.
33	17½	20½	32¼	...	?	Capt. P. Z. Cox.
–33	14	...	...	34	Western Ghats	J. D. Inverarity.
32½	...	27	...	...	Do.	Lieut.-Col. L. L. Fenton.
–32	19	27	...	...	Assam .	Major James Grant.
–32	18	...	...	...	Burma .	Indian Museum.
31⅞	17⅓	21⅜	32½	...	Travancore Hills	A. O. Hume, C.B.
–31½	18	29	...	43	?	Bombay Natural History Society (*Proceedings*).
–31½	17	21	32¼	...	?	Dublin Museum.
31¼	17½	22⅝	27½	40½	Pulny Hills, Madura District	J. D. Goldingham, Bethnal Green Museum.
31	19½	24¼	30¾	37½	Mysore . .	Viscount Powerscourt.

GAUR (Bos gaurus)—*continued.*

Length on outside curve of longest horn.	Circumference at base.	Tip to Tip.	Widest inside.	Widest outside.	Locality.	Owner.
30½	19½	16	...	35	Travancore	Lord Douglas Compton.
30¼	18½	22½	37¼	...	Do.	A. T. Mackenzie.
30	19¼	11	32⅛		Kuch Behar	H.H. the Maharaja of Kuch Behar.
-30	20	15	26	...	?	G. Beck.
-30	16	...	38	41	Central Provinces	Lieut.-Col. J. W. H. Flanagan.
-30	19	16	32	.	Travancore	J. D. Rees.
29⅞	18¼	30	34	...	?	Sir Edmund G. Loder, Bart.
29¾	18⅝	25¼	30⅜	...	Hassanoor Hills, S. India	Sir Victor Brooke's Collection. (Shot by the late Gen. Douglas Hamilton.)
-29¾	19	22⅛	31⅛	36⅞	Mysore . .	Captain M. M'Neill.
-29½	19¼	16¼	26½	...	Narbada Valley	Major-General Alexander A. A. Kinloch.
-29½	18	...	...	33	Central Provinces	J. D. Inverarity.
29½	17¾	28½	39	...	Siam	A. Waley.
29½	17	32½	43	...	Coimbatore, S. India	P. Church.
29¼	12⅞	...	18	...	Nepal	The late General Hardwicke, British Museum.
-29	22	..	...	...	?	Otho Shaw.
-29	17½	...	...	35	North Kanara .	Lieut.-Col. L. L. Fenton.
29	16	30	...	41½	Assam .	A. J. Walter.
28¾	18½	14¼	30	...	Travancore .	Lord Wenlock, G.C.I.E.
28¾	17¼	23¼	31	...	South India	Captain H. M'Micking.
28½	15¾	18⅝	28⅝	...	?	Major-General Sir Arthur Ellis, K.C.V.O.
28½	18	15¾	33½	...	Travancore	H. L. Cottingham.
28½	15¼	17	27	...	?	Hume Collection, British Museum.
-28¼	18½	28⅛	...	38⅝	Raipur, C.P.	Captain M. M'Neill.
28	18	22½	34¾	...	Assam .	Hon. S. Tollemache.
28	16	10¼	24	...	Central Provinces	Martyn Kennard.
28	19¾	34½	43	...	Upper Burma .	C. W. A. Bruce.
28	16½	15¾	...	31½	?	H. W. Keys.
28	15½	16¼	...	31	Khandesh	A. Cumine.
-28	17½	17	...	36½	Mysore	Veterinary-Captain G. H. Evans.

GAUR (Bos gaurus)—*continued.*

Length on outside curve of longest horn.	Circumference at base.	Tip to Tip.	Widest inside.	Widest outside.	Locality.	Owner.
27⅞	17⅛	32¼	32¾	...	Central Provinces	Major C. S. Cumberland.
27¾	19¾	37	41	...	Kalkerray, S. India	Captain W. E. Fairholme.
27¾	18¾	24⅜	30½	...	?	Major G. A. L. Carew, D.S.O.
-27½	20½	26¼	...	36½	?	Major-General W. Rice.
27½	17	26¼	36	...	Assam . .	L. Truninger.
27½	19	15	31¾	...	Travancore .	Captain Hon. E. Baring.
27½	17¼	20¼	35	...	Tezpore, Assam	A. Y. Thomson.
27½	18¼	20¼	34	...	Travancore .	Captain Hon. E. Baring.
-27	16¾	22	30½	...	South India .	H. W. Murray.
-27	15	...	17	...	Panarel, Central India	Captain A. Hicks-Beach.
26⅞	15⅞	16¼	27	...	?	Hon. Walter Rothschild.
26¾	14⅞	13⅝	24¼	...	Sahaydri Mountains, S. India	Captain W. Tompson, British Museum.
26½	17	17½	...	32½	Central Provinces	Surgeon-Captain A. Pearse.
26½	18¼	26¾	...	36½	?	Major R. H. Fraser.
26	18½	23⅜	32¾	...	Central Provinces	G. de H. Smith.
26	19	16½	32½	...	Do.	Captain C. F. Pinney.
26	17¼	19⅜	...	...	?	Lord Wolverton.
26	15	26¼	36	...	Central Provinces	Captain John Fuller.
26	15	33¼	...	40	Do.	C. F. Egerton.
26	17¼	27	36	...	Do.	Colonel M. M. Bowie.
26	18	23	35	...	Burma . .	Captain S. L. Robinson.
25½	17	21½	28¼	33½	S. India	Captain C. S. Timins.
25	18¾	18¼	29	...	?	Lord Elphinstone.
25	18	23¾	33¾	...	Kanara . .	Captain G. J. Fitzgerald.
25	17¼	18½	34	...	Central Provinces	Dr. W. P. Y. Bainbrigge.
24½	15¾	24⅝	34	...	?	H. De Prée.
-24	18	34	...	38⅜	?	J. D. Inverarity.
-24	19	27	34	...	Burma . .	W. F. Loftus-Tottenham.
23	15	22	33½	...	Assam .	Major E. T. Paul.

GAUR (Bos gaurus)—*continued.*

Length on outside curve of longest horn.	Circum- ference at base.	Tip to Tip.	Widest inside.	Widest outside.	Locality.	Owner.
♀ 22	10½	14⅝	27	.	?	H. De Prée.
♀ 20½	10½	12	..	...	Madras . .	Major J. W. M. Cotton.
- ♀ 19½	11½	...	...	...	N. Kanara .	Lieutenant-Colonel L. L. Fenton.
♀ 24	13¼	13	22	27	N. Travancore Hills	A. O. Hume, C.B. (See illustration.)

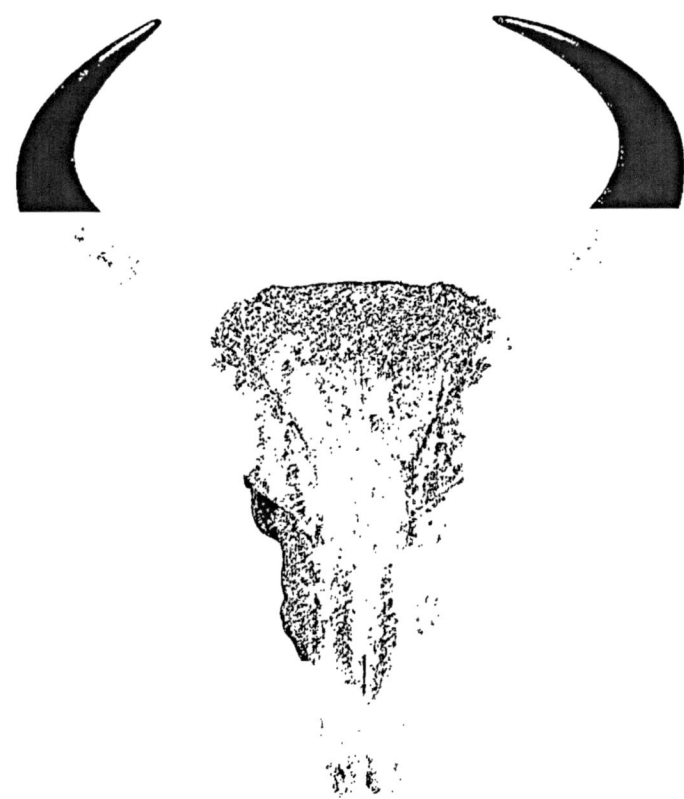

Skull and Horns of Cow Gaur, from A. O. Hume's specimen

Skull and Horns of Bull Gayal, from A. O. Hume's specimen.

GAYAL (Bos frontalis).

Chiefly known in a half-domesticated condition, the gayal is a rather smaller animal than the gaur, of a blacker colour, with a large dewlap, and with a straight line between the bases of the massive horns, which are more divergent, less curved upwards, more nearly cylindrical in section, and of a darker colour. The head, too, is much shorter, with the forehead very broad and flat.

Distribution.—Apparently the Tenasserim district in a wild state, but kept in a semi-domesticated condition by many of the hill-tribes of Assam and Chittagong. Gayal have been crossed with the American bison, the resulting progeny being fertile.

Length on outside curve.	Circumference.	Tip to Tip.	Locality.	Owner.
15	11½	26⅔	?	British Museum.
14½	13½	28	Tenasserim Hills .	A. O. Hume, C.B. (See illustration.)
−14	14	...	?	Indian Museum.
12⅝	13¼	27¾	?	British Museum.

Head of Male Burmese Banting. (From the *Proc. Zool. Soc.*, 1898.)

BANTING (Bos sondaicus).

The third and last member of the gaur group departs less widely from the type of the common ox than do the two others, the ridge on the withers being less developed, and the horns almost cylindrical. The cows, too, are always reddish coloured, although the bulls may be black, and in the latter sex at least there is always a large white patch on the rump.   Very distinctive of the species is the presence of a horny shield on the crown of the head between the bases of the horns. Height at shoulder about 5 feet 9 inches.

Distribution.—Burma, the Malay Peninsula, Borneo, Java, Bali, and perhaps Sumatra.   At least two distinct races of the banting are distinguishable.   First, the true banting, or Java ox (*Bos sondaicus typicus*), from Java, and perhaps some of the other Malayan islands and the Peninsula.   In this race the old bulls become of a deep blackish brown colour.   The same tint is characteristic of the old male banting in Borneo, but the horns are directed more uprightly.

The second well-defined race (*B. sondaicus birmanicus*) inhabits Burma, and may extend northwards to Manipur. Old bulls retain the reddish tint of the cows throughout life, showing more or less of gray on the head.

Skulls of Gaur and Banting.   Shot by Vet.-Capt. G. H. Evans.

Length on outside curve.	Circumference.	Tip to Tip.	Widest inside.	Locality.		Owner.
-33½	17	26⅞	35	Tammu, Burma	Upper	Surgeon-Capt. H. S. Wood.
-30	17	...	...	Java	. . .	Indian Museum.
-28½	17½	30½	36	Burma	. . .	Vet.-Capt. G. H. Evans.
28½	15	26½	36¾	Java	. . .	H. Van-Son.
26½	16½	21½	28	Do.	. . .	Sir Edmund G. Loder, Bart.
-26	18	17½	27	Burma	. . .	C. W. A. Bruce.
25¾	16⅜	20⅞	26¾	Siam	. . .	H. C. V. Hunter.
25½	13¼	29	32	Burma	. . .	W. H. Prendergast.

2 E

BANTING (Bos sondaicus)—*continued.*

Length on outside curve.	Circumference.	Tip to Tip.	Widest inside.	Locality.	Owner.
25½	19½	24½	30	Burma .	C. W. A. Bruce.
24¾	12¼	15¾	24¼	Java . . .	British Museum.
-24½	14½	30	35	Pegu	Vet.-Capt. G. H. Evans. (See illustration.)
21⅜	12¼	13⅛	19¼	Borneo	H. B. Low, British Museum.
20⅝	12¼	18⅛	22⅛	Do. . . .	Do.
20	16	22¾	24½	Kudah, B. N. Borneo	H. Ll. Davies.
♀ 20	12	21½	28	Upper Burma . .	C. W. A. Bruce.
-19¼	11¼	17	20	Borneo . .	Sir Edmund G. Loder, Bart.
19	11⅝	18	21⅜	Java .	The late H. J. H. Platt.
18	13½	12½	...	Borneo .	Sir Edmund G. Loder, Bart.
17⅝	10⅜	7⅛	14¼	British North Borneo	W. B. Pryer, British Museum.
17½	10⅛	17¼	20¾	Siam	H. C. V. Hunter.
16½	10¾	9½	13⅜	Sarawak .	British Museum.
16½	12¾	17½	18½	N. Borneo . .	A. D. Boden.
♀ 15½	7½	7½	16½	Tammu, Burma .	Surgeon-Capt. H. S. Wood.
♀ 7¼	7¼	6¾	...	Java . .	The late H. J. H. Platt.

DOMESTIC OXEN (Bos taurus and B. indicus).

The domesticated cattle of Europe are the descendants of the primitive wild ox, or aurochs (a name frequently misapplied to the bison), of Europe and North Africa (*Bos taurus primigenius*), now completely extinct in the wild state, although it survived on the continent till the Middle Ages. On the other hand, the humped oxen (zebu) of India and the Galla cattle of Africa (*Bos indicus*) appear to trace their origin to a totally distinct species, also extinct in the wild state.

Length on outside curve.	Circumference.	Tip to Tip.	Widest inside.	Locality.	Owner.
81¼	18¼	103½	...	N'gamiland . .	The late W. C. Oswell.
-?	17	100	124	Do. . .	A. Ohlsson.

DOMESTIC OXEN (Bos taurus and B. indicus)—*continued.*

Length on outside curve.	Circumference.	Tip to Tip.	Widest inside.	Locality.	Owner.
57	19½	82	...	Bechuanaland	Sir Edmund G. Loder, Bart.
56½	17½	76¼	...	South Africa .	R. A. Cooper.
47	15⅝	21⅛		Abyssinia (Galla Ox)	The late H. Salt, British Museum.
44	12⅞	70½ (about)	...	?	British Museum.
42⅛	23⅝	22⅛	...	Central Africa	The late Col. Denham, British Museum.
41¾	14	52¾	...	Madagascar .	Bethnal Green Museum.
40¼	12¼	60⅞	...	Vienna (Polish Bull)	British Museum.
38½	10½	54¾	...	Italy . .	Bethnal Green Museum.
35¾	12¾	59½	...	Cape of Good Hope	Do.
30⅛	12⅜	35	...	Spain .	Do.
29⅝	11⅛	28⅞	..	Gambia .	A late Earl of Derby, British Museum.
17½	10⅜	30½	...	Buenos Aires (Niata Cattle)	G. Claraz, British Museum.
17¼	10¼	25⅛	...	Gambia .	A late Earl of Derby, British Museum.
17⅛	10¾	25¼	...	India .	British Museum.
12⅛	8	16⅛	...	Angola	Sir Victor Brooke's Collection.
11½	7½	single horn	...	Nepal .	The late B. H. Hodgson, British Museum.

The following specimens belong to the so-called Wild Cattle of certain British parks, which are, however, certainly the descendants of at least partially domesticated breeds.

Length on outside curve.	Circumference.	Tip to Tip.	Widest Inside.	Locality.	Owner.
18½	9½	36½	...	Chartley Park	Hon. Walter Rothschild.
18½	7	34¾	...	Do.	Major James Grant.
18½	10⅜	20	21⅛	Chillingham Park	Earl of Tankerville, British Museum.
♀ 18¼	7	10⅛	15⅜	Do.	Do.
15¼	9⅝	17⅜	18⅛	Northumberland	Duke of Hamilton, British Museum.
15	7½	20¾	...	Chartley Park	Captain G. W. Hill, R.N.

HIPPOPOTAMUS (Hippopotamus amphibius).

Swahili name *Kiboko.*   Abyssinian name *Gumare.*
Danakil name *Dul.*   Boer name *Zee-koe.*
Galla name *Robi.*   Swazi name *Imvubu.*
                   Basuto name *Ikubu.*

Such a familiar animal as the uncouth and unwieldy hippopotamus—
the largest member of the swine group—requires but little in the way
of description here.   It is widely distinguished from the pigs and wart-
hogs by the broad and rounded muzzle, so unlike the disc-shaped snout
of the latter ; and consequently forms a family by itself.   The tusks
and molars are likewise of a totally different and distinctive type ;
while the feet have four sub-equal toes with symmetrical, rounded nails.
In all its organisation the hippopotamus is beautifully adapted for a
sub-aquatic life ; the eyes and nostrils forming the highest points of the
head, and thus allowing the creature to come up and breathe with the
least possible exposure of its body.   The weight of a full-grown bull
hippo is at least three tons.

Distribution.—Formerly this animal frequented most of the rivers of
    Africa south of the Sahara, but it has long since been exterminated
    from the lower reaches of the Nile, and is daily becoming scarcer
    in the South African rivers.   In the Zambesi, where it is less easily
    attacked than in the smaller rivers of Mashonaland, it is still
    abundant, as it also is in the Chobe and neighbouring rivers, as well as
    in Lake Ngami ; and even in the lower reaches of the Orange River
    a few are still to be met with.   North of the Zambesi these animals
    occur in great numbers.   Hippos are chiefly hunted for the sake
    of their hides, which are manufactured into sjamboks, or raw-hide
    whips.   Their tusks have also a certain commercial value, although
    not so great as formerly, when they were employed for artificial teeth.

In Liberia and some other parts of the West Coast there occurs the
much smaller pigmy hippopotamus (*H. liberiensis*), an animal measuring
only some six feet in length, and possessing more the habits of a pig.
It also differs from the common species by having, as a rule, only one,
instead of two, pairs of incisor teeth between the tusks.

A hippopotamus, shot on the Shiré River, British Central Africa,
by F. Vaughan Kirby, measured as follows :

	ft.	in.		ft.	in.
Total length, nose to tail	14	2	Length of tusks . .	2	5
Tail	1	8	Circumference of tusks .		$8\frac{1}{4}$
Vertical standing height	3	$10\frac{1}{2}$	Weight per pair ,, .		$14\frac{1}{2}$ lbs.

These tusks measured 31 and $30\frac{1}{4}$ inches, with circumference $8\frac{3}{4}$ inches, after they were extracted from the skull.

Length round outside curve of tusk.	Circumference.	Locality.	Owner.
[1]–51	9 (malformed)	S. E. Africa	J. Lamont.
[1]41	8 Do.	Tana River, East Africa	J. Benett Stanford.
[1]–38 protruding from jaw	...	Nyasaland	Major P. W. Forbes.
[1]$37\frac{1}{2}$	$8\frac{1}{4}$	Shiré River	Comdr. A. T. Hunt.
32	$9\frac{1}{2}$	Lualaba, Central Africa	S. L. Hinde.
$31\frac{3}{4}$	$10\frac{3}{8}$	?	Sir Clement Hill, Bart.
$31\frac{5}{8}$	$9\frac{1}{3}$	?	Sir Edmund G. Loder, Bart.
[2]$31\frac{1}{4}$	...	S. E. Africa	F. Vaughan Kirby.
$30\frac{1}{2}$	$9\frac{1}{8}$	St. Lucia Bay	Hon. Charles Ellis.
30	9 (weight 15 lbs. pair)	Do.	Do.
30	9	Shiré River	Staff-Surgeon J. Dowson, R.N.
30	9	Zambesia	E. W. Tompson.
–30	(weight 11 lbs.)	Katungas, Shiré River	E. B. Vertue.
$29\frac{3}{4}$	$8\frac{3}{4}$	Do.	F. C. Selous.
$29\frac{1}{4}$	8	Do.	Dr. W. P. Y. Bainbrigge.
29	8	Do.	Do.
29	$8\frac{1}{4}$	Shiré River	F. Vaughan Kirby.
29	$9\frac{1}{2}$	?	Rowland Ward.
$27\frac{1}{3}$	...	Atbara River, North-East Africa	W. D. James.
27	8	East Africa	E. Gedge.
$26\frac{1}{2}$	$8\frac{1}{2}$	Pungwe River	Earl of Dunmore.
$-26\frac{1}{2}$	$8\frac{1}{2}$	Zambesia	James J. Harrison.
$25\frac{1}{2}$	8	Nyasaland	Alex. R. Alston.
$19\frac{7}{8}$	...	Do.	Sir John Kirk, K.C.B.
$-11\frac{1}{4}$ protruding from jaw	$8\frac{1}{4}$	Shiré River	Dr. Percy Rendall.

[1] Malformed.   [2] Straight tusk 19 ins. long.

Lower Tusk of Wild Boar.

WILD BOAR (Sus scrofa and S. cristatus).

Most of the European and Asiatic species of wild swine, forming the typical group of the genus *Sus*, are so like each other, that it is often a matter of difficulty to discriminate between them, and naturalists are not yet in accord as to the number of species which should be recognised. The European wild boar is a large coarsely-haired species, with an undercoat of woolly fur, no warts on the face, and standing about 33 inches at the shoulder. It lacks the crest or mane of long black bristles running from the nape down the back in its Indian cousin ; and the last tooth in the lower jaw is of a rather less complex structure than in the latter. The wild boar of India (*S. cristatus*) is dear to the heart of the Indian sportsman, though he does contemptuously call its chase "pig-sticking."

"Pig-sticking" is considered quite as dangerous, if not more so than tiger-shooting. It is not a game of long bowls, but a close personal attack on a very fierce and pugnacious animal, endowed with strength, swiftness, and much tenacity of life. It takes a good horse and a good man to try conclusions satisfactorily with an old gray boar over nasty country, and the weapon used is only a spear. There are parts of the hilly country in India where it is impossible to ride, and here the rifle may take the place of the spear; but then there is not much glory in shooting a pig. A solitary boar is frequently a morose and dangerous animal.

A Spanish boar killed by H.R.H. le Duc d'Orléans weighed 302 lbs.

Distribution.—Europe, Asia Minor, and North-East Africa.

Length outside curve of tusk. Right.	Length outside curve of tusk. Left.	Length of tusk out of gum.	Locality.	Owner.
$-11\frac{1}{2}$	...	...	Caucasus .	Col. Veernhof.
$-11\frac{1}{4}$	...	...	Do. .	Capt. Robert Finnie.
$9\frac{3}{4}$	...	...	Asia Minor .	Admiral Sir Michael Culme Seymour, Bart.
[2] $9\frac{5}{8}$	...	...	Caucasus .	Prince Demidoff.
$9\frac{1}{2}$	...	...	Do. .	Do.
-9	...	...	Do.	Capt. Robert Finnie.
9	...	...	Albania . .	Sir Reginald Cathcart, Bart.
$-8\frac{5}{8}$	...	...	Algeria	Sir Edmund G. Loder, Bart.
[1] $-8\frac{1}{2}$	$8\frac{1}{8}$	3	Near Bona, Algeria .	Viscount Edmond de Poncins.
$-8\frac{1}{2}$	$8\frac{1}{2}$	$1\frac{5}{8}$	Do.	Do.
-8	...	...	Albania	Capt. Robert Finnie.
8	$2\frac{1}{2}$	...	Russia .	Count J. Potocki.

1 Weight 275 lbs. clean. 2 Weight 372 lbs.

Length outside curve of tusk.	Locality.	Owner.
$-14\frac{3}{4}$ (malformed)	Purneah, Lower Bengal . .	H. R. P. Carter, recorded in *Field*, 19th January 1895. (See illustration, p. 422.)
$-14\frac{3}{8}$	Hills above Jamu	Col. Sir Neville Chamberlain.
$-12\frac{3}{16}$	Java .	H. Van Son.
$-10\frac{5}{8}$	North Kanara . .	Bombay Natural History Society's Museum.
$-10\frac{1}{2}$	?	Meerut Tent Club.
-10	India	The late Sir Samuel Baker.
$-9\frac{3}{4}$	?	Meerut Tent Club.
$9\frac{3}{4}$	?	Dr. Travers.
$9\frac{1}{2}$	Burma . .	Langford Whitehouse.
$9\frac{3}{8}$	North Kanara	Lieut.-Col. L. L. Fenton.
$9\frac{3}{8}$	Central Provinces .	Major J. S. Ashby.

WILD BOAR (Sus scrofa and S. cristatus)—*continued.*

Length outside curve of tusks.	Locality.	Owner.
9¼	Central Provinces . . .	The late J. Moray-Brown.
-8¾	Do. . . .	Col. F. D. Lugard, C.B., D.S.O.
8½	Jumna Valley	Capt. F. C. Quicke.
8¼	Bengal	J. M'Kie.
-8.30	Assam	Viscount Edmond de Poncins.
-8¼	Bikanir	Maharaja of Bikanir.
-7.85	Assam	Viscount Edmond de Poncins.
8	?	Capt. P. A. Bainbridge.
7¼	Mhou	H. Dibble.
7¼	?	Maharaja of Bikanir.

Head of Wild Boar.

CAPE BUSH-PIG (Sus [Potamochœrus] chœropotamus).

Bosch-vark of the Boers.   *Ingulubi* of the Swazis and Zulus.

The bush-pigs, or river-hogs, of Africa and Madagascar form a peculiar group of swine characterised by having only 42, in place of 44, teeth, small tusks, and a large ridge-like prominence on each side of the face, due to the presence of a ridge of bone on the sheath of the tusk.   The ears may be surmounted with tufts of long hair.   The various species are best distinguished by the character of their skulls, colour forming a very uncertain guide.   The Cape bush-pig, or bosch-vark, is very generally gray, but the late Sir Andrew Smith stated that " scarcely any two specimens of this species exhibit the same colours ; some are a brownish black variegated with white, and others are almost entirely of a light reddish brown or rufous tint, without any white markings ; indeed, such are the varieties that it is scarcely possible to say what are the prevailing colours."   In British Central Africa, where they have been wrongly identified with the West African species, they are invariably reddish.   Height at shoulder about 31 inches ; weight, 35 lbs. Lower tusks average 6 to 7 inches long, and a good specimen shot by F. Vaughan Kirby has tusks protruding out of jaw $4\frac{3}{8}$ inches.

Distribution.—South and South-East Africa.

WEST AFRICAN BUSH-PIG or RED RIVER-HOG

(Sus [Potamochœrus] porcus).

In this species the colour is always some shade of rufous, either shining brownish red with a tinge of yellow, or dark reddish yellow with black on the forehead, ears, and limbs, the mane of the back, part of the margins of the ears, tips of the long tufts of hairs with which they are surmounted, and streaks above and below the eyes white.

Distribution.—West Africa, from Angola to Senegambia, and eastwards to Monbuttu.

Height at shoulder.	Weight.	Locality.	Owner.
-23¼	35 lbs.	Shiré River, British Central Africa	Dr. Percy Rendall.

BABIRUSA (Babirusa alfurus).

The pig-deer (to translate its Malay name) is not the least notable of several remarkable animals restricted to Celebes; the peculiar form and position of the upper tusks of the boars rendering them almost comparable to horns. Unlike other pigs, in which they curve upwards from the sides of the lips, the tusks grow from the centre of the muzzle, piercing through the skin, and as they are not worn by the lower pair, attain extraordinary dimensions. Both pairs are quite devoid of enamel; the lower ones growing from the sides of the jaw in the ordinary manner. The other teeth are somewhat less numerous than in ordinary pigs. In other parts of its organisation the babirusa is, however, very like the latter, although its nearly naked skin is remarkable for its coarse and rugged nature, being almost comparable to the bark of a tree. The height at the middle of the back, the highest point of the animal, is about 42 inches. Unlike the rest of its tribe, the female babirusa produces only a pair of young at a birth, which are of the same uniformly slaty hue as their parent. Babirusa are confined to the island of Celebes, where they afford good sport to the natives, who drive them into nets and then spear them.

Dr. F. H. H. Guillemard recorded in the *Cruise of the " Marchesa "* :

Weight, male, 128 lbs.; female, 85 lbs.
Height at shoulder, $27\frac{1}{2}$ in.; female, $25\frac{1}{2}$ in.

Length.		Locality.		Owner.
Upper tusks.	Lower tusks.			
-17	...	Celebes	.	H. Van Son.
-$14\frac{1}{2}$	...	Do.	.	Dr. F. H. H. Guillemard.
-$9\frac{1}{10}$	$7\frac{4}{10}$	Do.	. .	Dr. Percy Rendall.

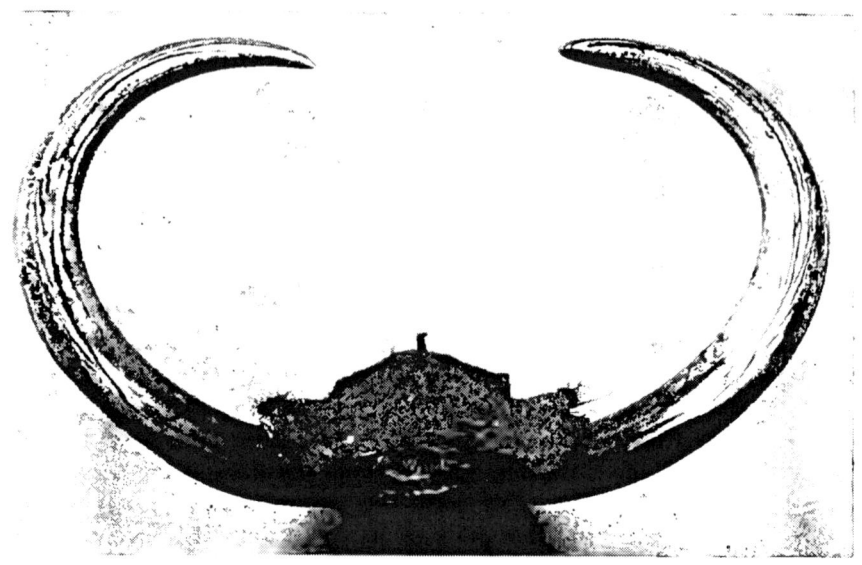

Tusks of Male Wart-Hog, F. H. Barber's specimen.

WART-HOG (Phacochœrus æthiopicus).

or *Nguruwe* of the Swahilis.
: of the Basutos.
izana of the Swazis and
ıs.
·y of the Somalis.
wi in the Barotse country.

Ngolobwi in the Lake Ngami
country.
Ngolobwi in the Chilala and
Chibisa countries.
Vlak-vark of the Boers.

r downright ugliness the African wart-hog is hard to beat, and as
ell armed and possesses a bad temper, it is in all respects an
·able acquaintance. The name is derived from the presence of
airs of wart-like protuberances on the sides of the face between
es and the tusks ; the head itself being characterised by the
ortionate length and flatness of the face. Unlike the true pigs,
ut upper tusks are longer than the lower pair ; the inferior
s of their basal halves being worn to smooth facets by the
of the latter. Another peculiarity of the upper tusks is that
ve no enamel, except at the extreme tips, which are soon worn
use. But a further peculiarity is presented by the last molar
f each jaw, which, together with the tusks, are often the only
emaining in very old animals. They are both long and tall,

consisting of a number of closely-packed cylindrical columns of enamel, which, when worn, present a characteristic pattern. Except along the neck and back, where it carries a mane of bristly hair, the skin is nearly naked; and the young differ from those of ordinary pigs in being neither striped nor spotted. Height at shoulder, 30 inches.

Distribution.—The wart-hog is typically an inhabitant of South and South-East Africa. Animals of the same genus extend, however, right through East and Central Africa to Abyssinia; those from the latter country having been described as a distinct species, under the name of *P. africanus*. Not improbably, however, the northern animal is only a local race of the southern form. Wart-hogs, possibly from their habit of going to ground when pursued, are but seldom hunted with the spear; "pig-sticking" being, in fact, a sport practically unknown in Africa. The lower tushes seldom exceed 6 inches on the front curve.

Length on outside curve.	Length exposed from gum.	Locality.	Owner.
-27 } 26	...	Annesley Bay.	Capt. Ralph Berners, R.N.
20	17¾	South Africa . .	F. H. Barber.
-16¼	13½	?	J. Whitaker.
-15½ } 15	13½	Matanari Bush . .	F. Vaughan Kirby.
-15	...	South-East Africa .	W. Russell Bowker.
14¾	...	British Central Africa	James Yule.
...	13¾	Zambesia . . .	R. J. Cuninghame.
13¹⁄₁₆	...	Somaliland	B. R. M. Glossop.
-13	...	Timbabti River, S.E. Africa	W. Russell Bowker.
...	13	South-East Africa	F. C. Selous.
...	11¾	Somaliland . .	Viscount Edmond de Poncins.
-12	...	South-East Africa .	James Meldrum.
-11½	...	Do.	Julius Jeppe.
-11½	...	Do. .	James J. Harrison.
-11¼	...	Somaliland . .	J. D. Inverarity.
...	10¾	Mashonaland . . .	S. Chillingworth.
-11	...	East Africa .	Count Scheibler.

WART-HOG (Phacochœrus æthiopicus)—*continued.*

Length on outside curve.	Length exposed from gum.	Locality.	Owner.
11	...	British Central Africa .	R. Skeffington Smyth.
...	$10\frac{5}{8}$	Sabi Flats, Transvaal .	Dr. Percy Rendall.
...	$10\frac{1}{4}$	Near Ruo River, South-east Africa	C. C. Bowring.
$10\frac{1}{2}$	...	Somaliland . . .	W. R. Bindloss.
$10\frac{1}{4}$	...	South-East Africa . .	F. Vaughan Kirby.
...	$9\frac{3}{8}$	...	W. W. Ashley.
...	9	Pungwe . . .	Count E. Hoyos.
...	9	Somaliland . . .	Prince Boris Czetwertynski.
...	9	Do. . . .	Capt. F. C. Quicke.

Lower Tusks.

$9\frac{1}{2}$	...	Somaliland . . .	J. D. Inverarity.
$9\frac{1}{2}$	...	Do. . . .	Viscount Edmond de Poncins.

Head of Male Wart-Hog.

Indian Rhinoceros (Rhinoceros Unicornis)
from Kuch Behar

GREAT INDIAN RHINOCEROS (Rhinoceros unicornis).

In addition to being the giant among its Asiatic kindred and possessing but a single horn, this huge rhino is specially characterised by the form of the folds in its hide, and the large tubercles on the fore- and hind-quarters, which look as though the skin had been fastened to the body by means of rivets. A fold before and behind the shoulder marks off one large triangular shield on each side, while another fold before each thigh separates a large rump-shield; the saddle-shaped body-shield being defined by the fold behind the shoulder and the one in front of the thigh, both of which extend across the back. Very characteristic, too, are the great folds which form heavy rings of skin round the neck. Although the tubercles are largest on the fore- and hind-quarters, they also occur on other parts of the body. Height at shoulder from 5 feet 8 inches to at least 6 feet; girth, 105 inches; length, 12 feet 10 inches, of body 11 feet.

MAHARAJA OF KUCH BEHAR'S SPECIMENS

Height at shoulder . .	6 ft. 4¼ ins.	6 ft. 1 in.	6 ft. ½ in.
Total length . .	14 ft. 1 in.	13 ft. 2 ins.	13 ft. 10 ins.
Body . . .	11 ft. 11 ins.	11 ft. 2 ins.	11 ft. 8 ins.
Girth behind shoulder .	119 ins.	112 ins.	
Biggest girth . .	144 ins.	142 ins.	
Round neck nearest body	90 ins.	84 ins.	
" " head	74 ins.	75 ins.	
Horn . . .	16¼ ins.	13⅞ ins.	

At one time this animal was found over the greater part of the Indian peninsula, as attested by fossil remains, but now it is restricted to Assam; its place farther east in the Sanderbans, Chittagong, and Burma being taken by the smaller *R. sondaicus.*

Distribution.—Chiefly the Assam plain at the present day.

Length on front curve.	Circumference.	Weight.	Locality.	Owner.
–24	...	...	?	The late Dr. T. C. Jerdon.
19⅛	22⅜	...	India . .	British Museum.
–19	18	...	Singpo, Burma .	Sir C. A. Elliot, Bart.
16¾	...	...	Belsire, Assam . .	W. C. Sherwill.
♀ 16¼	...	...	Kuch Behar .	Maharaja of Kuch Behar.
♀ 16	...	3½ lbs.	Nowgong, Assam .	L. Fabre Tonnerre.
14¼	21	...	Assam	Dr. W. P. Y. Bainbrigge.
♀ 14	22⅞	4½ lbs.	Nowgong, Assam .	L. Fabre Tonnerre.
–13⅞	...	...	Kuch Behar . .	Maharaja of Kuch Behar.
[1] 13	...	...	Do. .	Do.
13	20½	...	Assam . .	G. A. Dolby.
12¾	23	...	Do.	H. B. Firman.
12½	21⅝	...	Do.	H. C. Holland.
–12½	15½	...	Kuch Behar .	James J. Harrison.
12½	21	...	?	J. W. Grieve.
–12	...	...	Bhutan Duars .	Major-General Alexander A. A. Kinloch.
11	20	...	Kuch Behar . .	Capt. Hon. W. Lambton.
–10¾	21¾	...	Foot of Garro Hills .	A. O. Hume, C.B.
10½	17	...	?	Earl of Dunmore.
10	...	...	Kuch Behar .	Duke of Portland.
♀ –8¾	8	...	Do.	Countess Scheibler.
8⅜	15	...	Assam	Sir Peter Walker, Bart.
8¼	14⅞	...	Do.	Hugh G. Barclay.
8	17	...	Do. . . .	Major E. T. Paul.
6½	15	...	Tezpore, Assam . .	A. Y. Thomson.
5½	14½	...	Kuch Behar . .	Major Henry Streatfeild.

[1] Height at shoulder, 6 ft. 6 ins.

JAVAN or LESSER ONE-HORNED RHINOCEROS (Rhinoceros sondaicus).

A less gigantic and smaller-headed species than the last, with the skin divided up into a kind of mosaic pattern, and the fold in front of the shoulder continued right across the body like the two hinder folds. The neck also lacks the large ring-like masses of folded skin.   Horn never very large, and generally almost or completely wanting in the female.   A female has been measured which stood $5\frac{1}{2}$ feet at the shoulder, and it is probable that the male stands little less than the great Indian species, although it is of lighter build.

Distribution.—The Sanderbans and other parts of Eastern Bengal, to the Terai, Sikim, Assam, and thence through Burma and the Malay Peninsula to Sumatra, Java, and Borneo.

Length on front curve.	Circumference.	Locality.		Owner.
$10\frac{5}{8}$	$19\frac{5}{8}$	Java	.	British Museum.
$10\frac{5}{8}$	$19\frac{1}{2}$	Do.	.	H. Van Son.
$8\frac{1}{4}$	20	Do.		A. S. Campbell.

SUMATRAN RHINOCEROS (Rhinoceros sumatrensis).

The smallest of the Asiatic rhinos, and the only one with two horns ; differing, however, from the African members of the genus by the folds in the skin and the presence of teeth in the front of the jaws.   Only the fold behind the shoulders is continued across the back, and the brown or black skin is rough, granular, and more or less hairy. Height at shoulder from about 4 feet to $4\frac{1}{2}$ feet ; weight about 2000 lbs.

Distribution.—From Assam (where the species is very rare) to Siam, the Malay Peninsula, Sumatra, and Borneo.   Specimens from Chittagong are remarkable for the excessive development of the hair, which is long and very thick ; they may indicate that the Assamese form is a distinct local race (*R. sumatrensis lasiotis*).

Length on front curve.	Circumference.	Owner.
$32\frac{1}{8}$	$17\frac{3}{4}$	British Museum.
$27\frac{1}{8}$	$17\frac{7}{8}$	Do.

Common African Rhinoceros Skulls and Horns, from A. H. Neumann's specimens. The biggest horn of the three measures 40 inches on front curve.

COMMON AFRICAN RHINOCEROS (Rhinoceros bicornis).

Aurarisse of the Abyssinians.
Chipamberi of the Lower Zambesi natives.
Gurhu of the Danakil tribes.
Favu of the Swahilis.

Sipejana of the Swazis and Matonga.
Upelepe of the Basutos.
Upejana of the Matabeles and Zulus.
Weel of the Somalis.
Zwart Rhinoster of the Boers.

The African rhinoceroses are two-horned animals, readily distinguished from their Asiatic relatives by the absence of the folds of skin on the body which form such a characteristic feature of the latter ; as they also are by the lack of front teeth in both the upper and lower jaws. The hide, too, is almost completely naked, although there are some bristly hairs on the margins of the ears and the tip of the tail. Average height at shoulder, 5 feet.

Perhaps the most distinctive external feature of the black rhinoceros, as the present species is commonly called, is to be found in the prehensile tip to the upper lip, which is rounded and not very wide in front. Other points of distinction are, however, shown by the form of the horns and ears and the position of the eyes ; while in bodily size this animal is also considerably inferior to the next. If anatomical

2 F

characters be taken into account, the black rhinoceros is also well characterised by the comparative shortness of its skull, and the form and structure of the molar teeth, which are adapted for a diet of twigs and leaves.

Captain Edgar G. Harrison, writing in the *Field*, December 25, 1897, records the measurements of a five-horned Rhinoceros shot by him in East Africa as follows :—

Head of Common African Rhinoceros.

First Horn.—Counting from snout, measurement 14¾ in. ; is a normal front horn curving backwards.

Second Horn.—15¼ in., curving forwards instead of backwards or being straight, as is usual, and leaning considerably over to the off-side.

Third Horn.—11¼ in. long and 5½ in. wide half-way between base and apex ; is flat and perpendicular, and, though a distinct horn, grows out of the off-side of the base of No. 2.

Fourth Horn.—Is a stumpy, abortive horn, 9 in. long, growing partly from the base of No. 3, but quite separate and inclining slightly backwards.

Fifth Horn.—A distinct horn, 9¾ in. long, with its own base separated about 3 in. from No. 4.

Distribution.—From Abyssinia and Somaliland through East and Central Africa, in suitable localities, to the Cape. Now rare to the south of the Zambesi, and probably more abundant in the districts between the interior of Somaliland and Lake Rudolph than anywhere else. Although more alert and active than Burchell's rhinoceros, and thus a more dangerous animal, this species is by no means difficult to kill with modern weapons; and in the old days hunters frequently shot half-a-dozen in a single evening as they came to drink at a pool. In spite of its wide distribution, it has not been found possible to split up the species into local races; although this may perhaps be due to the want of sufficient specimens for comparison.

Length on outside curve.		Circumference.		Locality.	Owner.
Front Horn.	Rear Horn.	Front Horn.	Rear Horn.		
44	...	...	...	?	The late F. Holmwood.
43	...	21½	...	?	A. Beit.
41½	10	20½	16½	Zululand . . .	Lieut.-Col. Hon. W. Coke.
-41¼	...	22½	...	Orange River .	Major-Gen. Sir William Crossman, K.C.M.G.
-41	...	...	...	?	Carl Hagenbeck.
41	...	...	...	East Africa . .	The late F. Holmwood.
-40	...	22	...	Do. . .	Berlin Museum.
40	14¾	18½	20¼	Mt. Kenia, East Central Africa	A. H. Neumann.
-39⅛	...	21½	...	South Africa . .	J. Lamont.
38¾	...	21	...	?	Hon. Walter Rothschild.
38½	...	19	...	Masailand . . .	Sir John Kirk, K.C.B.
-38	11	24	21¾	South Africa . .	Earl of Dartmouth.
-36	...	...	...	East Africa . .	Sir Bartle Frere, Bart.
-35½	...	18	...	?	H. Murray.
♀ 33½	...	17½	...	Matabeleland . .	W. Van Ness.
-32½	21	19	15⅛	Portuguese Northern Zambesia	F. Vaughan Kirby.
-32	11¾	19⅞	19½	Athi Plains, East Africa	Count Scheibler.
31	...	18	...	East Africa . .	R. P. Carroll.
31	19½	16	16⅛	Do. . .	H. C. V. Hunter.
30½	...	21¼	...	Zambesi Valley . .	Sir John Kirk, K.C.B.

COMMON AFRICAN RHINOCEROS (Rhinoceros bicornis)—*continued.*

Length on outside curve.		Circumference.			
Front Horn.	Rear Horn.	Front Horn.	Rear Horn.	Locality.	Owner.
-29½	14½	...	...	Somaliland . .	A. H. Straker.
29	...	19	...	East Africa . .	Prince Boris Czetwertynski.
28½	...	18	...	South Africa . .	C. D. Rudd.
28¼	8¾	18⅛	...	Do. .	F. C. Selous.
-27½	12	...	...	Lake Njire .	T. E. Buckley.
27¼	10	21	17	Masailand . .	Capt. R. A. J. Montgomerie, C.B., R.N.
27	...	20½	...	East Africa .	E. Gedge.
27	16½	17⅞	17½	Do.	Sir Robert Harvey, Bart.
27	12	...	...	Do. .	Sir John Willoughby, Bart.
26¾	13¼	22	...	?	Sir Edmund G. Loder, Bart.
26½	10½	19½	15	East Africa .	Henry Charrington.
♀ 25¾	17	16	15	East shore of Lake Rudolph	A. H. Neumann.
25⅝	9⅛	17⅜	...	East Africa .	F. J. Jackson, C.B.
♀ 24½	12	16	17½	Masailand .	Capt. R. A. J. Montgomerie, C.B., R.N.
♀ 24	...	10¼	...	Kilimanjaro .	T. E. Buckley.
22¾	...	19¼	...	East Africa .	W. Astor Chanler.
22½	14½	17	16½	Somaliland . .	Julius Jeppe.
22¼	10	22¾	19	Do. .	Sir H. D. Tichborne, Bart.
-22	12·3	20·8	19·2	East Africa . .	Prince Henry of Liechtenstein.
21¾	11⅜	19	19	Somaliland . .	J. Kenneth Foster.
21⅜	17	14	16	Abyssinia . .	British Museum.
-20½	9¼	21¾	19⅞	Somaliland . .	Count E. Hoyos.
20	11½	21½	18	Do. . .	J. Byng Paget.
20	6¾	20½	19½	Do. .	Major H. G. C. Swayne.
-20	8¼	23½	21⅞	Do. . .	Count E. Hoyos.
-19½	8	...	...	Do. .	Capt. M. M'Neill.
-19¼	18⅛	8½	17½	Sabi Flats	Dr. Percy Rendall.
-19¼	6½	15½	14	E. C. Africa . .	James J. Harrison.
-19	22	18¼	20	B. E. Africa . .	Count Scheibler.

COMMON AFRICAN RHINOCEROS (Rhinoceros bicornis)—*continued.*

Length on utside curve.		Circumference.		Locality.	Owner.
ont Horn.	Rear Horn.	Front Horn.	Rear Horn.		
9	8	14	...	Somaliland	Count Grudzinski.
8¾	10½	18½	16½	Do.	A. S. Trevor.
8½	7	22	20½	Do.	P. H. G. Powell-Cotton.
8½	...	21½	...	Do.	Count T. Zamoyski.
8	12½	20	22	East Africa	Lord Delamere.
8	12	20	18	South Africa	Durban Museum.
8	7½	21	17	Somaliland	R. Wahrmann.
7½	7¾	19¼	19⅞	Abyssinia	British Museum.
17½	9¾	20	17½	Somaliland	Prince Nicolas Ghika.
17½	12¾	17	18½	Do.	W. W. Ashley.
17	6½	21	17	Do.	Prince Demeter Ghika.
17	13	16¼	18½	Do.	J. Benett-Stanford.
16¾	...	15⅞	...	Sudan	Col. Ralph Vivian.
16½	7½	17¼	15½	Somaliland	C. V. A. Peel.
16¼	8	20	18½	Do.	Count J. de Bylands.
16	...	...	...	Do.	Capt. M. M'Neill.
16	9½	14¾	16	Do.	Major V. M. Stockley.
15¾	6	18	15	Do.	A. Leslie Renton.
15¾	8	20	19	Do.	Count J. Potocki.
15	11½	15¼	16½	Athi Plains, East Africa	Countess Scheibler.
14½	6½	16	...	Somaliland	P. B. Vander-Byl.
11½	5¼	16½	15¾	Do.	Col. Arthur Paget.
10	6+3	(3 horns)	...	East Africa	Sir John Willoughby, Bart.

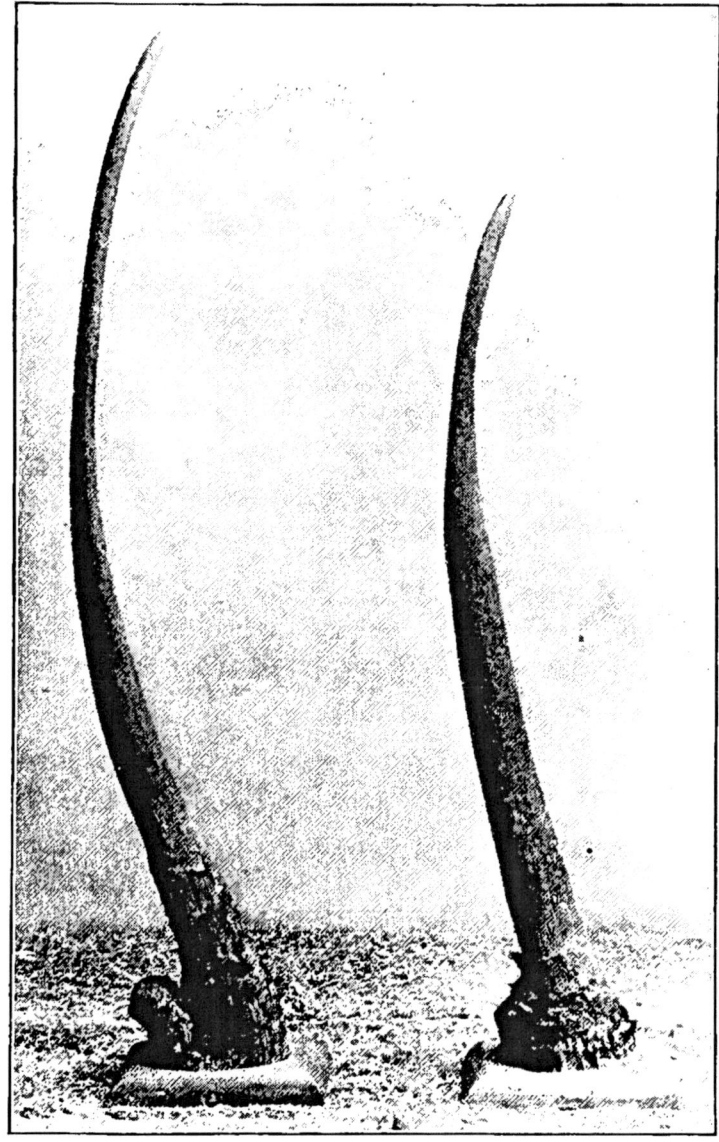

Front Horns of Burchell's Rhinoceros.
From specimens in the collection of the late Roualeyn Gordon Cumming, in the possession of
Col. W. Gordon Cumming.

BURCHELL'S RHINOCEROS (Rhinoceros simus).

Next to the Indian elephant this is the largest mammal that has trodden the earth in modern times ; and its practical extermination cannot fail to be a matter of lasting regret. Its huge bulk, bluntly truncate muzzle, which has no prehensile tip, the great length of the skull, and the enormous front horn, with its expanded base, form the most striking external characteristics of this species. And on looking at the skull it will be found that the molar teeth are of quite a different type of structure from those of the preceding species ; being, in fact, adapted for chewing grass. In walking, the animal carried its head low, so that in examples in which the front horn bends forward, its tip became worn by being pushed along the ground. It is difficult to surmise the reason for the application of the name " white rhinoceros " to this species, unless, indeed, it be that Cape specimens were lighter coloured than any seen in the districts to the north.

Distribution.—South and South-East Africa, in suitable localities, as far north as the Zambesi. Exterminated early in the century to the south of the Orange River ; and now represented at the most by a few survivors in North-East Mashonaland, and possibly by others in the reedy swamps at the junction of the Black and White Umvolosy rivers. Between the Zambesi and Orange rivers the species was abundant less than half a century ago ; Andersson alone having killed sixty in the course of a few months. Till a few years ago this rhinoceros was unrepresented by adult skins or skeletons in any British Museum ; and it is to the credit of Messrs. Coryndon, Eyre and Varndell that complete examples were secured before it became too late.

North of the Zambesi there exists a rhinoceros (*R. holmwoodi*) at present known only by single horns, which appears to be a near ally of this species, although it was at first regarded as a variety of the common rhinoceros.

Length on outside curve.		Circumference.		Locality.	Owner.
Front Horn.	Rear Horn.	Front Horn.	Rear Horn.		
-62½	...	22½	...	South Africa .	. Col. W. Gordon Cumming.
56½	...	23½ about	...	Do. .	. British Museum.
-52⅓	...	21½	...	Do. .	. Col. W. Gordon Cumming.
44	...	20	...	?	British Museum.
43¾	...	23¾	...	South Africa .	. A. Beit.

BURCHELL'S RHINOCEROS (Rhinoceros simus)—*continued.*

Length on outside curve. Front Horn.	Rear Horn.	Circumference. Front Horn.	Rear Horn.	Locality.	Owner.
42¾	...	...	25⅝	Limpopo, S. Africa .	The late W. C. Oswel
–41	...	...	...	South Africa . .	J. W. Fitzherbert.
40¾	...	29¾	...	Do. . .	Sir Edmund G. Loder
–40½	...	22½	...	Do. . .	Do.
40	...	15¾	...	Do. . .	British Museum.
–39	...	...	...	?	A. Ohlsson.
♀ 38⅝	...	24½	...	?	The late W. C. Oswel
38¼	...	22¼	...	?	J. B. Taylor.
37⅜	17⅞	27⅛	...	Mashonaland .	F. C. Selous.
37¼	...	24	...	South Africa . .	British Museum.
–36¾	...	20½	...	?	Berlin Museum.
36	...	28½	...	Mashonaland . .	C. D. Rudd.
36	...	25 lbs.	...	?	Rev. V. R. Carter.
35½ (mounted specimen)	7⅝	26	21	Mount Domo, Mashonaland	Cecil Rhodes, Cape Museum.
–33½	...	23	...	?	Julius Jeppe.
33	...	25½	...	?	Duke of Westminster.
33	13⅛	23¼	...	Mashonaland . .	F. C. Selous.
33	...	25½	...	?	Duke of Westminster.
32¾	...	27½	...	?	The late J. S. Jameso
♀ 32¾	...	27	...	Lake Ngami . .	The late W. C. Oswel
31⅛	...	19½	...	?	Mr. Justice Hopley.
31	...	24	...	Zululand . . .	Lieut.-Col. Hon. W.
–30¾	...	25¼	...	South Africa .	Col. H. B. H. Blunde
♀ 29¾	5½	23	20½	Zululand . .	Julius Jeppe, Pretoria
27⅝	12	22¾	18¼	Do. . .	Julius Jeppe.
27	...	20½	...	Do. .	Dr. W. P. Y. Bainbri
27	11¾	30⅜	25	Do. . .	Sir Edmund G. Lode
23⅛	...	26	...	?	Mr. Justice Hopley.
22½ (mounted specimen)	7½	26¼	...	Mashonaland .	Hon. Walter Rothsch
...	13	...	19½	?	Mr. Justice Hopley.
20¾ (mounted specimen)	7	28¾	...	Mashonaland . .	British Museum.
20	6	25½	18½	Zululand .	H.R.H. le Duc d'Orl

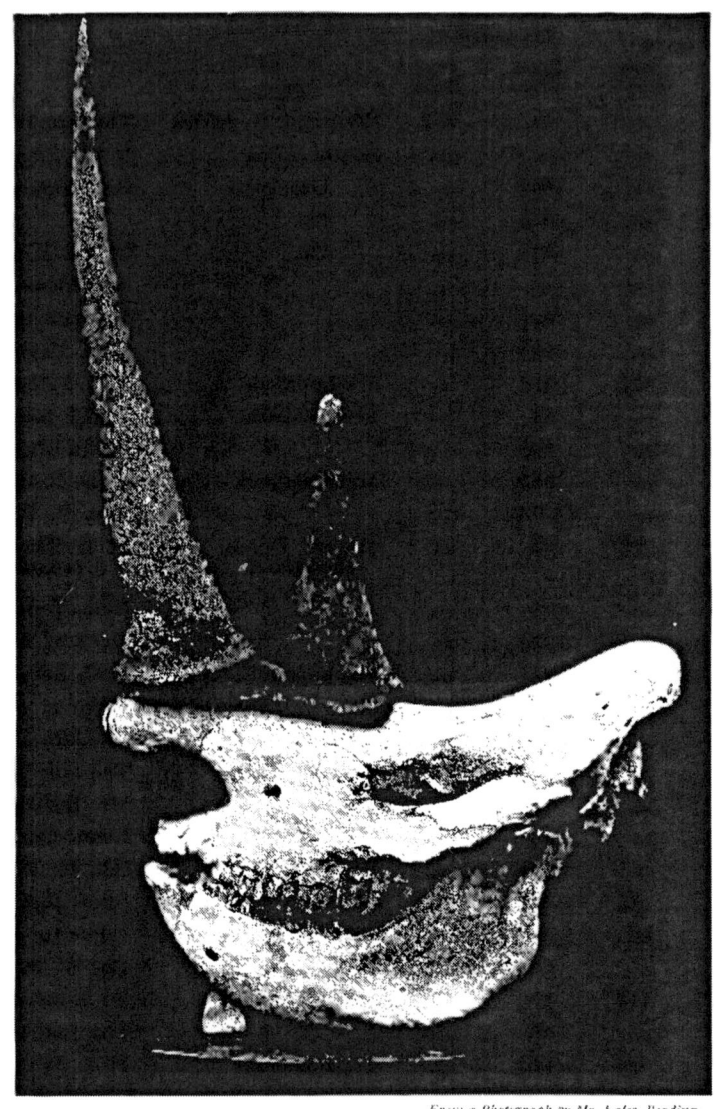

From a Photograph by Mr. Eales, Reading.

Skull and Horns of Burchell's Rhinoceros, Mashonaland, 1880.
Shot by F. C. Selous.

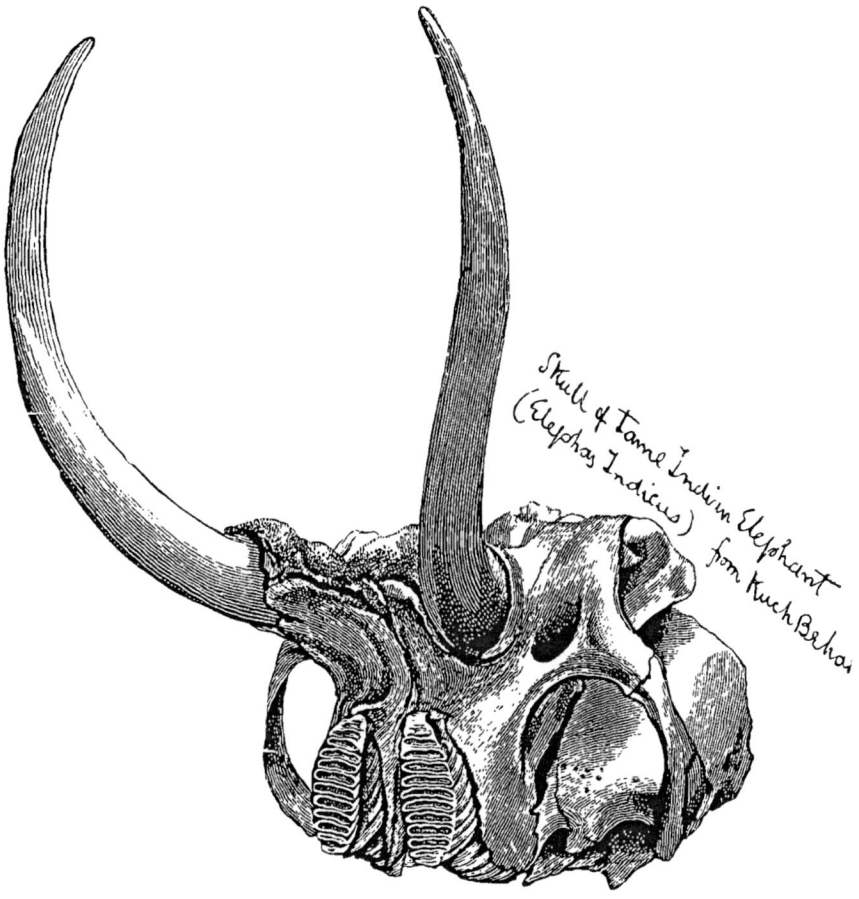

Skull of tame Indian Elephant
(Elephas Indicus) from Kuch Behar

INDIAN ELEPHANT (Elephas indicus).

In general a decidedly smaller animal, the Indian elephant differs
from its African relative not only in external form, but also in the
structure of its molar teeth, which are composed of a greater number of
much thinner vertical plates.   The females, as a rule, have only very
small tusks, not projecting beyond the jaw ; and in some cases those of
the males are equally poorly developed.   Five nails are usually present
on the fore-feet, and four on the hinder ones.   Externally, the most
characteristic distinction is the comparatively small size of the ears ;
next to which comes the presence of a finger-like process on the front
edge only of the tip of the trunk ; the African species having one in
front and a second behind.   The skin is nearly smooth ; and the

bristles on the tail are confined to the front and back edges for some distance above the tip. Other noticeable points are the comparative flatness of the forehead, and the regular convex form of the back. Although males do not generally exceed 9, and females 8 feet in height, specimens have been killed measuring 9 feet 10 inches, 10 feet 1 inch, and 10 feet 7½ inches, while one is stated to have reached 11 feet, and there is evidence of still larger individuals, perhaps of 12 feet.

Distribution.—The forest districts of India, Ceylon, Assam, Burma, Siam, Cochin China, Sumatra, and Borneo. The Sumatran elephant has been regarded as a distinct species, and it may possibly form a peculiar local race.

Height at Shoulder. ft.	in.	Locality.	Owner.
–11	0	Mysore . . .	Viscount Powerscourt.
–10	4	Gurhwal, N.W.P. . .	Col. J. E. Campbell.
–10	1	Ceylon	James J. Harrison.
–10	1	?	Major-General Alexander A. A. Kinloch.
–9	7	Mysore	The late Col. G. P. Sanderson.
–9	4	Ceylon .	Count Scheibler.

Tusks.

Length outside curve. ft.	ins.	Greatest circumference. ins.	Weight. lbs.	Locality.	Owner.
–8	9 R	17¼	81	Assam . .	Presented to the late Lord Lytton by Sir Steuart Bayley, K.C.S.I. Measured by A. O. Hume, C.B.
–8	2 L	...	80·2	Do. . .	Do.
...		...	100	Do.	The late Charles Redde, *P.Z.S.* 1886, p. 176.
8	0	16⅞	90	South India . .	Sir Victor Brooke's Collection.
[1] 7	3⅜	17½	102	Burma . .	Marquis of Waterford.
7	3¼	17⅛	97½	Do. . .	Marquis of Waterford.
6	10	17½	65⅝	India	J. D. Goldingham, Bethnal Green Museum.
–6	8	...	77¼	Madura District, South India	Col. G. M. Payne.
6	7½	14⅜	52½	Mysore	Viscount Powerscourt.
–6	7	12½	46½	Yala, S. Provinces, Ceylon	Capt. R. J. Marker.
–6	3½	...	73¼	Madura District .	Col. G. M. Payne.

[1] The tusks of the sacred white elephant which came out of King Thebaw's Palace, Burma.

INDIAN ELEPHANT (Elephas indicus). Tusks—*continued.*

Length outside curve.	Greatest circumference.	Weight.	Locality.	Owner.
ft. ins.	ins.	lbs.		
6 0	...	50	Madras . . .	J. Fortune.
−5 10	...	...	Borneo . . .	C. M. D. Stewart.
−5 3	15	42	Ceylon . . .	W. S. Murray.
−5 1½	15	35	Travancore . .	Hon. E. Stonor.
−5 0	...	...	Burma . . .	T. Mumford.
4 10	15¼	32½	Travancore .	Hon. E. Stonor.
−4 7	13	...	Do. . .	J. D. Rees.
4 6	15	...	Do. .	Lord Wenlock, G.C.I.E.
4 4½	15	...	Do. . .	Do
[1] 3 11¾	12¼	29¾	Yala, S. Provinces, Ceylon	Capt. R. J. Marker.

MEASUREMENTS PROTRUDING FROM SKULL.

3 11	...	...	India . . .	British Museum.
3 6⅞	...	...	Do. . .	Do.
3 3	...	...	Do. . .	Do.
2 5⅝	15	...	Do. . .	Do.
2 0½	...	...	Mysore . .	Viscount Powerscourt.
1 6	4⅜	...	Sumatra . .	British Museum.

[1] Broken end, pair to 6 ft. 7 ins.

Feet.

Circumference at base.	Width at bottom, back to front.	Locality.	Owner.
−67½	...	Measurement taken from living elephant under ch	Lieut.-Col. G. W. Hanson.
62½	...	South Arcot District .	J. Fortune.
61	20	Travancore . .	D. M. Lumsden.
60	18	Mysore . . .	Viscount Powerscourt.
−60	...	Gurhwal . . .	B. B. Osmaston.
−60½	...	India . .	Major-Gen. Alexander A. J
−59½	...	Gurhwal . . .	B. B. Osmaston.
58½	18	Travancore . .	H. L. Cottingham.

INDIAN ELEPHANT (Elephas indicus). **Feet**—*continued.*

ce	Width at bottom, back to front.	Locality.	Owner.
	18	Travancore	Hon. E. Stonor.
	19	Assam . . .	H. C. Holland.
	17	Ceylon . . .	R. Gordon Smith.
	18½	Assam . .	D. D. F. Hosack.
	...	Ceylon .	E. J. Brooke.
	17	Do. . .	G. M. Norrie.
	18	Do. .	Sir Peter Walker, Bart.
	17½	Do. . . .	T. H. Mann.
	18½	Travancore . .	Lord Wenlock, G.C.I.E.
	17¾	Ceylon . .	Rowland Ward.
	17	Gurhwal . . .	B. B. Osmaston.
	17	N.W. Provinces . .	Capt. G. O. Bigge.
	18	Pyinmana Tai . .	H. Partridge.
	17½	Ceylon . .	H. Storey.
	18¼	Do. . . .	W. H. Walker.
	17	Do. . . .	H. E. Lindsay.
	16½	Do. . . .	James J. Harrison.
	15	Do. . . .	Capt. R. J. Marker.
	16	Sumatra . . .	R. P. Carroll.
	15	?	G. A. Dolby.
	15½	Mysore .	W. G. Deeds.

· **Measurements** 54 ins. × 17 ins. when dried.　　　² **Measurements** 59½ when shot.

Head of African Elephant.

AFRICAN ELEPHANT (Elephas africanus).

Arba of the Gallas.

Dakana of the Abyssinians (Dan-akil).

Marodi of the Somalis.

Njovu in the Chilala and Chibisa countries.

Tlo in the Barotse country.

Thlo in the Lake Ngami country.

Zahon of the Abyssinians.

Zemba of the Swahilis.

The African elephant, although still abundant in many regions of Central Africa, in the southern part of the Continent is rapidly approaching extinction. A very remarkable exception to this melancholy process of extermination is, however, to be found in the south and east of Cape Colony, where, since the year 1830, wild elephants have been systematically preserved by Government. Strong troops of these protected elephants still roam the dense and impenetrable jungles of the Addo Bush and the Knysna and Zitzikamma forests. A permit to shoot one of these elephants—costing £20—is to be obtained at Cape Town. Farther inland the ivory-hunters have for a generation past been so actively employed, that, despite the vast numbers of these great mammals which forty or fifty years ago thronged the interior from the Orange River northwards, but a few troops are now left south of the Zambesi. In all Khama's country of Bamangwato, for instance, where Gordon Cumming, Oswell, and others shot most of their elephants, only one solitary troop remains !

ft.	in.		Owner.
10	7	" Jumbo " . . .	Barnum and Bailey.

Male shot by James J. Harrison in the Chiperoni Forest, Mozambique Province.

	ft.	in.		ft.	in.
Trunk-tip to crown . .	9	9	Girth of forearm	4	6
Crown to tail-tip . .	17	3	,, fore-foot	4	11
Vertical standing height .	11	1	The tusks were not very large.		

Estimated height of a huge tuskless male shot by Mr. F. Vaughan Kirby in the Chiringoma Forest, 10 feet 8 or 9 inches, circumference of forefoot 60 inches.

Male shot in Portuguese East Africa by F. Vaughan Kirby.

	ft.	in.		ft.	in.
Length from trunk-tip to crown .	9	7	Greatest height above ground as it		
,, crown to tail-tip . .	16	9	lay dead	5	4
Vertical shoulder height . . .	10	6½	Right tusk on the curve . . .	5	10
Perpendicular diameter of left ear			Left ,, ,, . . .	5	11½
over the flap	5	9	Greatest circumference . . .		19
Girth of left fore-foot . . .	4	10	Weight, right 77 lbs., left 81½ lbs.		

Mr. A. H. Neumann, in his *Elephant Hunting in East Equatorial Africa*, records the following among other dimensions :—

Male.	Height at shoulder in straight line.	Length from root of tail to eye, in straight line.	Girth of forearm below elbow.	Circum- ference of fore-foot.	Long diameter of hind-foot.	Girth of thickest tusk just outside lip.
	ft. in.	ft. in.	ft. in.	ft. in.	ft. in.	ft. in.
Shot at El Bogoi (foot of Lorogi Mountains), 30th Sept. 1894.	10 8 or 9 (at least)	12 6	4 6	4 8½	1 9	1 6½
Shot at Bumi (Lake Rudolph), 29th Dec. 1895.	10 5 (at least)	12 6	...	4 8½	...	1 6
Do. do.	10 9 (at least)	12 8 or 9	...	5 0	1 10	1 9¼
Shot at Janjai (near Kenia), 13th May 1894.	10 6 (at least)	...	...	...	...	...

The three first were old bulls of the type found, as a rule, in separate herds. The last was a "herd bull" or breeding male.

AFRICAN ELEPHANT (Elephas africanus)—*continued.*

Height at shoulder in straight line.		Total length (trunk to end of tail).		Girth of belly.		Girth of fore-foot.		Locality.	Owner.
ft.	in.	ft.	in.	ft.	in.	ft.	in.		
-10	6	...		...		...		S.E. Africa	F. C. Selous.
-10	3½	...		...		...		E. C. Africa	James J. Harrison.
10	3	21	0	18	0	5	1	Nyasaland	Sir John Kirk, K.C.B.
-10	0	23	5	16	6	...		South Africa	H.R.H. the Duke of Saxe-Coburg and Gotha.
-9	7¼	...		...		4	6½ (dried)	Somaliland	Viscount Edmond de Poncins.
-9	6½	...		...		...		Do.	Capt. M. M'Neill.
-9	3	24	6	...		...		?	Count E. Hoyos.
-9	2	...		...		...		Ruwenzori, E. C. Africa	Capt. C. Ashburnham.
-8	0	...		...		3	8½	?	Count Scheibler.

Tusks.

Length (outside curve).		Greatest circumference.	Weight.	Locality.	Owner.
ft.	in.	in.	lbs.		
9	5	22½	184	Africa	Sir Edmund G. Loder, Bart.
...		...	172	Do.	The late Sir Samuel Baker.

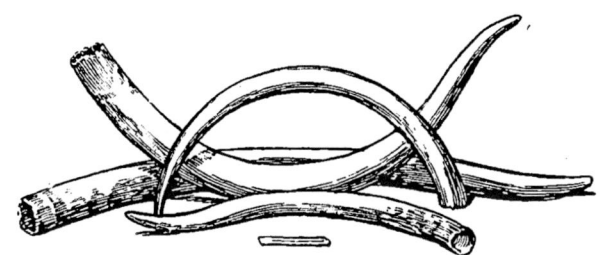

Specimens of A. H. Neumann's large Elephant Tusks.

9	4	20½	160	E. Africa	Sir John Kirk, K.C.B.
9	4 (tip broken)	18	110	Do.	Duke of Westminster.
-9	4	...	151	Elgayu, E. Africa	F. J. Jackson, C.B.
-9	3	...	129	?	Do.
9	0	18½	116	N. of Lake Rudolph, E. C. Africa	A. H. Neumann.
9	0	21	150	Africa	Sir Edmund G. Loder, Bart.
9	0	18½	116	N. of Lake Rudolph	A. H. Neumann.

AFRICAN ELEPHANT (Elephas africanus).   Tusks—*continued.*

Length (side curve).	Greatest circumference.	Weight.	Locality.	Owner.
ft. in.	in.	lbs.		
; 11	18⅝	...	Galla Country	Measured by Viscount Edmond de Poncins.
; 11	17¼	90	?	H.M. the Queen, Bethnal Green Museum.
; 10	18	105	East Africa	Lord Delamere.
; 8	18½	...	?	Sir H. B. Meux, Bart.

From a photograph by Mr. F. R. W. Pigott.

ie Big Tusk (8 ft. 7½ in., 165 lbs.) presented by the Officers serving in British East Africa to H.R.H. the Duke of York on the Occasion of his Marriage.

7½	22¾	165	East Africa	H.R.H. the Duke of York.
6	18¼	100	Do.	Lord Delamere.
3	18¾	81½	Do.	T. W. Greenfield.
2	18¾	80	Do.	Do.
1	20¼	114	N. of Lake Rudolph, E. C. Africa	A. H. Neumann.

2 G

AFRICAN ELEPHANT (Elephas africanus). Tusks—*continued.*

Length (outside curve).		Greatest circumference.	Weight.	Locality.	Owner.
ft.	in.	in.	lbs.		
7	10	19⅝	107	East Africa	A. H. Neumann.
7	8½	23½	160	Africa . .	Chalmers, Guthrie, and (
-7	8	...	108	Galla Country .	Dr. Donaldson Smith.
7	6	...	100	Do.	Do.
7	6	17	...	?	Duke of Westminster.
7	6½	21¼	...	South Africa .	The late W. C. Oswell.
7	3¼	19½	102	East Africa . .	Col. F. D. Lugard, C.B.,
7	o⅛	17⅛	60 (about)	Kilimanjaro, East Africa	F. J. Jackson, C.B.
7	o	18 (about)	...	South Africa .	Cetywayo's peace-offering to Lord Chelmsford.
6	9	17¼	...	Kilimanjaro	F. J. Jackson, C.B.
6	8	17	74	?	Julius Jeppe.
6	7	16⅛	...	South-East Africa .	F. C. Selous.
? 6	5½	12½	...	N. of Lake Rudolph, E. C. Africa	A. H. Neumann.
6	4½	17¼	...	East Central Africa .	H. S. H. Cavendish.
6 (spiral tusk)	1	7½	...	Masailand . .	Sir John Kirk, K.C.B.
-6	1	18	...	Somaliland .	Sir H. B. Meux, Bart.
5	10	16⅛	...	White Nile .	The late Sir Samuel Bak British Museum.
-5	9	18	70	Nyasaland . .	S. Pulley.
5	4	14½	...	East Central Africa .	G. E. Smith.
5	4	16½	78	Ruwenzori, E. C. Africa	Capt. C. Ashburnham.
4	11	15	26	Somaliland . .	A. H. Straker.
4	11	16	...	Ruwenzori, E. C. Africa	Capt. C. Ashburnham.
4	9½	14⅜	33½	Somaliland . .	E. W. S. Brooke.
4	8¼	13½	...	Do. . .	Sir Edmund G. Loder,]
4	5	12½	...	Do. . .	Lord Delamere.
4	5	10½	20	Do. .	P. R. Denny.
4	5	10	...	East Africa .	W. Astor Chanler.
4	4	13¾	26	Somaliland . .	Capt. J. M'Call Maxwe!
4	1	14½	60	Do. .	Digby Davies.

AFRICAN ELEPHANT (Elephas africanus). Tusks—*continued.*

Length (outside curve). ft.	in.	Greatest circumference. in.	Weight. lbs.	Locality.	Owner.
–4	1	13½	15¾	Somaliland . .	Capt. M. M'Neill.
4	8⅛	11	19¾	Do. . .	P. R. Denny.
–3	8⅛	14⅝	16⅛	Danakil . . .	Viscount Edmond de Poncins.
–3	4⅛	14⅝	16⅛	Do. .	Do.
–2	10¼	7¾	6$\frac{5}{16}$	Do. . .	Do.
–2	10	7¾	...	Somaliland . .	Dr. Donaldson Smith.
–2	10	...	...	Do. .	James J. Harrison.
				MEASUREMENTS PROTRUDING FROM SKULL.	
–4	8	...	...	Somaliland . .	Capt. M. S. Wellby.
–4	1	16¼	...	?	Julius Jeppe.
–3	11	16	...	?	Do.
3	5⅞	15⅛	...	South Africa . .	The late J. S. Jameson.

Feet.

Circumference at base.	Width at bottom, back to front.	Locality.	Owner.
–60¾	...	Somaliland . .	Capt. M. S. Wellby.
58½	19	E. C. Africa . .	H. S. H. Cavendish.
56	19	Somaliland . .	The late Col. E. Carrington.
54	18½	Do. . .	Major J. S. Ashby.
54	...	Kilimanjaro . .	F. J. Jackson, C.B.
–54	17	Somaliland . .	Count E. Hoyos.
53⅞	18½	South-East Africa .	The late J. S. Jameson.
53	17	Somaliland . .	Capt. J. M'Call Maxwell.
52½	19	Do. . .	Major J. S. Ashby.
52½	17	South Africa . .	Rowland Ward.
–51	...	Galla Country . .	Viscount Edmond de Poncins.
50	17	South Africa . .	F. C. Selous.
49½	17¼	Do. . .	Do.

AFRICAN ELEPHANT (Elephas africanus). Feet—*continued.*

Circumference at base.	Width at bottom, back to front.	Locality.	Owner.
-49½	...	East Central Africa .	James J. Harrison.
49½	17	Rhodesia . . .	W. W. Ashley.
49½	17	Masailand . .	Col. F. D. Lugard, C.B., D.
49¼	16½	East Africa . .	W. Astor Chanler.
48⅞	16⅛	East Africa .	H. C. V. Hunter.
-48¾	16¼	Somaliland . .	Capt. M. M'Neill.
48	...	Uganda . . .	Col. F. D. Lugard, C.B., D
48	16	B. E. Africa .	Col. Trevor Ternan.
44¾	14¾	Sudan .	Col. Ralph Vivian.
44¼	15½	Somaliland	Prince Demeter Ghika.

MAMMOTH or SIBERIAN ELEPHANT (Elephas primigenius

Nearly allied to the Indian elephant, but the plates of the still narrower and more numerous, the tusks spirally twisted, a skin clothed in woolly fur with long bristles intermixed.

Remains of this species occur in the superficial deposits of and Northern Asia. In the frozen soil of Siberia the skin, fle hair are frequently preserved, and the ivory is often suitable purposes of the turner.

Length (outside curve).	Greatest Circumference.	Weight.	Locality.	Owner.
11 ft.	20⅞ ins.	173 lbs.	Siberia	Sir Edmund G. Loder,

LION (Felis leo).

Ambassa of the Abyssinians.
Asced of the Arabs.
Imbubi of the Swazis and Zulus.
Lendja of the Gallas.
Libbah of the Somalis.
Libbaka of the Abyssinians (Danakil).

Mkango or *Nkalamo* in the Chilala and Chibisa countries.
Simba of the Swahilis.
Tau of the Basutos.
Tauw in the Barotse country.
Tauw in the Lake Ngami countries.

Any description of such a familiar animal as the lion (the only cat in which the male is furnished with a mane on the head and shoulders, and a tuft of long hair to the tip of the tail) would obviously be superfluous here. One of the great points of interest attaching to the species is its wide geographical distribution ; and it has not yet been determined that the Indian form can be separated as a distinct race, the alleged absence of the mane having been shown to be inconstant. Neither can black-maned and yellow-maned lions be regarded as distinct forms, since examples of both may be met with in one and the same litter. Somali lions seem, however, to run smaller than those from either the Cape or Algeria, although their manes are often very fine. Heights of 3 feet $4\frac{1}{2}$ and 3 feet 8 inches at the shoulder have been recorded in African specimens (the larger measurement by F. C. Selous), and 3 feet 6 inches in an Indian example (by Gen. W. Rice). Colonel Paget estimated the weight of a Somali lion at about 550 lbs. Wild lions never develop the enormous manes frequently seen in menagerie examples.

Distribution.—At the present day Africa from Algeria to the Cape, Mesopotamia on the west flanks of the Zagros range, Persia south of Shiraz, and India in the districts of Kathiawar, Sind, the Central Provinces, and Bundelcund. Now very rare in the latter country.

LION (Felis leo).

Total length before skinning.	Length from nose to root of tail.	Skin measurement from tip of nose to tip of tail.	Height at shoulder.	Girth of forearm.	Girth behind shoulder.	Weight.	Description.	Locality.	Owner.
ft. in.	ft. in.	ft. in.	ft. in.	in.	in.	lbs.			
10 5 (A)	...	10 10½ (raw)	3 7	...	...	...	Full black mane	S. E. Africa	F. Vaughan Kirby.
10 4	7 2	11 4	...	20	...	...	...	?	Do.
10 4	...	...	...	...	...	...	...	Somaliland	Count T. Zamoyski.
10 0	6 10	...	3 6	22 (upperarm)	57	434	Fine mane	Edmund's Menagerie	W. Yellowby.
9 11 (C)	...	11 9 (raw)	3 8	...	...	410	Do.	Hartley Hills, Mashonaland	F. C. Selous.
9 10½ (D)	6 8	10 8 (dressed)	3 6	19½	51½	516	Do.	British East Africa	Capt. R. A. J. Montgomerie, C.B., R.N.
9 10	...	...	...	...	...	...	Fair mane	Mashonaland	Sir John Willoughby, Bart.
9 10 (E)	...	...	...	...	...	...	Do.	Limpopo	T. E. Buckley.
9 10 (H)	...	12 1¼ (raw)	3 7	...	49⅝	...	Full black mane	Mushukulumbwe	Major A. St. H. Gibbons.
9 10	7 0½	10 10	...	...	...	...	Yellow and black mane	Somaliland	J. Johnston Stewart.
9 10 (K)	...	11 6	...	...	...	...	Do.	Do.	A. E. Leatham.
9 8	6 6½	...	3 4½	15¼	...	...	Full yellow mane	Zomba, B. C. Africa	R. G. Beswick.
9 8·13	6 10	...	...	...	...	...	...	East Africa	Prince Henry of Liechtenstein.
9 8	...	...	...	...	...	...	Yellow mane	Olipbant River	James J. Harrison.
9 7	...	11 3	...	...	...	...	Fine mane	North Somaliland	Norman B. Smith.
9 (?)	...	...	...	...	...	...	Do.	Kathiawar, India	Lord Harris, G.C.S.I.

9 7	6 8¼							East Africa	Prince Henry of Liechtenstein.
9 6	6						Fine lioness	Somaliland	Major A. E. Sandbach.
9 5	6 6						Do.	Kathiawar	Lieut.-Col. L. L. Fenton.
9 4½		10 11	3 11				Do.	Oliphant River	James J. Harrison.
9 4							...	Somaliland	A. E. Pease.
9 4		9 6						Do.	Count J. Potocki.
9 3	6 6	10 3	3 11	16	45		Well maned, partially black	Do.	Count Scheibler.
9 3		11 0						Do.	C. V. A. Peel.
9 2 (F)		10 0 (dressed)			48		Black mane	Do.	Major T. R. Harkness.
9 2		10 9¼						Do.	Capt. M. M'Neill.
9 2							Lioness	Do.	Lord Delamere.
9 1		11 0 (raw)	3 4	17	48½		Fair mane	Pungwe, S. E. Africa	F. C. Selous.
9 1	6 1	9 7½	3 6½	15	44		Light coloured mane	Somaliland	Count Scheibler.
9 1 (G)		10 4 (dressed)					Fine black mane	Do.	Capt. G. Campbell.
9 1		10 4 (dressed)					Good mane	Do.	Lord Delamere.
8 10	6 0¼	9 1¼					Lioness	Do.	J. Johnston Stewart.
8 9½						490		Central India	Capt. Smee.
....		9 5½						Somaliland	Count E. Hoyos.
8 7½		9 2 (raw)	3 3				Lioness	?	F. Vaughan Kirby.
8 6		9 7					Old lioness	British East Africa	Capt. R. A. J. Montgomerie, C.B., R.N.

In the accompanying list of skull measurements many will be found belonging to the skins on p. 454.

I have not yet seen a Somali skull measuring over 15 inches. A lion skull may be easily recognised when placed beside that of a tiger by observing that in the lion all the terminations of the sutures of the skull on the frontal are almost level ; in a tiger the nasal bones extend much further back—besides this a lion skull will stand much flatter on a table than that of a tiger.

Skulls.

Basil length from back to front.	Width across the zygomatic arches.	Weight cleaned.	Locality.	Owner.
16½ (A)	10	...	South-East Africa	F. Vaughan Kirby.
16 (end broken)	10¼	5 lbs.	East Africa . .	E. Gedge.
−15⅞	9¾	6 lbs.	South Africa .	J. Lamont.
15½ (D)	10½	5 lbs. 3 oz.	East Africa . .	Capt. R. A. J. Montgomerie, C.B., R.N.
15½	9¼	...	Pungwe . .	Hon. T. Thynne.
−15¼ (II)	9¾	...	Mushukulumbwe .	Major A. St. H. Gibbons.
15	10	...	Mashonaland	Basil H. Woodd.
−15	10	...	Somaliland .	J. D. Inverarity.
15	10	...	Benguela	G. W. Penrice.
15	9½	...	Beira . . .	H. T. and A. H. Glynn.
15	9½	...	Athi Plains .	C. F. S. Vandeleur, D.S.O.
15	10	...	Somaliland .	Col. Arthur Paget.
15 (C)	10	5½ lbs.	South-East Africa	F. C. Selous.
14¾	10½	...	East Africa .	Lord Delamere.
14¾	9	...	Matabeleland .	Capt. Sir K. Fraser, Bart.
14½	9¾	4 lbs.	South Africa .	Sir Edmund G. Loder, Bart.
−14⅜ (E)	9⅛	...	Limpopo .	T. E. Buckley.
14⁵⁄₁₆	9¼	...	Matabeleland	Capt. Sir K. Fraser, Bart.
14¼ (G)	9¾	...	Somaliland . .	Capt. G. Campbell.
−14¼	8¼	3½ lbs.	Nyasaland .	Dr. Percy Rendall.
14¼	9¾	...	Somaliland . .	Lieut.-Col. J. W. H. Flanagan.
14¼	9⅜	4½ lbs.	Do. .	Rowland Ward.

LION (Felis leo). Skulls—*continued.*

Basil length from back to front.	Width across the zygomatic arches.	Weight cleaned.	Locality.	Owner.
−14¼ (K)	9¼	...	Somaliland . .	A. E. Leatham.
14⅛	9	...	Matabeleland .	Col. R. S. S. Baden-Powell.
♀ 14⅛	8¾	...	South-East Africa	F. Vaughan Kirby.
14	10	...	Somaliland . .	Capt. C. J. Melliss.
−14	9⅝	...	Do. . .	H. W. Seton-Karr.
14	9½	...	Do. . ·.	Lord Delamere.
−14 (I)	9½	4 lbs.	British East Africa	Count Scheibler.
13¾	9½	...	Somaliland . .	Lord Wolverton.
13¾	9¼	...	Do. . .	E. W. S. Brooke.
−13¾	9¼	...	Do. . .	C. V. A. Peel.
−13½	8	...	South Africa .	Dr. W. P. Y. Bainbrigge.
13⅜	8⅝	...	Zomba . .	A. H. Sharp.
13¼	8⅛	...	Mashonaland .	Sir John Willoughby, Bart.
13¼	9	...	Kathiawar, India.	Lord Harris, G.C.S.I.

TIGER (Felis tigris).

A much less noisy animal than the lion, the great striped cat of Asia is also a more variable species, of which at least three local races may be recognised. First, we have the typical Bengal tiger, a large, long-limbed, lithe, and short-haired creature. A much smaller and rougher-haired race (*F. tigris virgata*) inhabits the Caspian provinces of Persia, and it is probably this form that extends into the Caucasus. Lastly, we have the Manchurian tiger (*F. tigris longipilis*), characterised by its large size, heavy build, short limbs, and the great length and thickness of the fur, which is often much less fully striped than in Indian specimens. The dimensions attained by tigers are given in the subjoined table.

Distribution.—From the Caucasus through Northern Persia, Afghanistan, India, Assam, Burma, the Malay Peninsula, Sumatra, Java, and China, to Manchuria and Amurland. In India ranging from an elevation of some 7000 feet in the Himalaya to Cape Comorin, but unknown in Ceylon.

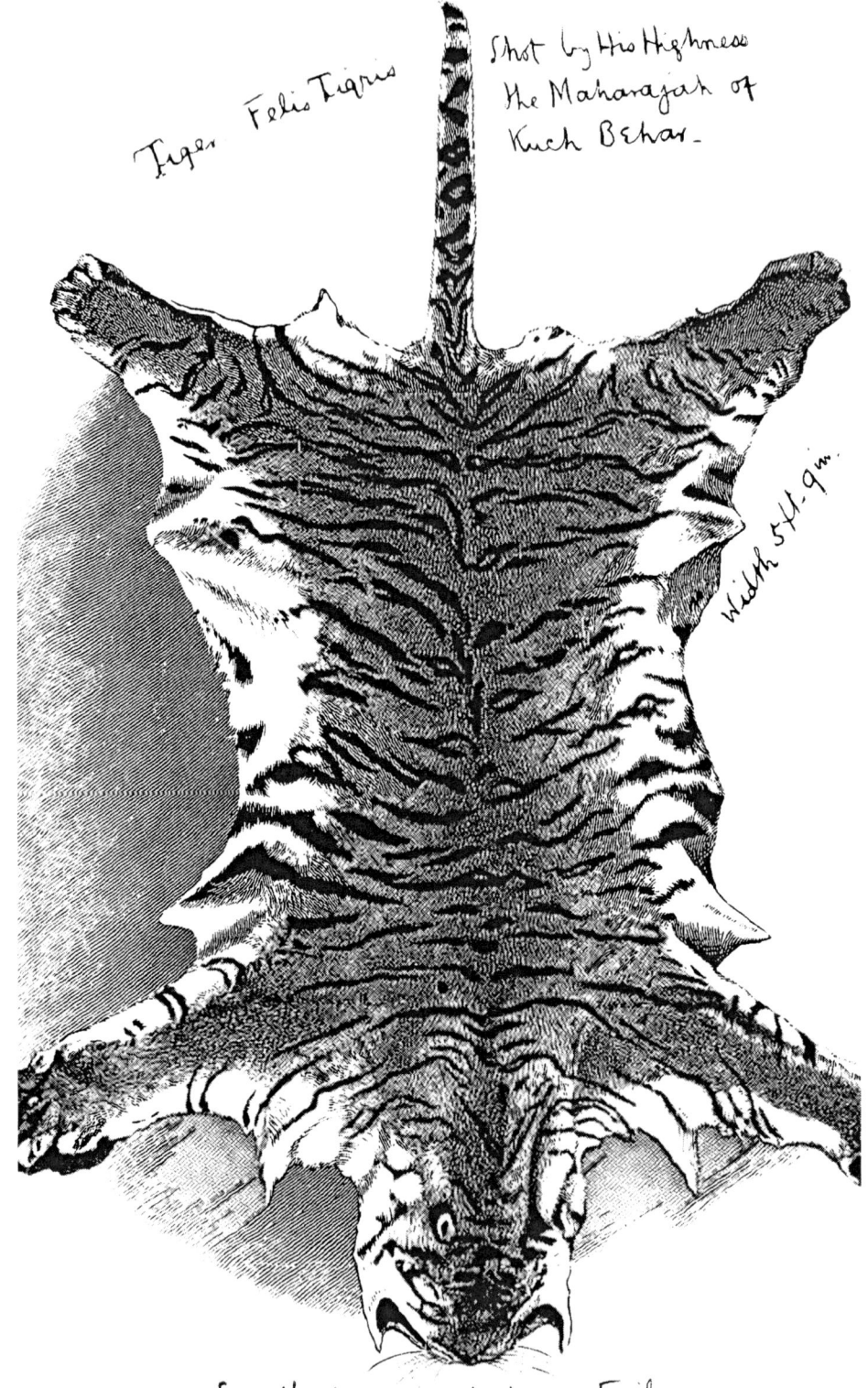

Tiger Felis Tigris

Shot by His Highness
the Maharajah of
Kuch Behar.

Width 5ft. 9in.

Length from nose to tip of tail
before skinning   10 ft 1½ in
dried skin   11 - 7 -

TIGER (Felis tigris)—*continued.*

Length before skinned.	Length of body.	Length dressed.	Girth of body.	Girth. Upper arm.	Girth. Fore arm.	Head.	Height at shoulder.	Weight.	Locality.	Owner.
ft. in.	ft. in.	ft. in.	inches.	ft.	ft.	ft.	ft. in.	lbs.		
–10 7(A)	7 0	12 1	56½	25	19½	36	3 4	491	Ramshai Hâb, Duars, Bengal	Col. Evans Gordon.
–10 6	...	11 8	...	...	...	...	...	...	Assam Frontier .	H.I.M. the Sultan of Turkey. (Shot by late Baron de Nolde.)
–10 5⅜	...	...	...	...	...	...	...	...	Central Provinces	Noel Fenwick.
–10 4	7 1½	12 2½	52	...	21	39	3 6	...	Bignor, N.W.P. .	A. M. Markham.
–10 4(D)	...	...	...	...	...	...	...	...	Kanara, B.P.	W. Holland.
–10 3	7 1½	12 1	52	29	19½	36½	3 4½	487	Kuch Behar .	Maharaja of Kuch Behar.
–10 3(C)	7 1	12 2	49	...	19½	32½	3 4	...	Balti Dun, N.W.P.	A. M. Markham.
–10 2½	7 0	...	48½	26½	20	38½	3 3½	530	Kuch Behar .	Maharaja of Kuch Behar.
–10 2½	...	...	...	...	...	...	...	...	Nepal Terai .	Sir E. L. Durand, Bart, C.B.
–10 2	...	...	...	...	...	...	...	...	Do. . .	Otho Shaw.
–10 1¾	6 10	12 4	51½	28½	13¾	38	3 4⅞	462	Kuch Behar	H.H. the Maharaja of Kuch Behar.
–10 1½	7 1⅓	11 7	54	29	21	40½	3 8¾	600	Do. .	Do.
–10 1	7 3	10 4½	...	...	...	...	...	...	...	Major J. W. M. Cotton.
–10 1	...	11 10	...	...	...	...	...	...	Kuch Behar .	Capt. Hugh Fraser.
–10 1	...	...	...	...	...	...	...	...	Central Provinces	James J. Harrison.
–10 0½	...	12 6	66	...	...	...	...	...	Rewa, C.P. . .	H. de Barreto.
–10 0½	...	11 11⅓	...	...	...	...	...	...	?	E. R. Henry.
–10	6 11	...	52	26	21	36	3 4	540	Kuch Behar .	Maharaja of Kuch Behar.
–10(E)	...	12 2	...	...	...	...	...	...	Terai Forests, Bengal	R. Nolan.
10 4(F)	...	...	...	...	...	...	...	...	Duars . . .	Capt. S. H. Pollen.

								Weight	Locality	Owner
10								…	Nilgiri Hills	Sir Edmund G. Loder, Bart.
9 11	6 9		50½	28¾	20¼	37	3 3¼	…	Kuch Behar	Count E. Hoyos.
9 11	6 6	11 2	54					…	Rewa, C.P.	Do.
9 11		11 1½						…	Nepal	A. E. Leatham.
9 10½	6 11		54	29	19½	39½	3 4	508	Kuch Behar	Maharaja of Kuch Behar.
9 10½	6 10½	12 10						500	Do.	Capt. S. H. Pollen.
9 10							3 9	…	Hyderabad	Capt. Hon. R. H. Marsham and Lieut. Sutton.
9 10	6 6							…	Nepal Terai	Major B. B. Russell.
9 10		11 8						…	Hyderabad, Deccan	A. M. Rotheram.
9 9								…	Central Provinces	James J. Harrison.
9 9	8½		48	24½	17	34½	3 3¼	…	Hyderabad, Deccan	Capt. C. E. G. Norton and Capt. Sir K. Fraser, Bart.
9 8½	8 8							…	Kuch Behar	Count E. Hoyos.
9 8			45					…	Terai	Lieut.-Col. B. D. Möller.
9 8								…	Philipil	Capt. J. H. Gwynne.
9 8	8 (B)							…	North Kanara	Lieut.-Col. L. L. Fenton.
9 8								…	?	Lieut.-Col. F. H. Whitby.
9 7	7							437	Rewa, C.P.	O. V. Bosanquet.
9 7	6 3	11 4						…	Do.	The late Sir Samuel Baker.
9 6								…	Do.	Count E. Hoyos.
9 6		10 9						…	Hyderabad, Deccan	Major G. A. L. Carew, D.S.O., and Capt. G. L. Holdsworth.
9 6								…	Deccan	Capt. Frank Lee.
9 5								…	Do.	J. D. Inverarity.
9 5	6 4	10 4½	49	26	18	32½	3 2½	420	Kuch Behar	Count Scheibler.

Length before skinned. ft. in.	Length of body. ft. in.	Length dressed. ft. in.	Girth of body. inches.	Upper arm. ft.	Girth. Fore arm. ft.	Head. ft.	Height at shoulder. ft. in.	Weight. lbs.	Locality.	Owner.
9 4½	...	11 6	...	...	...	...	...	...	Rewa, C. P.	C. C. Branch.
9 4	...	...	...	...	...	...	...	418	Kuch Behar	Capt. Hugh Fraser.
9 4	...	.	...	...	...	...	...	...	Mount Abu	Capt. H. B. Dalgety.
9 3½	6 0	...	44	...	...	...	...	...	Near Rewa, C.P.	Capt. H. P. Lane.
9 3½	...	...	...	...	...	...	...	...	Do.	H. de Barreto.
9 3	6 3	...	41	22	16	36	2 10	360	Kuch Behar	Maharaja of Kuch Behar.
9 3	...	...	...	...	...	...	...	...	Eastern Bengal	O. V. Bosanquet.
9 3	6 4	...	56	...	20½	39	...	over 563	Central Provinces	Capt. W. H. Hunter.
9 3	6 4½	...	...	...	...	...	...	448	Do.	Bombay Natural History Society's Journal.
9 3	...	9 3½	...	...	...	...	...	...	Chanda, C.P.	Capt. M. McNeill.
9 2	...	...	...	...	...	...	...	...	Nepal.	A. E. Leatham.
9 1	...	...	...	...	...	...	...	...	Ram Naydr, N.W.P.	Capt. B. H. Boucher.
9 9	...	...	...	...	...	...	...	...	North Kanara	Lieut.-Col. L. L. Fenton.
9 0	...	...	...	...	...	...	...	...	Deccan	Capt. Frank Lee.
8 10	...	...	...	...	...	...	...	...	Hyderabad, Deccan	Major G. A. L. Carew, D.S.O, and Capt. G. L. Holdsworth.
8 8	...	...	...	...	...	...	...	...	Gwalior	Viscount Edmond de Poncins.
8 7	...	...	...	...	...	...	...	...	Rewa, C.P.	C. C. Branch.
8 7	...	...	...	...	...	...	...	...	Do.	O. V. Bosanquet.
8 5½	...	...	...	...	...	...	...	345	Bignor District	Surgeon-Capt. E. McK. Williams.

TIGER (Felis tigris)—*continued.*

Skulls.

Basal length from back to front.	Breadth across tbe zygomatic arches.	Weight cleaned. lbs.	oz.	Locality.	Owner.
–15¾	...	...		Kuch Behar . .	Maharaja of Kuch Behar.
–15¼	10⅞	...		N.E. Bengal .	A. M. Murdoch.
–15¼	10½	...		Purneah .	R. A. Sterndale.
–15 (A)	10⅓	...		Bengal . . .	Col. Evans Gordon.
15	10¼	...		?	Rowland Ward.
14⅞ (F)	10	...		Duars . .	Capt. S. H. Pollen.
14½	9¾	4	10	Do. . .	Sir Edmund G. Loder, Bart.
14½	10⅜	...		Deccan . .	W. J. R. Wingfield.
–14½	10	...		Terai . .	Bombay Natural History Society's Museum.
14½	10⅛	...		Central Provinces .	Capt. W. H. Hunter.
–14½ (C)	10¼	...		Bignor District, C.P.	A. M. Markham.
14¼	10⅜	...		Central Provinces .	Capt. E. A. D'Arcy Thomas.
14¼ D)	9½	...		Kanara Jungles	W. Holland.
14¼ (E)	9½	...		Terai . . .	R. Nolan.
–14	10	...		?	J. D. Inverarity.
–14	10 9/16	...		Bignor District .	A. M. Markham.
13⅞	9¾	...		?	Capt. S. H. Pollen.
13¾	9¼	...		Indhaorèe, Nimar .	Lieut.-Col. H. Wade-Dalton.
13¾	9¾	...		?	Philip Wood.
13¾	9½	...		Madras . .	Col. J. Hinde.
–13¾ (B)	9¼	...		North Kanara .	Lieut.-Col. L. L. Fenton.
13·70	9	...		Duars . .	Mrs. Lawrie-Johnstone.
–13½	9½	3	14	?	Major J. W. M. Cotton.
13⅜	9⅞	...		Kumaun Terai .	H. J. Boas.
–12⅛	8 5/16	...		Bignor District, C.P.	A. M. Markham.

Skins.

Length of skin dressed. ft.	in.	Locality.	Owner.
13	6	Chinese Mongolia . .	A. Bignold.
12	6	Do. . .	Rowland Ward.
11	3½	Do. . .	W. H. Walker.
12	0	Do. .	H.R.H. le Duc d'Orléans.

A, B, C, D, E, F. For skins see p. 460.

LEOPARD (Felis pardus).

The leopard has an even larger range than the lion, and is probably the most widely distributed of all the cats. Sportsmen in India recognise a larger "panther" and a smaller "leopard," although naturalists fail to distinguish them as separate forms. The African and Indian leopards are also generally regarded as identical, but since the former has the spots on the body of smaller size than in the latter, and many of them without light centres, like those on the head, it is quite probable that it constitutes a different race. In Persia, Baluchistan, and the mountains of Sind is found a variety of the leopard (*F. pardus tulliana*) characterised by its pale colour, long fur, and thick tail; it is to some extent intermediate between the typical race and the ounce. Lastly, there is the Chinese leopard (*F. pardus fontanieri*), a very distinct animal, of heavy build, with a pale ground-colour to the fur, which is very long and thick, and the spots in the form of large complete rings, without any smaller spots in the centre. In the moist forest districts of Asia black leopards are by no means uncommon; and there is a tendency to darkening of a different type in some South African specimens. Height at shoulder from about 2 feet (India) to 2 feet 4 inches (Africa). A large leopard killed by Lieut.-Col. L. L. Fenton in the Gir forest, Kathiawar, measured 7 feet 8½ inches in length; the length of the tail being 35½ inches, the girth of the neck 21½ inches, of the forearm 11½ inches, and of the body behind the shoulder 35½ inches; weight, 160 lbs.

Distribution.—Africa, the Caucasus, Asia Minor, and Asia generally, with the exception of Northern Siberia, the Tibetan plateau, and perhaps Japan.

a.—Indian Specimens.

	Male		Female	
	ft.	in.	ft.	in.
Length from tip of nose to end of tail .	7	0	6	4
„ „ root of tail .	4	3½	3	7
Height at shoulder .	2	2½	1	9
Girth . . .	2	7	2	1
Circumference of upper arm .	0	13	0	10
„ forearm .	0	10¾	0	8½

Shot in Ceylon by Count Scheibler.

LEOPARD (Felis pardus).   Indian Specimens—*continued.*

Length before skinned.		Total length dressed.		Weight.	Locality.	Owner.
ft.	in.	ft.	in.	lbs.		
-8	4				Kuch Behar . .	Maharaja of Kuch Behar.
-8	2⅓	...		...	Do.	.	Do.
-8	1½	...		...	Do.	.	Do.
-8	o	...		154	Do.	Do.
-8	o	8	8½	...	India	Count J. Potocki.
-7	10	8	4¾	...	Ganges Kadir . .	See below.[1]
-7	9½	8	6	...	Central Provinces .	James J. Harrison.
-7	9	...		...	Nepal . .	C. H. H. B. Caldwell.
-7	9	...		...	Oudh	Mrs. Innes.
-7	8	...		...	Hyderabad, Deccan .	Capt. C. E. G. Norton and Capt. Sir K. Fraser, Bart.
-7	8	...		...	Ganges Kadir . .	Muttra Tent Club.[2]
-7	7	8	7½	...	Siwaliks . .	E. H. E. Green.
-...		7	10	...	?	Col. W. Gordon Cumming.
-7	6	...		...	Chaubattia .	.	Capt. R. B. Fell.
-7	1	7	10⅞	...	Rewa, C.P.	.	Count E. Hoyos.
-7	4½	...		...	Gujerat .	Capt. H. J. Morphy.
?7	4	8	1	145	Bignor District .	Surg.-Capt. E. McK. Williams.
-7	4	...		...	Kathiawar . .	Lieut.-Col. L. L. Fenton.
-7	3	...		...	?	Lieut.-Col. F. H. Whitby.
-7	1	7	11½	...	Kotah . . .	Maharaja of Bikanir.
-7	1	...		...	Hyderabad, Deccan .	Major G. A. L. Carew, D.S.O., and Capt. G. L. Holdsworth.
-7	o¼	8	3½	...	?	Maharaja of Bikanir.
7	o	...		...	?	Major A. E. Ward.
-6	10	7	10	140	Bignor District	Surg.-Capt. E. McK. Williams.
-6	10	...		...	Chaubattia .	.	Capt. R. B. Fell.
-6	8	...		110	?	M. Loam.
'6	5	...		...	Chaubattia .	.	Capt. R. B. Fell.

[1] Speared by Capt. H. Hoare (5th D.G.), Capt. J. G. Rotton (R.A.), and W. Gillman (R.H.A.)
[2] Major A. C. King and some officers of the 5th Lancers, when out with the Muttra Tent Club.

2 H

LEOPARD (Felis pardus).   Indian Specimens—*continued.*

Length before skinned.		Total length dressed.		Weight.	Locality.	Owner.
ft.	in.	ft.	in.	lbs.		
−...		7	8½	...	Kuch Behar .	Maharaja of Kuch Behar.
− ♀ 6	2	6	5	...	Gwalior . .	Viscount Edmond de Poncins.
− ♀ 5	11	...		...	Chaubattia . .	Capt. R. B. Fell.
− ♀ 5	10	6	8½	96	Bignor District	Surg.-Capt. E. McK. Williams.
− ♀ 5	8	6	4	80	Do.	Do.
−...		7	8	...	Kuch Behar .	Maharaja of Kuch Behar.
1...		7	8	...	?	Capt. A. G. Ferguson.
−...		7	6½	140	Kuch Behar	Maharaja of Kuch Behar.
−...		7	4½	...	?	Col. Howard.
−...		7	4	...	Nepal .	H. L. Heber-Percy.
−...		7	1	...	Do.	Sir E. L. Durand, Bart., C.B.
......		6	8	110	Madras . .	M. Loam.

b. AFRICAN SPECIMENS.

Length before skinned.		Weight.	Locality.	Owner.
ft.	in.	lbs.		
−7	3½	...	?	Count J. Potocki.
−7	3	...	Wadelai, E. C. Africa	Capt. W. P. Pulteney.
−7	2	...	Somaliland .	Count Scheibler.
−7	2	...	South-East Africa .	F. Vaughan Kirby.
−7	1½	...	?	C. V. A. Peel.
−7	0	..	Somaliland	J. Johnston-Stewart.
−6	11	...	E. C. Africa .	James J. Harrison.
−6	10	...	Somaliland	Count Scheibler.
−6	10	140	Nyasaland . . .	A. White.
−6	3	...	Somaliland . .	Norman B. Smith.
1−6	2	...	Jebba, Nigeria .	The late Capt. H. W. Baker.
−6	0	...	Somaliland .	Count E. Hoyos.
− ♀ 6	0	...	Do. . .	C. V. A. Peel.
2−5	7	...	Nigeria . .	Lieut.-Col. T. D. Pilcher.

1 Height at shoulder, 2 ft. 1⅛ in.   2 Height at shoulder, 22 in.; girth, 21¾ in.

The following specimens were shot and measured by F. Vaughan Kirby :—

(*a*) Nguanetsi River, S.E.A. (*b*) Matamiri Bush, S.E.A.

	Length, tip to tip in a straight line.		Length over all—'sportsman's' measurement.		Shoulder height.		Girth of neck.	Girth behind shoulder.	Girth of forearm.	Length of skull.	Zygomatic width.	Cleaned weight.	
	ft.	in.	ft.	in.	ft.	in.	in.	in.	in.	in.	in.	lbs.	oz.
(a)	6	11	7	2	2	7	22	$35\frac{1}{2}$	$12\frac{1}{2}$	$9\frac{7}{8}$	$6\frac{1}{8}$	1	8
(b)	6	9	7	2	2	7	20	$33\frac{1}{8}$	$11\frac{1}{4}$	9	$5\frac{1}{4}$	...	

Leopard Skulls.

Total length.	Width.	Weight.	Locality.	Owner.
in.	in.	lbs. oz.		
$-10\frac{1}{4}$	$6\frac{5}{8}$	...	Bignor District, N.W.P.	A. M. Markham.
$-10\frac{3}{16}$	$6\frac{1}{4}$	...	Gir Forest, Kathiawar .	Lieut.-Col. L. L. Fenton.
$-9\frac{13}{16}$	...	1 5 clean	Nyasaland .	Dr. Percy Rendall.
$-9\frac{3}{4}$	6	...	?	Julius Jeppe.
$-9\frac{1}{2}$	...	...	?	Do.
-9	$5\frac{1}{4}$	...	S.E. Africa .	F. Vaughan Kirby.
$-6\frac{7}{8}$	5	...	India .	. W. T. Blanford.

OUNCE or SNOW-LEOPARD (Felis uncia).

Although the Persian leopard is in some degree intermediate in respect to colour and the length of the coat, the ounce differs from the leopard by the ground-colour of the long and dense fur being dirty white, with the spots on the back, sides, and tail, in the form of large, irregular, ill-defined, and interrupted rings, and by the great thickness of the tail, which scarcely tapers, and is about three-quarters the length of the head and body. Height at shoulder about 2 feet 4 inches. Skull about 6 inches long.

Distribution.—The high ranges of Central Asia, including Gilgit, Hunza, Turkestan, Trans-Baikalia, Ladak, Tibet, Amurland and Western China, extending in the north-west to the Altai, and in the west, it is said, to Persia. In Prince Demidoff's *Hunting Trips in the Caucasus* a snow-leopard is figured as coming from that range, but whether the animal found there is *F. uncia* or *F. pardus tulliana* may be doubtful. Generally dwelling at elevations of over 8000 feet, descending in Gilgit during winter to 6000 feet.

Length dressed.		Weight.	Locality.	Owner.
ft.	in.			
8	7	...	Tibet .	. Rowland Ward.
-8	6	Skull, 7¾ + 5¼	Kashmir .	. R. Rankin.
8	2⅓	...	Baltistan	E. Langworthy.
-7	10	...	Near Leh .	Major S. Frewen.
-7	5¾	...	Pamir .	Viscount Edmond de Poncins.
7	5	...	?	Major F. J. Harden.
-7	4	(24 inches at shoulder)		R. A. Sterndale.
-7	3	...	?	Major A. E. Ward.

CLOUDED LEOPARD (Felis nebulosa).

The *arimau dahan*, as this species is called by the Malays, is the size of a small leopard, with a very long and thickly furred tail, and large upper tusks. The ground-colour of the fur varies from grayish brown to fulvous, upon which are large dark blotches, frequently bordered in part with black. In old specimens the blotches often disappear, leaving only the black borders.

Distribution.—From the Sikim and Bhutan Himalaya, through Assam, Burma, Siam, and the Malay Peninsula, to Sumatra, Java, and Borneo. Represented by a smaller variety (*F. nebulosa brachyurus*) in Formosa.

Length dressed.		Weight.	Locality.	Owner.
ft.	in.	lbs.		
-6	6	...	Assam .	. The late B. H. Hodgson.
-6	4	44½	?	R. A. Sterndale.
5	9	...	?	B. R. M. Glossop.
5	7½	...	Assam .	. The late B. H. Hodgson.
5	7½	...	Do. .	. P. Russel.

SKULL.

Basal length from back to front.	Breadth.	Locality.	Owner.
6.2 in.	4.75	Assam	. The late B. H. Hodgson.

JAGUAR (Felis onca).

This cat may be regarded as the American representative of the leopard, which it fully equals, even if it does not exceed, in size. The colour and markings are generally similar to those of the latter, but the dark rings are larger and arranged more definitely in groups, each ring usually enclosing one or more dark central spots, and the enclosed light area being of the same tint as the general ground-colour of the fur, which is typically of a rich tan. Usually seven or eight more or less distinct longitudinal rows of rosettes may be noticed on each side of the body.

Distribution.—America, from Louisiana, Texas, and Northern Mexico to about the Rio Negro, on the northern confines of Patagonia in lat. 40° S.

Length before skinning.		Length dressed.		Locality.	Owner.
ft.	in.	ft.	in.		
-9	3	9	3	Brazil	Count Henry Coudenhove.
-8	3¾		...	Do.	Do.
-6	11	7	9	Paraguay . .	James J Harrison.
	...	7	7	British Guiana .	Sir A. W. L. Hemming, K.C.M.G.

PUMA (Felis concolor).

With the exception of the much smaller and longer-tailed yaguarondi, the puma (pronounced pooma) is the only uniformly coloured cat found in America, where its range extends from British Columbia and Maine in the north to the Strait of Magellan in the south. The size is inferior to that of the jaguar, the height at the shoulder being about 2 feet, and the weight 150 lbs. The general colour of the fur is tawny, tending, like that of the Virginian deer, to reddish in summer, and to grayish in winter, with the middle of the back darker, and a whitish patch on the back of the otherwise black ears. But with such an enormous geographical range, it is inevitable there should be much local variation ; and American writers recognise more than one species. *F. concolor oregonensis*, of the north-west coast, may be admitted as a local race, as may *F. concolor puma* of South America.

Length in the field.		Weight.	Locality.	Owner.
ft.	in.	lbs.		
-8	6	about 150	...	A. Pendarves Vivian.
-7	6⅝	...	Brazil	Count Henry Coudenhove.
-7	5	...	Gallegos River, Patagonia .	W. Moncreiffe.
-7	3	...	Fraser River, British Columbia	J. Fannin.
-7	0	...	Wyoming . . .	J. L. Scarlett.
-5	9	...	South America .	James J. Harrison.

LYNXES (Felis lynx, etc.).

The lynxes form a well-marked group connected with the more typical members of the cat tribe by the jungle-cat (*F. chaus*), and distinguished by the tuft of long hairs at the summit of the ears, and the absence of the first upper cheek-tooth. From the others the caracal (*F. caracal*), of Africa and India, is broadly distinguished by its long tail and uniform rufous colour. The short-tailed lynxes are, however, a group in which it is very difficult to determine whether the variations indicate distinct species or local races. In the typical European lynx (*F. lynx*) the tail is very short, the throat has a ruff of long hair, and the coat is spotted with dark brown. The Tibet lynx (*F. lynx isabellina*) is certainly only a pale variety. Probably the Canadian lynx (*F. lynx canadensis*), which may be identical with the lynx of Northern Europe and Asia, should hold the same rank ; it ranges in America as far south as California. More doubt exists whether the red lynx (*F. rufa*), which is also widely extended in America, should be regarded as a separate race, but the so-called plateau lynx (*F. baileyi*) seems certainly only a variety of the former inhabiting the high grounds of Colorado, Utah, and Arizona. On the other hand, from differences in the form of the skull, the Spanish lynx (*F. pardina*), which is a fully spotted animal, seems rightly regarded as a distinct species. It ranges over a large portion of Southern Europe, including Turkey, Greece, Sicily, Sardinia, and Spain and Portugal. The ordinary lynx stands from 16 to 18 inches at the shoulder.

a. EUROPEAN LYNX.

Length on the field, nose to root of tail.	Locality.	Owner.
-42·9 in.	Eastern Carpathians .	Prince Henry of Liechtenstein.

b. TIBET LYNX.

Height at shoulder, 16 or 18 inches.

c. CANADIAN and RED LYNX.

Length on the field, nose to root of tail.	Height at shoulder.	Weight.	Locality.	Owner.
[1]-38 in.	25	60 lbs. (about)	Wyoming .	Capt. G. Dalrymple White.
[2]-32 ,,	22	40 lbs. (about)	Nova Scotia .	Do.

[1] Canadian Lynx.　　　　　[2] Bay Lynx.

d. CARACAL.

Flat skin.	Locality.	Owner.
46½ in.	Nr. Grahamstown, S. Africa	Dr. H. Smith.

HUNTING-LEOPARD or CHITA (Cynælurus jubatus).

Although this animal is commonly called chita (cheetah) by Anglo-Indian sportsmen, that name is at least as often applied in India to the leopard. From all the true cats and lynxes the hunting-leopard differs by the claws being capable of only partial withdrawal into their sheaths, so that their tips are always exposed. The body also is more slender, and the limbs are proportionately longer. The black spots on the skin are small and without light centres, like those on the head of the leopard. Length 7 feet or less, height at shoulder 30 to 39 inches. A specimen speared by Lieut.-Col. L. L. Fenton in Kathiawar measured 6 feet $\frac{1}{4}$ inch in length, the tail being 2 feet $2\frac{1}{4}$ inches.

The animal is the "Ihlose" of the Zulus and Swazis, and is distributed sparsely throughout S.E. Africa. They usually hunt in couples, and fairly stalk their game, securing it with a swift rush at the last. Mr. F. Vaughan Kirby says: "I have seen a party of six hunting together and another of eight. Though I have often tried, I have never yet succeeded in running into one on horseback; they are incredibly swift of foot. They invariably kill their prey by strangulation."

Distribution.—Africa and South-Western Asia, extending from Persia to Western Turkestan and the countries east of the Caspian, and eastwards into India; unknown in the latter country on the Malabar coast and to the north of the Ganges, as it also is in Ceylon. The African hunting-leopard is stated to differ by its more woolly coat, and if this be the case, should be known as *C. jubatus laneus.*

Shot in the Eastern Transvaal by F. Vaughan Kirby.

Total length in straight line.	Do. over all.	Tail.	Vertical height.	Girth of forearm.	Do. shoulders.
6 ft. 8 in.	7 ft. 7 in.	2 ft. 9 in.	2 ft. $11\frac{1}{2}$ in.	$8\frac{1}{4}$ in.	31 in.

Length.		Length of tail.		Height at shoulder.	Locality.	Owner.
ft.	in.	ft.	in.			
-7	0		...	...	India . . .	R. A. Sterndale.
-6	$0\frac{1}{4}$	2	$2\frac{1}{4}$	...	Near Rajkot, Kathiawar	Lieut.-Col. L. L. Fenton.
-6	$4\frac{3}{4}$	2	$3\frac{1}{2}$	$28\frac{1}{2}$	N.E. Transvaal . 90 lbs.	Dr. Percy Rendall.
-6	4		...	...	Somaliland .	J. Johnston-Stewart.
-6	$1\frac{1}{2}$		...	...	Do. .	C. V. A. Peel.
-6	0		...	...	Do. .	Do.

SPOTTED HYÆNA (Hyæna crocuta).

Somali *Uaraba*.	*Setongwani* in the Barotse country.
Danakil *Yangula*.	*Piri* in the Lake Ngami country.
Abyssinian *Jib*.	*Chimbwi* in the Chilala and Chibisa countries.

The hyænas form a small family of Carnivora allied in some respects to the cats, but distinguished by the form of the skull, the more numerous teeth (which are, however, to a considerable extent cat-like), and the four-toed feet, with non-retractile claws. The spotted hyæna is the largest of the three species, and takes its name from the large dark blotches on its tawny coat. Its carnassial teeth are more cat-like than those of the other species.

Distribution.—Africa, south of the Sahara.

Nose to root of tail in a straight line, 4 feet $9\frac{1}{2}$ inches. Length of tail, 1 foot 1 inch.

Extreme length over all, 6 feet 3 inches.

Vertical standing height, 3 feet.

Girth behind shoulders, $39\frac{1}{2}$ inches.

SKULLS.

Length.	Width.	Weight.		Locality.	Owner.
in.	in.	lbs.	oz.		
$-12\frac{1}{4}$	$7\frac{1}{4}$	2	8	South-East Africa	F. Vaughan Kirby.
$-12\frac{1}{4}$	$7\frac{3}{8}$	2	12	Zomba, B.C.A.	D. MacAlpine.
-11	$7\frac{1}{2}$		...	Somaliland .	Viscount Edmond de Poncins
-11	$6\frac{7}{8}$		...	South-East Africa .	F. Vaughan Kirby.
$-10\frac{5}{8}$	$6\frac{7}{8}$	2	3	East Africa . .	Capt. R. A. J. Montgomerie C.B., R.N.

Brown Bear.

BEARS (Ursidæ).

Bears are so unlike other animals and so like one another that no one has the slightest difficulty in recognising a member of the group when he sees it. They constitute a family of Carnivora—the *Ursidæ*— and are spread over the greater part of the globe, with the exception of Africa to the south of the Sahara desert, and the Australasian islands. As some of their leading characteristics may be mentioned their large bodily size, clumsy build, shaggy fur, generally uniform coloration, the very short tail, and the application of the whole sole of the foot to the ground in walking. The skull and teeth are likewise very peculiar and distinctive, although these need not be taken into consideration in this place.

In consequence of the marked similarity to one another of most members of the group, it is a matter of extreme difficulty to come to a definite conclusion as to the number of species of bears—not that this is a matter of very much importance one way or another. The typical member of the group is the familiar brown bear (*Ursus arctus*) of Europe, whose colour is generally a darker or lighter shade of brown, but occasionally tends to grayish. The Syrian bear (*U. arctus syriacus*), in which this grayish tinge predominates, may be regarded as a local variety, and the same is the case with the snow-bear of Kashmir (*U. arctus isabellinus*), in which the colour is generally a light creamy brown. European specimens probably seldom exceed eight feet, but the huge Kamschatkan bear (*U. arctus collaris*) grows to nine feet. Even more gigantic is the Kadiak bear (*U. arctus middendorfi*) of Kadiak Island, Alaska; while the Yezo bear (*U. arctus yesoensis*) of Japan is another large form, with much the external appearance of a grizzly. The Alaskan bear (*U. arctus dalli*), from the mainland of Alaska, is also a huge animal, slightly smaller than the one from Kadiak Island, with more resemblance to an ordinary brown bear than to a grizzly. The typical grizzly of the Rocky Mountains is a smaller animal, with longer and straighter claws, but scarcely entitled to rank as more than another local race (*U. arctus horribilis*), next to which comes the Barren Ground bear (*U. arctus richardsoni*). Finally, the last animal which can be included in this group of the genus is the African bear (*U. arctus crowtheri*), of North-Western Africa, still imperfectly known. The extinct cave-bear (*U. spelæus*) is a large species allied to the brown bear.

The little blue bear (*U. pruinosus*) of Tibet, with more or less of white on the head and shoulders, seems to form a distinct species. The same is the case with the American black bear (*U. americanus*), which is generally black, and exhibits distinctive features in the skull and teeth. Not improbably the Himalayan black bear (*U. torquatus*) is a relative of the last-named species; it may be recognised by the conspicuous white gorget on the breast. In Japan it is represented by the Japanese black bear (*U. japonicus*). The smallest species of the genus are the very distinct Malayan bear (*U. malayanus*), and the allied spectacled bear (*U. ornatus*) of the Peruvian Andes, the latter distinguished by the light-coloured rings around the eyes, from which it derives its name.

The most distinct of all the species included in the genus *Ursus* is the Polar bear (*U. maritimus*), so distinct, indeed, that many naturalists think it ought to form a group by itself. Externally its chief characteristics are its white coat, and the presence of a certain amount of hair on the soles of the feet; both these peculiarities being evidently adaptations to the Arctic habitat of the animal. It has been recently stated that very old Polar bears exhibit a tendency to the development of a brownish tinge in the fur. Last of all come the Indian sloth-bear (*Melursus ursinus*), and the parti-coloured bear (*Æluropus melanoleucus*) of Tibet, both of which are so different from the other kinds as each to form a genus by itself. The former is too well known an animal to need description, some of its characteristics being the long and bare snout, the ragged, wiry hair, extensile tongue, small cheek-teeth, and the diminished number of front teeth. From all its kindred the second differs by its pied fur, as it does by its remarkably-formed cheek-teeth, which are broader and shorter than in other bears.

a—SKULLS.

Basal length from back to front.	Width across the zygomatic arches.	Weight cleaned.		Race, or Species.	Locality.	Owner.
in.	in.	lbs.	oz.			
18¾	11⅜	12	0	Cave bear	Europe .	Sir Edmund G. Loder, Bart.
18	11	10	0	Kamschatkan	Siberia . .	Hon. Walter Rothschild.
–16½	...	...		...	Alaska . .	H. W. Seton-Karr.
16	9⅝	6	3	Polar .	Arctic Seas .	Rowland Ward.
16	9⅞	5	8	Do. .	Nova Zembla.	J. Lamont.
15½ (D)	9½	5	10	Grizzly .	Brit. Columbia	Sir Peter Walker, Bart.
15⅜	9¼	4	10	Kamschatkan	Kamschatka	Lieut. R. E. R. Benson, R.N.
15⅞	10½	5	13	Polar .	Polar Seas .	Sir Edmund G. Loder, Bart.
14½	9	5	14	Do. .	Franz Josef Land	Jackson-Harmsworth Expedition.
14½	8¼	4	8	Grizzly .	Brit. Columbia	S. B. Bennett.
14⅜ (C)	8¼	5	0	Do. .	New Mexico	Montague Stevens.
13	9⅛	...		Polar	Spitzbergen .	The late Capt. Townley Parker.
–12⅞	7	...		Sloth	Mysore . .	Capt. M. M'Neill.
12½	7⅜	...		Do. .	Cent. Prov. .	C. F Egerton.
12½	7	...		Grizzly	Wyoming .	J. L. Scarlett.
12½ (B)	6¾	...		Sloth .	Cent. Prov. .	Surgeon-Major M. O'C. Drury.
12⅜	7⅝	...		Snow .	Kashmir	A. Ezra.
12⅛	7⅝	...		Grizzly .	Wyoming	J. L. Scarlett.
12	7⅛	...		Sloth .	Cent. Prov. .	C. F. Egerton.
11¾	7½	...		Snow .	Kashmir	W. R. Bindloss.
11½ (A)	6¾	...		Brown .	W. Caucasus .	St. George Littledale.
–10	6.8	...		Black .	Nepal .	W. T. Blanford.
–8.5	8.3	...		Malayan .	Borneo	Do.

BEARS (Ursidæ)—*continued.*

b—SKINS.

Length from nose to tip of tail.		Height at shoulder.		Girth.		Weight.	Race, or Species.	Locality.	Owner.
ft.	in.	ft.	in.	ft.	in.	lbs.			
-13	6 [1]	...		...		1656	Kadiak Island	English Bay, Kadiak Island, Alaska	J. C. Tolman.
-11	6½ [1]	10	2 [2] (from one front paw to other)	...		1536	?	Nevada, 1881	W. F. Sheard.
9	10 [1]	...		...		...	Alaskan	Alaska . .	Rowland Ward.
9	8 [1]	...		...		...	Do.	Do. . .	Cape Town Museum.
9	5 [1]	...		...		...	Do.	Do. .	Dublin Museum.
9	5	4	6	...		...	Polar .	Baffin Bay .	W. Livingstone Learmonth.
9	5 [1]	...		...		...	Alaskan	Alaska . .	Hon. Walter Rothschild.
8	10 [1]	4	0 (mounted)	...		...	Do.	Do. . .	British Museum.
8	7	...		...		1600	Polar .	Arctic Seas .	Captain Lyon.
8	7	...		...		...	Do.	Spitzbergen .	A. Barclay Walker.
8	6	...		...		...	Do. .	Franz Josef Land	Dr. S. H. T. Armitage.
-8	5	...		...		...	Black	Kashmir .	Capt. W. Westropp White.
8	4	...		...		...	Do. .	?	Surg.-Capt. W. White.
8	3	...		...		...	Kamschatkan	Kamschatka .	Dr. F. H. H. Guillemard.
-8	0½	...		...		...	Grizzly .	Wyoming .	T. W. H. Clarke.
8	0	...		...		...	Polar .	Spitzbergen .	A. Barclay Walker.
8	0 (D)	3	11	...		...	Grizzly .	Brit. Columbia	Sir Peter Walker, Bart.
-8	0 (C)	...		...		735	Do. .	New Mexico	Montague Stevens.
-7	11	...		...		800 (about)	Brown .	Norway .	Capt. Gerard Ferrand.
-7	9	...		...		...	Snow .	Kashmir .	Major C. F. Blane.
7	5½	...		...		...	Black .	Wyoming .	T. W. H. Clarke.
-7	1	...		...		...	?	N.W. Territory	James J. Harrison.
-7	0¾	...		...		680 (about)	Brown .	Lithuania .	Prince Radziwill.
7	0	3	2	...		...	Do. .	India .	Major A. E. Ward.
-6	11	...		...		...	Black .	Wyoming .	James J. Harrison.

[1] Skin measurement.

[2] Measurement of head in the flesh from tip of nose to base of skull, 29 inches; between ears, 16 inches.

BEARS (Ursidæ). Skins—*continued.*

Length from nose to tip of tail.		Height at shoulder.		Girth.		Weight.	Species.	Locality.	Owner.
ft.	in.	ft.	in.	ft.	in.	lbs.			
-6	10	3	0	4	4½ forearm	423	Sloth .	Kuch Behar .	Maharaja of Kuch Behar.
-6	9½	...			25	...	Snow .	Kashmir	S. V. Occleston.
-6	8 (B)	...		...		...	Snow .	Do.	A. Ezra.
-6	6	...		...		...	Grizzly	Wyoming	Count E. Hoyos.
-6	5	...		...		...	Do.	Do. .	J. L. Scarlett.
-6	4½	...		...		...	Snow	?	Capt. H. M. Biddulph.
-6	3	...		...		...	Grizzly .	Wyoming .	J. L. Scarlett.
-6	2½	...		...		...	Black .	Brit. Columbia	Count E. Hoyos.
-?6	2	...		...		...	Grizzly	Cent. Prov. .	Capt. M. M'Neill.
-6	1½	...		...		...	Sloth .	Mandla, Cent. Provinces	Capt. B. H. Boucher.
-6	1	...		...		...	Cinnamon	Wyoming .	James J. Harrison.
-6	0½	...		...		...	Snow .	Chamba .	Do.
-6	0½	...		...		...	Sloth	Hyderabad .	Count E. Hoyos.
-6	0	3	0	...		280	Do.	?	The late Col. G. P. Sanderson.
-5	10½	3	0	3	4	...	Red	?	Capt. H. M. Biddulph.
-5	10	...		...		...	Black .	Kashmir .	Major C. F. Blane.
-5	9	...		...		...	Sloth .	Cent. Prov. .	Capt. M. M'Neill.
-5	8	...		...		...	Do.	Do.	James J. Harrison.
-5	5½	...		...		216	Do. .	?	Capt. H. M. Biddulph.
-5	5	2	5¾	2	10¾	250 about	Black	Brit. Columbia	Count Scheibler.
-?5	2½	2	11¼	4	4	600 about	Grizzly .	Do.	Do.
-5	2 (A)	...		...		...	Brown .	W. Caucasus	St. George Littledale.
5	2	...		...		...	Snow .	Chamba .	Capt. B. H. Boucher.
-5	1½	...		...		200 about	Brown	Wyoming .	Count Scheibler.
-?5	1·65	...		...		...	Snow	Kandgoot .	Viscount Edmond de Poncins.
-4	11	...		...		...	Sloth .	Ganjam District	M. Loam.
-4	9·65	...		...		...	Do. .	Odeypore .	Do.
-4	7	...		...		...	?	Asia Minor .	H. O. Whittall.

N.B.—Some of the specimens entered as " Grizzly " may be the barren ground bear.

WALRUS (Odobœnus rosmarus and O. obesus).

The unwieldy seal-like animals commonly known by a corruption of the Scandinavian name valross (whale-horse) form in some respects a connecting link between the true seals and the eared seals, although differing from both in the huge upper tusks which depend from the muzzle of males and females alike, as also by the thick yellow bristles covering the muzzle itself. Like the true seals, walrus have lost all traces of external ears, but, unlike the former, and like the eared seals, their huge hind-flippers are turned forwards beneath the body when on land. The molar teeth, which are adapted for crushing the shells on which these monsters feed, have simple flattened crowns, quite unlike those of seals. Although young and adolescent walrus have a fairly thick coat of yellowish fur, in old individuals the tough hide becomes almost bare, except for the aforesaid bristles. Walruses are estimated to attain a weight of from 2250 to 3000 lbs.

Walruses are exclusively confined to the Arctic seas, where they spend much of their time on the ice. There are two kinds, now generally regarded as separate species; the one confined to the North Atlantic, and the other to the North Pacific. The distribution of these animals is by no means of circumpolar extent, the Atlantic walrus (*O. rosmarus*) apparently not ranging on the Asiatic coast east of the mouth of the river Lena; while in America they do not appear to inhabit the vast extent of coast lying between the western shore of Hudson Bay and Alaska. The Pacific walrus, which is the larger animal of the two, with considerably the longer tusks, always had a restricted range, and is now becoming very scarce. In European museums it appears to be represented only by skulls and tusks, and even these are rare. Formerly the Atlantic walrus occurred in countless thousands, but in accessible situations its numbers have been greatly reduced, owing to incessant persecution for the sake of its valuable oil and ivory. Between 1870 and 1880 at least 100,000 of these animals are estimated to have been slain.

The largest walrus ever shot by Mr. W. Livingstone Learmonth measured 12 feet 8 inches in length, and the tusks when extracted measured $25\frac{1}{2}$ inches in length and $8\frac{1}{2}$ in circumference at the largest part, but, as is the case with nearly all old bull walrus, the tusks were much broken at the points.

WALRUS (Odobœnus rosmarus and O. obesus)—*continued.*

TUSKS.

Total length of tusk.	Weight. lbs. oz.	Girth.	Locality.	Owner.
36	...	...	?	Sir Thos. Hesketh, Bart.
32⅜	...	8⅜	?	Bethnal Green Museum.
-31	6 1	...	...	F. Gordon George.
29	...	9¼	Arctic North America	C. C. Branch.
28¾	...	9¾	Do.	Do.
-25½	...	8½	Baffin Bay .	W. Livingstone Learmonth.
-19	...	8½	Spitzbergen	Alex. R. Alston.
	Length from gum.			
...	22⅛	7¾	Do. .	Sir Edmund G. Loder, Bart.
...	20¾	7½	Do.	Sir Victor Brooke's Collection.
...	18½	7½	Do.	Arnold Pike.
...	18	7½	Do. .	Earl of Dunmore.
...	15¼	6	Kolguev .	A. Coats.
...	12½	7¾	Do. . .	Do.

NARWHAL (Monodon monoceros).

The narwhal is the only member of the Cetacean or whale order furnished with tusks. These are present only in the male, and generally the left one alone is developed. Occasionally, however, both grow, as exemplified in a specimen in the British, and a second in the Cambridge Museum. A model of the animal is exhibited in the British Museum.

Distribution.—Arctic Seas.

The following measurements refer to tusks:—

Length. ft.	in.	Circumference.	Weight. lbs.	Locality.	Owner.
8	8¼	8⅝	...	Arctic Seas .	Bethnal Green Museum.
8	7½	8¼	14	Do. .	Rowland Ward.
8	3¼	7⅜	...	Do.	Bethnal Green Museum.
8	3¼	7⅞	...	Do. .	Hon. Charles Ellis.
8	3	7¾	17	Do.	Rowland Ward.
7	10¾	8⅛	...	Do.	Hon. Charles Ellis.
7	9	8¾	12½	Do. .	Sir Edmund G. Loder, Bart
7	0	6¾	...	Do. .	Duke of Westminster.

Suggestions for Recording the Length of Animals in the Field.

As the animal lies on the ground, and where circumstances permit, proceed as follows :—

Length. Pull the nose and the tail so as to get it in as nearly as possible in a straight line. Fix four pegs in, one at the end of nose, one at end of tail, one at root of tail, and one at the nape of neck behind ears.

Height at shoulder. Put the leg or paw in a standing position and place a peg at top of withers and measure carefully standing height (a) with extended paw, (b) with spread paw, as well as length of fore and hind legs from pegs at the stomach line.

The columns in the game-book would thus be as follows :—

A to F. Straight length from nose to tip of tail.	P. Girth of head.
	D to G. Height of hind-quarters.
A to E. Length along curve to root of tail.	C to L. Height at shoulder.
	K to L. Length of fore-leg.
E to F. Length of tail.	H to G. Length of hind-leg.
A to B. Length of head to nape of neck.	Weight, cleaned.
N. Girth, upper arm.	„ not cleaned.
M. „ forearm.	Cleaned skull (length, breadth, height,
O. „ of body.	weight).

The above measurements together with the note of its sex, estimated age, where and when killed, condition of the animal, with any other features of interest, such as colour of the eyes and skin, length of the hoofs, condition of teeth, weapons used and effect of bullets, etc. etc., will be of interest.

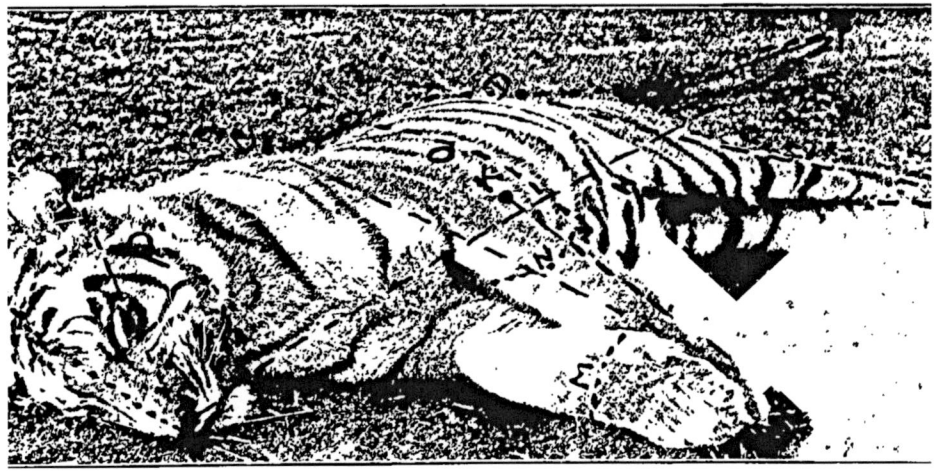

Tiger shot by Major H. G. C. Swayne, Central Provinces.

INDEX OF NAMES

INDEX OF SPECIES

THE END

Printed by R. & R. CLARK, LIMITED, *Edinburgh.*

ROWLAND WARD

LIMITED

𝔓ractical 𝔗axidermists

By Special Appointment to the Courts of Europe

"THE JUNGLE"

166 PICCADILLY, LONDON, W.

TELEPHONE 3644

PRACTICAL AND ARTISTIC TAXIDERMISTS, Designers of Trophies of Natural History, Preservers and Adapters of all Specimens of Animal Life. Natural Features of Animals adapted in Original Designs for Decorative Purposes and Every-day Uses. Furriers and Plumassiers, and Collectors in Natural History.

NOTICE.—ROWLAND WARD is the only member left in the profession of the Ward Family, long unrivalled for their accumulated experience and their skill in Practical Taxidermy, especially in its artistic department.

MEDALS AND DIPLOMAS OF HONOUR FOR ARTISTIC WORK

London International Exhibition, 1862.
Paris International Exhibition, 1862.
Vienna International Exhibition, 1873.
London International Fisheries, 1883.
Calcutta International Exhibition, 1883-84.

London International Health Exhibition, 1884.
London Colonial and Indian Exhibition, 1886.
The Anglo-Danish Exhibition, South Kensington, 1888.
The Royal Military Exbibition (Army Medical Department), 1890.

I

THE JUNGLE

AND INDIAN ANIMAL LIFE

WAS DESIGNED AND ARRANGED, AND THE ANIMALS MODELLED, BY

ROWLAND WARD, F.Z.S.

WHAT THE PRESS SAID:

" But everything else here is likely to be forgotten in presence of the wonderful jungle scene which Mr. Rowland Ward has constructed. . . . This will certainly be the first of the many attractions to which visitors will turn. . . . They will find themselves in presence of a scene which is likely to keep their gaze for some time. Mr. Ward has made the most of his limited space, into which he has collected the scenery and life which, in reality, is found scattered over an area of many thousand square miles. On the right we have a trophy from Kuch Bebar, formed by His Highness the Maharajah, the most prominent feature of which is a tiger hunt. We see a great group in the deep grass jungle. . . . Adjoining this are trophies designed to represent generally the Fauna and Flora of India, by representative animals and birds, picturesquely grouped in illustration of their life-habits."— *Times.*

" The visitors . . . were lost in admiration of Mr. Rowland Ward's masterly designs, modellings, and general arrangement. The novelty is already known as 'the Jungle.' . . . The deep grass jungle is occupied necessarily by many creatures which would not in their native wilds be found in such close companionship. . . . The scene is rendered with true tragic power."—*Daily News.*

" These numerous beasts . . . seem to illustrate the Fauna of India in a most vivid manner, and are very artistically prepared and arranged. . . . The entire trophy has been prepared by Mr. Rowland Ward. This group will unquestionably be one of the leading attractions of an exhibition which is already full of marvellous things."—*Morning Post.*

" Fitted up with the most perfect completeness—a jungle—the work of Mr. Rowland Ward. . . . The whole scene depicted is so life-like that one is startled by its vivid realism. . . . This jungle alone is almost enough to make an exhibition. . . . Besides, Mr. Rowland Ward has designed and arranged such other scenes in connection with several Colonial Courts."—*Daily Chronicle.*

" Mr. Rowland Ward, of Piccadilly, provides what will probably prove the most attractive feature of the exhibition, in the form of a series of picturesque trophies representing India, Ceylon, South Africa, Canada, and Queensland."—*Sportsman.*

" Perhaps the first place must be accorded to the jungle scene of Mr. Rowland Ward, which stands at the head of the Indian Courts, and which will certainly prove one of the favourite sights of the vast show."—*Daily Telegraph.*

EMPIRE OF INDIA EXHIBITION, 1895-96

THE JUNGLE

" A veritable triumph of the taxidermist's art—a tableau of jungle life which is entirely fresh and in every way remarkable."—*Daily Telegraph.*

" A series of scenes illustrative of jungle life, admirable alike in its artistic effect and fidelity to nature."—*Morning Advertiser.*

" 'The Jungle' will give the visitor vivid notions of Indian life."—*Times.*

" Will draw all eyes—gentle and simple, town-bred and country-bred ; is a wonderful exhibit. . . . such wealth of pelt and plumage, such glories of shikah . . the very combined essence of all jungles."—*Daily Chronicle.*

" A specially fine representation of an Indian jungle, with its characteristic vegetation and animals and wild scenery, to which Mr. Rowland Ward has contributed all his knowledge as a naturalist and his unrivalled skill as a taxidermist."—*Standard.*

" Most attractive . . . a comprehensive representation of animal life in the jungle and on the mountains of India . . . surpasses all former efforts . . . most realistic."—*Sporting Life.*

" Entirely fresh, and in every way remarkable."—*Graphic.*

" Rowland Ward's Jungle is the finest thing of the kind ever seen in this country, and should not be missed by any one."—*Court Journal.*

" A realisation of nature in its wildest and most tragic moods . . . provides instruction and amusement for the thousands in whose breast the love of nature and animal life is implanted."—*Globe.*

" Grand grouping of tropical life. Scrupulous attention to detail. . . . The hoarse coughing roar of the tiger closely imitated."—*South Africa.*

" Surpasses in interest any of the excellent exhibitions of the kind previously shown."—*Manchester Guardian.*

" The number of persons who visited Mr. Rowland Ward's Jungle was 10,500 making over 200,000 since the opening."—*Times* (August 6, 1895).

LONDON : ROWLAND WARD, LIMITED,

"THE JUNGLE," 166 PICCADILLY.

A SELECTED LIST OF BOOKS

OF

SPORT, TRAVEL

AND

NATURAL HISTORY

Rowland Ward   *Copyright*

THE JUNGLE

AT THE INDIAN AND COLONIAL EXHIBITION, 1886,
DESIGNED AND THE ANIMALS MODELLED
BY ROWLAND WARD, F.Z.S.

PUBLISHED BY

ROWLAND WARD, LIMITED

166 PICCADILLY, LONDON

4

5

Post 4to, 134 pp. Price 7s. 6d. net

THE
ENGLISH ANGLER

IN

FLORIDA

WITH SOME DESCRIPTIVE NOTES OF THE GAME, ANIMALS, AND BIRDS

BY

ROWLAND WARD, F.Z.S.

AUTHOR OF 'RECORDS OF BIG GAME,' 'SPORTSMAN'S HANDBOOK,' ETC.

WITH NUMEROUS ILLUSTRATIONS

" Mr. Rowland Ward, so widely known as a sporting publisher, has published a capital little book of his own writing. *The English Angler in Florida* gives an entertaining and eminently practical account of an angling trip he made to Florida last spring. Punta Gorda, on the western shore of the Peninsula, may be reached in nine days from Piccadilly, and, now that salmon fishings command fancy prices at home, English fishermen have been turning their attention to the tarpon. The tarpon is coming into notoriety, and promises to become the fashion, but it is only within the last ten or fifteen years that he has been persecuted. His flesh is worthless ; even the negro will not eat it, and nothing was suspected of the grand sport he gives with rod and line. As he runs ordinarily from 100 lbs. to 200 lbs., and is at least as vigorous in proportion as the salmon, the first consideration is a first-class outfit. Mr. Ward tells where it is best procured, and describes the short, stiff rod, the reel, the line, etc., and notably 'the friendly socket,' to be strapped round the waist, in which the butt of the rod is inserted ; for the strain upon back and arms is tremendous when fighting a 150 lb. fish for an hour or more. The tarpon is taken by gorge bait, and, unfortunately, the hook has yet to be invented which might be available for successful fly-fishing. For only here and there is the interior of the mouth vulnerable ; elsewhere, in Mr. Ward's words, it is impenetrable as a stone wall. He went in for his expedition almost regardless of expense, but he points out how it can be done as well and more economically ; and in particular he recommends chartering a sailing schooner instead of a steam launch. Sharks infest the fishing-grounds, snapping off the baits ; ' the slimy and filthy catfish ' swarm, and are even more troublesome ; and there is an interesting chapter on other eccentric marine monsters. He heard doubtful talk of a devil's ray, said to be 20 feet in diameter ; there is the sawfish, which with its formidable serrated proboscis is photographed as about twice and a half the height of a man ; and even that monstrosity is surpassed by the sawfish of the Mexican Gulf, which has been weighed up to nearly 800 lbs."—*Times.*

LONDON : ROWLAND WARD, LIMITED

'" THE JUNGLE," 166 PICCADILLY

Demy 8vo, 448 pp. Price 21s. net

ELEPHANT-HUNTING

IN

EAST EQUATORIAL AFRICA

BEING

AN ACCOUNT OF THREE YEARS' IVORY-HUNTING UNDER
MOUNT KENIA AND AMONG THE NDOROBO SAVAGES
OF THE LOROGI MOUNTAINS, INCLUDING A
TRIP TO THE NORTH END OF
LAKE RUDOLPH

BY

ARTHUR H. NEUMANN

WITH NUMEROUS ILLUSTRATIONS BY J. G. MILLAIS, E. CALDWELL
AND G. E. LODGE

COLOURED PLATE AND MAP

" It may be said that Mr. Neumann's volume is one of the most interesting books of African sport, adventure, and natural history that has appeared since that of Mr. Selous, and the illustrations are worthy of the text."—*Scotsman.*

"There is no lack of adventures throughout the book, and accounts of many narrow escapes from elephants. In addition to this, the author gives many interesting notes on the country traversed, and the manners and customs of the people with whom he came in contact. . . . Mr. Neumann may be congratulated on having produced a book which will be read with interest by sportsmen and geographers.

"The illustrations which the book contains are worthy of special commendation, and the map with which it is furnished will enable the reader to follow Mr. Neumann in his wanderings through a country very little of which, indeed, is known."—*Field.*

"This handsome volume, well written, well printed, well illustrated, and filled with such experiences of wild-forest life as few other men could boast, will delight the sportsman, geographer, the ethnologist, and the general reader. . . . He took his full share of fevers, thirst, lost roads, dangers by field and flood, and even as regards his principal prey, the elephant, was once as near to a dreadful death as any man who ever lived to tell the tale of having been charged and caught by a wounded elephant."—*Daily Telegraph.*

LONDON : ROWLAND WARD, LIMITED

"THE JUNGLE," 166 PICCADILLY

Demy 8vo, 506 pp.   Price 21s. net

SPORT IN THE HIGHLANDS

OF

KASHMIR

BEING

A NARRATIVE OF AN EIGHT MONTHS' TRIP
IN BALTISTAN AND LADAK, AND A LADY'S
EXPERIENCES IN THE LATTER COUNTRY;
TOGETHER WITH HINTS FOR THE GUID-
ANCE OF SPORTSMEN

BY

HENRY ZOUCH DARRAH

INDIAN CIVIL SERVICE

*WITH FIFTY-TWO ILLUSTRATIONS (FROM PHOTOGRAPHS BY
THE WRITER) AND TWO MAPS*

"Mr. Darrah's narrative of his visit to Kashmir and its outlying provinces Baltistan and Ladak has many merits.   It has the excellent foundation of notes 'generally recorded on the evenings of the days on which the events described occurred,' and of a diary kept whilst memory was fresh, the result being a book faithful and accurate in description of country and people . . . eminently trustworthy of the sport which may be enjoyed."—*Athenæum.*

"Mr. Henry Zouch Darrah's sumptuous volume *Sport in the Highlands of Kashmir* is the best book we have seen on sport beyond the Himalayas since General Macintyre's, nearly twenty years ago."—*Times.*

LONDON: ROWLAND WARD, LIMITED,

"THE JUNGLE," 166 PICCADILLY.

9

Medium 8vo, 336 pages.   Price 21s. net

HUNTING TRIPS

IN

THE CAUCASUS

BY

E. DEMIDOFF

PRINCE SAN DONATO

"*Hunting Trips in the Caucasus*, by Prince Demidoff, will be of interest not only to sportsmen, but to the general reader.   In his preface the author, as a foreigner, appeals to English sportsmen for indulgence.   We do not, however, think that there is any necessity for him to do so, as, in our opinion, the most interesting portion of the book is contained in his chapter on the game of the Caucasus, and the description of the first hunting trip, both of which have been written by himself.   The book is well got up, contains numerous excellent illustrations, and is furnished with a good map."—*Field.*

WITH 96 ILLUSTRATIONS AND MAP

LONDON

ROWLAND WARD, LIMITED

166 PICCADILLY

10

Medium 4to, 350 pp.   Price £5 : 5 : 0 net

THE DEER OF ALL LANDS

A HISTORY OF THE FAMILY CERVIDÆ.
LIVING AND EXTINCT

By R. LYDEKKER

Illustrated by Twenty-four Hand-Coloured Plates, drawn by J. SMIT ;
also a number of Process-Drawings of Horns, as well as
Photographic Reproductions of living Deer in the
Woburn and other Collections

"Mr. Lydekker's beautiful volume will, of course, find its way into the hands of every sportsman who can afford to indulge in the fascinating pursuit of 'big game' shooting, but it will also form an authoritative work of reference for naturalists of all countries, who will find in its pages a fund of useful information."—

LONDON: ROWLAND WARD, LIMITED,
"THE JUNGLE," 166 PICCADILLY.

Uniform with the above.   Price £5 : 5 : 0 net.

WILD

OXEN, SHEEP, AND GOATS
OF ALL LANDS

By R. LYDEKKER

Illustrated by Twenty-eight Coloured Plates, drawn by J. SMIT
and JOSEPH WOLF ; and a number of Drawings of Horns,
as well as Photographic Reproductions of
living Specimens

LONDON: ROWLAND WARD, LIMITED,
"THE JUNGLE," 166 PICCADILLY.

SUBSCRIPTION PRICE, £5 : 5s.

THE

GREAT & SMALL GAME OF AFRICA

Being a full Account of their Distribution, Habits, and Natural History, with Numerous Experiences of their Pursuit in the Field

WITH NUMEROUS HAND-COLOURED AND OTHER ILLUSTRATIONS

CONTRIBUTORS

Major A. J. ARNOLD
H. A. BRYDEN
T. E. BUCKLEY
T. W. H. CLARKE
Lord DELAMERE
Dr. D. G. ELLIOTT
Capt. B. T. FFINCH
H. C. V. HUNTER
J. D. INVERARITY
F. J. JACKSON
Sir HARRY JOHNSTON
F. VAUGHAN KIRBY
R. LYDEKKER

Capt. JOHN MARRIOTT
A. H. NEUMANN
A. E. PEASE
G. W. PENRICE
Viscount EDMOND DE PON-
CINS
Dr. PERCY RENDALL
F. C. SELOUS
ALFRED SHARPE
Lt.-Col. WILLIAM SITWELL
A. H. STRAKER
Major H. G. C. SWAYNE
POULETT-WEATHERLEY

General Editor.—H. A. BRYDEN

LONDON

ROWLAND WARD, LIMITED

"THE JUNGLE," 166 PICCADILLY

12

ImTheStory.com

CPSIA information can be obtained at www.ICGtesting.com
Printed in the USA
BVOW03s0835021213

337891BV00019B/865/P